5/18

lonely planet

Denmark

D0964060

**Northern
Jutland**
p248

Central Jutland
p213

Zealand
p94

✪ **Copenhagen**
p42

**Southern
Jutland**
p192

Funen
p160

Bornholm
p144

**Møn,
Falster &
Lolland**
p128

Mark Elliott
Carolyn Bain, Cristian Bonetto

Contents

BORNHOLM P144

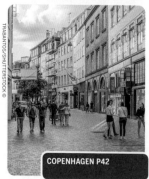

COPENHAGEN P42

Contents

Welcome to Denmark

Chart-topping contentment and quality of life, blockbuster dining and design, and a cheerful emphasis on hygge (cosiness) – explore (and envy) what makes Denmark tick.

Happiness & Hygge

It's heart-warming to know there's still a country where the term 'fairy tale' can be used freely – from enduring literary legacies to textbook castles. In a nutshell, Denmark gets it right: old-fashioned charm embraces the most avowedly forward-looking design and social developments. The country wins a regular place on lists of both the most liveable *and* the happiest nations on earth. You won't have to search hard to find *hygge* (pronounced hoo-gah or hue-guh), a unique-ly Danish trait that has a profound influence on the locals' inestimable happiness. *Hygge* is Denmark's social nirvana: a sense of cosiness, camaraderie and contentment.

History & Impact

The world first took notice of Denmark more than a millennium ago, when Danish Vikings took to the seas and ravaged vast tracts of Europe. How things have changed. These days Denmark captures global imaginations as the epitome of a civilised society. It punches above its weight on progressive politics, urban planning, sustainability, work-life balance, design and architecture. Recent global crushes, freshly exported from Copenhagen, include city cycling culture, the New Nordic culinary movement, and brilliantly addictive TV drama series.

Quality of Life

While many countries are noticeable for the ever-increasing gap between the 'haves' and 'have-nots', Denmark seems to be populated by the 'have enoughs', and the obviously rich and obviously poor are few and far between. This egalitarian spirit allows the best of the arts, architecture, eating and entertainment to be within easy reach of everyone. Indeed, the best catchword for Denmark might be 'inclusive' – everyone is welcome and everyone is catered to, be they young, old, gay or straight, and whether they travel with kids, pets or bikes in tow. Cities are compact and user-friendly, infrastructure is modern, and travel is a breeze.

The Danish Aesthetic

Denmark might lack the stop-you-in-your-tracks natural grandeur of its neighbours, but its understated landscapes – pure, simple and infused with ethereal Nordic light – are reflected in Danish design philosophy in fashion, food, architecture, furniture and art. Simplicity of form and function come first but not at the expense of beauty. And so you'll find moments of quintessential Danish loveliness on a long sandy beach, beside a lake, admiring a Renaissance castle, on quiet bike lanes or in a candlelit cafe that has perfected the art of *hygge*.

Why I Love Denmark

By Carolyn Bain, Writer

My first experience of Denmark came as a teenager, living there for a year as an exchange student. My first youthful Danish loves were the pastries and the long summer nights. These days I return with the same passions, enriched with an adult appreciation for Denmark's egalitarianism, its belief that cities belong to people not cars, and its endless quest for *hygge*. It helps that everything is easy on the eye – the unfairly attractive locals, yes, but also the architecture, the landscapes and the interior design. I think that, secretly, most cities want to grow up to be Copenhagen – and if they don't, they should.

For more about our writers, see p320

Above: Frederiksholms Kanal, Copenhagen (p42)

Denmark

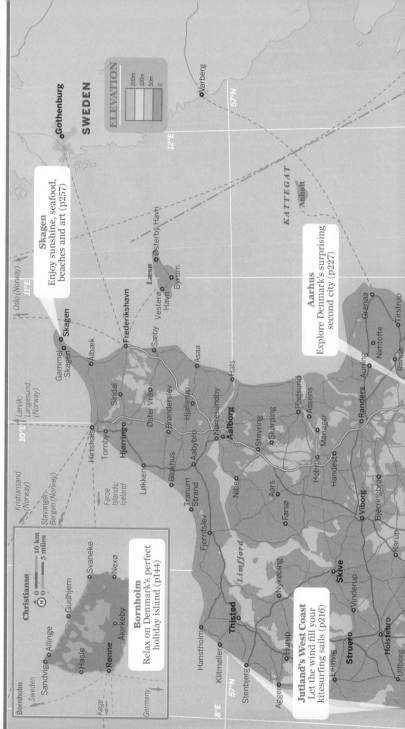

100 km
50 miles

N

Skagen
Enjoy sunshine, seafood, beaches and art (p257)

Aarhus
Explore Denmark's surprising second city (p227)

Bornholm
Relax on Denmark's perfect holiday island (p144)

Jutland's West Coast
Let the wind fill your kitesurfing sails (p216)

SWEDEN

ELEVATION
200m
100m
50m
0

Gothenburg

Varberg

Anholt

KATTEGAT

Læsø

Østerby Havn

Byrum

Vesterø Havn

Oslo (Norway)

Larvik;
Langesund
(Norway)

Kristiansand
(Norway)

Stavanger;
Bergen (Norway)

Faroe
Islands;
Iceland

12°E
11°E
10°E
8°E
57°N
57°N

Skagen
Gammel Skagen
Albæk
Frederikshavn
Sæby
Asaa
Hals
Sindal
Øster Vrå
Brønderslev
Hjallerup
Nørresundby
Aalborg
Stovring
Skørping
Hadsund
Assens
Hobro
Mariager
Handest
Randers
Auning
Grenaa
Nimtofte
Rønde
Tirstrup
Hjørring
Tornby
Hirtshals
Blokhus
Aabybro
Nibe
Aars
Farsø
Løkken
Tranum Strand
Fjerritslev
Nykøbing
Skive
Vinderup
Viborg
Bjerringbro
Karup
Limfjord
Klitmøller
Stenbjerg
Thisted
Hurup
Aggersund
Hanstholm
Struer
Lemvig
Holstebro
Ulfborg

Bornholm
Sweden
Sandvig
Allinge
Hasle
Gudhjem
Svaneke
Nexø
Akirkeby
Rønne
Køge
Germany

Christiansø

10 km
5 miles

N

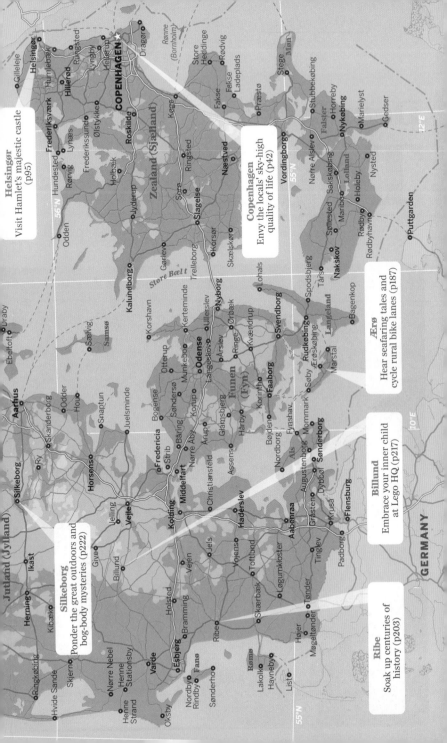

Helsingør
Visit Hamlet's majestic castle (p95)

Copenhagen
Envy the locals' sky-high quality of life (p42)

Ærø
Hear seafaring tales and cycle rural bike lanes (p187)

Billund
Embrace your inner child at Lego HQ (p217)

Silkeborg
Ponder the great outdoors and bog-body mysteries (p222)

Ribe
Soak up centuries of history (p203)

Jutland (Jylland)

Zealand (Sjælland)

Funen (Fyn)

Langeland

COPENHAGEN

GERMANY

Store Bælt

55°N

12°E

10°E

Denmark's
Top 15

Danish Dining

1 In recent times, the New Nordic movement has relaxed a little and become more accessible, while world-conquering Noma has travelled and reinvented itself. Michelin reviewers have cast their net wider to celebrate regional dining standouts, and modern Danish food (p283) continues to evolve. Emboldened by the attention and praise lavished on local produce and innovative chefs, food producers continue to embrace and modernise old-school culinary delights. Expect new spins on beloved rye breads and pastries, smørrebrød (open sandwiches; pictured below left), smoked fish, and even humble pork-and-potato dishes, and to eat damn well in unexpected corners of the country.

Copenhagen

2 You may find it hard to suppress your envy for residents of Scandinavia's coolest capital (p42). While this 850-year-old harbour town retains much of its historic good looks (think copper spires, cobbled squares and pastel-coloured gabled abodes), the focus here is on the innovative. Denmark's high-achieving capital is home to a thriving design scene, a futuristic metro system, and clean, green developments. Its streets are awash with effortlessly hip shops, cafes and bars; world-class museums and art collections; brave new architecture; and no fewer than 15 Michelin-starred restaurants.

Bottom right: Det Kongelige Bibliotek (p54)

NOVEMBER OSCAR KILO/SHUTTERSTOCK ©

VLADIMIR MUCIBABIC/SHUTTERSTOCK ©

Danish Design

3 Denmark is a world leader in applied design, characterised by cool clean lines, graceful shapes and streamlined functionality – visit the capital's revitalised Designmuseum Danmark (p52; pictured) to learn more. Danish design concepts have been applied to everything from concert halls to coffee pots to Lego blocks. The result has not just been great artistic acclaim but also big business: iconic brands include Bang & Olufsen (sleek stereos), Bodum (kitchenware), Georg Jensen (silverware and jewellery) and Royal Copenhagen Porcelain. Then there are the furniture designers and fashion houses.

Viking History

4 The Vikings ensured that the Danes were known and feared throughout northern Europe from the 8th to 11th centuries, but battle and bloodlust is far from the whole story. The Vikings were not just plunderers but successful traders, extraordinary mariners and insatiable explorers. Getting a feel for the Viking era is easy, whether visiting the ship burial ground of Ladby (p173), the Viking forts of Zealand (p125), the longship workshops at Roskilde (p110; pictured) or the many museums that seek to recreate the era with live re-enactments.

WILLIAM PERUGINI/SHUTTERSTOCK ©

VALERIIAARNAUD/SHUTTERSTOCK ©

Bornholm

5 Bornholm (p144) is a Baltic beauty lying some 200km east of the Danish mainland, located closer to Germany and Sweden than to the rest of Denmark. This magical island holds a special place in the hearts of most Danes, and is beloved for its plentiful sunshine, glorious sandy beaches, endless cycle paths, iconic *rundekirke* (round churches; pictured above left), artistic communities, fish smokehouses and idyllic harbourside villages. If that's not enough to lure you, the island has developed a reputation for outstanding restaurants and local edibles.

Cycling

6 Is Denmark the world's best nation for cycling? Probably, thanks to its extensive national network of cycle routes, terrain that is either flat or merely undulating, and a culture committed to two-wheeled transport. But you needn't embark on lengthy tours of the country to enjoy cycling here. The cities are a breeze to pedal around, and many have public bike-sharing schemes. More than 50% of Copenhagen (p42) commuters travel by cycle – it's easy to follow their lead, especially with new cycling bridges like Inderhavnsbroen and Cirkelbroen popping up around the city.

Ærø

7 Denmark has been likened to a china plate that's been dropped and smashed into pieces. Each fragment represents an island – and there are 406 of them. The midsized islands, each with their own distinctive character, are the most fun to explore, and south of Funen there's a whole archipelago of them, making it a prime sailing destination. Steeped-in-time Ærø (p187) is an idyllic slice of Danish island life: visit for seafaring heritage, rural bike lanes, cobblestoned villages, sandy beaches and photogenic bathing huts. Above bottom: Ærøskøbing (p188)

MARINA SPIRONETTI/ALAMY ©

Aarhus

8 Always the brides-maid, never the bride – Aarhus (p227), the second-largest city in Denmark, has laboured in the shadow of Copenhagen, but is now enjoying some well-earned time in the spotlight. This is a terrific city to explore. It has a booming dining scene, thriving nightlife (much of it catering to the large student population), a transformed waterfront, picturesque woodland trails and beaches along the city outskirts, and one of the country's finest art museums, turning heads thanks to its crowning glory, *Your Rainbow Panorama* (p230). Top left: Aarhus Street Food (p236)

Ribe

9 Compact, postcard-perfect Ribe (p203) is Denmark's oldest town, and it encapsulates the country's golden past in style, complete with imposing 12th-century cathedral, cobblestoned streets, skewed half-timbered houses and lush water meadows. Stay overnight in atmospheric lodgings that exude history (low-beamed rooms in a wonky 1600s inn, or in converted jail cells), and take a free walking tour narrated by the town's night watch-man – the perfect way to soak up the streetscapes as well as tall tales of local characters.

Lego in Billund

10 Unassuming Billund (p217) is the home town of the Lego Company and unofficial HQ for happy wholesome families. Here, the LEGOLAND® Billund Resort theme park (pictured opposite top right) and the inspired new Lego House (designed to resemble gigantic Lego bricks) are geared to celebrate the 'toy of the century' (as adjudged by *Fortune* magazine in 2000) in detail-rich ways that will delight your child, and your inner child. They're indicative of a country that's overflowing with child-friendly attractions, from Tivoli Gardens in the capital to first-rate aquariums, animal parks and waterparks.

Beaches

11 Having been cooped up for the winter, Denmark comes alive in summer, and the country's 7314km of coastline and its smorgasbord of islands draw the locals for wholesome pursuits and a dose of vitamin D. True, water temperatures may be a little unkind, but long sandy strands such as Bornholm's Dueodde (p150; pictured right), Marielyst (p139) on Falster, and northern Jutland's Skagen (p257) easily fulfil seaside-holiday fantasies. Other stretches, especially at towns like Hvide Sande and Klitmøller along Jutland's wild west coast, crank up activities harnessing the wind's power.

Kronborg Slot

12 Something rotten in the state of Denmark? Not at this fabulous 16th-century castle (p95; pictured below left) in Helsingør, made famous as the Elsinore Castle of Shakespeare's *Hamlet*. Kronborg's primary function was as a grandiose toll house, wresting taxes from ships passing through the narrow Øresund between Denmark and Sweden for more than 400 years. The fact that Hamlet, Prince of Denmark, was a fictional character hasn't deterred legions of sightseers from visiting the site. It's the venue for glorious summer performances of Shakespeare's plays during the HamletScenen festival (p100).

Skagen

13 Skagen (p257) is an enchanting place, both bracing and beautiful. It lies at Denmark's northern tip and acts as a magnet for much of the population each summer, when the town is full to capacity yet still manages to charm. In the late 19th century, artists flocked here, infatuated with the radiant light's impact on the rugged landscape. Now tourists flock to enjoy the output of the 'Skagen school' artists, soak up that luminous light, devour the plentiful seafood and laze on the fine sandy beaches.

MIKLUHA_MAKLAI/SHUTTERSTOCK ©

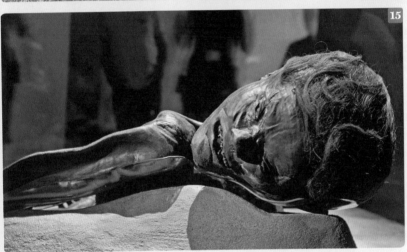

Summer Music Festivals

14 There's a fat calendar of summer festivals countrywide, from folk music in Tønder to riverboat jazz in the Lake District around Silkeborg. The capital lets loose at its largest event, Copenhagen Jazz Festival (p66), and celebrates electronic beats at Strøm. Meanwhile, NorthSide (p234) is augmenting Aarhus' music-fest street cred, and Tinderbox (p165) is doing the same for Odense. But it's the festivals outside the cities that draw the biggest crowds: Roskilde rocks with Scandinavia's largest music festival (p113; pictured), and Skanderborg hosts Denmark's 'most beautiful' event, lakeside Smukfest (p234).

Bog Bodies

15 Relics and monuments from Denmark's illustrious past abound. Two stars of the early Iron Age are the intact bodies of men who lived around 300 BC and were exhumed from Denmark's peat bogs after their two-millennia-long slumber; their discovery brings us tantalisingly close to ancient societies. The bodies also provide compelling historical who- and why-dunnits: were they human sacrifices, executed prisoners, or victims of murder perhaps? Tollund Man (p223) rests in a museum in bucolic Silkeborg; Grauballe Man (p233; pictured) lies in Aarhus' magnificent Moesgaard Museum.

Need to Know

For more information, see Survival Guide (p293)

Currency
Danish krone
(DKK or kr)

Language
Danish

Visas
Not required for members of EU or Schengen countries. More than 60 other nationalities including US, Canadian, Australian and New Zealand citizens can stay up to 90 days without a visa. Full listing on www.newtodenmark.dk.

Money
ATMs are widely available. Credit cards are accepted in most hotels, restaurants and shops.

Mobile Phones
Mobile coverage is widespread. Non-EU residents should bring a GSM-compatible phone; local SIM cards are available.

Time
Central European Time (GMT/UTC plus one hour)

When to Go

Warm summers, cool winters
Mild summers, cold winters

Aalborg
GO May–Sep

Aarhus
GO year-round

Copenhagen
GO year-round

Odense
GO May–Sep

Bornholm
GO Jun–mid-Sep

High Season
(mid-Jun–mid-Aug)

➡ Long daylight hours, with A-list concerts, festivals and theme parks in full swing.

➡ Busy camping grounds, beaches, sights and transport.

➡ Accommodation prices peak.

Shoulder
(May–mid-Jun, mid-Aug–Sep)

➡ A good time to travel, with generally mild weather and lighter crowds.

➡ Spring offers local produce, flowers and a few festivals.

➡ Autumn has golden landscapes and cosy nights.

Low Season
(Oct–Apr)

➡ Cool and wet with short daylight hours, but *hygge* (cosiness) is in full swing.

➡ Big cities have Christmas lights, ice-skating rinks and *gløgg* (mulled wine).

➡ Reduced hours for sights; outdoor attractions closed.

Useful Websites

Visit Denmark (www.visit denmark.com) Info ranges from the practical to the inspirational.

Visit Copenhagen (www.visitcopenhagen.com) All the capital's highlights.

Rejseplanen (www.rejseplanen.dk) Great journey planner.

Denmark.dk (www.denmark.dk) Hugely informative on diverse subjects.

Lonely Planet (www.lonelyplanet.com/denmark) Destination information, hotel bookings, traveller forum and more.

Important Numbers

There are no area codes in Denmark.

Denmark country code	45
International access code	00
Emergency (police, fire, ambulance)	112
Directory assistance (local)	118
Directory assistance (international)	113

Exchange Rates

Australia	A$1	5.00kr
Canada	C$1	5.00kr
Euro zone	€1	7.40kr
Japan	¥100	5.80kr
New Zealand	NZ$1	4.60kr
UK	UK£1	8.10kr
USA	US$1	6.30kr

For current exchange rates see www.xe.com.

Daily Costs

Budget: Less than 800kr

➡ Dorm bed: 150–300kr

➡ Double room in budget hotel: 500–700kr

➡ Cheap meal: under 125kr

➡ Bike hire: free, or per day 100kr

➡ 24-hour City Pass for Copenhagen transport: 80kr

Midrange: 800–1500kr

➡ Double room in midrange hotel: 700–1500kr

➡ Three-course menu in restaurant: 300–400kr

➡ Train ticket Aarhus–Copenhagen: 388kr

➡ Museum admission: 50–120kr

➡ Adult entry to major attractions: 120–380kr

Top End: More than 1500kr

➡ Double room in top-end hotel: from 1500kr

➡ Main course in top-end restaurant: from 250kr

➡ Car hire: per day around 600kr

Opening Hours

Opening hours vary throughout the year, especially for sights and activities.

Banks 10am–4pm Monday to Friday

Bars & Clubs 4pm–midnight, to 2am or later Friday and Saturday (on weekends clubs may open until 5am)

Cafes 8am–5pm or midnight

Restaurants noon–10pm (maybe earlier on weekends for brunch)

Shops 10am–6pm Monday to Friday, to 4pm Saturday, some larger stores may open Sunday

Arriving in Denmark

From **Copenhagen International Airport** (www.cph.dk):

Trains Every 10 minutes (36kr, 12 minutes) to Copenhagen Central Station.

Taxi Around 20 minutes to the city centre, 250kr to 300kr.

Metro Line M2 runs 24 hours from the airport station (Lufthavnen) to neighbourhoods including Christianhavn, Nørreport and Frederiksberg, but doesn't go via Copenhagen Central Station.

Getting Around

Public transport in Denmark is well organised and wide-reaching. Your best friend is the journey-planning website www.rejseplanen.dk available as a useful downloadable phone app.

Train Fast, sensibly priced, with extensive routes and frequent departures, trains are usually the best option for inter-city travel.

Car Quiet roads, few tolls and generally easy parking make Denmark delightful for touring by car. Drive on the right.

Bike Extensive bike paths link towns and villages throughout the country. Bikes can be hired in virtually every town.

Bus All large cities and towns have a local and regional bus system. Long-distance buses run a distant second to trains but are often cheaper.

Ferries Regular boats access virtually all of Denmark's populated islands that lack bridges.

For much more on **getting around**, see p303

What's New

Far-Flung Food Stars

The stellar food scene has spread from Copenhagen to the bigger cities, and to some surprising corners of the country. In recognition, Michelin now awards stars beyond the capital, thereby compiling a bucket list for travelling foodies that spans from Henne Kirkeby Kro (p217) on Jutland's west coast to Kadeau (p149) on Bornholm.

Second-City Spotlight

Aarhus, Denmark's second city, is enjoying some well-earned time in the spotlight. In the lead-up to its year as European Capital of Culture in 2017, its list of cultural offerings and big-city attractions boomed, and it continues to impress. (p227)

Setting the Standard for Cycling

In Copenhagen, the opening of cycling bridges Inderhavnsbroen and Cirkelbroen now makes it possible to cycle, walk or jog around the 13km-long Harbour Circle route. Another bridge is scheduled to open just south of the Royal Library. (p56)

Billund Blockbuster

The rise of Lego continues, with the new Lego House ('The Home of the Brick') opening its doors in September 2017 in Billund (Lego HQ). Its design is superb, its displays both playful and meaningful. (p217)

A New Story in Odense

Odense is in a cocoon of brilliance partway through its transformation into an urban butterfly. Work continues on a light railway plus the pedestrianisation and beautification of the centre; the harbour area is already revamped. (p162)

Roskilde Rocks

Roskilde's post-industrial Musicon district is a crucible of creativity; here, the inspired Ragnarock houses a super-interactive rock-and-roll museum that plays to a virtual Roskilde Festival crowd. (p110)

Capital Digs

Copenhagen's accommodation scene has a string of new options, including vintage-inspired Hotel Danmark. Most extraordinary is **The Krane** (https://thekrane.dk), a luxury retreat in a former coal crane. (p67)

Nyborg Reborn

Disputing the title of 'Denmark's first capital' with Roskilde, Nyborg is making a concerted effort to gain attention and has started the country's first castle (re)building project for centuries. (p171)

West Coast Action

Klitmøller (p263), aka Cold Hawaii, has seen a spike in interest, while the Wadden Sea area is winning more fans thanks to its Unesco World Heritage status. New museum showstoppers reside near Ribe (p203) and at Tirpitz (p209).

Architectural Prowess

In Copenhagen, Blox is a striking harbourside complex designed by Dutch architect Rem Koolhaas. One of its new residents is the Dansk Arkitektur Center, which runs modern-architecture tours of the city. (p46)

For more recommendations and reviews, see lonelyplanet.com/denmark

If You Like...

Viking History

Roskilde Compare the museum's five genuine Viking ship remains with seaworthy reconstructions moored outside. (p110)

Lejre Explore the fascinating experimental archaeology centre 'Land of Legends'. (p116)

Ladby Discover an unearthed ship grave, where a chieftain was laid to rest in a splendid warship. (p173)

Trelleborg See an enigmatic circular fortress constructed in the 10th century and built to a precise mathematical plan. (p125)

Ribe An informative museum as well as a fun village recreation – with warrior training! (p205)

Jelling The royal seat of King Gorm during the Vikings' most dominant era. (p221)

Aalborg The atmospheric Viking burial ground at Lindholm Høje. (p250)

Copenhagen Rune stones and unearthed Viking loot on show at Nationalmuseet. (p45)

Architecture & Design

Amager Bakke Copenhagen is already Denmark's architecture and design mother lode. Now comes this mad-genius waste-to-energy plant, soon to feature a ski slope and hiking on its roof. (p58)

Aalborg Visit Jørn Utzon's striking waterfront centre plus an art museum designed by Finnish great Alvar Aalto. (p250)

Kolding The Trapholt modern art and design museum incorporates Arne Jacobsen's one-of-a-kind prototype summerhouse. (p194)

Tønder A converted water tower showcases the fabulous chairs of home-grown design hero Hans Wegner. (p198)

Aarhus A modernist, Jacobsen-designed town hall, an art museum topped by a rainbow walkway, and apartments that resemble an iceberg. (p227)

Bilund Behold the new Lego House – a genius design that resembles a stack of gigantic Lego bricks. (p217)

Helsingør Prolific Bjarke Ingels' maritime museum, cleverly built into a dry dock. (p95)

Islands

Bornholm Lose yourself in nature and nosh on this Baltic summer playground. (p144)

Møn Find lesser-visited approaches to the famous white cliffs of Møns Klint. (p134)

Læsø Check out salty traditions and unwind in a restorative salt bath. (p255)

Nyord Watch stars or birds from the free observation tower of this charming one-village getaway. (p133)

Ærø Cycle between character-filled towns rich in seafaring tradition. (p187)

Fanø Observe the metaphorical distance between industrial Esbjerg and beguiling Fanø. (p211)

Rømø Choose your pace – gentle (horse riding) or wind-whipped (blokarts and kite buggies). (p200)

Mandø Take a tractor ride to this tiny island in the Wadden Sea National Park. (p203)

Outdoor Activities

Copenhagen City jogging tours, cycling tours and kayaking tours, plus stylish swimming spots on the main canal. (p61)

Lake District Hire canoes to paddle lakes and rivers between rolling hills and lovely beech forests. (p222)

Bornholm An island full of worthy destinations linked by cycling trails. (p143)

Hvide Sande Fill your surfing sails with the wild winds or learn to water ski. (p216)

Rebild Bakker Walking trails and mountain-bike tracks in rolling rural forests. (p245)

Klitmøller Waves to conquer and winds to tame thanks to well-organised surfing and windsurfing schools. (p263)

Rømø Horse rides along the island's shoreline, or kite buggies and blokarts zipping across the sand. (p201)

Svendborg Kayaking, scuba diving and sailing on old wooden schooners in the pretty sounds around the South Funen Archipelago. (p182)

Wadden Sea National Park Bird-watch, harvest oysters and explore mudflats in this fun natural playground. (p202)

Møn Hiking the extensive web of Camønoen trails is a great way to see the island. (p130)

Esrum Sø Go kayaking or boating on the lake then meander the nearby woodland trails of glorious Gribskov. (p106)

Family Attractions

Copenhagen Headliners are Tivoli amusement park and Den Blå Planet aquarium. (p93)

Billund Plastic-fantastic LEGOLAND Billund plus Lalandia waterpark. (p217)

Odense The city that gave birth to children's literature by way of Hans Christian Andersen. (p162)

Vordingborg Hunt down virtual ghosts amid castle ruins. (p123)

Randers Home to a magnificent man-made rainforest. (p244)

Djursland A plethora of amusement parks, theme parks, safari parks and beaches. (p241)

Knuthenborg One of northern Europe's best safari parks. (p141)

Top: HC Andersens Hus, birthplace of Hans Christian Andersen (p162), Odense
Bottom: Jogging around Copenhagen (p66)

Month by Month

TOP EVENTS

Roskilde Festival, July

Copenhagen Jazz Festival, July

Aarhus Festival, August

Kulturnatten, October

Christmas Fairs, December

February

Midwinter in Denmark can be scenic under snow and in sunshine, but more likely grey and gloomy, with a few events to brighten the mood. A midterm school holiday sees many locals head north to ski.

☆ Vinterjazz

Danes love their summer jazz festivals; in February, those suffering from jazz withdrawal can get their fix from this smaller-scale event (www.jazz.dk) held at cosy venues countrywide.

Winter in Tivoli

New in 2018, Copenhagen's Tivoli (www.tivoligardens. com) will get its winter sparkle on, opening for three weeks and covering the local school break, plus Valentine's Day. Visit for *hyggelig* charm, ice-skating and fairy lights.

April

Spring has sprung! Warmer, drier days bring out the blossoms, and attractions that were closed for the winter reopen (including LEGOLAND Billund at the start of the month).

🏃 Sort Sol

The marshlands of the west-coast Wadden Sea provide food and rest for millions of migratory birds, and in late March and April (and again in September and October) huge formations of starlings put on a brilliant natural show known as the 'Sort Sol' (Black Sun; p203).

May

The sun comes out on a semi-permanent basis, more warm-weather attractions open, and the events calendar starts filling as Danes throw off winter's gloom. Tourists have yet to arrive in great numbers.

3 Days of Design

Copenhagen's design fest (www.3daysofdesign.dk) celebrates the country's uncanny knack for producing clever, functional, easy-on-the-eye pieces. There are special events, exhibitions and product launches, plus access to design studios and showrooms.

Aalborg Carnival

In late May, Aalborg kicks up its heels hosting the biggest carnival celebrations in northern Europe (www.aalborgkarneval.dk), when up to 100,000 participants and spectators shake their maracas and paint the town red.

🍷 Ølfestival

Specialist beer and microbrewing are booming in Denmark. This is the country's largest beer festival (http://beerfestival.dk), held over three days in mid-May in the capital and drawing thousands of thirsty attendees.

June

Hello summer! Denmark's festival pace quickens alongside a rising temperature gauge and longer daylight hours. The main tourist season begins in earnest in late June, when schools break for a seven-week vacation.

Distortion

Known to get a little crazy, Distortion (www.cphdis

tortion.dk) is a celebration of the capital's nightlife, with the emphasis on clubs and DJs. It's a five-day mobile street party, rolling through a different Copenhagen neighbourhood each day.

 Fanø Kite-Flying

In mid-June, the beaches of windy Fanø host a super-photogenic festival attracting kite-fliers from all over the world (www.kitefliers meetingfanoe.de).

Midsummer Eve

The Danes let rip on the longest day of the year (23 June), known as Sankt Hans Aften (St Hans Evening), with bonfires in parks, gardens and, most popular of all, on the beaches. They burn an effigy of a witch on the pyre, sing songs and get merry.

☆ NorthSide

A three-day midmonth music event (www.north side.dk) in Aarhus that's building a big reputation – line-ups rival the legendary Roskilde Festival.

☆ Riverboat Jazz Festival

Jutland's bucolic Lake District, centred on Silkeborg, comes alive with five days of jazz (www.riverboat.dk). It's not quite New Orleans but you can buy a ticket and take a cruise down the river, or stroll the streets and enjoy the free performances.

Sol over Gudhjem

Bornholm is home to Denmark's biggest one-day cook-off (the name translates as 'Sun over Gudhjem'; www.sogk.dk). It sees some of the country's best chefs battle it out using fine local produce. It's a growing hit with visitors and is broadcast on TV.

☆ Tinderbox

Not to be outdone by Copenhagen and Aarhus, Odense now hosts its own three-day music fest (www.tinderbox.dk), bringing big-name international acts to 35,000 fans in a woodland venue on the town's outskirts.

◉ Esrum Fair

At the end of June, the grounds of Esrum Kloster (www.esrum.dk), once one of Denmark's greatest monasteries, hosts a major medieval fair full of activities and costumed players.

July

Many Danes take their main work holiday during the first three weeks of July, so expect busy seaside resorts, chock-a-block camping grounds and near-full coastal hotels – book ahead to join in on the beachy summer-holiday vibe.

☆ Copenhagen Jazz Festival

This swingin' party (www.jazz.dk) is the biggest annual entertainment event in the capital. For your sensory pleasure there are 10 days of Danish and international jazz, blues and fusion music. In 2017, 1400 concerts were staged at more than 120 venues.

Rebild Festival

One for the Americans, the Rebild Festival (www.rebildfesten.dk) is an annual July 4th celebration (held since 1912) that is among the biggest outside the USA. It's held in the forested hills of Rebild Bakker and features musicians and high-profile guest speakers (Danish and American).

☆ Roskilde Festival

Roskilde is rocked by Scandinavia's largest music festival for a week in early July, with major international acts and some 130,000 music fans (many camping on-site). It's renowned for its relaxed, friendly atmosphere. (p113)

Skagen Festival

Skagen acts as a magnet in summer, drawing well-heeled holidaymakers to Jutland's far-northern tip. Held over four days in early July, this festival (www.skagenfestival.dk) entertains with quality folk and world music.

◉ Viking Moot

You can unleash your inner pillager at a Viking-style market (www.moesgaard museum.dk) outside Aarhus in late July. There are crafts, food and equestrian events, plus Vikings of all nationalities competing to outfight each other.

August

Summer continues unabated, with beaches and theme parks packed to the gills, and the populace determined to wring every last ray of sunshine out of the season. School resumes around midmonth.

✸ Aarhus Festival

Denmark's second city dons its shiniest party gear at the end of August, when this festival (www.aarhus festival.com) transforms the town for 10 days, celebrating music, food, short film, theatre, visual arts and outdoor events for all ages (many of which are free).

✖ Copenhagen Cooking & Food Festival

The world's foodie lens seems trained on Copenhagen of late, and this 10-day food festival (Scandinavia's largest) focuses on the gourmet end of the food spectrum and is held in venues and restaurants throughout the city. See www.copen hagencooking.dk.

✸ Copenhagen Pride

Out and proud since 1996, this week-long festival (www.copenhagenpride.dk) brings Carnival-like colour to the capital, culminating in a gay-pride march. Needless to say, there's lots of dancing and flirting.

✸ HC Andersen Festivals

Of course Odense honours its home-grown literary hero – this week-long program (www.hcafestivals. com) in mid-August features plenty of Hans Christian Andersen performances and lectures, plus concerts, comedy and family-friendly events.

☆ Shakespeare Festival

Helsingør's grand Kronborg Slot was made famous as the Elsinore Castle of Shakespeare's *Hamlet*. Every summer it hosts outdoor productions – the festival does more than just perform *Hamlet,* with different plays by the Bard each year (www.hamlet scenen.dk).

☆ Smukfest

This midmonth music marvel in Skanderborg bills itself as Denmark's most beautiful festival (www. smukfest.dk; p234), and is second only to Roskilde in terms of scale. It takes place in lush parkland in the scenic Lake District.

☆ Strøm

Copenhagen's four-day electronic music festival (www. stromcph.dk) is considered the best of its kind in Scandinavia. Events include workshops and masterclasses, concerts, raves and parties across the city.

☆ Tønder Festival

Regarded as one of Europe's best folk-music festivals, this south Jutland shindig (www.tf.dk) draws some 20,000 attendees to its celebration of folk and roots music, and is renowned for its friendly, fun atmosphere.

September

The summer madness drops off as abruptly as it began, and crowds have largely disappeared. Good weather is still a possibility, but by month's end many big outdoor attractions have wrapped things up for another year.

☆ CPH PIX

Held over two weeks from late September, this is Copenhagen's feature-film festival (www.cphpix.dk). Expect flicks from Denmark and abroad, as well as a busy program of film-related events.

◉ Code Art Fair

This major art fair (www. codeartfair.dk) in Copenhagen sees the participation of around 60 leading international art galleries, and showcases a number of contemporary artists from Nordic Europe.

October

Summer is a distant memory, with the weather crisp and cool and the countryside taking on a golden tinge. Business travellers outnumber those travelling for pleasure.

☆ Copenhagen Blues Festival

If the shorter days have you feeling blue, this five-day international event (www. copenhagenbluesfestival. dk) should suit, with dozens of toe-tapping concerts staged at venues around the capital.

✸ Kulturnatten (Culture Night)

Usually held on the second Friday in October, this wonderful, atmospheric event (www.kulturnatten. dk) sees Copenhagen's museums, theatres, galleries, libraries, churches and even palaces throw open their doors through the night with a wide range of special events.

November

Winter is coming, daylight hours are shorter, but to offset the gloom, Christmas festivities are under way by the end of the month.

👁 Tivoli

Copenhagen's Tivoli (p44) reopens for Christmas (in mid-November) with a large market and buckets of schmaltz. Attractions include special Christmas tableaus, costumed staff and theatre shows. Fewer rides are operational but the traditional *gløgg* (mulled wine) and *æbleskiver* (spherical pancakes) ought to be ample compensation.

December

Sure, the weather is cold and damp, but Denmark cranks up the *hygge* (cosiness) and celebrates Christmas in style: twinkling lights, ice-skating rinks and gallons of warming *gløgg* (mulled wine).

🔒 Christmas Fairs

Fairs are held countrywide throughout December, with booths selling sometimes-kitschy arts and crafts, and traditional Yuletide foodie treats. For an idyllic, olden-days atmosphere, visit somewhere with a strong connection to the past: Den Gamle By in Aarhus, or historic Ribe in southern Jutland.

Top: Copenhagen Pride (p67)

Bottom: Carpark North performs at Smukfest (p234), Skanderborg

Itineraries

 Denmark's Classic Hits

Denmark's compact size means that it never takes too long to get from A to B. To cover the classic sites, start in **Copenhagen** and soak up the riches (cultural, culinary, retail) of the capital. From there, it's a short hop west to **Roskilde** to investigate Denmark's royal and Viking heritage. Further west, **Odense** offers up fairy-tale charm in abundance and plenty of ways to connect with the city's famous native son, Hans Christian Andersen.

Stop in **Kolding** for a polished mix of the old and the cutting-edge, en route to history-soaked **Ribe**, Denmark's oldest town, oozing with chocolate-box appeal. Pause on the history lessons with a hefty dose of childhood nostalgia investigating Lego-themed treats in **Billund**, then some lakeside R&R in **Silkeborg** – go canoeing or take a cruise through the area's picturesque lakes. Squeeze in a quick hop north to luminous **Skagen** for art, beaches and fresh seafood.

Finish up in cosmopolitan **Aarhus**. The country's second city holds a few surprises, not least its rainbow-topped art museum. From Aarhus you could take a ferry back to northwestern Zealand.

 Denmark in Detail

Got some time up your sleeve and a desire to delve deep into Denmark?

Allocate **Copenhagen** some quality time, adding day trips outside the capital to see superb modern art at the Louisiana Museum in **Humlebæk** and magnificent castles such as Kronborg Slot at **Helsingør** and Frederiksborg at **Hillerød**. Heading south, potter about pretty, historic **Køge**, then catch a ferry out to the Baltic bombshell of **Bornholm** – spend a few days exploring the island's bike trails, sandy beaches and gastronomic treats. Return via Zealand to **Møn**, an enchanting island whose exalted white-chalk cliffs rise sharply above a jade-green sea.

Re-cross southern Zealand to Funen, where **Odense** celebrates home-town hero Hans Christian Andersen. Take time to visit the Viking-ship grave at **Ladby** and the Renaissance treats of **Egeskov Slot**, then sail to the friendly old seafaring island of **Ærø** where a day or two will recharge your batteries.

West-bound ferries via **Als** lead on to southern Jutland, where **Ribe** provides history lessons with a decidedly friendly face (mock Viking settlements, a night watchman's tour of the cobbled streets), plus some great birdwatching and fresh-air fun at the Wadden Sea National Park. Jump on a boat out of Esbjerg for the 12-minute trip to idyllic **Fanø**, and take a pause in the idyllic hamlet of Sønderho.

LEGOLAND Billund and the new Lego House at **Billund** squeeze remarkable creativity from the humble plastic brick. Then it's back to the west coast for North Sea kitesurfing at **Hvide Sande**.

From here, wend your way east via leafy, lakeside **Silkeborg** to **Aarhus** for top-notch museum-mooching and gourmet treats. The rejuvenated northern city of **Aalborg** warrants a stop for its Utzon architecture and a Viking burial ground. But arguably the best comes last at cinematic **Skagen**, hugging Denmark's northernmost tip. Make time to admire the artwork, indulge in fine seafood, soak in the mesmerising northern light and dip a toe in the angry seas.

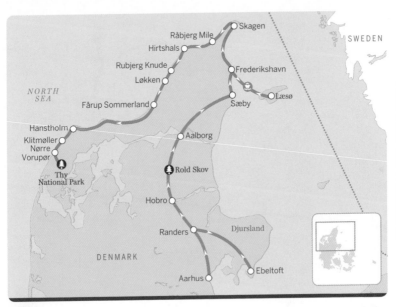

Northern Exposure

For some off-the-beaten-track seaside R&R, the underrated further reaches of northern Jutland beckon, with plenty of quirky treats complementing sun, sea, sand and seafood. Start from **Aarhus,** with its fine dining, ace festivals and snazzy museums (particularly rainbow-topped ARoS and head-turning Moesgaard), and head north, stopping in **Randers** for a man-made rainforested dome and a left-field dose of Elvis kitsch courtesy of a replica Graceland. With kids in tow, a detour to the safari parks and sandy beaches of Djursland is a must – but there's lots for grown-ups here too, particularly in the gourmet hotspots at Femmøller outside **Ebeltoft**.

Sleepy **Hobro** offers history in the shape of a 10th-century Viking ring fortress, while **Rold Skov** lets you cut loose on forested mountain-bike trails. **Aalborg** puts on its best face to impress you with a rejuvenated waterfront and the final design from revered architect Jørn Utzon. At sweet **Sæby** you can connect with Danish literature and go back for seconds at bountiful seafood buffets.

From **Frederikshavn**, catch a ferry to the island of **Læsø** to take a step back in time (salt baths optional). Next is **Skagen**, a delightful slice of seaside life with a stellar art museum, boutique hotels and alfresco dockside dining. Southwest of Skagen, the walkabout sand dunes of **Råbjerg Mile** let you know Mother Nature is still in charge, while in **Hirtshals** you can admire more of her handiwork at a huge aquarium. Check out the photogenic strand at **Løkken** and the precarious lighthouse at windswept **Rubjerg Knude**, then get your heart pumping with amusement rides and a waterpark at **Fårup Sommerland**.

Heading south, stop to inspect WWII-era bunkers and devour a fab lunch in **Hanstholm** before a visit to quirky 'Cold Hawaii' – the celebrated surfing village of **Klitmøller**, where you can get wet and windblown in various ways. Stop by the sea baths at nearby **Nørre Vorupør** and take to some walking or cycling trails through the dune heaths of **Thy National Park**. You'll return to Aarhus with the cobwebs well and truly blown away.

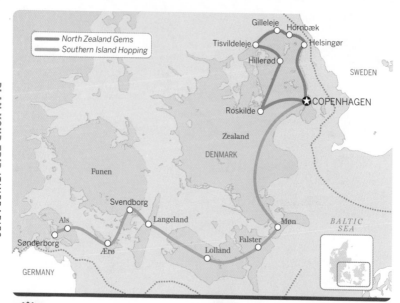

1 WEEK Southern Island Hopping

This meandering, slow-travel option offers rural retreats, quiet villages and plenty of salty island-hopping opportunities. From **Copenhagen** make a beeline for **Møn**, then cross **Falster** to **Lolland**. This trio known as Denmark's 'South Sea Islands' might lack any hint of a coconut palm, but they do offer a fine glimpse of rural Scandinavian island life: rolling fields, sandy beaches and rustic manor houses. Don't miss Møn's chalky cliffs, Falster's glorious Marielyst beach, and Lolland's family-focused parks and great farming estates.

A ferry brings you to **Langeland**, a sleepy stretch of green connected by road to Funen. From pretty Faaborg and from the yacht-filled harbour at **Svendborg**, a plethora of routes link the pint-sized islands of the South Funen Archipelago. The most enchanting is **Ærø**, well worth a visit for its maritime history, bike lanes, thatched farmhouses and postcard-perfect bathing huts. When you've had your fill, yet another ferry sails on from Ærø to **Als**, connected by road to **Sønderborg**. Now you're in the southeast corner of Jutland, with a whole peninsula to explore...

1 WEEK North Zealand Gems

This easy, accessible circuit of north Zealand offers glam beaches, royal remains, fairy-tale castles, Viking ships and cutting-edge architecture.

Start in fjord-side **Roskilde** with its Viking longships and a millennium's worth of Danish kings and queens buried within the country's finest cathedral. North from here, magnificent Frederiksborg Slot dominates the unassuming town of **Hillerød**. It's hard to decide which is more impressive, the baroque interiors or the regal grounds.

For northern light and sunbathing Scandi-style, head to the chic bathing hotels of **Tisvildeleje**, the seafood restaurants of **Gilleleje** and the kitesurfing beaches of **Hornbæk**, where the young and gorgeous go to appreciate beauty, both natural and their own. Historic port **Helsingør** offers much more than simply the castle-home of existential ditherer Hamlet: don't miss its stunningly designed national maritime museum. A short, picturesque coastal drive along the 'Danish Riviera' leads back to **Copenhagen** via the Louisiana Museum, noted for its architecture as much as for its vast collection of contemporary art.

Top: Cycling around Copenhagen (p42)

Bottom: Harbour at Svendborg (p179)

Plan Your Trip

The Great Outdoors

Denmark offers diverse activities, from island-hopping cycling adventures to Lake District canoeing. The sea, never far away, offers fishing, sailing and wind- and kitesurfing, while hiking trails are abundant. The cycling opportunities are outstanding, with more than 12,000km of signposted cycle routes, most of which traverse relatively quiet country roads.

Best of Outdoor Denmark

Best Time to Go

June to August. Having been cooped up in the cold weather, Denmark comes alive in summer, shaking off winter's grey blanket to catch a Scandi tan. May and September can also be good, weather-wise.

Best Cycling

For long-distance pedalling, any of the 11 national cycling routes is a fine choice. Leisurely island cycling is outstanding on Bornholm and Ærø. Looking to catch some air? Forested Rold Skov has mountain-biking tracks.

Best Walking

Scenic short walks take in the white cliffs of Møns Klint or the bucolic Lake District. For a longer ramble, the Hærvej Route covers Jutland's spine, while Øhavssti incorporates the South Funen Archipelago.

Best on the Water

Sailors flock to Svendborg – from here there's an archipelago to explore. Canoeists will love the lakes and rivers of the Lake District (regional hub: Silkeborg). Wind-powered water sports are big on the west coast – try Hvide Sande or Klitmøller.

Cycling

Denmark is a superb country for cyclists, with more than 12,000km of signposted cycle routes and relatively quiet country roads that wend through attractive, gently undulating landscapes.

As well as the Danes' use of cycling as a widespread means of commuting, you'll also see locals (and tourists) enjoying cycling holidays. The big draw for touring cyclists are the 11 national routes, which are in excellent condition, but there are oodles of regional and local routes to get you pedalling. The routes are well suited to recreational cyclists, including families with children.

Danish cyclists enjoy rights that, in most other countries, are reserved for motorists. There are bicycle lanes along major city roads and through central areas; road signs are posted for bicycle traffic; and bicycle racks can be found at grocery shops, museums, train stations and many other public places. Overall, cyclists and drivers coexist remarkably well.

When bicycle touring, accommodation is easy to find, be it at a small country inn or camping ground. One advantage of Denmark's small scale is that you're never far from a bed and a hot shower.

For quality rental bikes, Copenhagen and Aarhus are your best starting points, but you can generally rent bikes in every town – enquire locally. Note: you are not legally required to wear a helmet. Bikes are allowed on most trains, some buses and all ferries.

Cycling Routes

Signs along cycling routes are blue, with a white bike symbol. Note that many routes criss-cross each other, so it's possible to combine routes.

➡ **National routes** White route number in a red square. North–south routes have uneven numbers; east–west routes are even. There are two circular routes (10 and 12).

➡ **Regional routes** White route number on a blue background, with numbers 16 to 99.

➡ **Local routes** White route number on a blue background, with numbers 100 to 999.

Planning & Resources

The best way to tour Denmark by bike is by grabbing a map and planning it yourself. Tours are also available and are well run, although they tend to be rather pricey.

You can view a digital map of Denmark's cycle routes on the Danish Road Directorate's website (www.vejdirektoratet.dk), and download routes to GPS devices and your phone from www.denmarkbybike.dk. Visit Denmark produces the Bike & Stay app in four languages (Danish, English, Dutch and German). I Bike CPH is an app produced by the City of Copenhagen.

A newly updated series of eight cycle touring maps together cover all of Denmark. These are detailed 1:100,000 maps, accompanied by booklets detailing accommodation, sights and other local information. The maps are in Danish, German and English, cost around 149kr, and are available at tourist offices or online via the Danish Cycling Federation, Dansk Cyklist Forbund (its shop is at www.1905.dk). The 1:500,000-scale Cycling Map of Denmark (95kr), showing all the national routes, is very useful for general planning, but not detailed enough to use on the trail.

Websites

Cyclistic (http://cyclistic.dk/en/) Fabulous resource, combining route-finding for cyclists with attractions and practical information along the way (sights, accommodation, food etc).

CYCLING BORNHOLM

Out in the Baltic, the magical island of Bornholm is ideal for exploring by bike. Some 235km of bike trails cover main roads, extensive forests, former train routes and fine sandy beaches. There are picturesque coastal hamlets, medieval round churches and top-notch museums, and the excellent local food and drink are a great reward for pedalling.

Consider burning some calories from Gudhjem to Østermarie and on to Svaneke, stopping at shops producing chocolates, toffees and sweets; smokehouses; farm shops; a super cake cafe and a microbrewery.

The island's tourist offices stock a free cycling booklet, outlining routes of varying difficulty across the island.

Cycling Embassy of Denmark (www.cycling-embassy.dk) Has great info on cycling culture and some cool stats too – for example, nine out of 10 Danes own a bicycle, and 75% of bicycle traffic continues through the winter.

Dansk Cyklist Forbund (www.cyklistforbundet.dk) Website of the Danish Cycling Federation, with a helpful compilation of info and links.

Denmark by Bike (www.denmarkbybike.dk) Lots of assembled info: long and short routes, map recommendations, advice for families.

Visit Denmark (www.visitdenmark.com/cycling) A good starting point, with loads of useful information on its cycling-dedicated pages (including cycling with kids). It outlines 26 great 'panorama cycling routes' of 15km to 40km length, broken into east coast and west coast Denmark. Download its Bike & Stay app.

Swimming

Although the water temperature would worry even brass monkeys most of the year, enjoyable seaside swimming can be had in the warmer months (July and August). The quality of the beaches is outstanding as the majority have clean water, silky sand and plenty of room.

Generally speaking the Baltic waters (east coast) will be a degree or two warmer than those of the North Sea (west coast). If you're swimming on the west coast of

DENMARK'S NATIONAL CYCLING ROUTES

ROUTE NO	ROUTE NAME	DISTANCE	DESCRIPTION
1	Vestkystruten (West Coast Route)	560km (70% sealed)	Begins in Rudbøl (by the German border) and runs to Skagen along the windswept west coast of Jutland, taking in sandy beaches, tidal flats and dunes. See also www.northseacycleroute.dk.
2	Hanstholm-Copenhagen	420km (80% sealed)	Begins in the north Jutland fishing port of Hanstholm and runs southeast across central Jutland to Ebeltoft. The Ebeltoft–Odden ferry allows you to pick up the route again through northern Zealand to Copenhagen.
3	Hærvejsruten (Hærvej Route)	450km (78% sealed)	Heads from Skagen along the backbone of Jutland to Padborg on the German border. From Viborg it follows the Hærvej, an ancient trackway. See also www.haervej.dk.
4	Søndervig-Copenhagen	310km (90% sealed)	Runs from Søndervig on the west Jutland coast, east to Hou, then by ferry (via Samsø) across to Kalundborg, and east across Zealand to finish in Copenhagen.
5	Østkystruten (East Coast Route)	650km (90% sealed)	The longest route begins in Skagen and runs the length of Jutland, hugging the east coast to finish at Sønderborg.
6	Esbjerg-Copenhagen	330km (92% sealed)	Begins in Esbjerg and runs east through Funen and Zealand to finish in Copenhagen. Note: cyclists are not permitted on the 18km Storebælt bridge linking Funen and Zealand; you will need to take a train.
7	Sjællands Odde-Rødbyhavn	240km (90% sealed)	A family-friendly route that begins at Odden in northwest Zealand and travels south through north Falster and Lolland to end at Rødbyhavn.
8	Sydhavsruten (South Sea Route)	360km (95% sealed)	This trail sweeps across southern Denmark and requires a couple of island-hops. It begins in Rudbøl, traverses Jutland to Als, crosses to southern Funen, Langeland, Lolland, Falster and ends at Møns Klint.
9	Helsingør-Gedser	290km (92% sealed)	This route has links with Sweden and Germany thanks to ferry connections at its start (Helsingør) and end (Gedser) points. It follows the east coast of Zealand before tracking south through Møn and Falster.
10	Bornholm Rundt (Around Bornholm)	105km (90% sealed)	Bornholm is an idyllic island encircled by a popular cycling route.
12*	Limfjordsruten (Limfjord Route)	610km (90% sealed)	The route hugs both sides of the Limfjord in northern Jutland, from the Kattegat to the North Sea. Ferry and bridge 'shortcuts' across the fjord are possible.

*Note: there is no route 11.

Jutland, caution needs to be taken with currents and undertows; otherwise the waters are generally calm and child-friendly.

Aside from the miles of beaches (no place in Denmark is more than 52km from the coast), most towns have a family-focused aqua centre with heated pool – look for the *svømmehal* (swimming hall). These are becoming more grandiose, offering plenty of ways to wrinkle your skin (water slides, jacuzzis, saunas, kids' play area, day spas).

There are also summertime waterparks – incredibly popular are the aqua playlands of Lalandia, at Billund (p218) and Lolland (p143), and Sommerland, attached to amusement parks at Fårup (p263), near Løkken, and Djursland (p244).

Water Sports

The wild winds of Jutland's west coast have gained plenty of attention from windsurfers and kitesurfers, and the consistently good conditions attract many European enthusiasts to Klitmøller (aka 'Cold Hawaii', a nickname we love) and Hvide Sande.

Not only do these towns hold numerous contests each year, but they have great options for all skill levels. Experts can carve up the wild North Sea breakers, while beginners can master the basics on the inland fjords.

At both Klitmøller and Hvide Sande, outfits offer gear rental and lessons in windsurfing and kitesurfing. There are other water sports on offer, too – surfing

and stand-up paddle boarding. At Hvide Sande there's also a cool water-skiing course, which skiers navigate using cable rope-tows.

Other summer strands have fun options – you can learn to surf at Løkken, and sign up for courses to harness the wind in kites and sails at places like Hornbæk in northern Zealand, Balka on Bornholm, Marielyst on Falster and Sønderstrand on Rømø.

Sailing

Denmark's long (7314km) and varied coastline and 406 islands are made for sailing, something the Danes embrace enthusiastically.

The island-speckled, sheltered cruising area between Jutland's east coast and Sweden is very popular. The mixture of sea, calmer inshore waters and still fjords, combined with scores of pretty, cobbled and often historic harbours (more than 350 marinas) makes sailing a perfect way to explore the country. Yachts and motorboats equipped with all the necessary safety, living and navigational equipment can be hired – prices vary considerably by season and size of craft.

Charter a yacht through **Scancharter** (www.scancharter.com) or **JIM Søferie**

TOP BEACHES

Our writers have travelled the length and breadth of Denmark to bring you their favourite spots to take a dip.

Copenhagen (Islands Brygge; p65) Not technically a beach, but slap-bang in Copenhagen's main canal, this designer outdoor pool comes with downtown views and delectable eye candy.

Zealand (Tisvildeleje; p108) Sandbars, shallows and chic hotels on Zealand's north-coast 'riviera'.

Møn, Falster & Lolland (Marielyst, Falster; p139) Endless sandy beaches and a family-friendly holiday vibe.

Bornholm (Dueodde; p150) Soft endless sand, epic skies and a forest backdrop.

Funen (Vesterstrand, Ærø; p189) Swim and/or sunset-watch among the brightly painted bathing huts outside Ærøskøbing.

Southern Jutland (Rømø; p200) Miles of west-coast emptiness, plus hair-raising speed-machine activities down south.

Central Jutland (Hvide Sande; p216) Colourful wind- and kitesurfers harnessing the North Sea wind.

Northern Jutland (Skagen; p257) Wild winds and shifting sands to the west, calm family-friendly waters to the east, and everywhere are the blue hues that have inspired many artists.

'TIS THE SEASON

If you're thinking about visiting Denmark to partake of the outdoors, it's worth bearing in mind a few things. There's an old joke that Denmark has two winters – a green one and a white one – but that is rather unkind. While it's true the weather can be fickle, the summer season most reliably runs from mid-June to mid-August. That's when there are enough travellers around to ensure regular departures of boat cruises or frequent schedules of windsurfing classes etc, and hence there's a wider range of activity options during this two-month window. Depending on weather and demand, however, many operators may open in May and remain open until mid/late September.

And in winter...? Denmark is *not* a destination for winter-sports enthusiasts. The country's highest post is a trifling 171m. That's not to say that Danes don't love (or excel at) snowbound activity – it's just that many of them head north to Norway to engage in it.

(www.jim-soeferie.dk). The latter website also has a few tour suggestions. If hiring your own craft sounds too much like hard work, major towns along Funen's southern coast offer sailing cruises around the islands of the South Funen Archipelago. Svendborg is an excellent yachting hub.

Canoeing & Kayaking

Canoeists and kayakers can paddle the extensive coastline and fjords or the rivers and lakes. White water is about the only thing that's missing in mountain-free Denmark.

The country's best canoeing and kayaking can be experienced along the rivers Gudenå (in Jutland) and Suså (in Zealand). The idyllic forests and gentle waterways of central Jutland's prized Lake District are perfect for cycling, rambling and, especially, canoeing – multiday canoeing-and-camping adventures are possible here. You can hire canoes and equipment in Silkeborg. The lakes are generally undemanding as far as water conditions go, although some previous experience is an advantage.

Canoeing the small coves, bays and peninsulas of several Danish fjords is also an option, including Limfjorden in northern Jutland, Stege Fjord on Møn and the fjords of Zealand: Roskilde Fjord, Holbæk Fjord and Isefjord. Kayaking Svendborg Sound is also an intriguing option.

Walking

There's not much wilderness in wee Denmark (especially in comparison to its larger, more mountain-endowed neighbours), and walking or hiking is not as widespread a phenomenon as cycling. But rambling is popular nonetheless, and all local tourist offices will be able to point you in the direction of a local area with walking trails.

In Jutland, there are some picturesque trails through the forested Rold Skov area, the Mols Bjerge and Thy National Parks, and the bucolic Lake District.

The 220km Øhavssti (Archipelago Trail; p175) is a long-distance walking trail spanning Funen and the islands to its south. It snakes its way from west to east Funen along the southern coast, then traverses northern Langeland. It concludes with a delightful 36km stretch across Ærø's countryside.

An increasing number of hikers are heading to Møn to walk the well-organised network of trails known as **Camønoen** (www.camoenoen.dk), named with a punning nod to the classic Camino pilgrim trail.

Shorter walks at or around scenic landmarks include the base of the chalk cliffs at Møns Klint; along the coast at Stevns Klint; to Grenen sand spit, Denmark's northernmost point; along Hammeren's heather-lined trails at the northern tip of Bornholm; and in the forests around 147m Himmelbjerget, one of Denmark's highest peaks.

Plan Your Trip
Travel with Children

Denmark is prime family holiday territory, especially in high season when family-filled camper vans hit the road to celebrate the summer break. Theme parks, amusement parks, zoos and child-friendly beaches are just part of the story – businesses go out of their way to woo families, and children are rarely made to feel unwelcome.

Denmark for Kids

Entry to most museums is free for kids, and you won't have to minimise your time in cultural attractions lest your offspring start climbing the walls – almost everywhere has displays and activities designed especially to keep kids entertained.

Travellers with children should enquire at local tourist offices – all regions have places where kids are king, from huge indoor swim centres to play centres and petting farms.

The larger theme parks and animal parks aren't particularly cheap, but most attractions have family passes and packages. Free entertainment can come in the form of long sandy beaches, parks and playgrounds.

Children's Highlights
Cultural Kids

Copenhagen Nationalmuseet (p45) has a brilliant hands-on children's section, while kids are spoiled at Louisiana (p92) with a wing of their own, where they can create artistic masterpieces.

Zealand The superb Viking Ship Museum (p110) in Roskilde displays five Viking ships; there's also Viking shipbuilding and the chance to go on a longboat cruise. M/S Museet for Søfart (p95), the

Best Regions for Kids
Copenhagen

Capital attractions include funpark-meets-fairy-tale Tivoli (p44), the swimming polar bears at the zoo (p61) and the insanely colourful fish of Den Blå Planet (p93).

Møn, Falster & Lolland

Chalk cliffs and a mind-bending geology centre (p134) on Møn, long beaches and a medieval village (p137) on Falster, and a safari park (p141) and waterpark (p143) on Lolland.

Funen

Odense pays homage to the tales of Hans Christian Andersen (p162). Plus there's a moat-encircled castle (p178) with mazes and marvels, and bunkers and battleships at a 1950s fort (p186).

Jutland

Plastic fantastic LEGOLAND Billund (p218) and new Lego House (p217) – need we say more? Close by are a waterpark and safari park, plus family canoeing opportunities and loads more amusement parks. Further north are endless sandy strands and shifting dunes that will put your sandcastles to shame, plus a mega-aquarium (p262) that reveals just what lies beneath.

36

PLAN YOUR TRIP TRAVEL WITH CHILDREN

national maritime museum in Helsingør, has vivid interactive exhibitions.

Funen At Fyrtøjet (p163), in Odense, kids get to explore the world of Hans Christian Andersen through storytelling and music. Egeskov Slot (p178) is a must – the summer program includes evening concerts, ghost hunts and fireworks.

Central Jutland Aarhus' art museum (p230) will wow kids with its giant *Boy* sculpture and awesome rooftop rainbow walkway. Kvindemuseet (p232) has hands-on kids' exhibits in its 'History of Childhood' section.

Fun Parks & Theme Parks

Copenhagen Tivoli (p44) is a charming combination of amusement rides, flower gardens, food pavilions, carnival games and open-air stage shows. Bakken (p61) is its poorer relation but still provides loads of old-fashioned fun.

Møn, Falster & Lolland Lalandia (p143) on Lolland undersells itself with the label 'waterpark'.

Central Jutland LEGOLAND Billund (p218) is the big daddy of Danish theme parks, joined by Lalandia (p218) as its neighbour. Aarhus has Tivoli Friheden (p233) for rides and games, and Djurs Sommerland (p244) has the blockbuster combo of waterpark and amusement park in one super-popular attraction.

Northern Jutland Djurs Sommerland's northern sister is Fårup Sommerland (p263), equally popular and home to a waterpark and amusement rides.

Animal Encounters

Copenhagen The zoo (p61) houses a multitude of critters, and some lovely architect-designed homes for them – including a polar bear enclosure with glass tunnel. Den Blå Planet (p93) takes its fishy business seriously.

Møn, Falster & Lolland Knuthenborg Safari Park (p141) on Lolland has a drive-through savannah area for a taste of Africa (but with lousier weather).

Bornholm The Sommerfuglepark (p150) showcases jungle climates and has more than 1000 butterflies.

Funen Odense Zoo (p165) has an African area for junior explorers.

Central Jutland Randers Regnskov (p244) is a sultry, dome-enclosed tropical zoo taking you to Africa, Asia and South America. At Skandinavisk Dyrepark (p244) you can assess a full collection of

Scandi species, including polar bears and brown bears. Silkeborg's Aqua (p223) has an abundance of fish and cute otters.

Northern Jutland Aalborg has a quality zoo (p250), while Hirtshals is home to one of the largest aquariums (p262) in northern Europe.

Time Travel

The Danes have a seemingly limitless enthusiasm for dressing up and recreating history, and they do it well in countless open-air museums and recreated Viking camps and medieval villages, all with activities for youngsters.

Zealand The experimental archaeology centre of Sagnlandet Lejre (p116), 'Land of Legends', is fascinating. Danmarks Borgcenter (p123) in Vordingborg lets kids explore medieval castle life and the world of kings using iPad technology.

Møn, Falster & Lolland Falster's Middelaldercentret (p137) recreates an early-15th-century medieval village.

Bornholm Oh look, it's another ye-olde village: Bornholms Middelaldercenter (p156) recreates a medieval fort and village.

Funen Den Fynske Landsby (p163) is a recreated olden-days country village with the requisite costumes and farmyard animals.

Southern Jutland Ribe VikingeCenter (p205) recreates the Viking era in Denmark's oldest town; finish the day with a walk alongside the town's nightwatchman (p207).

Central Jutland Den Gamle By (p231), 'The Old Town', in Aarhus is a photogenic open-air museum. Hobro has a Viking-era farmstead (p246) to complement its Viking fortress.

Fresh-Air Fun

Copenhagen Amager Strandpark (p65) is a sand-sational artificial lagoon, with acres of sandy beach. Playground facilities and shallow water make it ideal for children. Plus, you can't visit Copenhagen and *not* take a canal boat trip (p61).

Zealand Roskilde's Viking Ship Museum (p110) runs sailing trips on the fjord. The beautiful beaches of northern Zealand are great for summertime fun.

Møn, Falster & Lolland On Falster, Marielyst (p139) is home to family-oriented activities as well as a seemingly endless sandy beach; take a boat trip to see the white cliffs of Møns Klint (p134).

Bornholm The calm and shallow waters of the sweeping beach at Dueodde (p150) suit families to a T.

Funen The grounds of Egeskov Slot (p178) are full of fun diversions, while Svendborg offers sailing trips and a forested park (p179) full of ropeways and zip lines.

Southern Jutland The Wadden Sea National Park (p203) has ace tidal tours exploring the mudflats, while for older kids, Rømø's southern beach (p201) is full of windblown speed treats.

Central Jutland Canoeing and camping in the picturesque Lake District (p222) make for undeniably wholesome family fun.

Northern Jutland Loads of beaches, mega sand dunes at Rubjerg Knude (p263) and Råbjerg Mile (p257), and a tractor-pulled bus ride (p258) to Denmark's northernmost tip.

Planning

Transport

➡ Having your own set of wheels will make life easier, but public transport shouldn't be dismissed – on trains, children under 12 years travel free if they are with an adult travelling on a standard ticket (each adult can take two children free).

➡ A cycling holiday may be doable with slightly older kids, as the terrain is flat and distances between towns are not vast. Larger bicycle-rental outfits have kids trailers and kids bikes for rent.

Useful Websites

The official websites visitdenmark.com and visitcopenhagen.com have pages dedicated to family holidays – lists of kid-approved attractions, child-friendly restaurants, ace playgrounds in the capital and much more.

When to Go

The best time for families to visit Denmark is the best time for any traveller – between May and September. Local school holidays run from late June to mid-August. On the plus side, at this time, good weather is likely (though never assured), all attractions and activities are in full swing, and your kids are likely to meet other kids. On the downside, beaches and attractions are busy, and camping grounds and hostels are heavily in demand (and also charge peak prices).

Where to Eat

On the whole, Danish restaurants welcome children with open arms. Virtually all offer high chairs, many have a *børnemenu* (children's menu) or will at least provide children's portions, and some have play areas. Two family-focused chains to look for are the steak chain **Jensen's Bøfhus** (www.jensens.com) and the US-influenced **Bone's** (www.bones.dk), with a menu of spare ribs, burgers and barbecued chicken. Both chains offer extensive kids menus and all-you-can-eat ice-cream bars – bonus! Food halls are a good choice, too, as they cater to all diners.

Self-catering will be a breeze if you are staying somewhere with kitchen facilities – larger supermarkets will stock all you'll need (including baby items). There are oodles of prime picnic spots.

Where to Stay

In high season (mid-June to mid-August) camping grounds are hives of activity, and many put on entertainment and activity programs for junior guests.

Hostels are exceedingly well set up for, and welcoming to, families. Rooms often sleep up to six (usually in bunks); there will invariably be a guest kitchen and lounge facilities. Farm stays may offer a rural idyll and/or the chance to get your hands dirty.

In resorts, summer houses are available at a reasonable price (usually by the week). In cities that are emptier due to the summer exodus, business hotels may drop their rates and add bunks to rooms to woo family business.

Regions at a Glance

Copenhagen

....

Food
Design
Museums & Galleries

....

New Nordic or Old Danish

Copenhagen is one of the world's hottest culinary destinations, home to visionary chefs concocting uniquely Nordic dishes. At the other end of the spectrum, old-school cafes and historic restaurants allow you to (re)discover classic like traditional smørrebrød.

Top Marks for Design

Check out architectural show-stealers like the Black Diamond library extension and Operaen; admire town planning that makes this city so damn user-friendly; and browse museums dedicated to local output that changed the way the world designs and decorates.

Calling Culture Vultures

For a whistle-stop tour through the country's history, nothing beats the Nationalmuseet; fine art excels at Statens Museum for Kunst and Ny Carlsberg Glyptotek. Out of town you can ogle modern art in modern architectural marvels, then take the pulse of the current art scene in fab city galleries.

p42

Zealand

....

Castles
Viking History
Beaches

....

Crowning Glories

Most visitors gravitate to Helsingør's magnificent Kronborg Slot, otherwise known as Elsinore, home of Shakespeare's indecisive anti-hero, Hamlet. But don't ignore Frederiksborg Slot, a glorious Dutch Renaissance–style confection. Divine Dragsholm Slot combines food and finery with aplomb.

Investigate the Viking Era

Got a thing for rugged, hirsute marauders? Be wowed by Viking ships at Roskilde, ponder the enigmatic ring fortress at Trelleborg, and get swept into the Iron Age lifestyle at the experimental archaeology centre outside Lejre.

Coastal Capers

Gorgeous white-sand beaches attract summer bathers and kitesurfers to northern escapes like Hornbæk and Tisvildeleje. Coastal trails lead past the cliffs of Stevns Klint to a fascinating Cold War–era fortress-museum.

p94

Møn, Falster & Lolland

Landscapes
Family Attractions
Arts & Crafts

Elevated Heights

You may notice that Denmark is rather flat. So Møn's striking white-chalk cliffs, rising 128m above a milky sea, are beloved of scenery-seekers. The cliffs are one of Denmark's most famous landmarks – take a hike or boat trip to check them out.

Family Fun

This predominantly agricultural island trio also draws summer-sun-seeking families with a family 'activity' beach zone, a re-created medieval village experience, a waterpark and an excellent safari park.

Møn Artistry

Møn is a magnet for artists and potters, keen to tap into the inspiration offered by cliffs, coastline and clay soils. Their works are on display in various studios and galleries, and you can admire wondrous art from an altogether different era in ancient, fresco-adorned churches.

p128

Bornholm

Beaches
Food
Cycling

Bathing Beauties

This Baltic outpost is encircled by beaches, but Dueodde justifiably hogs the limelight: a vast stretch backed by pine trees and expansive dunes. Its soft sand is so fine-grained it was once used in hourglasses and ink blotters.

Culinary Offerings

The productive island is home to historic fish smokehouses, first-class organic produce, a brace of fine-dining restaurants (Kadeau is Michelin-starred), and an ever-expanding league of food artisans, creating treats from ice creams and caramels, to hams and microbrews.

Cycling Bliss

More than 230km of bike trails cover main roads, forests, former train routes and beaches. There are a multitude of picturesque coastal hamlets and medieval round churches, and the excellent local food and drink are your reward for pedalling some gently undulating landscape.

p144

Funen

Castles
Fairy Tales
Islands

To the Manor Born

Dozens of castles and manor houses dot Funen. The big daddy of them all is splendid Egeskov Slot, complete with moat and drawbridge, and summertime evening fireworks. Need more? Broholm Castle is an antique-filled moated masterpiece you can sleep in.

Once upon a Time...

A baby was born to a cobbler and a washerwoman, in 1805 in Odense. That baby went on to write fairy tales known and loved the world over. Odense honours home-grown Hans Christian Andersen in all manner of ways, including museums dedicated to the man and sculptures of his most famous stories.

Island-Hopping

This region includes a bevy of islands (90 of 'em!), some home to people, some just to birds, rabbits and deer. Island-hopping by ferry or yacht is a salt-sprayed pleasure, as is exploring nautical-but-nice Ærø.

p160

Southern Jutland

Historic Villages
Nature
Design

Picture-book Destinations

You want thatch-roofed houses, blooming gardens and cobblestone streets lined with boutiques, galleries and cafes? You need Ribe (Denmark's oldest town), Møgeltønder and the island of Fanø on your itinerary. Careful, you might overdose on *hygge* (cosiness).

Birdwatching Bliss

Stretching along Jutland's west coast is the marshy Wadden Sea National Park, ripe for exploration. Its tidal rhythms provide opportunities for seal-spotting, winter oyster-collecting and bountiful birdwatching.

Unlikely Designer Destinations

Admire Utzon architecture in modern Esbjerg, a brilliant design museum in suburban Kolding and, in a converted water tower in Tønder, a Wegner chair collection that will have design buffs drooling.

p192

Central Jutland

Activities
Family Attractions
Art

The Great Outdoors

Truly something for everyone: the Lake District has canoeing and rambling; the wild west coast offers first-class wind- and kitesurfing; and Rold Skov has excellent mountain biking. Aarhus is perfect for city cycling, while Djursland has long, pristine beaches.

Lego & Loads More

Did someone say Lego? Yes, Billund is the birthplace of the wondrous plastic brick. There's also some cool kid-oriented stuff in Aarhus, Randers has a brilliant man-made rainforest, and Djursland is prime holiday turf, brimming with amusement and safari parks.

Modern Art Marvels

Modern art struts its stuff in this region – prime viewing is *Your Rainbow Panorama* atop Aarhus' outstanding ARoS. You can admire gobsmacking glass-works in Ebeltoft, appreciate Asger Jorn's repertoire in Silkeborg, and ponder conceptual art in Herning.

p213

Northern Jutland

Landscapes
Beaches
Food

Mother Nature's Finest

Visitors can witness the region's natural beauty without needing to rough it: the shifting sands, the luminous light, the raging winds, the clashing waters. You'll understand why artists and writers have felt inspired here.

Beachy Keen

Both the east and west coasts draw holidaymakers to long sandy stretches – sometimes windy and woolly on the west, more sheltered on the east. Northernmost Skagen combines the best of both worlds, while surfers love Løkken and Klitmøller's celebrated waves.

Fresh Catch

At the *røgeri* (smokehouse) in Hanstholm, the harbourside buffets of Sæby, the chic restaurants of Skagen and the smart menus around Aalborg, you're left in little doubt – seafood is king here. And it's a worthy monarch, fresh as can be.

p248

On the
Road

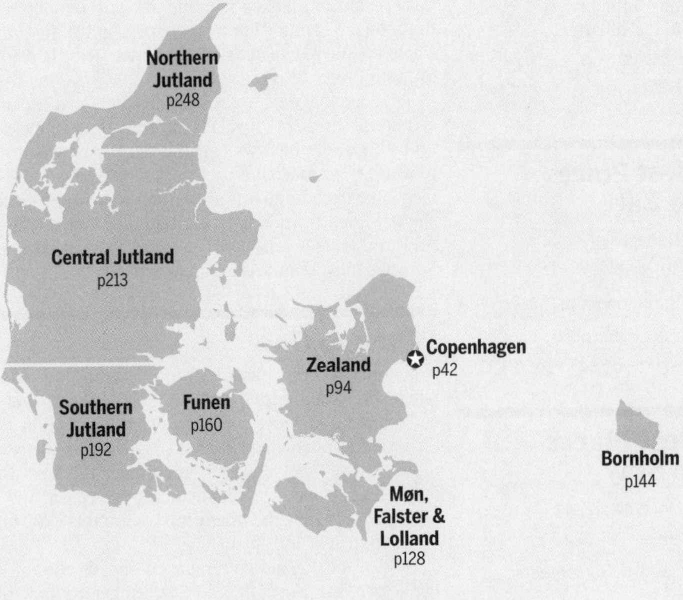

Northern
Jutland
p248

Central Jutland
p213

Southern
Jutland
p192

Funen
p160

Zealand
p94

Copenhagen
p42

Møn,
Falster &
Lolland
p128

Bornholm
p144

Copenhagen

AREA 1980 SQ KM / POP 1.7 MILLION

Best Places to Eat

➡ Kadeau (p77)

➡ Höst (p74)

➡ Schønnemann (p72)

➡ Paté Paté (p80)

➡ Manfreds og Vin (p78)

Best Places to Stay

➡ Hotel Alexandra (p68)

➡ Hotel Nimb (p68)

➡ Babette Guldsmeden (p69)

➡ Hotel Danmark (p68)

➡ Ibsens Hotel (p67)

Why Go?

Copenhagen is the coolest kid on the Nordic block. Edgier than Stockholm and worldlier than Oslo, the Danish capital gives Scandinavia the X factor. Just ask style bibles *Monocle* and *Wallpaper* magazines, which fawn over its industrial-chic bar, design and fashion scenes, and culinary revolution. This was home to world-famous New Nordic pioneer Noma (due to reopen in 2018), just one of 15 Michelin-starred restaurants in town – not bad for a city of 1.2 million.

Yet Copenhagen is more than just seasonal cocktails and geometric threads. A royal capital with almost nine centuries under its svelte belt, it's equally well versed when it comes to world-class museums and storybook streetscapes. Its cobbled, bike-friendly streets are a *hyggelig* (cosy) concoction of sherbet-hued town houses, craft studios and candlelit cafes. Add to this its compact size, and you have what is possibly Europe's most seamless urban experience.

When to Go

Arguably, the best time to drop by is from May to August, when the days are long and the mood upbeat. Events such as Distortion in June, Copenhagen Jazz Festival in July, and Strøm and Copenhagen Pride in August give the city a fabulous, festive vibe. However, in summer the tourist crowds are at their worst, accommodation prices peak, and gastronomes should note that many top restaurants close for several weeks in July and August.

Golden foliage and cultural events make autumn appealing, while late November and December counter the chill with Yuletide markets, twinkling lights and *gløgg* (mulled wine).

History

Copenhagen was founded in 1167 by tough-as-nails Bishop Absalon, who erected a fortress on Slotsholmen island, fortifying a small and previously unprotected harbour-side village.

After the fortification was built, the village grew in importance and took on the name Kømandshavn (Merchant's Port), which was later condensed to København. Absalon's fortress stood until 1369, when it was destroyed in an attack on the town by the powerful Hanseatic states.

In 1376 construction began on a new Slotsholmen fortification, Copenhagen Castle, and in 1416 King Erik of Pomerania took up residence at the site, marking the beginning of Copenhagen's role as the capital of Denmark.

Still, it wasn't until the reign of Christian IV, in the first half of the 17th century, that the city was endowed with much of its splendour. A lofty Renaissance designer, Christian IV began an ambitious construction scheme, building two new castles and many other grand edifices, including the Rundetårn observatory and the glorious Børsen, Europe's first stock exchange.

In 1711 the bubonic plague reduced Copenhagen's population of 60,000 by one-third. Tragic fires, one in 1728 and the other in 1795, wiped out large tracts of the city, including most of its timber buildings. However, the worst scourge in the city's history is generally regarded as the unprovoked British bombardment of Copenhagen in 1807, during the Napoleonic Wars. The attack targeted the heart of the city, inflicting numerous civilian casualties and setting hundreds of homes, churches and public buildings on fire.

Copenhagen flourished once again in the 19th and 20th centuries, expanding beyond its old city walls and establishing a reputation as a centre for culture, liberal politics and the arts. Dark times were experienced with the Nazi occupation during WWII, although the city managed to emerge relatively unscathed.

During the war and in the economic depression that had preceded it, many Copenhagen neighbourhoods had deteriorated into slums. In 1948 an ambitious urban renewal policy called the 'Finger Plan' was adopted; this redeveloped much of the city, creating new housing projects interspaced with green areas of parks and recreational facilities that spread out like fingers from the city centre.

A rebellion by young people disillusioned with growing materialism, the nuclear arms race and the authoritarian educational system took hold in Copenhagen in the 1960s. Student protests broke out on the university campus and squatters occupied vacant buildings around the city. It came to a head in 1971 when protesters tore down the fence of an abandoned military camp at the east side of Christianshavn and began an occupation of the 41-hectare site, naming this settlement Christiania.

In recent decades, major infrastructure projects, enlightened city planning and a wave of grassroots creativity have helped transform Copenhagen from a provincial Scandinavian capital into an enlightened international trendsetter. Not surprisingly, the city never fails to rank highly in quality-of-life surveys; in 2016 influential New York–based magazine *Metropolis* declared it the world's most liveable city.

Sights

One of the great things about Copenhagen is its size. Virtually all of Copenhagen's major sightseeing attractions – Tivoli Gardens, Nationalmuseet, Statens Museum for Kunst, Ny Carlsberg Glyptotek, Christiansborg, Christiania, Nyhavn, Marmorkirken, Amalienborg and Rosenborg – are in or close to the medieval city centre. Only the perennially disappointing Little Mermaid lies outside of the city proper, on the harbourfront.

Central Copenhagen

The eminently walkable central area stretches from the historic **Tivoli** pleasure garden to **Kongens Nytorv** and classic canal-side Nyhavn (p52). Crossing the centre west–east is a long string of five brashly commercial pedestrianised shopping streets known collectively as **Strøget**. Strøget starts from statue-rich **Rådhuspladsen**, a busy square where Copenhagen's former west gate once stood. To the north of Strøget is the atmospheric **Latin Quarter** (Map p48; 5C, 6A, 14, Nørreport, Nørreport), so nicknamed for the old campus of **Copenhagen University** (founded 1479) where Latin was once widely spoken. Here you'll find many historical sights, old pastel-hued buildings and postcard-pretty nooks like mid-17th century **Gråbrødretorv** (Grey Friars' Square). For panoramic city views, climb Rundetårn (p45), Europe's oldest functioning observatory-tower. North of the Latin Quarter are the parks and art

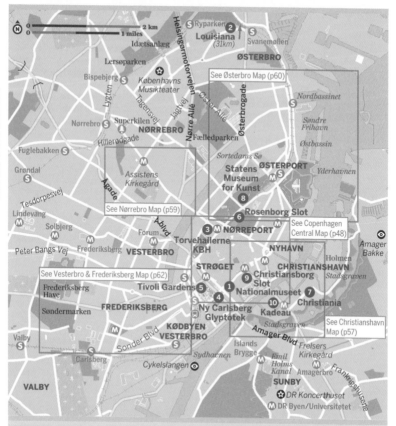

Copenhagen Highlights

1 Nationalmuseet
(p45) Learning about the Vikings at Denmark's National Museum.

2 Louisiana (p92)
Getting inspired at this extraordinary museum of modern and contemporary art.

3 Torvehallerne KBH
(p71) Enjoying all things seasonal, artisanal and scrumptious at this celebrated market.

4 Ny Carlsberg Glyptotek
(p45) Understanding the classical and the classics at this glorious art museum.

5 Tivoli Gardens (p44)
Indulging in thrills and spills at this vintage amusement park.

6 Rosenborg Slot
(p47) Believing that fairy tales can come true at this magnificent Renaissance palace.

7 Christiania (p56)
Letting your hair down in this free-spirited neighbourhood.

8 Statens Museum for Kunst (p47) Seeking out an impressive collection of paintings at Denmark's preeminent art museum.

9 Christiansborg Slot
(p53) Checking out Copenhagen's architectural phoenix.

10 Culinary Thrills Treating your taste buds at restaurants like **Kadeau** (p77).

collections of Nørreport (p47). South of Strøget, cross the canal to the attraction-packed Slotsholmen (p53) area.

★**Tivoli Gardens**   AMUSEMENT PARK
(Map p48; ☑ 33 15 10 01; www.tivoli.dk; Vesterbrogade 3; adult/child under 8yr 120kr/free, Fri after 7pm 160kr/free; ⊙ 11am-11pm Sun-Thu, to midnight

Fri & Sat early Apr-late Sep, reduced hours rest of year; ⓘ; 🚌2A, 5C, 9A, 12, 14, 26, 250S, Ⓢ København H) Dating from 1843, tasteful Tivoli wins fans with its dreamy whirl of amusement rides, twinkling pavilions, carnival games and open-air stage shows. Visitors can ride the renovated, century-old **roller coaster**, enjoy the famous Saturday evening **fireworks display** or just soak up the storybook atmosphere. A good tip is to go on Friday during summer when the open-air Plænen stage hosts free rock concerts by Danish bands (and the occasional international superstar) from 10pm – go early if it's a big-name act.

Indeed, Tivoli is at its most romantic after dusk, when the fairy lights are switched on, cultural activities unfold and the clock tower of the neighbouring Rådhus soars in the moonlight like the set of a classic Disney film.

Each of Tivoli's numerous entertainment venues has a different character. Perhaps best known is the open-air Pantomime Theatre, built in 1874 by Vilhelm Dahlerup, the Copenhagen architect who also designed the royal theatre. Tivoli's large concert hall features performances by international symphony orchestras and ballet troupes, as well as popular musicians. While the numerous open-air performances are free of charge, there's usually an admission fee for the indoor performances – check the website for venue details, line-ups and prices.

Amusement ride tickets cost 25kr (some rides require up to three tickets), making the unlimited-ride wristband (230kr) better value in most cases.

Outside the main summer season, Tivoli also opens for approximately three weeks around Halloween and from mid-November to early January for Christmas. For up-to-date opening times, see the Tivoli website.

★**Ny Carlsberg Glyptotek** MUSEUM
(Map p48; ☏33 41 81 41; www.glyptoteket.dk; Dantes Plads 7, HC Andersens Blvd; adult/child 95kr/free, Tue free; ◷11am-6pm Tue-Sun, until 10pm Thu; 🚌1A, 2A, 9A, 37, Ⓢ København H) Fin de siècle architecture meets with an eclectic mix of art at Ny Carlsberg Glyptotek. The collection is divided into two parts: Northern Europe's largest booty of antiquities, and a collection of 19th-century Danish and French art. The latter includes the largest collection of Rodin sculptures outside of France and no less than 47 Gauguin paintings. These are displayed along with works by greats like Cézanne, Van Gogh, Pissarro, Monet and Renoir.

At the museum's heart is a delightful glass-domed conservatory, replete with palm trees and a gorgeous cafe that's especially welcoming in the Danish winter.

An added treat for visitors is the August/September Summer Concert Series (admission around 75kr). Classical music is performed in the museum's concert hall, which is evocatively lined by life-size statues of Roman patricians. Concerts usually commence at noon on Sunday.

★**Nationalmuseet** MUSEUM
(National Museum; Map p48; ☏33 13 44 11; www.natmus.dk; Ny Vestergade 10; adult/child 75kr/free; ◷10am-5pm Tue-Sun, also open Mon Jul & Aug; ⓘ; 🚌1A, 2A, 9A, 14, 26, 37, Ⓢ København H) For a crash course in Danish history and culture, spend an afternoon at Denmark's National Museum. It has first claims on virtually every antiquity uncovered on Danish soil, including Stone Age tools, Viking weaponry, rune stones and medieval jewellery. Among the many highlights is a finely crafted 3500-year-old Sun Chariot, as well as bronze *lurs* (horns), some of which date back 3000 years and are still capable of blowing a tune.

You'll find sections related to the Norsemen and Inuit of Greenland, and an evocative exhibition called *Stories of Denmark,* covering Danish history from 1660 to 2000. Among the highlights here are recreated living quarters (among them an 18th-century Copenhagen apartment) and a whimsical collection of toys, including a veritable village of doll houses. The museum also has an excellent **Children's Museum** (Map p48; www.natmus.dk; Nationalmuseet, Ny Vestergade 10; ◷10am-4.30pm Tue-Sun; ⓘ; 🚌1A, 2A, 9A, 14, 26, 37, Ⓢ København H), as well as a classical antiquities section complete with Egyptian mummies.

Rådhuspladsen, the square outside, features several statues. Top-hatted Hans Christian Andersen sits gazing towards Tivoli. A fountain features a dragon-versus-bull fight. And on a tall pillar are a pair of Viking statues playing the *lur*, a ceremonial Norse Bronze Age instrument.

Rundetårn HISTORIC BUILDING
(Round Tower; Map p48; ☏33 73 03 73; www.rundetaarn.dk; Købmagergade 52; adult/child 25/5kr; ◷10am-8pm May-Sep, reduced hours rest of year, observatory times vary; 🚌14, Ⓜ Nørreport, Ⓢ Nørreport) Haul yourself to the top of the 34.8m-high red-brick 'Round Tower' and you will be following in the footsteps of such

COPENHAGEN SIGHTS

ℹ️ COPENHAGEN FOR FREE

Copenhagen has a reputation for being heavy on the budget, but many of its top sights are free for at least one day of the week. So zip up the wallet and head to the following spots, all of which are free all week unless a particular day is specified.

Assistens Kirkegård (p58)

Christiania (p56)

Churches, including **Vor Frue Kirke** (p46) and **Marmorkirken** (p53)

Davids Samling (p47)

Folketinget (p56)

Ny Carlsberg Glyptotek (p45) (free on Tuesday only)

Thorvaldsens Museum (p54) (free on Wednesday only)

V1 Gallery (p59)

luminaries as King Christian IV, who built it in 1642 as an observatory for the famous astronomer Tycho Brahe. You'll also be following in the hoofsteps of Tsar Peter the Great's horse and, according to legend, the track marks of a car that made its way up the tower's spiral ramp in 1902.

Rådhus
HISTORIC BUILDING

(City Hall; Map p48; ☎ 33 66 25 86; www.kk.dk; Rådhuspladsen; ⊙ 9am-4pm Mon-Fri, 9.30am-1pm Sat; 🚌 2A, 12, 14, 26, 33, 250S, 🚇 København H) **FREE** Completed in 1905, Copenhagen's national Romantic-style city hall is the work of architect Martin Nyrop. Inside is the curious **Jens Olsen's World Clock** (Map p48; ⊙ 9am-4pm Mon-Fri, 9.30am-1pm Sat) **FREE**, designed by astro mechanic Jens Olsen (1872–1945) and built at a cost of one million kroner. Not only does it display local time, but also solar time, sidereal time, sunrises and sunsets, firmament and celestial pole migration, planet revolutions, the Gregorian calendar and even changing holidays! You can also climb the 105m city hall **tower** (Map p48; 30kr; ⊙ tour 11am & 2pm Mon-Fri, noon Sat, minimum 4 people) for a commanding view.

Vor Frue Kirke
CATHEDRAL

(Map p48; ☎ 33 15 10 78; www.koebenhavnsdom kirke.dk; Nørregade 8; ⊙ 8am-5pm, closed during services & concerts; 🚌 14, 🚇 Nørreport, 🚊 Nørreport) Founded in 1191 and rebuilt three times after devastating fires, Copenhagen's neoclas-

sical cathedral dates from 1829. Designed by CF Hansen, its lofty, vaulted interior houses Bertel Thorvaldsen's statues of Christ and the apostles, completed in 1839 and considered his most acclaimed works. In fact, the sculptor's depiction of Christ, with comforting open arms, remains the most popular worldwide model for statues of Jesus. In May 2004, the cathedral hosted the wedding of Crown Prince Frederik to Australian Mary Donaldson.

Dansk Arkitektur Center
GALLERY

(Danish Architecture Centre; DAC; Map p57; ☎ 32 57 19 30; www.dac.dk; Frederiksholms Kanal 30; exhibition adult/child 40kr/free, 5-9pm Wed free; ⊙ exhibition & bookshop 10am-5pm Mon, Tue & Thu-Sun, to 9pm Wed, cafe from 11am Mon-Fri, 10am-4pm Sat & Sun; 🚌 66, 🚊 Det Kongelige Bibliotek) From May 2018, you will find the Danish Architecture Centre inside the new, harbourside Blox building, designed by Dutch 'starchitect' Rem Koolhaas. Aside from its excellent book- and design-shop, the centre will host changing exhibitions on Danish and international architecture. On weekends from late May to September, DAC also runs 90-minute **walking tours** of the city's contemporary architecture (125kr). See the website for updates.

Nikolaj Kunsthal
GALLERY

(Map p48; ☎ 33 18 17 80; www.nikolajkunsthal. dk; Nikolaj Plads 10; adult/child 60kr/free, Wed free; ⊙ noon-6pm Tue-Fri, 11am-5pm Sat & Sun; 🚌 1A, 2A, 9A, 26, 37, 66, 350S, 🚇 Kongens Nytorv) Built in the 13th century, the church of Sankt Nikolaj is now home to the **Copenhagen Contemporary Art Centre**, which hosts around half a dozen exhibitions annually. Exhibitions tend to focus on modern-day cultural, political and social issues, explored in mediums as diverse as photography and performance art. The centre also houses a snug, well-regarded Danish restaurant called **Maven**.

Sankt Petri Kirke
CHURCH

(Map p48; ☎ 33 13 38 33; www.sankt-petri.dk; Sankt Pedersstræde 2; ⊙ 11am-3pm Wed-Sat; 🚌 5C, 6A, 14, 🚇 Nørrebro, 🚊 Nørrebro) A handsome place of worship in the Latin Quarter is the German church of Sankt Petri Kirke. Dating from the 15th century, this is the oldest church building in the city. A child's coffin in the crypt is believed to hold the bones of Johan Friedrich Struensee, Christian VII's German physician. Struensee was beheaded, dismembered and buried on Gallows Hill in 1772 for bedding Queen Caroline Mathilde.

☉ Nørreport

North of the Latin Quarter, featuring some distinguished art collections and museums, is an area of parks including castle-skirting Kongens Have (p50), one of Copenhagen's oldest and most beautiful.

★**Rosenborg Slot**   CASTLE

(Map p48; ☎ 33 15 32 86; www.kongernessamling. dk/en/rosenborg; Øster Voldgade 4A; adult/child 110kr/free, incl Amalienborg Slot 145kr/free; ☉ 9am–5pm mid-Jun–mid-Sep, reduced hours rest of year; ⬚ 6A, 42, 184, 185, 350S, Ⓜ Nørreport, Ⓢ Nørreport) A 'once-upon-a-time' combo of turrets, gables and moat, the early-17th-century Rosenborg Slot was built in Dutch Renaissance style between 1606 and 1633 by King Christian IV to serve as his summer home. Today, the castle's 24 upper rooms are chronologically arranged, housing the furnishings and portraits of each monarch from Christian IV to Frederik VII. The pièce de résistance is the basement Treasury, home to the dazzling crown jewels, among them Christian IV's glorious crown and Christian III's jewel-studded sword.

★**Statens Museum for Kunst**   MUSEUM

(Map p60; ☎ 33 74 84 94; www.smk.dk; Sølvgade 48-50; adult/child 110kr/free; ☉ 11am-5pm Tue & Thu-Sun, to 8pm Wed; ⬚ 6A, 26, 42, 184, 185) FREE Denmark's National Gallery straddles two contrasting, interconnected buildings: a late-19th-century 'palazzo' and a sharply minimalist extension. The museum houses medieval and Renaissance works and impressive collections of Dutch and Flemish artists, including Rubens, Breughel and Rembrandt. It claims the world's finest collection of 19th-century Danish 'Golden Age' artists, among them Eckersberg and Hammershøi, foreign greats like Matisse and Picasso, and modern Danish heavyweights including Per Kirkeby.

★**Davids Samling**   MUSEUM

(Map p48; ☎ 33 73 49 49; www.davidmus.dk; Kronprinsessegade 30; ☉ 10am-5pm Tue & Thu-Sun, to 9pm Wed; ⬚ 26, 350S, Ⓜ Kongens Nytorv) FREE Davids Samling is a wonderful curiosity of a gallery housing Scandinavia's largest collections of Islamic art, including jewellery, ceramics and silk, and exquisite works such as an Egyptian rock crystal jug from AD 1000 and a 500-year-old Indian dagger inlaid with rubies. And it doesn't end there, with an elegant selection of Danish, Dutch, English and French art, porcelain, silverware and furniture from the 17th to 19th centuries.

COPENHAGEN IN...

Two Days

Start with a canal and harbour tour, then soak up the salty atmosphere of Nyhavn on your way to **Designmuseum Danmark** (p52). Lunch on celebrated smørrebrød at **Schønnemann** (p72) before heading up the historic **Rundetårn** (p45) for a bird's-eye view of the city. That done, stock up on Danish design at **Illums Bolighus** (p88), **Hay House** (p89) or **Stilleben** (p89), then pick a restaurant in Vesterbro's buzzing Kødbyen (literally 'Meat City') precinct. Once fed, cap the night with shameless fun and Danish *hygge* (cosiness) at **Tivoli** (p44).

On day two, brush up on your Danish history at **Nationalmuseet** (p45), lunch at produce market **Torvehallerne KBH** (p71), break free from the rat race at **Christiania** (p56) before New Nordic feasting at **Kadeau** (p77) or **108** (p77). If the night is still young, kick on with cocktails at **Ruby** (p81) or **1105** (p81), or late-night sax at **La Fontaine** (p86).

Four Days

If you have a third day, escape the city with a trip to art museum **Louisiana** (p92). Lunch there before heading back into the city to snoop around **Rosenborg Slot** (p47), then head straight to **Ved Stranden 10** (p81) for a well-earned glass of vino. Fine-dine at **Höst** (p74) or keep it simple and juicy at **Cock's & Cows** (p72).

Kick-start day four with masterpieces at **Statens Museum for Kunst** (p47) or **Ny Carlsberg Glyptotek** (p45), then spend the rest of the day treading the grit-hip streets of Nørrebro, home to street art, eclectic bars and the city's most beautiful cemetery, **Assistens Kirkegård** (p58). If you get hungry, slip into **Manfreds og Vin** (p78) for local produce cooked simply and skillfully.

Copenhagen Central

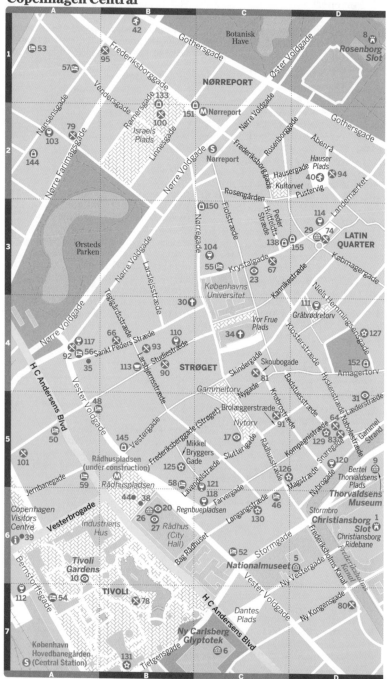

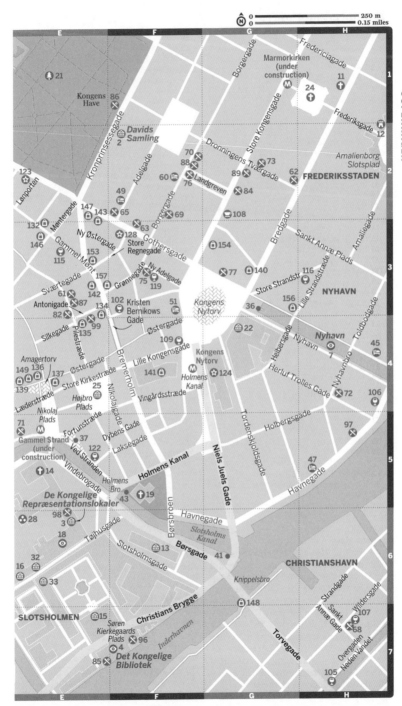

0 250 m
0 0.15 miles

21

Fredericiagade

Borgergade

Marmorkirken
(under
construction)

11

24

Frederiksgade

12

Kongens
Have

86

Davids
Samling

2

Kronprinsessegade

Adelgade

Dronningens Tværgade

Store Kongensgade

70

88

73

89

62

Amalienborg
Slotsplad

FREDERIKSSTADEN

123

Lønporten

Borgergade

60

76

Landgreven

84

Amaliegade

132

146

Møntergade

147

143

65

49

69

108

Gammel Mønt

115

63

128

Store
Regnegade

Gothersgade

154

Bredgade

Sankt Annæ Plads

116

NYHAVN

153

157

Ny Adelgade

Grønnegade

75

119

77

140

Store Strandstr

Lille Strandstræde

Sv/ærtegade

61

142

134

102

Kristen
Bernikows
Gade

51

Kongens
Nytorv

36

156

Antonigade

87

82

99

Silkegade

135

Pilestræde

Østergade

109

22

Nyhavn

45

Amagertorv

149

136

137

Østergade

25

141

Kongens
Nytorv

124

Holmens
Kanal

Herluf Trolles Gade

72

106

97

139

Store Kirkestræde

Nikolajgade

Bremerholm

Vingårdsstræde

Læderstræde

Nikolaj
Plads

71

37

122

Fortunstræde

Dybens Gade

Laksegade

Holbergsgade

47

Gammel Strand
(under
construction)

14

Ved Stranden

Holmens Kanal

Niels Juels Gade

Tordenskjoldsgade

Havnegade

Vindebrogade

De Kongelige
Repræsentationslokaler

Holmens
Bro

43

19

Havnegade

28

98

3

18

Tøjhusgade

13

Børsgade

Slotsholms
Kanal

CHRISTIANSHAVN

32

16

33

Slotsholmsgade

Børsgade

41

Knippelsbro

Strandgade

Wildersgade

SLOTSHOLMEN

15

Christians Brygge

148

107

Søren
Kierkegaards
Plads

96

Inderhavnen

Sankt Annæ Gade

68

Overgaden Neden Vandet

4

Det Kongelige
Bibliotek

85

Torvegade

105

Copenhagen Central

Kongens Have PARK

(King's Gardens; Map p48; http://parkmuseerne.
dk/kongens-have; Øster Voldgade; ⏰7am-11pm
Jul–mid-Aug, to 10pm May–mid-Jun & mid-late Aug,
reduced hours rest of year; 🚻; 🚌26, Ⓜ Nørreport,
Ⓢ Nørreport) FREE The oldest park in Copenhagen was laid out in the early 17th century
by Christian IV, who used it as his vegetable
patch. These days it has a little more to offer,
including wonderfully romantic paths, a fra-
grant rose garden, some of the longest mixed
borders in northern Europe and a mario-
nette theatre with free performances.

Located on the northeastern side of the
park, the theatre occupies one of the neoclassical pavilions designed by Danish architect
Peter Meyn.

Botanisk Have GARDENS

(Botanic Garden; Map p60; http://botanik.snm.
ku.dk; Gothersgade 140, Nørreport; ⏰8.30am-6pm
Apr-Sep, to 4pm Tue-Sun Oct-Mar; 🚻; 🚌6A, 42,
150S, 184, 185, Ⓜ Nørreport, Ⓢ Nørreport) Restorative and romantic, Copenhagen's Botanic
Garden lays claim to around 13,000 species
of plant life – the largest collection in Denmark. You can amble along tranquil trails,

escape to warmer climes in the 19th-century **Palmehus** (Map p60; ⊙10am-5pm daily Apr-Sep, 10am-3pm Tue-Sun Oct-Apr; 🚌6A, 14, 37, 150S, 184, 185, Ⓜ Nørreport, Ⓢ Nørreport) glasshouse and even pick up honey made using the garden's own bees at the gorgeous little gift shop.

Just east of the Palmehus is the Botanisk Have's Danish Quarter, a garden with rotating themes. From spring 2018, the theme will be Nordic beer, with a series of plants used in its production, including unique and historical hops. At the garden's northwest corner lies the **Geologisk Museum** (Geology Museum; Map p60; ☑35 32 22 22; http://geologi. snm.ku.dk; Øster Voldgade 5-7; adult/child 75/50kr; ⊙10am-4pm Tue-Sun; 🚌6A, 26, 184, 185), worth a trip for its exhibition of botanical drawings and dazzling mineral displays.

Hirschsprung   MUSEUM
(Map p60; ☑35 42 03 36; www.hirschsprung.dk; Stockholmsgade 20; adult/child 75kr/free; ⊙11am-4pm Wed-Sun; 🚌6A, 14, 37, 42, 150S) Dedicated to Danish art of the 19th and early 20th centuries, Hirschsprungske is a little jewel-box of a gallery, full of wonderful surprises for art lovers unfamiliar with the classic era of Danish oil painting. Originally the private holdings

of tobacco magnate Heinrich Hirschsprung, it contains works by 'Golden Age' painters such as Christen Købke and CW Eckersberg, a notable selection by Skagen painters PS Krøyer and Anna and Michael Ancher, and also works by the Danish symbolists and the Funen painters.

◉ Nyhavn & the Royal Quarter

Ideal for sunny-day quayside cafe-hopping, the canal-side of Nyhavn (pronounced 'new-hown') also seduces tourists with its ship masts, canal tours (p63) and colourful gabled town houses. Nearby Frederiksstaden is one of Copenhagen's most elegant quarters, home to the royal palace, Marmorkirken (Marble Church) and, further north, the altogether less impressive Little Mermaid.

★ Nyhavn   CANAL
(Map p48; Nyhavn; 🚌 1A, 26, 66, 350S, Ⓜ Kongens Nytorv) There are few nicer places to be on a sunny day than sitting at the outdoor tables of a cafe on the quayside of the Nyhavn canal. The canal was built to connect Kongens Nytorv to the harbour and was long a haunt for sailors and writers, including Hans Christian Andersen. He wrote *The Tinderbox, Little Claus and Big Claus* and *The Princess and the Pea* while living at number 20, and also spent time living at numbers 18 and 67.

The oldest house on the canal is number 9, remarkably unaltered since its construction

in 1681. Today, Nyhavn is a tourist magnet of brightly coloured gabled town houses, salty boats and foaming beers. It's also a handy place to hop on a boat ride with Canal Tours Copenhagen (p63).

★ Designmuseum Danmark   MUSEUM
(Map p60; www.designmuseum.dk; Bredgade 68; adult/child 100kr/free; ⊙ 11am-5pm Tue & Thu-Sun, to 9pm Wed; 🚌 1A, Ⓜ Kongens Nytorv) The 18th-century Frederiks Hospital is now the outstanding Denmark Design Museum. A must for fans of the applied arts and indus-trial design, its fairly extensive collection includes Danish textiles and fashion, as well as the iconic design pieces of modern inno-vators like Kaare Klint, Poul Henningsen and Arne Jacobsen.

Amalienborg Slot   PALACE
(Map p48; ☎ 33 15 32 86; www.kongernessamling. dk/amalienborg; Amalienborg Plads; adult/child 95kr/free; ⊙ 10am-5pm daily mid-Jun–mid-Sep, reduced hours rest of year; 🚌 1A, 26) Home of the current queen, Margrethe II, Amalienborg Slot consists of four austere 18th-century palaces around a large cobbled square. The changing of the guard takes place here dai-ly at noon, the new guard having marched through the city centre from the barracks on Gothersgade at 11.30am.

One of the palaces features exhibits of the royal apartments used by three generations of the monarchy from 1863 to 1947, its recon-structed rooms decorated with gilt-leather

---

THAT LITTLE MERMAID

New York has its Lady Liberty, Sydney its (Danish-designed) Opera House. When the world thinks of Copenhagen, chances are they're thinking of the **Little Mermaid** (Den Lille Havfrue; Map p60; Langelinie, Østerport; 🚌 1A, 🚢 Nordre Toldbod). Love her or loathe her (watch Copenhageners cringe at the very mention of her), this small, underwhelming statue is arguably the most photographed sight in the country, as well as the cause of countless 'is that it?' shrugs from tourists who have trudged the kilometre or so along an often windswept harbourfront to see her.

She was commissioned in 1909 by Danish beer baron Carl Jacobsen, who had been moved by a ballet performance based on Hans Christian Andersen's *Little Mermaid* fairy tale. Sculptor Edvard Eriksen modelled the body on his wife Eline, the face on ballerina Ellen Price. The statue survived Copenhagen's WWII occupation unscathed, but modern times haven't been so kind: Denmark's leading lady has suffered a series of decapita-tions and lost limbs at the hands of vandals, pranksters and protesters trying to make various political points.

Partly in response to these attacks, Carlsberg commissioned Danish artist Bjørn Nør-gaard to create a second Little Mermaid in 2006. Sitting only a few hundred metres from the original, this 'genetically altered' sister is a misshapen creation that's arguably truer in spirit to Andersen's rather bleak, twisted fairy tale, in which the fish-tailed protagonist is physically and emotionally tormented. Then, since 2012 there's also Han (p99) in Helsingør, a third iteration that's contrastingly gleaming, tail-less... and male.

tapestries, trompe l'oeil paintings, family photographs and antiques. They include the study and drawing room of Christian IX (1863–1906) and Queen Louise, whose six children wedded into nearly as many royal families – one ascending to the throne in Greece and another marrying Russian Tsar Alexander III. The grand, neoclassical Gala Hall houses statues of Euterpe and Terpsichore created by a young Bertel Thorvaldsen.

Marmorkirken
CHURCH

(Marble Church; Map p48; ☎ 33 15 01 44; www.marmorkirken.dk; Frederiksgade 4; dome adult/child 35/20kr, church admission free; ☺ church 10am-5pm Mon-Thu & Sat, from noon Fri & Sun, dome 1pm daily mid-Jun–Aug, 1pm Sat & Sun rest of year; ☐ 1A) Consecrated in 1894, the neo-baroque Marble Church (officially Frederikskirken) is one of Copenhagen's most imposing architectural assets. Its grandiose dome – inspired by St Peter's in Rome and the largest church dome in Scandinavia – offers an impressive view over the city. The church was ordered by Frederik V and drawn up by Nicolai Eigtved. Construction began in 1749 but spiralling costs saw the project mothballed. Salvation came in the form of Denmark's wealthiest 19th-century financier CF Tietgen, who bankrolled the project's revival.

Kunsthal Charlottenborg
MUSEUM

(Map p48; ☎ 33 74 46 39; www.kunsthalcharlottenborg.dk; Nyhavn 2; adult/child 75kr/free, after 5pm Wed free; ☺ noon-8pm Tue-Fri, 11am-5pm Sat & Sun; ☐ 1A, 26, 350S, Ⓜ Kongens Nytorv) Fronting Kongens Nytorv, Charlottenborg was built in 1683 as a palace for the royal family. Home to Det Kongelige Kunstakademi (Royal Academy of Fine Arts) since 1754, it is also a spacious venue for topical contemporary art from homegrown and international names. Expect anything from site-specific installations and video art to painting and sculpture. Admittedly, shows here can be a little hit or miss, so check what's on before heading in.

Kastellet
FORTRESS

(Map p60; ☐ 1A, ☻ Nordre Toldbod) The star-shaped fortress of Kastellet was originally commissioned by Frederik III in 1662. Today, it is one of the most historically evocative sites in the city, its grassy ramparts and moat surrounding some beautiful 18th-century barracks, as well as a chapel occasionally used for concerts. On the ramparts is a historic windmill, and you get some excellent views of the harbour and Marmorkirken's Vatican-like dome.

THE CYCLING SNAKE

Two of the Danes' greatest passions – design and cycling – meet in spectacular fashion with **Cykelslangen** (Map p93), an elevated, 235-metre-long cycling path that evokes a slender ribbon, its gently curving form contrasting dramatically with a block-like architectural backdrop. It winds its whimsical way west from Bryggebro (Brygge Bridge) to Fisketorvet Shopping Centre (bus 34). It's only accessible by bicycle.

Just beyond the fortress' southeastern edge is Anders Bundgaard's monumental **Gefion Fountain** (Gefionspringvandet; Map p60; ☐ 1A, ☻ Nordre Toldbod), depicting the Norse goddess Gefion steering some rather stoic oxen.

Aleksander Nevskij Kirke
CHURCH

(Map p48; ☎ 33 13 60 46; www.ruskirke.dk; Bredgade 53; ☺ only for services; ☐ 1A) Completed in 1883, golden-domed, granite-and-brick Alexander Newsky Kirke flaunts a Russian Byzantine style, complete with marble staircase, mosaic floors and Byzantine-style frescoes. This Byzantine influence is not surprising given that its Russian designer, David Ivanovich Grimm, was a respected Neo-Byzantine architect. The church's bronze chandelier was a gift from Tsar Alexander III, who commissioned the church.

◉ Slotsholmen

Separated from the city centre by a moat-like canal, Slotsholmen is a compact, spire-spiked island heaving with history, culture and arresting architecture, both old and cutting edge. At its heart is Christiansborg Slot, home to the national government, a glorious Renaissance hall and commanding tower views. Beneath it lie Copenhagen's medieval traces, while around it, museums include Thorvaldsens Museum, an ode to Denmark's greatest sculptor. Adding sharp relief is Det Kongelige Bibliotek. Copenhagen's royal library, its leaning 'Black Diamond' extension is one of Scandinavia's most applauded contemporary buildings.

★ Christiansborg Slot
PALACE

(Christiansborg Palace; Map p48; ☎ 33 92 64 92; www.christiansborg.dk; Prins Jørgens Gård 1; adult/child 90kr/free, joint ticket incl royal reception rooms, ruins, kitchen & stables 150kr/free; ⊘10am-5pm daily May-Sep, closed Mon Oct-Apr; ♿; 🚍1A, 2A, 9A, 26, 37, 66, 🚇Det Kongelige Bibliotek, Ⓜ Christianshavn) Christiansborg Slot is home to the Folketinget (the Danish parliament), Prime Minister's office and the Supreme Court. Visitor highlights include the glorious royal reception rooms, 11th-century ruins and royal kitchen, all of which can be visited separately or as part of a joint ticket. The palace is free to visit and offers sweeping views of the Danish capital.

Several short bridges link Slotsholmen to the rest of Copenhagen. If you walk into Slotsholmen from Ny Vestergade, you'll cross the western part of the canal and enter the large main courtyard of Christiansborg Slot, which was once used as royal riding grounds and still maintains a distinctively equestrian feel, overseen by a statue of Christian IX (1863–1906) on horseback and flanked to the north by stables and to the south by carriage buildings.

The stables and buildings surrounding the main courtyard date back to the 1730s when the original Christiansborg palace was built by Christian VI to replace the more modest Copenhagen Castle that previously stood there. The grander west wing of Christian VI's palace went up in flames in 1794, was rebuilt in the early 19th century and was once again destroyed by fire in 1884. In 1907 the cornerstone for the third (and current) Christiansborg palace was laid by Frederik VIII and, upon completion, the national parliament and the Supreme Court moved into new chambers there.

In addition to the sights listed here, visitors can enter **Christiansborg Slotskirke** (Map p48; ⊘10am-5pm Sun, daily Jul; 🚍1A, 2A, 9A, 26, 37, 66), the castle's domed church, which was set ablaze by stray fireworks in 1992 and has since been painstakingly restored. You can also hop on the elevator and take a ride to the top of the tower for spectacular panoramic city views.

★ **De Kongelige Repræsentationslokaler**   HISTORIC BUILDING
(Royal Reception Rooms at Christiansborg Slot; Map p48; www.christiansborg.dk; Slotsholmen; adult/child 90kr/free; ⊘10am-5pm daily May-Sep, closed Mon Oct-Apr, guided tours in Danish/English 11am/3pm; 🚍1A, 2A, 9A, 26, 37, 66, 🚇Det Kongelige Bibliotek) The grandest part of Christiansborg is De Kongelige Repræsentationslokaler, a series of palace rooms and halls used by the queen to hold royal banquets and entertain

heads of state. The Queen's Library is especially memorable, a gilded wonderland adorned with dripping chandeliers, ornate stucco, ceiling storks and a small part of the royal family's centuries-old book collection. Top billing goes to the Great Hall, home to riotously colourful wall tapestries depicting 1000 years of Danish history.

Created by tapestry designer Bjørn Nørgaard over a decade, the works were completed in 2000. Keep an eye out for the Adam and Eve–style representation of the queen and her husband (albeit clothed) in a Danish Garden of Eden.

★ **Thorvaldsens Museum**   MUSEUM
(Map p48; ☑33 32 15 32; www.thorvaldsens museum.dk; Bertel Thorvaldsens Plads 2; adult/child 70kr/free, Wed free; ⊘10am-5pm Tue-Sun; 🚍1A, 2A, 26, 37, 66) What looks like a colourful Greco-Roman mausoleum is in fact a museum dedicated to the works of illustrious Danish sculptor Bertel Thorvaldsen (1770–1844). Heavily influenced by mythology after four decades in Rome, Thorvaldsen returned to Copenhagen and donated his private collection to the Danish public. In return the royal family provided this site for the construction of what is a remarkable complex housing Thorvaldsen's drawings, plaster moulds and statues. The museum also contains his own collection of Mediterranean antiquities.

★ **Det Kongelige Bibliotek**   LIBRARY
(Royal Library; Map p48; ☑33 47 47 47; www. kb.dk; Søren Kierkegaards Plads; ⊘8am-7pm Mon-Fri, from 9am Sat Jul & Aug, 8am-9pm Mon-Fri, 9am-7pm Sat rest of year; 🚍66, 🚇Det Kongelige Bibliotek) FREE Scandinavia's largest library consists of two very distinct parts: the original 19th-century red-brick building and the head-turning 'Black Diamond' extension, the latter a leaning parallelogram of sleek black granite and smoke-coloured glass. From the soaring, harbour-fronting atrium, an escalator leads up to a 210 sq metre ceiling mural by celebrated Danish artist Per Kirkeby. Beyond it, at the end of the corridor, is the 'old library' and its Hogwarts-like northern Reading Room, resplendent with vintage desk lamps and classical columns.

Aside from housing a complete collection of all Danish printed works produced since 1482, Denmark's national library is also home to the **National Museum of Photography**, which hosts rotating exhibitions of historical and contemporary photography sourced from its rich collection.

The library is also home to decent cafe **Øieblikket** (Map p48; ☑ 33 47 41 06; Søren Kierkegaards Plads 1; soup & salads 40-45kr, sandwiches 50-55kr; ☺ 8am-7pm Mon-Fri, 9am-6pm Sat; 🖥🖉; ⬛ 9A, ⬛ Det Kongelige Bibliotek) and modern Danish restaurant **Søren K** (Map p48; ☑ 33 47 49 49; http://soerenk.dk; Søren Kierkegaards Plads 1; 1/5 courses 120/500kr; ☺ noon-3pm & 5.30-10pm Mon-Sat; 🖥; ⬛ 66, ⬛ Det Kongelige Bibliotek).

Ruinerne under Christiansborg   RUINS

(Ruins under Christiansborg; Map p48; ☑ 33 92 64 92; www.christiansborg.dk; adult/child 50kr/free, joint ticket incl royal reception rooms, kitchen & stables 150kr/free; ☺ 10am-5pm daily May-Sep, closed Mon Oct-Apr; ⬛ 1A, 2A, 9A, 26, 37, 66, ⬛ Det Kongelige Bibliotek, Ⓜ Christianshavn) A walk through the crypt-like bowels of Slotsholmen, known as Ruinerne under Christiansborg, offers a unique perspective on Copenhagen's well-seasoned history. In the basement of the current palace are the ruins of Slotsholmen's original fortress – built by Bishop Absalon in 1167 – and its successor, Copenhagen Castle. Among these remnants are each building's ring walls, as well as a well, baking oven, sewerage drains and stonework from the castle's Blue Tower.

The tower is infamously remembered as the place in which Christian IV's daughter, Leonora Christina (p141), was incarcerated for treason from 1663 to 1685. Guided tours at noon on Saturday/Sunday in English/Danish.

Dansk Jødisk Museum   MUSEUM

(Map p48; ☑ 33 11 22 18; www.jewmus.dk; Proviantpassagen 6, Kongelige Bibliotekshave (Royal Library Garden); adult/child 60kr/free; ☺ 10am-5pm Tue-Sun Jun-Aug, 1-4pm Tue-Fri, noon-5pm Sat & Sun rest of the year; ⬛ 66, ⬛ Det Kongelige Bibliotek) Designed by Polish-born Daniel Libeskind, the Danish Jewish Museum occupies the former Royal Boat House, an early 17th-century building once part of Christian IV's harbour complex. The transformed interior is an intriguing geometrical space, home to a permanent exhibition documenting Danish Jewry. Historical events covered include the Rescue of the Danish Jews in WWII, in which most of the country's Jewish population managed to flee to neutral Sweden with the help of the Danish resistance movement and ordinary Danish citizens.

You'll find the museum entrance in the gorgeous Royal Library Garden, right behind the Kongelige Bibliotek (Royal Library).

Teatermuseet   MUSEUM

(Theatre Museum; Map p48; ☑ 33 11 51 76; www.teatermuseet.dk; Christiansborg Ridebane 18; adult/child 40kr/free; ☺ noon-4pm Tue-Sun; ⬛ 1A, 2A, 9A, 26, 37, 66) Dating from 1767, the wonderfully atmospheric Hofteater (Old Court Theatre) has hosted everything from Italian opera to local ballet troupes, one of which included fledgling ballet student Hans Christian Andersen. Taking its current appearance in 1842, the venue is now the Theatre Museum, and visitors are free to explore the stage, boxes and dressing rooms, along with displays of set models, drawings, costumes and period posters tracing the history of Danish theatre.

Royal-watchers will enjoy peeking into the royal boxes – Christian VIII's entertainment area comes equipped with its own commode.

Holmens Kirke   CHURCH

(Church of the Royal Danish Navy; Map p48; ☑ 33 13 61 78; www.holmenskirke.dk; Holmens Kanal 9; ☺ 10am-4pm Mon, Wed, Fri & Sat, to 3.30pm Tue & Thu, noon-4pm Sun; ⬛ 1A, 26, 66) Queen Margrethe II took her marriage vows here in 1967, and while much of the present Dutch Renaissance–style structure dates from 1641, the church's nave was originally built in 1562 to be used as an anchor forge. Converted into a church for the Royal Navy in 1619, the building's burial chapel contains the remains of Admiral Niels Juel, who beat back the Swedes in the crucial 1677 Battle of Køge Bay. Other highlights include an intricately carved 17th-century oak altarpiece and pulpit.

De Kongelige Stalde   MUSEUM

(Royal Stables; Map p48; ☑ 33 40 10 10; www.kongehuset.dk; adult/child 50kr/free; ☺ 1.30-4pm daily May-Sep, closed Mon Oct-Apr, guided tours in English 2pm Sat; ⬛ 1A, 2A, 9A, 26, 37, 66) Completed in 1740, the two curved, symmetrical wings behind Christiansborg belonged to the original baroque palace, destroyed by fire in 1794. The wings still house the royal stables and its museum of antique coaches, uniforms and riding paraphernalia, some of which are still used for royal receptions. Among these is the 19th-century Gold Coach, adorned with 24-carat gold leaf and still used by the queen on her gallop from Amalienborg to Christiansborg during the New Year's levee in January.

Børsen   HISTORIC BUILDING

(Map p48; Børsgade; ⬛ 2A, 9A, 37, 66) Not many stock exchanges are topped by a 56m-tall spire formed from the entwined tails of four dragons. Børsen is one. Constructed in the bustling early-17th-century reign of Christian IV, the building is considered one of the finest examples of Dutch Renaissance architecture in Denmark, with richly embellished gables. Its still-functioning chamber of commerce is the oldest in Europe, though the building is not generally open to the public

Folketinget
NOTABLE BUILDING

(Map p48; ☑ 33 37 32 21; www.thedanishparliament. dk; Rigsdagsgården; ⊙ 45min guided tours in English 1pm Sun-Fri late Jun–mid-Aug, reduced hours rest of year; ⚇ 1A, 2A, 9A, 26, 37, 66) FREE Folketinget is where the 179 members of the Danish parliament debate national legislation. Guided tours also take in Wanderer's Hall, which contains the original copy of the Constitution of the Kingdom of Denmark, enacted in 1849. Outside the summer high season, the guided tours generally take place at 1pm on selected Sundays and public holidays.

Tøjhusmuseet
MUSEUM

(Royal Danish Arsenal Museum; Map p48; ☑ 33 11 60 37; www.natmus.dk; Tøjhusgade 3; adult/child 65kr/free; ⊙ 10am-5pm Tue-Sun; ⚇ 1A, 2A, 9A, 14, 26, 37, 66) The Royal Arsenal Museum houses an impressive collection of historic weaponry, from canons and medieval armour to pistols, swords and even a WWII flying bomb. Built by Christian IV in 1600, the 163m-long building is Europe's longest vaulted Renaissance hall.

⊙ Christianshavn

Established in the early 17th century as a commercial centre and military buffer for the expanding city, Christianshavn recalls Amsterdam, both with its network of boat-lined waterways and with its hyper-liberal, free-spirited neighbourhood of Christiania. The area also sports several historic churches and a gigantic 2005 opera house (p87) that cost a billion euros to build.

Nyhavn and Christianshavn are handily linked by the 2016 car-free **Inderhavnsbroen** (Map p57), nicknamed *Kyssebroen* (Kissing Bridge) as it looks likes two tongues meeting.

★ Christiania
AREA

(Map p57; www.christiania.org; Prinsessegade; ⚇ 9A, Ⓜ Christianshavn) Escape the capitalist crunch at Freetown Christiania, a hash-scented commune straddling the eastern side of Christianshavn. Since its establishment by squatters in 1971, the area has drawn non-conformists from across the globe, attracted by the concept of collective business, workshops and communal living. Explore beyond the settlement's infamous 'Pusher St' – lined with shady hash and marijuana dealers who do not appreciate photographs – and you'll stumble upon a semi-bucolic wonderland of whimsical DIY homes, cosy garden plots, eateries, beer gardens and music venues.

Before its development as an alternative enclave, the site was an abandoned military camp. When squatters took over, police tried to clear the area. They failed. The hippie revolution was at its peak and wave after wave of alternative folk continued to pour in.

Bowing to public pressure, the government allowed the community to continue as a social experiment. Self-governing, ecology-oriented and generally tolerant, Christiania residents did, in time, find it necessary to modify their 'anything goes' approach. A new policy was established that outlawed hard drugs, and the heroin and cocaine pushers were expelled.

The main entrance into Christiania is on Prinsessegade, 200m northeast of its intersection with Bådsmandsstræde. From late June to the end of August, 60- to 90-minute guided tours (40kr) of Christiania run daily at 11am and 3pm (weekends only September to late June). Tours commence just inside Christiania's main entrance on Prinsessegade.

Vor Frelsers Kirke
CHURCH

(Map p57; ☑ 41 66 63 57; www.vorfrelserskirke. dk; Sankt Annæ Gade 29; church free, tower adult/child 40/10kr; ⊙ 11am-3.30pm, closed during services, tower 9.30am-7pm Mon-Sat, 10.30am-7pm Sun May-Sep, reduced hours rest of year; ⚇ 2A, 9A, 37, 350S, Ⓜ Christianshavn) It's hard to miss this 17th-century church and its 95m-high spiral tower. For a soul-stirring city view, make the head-spinning 400-step ascent to the top – the last 150 steps run along the outside rim of the tower, narrowing to the point where they literally disappear at the top. Inspired by Borromini's tower of St Ivo in Rome, the spire was added in 1752 by Lauritz de Thurah. Inside the church, highlights include an ornate baroque altar and elaborately carved pipe organ from 1698.

Overgaden
GALLERY

(Map p57; ☑ 32 57 72 73; www.overgaden.org; Overgaden Neden Vandet 17; ⊙ 1-5pm Tue, Wed & Fri-Sun, to 8pm Thu; ⚇ 2A, 9A, 37, 350S, Ⓜ Christianshavn) FREE Rarely visited by tourists, this non-profit art gallery runs about 10 exhibitions annually, putting the spotlight on

Christianshavn

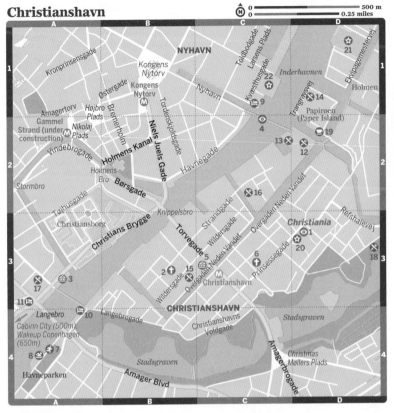

Christianshavn

contemporary installation art and photography, usually by younger artists, both Danish and international. The gallery also runs a busy calendar of artist talks, lectures, performances, concerts and film screenings. See the website for upcoming events.

AMAGER BAKKE

East of Christianshavn, **Amager Bakke** (www.a-r-c.dk/amager-bakke; Vindmøllevej 6; 🚊 37) is a highly ambitious waste-to-energy plant whose skyscraping chimney blows visible 'smoke rings' (water vapour, actually) for every 250kg of carbon dioxide released into the atmosphere. When completed in 2018, its spectacular sloping roof will feature a year-round ski run, and hiking trails.

Christians Kirke   CHURCH
(Map p57; ✆ 32 54 15 76; www.christianskirke. dk; Strandgade 1; ⊙ 10am-4pm Tue-Fri; 🚊 2A, 9A, 37, 350S, Ⓜ Christianshavn) Named in honour of Christian IV – who founded Christianshavn in the early 17th century – Christians Kirke is well known for its unusual rococo interior. This includes tiered viewing galleries more reminiscent of a theatre than a place of worship. The church was built between 1754 and 1759, serving Christianshavn's sizeable German congregation until the end of the 19th century.

◉ Nørrebro & Østerbro

Østerbro is a white-bread neighbourhood where chi-chi boutiques and bistros mingle with some of Copenhagen's most fascinating domestic architecture. Contrastingly bohemian, Nørrebro offers a sexy funk of art-clad 19th-century tenements, kaleidoscopic street life, multicultural crowds and thronging cafe-bars. Plus there's celebrity cemetery Assistens Kirkegård. For views, climb to the playground-rooftop of the imaginative, eight-storey car park **Konditaget Lüders** (Map p60; Helsinkigade 30, Nordhavn; ⊙ 24hr; 🚊 3A, 8A, 37, Ⓢ Nordhavn). Or gaze forth from the 1887 bridge, **Dronning Louises Bro** (Map p59; 🚊 5C, Ⓜ Nørreport, Ⓢ Nørreport), to survey Nørrebrø's famous neon lights.

Assistens Kirkegård   CEMETERY
(Map p59; ✆ 35 37 19 17; http://assistens.dk; Kapelvej 4, Nørrebro; ⊙ 7am-10pm Apr-Sep, to 7pm Oct-Mar; 🚊 5C, 8A) You'll find some of Denmark's most celebrated citizens at this famous cemetery, including philosopher Søren Kierkegaard, physicist Niels Bohr, author Hans Christian Andersen, and artists Jens Juel, Christen Købke and CW Eckersberg. It's a wonderfully atmospheric place to wander around – as much a park and garden as it is a graveyard. A good place to start is at the main entrance on Kapelvej, where you can usually find fold-out maps of the cemetery and its notable burial sites.

Superkilen   PARK
(Nørrebrogade 210, Nørrebro; 🚊 5C, Ⓢ Nørrebro) This fascinating 1km-long park showcases objects sourced from around the globe with the aim of celebrating diversity and uniting the community. Items include a tile fountain from Morocco, bollards from Ghana and swing chairs from Baghdad, as well as neon signs from Russia and China. Even the benches, manhole covers and rubbish bins hail from foreign lands.

◉ Vesterbro & Frederiksberg

It is hard to imagine two more disparate neighbours than hip, gritty Vesterbro and middle-class Frederiksberg, yet both promise intriguing sights, atmosphere and hangouts. **Vesterbro** is the epicentre of Copenhagen cool, a place where sharply curated shelves, menus and drink lists share the limelight with street art, sex shops and old-school grocers and barbers. At its southern end is Kødbyen, a mid-century 'Meatpacking District' turned eating-and-drinking hotspot. Respectable **Frederiksberg** is all about genteel diversions, from royal gardens and subterranean art, to Copenhagen Zoo and a world-famous brewery.

★**Frederiksberg Have**   GARDENS
(Map p62; Frederiksberg Runddel, Frederiksberg; ⊙ 7am-11pm mid-Jun–mid-Aug, to 10pm May–mid-Jun & mid-late Aug, reduced hours rest of year; 🚊 6A, 8A, 71, 72, Ⓜ Frederiksberg) This is Copenhagen's most romantic park, with lakes, woodlands and lovely picnic lawns. Guarding the main entrance is 19th-century royal Frederik VI, who would thrill his loyal subjects by taking boat rides along Frederiksberg Have's canals. The park's imposing baroque palace, Frederiksborg Slot, was the royal family's summer residence until the mid-19th century. These days it houses the Royal Danish Military Academy. The Chinese Pavilion is another regal relic, built in 1799 as a royal tea house.

Frederiksberg Have's most unusual attraction is its *suttetræet* (sucky tree), located north of the Chinese Pavilion. The 250-year-old tree is hard to miss, its branches hung with hundreds of colourful ribbons tied to baby pacifiers. According to Danish tradition, when a toddler turns three it is time to give up their pacifier. To make the separation

Nørrebro

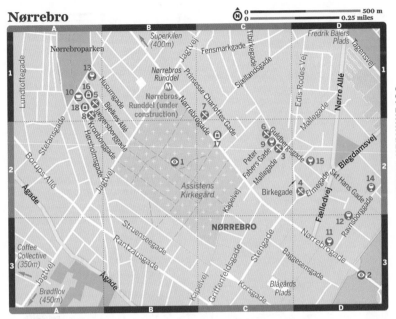

Nørrebro

easier, parents and children entrust the pacifier to their local *suttetræet*, along with a note on behalf of the toddler asking the tree to take good care of it.

Cisternerne　　　　　　　　　GALLERY
(Map p62; ☑30 73 80 32; www.cisternerne.dk; Søndermarken, Frederiksberg; adult/child 60kr/free; ☉vary; ☐6A, 72) Below elegant Søndermarken Park lurks Copenhagen's damp, dripping 19th-century reservoir. These days it's best known as Cisternerne, one of Copenhagen's most unusual and atmospheric art spaces. Each year, a renowned artist is given the opportunity to transform the reservoir into

a huge, immersive installation. Artists have included Denmark's Eva Koch and German-born Christian Lemmerz, as well as Japanese architect Hiroshi Sambuichi.

V1 Gallery　　　　　　　　　GALLERY
(Map p62; ☑33 31 03 21; www.v1gallery.com; Flæsketorvet 69-71, Vesterbro; ☉noon-6pm Wed-Fri, to 4pm Sat during exhibitions; ☐1A, 10, 14, ⑤Dybbølsbro) **FREE** Part of the Kødbyen (Vesterbro's 'Meatpacking District'), V1 is one of Copenhagen's most progressive art galleries. Cast your eye on fresh work from emerging and established local and foreign artists. Some of the world's hottest names in street

Østerbro

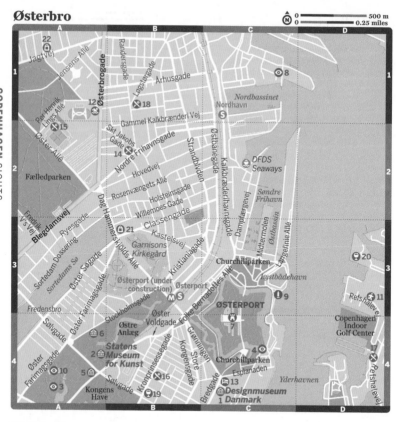

N 0 ———— 500 m
0 ———— 0.25 miles

Østerbro

◉ Top Sights
1 Designmuseum Danmark C4
2 Statens Museum for Kunst A4

◉ Sights
3 Botanisk Have A4
4 Gefion Fountain C4
5 Geologisk Museum A4
6 Hirschsprung A4
7 Kastellet C4
8 Konditaget Lüders C1
9 Little Mermaid C3
10 Palmehus A4

◎ Activities, Courses & Tours
11 Duffy Boat D3
12 Øbro-Hallen A1

◎ Sleeping
13 Babette Guldsmeden C4

◎ Eating
14 Fischer B2
15 Geranium A2
16 Kokkeriet B4
17 La Banchina D4
18 Pixie B1

◎ Drinking & Nightlife
19 Culture Box B4
20 Halvandet D3

◎ Shopping
21 Hoff B3
    Stine Goya .... (see 21)
22 Vintage 199 .... A1

and graffiti art have exhibited here, from Britain's Banksy to the USA's Todd James and Lydia Fong (aka Barry McGee).

Visit Carlsberg   BREWERY
(Map p62; ☎ 33 27 12 82; www.visitcarlsberg. dk; Gamle Carlsberg Vej 11, Vesterbro; adult/child

100/70kr; ☉10am-8pm May-Sep, to 5pm rest of year; 🚇1A, 26, Ⓢ Carlsberg) Adjacent to the architecturally whimsical Carlsberg brewery, Visit Carlsberg explores the history of Danish beer from 1370 BC (yes, they carbon-dated a bog girl who was found in a peat bog caressing a jug of well-aged brew). Dioramas give the lowdown on the brewing process, and en route to your final destination you'll pass antique copper vats and the stables with a dozen Jutland dray horses.

The self-guided tour ends at the bar, where you can knock back two beers (or soft drinks), included in the admission price. Guided tours (50kr) are also available every hour from 11am.

From April to September, a free shuttle bus service runs between the Visit Carlsberg and the Royal Hotel at Vesterbrogade 6 (right beside Central Station). Buses run hourly from 11am to 5pm.

Copenhagen Zoo ZOO
(Map p62; ☎72 20 02 00; www.zoo.dk; Roskildevej 32, Frederiksberg; adult/child 180/100kr; ☉10am-6pm Jun & mid-late Aug, to 8pm Jul–mid-Aug, reduced hours rest of year; 🚌6A, 72) Located up on Frederiksberg (Frederik's Hill), Copenhagen Zoo rustles and rumbles with more than 2500 critters, including lions, zebras, hippos and gorillas. The zoo's state-of-the-art elephant enclosure was designed by English architect Sir Norman Foster, while the Arctic Ring enclosure allows visitors to walk right through the polar-bear pool for some spectacular close encounters with those deceptively cuddly-looking beasts.

🏃 Activities

★Mystery Makers WALKING
(☎30 80 30 50; http://mysterymakers.dk; Mystery Hunt per person 250-400kr; ☉hours vary) Bring out your inner Detective Sarah Lund with Mystery Makers' interactive mystery hunts. Offered at numerous historical sites around town – including Kastellet (p53) – players are given fictional identities and a mystery to solve, with a series of riddles and clues along the way. Suitable for adults and kids aged 12 and above, it's a stimulating, engaging way to explore Copenhagen's backstory.

You will need a minimum of four people to form a team. See the website for pricing, which varies according to the day of the week and time of day (Sunday to Wednesday before 3pm is cheapest). Mystery Makers also runs a series of excellent, one-hour Escape Room games (from 200kr).

Bakken AMUSEMENT PARK
(Map p93; ☎39 63 35 44; www.bakken.dk; Dyrehavevej 62, Klampenborg; multiride wristband adult/child 269/189kr; ☉late Mar-early Sep; Ⓢ Klampenborg) An 800m walk west from Klampenborg station is Bakken, established in the 16th century and now the world's oldest amusement park. A blue-collar version of Tivoli, it's a honky-tonk carnival of bumper cars, roller coasters, slot machines and beer halls.

Københavns Cyklerbørs CYCLING
(Map p48; ☎33 14 07 17; www.cykelboersen.dk; Gothersgade 157; bicycles per day/week 90/450kr; ☉10am-5.30pm Mon-Fri, to 2pm Sat, also 10am-2pm Sun May-Aug; 🚇5C, 37, 350S, Ⓜ Nørreport, Ⓢ Nørreport) Bicycle rental close to the Botanisk Have (Botanic Garden) on the northwest edge of the city centre.

Baisikeli CYCLING
(Map p62; ☎26 70 02 29; http://baisikeli.dk; Ingerslevsgade 80, Vesterbro; bicycles per 6hr/week from 50/270kr; ☉10am-6pm; 🚇1A, Ⓢ Dybbølsbro) Baisikeli is Swahili for bicycle, and the profits from this rental outlet are used to ship much-needed bikes to African communities annually. It's located beside Dybøllsbro S-train station and just south of the Kødbyens Fiskebar restaurant and bar precinct in Vesterbro.

Hauser Plads PLAYGROUND
(Map p48; ⛲; 🚌6A, 150S, 184, 185, 350S, Ⓜ Nørreport, Ⓢ Nørreport) With its mini green hills and surreal climbing structures, the playground on Hauser Plads looks straight off *Teletubbies*. In reality, it's the work of Dutch landscape architects Karres en Brands and Danish firm Polyform, who together turned a forlorn city square into a magnet for energetic kids, their adult keepers, lunching office workers and the odd design fan.

You'll find swings, a sandpit and water fountains, plus a giant amoeba-shaped opening looking down at subterranean offices. How's that for clever storage space?

Boating
★GoBoat BOATING
(Map p57; ☎40 26 10 25; www.goboat.dk; Islands Brygge 10; boat hire 1/2/3hr 399/749/999kr; ☉9.30am-sunset; ⛲; 🚌5C, 12, Ⓜ Islands Brygge) 🚤 What could be more 'Copenhagen' than sailing around the harbour and canals in your own solar-powered boat? You don't need prior sailing experience, and each boat or vessel comes with a built-in picnic table (you can buy supplies at GoBoat or bring your

COPENHAGEN

Vesterbro & Frederiksberg

500 m
0.25 miles

KØDBYEN

VESTERBRO

FREDERIKSBERG

Frederiksberg Have

Frederiksberg Have

Frederiksberg Rundel

Søndermarken

Sankt Jørgens Sø

Hammerichsgade
Vester Farimagsgade
Ved Vesterport
Vesterport
Reventlowsgade
Colbjørnsensgade
Helgolandsgade
Abel Cathrines Gade
Istedgade
Halmtorvet
Gasværksvej
Eskildsgade
Absalonsgade
Dannebrogsgade
Oehlenschlægersgade
Matthæusgade
Sundevedsgade
Kingosgade
Flensborggade
Haderslevgade
Valdemarsgade
Enghavevej
Skelbækgade
Sønder Blvd
Dybbølsgade
Ingerslevsgade
Dybbølsbro
Vestbanegade
Kvægtorvsgade
Tietgensgade
Slagterboderne
Flæsketorvet
Kødboderne
Slagterhuset
Vodroffsvej
Forchhammersvej
Skt Knuds Vej
Værnedamsvej
Gammel Kongevej Amend
Gammel Kongevej
Vesterbrogade
Alhambravej
Mynstersvej
Gammel Kongevej Amend
Frederiksberg Allé
Madvigs Allé
Pile Allé
Nyvej
Amicisvej
Henrik Ibsens Vej
Kochsvej
Platanvej
Jacobys Allé
Rahbeks Allé
Ny Carlsberg Vej
Vesterfælledvej
Enghave Plads
Enghave Plads (under construction)
Alsgade
Sønder Blvd
Ny Carlsberg Vej
Pasteursvej
Bohrsgade
Carlsberg
Olivia Hansens Gade
Gamle Carlsberg Vej
Valby Langgade
Vigerslev Allé
Roskildevej
Vesterbrogade

Vesterbro & Frederiksberg

own). Boats seat up to eight people and rates are per boat, so the more in your group, the cheaper per person.

The rental kiosk sits right beside Islands Brygge Havnebadet.

Duffy Boat BOATING
(Map p60; ☑42 36 36 00; http://duffyboats. dk; Refshalevej 163B; 2hr 9-person boat rental with captain 2500kr; ⊙noon-4pm Mon-Fri, from 10am Sat mid-Apr–Sep; ☐9A, ☒Refshaleøen) ✎ Ideal for larger groups, these super-comfy, electric-powered boats can be hired for two-, three- and four-hour tours of the harbour. A captain is included in the rental price, and guests have the option of ordering a drinks package (one beer, bottle of wine, soft drink and snack for 110kr per person). That said, you're also welcome to bring your own drinks and snacks.

Canal Tours Copenhagen BOATING
(Map p48; ☑32 96 30 00; www.stromma.dk; Ny-havn; adult/child 80/40kr; ⊙9.30am-9pm late Jun–mid-Aug, reduced hours rest of year; ⊕; ☐1A, 26, 66, 350S, Ⓜ Kongens Nytorv) Canal Tours Copen-hagen runs one-hour cruises of the city's ca-nals and harbour, taking in numerous major

sights, including Christiansborg Slot, Chris-tianshavn, the Royal Library, Opera House, Amalienborg Palace and the Little Mermaid. Embark at Nyhavn or Ved Stranden. Boats depart up to six times per hour from late June to late August, with reduced frequency the rest of the year.

Netto-Bådene BOATING
(Map p48; ☑32 54 41 02; www.havnerundfart.dk; Holmens Bro; adult/child 40/15kr; ⊙tours 2-5 per hour, 10am-7pm Jul & Aug, reduced hours rest of year; ☐1A, 2A, 9A, 26, 37, 66) Netto-Bådene operates good-value one-hour cruises of Copenhagen's canals and harbour. Embarkation points are at Holmens Kirke and Nyhavn. From Octo-ber to March, tours are conducted in heated, glass-roofed boats.

Swimming

DGI-byen SWIMMING
(Map p62; www.dgi-byen.dk; Tietgensgade 65, Vesterbro; day pass adult/child Mon-Fri 65/45kr, Sat & Sun 75/50kr; ⊙6am-10pm Mon-Thu, to 7.30pm Fri, 8am-7pm Sat, 8am-6pm Sun; ⊕; ☐1A, 32, ⓢKøbenhavn H) An extravagant indoor swim centre with several pools, including a grand ellipse-shaped affair with 100m lanes, a

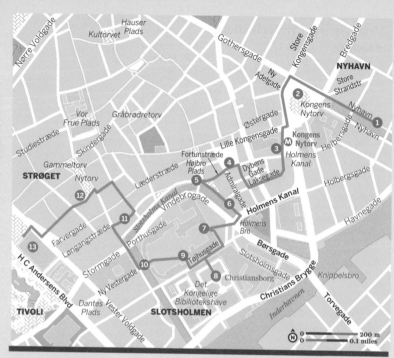

City Walk
Copenhagen: Cobbles & Cosiness

START NYHAVN
FINISH RÅDHUSPLADSEN
LENGTH 2.7 KILOMETRES; TWO HOURS

Start your stroll at iconic canal-side **1 Ny-havn** (p52), eyeing up its crayon-coloured townhouses and imagining a past filled with rowdy sailors and women of 'ill repute'. Commissioned by Christian V, the canal was constructed by Swedish war prisoners in the 17th century to connect the harbour to **2 Kongens Nytorv**, Copenhagen's largest square. At the southern end of the square stands the **3 Magasin department store** (p88), a commanding example of French Renaissance Revival architecture. Built in 1894, it replaced the Hotel du Nord, which was home to Hans Christian Andersen between 1838 and 1847.

Continue south into Laksegade, turning right into Nikolajgade. The street leads to **4 Nicolaj Kunsthal** (p46), a contemporary art space set inside Copenhagen's third-oldest church. Head west down Fortunstræde to **5 Højbro Plads**, home to a statue of Copenhagen's founder, Bishop Absalon.

Close by is superlative wine bar **6 Ved Stranden 10** (p81). Stop for a swill, then cross the canal at Holmens Bro. In front of you is **7 Christiansborg Slot** (p53), home to the Danish parliament. Head through the archway to the left of the palace, then through the second archway on your left. Awaiting is the **8 Royal Library Garden**, built on top of Christian IV's old naval port, Tøjhushavnen. Head back through the archway, continuing south to the late-baroque **9 Riding Ground Complex**, the only surviving remnant from the original Christiansborg Palace. The riding ground leads out to the 18th-century **10 Marble Bridge**. Cross it, turning right into Frederiksholms Kanal until you reach **11 Magstræde**, Copenhagen's oldest street. Wander down it, turning left into Knabrostræde and then left again at Brolæggerstræde. The street spills into Nytorv, home to Copenhagen's pink-stucco court house **12 Domhuset** (Map p48). Head down Slutterigade to the left of the building, at the very end of which soars the architectural flourish that is **13 Rådhus** (p46).

deep 'mountain pool' with a climbing wall, a hot-water pool and a children's pool. If you've forgotten your togs or towels, they can be hired for 25kr each (bring photo ID as a deposit). Admission is cheapest on weekdays before 9am (adult/child 45/30kr).

Øbro-Hallen SWIMMING
(Map p60; ☑82 20 51 50; http://teambade.kk.dk/indhold/oebro-hallen; Gunnar Nu Hansens Plads 3, Østerbro; adult/child 40/20kr; ☺7am-8pm Mon, Tue & Fri, from 8am Wed, from 6.30am Thu, 9am-3pm Sat & Sun; ☻; ▣1A) Inspired by ancient Roman baths and dating back to 1929–30, Øbro-Hallen is Denmark's oldest indoor public pool complex. It's also one of its most beautiful, its three pools – a 25m lap pool, a children's pool and an infant pool – awash with natural light from the elegant glass ceiling.

Islands Brygge Havnebadet SWIMMING
(Map p57; http://teambade.kk.dk/indhold/havnebade-0; Islands Brygge; ☺24hr Jun-Sep, lifeguards on duty 11am-7pm; ☻; ▣5C, 12, Ⓜ Islands Brygge) FREE Copenhagen's coolest outdoor pool complex comprises three pools and sits right in the central city's main canal. Water quality is rigorously monitored, and the lawns, BBQ facilities and eateries make it a top spot to see and be seen on a warm summer day, whether you get wet or not.

Havnebadet Sluseholmen SWIMMING
(Map p93; ☑51 82 63 79; http://teambade.kk.dk/indhold/havnebade-0; Ben Websters Vej 69; ☺11am-7pm Jun-Sep; ☻; ▣14, 34, ⚓Teglholmen) FREE With a striking design inspired by coral, this free outdoor bathing complex sits at the southern end of Copenhagen Harbour. Facilities include two shallow pools for young children and adolescents, and a deep pool designed for swimming and diving. Lifeguards are on hand, and the complex is wheelchair-accessible.

Amager Strandpark BEACH
(Map p93; www.kk.dk/amagerstrandpark; ☻; Ⓜ Øresund, Amager Strand) A sand-sational artificial lagoon southeast of the city centre, with acres of beach and, during summer, a festive vibe most days, with cafes and bars. Playground facilities and shallow water make it ideal for kids. The beach is also home to Helgoland (Map p93; ☺24hr daily May-Aug; Ⓜ Øresund, Amager Strand) FREE, a vintage-inspired sea bathing complex with multiple pools open to nonmembers from late June to the end of August.

☞ Tours

Kayak Republic KAYAKING
(Map p48; ☑22 88 49 89; www.kayakrepublic.dk; Børskaj 12; 1/2/3hr rental 175/275/375kr, 2hr guided tour 395kr; ☺10am-9pm Jun-Aug, reduced hours rest of year; ▣2A, 9A, 37, 350S) ⚓ Kayak Republic runs daily two-hour kayaking tours through the city's canals, as well as less frequent three-hour tours that focus on Nordic food (695kr) or architecture (525kr). While no previous kayaking experience is necessary for the guided tours, only people with an EEP 2 or BCU 2 certificate (and ID) are able to rent sea kayaks for unaccompanied exploration.

Bike Copenhagen with Mike CYCLING
(Map p48; ☑26 39 56 88; www.bikecopenhagenwithmike.dk; Sankt Peders Stræde 47; per person 299kr; ▣2A, 5C, 6A, 14, 250S) If you don't fancy walking, Bike Mike runs three-hour cycling tours of the city, departing Sankt Peders Stræde 47 in the city centre, just east of Ørstedsparken (which is southwest of Nørreport station). The tour cost includes bike, helmet rental and Mike himself, a great character with deep, attention-grabbing knowledge of the city. Cash only.

Note that tours must be booked online and in advance; the office is not usually manned, aside from bike pick-up and departure times. Seasonal and private tours are also available.

Copenhagen City Sightseeing TOUR
(Map p48; ☑32 96 30 00; www.citysightseeing.dk; tickets adult/child from 158/79kr; ☺departures every 30-60min, 9.30am-4.30pm daily late Apr–mid-Sep, shorter hours & routes rest of year) A hop-on/hop-off double-decker bus tour, with three themed tours: Mermaid, Carlsberg and Christiania. Multilingual tape recordings make sure everyone gets the picture. The two-day 'Bus & Boat combo' (adult/child 245/123kr) also covers Canal Tours Copenhagen. There's a ticket booth on Ved Stranden, opposite Christiansborg Slotskirke.

Copenhagen Free Walking Tours WALKING
(Map p48; www.copenhagenfreewalkingtours.dk; Rådhuspladsen) This outfit runs free daily walking tours of the city. The three-hour Grand Tour of Copenhagen departs daily at 10am, 11pm and 3pm from outside Rådhus (City Hall), taking in famous landmarks and featuring interesting anecdotes. There's also a 90-minute Classical Copenhagen Tour, departing daily at noon. A 90-minute tour of Christianshavn departs daily at 4pm from Højbro Plads. A tip is expected.

Nordic Noir Tours WALKING

(Map p62; www.nordicnoirtours.com; per person 150kr, if booked online 100kr; ⊙The Killing/ The Bridge tour 4pm Sat, pre-booked Borgen tour 2pm Sat; ⓢVesterport) Fans of Danish TV dramas *The Bridge* and *The Killing* can visit the shooting locations on these themed 90-minute walks. Tours start at Vesterport S-train station. Bookings are not required, though tickets purchased online at least 48 hours in advance are 50kr cheaper. A 90-minute *Borgen* tour is also offered, though advance booking is necessary. Check website for open tour months.

CPH:cool WALKING

(Map p48; ✆50 58 28 24; www.cphcool.dk; Vesterbrogade 4A; tour 1-6 people from 1650kr; ▣2A, 6A, 12, 14, 26, 250S, ⓢKøbenhavn H) Running between two and 2½ hours, these niche walking tours cover themes like shopping, architecture, design, gastronomy and beer. There are also a couple of cycling tours. Prices vary according to the number of participants, and all tours start outside the Copenhagen Visitors Centre at Vesterbrogade 4A, opposite Tivoli amusement park.

Running Tours Copenhagen RUNNING

(Map p48; ✆50 59 17 29; www.runningtours.dk; 1-2 people 350kr, each additional person 100kr; ▣2A, 12, 14, 26, 33, 250S, ⓢKøbenhavn H) Run (or jog) around town for a cardio-friendly sightseeing session. Choose from various themes, including the Grand Tour, the Night Run, and our favourite, the Pub Run. Tours begin from Rådhuspladsen, though hotel pick-ups can be arranged.

★☆ Festivals & Events

★Copenhagen Jazz Festival MUSIC

(www.jazz.dk; ⊙Jul) Copenhagen's single largest event, and the biggest jazz festival in northern Europe, hits the city over 10 days in early July. The program covers jazz in all its forms, with an impressive line-up of local and international talent.

Fredagsrock at Plænen MUSIC

(www.tivoli.dk; Tivoli Gardens, Vesterbrogade 3; ⊙Apr-Sep) From mid-April to late September, Tivoli Gardens runs its hugely popular 'Friday's Rock'; open-air, Friday-night concerts featuring top-notch music acts from Denmark and around the world. Past performers have included Lil Wayne, 5 Seconds of Summer, Brian Wilson and Erykah Badu. Concerts are free with normal Tivoli Gardens admission.

Ølfestival BEER

(http://beerfestival.dk; ⊙May) A three-day beer fest in May, showcasing more than 800 brews from Danish and international producers. Events – which take place in a converted train workshop south of Vesterbro – include tastings, demonstrations and live music.

CPH:PIX FILM

(www.cphpix.dk; ⊙Sep/Oct) Copenhagen's feature film festival runs over two weeks in September and October. Expect a comprehensive program of cinema from Denmark and abroad, as well as numerous film-related events, including director and actor Q&As.

CPH:DOX FILM

(www.cphdox.dk; ⊙Mar) CPH:DOX is an acclaimed international documentary film festival, the third largest of its kind in the world. Taking place over 11 days in March, its diverse program takes to cinemas across the city. Screenings aside, the event also includes concerts, art exhibitions and seminars.

Tivoli Christmas Market CULTURAL

(www.tivoli.dk; ⊙Nov-Dec) From mid-November to late December, Tivoli gets into the Christmas spirit with a large Yuletide market, costumed staff and theatre shows. Fewer rides are operational but the mulled wine and *æbleskiver* (small doughnuts) are ample compensation.

Copenhagen Cooking & Food Festival FOOD & DRINK

(www.copenhagencooking.dk; ⊙Aug) Scandinavia's largest food festival serves up a gut-rumbling program spanning cooking demonstrations from A-list chefs to tastings and foodie tours of the city. Events are held in venues and restaurants across town, usually in August.

Distortion MUSIC

(www.cphdistortion.dk; ⊙May/Jun) Taking place over five heady days in late May and early June, Copenhagen Distortion celebrates the city's street life and club culture. Expect raucous block parties and top-name DJs spinning dance tracks in bars and clubs across town.

Strøm MUSIC

(www.stromcph.dk; ⊙Aug) Copenhagen's electronic music festival runs for five days in August. Considered the top festival of its kind in Scandinavia, its events include masterclasses, concerts, raves and parties across the city, many of them free.

3 Days of Design
CULTURAL
(http://3daysofdesign.dk; ⊙ May/Jun) Held in late May or early June, Copenhagen's three-day lifestyle and interior-design event sees dozens of venues, from furniture and design stores to cafes and Designmuseum Danmark, host special events open to the public. These include design-themed talks, tours and product launches.

CPH Opera Festival
MUSIC
(http://operafestival.dk; ⊙ Jul/Aug) An 11-day celebration of opera in unconventional locations across the city, from historic buildings to boats in the harbour. The festival usually runs from late July to early August.

Kulturhavn
CULTURAL
(www.kulturhavn.dk; ⊙ Aug) For three days in August, Copenhagen takes culture to the harbour and waterways with a wide program of theatre, dance, music, sports and parades on the 'beach' at Islands Brygge, as well as at Sydhavnen, Papirøen, Refshaleøen and other waterside locations. Events are free.

Mix Copenhagen
LGBT
(www.mixcopenhagen.dk; ⊙ Oct-Nov) Copenhagen's dedicated LGBT film festival runs over 10 days, usually in late October and early November. Screenings of homegrown and foreign films are held at various venues across the city.

Copenhagen Pride
LGBT
(www.copenhagenpride.dk; ⊙ Aug) Rainbow flags fly high during the city's six-day queer fest in August. Expect live music and merry revellers in the city centre, fabulous club parties, and film screenings, as well as cultural and political forums. The Pride parade takes place on the Saturday afternoon, starting in Frederiksberg and ending in Rådhuspladsen in the city centre.

🛏 Sleeping

Copenhagen's accommodation continues to smarten up, with a string of svelte, on-point hotels either recently opened or in the pipeline. These are a refreshing antidote to the city's plethora of soulless, business-geared hotels and 'boutique' digs in need of a refresh. Budget accommodation has also received a boost in recent years with hip, low-frill chains WakeUp Copenhagen and Generator Hostel. Reserve rooms in advance, especially during the busy summer season.

🏨 Central Copenhagen

There's abundant, varied accommodation in the central area if you can cope with busy roads, tourist crowds and a general lack of cosiness. Waterside Christianshavn has contrastingly limited choice.

Copenhagen Downtown Hostel
HOSTEL €
(Map p48; ☑ 70 23 21 10; www.copenhagendowntown.com; Vandkunsten 5; dm from 210kr; ☎; 🖳 1A, 2A, 9A, 14, 26, 37, Ⓢ København H) Centrally located in the city's historic core, this hostel is the perfect jumping-off point for exploring Copenhagen on foot. It's a lively, retro-style place with a community feel, along with a colourful bar and cafe with happy-hour offerings and free dinner nightly (when you book accommodation via the hostel website). Other freebies include live music and social events. Bike rental is available, and the optional breakfast buffet will set you back 70kr.

Cabinn City
HOTEL €
(☑ 33 46 16 16; www.cabinn.com; Mitchellsgade 14; s/d 495/645kr; @ ☎; 🖳 5C, 34, 66, 250S, Ⓢ København H) If you're not intent on surrounding yourself with fancy Danish design, but just want somewhere clean and relatively comfortable to lie your head, Cabinn may be your hotel in shining armour. Rooms are small but functional, making clever use of the limited space. And it's close to the action.

Danhostel Copenhagen City
HOSTEL €
(Map p57; ☑ 33 11 85 85; www.danhostel.dk; HC Andersens Blvd 50; dm/d from 205/590kr; @ ☎; 🖳 5C, 250S, Ⓢ København H) Step into the lobby here with its cafe-bar and it looks more like a hotel than a hostel. Set in a tower block overlooking the harbour just south of Tivoli Gardens (did we mention the views?), the dorms and private rooms are all bright, light and modern, each with bathroom.

★ Ibsens Hotel
BOUTIQUE HOTEL €€
(Map p48; ☑ 33 13 19 13; www.ibsenshotel.dk; Vendersgade 23; d from 975kr; @ ☎; 🖳 5C, 37, 350S, Ⓜ Nørreport, Ⓢ Nørreport) Ibsens is a sound choice for discerning sophisticates. Local creativity underscores everything from the striking textiles to the artwork; the inviting lobby comes complete with industrial French lamps and timber tables from veteran Copenhagen cabinetmakers Jul. Møller & Søns. The rooms themselves are minimalist yet plush, with muted tones, designer fixtures and blissful beds. Book early for the best rates.

★**Hotel Alexandra** BOUTIQUE HOTEL €€

(Map p48; ☑ 33 74 44 44; www.hotelalexandra.dk; HC Andersens Blvd 8; d from 1180kr; P @ 🛜; 🚇 2A, 10, 250S, Ⓢ Vesterport) The furniture of Danish design deities such as Arne Jacobsen, Ole Wanscher and Kaare Klint graces the interiors of the crisp, refined yet homey Alexandra. Rooms are effortlessly cool, each decked out in a mix of mid-century Danish pieces. Purists can opt for one of the suites, which are dedicated to single Danish designers. On-site parking costs 180kr per day.

Although the hotel faces a busy road, it's a quick walk from the cosy Latin Quarter.

★**Hotel Danmark** BOUTIQUE HOTEL €€

(Map p48; ☑ 33 11 48 06; www.brochner-hotels. com; Vester Voldgade 89; d from 1210kr; P 🛜; 🚇 12, 33, Ⓢ København H) The revamped Danmark is a svelte boutique hideaway steps away from major sights. Though most of its 88 rooms are rather petite, they're all flawlessly chic and ensconcing, with heavenly beds, tactile fabrics and restrained, elegant Danish furniture. Interestingly, the muted colour accents – which range from sage green to cobalt blue – are inspired by the nearby Thorvaldsen Museum.

The hotel's entry-level bunk-bed rooms offer the same luxe style and amenities featured in higher-category rooms, and the optional breakfast (195kr, half-price for children) is delicious and mostly organic. Extra perks include complimentary evening wine and a rooftop terrace. Rooms are generally cheaper on weekends. On-site parking costs 215kr per day.

Hotel Kong Arthur HOTEL €€

(Map p48; ☑ 33 11 12 12; www.kongarthur.dk; Nørre Søgade 11; d from 1180kr; P @ 🛜; 🚇 5C, 37, Ⓜ Nørreport, Ⓢ Nørreport) The 155-room Kong Arthur merges understated elegance with quirky period details, such as suits of armour. Rooms are a soothing white, splashed with contemporary art and include attractive bathrooms. Some overlook the waters of Peblinge Sø. The in-house spa – complete with hot tub, sauna and aroma steam bath – is free for guests who book directly on the hotel website.

Hotel SP34 BOUTIQUE HOTEL €€

(Map p48; ☑ 33 13 30 00; www.brochner-hotels. com; Sankt Peders Stræde 34; d from 1140kr; 🛜; 🚇 5C, 6A, Ⓢ Vesterport) A popular choice for design-savvy urbanites. Tans and subtle pastels underline the communal areas, among them a plush, light-drenched lounge, modernist-inspired reading room and svelte lobby bar. The 118 rooms are smart yet simple, with an austere, grey-on-grey colour palette warmed by timber, brass and leather accents. Nibble on organic produce at breakfast, and sip complimentary vino between 5pm and 6pm.

On-site facilities also include a small movie-screening room and the commendable Nordic restaurant Väkst. Best of all, the property sits on the edge of the vibrant Latin Quarter. Book well ahead.

Square HOTEL €€

(Map p48; ☑ 33 38 12 00; www.thesquarecopen hagen.com; Rådhuspladsen 14; d from 1225kr; ❄ @ 🛜; 🚇 2A, 12, 26, 250S, Ⓢ Vesterport) Fitted out with Arne Jacobsen chairs and red leather, the Square is an excellent three-star hotel with designer flair and amenities generally associated with greater expense and more stiffness. Standard rooms are a little small but well equipped, and some have sterling views of Rådhuspladsen – plus all the city's main sights are within walking distance.

First Hotel Kong Frederik HOTEL €€

(Map p48; ☑ 33 12 59 02; www.firsthotels.com; Vester Voldgade 25; d from 1160kr; @ 🛜; 🚇 2A, 10, 250S, Ⓢ Vesterport) There's something rather baronial about black-and-gold Kong Frederik, its interiors a mix of dark woods, antique furnishings, and paintings of Danish royalty and hunting scenes. The well-appointed rooms include wonderfully comfortable beds with fluffy duvets and free bottled water and soft drinks in the mini bar. Staff are friendly and helpful, and it's within easy walking distance of the lively Latin Quarter.

Hotel Skt Petri HOTEL €€

(Map p48; ☑ 33 45 91 00; www.hotelsktpetri. com; Krystalgade 22; rm from 1125kr; @ 🛜; 🚇 14, 150S, Ⓜ Nørreport, Ⓢ Nørreport) What was once a department store is now the Skt Petri. Despite its size – the lobby looks like a furniture showroom – the place radiates warmth. The rooms are snug and comfortable, with tactile materials and a charcoal palette softened by blonde-timber flooring and rich splashes of deep green, purple, blue and bronze. Request a room on level four or higher for the best views.

★**Hotel Nimb** BOUTIQUE HOTEL €€€

(Map p48; ☑ 88 70 00 00; www.nimb.dk; Bernstorffsgade 5; r from 2800kr; P @ 🛜; 🚇 2A, 5C, 9A, 250S, Ⓢ København H) Part of historic Tivoli

Gardens, this boutique belle offers 17 individually styled rooms and suites that fuse clean lines, beautiful art and antiques, luxury fabrics and tech perks, such as Nespresso coffee machines and Bang & Olufsen TVs and sound systems. All rooms except three also feature a fireplace, while all bar one come with views over the amusement park.

In-house perks include a savvy cocktail lounge with crackling fire and herbivore-focused hotspot restaurant **Gemyse** (Map p48; 6-course menu 250kr, add meat/fish per serving 105kr; ☺noon-11pm; 🖂🖉). Book rooms well in advance for the best prices.

Hotel d'Angleterre   HOTEL €€€
(Map p48; ☑33 12 00 95; www.dangleterre.com; Kongens Nytorv 34; r from 3250kr; ✳@🖂≋; Ⓜ Kongens Nytorv) Hitting the scene in 1755, the neoclassical d'Angleterre is Copenhagen's most glamorous slumber palace. Renovated in 2013, it's once again fit for royalty and mere mortal sybarites. Regal portraits, fireplaces and art nouveau flourishes keep things suitably posh in the public areas, while the hotel's rooms and suites deliver contemporary twists on classic luxury, with powdery accents, luxurious fabrics and marble bathrooms.

The hotel's rebirth also includes an extraordinary 2,000 sq ft tile-and-marble pool, part of the hotel's luxury spa. Other hotel perks include the city's first dedicated **champagne bar**, and Michelin-starred nosh spot **Marchal**.

Scandic Palace Hotel   HOTEL €€€
(Map p48; ☑33 14 40 50; www.scandichotels.com; Rådhuspladsen 57; d from 1500kr; ✳@🖂; Ⓠ10,12,14,26,33, Ⓢ København H) Bang on Rådhuspladsen and housed in a landmark 1910 Anton Rosen–designed building, the Palace skillfully balances historic architecture with contemporary detailing. Rooms are elegantly pared back, with sleek bathrooms and shades of pastel or grey breaking up the Scandinavian white.

🛏 Nyhavn & the Royal Quarter

★Generator Hostel   HOSTEL €
(Map p48; ☑78 77 54 00; www.generatorhostel.com; Adelgade 5-7; dm/d from 130/595kr; @🖂; Ⓠ350S,1A,26, Ⓜ Kongens Nytorv) A solid choice for 'cheap chic', upbeat, design-literate Generator sits on the edge of the city's medieval core. It's kitted out with designer furniture, slick communal areas (including a bar and outdoor terrace) and friendly, young staff. While the rooms can be a little small, all are bright and modern, with bathrooms in private rooms and dorms.

Bedwood Hostel   HOSTEL €
(Map p48; ☑61 42 61 46; www.bedwood.dk; Nyhavn 63C; dm from 200kr; 🖂; Ⓠ1A, 26, 66, 350S, Ⓜ Kongens Nytorv) Located on the famous Nyhavn waterfront, this cosy hostel occupies a historic wood-beamed warehouse dating from 1756. The dorms range in size from six to 12 beds, and each bed is handmade with a nifty curtain for privacy and bedside power socket. On-site facilities include a small communal kitchen, laundry and bike rental (handy for cycling the nearby Harbour Circle route). The optional breakfast costs 55kr, and reception is open around the clock.

★Babette Guldsmeden   BOUTIQUE HOTEL €€
(Map p60; ☑33 14 15 00; www.guldsmedenhotels.com; Bredgade 78; d from 995kr; @🖂≋; Ⓠ1A) 🖉 The 98-room Babette is part of the superb Guldsmeden hotel chain, with the same (unexpectedly) harmonious blend of Nordic and Indonesian design aesthetics. Though on the smaller side, the rooms are inviting and tactile, with four-poster beds, sheepskin throws and vibrant artworks. There's a Balinese-inspired rooftop spa and sauna, tranquil leafy courtyard, buzzing bar popular with locals, as well as a good, mostly organic restaurant.

Copenhagen Strand   HOTEL €€
(Map p48; ☑33 48 99 00; www.copenhagenstrand.dk; Havnegade 37; r from 1035kr; @🖂; Ⓠ66, Ⓜ Kongens Nytorv) 🖉 In a converted 19th-century warehouse, the appealing Strand overlooks Copenhagen Harbour. Rooms are classically styled in wood, brass and shades of greys and blue. Standard rooms are smallish but cosy; the executive rooms and suites come with water views. Bike rental available.

Wakeup Copenhagen   HOTEL €€
(Map p48; ☑44 80 00 00; www.wakeupcopenhagen.com; Borgergade 9; r 450-1500kr; 🖂; Ⓠ1A, 26, Ⓜ Kongens Nytorv) An easy walk from Nyhavn, Rosenborg Slot and some of the city's best shopping, this is one of two Wakeup Copenhagen branches in town, well known for offering style on a budget (assuming you've booked online and in advance). The foyer is spacious and design-literate, while the 498 rooms are small yet quiet, clean and sharp, with flat-screen TVs and capsule-like showers.

Wakeup's original **branch** (☑44 80 00 00; www.wakeupcopenhagen.com; Carsten Niebuhrs Gade 11; r 450-1500kr; @🤶; 🚊34, 66, Ⓢ København H) is located closer to Tivoli Gardens.

71 Nyhavn Hotel
HOTEL €€€

(Map p57; ☑33 43 62 00; www.71nyhavnhotel. com; Nyhavn 71; r from 1700kr; ✳@🤶🐕; 🚊66, Ⓜ Kongens Nytorv) Housed in two striking 200-year-old canal-side warehouses, atmospheric 71 Nyhavn offers great views of both the harbour and Nyhavn canal. Rooms facing Nyhavn are quite small, while those without the view compensate with more space. The hotel is popular with business travellers, and therefore can be a bargain on weekends.

🛏 Christianshavn

CPH Living
BOUTIQUE HOTEL €€

(Map p57; ☑61 60 85 46; www.cphliving.com; Langebrogade 1A; r incl breakfast from 1380kr; 🤶; 🚊5C, 12, Ⓜ Christiania) Located on a converted freight boat, Copenhagen's only floating hotel consists of 12 stylish, contemporary rooms with harbour and city views. Perks include modern bathrooms with rain shower head, heated floors and a communal sun deck for summertime lounging. Breakfast is a simple affair, while the central location makes it walkable to the city centre, Christianshavn and the harbour pools at Islands Brygge.

🛏 Vesterbro

Handily close to Central Station, Vesterbro has hotspot restaurants, cafes and bars, though its eastern section feels more seedy. There are two Cabinn-chain budget hotels near Forum Metro.

★ Urban House
HOSTEL, HOTEL €

(Map p62; ☑89 88 32 69; www.urbanhouse. me; Colbjørnsensgade 5-11, Vesterbro; dm/d from 140/530kr; @🤶; 🚊2A, 5C, 9A, 10, 14, 250S, Ⓢ København H) This huge hostel spans a trio of historic buildings close to Central Station and Vesterbro's on-trend venues. Slumber options range from single rooms to dorms with bunks for up to 12 people; all have private bathrooms. Bed linen and towels are included in the price, while in-house facilities include a communal kitchen, laundry, games room, small cinema and even a tattoo parlour!

Bike rental is available, and regular activities include free daily guided walks, early morning jogs, salsa nights and live music. Note that there is no reception; check-in is automated.

Andersen Hotel
HOTEL €€

(Map p62; ☑33 31 43 44; www.andersen-hotel. dk; Helgolandsgade 12, Vesterbro; d from 1210kr; 🤶; 🚊6A, 26, Ⓢ København H) White-on-white gives way to bold, playful design at Andersen. Rooms are simple yet skilfully fitted out with smile-inducing details, from geometric blankets and cushions, to *Mad Men*–style rugs and chairs, and text wall murals. We also love the Molten Brown bathroom amenities and complimentary evening wine (between 5pm and 6pm). If you're a light sleeper, request a room facing the internal courtyard.

The hotel is a quick walk from Central Station and Vesterbro's popular bars, restaurants and boutiques.

Bertrams Guldsmeden
BOUTIQUE HOTEL €€

(Map p62; ☑70 20 81 07; www.guldsmedenhotels. com; Vesterbrogade 107, Vesterbro; d from 1190kr; @🤶; 🚊3A, 6A) 🌱 Like the rest of the gorgeous Guldsmeden hotels (there are several in town), Bertrams features raw stone, bare wood, crisp white linen, spectacular bath tubs and exotic Bali-style decor. The hotel is eminently comfortable, with underfloor heating and plenty of squishy sofas and comfortable seating spaces; the breakfast is also a slice above the norm.

The Guldsmeden hotels are all Green Globe certified, which means tasty organic food and an active recycling policy.

Hotel Ansgar
HOTEL €€

(Map p62; ☑33 21 21 96; www.ansgarhotel. dk; Colbjørnsensgade 29, Vesterbro; d from 945kr; 🅿@🤶🐕; 🚊2A, 5C, 9A, 10, 14, 250S, Ⓢ København H) Around the corner from the main train station, rooms here have a white-on-white, somewhat clinical look, though most are spacious with large bathrooms. Several rooms overlook the attractive outside terrace with its bubbling fountain; from others you can spy nearby Tivoli. Bikes are available to rent, and the management go out of their way to advise and assist.

Tiffany
HOTEL €€

(Map p62; ☑33 21 80 50; www.hoteltiffany.dk; Colbjørnsensgade 28, Vesterbro; d from 895kr; @🤶; 🚊2A, 5C, 9A, 10, 14, 250S, Ⓢ København H) The Tiffany, which proudly bills itself as a 'Sweet Hotel', is a pleasant little place filled with character. Extras in the 30 rooms include Nespresso machine and kitchenette equipped with fridge, microwave oven and toaster. Service is kind and considerate, and it's an easy walk from Central Station, Tivoli Gardens and the cool and fashionable Vesterbro.

Axel Guldsmeden   BOUTIQUE HOTEL **€€€**
(Map p62; ☑ 33 31 32 66; www.guldsmedenhotels.
com; Helgolandsgade 7-11, Vesterbro; d from 1395kr;
@ 🛜; 🚌 6A, 26, 🚇 København H) 🏊 Part of the
reputable ecohotel chain, Axel Guldsmeden
puts a Nordic spin on Balinese chic. Rooms
are spacious and plushly decorated, oriental
carpets contrasting against parquet flooring
and pale paintwork. There's a luxe spa on site
with sauna, Jacuzzi, steam bath and cold tub,
plus lushly planted garden and fireplace for
warming your toes on chilly evenings. The
breakfast buffet is organic.

Always check for last-minute deals, which
can see rooms offered for as low as 895kr.

🍴 Eating

Beneath Copenhagen's galaxy of Michelin
stars is a growing number of hotspots serving innovative contemporary Danish fare
at affordable prices. The international food
scene is also lifting its game, with a spate of
new places serving authentic dishes like pho,
ramen and tacos made using top-notch produce. Keeping them company are veritable
city institutions serving classic Danish fare,
including smørrebrød.

Central Copenhagen

★ Café Halvvejen   DANISH **€**
(Map p48; ☑ 33 11 91 12; www.cafehalvvejen.dk;
Krystalgade 11; dishes 55-125kr; ⊙ 11am-2am Mon-
Thu, to 3am Fri & Sat; 🚌 5A, 6A, 14, 150S, 🚇 Nørreport, 🚇 Nørreport) Cosy, creaky, wood-panelled
Café Halvvejen channels a fast-fading Copenhagen. The menu is unapologetically hearty,
generous and cheap for this part of town,
with faithful open sandwiches, *frikadeller*
(Danish meatballs) and *pariserbøf* (minced
beef steak with egg and onions). The deceptively named *miniplatte* offers a satisfying
overview of classic Nordic flavours. Whatever you choose, wash it down with a (very
generous) shot of *akvavit*.

Café Halvvejen has just a handful of tables
(book or go early) and the kitchen is only
open between noon and 3pm.

★ Torvehallerne KBH   MARKET **€**
(Map p48; www.torvehallernekbh.dk; Israels Plads,
Nørreport; dishes from around 50kr; ⊙ 10am-7pm
Mon-Thu, to 8pm Fri, to 6pm Sat, 11am-5pm Sun;
🚌 15E, 150S, 185, 🚇 Nørreport, 🚇 Nørreport) Food
market Torvehallerne KBH is an essential
stop on the Copenhagen foodie trail. A delicious ode to the fresh, the tasty and the
artisanal, the market's beautiful stalls peddle

everything from seasonal herbs and berries
to smoked meats, seafood and cheeses, smørrebrød, fresh pasta and hand-brewed coffee.
You could easily spend an hour or more exploring its twin halls.

As well as a market, you can eat here too;
several of the vendors also prepare inexpensive meals.

★ Gasoline Grill   BURGERS **€**
(Map p48; www.facebook.com/gasolinegrill; Landgreven 10; burgers 75kr; ⊙ 11am-until sold out; 🚌 1A,
26, 🚇 Kongens Nytorv) Some of the city's most
famous chefs join the queue at Gasoline, a
petrol station-turned-burger takeaway. The
menu is refreshingly straightforward: four
burgers (one vegetarian), fries with a choice
of toppings and homemade dips, and two
desserts. The meat is organic and freshly
ground daily, the buns brioche, and the flavour rich and decadent without the post-feed
grease and guilt. The place closes when the
burgers run out; usually around 6pm. (Go at
lunch to avoid disappointment.)

Atelier September   CAFE **€**
(Map p48; ☑ 26 29 57 53; www.atelierseptember.
dk; Gothersgade 30; dishes 30-125kr; ⊙ 7.30am-
4pm Mon-Fri, from 9am Sat, from 10am Sun; 🚌 350S,
🚇 Kongens Nytorv) It might look like a *Vogue*
photo shoot with its white-on-white interior and vintage glass ceiling (typical of old
Danish pharmacies), but Atelier September
is very much a cafe. Kitted out in vintage
exhibition posters and communal tables, it
sells gorgeous espresso and simple, inspired
edibles. Standouts include sliced avocado on
rye bread, topped with lemon zest, chives, pa-
prika and peppery olive oil.

Palæo   HEALTH FOOD **€**
(Map p48; ☑ 73 70 97 01; www.palaeo.dk;
Pilestræde 32; dishes 59-85kr; ⊙ 8am-8pm Mon-Fri,
9am-7pm Sat, 9am-5pm Sun; 🛜; 🚌 1A, 26, 350S,
🚇 Kongens Nytorv) Fast-food, Flintstones-style
is what you get at Palæo, a trendy eat-in/take-
away joint peddling so-called 'primal gastronomy'. Dishes are inspired by the Paleolithic
diet, which means carb-light creations like
hot dogs and especially popular wraps which
ditch bread for egg-based wrappers. But if
you're thinking mung-bean mediocrity, think
again: behind the menu is Michelin-starred
chef Thomas Rode Andersen.

Far's Dreng   DANISH **€**
(Map p48; ☑ 30 86 89 89; www.farsdreng.com;
Ny Adelgade; smørrebrod 70kr, salad from 55kr;
⊙ 8am-6pm Mon-Fri, 9.30am-6pm Sat, 9.30am-

4pm Sun; 🖥; Ⓜ Kongens Nytorv) On two snug floors decorated with low-slung lamps and sheepskin-covered chairs, bustling Far's Dreng pulls in young, hip crowds with affordable, tasty cafe grub that's freshly made. The menu is a short, straightforward affair, with an emphasis on smørrebrod made using quality, often organic ingredients. Simply tick your choices on the menu and hand it over at the counter.

Lillian's Smørrebrød
DANISH €

(Map p57; 🖥 33 14 20 66; www.facebook.com/lillianssmorrebrod; Vester Voldgade 108; smørrebrød from 17kr; ⊙ 6am-2pm Mon-Fri; 🚇 1A, 2A, 9A) Tiny 1970s throwback Lillian's is one of the best and least costly smørrebrød places in town. Decked out in white deli-style tiles, with kitsch artwork and just a handful of tables, its generous, open-face sandwiches are classic: think marinated herring, chicken salad and roast beef with remoulade. However, while the coffee here is also a bargain, you'll get a much better cup elsewhere.

Restaurant Kronborg
DANISH €

(Map p48; 🖥 33 13 07 08; www.restaurantkronborg.dk/en; Brolæggerstræde 12; smørrebrød 69-139kr; ⊙ 11am-5pm; 🖥; 🚇 14) Behind its hulking, centuries-old walls, cosy, wood-beamed Kronborg serves up classic Danish fare. Head here for the impressive choice of lunchtime smørrebrød, appropriately served on Royal Copenhagen china. Favourites include the sweet, succulent Brantevik herring, marinated in sugar, vinegar and allspice and topped with fresh herbs. Toast to tradition with an *akvavit* or a craft brew from Copenhagen's own Nørrebro Bryghus.

Cock's & Cows
BURGERS €

(Map p48; 🖥 69 69 60 00; www.cocksandcows.dk; Gammel Strand 34; burgers 89-129kr; ⊙ 11.30am-9.30pm Sun-Thu, to 10.30pm Fri & Sat; 🖥; 🚇 1A, 2A, 9A, 26, 37, 66) When burger lust hits, satiate your urges at Cock's. In a setting best described as American diner meets Danish modernist (red leather booths against Poul Henningsen lamps), energetic staff deliver fresh, made-from-scratch burgers. The meat is Danish and charcoal-grilled, and there's both a veggie and a vegan burger.

DØP
HOT DOGS €

(Map p48; 🖥 30 20 40 25; www.døp.dk; Købmagergade 50; hot dogs from 35kr; ⊙ 11am-6.30pm Mon-Sat; 🚇 14, Ⓜ Nørrebro, Ⓢ Nørrebro) 🍴 Danes love a good *pølse* (sausage), and hot-dog vans are ubiquitous across Copenhagen. DØP is

the best, with a van right beside Rundetårn (Round Tower). Everything here is organic, from the meat and vegetables to the toppings. Options range from a classic Danish roasted hot dog with mustard, ketchup, remoulade, pickles and onions both fresh and fried, to a new-school vegan tofu version.

★ Schønnemann
DANISH €€

(Map p48; 🖥 33 12 07 85; www.restaurantschonnemann.dk; Hauser Plads 16; smørrebrød 75-185kr; ⊙ 11.30am-5pm Mon-Sat; 🖥; 🚇 6A, 42, 150S, 184, 185, 350S, Ⓜ Nørreport, Ⓢ Nørreport) A veritable institution, Schønnemann has been lining bellies with smørrebrød and snaps since 1877. Originally a hit with farmers in town selling their produce, the restaurant's current fan base includes revered chefs like René Redzepi; try the smørrebrød named after him: smoked halibut with creamed cucumber, radishes and chives on caraway bread.

★ Pluto
DANISH €€

(Map p48; 🖥 33 16 00 16; http://restaurantpluto.dk/forside; Borgergade 16; mains 135-225kr; ⊙ 5.30pm-midnight Mon-Thu, to 2am Fri & Sat, to 11pm Sun; 🖥; 🚇 1A, 26, Ⓜ Kongens Nytorv) Loud, convivial Pluto is not short of friends for good reason: super-fun soundtrack, attentive staff and beautiful, simple dishes by respected local chef Rasmus Oubæk. Whether it's flawlessly seared cod with seasonal carrots or a side of new potatoes, funky truffles and green beans in a mussel broth, the family-style menu is all about letting the produce sing.

The bistro has a solid selection of charcuterie and smoked meats, and some interesting natural wines, as well as bar seating (especially great for solo diners).

★ Slurp Ramen Joint
RAMEN €€

(Map p48; 🖥 53 70 80 83; http://slurpramen.dk; Nansensgade 90; ramen 130-135kr; ⊙ 5-10pm Tue-Sat, also noon-2.30pm Fri & Sat; 🚇 5C, 350S, Ⓜ Nørreport, Ⓢ Nørreport) That white-tile, pink-neon Slurp serves Copenhagen's best ramen makes sense: head chef Philipp Inreiter once worked at cult-status Tokyo ramen joint Hototogisu. The deeply flavoursome chicken-and-pork bone broth is cooked for more than eight hours, while noodles are made in-house with a pinch of freshly ground rye for added depth. Best of the trio of options (which includes a vegetarian ramen) is the shoyu.

Slurp is small, hugely popular and has a no-reservations policy: go as close to opening as possible, get your name on the waiting list and grab a pre-feed drink at one of the bars further down the street.

Royal Smushi Café
DANISH €€

(Map p48; ☑33 12 11 22; www.royalsmushicafe.
dk; Amagertorv 6; 2/3/4 pieces of smushi
98/148/195kr; ◷9am-7pm Mon-Thu, to 8pm Fri &
Sat, to 6pm Sun; ◨1A, 2A, 9A, 26, 37, 350S, Ⓜ Kongens Nytorv) Here, the traditional compo-
nents of the hearty Danish smørrebrød are
reimagined in a delicate and intricate style,
inspired by sushi. Breakfast and stunning
desserts are also available, as well as a range
of teas and speciality coffees. The cafe is accessed through a charming stone courtyard,
which is a lovely spot in warmer weather.

The Market
ASIAN €€

(Map p48; ☑70 70 24 35; http://themarketcph.
dk; Antonigade 2; mains 155-350kr, 12-course menu
595kr; ◷11.30am-4pm & 5-10pm Mon-Thu, to
10.30pm Fri & Sat, to 9.30pm Sun; ◨1A, 26, Ⓜ Kongens Nytorv) Dark, svelte and contemporary
(we love the dramatically back-lit bar and
organically shaped crockery), The Market
pumps out vibrant pan-Asian dishes like delicate brown-crab salad with apple, dashi and
avocado, or expertly grilled poussin dressed
in coconut sauce and fresh mango slithers.
The sushi is commendable, particularly the
maki.

Cantina
ITALIAN €€

(Map p48; ☑88 16 99 95; http://cantinacph.dk;
Borgergade 2; mains 225-265kr, pizzas 125-185kr;
◷11am-midnight Sun-Wed, to 1am Thu, to 2am Fri
& Sat; ☎; ◨1A, 26, Ⓜ Kongens Nytorv) Prolific
restaurateurs Henrik Laszlo and Mikkel Ege-
lund are behind this buzzing, semi-industrial
space. A hybrid Italian bistro-bar, its small
plates and pastas are especially good, the
latter offering the likes of properly al den-
te macaroni with slow-cooked rabbit, sage
and parmesan. The decent, Neapolitan-style
wood-fired pizzas are served all day – handy
if you're having a super-late lunch or very
early dinner.

Kanal Caféen
DANISH €€

(Map p48; ☑33 11 57 70; www.kanalcafeen.dk;
Frederiksholms Kanal 18; smørrebrød 64-127kr, platters per person from 205kr; ◷11am-5pm Mon-Fri,
11.30am-3pm Sat; ◨1A, 2A, 9A, 14, 26, 37) Famed
for its gruff staff and excellent herring, this
cosy, nautically themed old-timer comes
with a shaded summertime pontoon right on
the canal. Order some Linie Aquavit (*snaps*
matured at sea in oak-sherry casks) and the
Kanal Platter, an epic, hunger-busting feast
of Danish classics, including pickled herring,
crumbed plaice, and roast pork with pickled
red cabbage.

Bistro Pastis
FRENCH €€

(Map p48; ☑33 93 44 11; http://bistro-pastis.
dk; Gothersgade 52; salads & sandwiches 115-145kr,
mains 165-275kr; ◷11am-midnight Sun-Wed, to
1am Thu, to 2am Fri & Sat; ☎; ◨350S, Ⓜ Kongens
Nytorv) Paging both Paris and NYC with its
lipstick-red banquettes and white subway
tiles, upbeat Pastis is perfect for a post-
shopping Gallic bite or a more substantial
dinner. Feel fancy over a light *salade chévre
chaud* (grilled goat's cheese salad with pickled walnuts and raisins) or delve into bistro
mains like cognac-laced steak tartare or
warming bouillabaisse (fish soup). Great
house-made *pommes frites*, too.

42° Raw
VEGETARIAN €€

(Map p48; ☑32 12 32 10; www.42raw.com;
Pilestræde 32; meals 79-139kr; ◷8am-8pm Mon-Fri,
9am-6pm Sat & Sun; ☎◢; ◨350S, Ⓜ Kongens Nytorv) ◢ Treat your body at this hip, healthy
eat-in or takeaway. The deal is raw food,
served in vibrant, textured dishes like 'raw'
lasagne, Thai noodles, and burgers made with
organic, gluten-free buns. If it's still AM, fuel
up with one of the breakfast bowls.

Restaurant Krebsegaarden
INTERNATIONAL €€

(Map p48; ☑20 12 40 15; http://krebsegaarden.
dk/en/home; Studiestræde 17; mains 195-225kr;
◷6-10pm Tue-Sat; ◨5A, 6A, 10, 14, Ⓜ Nørreport,
Ⓢ Nørreport) Petite Krebsegaarden offers a
unique dining experience by drawing its culinary inspiration from the works displayed
in Gallery Krebsen, located in the beautiful
adjoining courtyard. The result is rotating
menus directly influenced by the current
exhibition as well as the nationality, heritage and preferred flavours of the artist on
show. Indeed, even the decor is affected by
the exhibitions, meaning an ever-changing
atmosphere.

★Bror
NEW NORDIC €€€

(Map p48; ☑32 17 59 99; www.restaurantbror.
dk; Sankt Peders Stræde 24A; 4-/5-course menu
450/625kr; ◷5.30pm-midnight Wed-Sun; ☎;
◨2A, 5C, 6A, 250S, Ⓜ Nørreport, Ⓢ Nørreport)
Founded by former Noma sous-chefs Sam
Nutter and Viktor Wågam, this tiny, split-
level bolthole mightn't look like much, but
it delivers technically brilliant dishes using
superlative Nordic produce. Wines are natural, organic or biodynamic, and expertly
paired with beautifully balanced creations
like Danish peas with crab meat, crab gel and
kombucha, or chocolate mousse with chamomile gel and sorbet, blackberries and tuile.

★ Restaurant Mes
DANISH €€€

(Map p48; ☑ 25 36 51 81; https://restaurant-mes.dk; Jarmers Plads 1; 5-course menu 350kr; ⊙ 5.30pm-midnight Mon-Sat; ☎; 🚇 2A, 5C, 6A, 250S, Ⓢ Vesterport) This rising star burst onto the Copenhagen dining scene in 2017. Owned by chef Mads Rye Magnusson (former chef at Michelin-three-starred Geranium), it's an intimate, refreshingly whimsical space, complete with moss feature wall and graffiti-soaked restrooms by local artist Fy. Most impressive is the menu, driven by market produce and the creative whims of its young, highly talented head chef.

★ Höst
NEW NORDIC €€€

(Map p48; ☑ 89 93 84 09; www.hostvakst.dk; Nørre Farimagsgade 41; 3-/5-course menu 350/450kr; ⊙ 5.30pm-midnight, last order 9.30pm; 🚇 37, Ⓜ Nørreport, Ⓢ Nørreport) Höst's phenomenal popularity is easy to understand: award-winning interiors and New Nordic food that's equally fabulous and filling. The set menu is superb, with three smaller 'surprise dishes' thrown in and evocative creations like baked flounder with roasted chicken skin, shrimp, peas and an apple-vinegar fish stock, or a joyful rose-hip sorbet paired with Danish strawberries, a green strawberry puree, meringue and herbs.

If you're watching your pennies, keep an eye on the price of the wines by the glass, some of which can add significantly to the bill.

Orangeriet
DANISH €€€

(Map p48; ☑ 33 11 13 07; www.restaurant-orangeriet.dk; Kronprinsessegade 13; smørrebrod 75kr, 3-/4-/5-course dinner 395/475/525kr; ⊙ 11.30am-3pm & 6-10pm Mon-Sat, noon-4pm Sun; 🚇 350S, 26) Take an airy, vintage conservatory, add elegant, seasonal menus, and you have Orangeriet. Skirting the eastern edge of Kongens Have, its contemporary creations focus on simplicity and premium produce. Savour clean, intriguing dishes like smoked mackerel with horseradish mayonnaise, pickled green strawberries, lettuce and herbs. Lunch is a simpler affair of picture-perfect smørrebrød, best nibbled in the restaurant garden when the weather behaves. Book ahead.

Marv & Ben
NEW NORDIC €€€

(Map p48; ☑ 33 91 01 91; www.marvogben.dk; Snaregade 4; small dishes 85-135kr, 4/6-course menu 400/600kr; ⊙ 5.30pm-1am Tue-Sat; ☎; 🚇 1A, 2A, 9A, 14, 26, 37) Cellar restaurant 'Marrow & Bone' has been repeatedly awarded a Michelin Bib Gourmand in recognition of its

value for money. Its New Nordic menu can be approached in various ways: a la carte or as four- or six-course tasting menus. Dishes are imaginative and evocative, celebrating Nordic landscapes and moods in creations like hay-smoked mackerel with chamomile or squid with kelp and buttermilk.

Uformel
NEW NORDIC €€€

(Map p48; ☑ 70 99 91 11; www.uformel.dk; Studiestræde 69; dishes 120kr; ⊙ 5.30pm-midnight Sun-Thu, to 2am Fri & Sat; ☎; 🚇 2A, 10, 12, 250S, Ⓢ Vesterport) The edgy younger brother of Michelin-starred restaurant Formel B, Uformel (Informal) offers a casual take on New Nordic cuisine. Expect an ever-changing menu of local, seasonal ingredients transformed into impressive dishes. Diners can choose several small plates to create their own tasting menu, or opt for the set menus, which includes a four-course option with matching wines (800kr).

Clou
DANISH €€€

(Map p48; ☑ 36 16 30 00; http://restaurant-clou.dk; Borgergade 16; tasting menu 1200kr, wine pairings 1100kr; ⊙ 6-9pm Tue-Sat; 🚇 1A, 26, Ⓜ Kongens Nytorv) Michelin-starred Clou luxuriates in its large, linen-clad tables and upholstered armchairs. That said, the menu is a contemporary affair, with both Nordic and Italo-French influences driving seasonal concoctions like brown crab with cucumber, sea salad and mint, or artichoke with dried corn, orange zest and aged cheese. À la carte options are available, though the tasting menu offers a fuller appreciation of Clou's brilliance.

If the budget permits, succumb to the exceptional wine parings. Heading the kitchen is talented young chef Jonathan K Berntsen, who opened the restaurant with his twin brother Alexander, a self-taught sommelier.

Madklubben
STEAK €€€

(Map p48; ☑ 33 13 33 34; www.madklubben.dk; Pilestræde 23; 3-course menu 300kr; ⊙ 5pm-midnight Mon-Sat; ☎; 🚇 1A, 26, 350S, Ⓜ Kongens Nytorv) Looking super-cute with its black-and-salmon booths, exposed brickwork and subway-tiled walls, Madklubben puts a fun, fashionable twist of the steakhouse. Succulent slabs of beef – either corn or grass fed – are the house speciality, glazed in brown butter, lard and garlic, cooked medium (unless requested otherwise) and served with your choice of sauce. Pescatarians needn't fret, with options like shellfish bisque and pan-fried fish.

☒ Nyhavn & the Royal Quarter

★ District Tonkin
VIETNAMESE €

(Map p48; ☎60 88 86 98; http://district-tonkin.com; Dronningens Tværgade 12; baguettes 54-62kr, soups & salads 68-120kr; ⏰11am-9.30pm Sun-Wed, to 11pm Thu-Sat; ⊒1A, 26, Ⓜ Kongens Nytorv) With a playful interior channelling the streets of Vietnam, casual, convivial District Tonkin peddles fresh, gut-filling *bánh mì* (Vietnamese baguettes), stuffed with coriander, fresh chilli and combos like Vietnamese sausage with marinated pork, homemade pâté and BBQ sauce. The menu also includes gorgeous, less-common Vietnamese soups, among them tomato-based *xíu mai* (with pork and mushroom meatballs).

★ AOC
NEW NORDIC €€€

(Map p48; ☎33 11 11 45; www.restaurantaoc.dk; Dronningens Tværgade 2; tasting menus 1500-1800kr; ⏰6.30pm-12.30am Tue-Sat; ☎1A, 26, Ⓜ Kongens Nytorv) In the vaulted cellar of a 17th-century mansion, this intimate, two-starred Michelin standout thrills with evocative, often surprising Nordic flavour combinations, scents and textures. Here, sea scallops might conspire with fermented asparagus, while grilled cherries share the plate with smoked marrow and pigeon breast. Diners choose from two tasting menus, and reservations should be made around a week in advance.

★ Geist
DANISH €€€

(Map p48; ☎33 13 37 13; http://restaurantgeist.dk; Kongens Nytorv 8; plates 85-225kr; ⏰6pm-1am; ⊒1A, 26, Ⓜ Kongens Nytorv) Chic, monochromatic Geist is owned by celebrity chef Bo Bech, a man driven by experimentation. His long list of small plates pairs Nordic and non-Nordic ingredients in unexpected, often thrilling ways. Create your tasting menu from dishes like grilled avocado with green almonds and curry, turbot and fennel ravioli with Gruyère, or out-of-the-box desserts like summer blueberries with black olives and vanilla ice cream.

★ Studio
DANISH €€€

(Map p48; ☎72 14 88 08; www.thestandardcph.dk; Havnegade 44; degustation menus from 1000kr; ⏰7pm-midnight Tue-Sat, also noon-3.30pm Sat; ⊒66, ⌑Nyhavn, Ⓜ Kongens Nytorv) Brainchild of Noma co-founder Claus Meyer and former Noma sous-chef Torsten Vildgaard, Studio bagged its first Michelin star within months of opening. Rooted in Nordic tradi-

SØLLERØD KRO

Not all of Copenhagen's Michelin stars are inner-city dwellers. In Holte, an unassuming outer suburb 19km north of the city centre, **Søllerød Kro** (Map p93; ☎45 80 25 05; www.soelleroed-kro.dk; Søllerødvej 35, Holte; 2-/3-course lunch 395/495kr, 4-/6-course dinner 875/1095kr; ⏰noon-2.30pm & 6-9.30pm Wed-Sun; ⊒195, Ⓢ Holte, then) is a one-star Michelin restaurant set in a beautiful 17th-century thatched-roof inn. The kitchen's creations are nothing short of extraordinary, pushing superlative produce to enlightened heights.

(side text: COPENHAGEN EATING)

tions, the open kitchen revels in ingredients and influences from further afield. Whether its sourdough *æbleskiver* (Danish pancake puffs) filled with truffle and cheese, or grilled pigeon paired with warm cherries cooked in foraged spices, Studio smashes it.

★ Rebel
DANISH €€€

(Map p48; ☎33 32 32 09; www.restaurantrebel.dk; Store Kongensgade 52; small dishes 115-175kr; ⏰5.30pm-midnight Tue-Sat; ⊒1A, 26, Ⓜ Kongens Nytorv) Smart, split-level Rebel dishes out arresting, modern Danish grub without the fanfare. The dining space is relatively small, simple and unadorned, giving all the attention to inspired creations like braised octopus with crispy chicken, sage and mushroom foam, or a ravioli of fried wild mushrooms, snail, ginger and soy. Trust the sommelier's wine choices, which include extraordinary Old and New World drops.

Damindra
JAPANESE €€€

(Map p48; ☎33 12 33 75; www.damindra.dk; Holbergsgade 26; lunch dishes 125-398kr, dinner tasting menu min 2 people 750kr; ⏰11am-3pm & 5-10pm Tue-Sat; ☎; ⊒66, Ⓜ Kongens Nytorv) One of Copenhagen's lesser-known talents, chef Taka Nishimura (formerly of Nobu in Melbourne) turns raw Nordic ingredients into obscenely fresh, arresting Japanese morsels. The evening 'Chef's Choice' set sushi menu offers a satisfying window into the kitchen's prowess, though cashed-up foodies should seriously consider the eight-course tour de force.

Kokkeriet
DANISH €€€

(Map p60; ☎33 15 27 77; www.kokkeriet.dk; Kronprinsessegade 64; small/large tasting menu 900/1200kr; ⏰6pm-1am Mon-Sat; ⊒1A, 26)

CAKES & BAKES

Where to head for fresh bread or the most heavenly cinnamon rolls? There's so much choice. Small cosy **Sankt Peders Bageri** (Map p48; ☑ 33 11 11 29; Sankt Pedersstræde 29; baked goods 6-45kr; ⊙ 6am-5:30pm Mon-Fri, from 6am Sat; ☐ 5A, 6A, 14, 10) goes with tradition dating back to 1652, **Brødflov** (☑ 31 31 97 10; www.broedflov.dk; Falkoner Alle 34, Frederiksberg; pastries from 20kr, sandwiches from 50kr; ⊙ 6am-7pm Mon-Fri, to 6pm Sat & Sun; ☐ 8A, Ⓜ Frederiksberg) ⫸ is a fine Frederiksberg choice, while multi-branch organic bakery **Meyers Bageri** (Map p48; www.clausmeyer.dk; Store Kongensgade 46; pastries from 14kr; ⊙ 7am-6pm Mon-Fri, to 4pm Sat & Sun; ☐ 1A, 26, Ⓜ Kongens Nytorv) gains from celebrity ownership – Claus Meyers being the founding father of the New Nordic food movement. Compromising waistlines since 1870, patisserie **La Glace** (Map p48; ☑ 33 14 46 46; www.laglace.dk; Skoubogade 3; cake slices 57kr, pastries from 36kr; ⊙ 8.30am-6pm Mon-Fri, 9am-6pm Sat, 10am-6pm Sun; 🛜 👶; ☐ 14) tempts with classic *valnøddekage* (walnut cake slices). And **Bertels Salon** (Map p48; ☑ 33 13 00 33; www.bertelskager.dk; Kompagnistrædet 5; ⊙ 11am-9pm Sun-Thu, to 10pm Fri & Sat; 🛜; ☐ 14) is reckoned to serve the city's best cheesecake (card payment only).

Tucked away in Copenhagen's historic Nyboder neighbourhood, intimate, stylish Kokkeriet proudly holds one Michelin star. Beautiful local ingredients drive the tasting menus, which offer contemporary, sharply executed takes on traditional Danish cooking. Herbivores don't miss out either, with a dedicated vegan tasting menu. On Tuesday evenings, the restaurant serves a menu comprising experimental dishes the chefs are testing out.

🍴 Slotsholmen

★ Tårnet
DANISH €€

(Map p48; ☑ 33 37 31 00; http://taarnet.dk/restauranten; Christiansborg Slotsplads, Christiansborg Slot; lunch smørrebrød 85-135kr, dinner mains 235kr; ⊙ 11.30am-11pm Tue-Sun, kitchen closes 10pm; 🛜; ☐ 1A, 2A, 9A, 26, 37, 66, 🚇 Det Kongelige Bibliotek) Book ahead for lunch at Tårnet, owned by prolific restaurateur Rasmus Bo Bojesen and memorably set inside Christiansborg Slot's commanding tower. Lunch here is better value than dinner, with superlative, contemporary smørrebrød that is among the city's best. While the general guideline is two smørrebrød per person, some of the a la carte versions are quite substantial (especially the tartare), so check before ordering.

🍴 Christianshavn

★ La Banchina
CAFE €

(Map p60; ☑ 31 26 65 61; www.labanchina.dk; Refshalevej 141A; mains 70-90kr; ⊙ 8am-11pm Mon-Fri, from 9am Sat & Sun May-Sep, reduced hours rest of year; ☐ 9A, 🚢 Refshaleøen) There are only two daily mains at this tiny lo-fi shack, cooked

beautifully and served on paper plates with little fanfare. The real magic is the setting, in a small harbour cove with picnic tables and a wooden pier where diners dip their feet while sipping decent vino, tucking into grub like tender barbecued salmon, and watching the summer sun sink over Copenhagen.

Copenhagen Street Food
STREET FOOD €

(Map p57; www.copenhagenstreetfood.dk; Warehouse 7 & 8, Trangravsvej 14; dishes from 50kr; ⊙ noon-9pm Mon-Wed & Sun, to 10pm Thu-Sat; 🍴; ☐ 66, 🚢 Operaen) ⫸ Take a disused warehouse, pack it with artisan food trucks and stalls, hipster baristas and a chilled-out bar or two, and you have this hot little newcomer. The emphasis is on fresh, affordable grub, from handmade pasta and tacos, to pulled-pork burgers and organic *koldskål* (cold buttermilk dessert).

A re-imagined version of the Copenhagen Street Food (complete with cultural events) is due to open 2.5km further north at Refshalevej 167A at Easter 2018.

Morgenstedet
VEGETARIAN €

(Map p57; Fabriksområdet 134, Christiania; dishes 50-110kr; ⊙ noon-9pm Tue-Sun; 🛜 🍴; ☐ 9A, Ⓜ Christianshavn) ⫸ A homey, hippy bolthole in the heart of Christiania, Morgenstedet offers a short, simple blackboard menu. There's usually one soup, plus two or three mains with a choice of side salads. Whether it's cauliflower soup with chickpeas and herbs or creamy potato gratin, options are always vegetarian, organic and delicious, not to mention best devoured in the blissful cafe garden. Cash only.

108　　　　　　　　　　DANISH €€

(Map p57; ☑32 96 32 92; www.108.dk; Strandgade 108; dishes 95-185kr, sharing dishes for 2 people 300-450kr; ⊙restaurant 5pm-midnight, cafe 8am-midnight Mon-Fri, from 9am Sat & Sun; ☎; ☐9A) ⬮ In a soaring, concrete-pillared warehouse, 108 offers a more casual, accessible take on New Nordic cuisine than its world-renowned sibling Noma. The family-style sharing-plate menu is all about seasonal, locally sourced ingredients, farmed or foraged, preserved, fermented and pickled. While not all dishes hit the mark, many leave a lasting impression. Three dishes per diner should satiate most appetites.

Although the glazed pork here is legendary, don't overlook the seafood dishes, which might include silky crayfish served in a green tomato and crayfish-head broth, or fluffy monkfish glazed in a piquant, earthy sauce of fermented bread and mushrooms. Attached to the restaurant is 108's small cafe, The Corner, serving coffee and house-made pastries in the morning, a short lunch menu and one main in the evening.

Cafe Wilder　　　　　　　DANISH €€

(Map p48; ☑32 54 71 83; www.cafewilder. dk; Wildersgade 56; lunch 119-149kr, dinner mains 179-209kr; ⊙9am-11pm Mon-Thu, to midnight Fri & Sat, to 10.30pm Sun; ☎; ☐2A, 9A, 37, 350S, Ⓜ Christianshavn) With its crisp white linen and circular sidewalk tables, this corner classic feels like a Parisian neighbourhood bistro. It's actually one of Copenhagen's oldest cafes, featured several times in the cult TV series *Borgen*. Relive your favourite scenes over beautiful lunchtime smørrebrød (open sandwiches) or Franco-Danish dinner mains like tender Danish pork with sweet-potato croquette and a blackcurrant sauce.

★Kadeau　　　　　　　NEW NORDIC €€€

(Map p57; ☑33 25 22 23; www.kadeau.dk; Wildersgade 10B; tasting menu 1800kr; ⊙6.30pm-midnight Wed-Fri, noon-4pm & 6.30pm-midnight Sat; ☐2A, 9A, 37, 350S, Ⓜ Christianshavn) The big-city spin-off of the Bornholm original, this Michelin-two-starred standout has firmly established itself as one of Scandinavia's top New Nordic restaurants. Whether it's salted and burnt scallops drizzled in clam bouillon, or an unexpected combination of toffee, crème fraiche, potatoes, radish and elderflower, each dish evokes Nordic flavours, moods and landscapes with extraordinary creativity and skill.

Barr　　　　　　　SCANDINAVIAN €€€

(Map p57; ☑32 96 32 93; http://restaurantbarr. com; Strandgade 93; small dishes 75-240kr, 4-course menu 600kr; ⊙5pm-midnight Tue-Thu, from noon Sat & Sat; ☎; ☐9A, 66, ⓔNyhavn) ⬮ Meaning 'barley' in old Norse, oak-lined Barr offers polished, produce-driven takes on old North Sea traditions. The small plates are a little hit and miss, with standouts including sourdough pancakes with caviar. You'll need about four small plates per person; a better-value option is to savour the pancakes and fill up on the fantastic schnitzel or *frikadeller* (Danish meatballs).

The selection of craft beers is outstanding, as are the attentive, well-trained staff. The restaurant is a joint venture between renowned New Nordic chefs René Redzepi and Thorsten Schmidt.

Kanalen　　　　　　　DANISH €€€

(Map p57; ☑32 95 13 30; www.restaurant-kanalen. dk; Wilders Plads 2; lunch dishes 95-195kr, dinner mains 225kr; ⊙11.30am-3pm & 5.30-10pm Mon-Sat; ☐2A, 9A, 37, 66, 350S, Ⓜ Christianshavn) Kanalen offers an irresistible combination: beautiful, modern Danish food and a canal-side location. While the lunch menu delivers competent renditions of Danish classics, it's the dinner menu that really stands out. Expect seamless, sophisticated dishes where tender pork finds new complexity with green peaches and foie gras, or where summertime blackberries intrigue in the company of liquorice and estragon. Book ahead.

Nørrebro & Østerbro

Mirabelle　　　　　　　CAFE €

(Map p59; ☑35 35 47 24; http://mirabelle-bakery. dk; Guldbergsgade 29, Nørrebro; pastries from 28kr, sandwiches 65kr, lunch & dinner dishes 115-175kr; ⊙7am-10pm; ☎; ☐3A, 5C) Decked out with bold geometric floor tiles, artisan bakery-cafe Mirabelle is owned by Michelin-lauded chef Christian Puglisi, who also owns popular restaurant Bæst next door. It's a slick, contemporary spot for made-from-scratch pastries, simple breakfast bites like eggs Benedict, and a short menu of Italo-centric lunch and dinner dishes, including house-made charcuterie, cheeses and organic-flour pasta.

★Oysters & Grill　　　　　SEAFOOD €€

(Map p59; ☑70 20 61 71; www.cofoco.dk/da/restauranter/oysters-and-grill; Sjællandsgade 1B, Nørrebro; mains 165-245kr; ⊙5.30pm-midnight; ☐5C) Finger-licking surf and turf is what you get at this rocking, unpretentious neighbourhood favourite, complete with kitsch vinyl tablecloths and a fun, casual vibe. The shellfish is fantastically fresh and, unlike most places, ordered by weight, which means you don't need to pick at measly servings. Meat lovers won't to be disappointed either, with cuts that are lustfully succulent. The kitchen closes at 9.45pm; book ahead.

★ Manfreds og Vin
DANISH €€

(Map p59; ☑ 36 96 65 93; www.manfreds.dk; Jægersborggade 40, Nørrebro; small plates 75-90kr, 7-course tasting menu 285kr; ⊙ noon-3.30pm & 5-10pm; 🖘 🖍; 🖵 8A) 🍴 Convivial Manfreds is the ideal local bistro, with passionate staffers, boutique natural wines and a regularly changing menu that favours organic produce (most from the restaurant's own farm) cooked simply and sensationally. Swoon over nuanced, gorgeously textured dishes like grilled spring onion served with pistachio puree, crunchy breadcrumbs and salted egg yolk. If you're hungry and curious, opt for the good-value seven-dish menu.

Fischer
ITALIAN €€

(Map p60; ☑ 35 42 39 64; www.hosfischer.dk; Victor Borges Plads 12, Østerbro; lunch mains 129-189kr, dinner mains 239kr; ⊙ 8am-midnight Mon-Fri, from 10am Sat & Sun; 🖘; 🖵 3A) A reformed workingmen's bar, neighbourly Fischer serves Italian-inspired soul food like grilled flatbread topped with tomato, goat's cheese, dates and basil, or house-made *maltagliati* pasta with rabbit, mint and chilli. That it's seriously good isn't surprising considering that owner and head chef David Fischer worked the kitchen at Rome's Michelin-starred La Pergola. Breakfast options feature some over-the-border dishes, including a hearty croque madame.

Pixie
CAFE €€

(Map p60; ☑ 39 30 03 05; www.cafepixie.dk; Løgstørgade 2, Østerbro; dishes 55-195kr; ⊙ 8am-midnight Mon-Thu, to 4am Fri & Sat, 10am-11pm Sun; 🖘; 🖵 1A) Strung with colourful lights, low-rise boho cafe Pixie looks straight out of the streets of Buenos Aires. Inside it's a *hyggelig* affair, with mismatching furniture, candlelight and soulful tunes on the speakers. Grub is fresh, unfussy cafe fare, from organic scrambled eggs with pico de gallo to salads, an organic-beef burger and home-baked cookies.

Laundromat Cafe
CAFE €€

(Map p59; ☑ 35 35 26 72; www.thelaundromatcafe. com; Elmegade 15, Nørrebro; dishes 48-128kr; ⊙ 8am-10pm Mon-Fri, from 9am Sat & Sun; 🖘; 🖵 3A, 5C, 350S) A cosy cafe and laundrette in one, this retro-licious Nørrebro institution is never short of loyal locals. It's a popular brunch spot, with both 'clean' (vegetarian) and 'dirty' (carnivorous) brunch platters, strong coffee and fresh juices. Breakfast options include oatmeal, spinach omelette, and pancakes with homemade maple syrup, while all-day comforters span hamburgers (veggie option included), sandwiches, soup and chilli con carne.

★ Relæ
NEW NORDIC €€€

(Map p59; ☑ 36 96 66 09; www.restaurant-relae. dk; Jægersborggade 41, Nørrebro; 4-/7-course menu 475/895kr; ⊙ 5-10pm Tue-Sat, also noon-1.30pm Fri & Sat; 🖵 8A, 5C) Established by prolific chef Christian Puglisi, Relæ was one of the first restaurants in town to offer superlative New Nordic cooking without all the designer fanfare. One Michelin star later, it remains a low-fuss place, where diners set their own table, pour their own wine and swoon over soul-lifting dishes focused on seasonality, simplicity and (mostly) organic produce. Book ahead.

★ Geranium
NEW NORDIC €€€

(Map p60; ☑ 69 96 00 20; www.geranium.dk; Per Henrik Lings Allé 4, Østerbro; lunch/dinner tasting menu 2000kr, wine/juice pairings 1400/700kr; ⊙ noon-3.30pm & 6.30pm-midnight Wed-Sat; 🖘 🖍; 🖵 14) 🍴 On the 8th floor of Parken Stadium, Geranium is the only restaurant in town sporting three Michelin stars. At the helm is Bocuse d'Or prize-winning chef Rasmus Kofoed, who transforms local ingredients into edible Nordic artworks like lobster paired with milk and the juice of fermented carrots and sea buckthorn, or cabbage sprouts and chicken served with quail egg, cep mushrooms and hay beer.

The tasting menu comprises more than 20 dishes, and those not wanting to sample the award-winning wine list can opt for equally enlightened juice pairings.

Kiin Kiin
THAI €€€

(Map p59; ☑ 35 35 75 55; www.kiin.dk; Guldbergsgade 21, Nørrebro; 4-/6-course menu 495/975kr, wine/juice menu 255/195kr; ⊙ 5.30pm-midnight Mon-Sat, latest reservation 8.30pm; 🖵 5C) Kiin Kiin serves clever, contemporary Thai. It's the only Thai restaurant in Europe to hold a Michelin star, and one of the few Michelin-starred restaurants in Copenhagen open on Mondays. The dining experience begins with street-food-style snacks in the lounge, then continues in the dining room with six beautifully and sometimes unusually presented courses packed with vibrant flavours like tamarind, lemongrass and galangal.

Kiin Kiin offers a set menu only, with the option of wine or juice accompaniments. The regular menu is six courses, and the early bird theatre menu (from 5.30pm to 7.30pm) consists of four courses – both menus include pre-meal nibbles.

✖ Vesterbro & Frederiksberg

★ WestMarket
MARKET €

(Map p62; ☏70 50 00 05; www.westmarket. dk; Vesterbrogade 97, Vesterbro; meals from 50kr; ⊙bakeries & coffee shops 8am-7pm, food stalls 10am-10pm; 🛜 ♿; 🚌6A) From dodgy shopping arcade to cool street-food hub, WestMarket peddles grub from all corners of the globe, from ramen, bao and lobster rolls to risotto, bubbling pizza and tapas. For a Scandi experience, hit **Kød & Bajer** (Map p62; ☏30 54 60 88; www.koedogbajer.dk; Vesterbrogade 97, Stall C12 ⊙11am-9pm; 🚌6A) for harder-to-find Nordic craft beers and snacks like dried moose, bear and elk sausages, then settle down at **Gros** (Map p62; ☏60 45 11 02; www.groshverdag skost.dk; Vesterbrogade 97, Stall C6, meals 98kr; ⊙11am-9pm; 🛜🍴; 🚌6A) 🌿 for modern takes on retro Danish dining classics.

Abundant seating and space make WestMarket more family-friendly than its city-centre rival, Torvehallerne KBH.

Hija de Sanchez
MEXICAN €

(Map p62; ☏31 18 52 03; www.hijadesanchez.dk; Slagterboderne 8, Vesterbro; 3 tacos 100kr; ⊙11am-8pm Mon-Thu, to 10pm Fri & Sat, to 6pm Sun; 🚌1A, 10, 14, 🚇Dybbølsbro) Hija de Sanchez serves up fresh, authentic tacos in the Meatpacking District. Expect three rotating varieties daily, from traditional choices like carnitas and al pastor to 'El Paul' – crispy fish skin with gooseberry salsa. There's always a vegetarian option, as well as homemade Mexican beverages like *tepache* (fermented pineapple juice). Chicago-native chef-owner Rosio Sánchez hails from renowned restaurant Noma, ie serious culinary cred.

Her original Hija de Sanchez location at Torvehallerne market operates from April to October.

Siciliansk Is
ICE CREAM €

(Map p62; ☏30 22 30 89; http://sicilianskis.dk; Skydebanegade 3, Vesterbro; ice cream from 25kr; ⊙noon-9pm mid-May–Aug, 1-6pm Apr–mid-May & Sep; 🚌10, 14) Having honed their skills in Sicily, gelato meisters Michael and David churn out Copenhagen's (dare we say Denmark's) best gelato. Lick yourself out on smooth, naturally flavoured options like strawberry, Sicilian blood orange and coconut. For a surprisingly smashing combo, try the *lakrids* (liquorice) with the Sicilian mandarin.

Chicky Grill
DANISH €

(Map p62; ☏33 22 66 96; Halmtorvet 21, Vesterbro; mains from 65kr; ⊙11am-8pm Mon-Sat; 🚌10, 14, 🚇København H) Despite its hip Kødbyen location, this unceremonious, wood-panelled, super-local bar and grill flies the flag for old-school comfort grub. Prices are low and portions are generous, from fried chicken and burgers to classic Danish staples like *flæskesteg* (roast pork), *pariserbøf* (minced beef patty, fried egg, onion, capers and pickled beetroot on rye bread) and *stjerneskud* (breaded and steamed fish fillets on white bread).

Mad & Kaffe
CAFE €

(Map p62; www.madogkaffe.dk; Sønder Blvd 68, Vesterbro; breakfast 78-148kr; lunch 65-124kr; ⊙8.30am-8pm; 🛜; 🚌1A, 10, 14, 🚇Dybbølsbro) With its string of cosy rooms and summertime outdoor tables, casual 'Food & Coffee' is especially popular for its breakfast; choose three, five or seven items to create your morning meal. We prefer lunching here; the smørrebrød options are gorgeous and generous.

Beer fans will appreciate the handful of interesting local brews. Consider avoiding weekends, when the wait for a table can be painfully long.

Dyrehaven
DANISH €

(Map p62; www.dyrehavenkbh.dk; Sønder Blvd 72, Vesterbro; breakfast 30-140kr, lunch 70-95kr, dinner mains 120-195kr; ⊙8.30am-2am Mon-Fri, from 9am Sat & Sun; 🛜; 🚌1A, 10, 14) Once a spit-and-sawdust working-class bar (the vinyl booths tell the story), Dyrehaven is now a second home for Vesterbro's cool young bohemians. Squeeze into your skinny jeans and join them for cheap drinks, simple tasty grub (the 'Kartoffelmad' egg open sandwich is a classic, with home-made mayo and fried shallots) and DJ-spun tunes on Friday and Saturday nights (summer excepted).

★ Paté Paté
INTERNATIONAL €€

(Map p62; ☑ 39 69 55 57; www.patepate.dk; Slagterboderne 1, Vesterbro; small dishes 95-150kr, 7/9-plate tasting menu 325/385kr; ⊙ 9am-10pm Mon-Thu, 9am-11pm Fri, 11am-11pm Sat; ☏; ☐ 10, 14) This pâté factory-turned-restaurant/wine bar gives Euro classics modern twists. The competent, regularly changing menu is designed for sharing, with smaller dishes like organic Danish burrata with salted courgette, spring onions, chilli, basil and walnuts, or veal tartare with harissa, mustard-pickled shallots and dukkah. Hip and bustling, yet refreshingly convivial, bonus extras include clued-in staff, a diverse wine list, and solo-diner-friendly bar seating.

Øl & Brød
DANISH €€

(Map p62; ☑ 33 31 44 22; www.ologbrod.dk; Viktoriagade 6; smørrebrod 85-165kr, dinner mains 150-250kr; ⊙ noon-5pm Tue & Wed, to 10pm Thu & Sun, to 11pm Fri & Sat Apr-Dec, reduced hours Jan-Mar; ☏; ☐ 6A, 9A, 10, 14, 26, ⑤ København H) Modernist Danish furniture and a muted palette of greys and greens offer the perfect backdrop to high-end, contemporary lunchtime smørrebrod. Raise your glass of (craft) beer to beautiful combinations like smoked mackerel with scrambled egg and chives or dill-pickled herring with potatoes and mustard. The dinner menu offers revisited Danish mains; think whole butter-fried flounder with parsley sauce and potatoes.

The restaurant claims Denmark's largest collection of *akvavit* and *snaps*.

Pony
NEW NORDIC €€

(Map p62; ☑ 33 22 10 00; www.ponykbh.dk; Vesterbrogade 135, Vesterbro; 3/4-course menu 325/425/485kr; ⊙ 5.30-10pm Tue-Sun; ☐ 6A) This is the cheaper bistro spin-off of Copenhagen's Michelin-starred Kadeau. While the New Nordic grub here is simpler, it's no less nuanced and seasonal; think cured brill with gooseberries and dried brill roe, or roasted wolf fish with summer cabbage, black cabbage, nasturtium and crispy grains. The wines are organic and from smaller producers, and the vibe intimate and convivial. Book ahead, especially on Friday and Saturday.

WarPigs
BARBECUE €€

(Map p62; ☑ 43 48 48 48; http://warpigs. dk; Flæsketorvet 25; meat per ¼lb from 45kr; ⊙ 11:30am-midnight Mon-Thu, 11am-2am Fri & Sat, 11am-11pm Sun; ☏; ☐ 10, 14, ⑤ Dybbølsbro) Loud, rocking WarPigs satiates carnivores with lusty, American-style barbecue from Europe's biggest meat smokers (capable of smoking up to two tons of meat a day!). Order at the counter, where you can mix and match meats and sides to create a personalised feed. There's also a kicking selection of beers brewed in-house; the place doubles as a brewpub part-owned by local microbrewery **Mikkeller**.

Cofoco
EUROPEAN €€

(Map p62; ☑ 33 13 60 60; http://cofoco.dk; Abel Cathrines Gade 7, Vesterbro; 4/5/6-course menu 295/335/375kr; ⊙ 6pm-midnight Mon-Sat; ☐ 6A, 26, 10, 14, ⑤ København H) One of several high-quality, design-savvy, affordable restaurants owned by the same team, Cofoco offers a glam setting and a selection of creative Nordic-Mediterranean dishes to customise your own set menu. Expect nuanced, artfully presented creations like mussel soup with baked hake and pickled gooseberries or flank of turkey with mushroom risotto and burnt corn. Perfect for gourmands on a (relative) budget. The kitchen closes at 9.45pm.

Granola
CAFE €€

(Map p62; ☑ 40 82 41 20; www.granola.dk; Værndemsvej 5, Frederiksberg; lunch 80-165kr, dinner mains 145-220kr; ⊙ 7am-midnight Mon-Fri, 9am-midnight Sat, 9am-4pm Sun; ☐ 9A, 26, 31, 71) On one of Copenhagen's most continental streets, Granola packs a cool Vesterbro crowd with its retro mix of industrial lamps, terrazzo flooring and 'General Store' cabinets. While the menu doesn't pack any serious punches, it does offer reliable comfort grub, from morning oatmeal, croque monsieur and pancakes to bistro staples like *salade au chèvre chaud* and steak-frites. Head in early on weekends.

Kødbyens Fiskebar
SEAFOOD €€€

(Map p62; ☑ 32 15 56 56; www.fiskebaren.dk; Flæsketorvet 100; mains 195-275kr; ⊙ 5.30pm-midnight Mon-Thu, 11.30am-2am Fri & Sat, 11.30am-midnight Sun; ☏; ☐ 10, 14, ⑤ Dybbølsbro) Concrete floors, industrial tiling and a 1000-litre aquarium meet impeccable seafood at this ever-popular, buzzy haunt, slap bang in Vesterbro's trendy Kødbyen (Meatpacking District). Ditch the mains for three or four starters. Standouts include the oysters and lobster with beer meringue, as well as the dainty, delicate razor clams, served on a crisp rice-paper 'shell'.

Mielcke & Hurtigkarl
INTERNATIONAL €€€

(Map p62; ☑ 38 34 84 36; www.mielcke-hurtigkarl. dk; Frederiksberg Runddel 1, Frederiksberg; tasting menus 950-1100kr; ⊙ 6-9pm Tue-Sat; ☏ ☑; ☐ 6A,

8A, 18, 26) Set in a former royal summer house adorned with contemporary, botanical murals, Mielcke & Hurtigkarl is as ethereal as its menu is heavenly. Executive chef Jakob Mielcke's inspired approach to local and global ingredients shines through in bold, whimsical creations that fuse Western and Eastern flavours.

Drinking & Nightlife

Vibrant drinking areas include the historic Latin Quarter; Vesterbro's Kødbyen (Meatpacking District), Istedgade and the northern end of Viktoriagade; Nørrebro's Ravnsborggade, Elmegade, Sankt Hans Torv and Jægersborggade. On a sunny day, there's always touristic Nyhavn, although prices are higher and the best places are away from the water.

Central Copenhagen

Taphouse   BAR
(Map p48; ☑88 87 65 43; http://taphouse.dk; Lavendelstræde 15; ⊙3pm-2am Mon-Thu, 3am Fri & Sat, noon-midnight Sun; 🛜; 🚇2A, 12, 14, 26, 33, Ⓢ København H) A firm favourite among Copenhagen's beer aficionados, Taphouse serves up drafts from an incredible 61 taps. Its ever-changing selection is one of the largest in Europe, and features craft beers from microbreweries around the world. Choices range from the mainstream to the totally unique, and knowledgeable, affable staff are on hand to guide customers towards their perfect brew.

★ Coffee Collective   CAFE
(Map p48; www.coffeecollective.dk; Stall C1, Hall 2, Torvehallerne KBH; ⊙7am-8pm Mon-Fri, 8am-7pm Sat, 8am-6pm Sun) 🍃 Save your caffeine fix for Copenhagen's most respected micro-roastery. The beans here are sourced ethically and directly from farmers. These guys usually offer two espresso blends, one more full-bodied and traditional, the other more acidic in flavour. If espresso is just too passé, order a hand-brewed cup from the Kalita Wave dripper. There are three other outlets, including in Nørrebro (p84) and Frederiksberg (p85).

★ Bastard Café   CAFE
(Map p48; ☑42 74 66 42; https://bastardcafe. dk; Rådhusstræde 13; ⊙noon-midnight Sun-Thu, to 2am Fri & Sat; 🚇1A, 2A, 9A, 14, 26, 37) A godsend on rainy days, this hugely popular, supercosy cafe is dedicated to board games, which line its rooms like books in a library. Some

are free to use, while others incur a small 'rental fee'. While away the hours playing an old favourite or learn the rules of a more obscure option.

★ Mother Wine   WINE BAR
(Map p48; ☑33 12 10 00; http://motherwine. dk; Gammel Mønt 33; ⊙10am-7pm Mon-Wed, to 10pm Thu & Sat, to late Fri; 🛜; 🚇350S, Ⓜ Kongens Nytorv) A *hyggelig* (cosy) wine bar/shop with some very prized Finn Juhl chairs, Mother Wine showcases natural, organic and lesser-known Italian drops. From organic Veneto Prosecco to Puglian Negroamaro, guests are encouraged to sample the day's rotating offerings before committing to a glass. Wines start at a very palatable 55kr and come with a small complimentary serve of Italian nibbles.

From Thursday to Saturday, the bar's upper floor hosts proper aperitivo sessions, where vino is offered with bites like couscous, Italian cheeses and *salsiccia* (sausage).

★ Ved Stranden 10   WINE BAR
(Map p48; ☑35 42 40 40; www.vedstranden10. dk; Ved Stranden 10; ⊙noon-10pm Mon-Sat; 🛜; 🚇1A, 2A, 9A, 26, 37, 66, 350S, Ⓜ Kongens Nytorv) Politicians and well-versed oenophiles make a beeline for this canal-side wine bar, its enviable cellar stocked with classic European vintages, biodynamic wines and more obscure drops. With modernist Danish design and friendly, clued-in staff, its string of rooms lend an intimate, civilised air that's perfect for grown-up conversation.

★ 1105   COCKTAIL BAR
(Map p48; ☑33 93 11 05; www.1105.dk; Kristen Bernikows Gade 4; ⊙8pm-2am Wed, Thu & Sat, 4pm-2am Fri; 🚇1A, 26, 350S, Ⓜ Kongens Nytorv) Head in before 11pm for a bar seat at this dark, luxe lounge. Named for the local postcode, its cocktail repertoire spans both the classic and the revisited. You'll also find a fine collection of whiskeys, not to mention an older 30- and 40-something crowd more interested in thoughtfully crafted drinks than partying hard and getting wasted.

★ Ruby   COCKTAIL BAR
(Map p48; ☑33 93 12 03; www.rby.dk; Nybrogade 10; ⊙4pm-2am Mon-Sat, from 6pm Sun; 🛜; 🚇1A, 2A, 14, 26, 37, 66) Cocktail connoisseurs raise their glasses to high-achieving Ruby, hidden away in an unmarked 18th-century townhouse. Inside, suave mixologists whip up near-flawless, seasonal libations created with craft spirits and homemade syrups,

while a lively crowd spills into a labyrinth of cosy, decadent rooms. For a gentlemen's club vibe, head downstairs among chesterfields, oil paintings and cabinets lined with spirits.

★ Forloren Espresso   CAFE

(Map p48; www.forlorenespresso.dk; Store Kongensgade 32; ⊙ 8am-4pm Mon-Wed, to 5pm Thu & Fri, 9am-5pm Sat; 🕾; 🖵 1A, 26, Ⓜ Kongens Nytorv) Coffee snobs weep joyfully into their nuanced espressos and third-wave brews at this snug, light-filled cafe. Bespectacled owner Niels tends to his brewing paraphernalia like an obsessed scientist, turning UK- and Swedish-roasted beans into smooth, lingering cups of Joe. If you're lucky, you'll score the cosy back nook, the perfect spot to browse Niels' collection of photography tomes.

Jane   CLUB

(Map p48; www.thejane.dk; Gråbrødretorv 8; ⊙ 8pm-late Thu-Sat; 🖵 5C, 6A, 14, 150S, 350S, Ⓜ Nørreport, Ⓢ Nørreport) With its plush armchairs, chesterfield sofas and soundtrack of jazz and blues, you'd be forgiven for thinking your name is Don Draper. But it probably isn't and you're definitely not on the set of *Mad Men*. You're at Jane, a hotspot, speakeasy-style bar with craft cocktails and a craftier bookshelf. As the night progresses, watch it open to reveal a hidden dance floor.

Bankeråt   BAR

(Map p48; 🕾 33 93 69 88; www.bankeraat.dk; Ahlefeldtsgade 27; ⊙ 9.30am-11pm Mon & Tue, to midnight Wed-Fri, 10.30am-midnight Sat, 10.30am-8pm Sun; 🕾; 🖵 37, 5C, 350S, Ⓜ Nørrebro, Ⓢ Nørrebro) A snug spot to get stuffed (literally), kooky, attitude-free Bankeråt is decorated with taxidermic animals in outlandish get-ups – yes, there's even a ram in period costume. The man behind it all is local artist Filip V Jensen. But is it art? Debate this, and the mouth-shaped urinals, over a local craft beer.

Living Room   CAFE

(Map p48; 🕾 33 32 66 10; www.facebook.com/thelivingroomdk; Larsbjørnsstræde 17; ⊙ 9am-11pm Mon-Thu, to 2am Fri, 10am-2am Sat, 10am-7pm Sun; 🕾; 🖵 5C, 6A, 10, 14, Ⓜ Nørreport, Ⓢ Nørreport) Spread over three levels and decked out in vintage decor and a Moroccan-themed tea room, the aptly titled Living Room is a super-cosy (albeit often busy) spot to settle in with a speciality coffee, tea, homemade smoothie or lemonade. Cocktails and other alcoholic libations are also served late into the evening.

Boulebar   BAR

(Map p48; 🕾 82 82 08 00; www.boulebar.dk; Nørregade 18; ⊙ 4-11.30pm Mon-Thu, 11am-1am Fri, 10:30am-1am Sat, to 11pm Sun; 🖵 14, 150S, Ⓜ Nørreport, Ⓢ Nørreport) Why merely sip French bubbles when you can do so over a game of oh-so-Gallic pétanque? This out-of-the-box

---

GAY & LESBIAN COPENHAGEN

Copenhagen is one of the world's most gay-friendly cities. Highly inclusive festival Copenhagen Pride (p67) takes place in August, and LGBT film festival Mix Copenhagen (p67) hits screens in October. Useful websites include www.out-and-about.dk, www.lgbt.dk and (in English) http://rainbowbusinessdenmark.dk.

Many of the LGBT-specific cafes, bars and clubs are located in the Latin Quarter and just off Rådhuspladsen in the city centre.

Oscar Bar & Cafe (Map p48; 🕾 33 12 09 99; www.facebook.com/oscarbarcafe; Regnbuepladsen 77; ⊙ 11am-midnight Sun-Thu, to 2am Fri & Sat; 🕾; 🖵 12, 14, 26, 33, Ⓢ København H) In the shadow of Rådhus, this friendly corner cafe-bar remains the most popular gay in the village. There's food for the peckish and a healthy quota of eye-candy locals and out-of-towners of all ages. In the warmer months, its alfresco tables are packed with revellers with one eye on friends, the other on Grindr.

Never Mind (Map p48; www.facebook.com/nevermindbar.dk; Nørre Voldgade 2; ⊙ 10pm-6am; 🖵 2A, 5C, 6A, 250S) If you can't take crowds and cigarette smoke, keep moving. If you can, this tiny, loud, often packed gay bar is a seriously fun spot for shameless pop and late-night flirtation.

Jailhouse CPH (Map p48; www.jailhousecph.dk; Studiestræde 12; ⊙ 3pm-2am Sun-Thu, to 5am Fri & Sat; 🕾; 🖵 5C, 6A, 14) Friendly, attitude-free and particularly popular with an older male crowd, this small, themed bar promises plenty of penal action, with uniformed 'guards' and willing guests. Skip the mediocre restaurant upstairs.

bar and restaurant comes with 15 pétanque lanes. If you're feeling hungry, channel Paris over classics like mussels, steak-frites and beef tartare. The bar also offers food-and-pétanque packages, combining 90 minutes of play with selected offerings from the kitchen.

Library Bar   BAR
(Map p48; ☑33 14 92 62; www.librarybar.dk; Bernstorffsgade 4; ⊙4pm-midnight Mon-Thu, to 1am Fri & Sat; 🖘; ☐2A, 5C, 6A, 9A, 26, 250S, ⑤København H) The Copenhagen Plaza's intimate hotel bar mimics a classic London gentlemen's club, with leather chairs, shelves lined with books and a stained-glass ceiling. Adding atmosphere is the live jazz, a regular fixture on Friday and Saturday nights from 9.30pm.

Hviids Vinstue   PUB
(Map p48; ☑33 93 07 60; www.hviidsvinstue.dk; Kongens Nytorv 19; ⊙10am-1am Mon-Thu, to 2am Fri & Sat, to 8pm Sun; ☐9A) One of the oldest bars in Copenhagen, Hviids Vinstue has been putting a wobble in people's steps since 1723. The interior is a suitably brooding combo of dark timber and leather. The place is famous for its *gløgg* (Danish mulled wine). Production begins in May, with the bar's annual *gløgg* season starting at 11am on 11 November, just in time for the biting Danish winter.

Palæ Bar   PUB
(Map p48; ☑33 12 54 71; www.palaebar.dk; Ny Adelgade 5; ⊙11am-1am Mon-Wed, to 3am Thu-Sat, 4pm-1am Sun; ☐1A, 26, 350S, Ⓜ Kongens Nytorv) The air may no longer be thick with tobacco, but the intriguing conversations continue at this unapologetically old-school drinking den. A traditional hit with journalists, writers and politicians, it draws an older local crowd, here to catch up, debate, play chess or tap their fingers to free live jazz, the latter usually offered once a month on Sunday.

🍷 Nyhavn & the Royal Quarter
Many locals avoid the touristy bars lining Nyhavn, instead buying their liquor from small, seasonal convenience store **Turs Havneproviant** (Map p48; ☑33 13 40 47; Lille Strandstræde 3; ☐1A, 26, Ⓜ Kongens Nytorv) and drinking it by the canal.

★Nebbiolo   WINE BAR
(Map p48; ☑60 10 11 09; http://nebbiolo-winebar. com; Store Strandstræde 18; ⊙3pm-midnight Sun-Thu, to 2am Fri & Sat; 🖘; ☐1A, 66, Ⓜ Kongens Nytorv) Just off Nyhavn, this smart, contemporary wine bar and shop showcases wines from

smaller, inspiring Italian vineyards. Wines by the glass are priced in one of three categories (75/100/125kr) and even those in the lowest price range are often wonderful.

★Den Vandrette   WINE BAR
(Map p48; ☑72 14 82 28; www.denvandrette.dk; Havnegade 53A; ⊙4-11pm Tue-Thu & Sun, to midnight Fri, 2pm-midnight Sat; ☐66, 🚢 Nyhavn) This is the harbourside wine bar for lauded wine wholesaler **Rosforth & Rosforth** (Map p48; ☑33 32 55 20; www.rosforth.dk). The focus is on natural and biodynamic drops, its short, sharply curated list of wines by the glass often including lesser-known blends. Guests are welcome to browse the cellar and pick their own bottle. Come summer, it has alfresco waterside tables and deckchairs.

🍷 Christianshavn

Christianshavns Bådudlejning og Café   BAR
(Map p48; ☑32 96 53 53; www.baadudlejningen. dk; Overgaden Neden Vandet 29; ⊙9am-midnight Jun-Aug, reduced hours rest of year; 🖘; ☐2A, 9A, 37, 350S, Ⓜ Christianshavn) Right on Christianshavn's main canal, this festive, wood-decked cafe-bar is a wonderful spot for drinks by the water. It's a cosy, affable hang-out, with jovial crowds and strung lights. There's grub for the peckish and gas heaters and tarpaulins to ward off any northern chill.

Eiffel Bar   BAR
(Map p48; ☑32 57 70 92; www.eiffelbar.dk; Wildersgade 58; ⊙9am-3am; 🖘; ☐2A, 9A, 37, 350S, Ⓜ Christianshavn) Don't be fooled by the name: dark, wood-panelled Eiffel Bar is a red-blooded Danish dive bar, and all the better for it. The joint dates back from 1737, when it was a hit with local sailors. The beer here is cheap, with all the standard local brews available on tap, plus a few Danish craft ales. A solid choice for an animated, amiable, old-school vibe.

Den Plettede Gris   CAFE
(Map p57; Trangravsvej 5; ⊙9am-6pm Mon-Fri, from 10am Sat & Sun; 🖘; ☐9A, 🚢 Papirøen) The pocket-sized 'Spotted Pig' on Papirøen (Paper Island) belongs to Danish designer, artist, musician and all-round avantgardiste Henrik Vibskov. Inside, the space is pure Vibskov, with elastic-band wall sculptures, splashes of pink and red, and a cool, chilled-out vibe. Stop by for Swedish-roasted coffee or organic tea, or guzzle boutique beers with ingredients like elderflower.

URBAN BEACH BAR

Copenhagen meets Ibiza at **Halvandet** (Map p60; ☑70 27 02 96; www.halvandet. dk; Refshalevej 325, Refshaleøen; ◷4.30pm-late Wed & Thu, from noon Fri-Sun mid-Jun–Aug, reduced hours mid-Apr–mid-Jun; ⛴Refshaleøen), a seasonal, harbourfront bar-lounge and activity centre (yes, you can play beach volleyball). Order a mojito and tan away to sexy lounge tunes. Edibles include sandwiches, grilled meats, seafood and salads, but the real reason to head in is the vibe and music. Opening times are weather-dependent, so always check Halvandet's Facebook page before heading in.

Nørrebro & Østerbro

★Coffee Collective   COFFEE

(Map p59; www.coffeecollective.dk; Jægersborggade 57, Nørrebro; ◷7am-8pm Mon-Fri, 8am-7pm Sat & Sun; ☐8A) Copenhagen's most prolific micro-roastery, Coffee Collective has helped revolutionise the city's coffee culture in recent years. Head in for rich, complex cups of caffeinated magic. The baristas are passionate about their single-origin beans, and the venue itself sits at one end of creative Jægersborggade in Nørrebro. There are three other outlets, including at gourmet food market Torvehallerne KBH (p71) and in Frederiksberg (p85).

★Brus   MICROBREWERY

(Map p59; ☑75 22 22 00; http://tapperietbrus. dk; Guldbergsgade 29F, Nørrebro; ◷3pm-midnight Mon-Thu, noon-3am Fri & Sat, noon-midnight Sun; ☎; ☐5C) What was once a locomotive factory is now a huge, sleek, hip brewpub. The world-renowned microbrewery behind it is To Øl, and the bar's 30-plus taps offer a rotating selection of To Øl standards and small-batch specials, as well as eight on-tap cocktails. The barkeeps are affable and happy to let you sample different options before you commit.

★Mikkeller & Friends   MICROBREWERY

(Map p59; ☑35 83 10 20; www.mikkeller.dk/ location/mikkeller-friends; Stefansgade 35, Nørrebro; ◷2pm-midnight Sun-Wed, to 2am Thu & Fri, noon-2am Sat; ☎; ☐5C, 8A) Looking suitably cool with its turquoise floors and pale ribbed wood, Mikkeller & Friends is a joint venture of the Mikkeller and To Øl breweries. Beer geeks go gaga over the 40 artisan draft beers and circa 200 bottled varieties, which might include a chipotle porter or an imperial stout aged in tequila barrels. Limited snacks include dried gourmet sausage and cheese.

A sneaky passageway at the back of the venue leads into Koelschip, a wonderfully snug, vintage-style beer bar with around 250 Belgian and Belgian-style brews.

Rust   CLUB

(Map p59; ☑35 24 52 00; www.rust.dk; Guldbergsgade 8, Nørrebro; ◷hours vary, club usually 8.30pm-5am Fri & Sat; ☎; ☐3A, 5C, 350S) A smashing, multilevel place attracting one of the largest, coolest, most relaxed crowds in Copenhagen. Live acts focus on alternative or upcoming indie rock, hip-hop or electronica. At 11pm, the venue transforms into a club, with local and international DJs pumping out anything from classic hip-hop to electro, house and more.

Nørrebro Bryghus   BREWERY

(Map p59; ☑35 30 05 30; www.noerrebrobry ghus.dk; Ryesgade 3, Nørrebro; ◷noon-11pm Mon-Thu, to 1am Fri & Sat, to 10pm Sun; ☐3A, 5C, 350S) This now-classic brewery kick-started the microbrewing craze more than a decade ago. While its in-house restaurant serves a decent lunchtime burger as well as fancier New Nordic dishes in the evening, head here for the beers, including the brewery's organic draught beer and a string of fantastic bottled options, from pale and brown ales to 'The Evil', a malty, subtly smokey imperial porter.

Kassen   BAR

(Map p59; ☑42 57 22 00; http://kassen.dk; Nørrebrogade 18B, Nørrebro; ◷8pm-late Wed, Thu & Sat, from 4pm Fri; ☐5C) Loud, sticky Kassen sends livers packing with its dirt-cheap drinks and happy-hour specials (80kr cocktails, anyone?). Guzzle unlimited drinks on Wednesdays for 250kr, with two-for-one deals running the rest of the week: all night Thursdays, 4pm to 10pm Fridays and 8pm to 10pm Saturday. Cocktail choices are stock-standard and a little sweet, but think of the change in your pocket.

Kind of Blue   BAR

(Map p59; ☑26 35 10 56; www.kindofblue. dk; Ravnsborggade 17, Nørrebro; ◷4pm-midnight Mon-Wed, to 2am Thu-Sat; ☎; ☐5A, 350S) Chandeliers, heady perfume and walls painted a hypnotic 1950s blue: the spirit of the Deep South runs deep at intimate Kind of Blue.

Named after the Miles Davis album, it's never short of a late-night hipster crowd, kicking back porters and drinking in owner Claus' personal collection of soul-stirring jazz, blues and folk. You'll find it on Nørrebro's bar-packed Ravnsborggade.

Vesterbro & Frederiksberg

★ Mikkeller Bar   BAR

(Map p62; ☑ 33 31 04 15; http://mikkeller.dk; Viktoriagade 8B-C, Vesterbro; ⊘ 1pm-1am Sun-Wed, to 2am Thu & Fri, noon-2am Sat; ☎; ☐ 6A, 9A, 10, 14, 26, Ⓢ København H) Low-slung lights, milk-green floors and 20 brews on tap: cool, cult-status Mikkeller flies the flag for craft beer, its rotating cast of suds including Mikkeller's own acclaimed creations and guest drops from microbreweries from around the globe. Expect anything from tequila-barrel-aged stouts to yuzu-infused fruit beers. The bottled offerings are equally inspired, with cheese and snacks to soak up the foamy goodness.

★ Lidkoeb   COCKTAIL BAR

(Map p62; ☑ 33 11 20 10; www.lidkoeb.dk; Vesterbrogade 72B, Vesterbro; ⊘ 4pm-2am Mon-Sat, from 8pm Sun; ☎; ☐ 6A, 26) Lidkoeb loves a game of hide-and-seek: follow the 'Lidkoeb' signs into the second, light-strung courtyard. Once found, this top-tier cocktail lounge rewards with passionate barkeeps and clever, seasonal libations. Slip into a Børge Mogensen chair and toast to Danish ingenuity with Nordic bar bites and seasonal drinks like the Freja's Champagne; a gin-based concoction with muddled fresh ginger, lemon and maraschino liqueur.

LATE-NIGHT ELECTRONICA

Electronica connoisseurs swarm to **Culture Box** (Map p60; ☑ 33 32 50 50; www.culture-box.com; Kronprinsessegade 54A; ⊘ Culture Box Bar 6pm-1am Thu-Sat, Red Box 11pm-late Fri & Sat, Black Box midnight-late Fri & Sat; ☐ 26), known for its impressive local and international DJ line-ups and sharp sessions of electro, techno, house and drum'n'bass. The club is divided into three spaces: pre-clubbing Culture Box Bar, intimate club space Red Box, and heavyweight Black Box, where big-name DJs play the massive sound system.

★ Coffee Collective   COFFEE

(☑ 60 15 15 25; https://coffeecollective.dk; Godthåbsvej 34b, Frederiksberg; ⊘ 7.30am-6pm Mon-Fri, from 9am Sat, from 10am Sun) It's right here that Copenhagen's coffee heavyweight roasts its prized, specialty beans, used for its espresso and third wave brews. On the first Friday of the month, the roast-master offers popular roastery tours and cupping sessions (150kr). The price includes a bag of the good stuff to take home and brew.

Fermentoren   CRAFT BEER

(Map p62; ☑ 23 90 86 77; http://fermentoren.com; Halmtorvet 29C, Vesterbro; ⊘ 3pm-midnight Mon-Wed, 2pm-1am Thu & Fri, 2pm-2am Sat, 2pm-midnight Sun; ☎; ☐ 1A, 10, 14, Ⓢ Dybbølsbro) Serious local beer fans flock to this cosy, candlelit basement bar. Its 24 taps pour an ever-changing cast of in interesting craft brews, both traditional and edgy. Look out for local brews from the likes of Evil Twin, Ghost and Gamma, as well as Fermentoren's own pale ale.

Falernum   WINE BAR

(Map p62; ☑ 33 22 30 89; www.falernum.dk; Værnedamsvej 16, Vesterbro; ⊘ noon-midnight Sun-Thu, to 2am Fri & Sat; ☎; ☐ 6A, 9A, 31) Worn floorboards, mismatched vintage chairs and a grown-up crowd give Falernum a deliciously snug, familial air. You'll find around 40 wines by the glass alone, as well as boutique beers, coffee, and a seasonal menu of soulful sharing plates; standouts include mushroom toast with egg yolk and fermented garlic.

Mesteren & Lærlingen   BAR

(Map p62; www.facebook.com/Mesteren-Lærlingen-215687798449433; Flæsketorvet 86, Vesterbro; ⊘ 8pm-3am Wed & Thu, to 3.30am Fri & Sat; ☎) In a previous life, Mesteren & Lærlingen was a slaughterhouse bodega. These days it's one of Copenhagen's in-the-know drinking holes, its tiled walls packing in an affable indie crowd of trucker caps and skinny jeans. Squeeze in and sip good spirits to DJ-spun soul, reggae, hip-hop and dance hall.

KBIII   CLUB

(Map p62; ☑ 33 23 45 97; www.kb3.dk; Kødboderne 3, Vesterbro; ⊘ bar 8pm-late Thu-Sat, club 11pm-4am Fri & Sat; ☐ 1A, Ⓢ Dybbølsbro) KBIII is the biggest club in the kicking Kødbyen (Meatpacking District), aptly occupying a giant former meat freezer. Although events span film screenings, live acts, burlesque and release parties, the emphasis is on thumping club tunes from resident and global DJs.

Bakken
BAR

(Map p62; Flæsketorvet 19-21; ⊘9pm-5am Thu, from 6pm Fri & Sat; 🚌10, 14, Ⓢ Dybbølsbro) Affordable drinks, DJ-spun disco and rock, and a Meatpacking District address make intimate, gritty Bakken a magnet for revellers.

☆ Entertainment

Copenhagen's entertainment offerings are wide, varied and sophisticated. On any given night choices will include ballet, opera, theatre, clubbing and live tunes spanning indie and blues to pop. The city has a world-renowned jazz scene, with numerous jazz clubs drawing top talent. Most events can be booked through **Billetten** (📲70 15 65 65; www. billetnet.dk), which has an outlet in Tivoli. You can also try **Billetlugen** (📲70 26 32 67; www. billetlugen.dk).

Cinema

You'll find a handful of cinemas just north of Tivoli Gardens near Vesterport train station, among them multiscreen **Dagmar Teatret** (www.nfbio.dk/biografer/dagmar), which screens a mix of first-release mainstream and independent films. Popular art-house cinemas include the historic **Grand Teatret** (Map p48; 📲33 15 16 11; www.grandteatret.dk; Mikkel Bryggers Gade 8; ⊘11am-10.30pm; 🐟; 🚌12, 14, 26, 33, Ⓢ København H) and the Danish Film Institute's **Cinemateket** (Map p48; 📲33 74 34 12; www.dfi.dk; Gothersgade 55; ⊘9.30am-10pm Tue-Fri, noon-10pm Sat, noon-7.30pm Sun; 🚌350S). As in the rest of Denmark, films are generally shown in their original language with Danish subtitles.

Dance, Opera, Theatre & Classical Music

Copenhagen's landmark Operaen (Opera House) hosts world-class seasons of works spanning time-honoured classics and contemporary operas (subtitled in Danish). Across the water, the equally state-of-the-art Skuespilhuset delivers Danish and non-Danish theatre, again both classic and freshly minted. The grand old Det Kongelige Teater focuses on top-tier ballet and opera, while across town, contemporary dance is served up at Dansehallerne. On the island of Amager is DR Koncerthuset, home of the Danish National Symphony Orchestra and National Chamber Orchestra, and the venue for an eclectic mix of concerts spanning classical, chamber, jazz, rock and experimental.

Det Kongelige Teater
BALLET, OPERA

(Royal Theatre; Map p48; 📲33 69 69 69; https:// kglteater.dk; Kongens Nytorv; 🚌1A, 26, 350S, Ⓜ Kongens Nytorv) These days, the main focus of the opulent Gamle Scene (Old Stage) is world-class opera and ballet, including productions from the Royal Danish Ballet. The current building, the fourth theatre to occupy the site, was completed in 1872 and designed by Vilhelm Dahlerup and Ove Petersen.

Skuespilhuset
THEATRE

(Royal Danish Playhouse; Map p57; 📲33 69 69 69; https://kglteater.dk; Sankt Anne Plads 36; 🚌66, 🚢Nyhavn, Ⓜ Kongens Nytorv) Copenhagen's harbourside playhouse is home to the Royal Danish Theatre and a world-class repertoire of homegrown and foreign plays. Productions range from the classics to provocative

---

ALL THAT JAZZ

Copenhagen has been the jazz capital of Scandinavia since the 1920s, when the Montmartre Club was one of the most famous in Europe. Revived in 2010 after a long hiatus, the rebooted **Jazzhus Montmartre** (Map p48; 📲70 26 32 67; www.jazzhusmontmartre. dk; Store Regnegade 19A; ⊘6pm-midnight Thu-Sat; 🚌350S, 1A, 26, Ⓜ Kongens Nytorv) is in good company, with top venues such as **La Fontaine** (Map p48; 📲33 11 60 98; www. lafontaine.dk; Kompagnistræde 11; ⊘7pm-5am daily, live music from 10pm Fri & Sat, from 9pm Sun; 🚌14), the city's most 'hardcore' jazz club, and **Jazzhouse** (Map p48; 📲33 15 47 00; www.jazzhouse.dk; Niels Hemmingsensgade 10; ⊘from 7pm Mon-Thu, from 8pm Fri-Sat; 🐟; 🚌1A, 2A, 9A, 14, 26, 37), the largest and most popular, ensuring that legacy remains alive and kicking. Several bars have low-key live jazz and blues too, including most Thursdays at **Lo-Jo's Social** (Map p48; 📲53 88 64 65; www.lojossocial.com; Landemærket 7; ⊘bar 11.30am-midnight Mon-Wed, to 2am Thu-Sat, kitchen; 🚌350S, Ⓜ Nørreport, Ⓢ Nørreport) and roughly monthly at **Palæ** (p83)

Copenhagen's 10-day **Jazz Festival** (p66), first launched in 1978, has become *the* biggest entertainment event in the city's calendar, mushrooming into one of Europe's leading jazz events. Over the years it has attracted countless great performers.

contemporary works. Tickets often sell out well in advance, so book ahead if you're set on a particular production. English-language tours (120kr) are available in July and August; see the website for details.

Operaen
OPERA

(Copenhagen Opera House; Map p57; ☑ box office 33 69 69 69; www.kglteater.dk; Ekvipagemestervej 10; ▣ 9A, ☖ Operaen) Designed by the late Henning Larsen, Copenhagen's state-of-the-art opera house has two stages: the Main Stage and the smaller, more experimental Takkeløftet. The repertoire runs the gamut from blockbuster classics to contemporary opera. While the occasional opera is sung in English, all subtitles are in Danish only.

Dansehallerne
DANCE

(Map p62; ☑ box office 33 88 80 08; www.dansehallerne.dk; Bohrsgade 19, Vesterbro; ▣ 1A, ☒ Carlsberg) Dansehallerne is Copenhagen's leading contemporary-dance venue. Located in a disused Carlsberg mineral-water factory, its stages showcase a busy season of works from international ensembles as well as Danish artists. Some performances take place off-site, in unusual locations across the city. Purchase tickets online or at the box office.

Københavns Musikteater
THEATRE

(☑ 33 32 55 56; www.kobenhavnsmusikteater.dk; Emblasgade 175, Nørrebro; ▣ 4A, 42) Push your boundaries at Copenhagen's avant-garde music theatre venue, delivering a wide range of artistic crossover performances. All works include newly composed or reinterpreted compositions, with genres including classical and chamber music, electronica, poetic pop and rock.

DR Koncerthuset
CONCERT VENUE

(☑ 35 20 62 62; www.dr.dk/Koncerthuset; Emil Holms Kanal 20, Amager; Ⓜ DR Byen) Home of the National Symphony Orchestra and National Chamber Orchestra, Jean Nouvel's bold blue box hosts world-class concerts spanning from classical, chamber and choral music to rock, pop, jazz and experimental sounds. Check the website for a list of upcoming events.

Tivoli Koncertsal
CONCERT VENUE

(Concert Hall; Map p48; www.tivoli.dk; Tietgensgade 30; ▣ 1A, 2A, 5C, 9A, 37, 250S, ☒ København H) The Tivoli concert hall hosts Danish and international symphony orchestras, string quartets and other classical-music performances, not to mention contemporary music artists and dance companies. Purchase tickets online or at the Tivoli Box Office.

Live Music

Huset-KBH
LIVE MUSIC

(Map p48; ☑ 21 51 21 51; www.huset-kbh.dk; Rådhusstræde 13; ⊙ hours vary; ☎; ▣ 1A, 2A, 9A, 14, 26, 37) Huset KBH is a local institution, churning out almost 1500 annual events spanning live music, theatre and art-house film, to poetry slams, cabaret and stand-up comedy. The complex also houses Bastard Café (p81), a popular cafe-bar jam-packed with a massive selection of board games.

Vega Live
LIVE MUSIC

(Map p62; ☑ 33 25 70 11; www.vega.dk; Enghavevej 40, Vesterbro; ☎; ▣ 3A, 10, 14, ☒ Dybbølsbro) The daddy of Copenhagen's live-music venues, Vega hosts everyone from big-name rock, pop, blues and jazz acts to underground indie, hip-hop and electro up-and-comers. Gigs take place on either the main stage (Store Vega), small stage (Lille Vega) or the ground-floor Ideal Bar. Performance times vary; check the website. Interestingly, the venue is a 1950s former trade union HQ revamped by leading Danish architect Vilhelm Lauritzen.

Loppen
LIVE MUSIC

(Map p57; ☑ 32 57 84 22; www.loppen.dk; Sydområdet 4B; ⊙ 8.30pm-late Sun-Thu, 9pm-late Fri & Sat; ☎; ▣ 9A, 2A, 37, 350S, Ⓜ Christianshavn) Rocking out in a wooden-beamed warehouse in live-and-let-live Christiania, Loppen delivers both established and emerging acts from Denmark and beyond. Music styles are as eclectic as the crowds, with anything from rock and funk to post-punk, jazz and electronic.

Mojo
BLUES

(Map p48; ☑ 33 11 64 53; www.mojo.dk; Løngangstræde 21C; ⊙ 8pm-5am; ▣ 1A, 2A, 9A, 12, 14, 26, 33, 37, ☒ København H) East of Tivoli, this is a great spot for deep, soulful blues and its associated genres, from bluegrass and zydeco to soul. There are live acts nightly, followed by DJ-spun tunes. The vibe is warm, convivial and relaxed, and there's draught beer aplenty.

🔒 Shopping

Strøget is the city's retail ground zero for everything from clothing to design to food, with parallel **Strædet** (Map p48; ▣ 1A, 2A, 9A, 14, 26, 37, 66) (combining Kompagnistræde and Læderstræde streets) good for antiques and local ceramics. In Vesterbro, look around Værndamsvej and gritty-turned-vibrant Istedgade for an eclectic mix of in-the-know fashion, art and design. Arty Nørrebro has interesting independent shops on Elmegade and Jægersborggade,

FINDING FASHION

Danish style is a global phenomenon; the fashion institute organises a global 'summit' pushing for sustainability in the industry, and Copenhagen has a fashion week as well as a truly outstanding range of designer boutiques.

Leading the way in women's apparel, model-turned-designer **Stine Goya** (Map p60; ✔️32 17 10 10; https://stinegoya.com) marries clean Nordic simplicity with quirky details including svelte bee-print jumpsuits and canary-yellow bomber jackets featuring contemporary local artwork. She has a second branch at Gothersgade 58. At respected Danish brand **Baum und Pferdgarten** (Map p48; ✔️35 30 10 90; www.baumundpferdgarten. com; Vognmagergade 2), collections by designers Rikke Baumgarten and Helle Hestehave inject a sense of quirkiness to structured silhouettes and beautiful fabrics. **Day Birger et Mikkleson** (Map p48; ✔️33 45 88 80; www.day.dk; Pilestræde 16) offer understated chic, bohemian spirit and subtle ethnic accents, and around the corner Malene Birger has her own **shop** (Map p48; ✔️35 43 22 33; www.bymalenebirger.dk; Antongata 10) too. Crown Princess Mary is said to ride her bicycle to shop for hats at milliner **Susanne Juul** (Map p48; ✔️33 32 25 22; www.susannejuul.dk; Store Kongensgade 14).

NN07 (Map p48; ✔️38 41 11 41; www.nn07.com; Gammel Mønt 7) gains plaudits for understated, contemporary Danish menswear in easy-to-match block colours. Guys and girls can find comfortable sweat tops, T-shirts and denim, as well as sharper contemporary threads at **Samsøe & Samsøe** (Map p62; ✔️35 28 51 02; www.samsoe.com; Værnedamsvej 12, Vesterbro), a label that's not afraid of unique patterns, colour and detailing. **Storm** (Map p48; ✔️33 93 00 14; www.stormfashion.dk; Store Regnegade 1) carries trendsetting labels with a youthful, urban vibe that attracts a cashed-up, street-smart style crew. **Wood Wood** (p89) also provides distinctive street fashion, and **Pop Copenhagen** (Map p48; ✔️23 47 36 84; www.popcph.dk; Møntergade 5) has sharp, youthful collections with inspirations from old-school rockers to contemporary club culture. Danish enfant terrible **Henrik Vibskov** (Map p48; ✔️33 14 61 00; www.henrikvibskov.com; Krystalgade 6) peddles boldly creative garb ranging from mid-century glamour to sculptural frocks inspired by geishas. **Kyoto** (Map p62; ✔️33 31 66 36; http://kyoto.dk; Istedgade 95, Vesterbro) is a top choice for multibrand, unisex gear, and don't overlook **Magasin** (Map p48; ✔️33 11 44 33; www.magasin.dk; Kongens Nytorv 13) – Copenhagen's biggest and oldest department store. There's plenty of fabulous vintage clothing too – try **Vintage 199** (Map p60; ✔️39 27 00 41; Jagtvej 199) in Østerbro, **Prag** (Map p62; ✔️33 79 00 50; www.pragcopenhagen.com; Vesterbrogade 98A) in Vesterbro and **Time's Up** (Map p48; ✔️33 32 39 30; www.times-up.dk; Krystalgade 4) in the Latin Quarter.

For accessories, **The Last Bag** (Map p48; ✔️42 32 73 91; www.pietbreinholm.dk; Nansensgade 48) features musician-turned-designer Piet Breinholm's classic leather satchels made with high-quality leather sourced from an ecofriendly Brazilian tannery. Leading silversmith **Georg Jensen** (Map p48; ✔️33 11 40 80; www.georgjensen.com; Amagertorv 4) has a flagship Copenhagen store, while **Hoff** (Map p60; ✔️33 15 30 02; www.gallerihoff.dk; Østerbrogade 44, Østerbro) is also a treasure-trove of innovative jewellery in which each item is a veritable conversation piece to covet for a lifetime.

affordable bric-a-brac along Ravnsborggade and, held on Saturdays, April to October, **Nørrebro Loppemarked** (Map p59; www. berling-samlerting.dk/32693948; Nørrebrogade, Nørrebro; ⏰8am-3pm Sat Apr-Oct; 🚌5C, 8A, 350S) is Denmark's biggest flea-market. Head to Nørreport for gourmet food and drink, handcrafted bags and more top fashion. Right on Rådhuspladsen, **Politikens Boghal** (Map p48; ✔️30 67 28 06; https:// politikensforlag.dk/politikens-boghal/c-9; Rådhuspladsen 37; ⏰9am-7pm Mon & Tue, to 8pm Wed-Fri,

10am-6pm Sat, 11am-6pm Sun; 🚌2A, 5C, 6A, 10, 250S) is the city's biggest bookshop, while **Posterland** (Map p48; ✔️33 11 28 21; www. posterland.dk; Gothersgade 45; ⏰9.30am-6pm Mon-Thu, to 7pm Fri, to 5pm Sat; 🚌350S, Ⓜ Kongens Nytorv) is great for postcards, calendars and fridge magnets as well as posters.

⭐**Illums Bolighus**   DESIGN
(Map p48; ✔️33 14 19 41; www.illumsbolighus. dk; Amagertorv 8-10; ⏰10am-7pm Mon-Thu & Sat, to 8pm Fri, 11am-6pm Sun; 🚇; 🚌1A, 2A, 9A, 14, 26,

37, 66, Ⓜ Kongens Nytorv) Design fans hyperventilate over this sprawling department store, its four floors packed with all things Nordic and beautiful. You'll find everything from ceramics, glassware, jewellery and fashion to throws, lamps, furniture and more.

★ **Designer Zoo** DESIGN
(Map p62; ☑ 33 24 94 93; www.dzoo.dk; Vesterbrogade 137, Vesterbro; ⊙ 10am-6pm Mon-Fri, to 3pm Sat; ☑ 6A) If you find yourself in Vesterbro – and you should – make sure to drop into this super-cool design hub. A store, gallery and workshop complex in one (the staff are actual designers and artisans), it's a platform for independent Danish design talent. Scan both floors for locally made limited-edition objects spanning jewellery, soft furnishings and furniture to ceramics and glassware.

★ **Hay House** DESIGN
(Map p48; ☑ 42 82 08 20; www.hay.dk; Østergade 61; ⊙ 10am-6pm Mon-Fri, to 5pm Sat; ☑ 1A, 2A, 9A, 14, 26, 37, 66, Ⓜ Kongens Nytorv) Rolf Hay's fabulous interior-design store sells its own coveted line of furniture, textiles and design objects, as well as those of other fresh, innovative Danish designers. Easy-to-pack gifts include anything from notebooks and ceramic cups, to building blocks for style-savvy kids. There's a **second branch** at Pilestræde 29-31.

★ **Stilleben** DESIGN
(Map p48; ☑ 22 45 11 31; https://stilleben.dk; Frederiksborggade 22; ⊙ 10am-6pm Mon-Fri, to 5pm Sat; ☑ 350S, Ⓜ Nørreport, Ⓢ Nørreport) One of Copenhagen's top design stores, Stilleben is famed for its graphic prints, not to mention its stock of unique objects from mostly smaller-scale Scandi designers. Go gaga over all things beautiful and kooky, from boldly patterned cups, jugs, vases and tea cosies to striking sofa cushions, sculptural candle holders, jewellery, bags, socks and more.

There's another location just off **Strøget** (Map p48; ☑ 33 91 11 31; www.stilleben.dk; Niels Hemmingsensgade 3; ⊙ 10am-6pm Mon-Fri, to 5pm Sat; ☑ 1A, 2A, 9A, 14, 26, 37, 66, Ⓜ Kongens Nytorv).

Royal Copenhagen CERAMICS
(Map p48; ☑ 38 14 96 05; www.royalcopenhagen.com; Amagertorv 6; ⊙ 10am-7pm Mon-Fri, to 6pm Sat, 11am-4pm Sun; ☑ 1A, 2A, 9A, 14, 26, 37, 66, Ⓜ Kongens Nytorv) This is the main showroom for the historic Royal Copenhagen porcelain, one of the city's best-loved souvenir choices. Its 'blue fluted' pattern is famous around the world, as is the painfully expensive Flora Danica dinner service, its botanical illustrations the work of 18th-century painter Johann Christoph Bayer.

Wood Wood FASHION & ACCESSORIES
(Map p48; ☑ 35 35 62 64; www.woodwood.dk; Grønnegade 1; ⊙ 10.30am-6pm Mon-Thu, to 7pm Fri, to 5pm Sat, noon-4pm Sun; ☑ 1A, 26, 350S, Ⓜ Kongens Nytorv) Unisex Wood Wood's flagship store is a solid spot for distinctive street fashion. Top of the heap are Wood Wood's own playful creations, made with superlative fabrics and attention to detail. The supporting cast includes sneakers, unconventional threads from designers like Comme des Garçons Play, Peter Jansen and Gosha Rubchinskiy, as well as accessories spanning fragrances and wallets to quirky eyewear.

Vanishing Point HANDICRAFTS
(Map p59; ☑ 25 13 47 55; www.vanishing-point.dk; Jægersborggade 45, Nørrebro; ⊙ 11am-5.30pm Mon-Fri, to 6pm Sat, to 3pm Sun; ☑ 8A) On trendy Jægersborggade, Vanishing Point is a contemporary craft shop and studio showcasing quirky ceramics, unique jewellery, handmade knits and quilts, as well as engaging, limited-edition prints. Most items are created on-site, while some are the result of a collaboration with non-profits around the world. The aim: to inspire a sustainable and playful lifestyle through nature, traditional craft techniques and humour.

Klassik Moderne Møbelkunst DESIGN
(Map p48; ☑ 33 33 90 60; www.klassik.dk; Bredgade 3; ⊙ 11am-6pm Mon-Fri, 10am-4pm Sat; ☑ 1A, 26, 350S, Ⓜ Kongens Nytorv) Close to Kongens Nytorv, Klassik Moderne Møbelkunst is Valhalla for lovers of Danish design, with a trove of classics from greats like Poul Henningsen, Hans J Wegner, Arne Jacobsen, Finn Juhl and Nanna Ditzel – in other words, a veritable museum of Scandinavian furniture from the mid-20th century.

Bornholmer Butikken FOOD & DRINKS
(Map p48; ☑ 30 72 00 07; www.bornholmerbutikken.dk; Stall F6, Hall 1, Torvehallerne KBH; ⊙ 10am-7pm Mon-Thu, to 8pm Fri, to 6pm Sat, 11am-5pm Sun; ☎; ☑ 15E, 150S, 185, Ⓜ Nørreport, Ⓢ Nørreport) The Bornholm Store in Torvehallerne Market peddles specialties from the Danish island of Bornholm, famed for its prized local edibles. Tasty treats to bring home include honeys, relishes and jams, Johan Bülow liquorice, charcuterie, cheeses, herring, liquors and craft beers.

Ostekælderen
CHEESE

(Map p48; ☑33 13 64 18; Gothersgade 41; ◷10am-5.30pm Tue-Thu, to 5pm Fri; ⬛350S, Ⓜ Kongens Nytorv) Complete with sawdust floors, this charming basement cheese shop is the city's oldest, dating from 1888. Although its long-time owners Vivvi and Hesluf retired in 2017, the tradition continues and the place remains a top spot to pick up well-priced, interesting Danish cheeses like Samsø, a cow's-milk variety with Swiss-cheese-like consistency and a nutty, pungent flavour.

Sømods Bolcher
FOOD

(Map p48; ☑33 12 60 46; www.soemods-bolcher. dk; Nørregade 36; ◷9.15am-5.30pm Mon-Thu, to 6pm Fri, 10am-3.30pm Sat; ⬛15E, 150S, 185, Ⓜ Nørreport, Ⓢ Nørreport) An official Danish 'Royal Purveyor', Sømods Bolcher has been producing *bolcher* (hard candies) since 1891. The original techniques and recipes are still in use, passed down through four generations of the Sømod family. Pearl sugar is heated to 180°C and then shaped by hand, producing more than 70 varieties of sweets.

Gågron!
HOMEWARES

(Map p59; ☑42 45 07 72; www.gagron.dk; Jægersborggade 48, Nørrebro; ◷11am-5.30pm Mon-Fri, 10am-3.30pm Sat, 11am-3pm Sun; ⬛8A) Gågron! peddles design-literate products with a conscience. The focus is on natural fibers and sustainable, recycled and upcycled materials, transformed into simple, stylish products for everyday use.

Playtype
GIFTS & SOUVENIRS

(Map p62; ☑60 40 69 14; www.playtype.com; Værnedamsvej 6, Vesterbro; ◷noon-6pm Mon-Fri, 11am-3pm Sat; ⬛6A, 9A, 26) Print is alive, well and making font fans freak at Playtype, an online type foundry with its own real-life, hard-copy shop. The theme is Danish-designed fonts, showcased as letters, numbers and symbols on everything from posters and notebooks to postcards.

ⓘ Information

INTERNET ACCESS

Free wi-fi is available at many museums, cafes and restaurants, as well as the overwhelming majority of accommodation options, from hotels and hostels to self-catering apartments. It's also offered at the **Copenhagen Visitors Centre** (Map p48; ☑70 22 24 42; www.visitcopen hagen.com; Vesterbrogade 4A, Vesterbro; ◷9am-8pm Mon-Fri, to 6pm Sat & Sun Jul & Aug, reduced hours rest of year; ☎; ⬛2A, 6A, 12, 14, 26, 250S, Ⓢ København H) and the main

public library, **Københavns Hovedbibliotek** (☑33 66 30 00; https://bibliotek.kk.dk; Krystalgade 15; ◷8am-9pm Mon-Fri, 9am-5pm Sat; ☎; ⬛14, Ⓜ Nørreport, Ⓢ Nørreport). The library also has computer terminals with internet access.

LEFT LUGGAGE

Central Station has a **left-luggage office** (☑24 68 31 77; per 24hr luggage per piece 70-80kr, max 10 days; ◷5.30am-1am Mon-Sat, 6am-1am Sun) and **luggage lockers** (per 24hr small/large 65/75kr, max 72hr). Both are located at the back of the station, near the exit into Reventlowsgade.

Copenhagen Airport offers three sizes of **luggage lockers** (24hr locker rental 80-120kr) in car park 4 (P4). Payment is by Visa or MasterCard only. Maximum rental period is seven consecutive days.

MEDICAL SERVICES

Private doctor and dentist visits vary but usually cost from around 1400kr. To contact a doctor, call ☑60 75 40 70.

Call ☑1813 before going to a hospital emergency department to save waiting time. The following hospitals have 24-hour emergency wards:

Amager Hospital (☑32 34 32 34; www. amagerhospital.dk; Italiensvej 1, Amager; ⬛2A, 4A, 12, Ⓜ Amager Strand) Southeast of the city centre.

Bispebjerg Hospital (☑35 31 23 73; www. bispebjerghospital.dk; Bispebjerg Bakke 23; Ⓢ Bispebjerg, Emdrup) Northwest of the city centre.

Frederiksberg Hospital (☑38 16 38 16; www. frederiksberghospital.dk; Nordre Fasanvej 57, Frederiksberg; ◷24hr; ⬛4A, Ⓜ Fasanvej) West of the city centre.

Tandlægevagten (☑1813; www.tandlægevag ten.dk; Oslo Plads 14; ⬛1A, Ⓢ Østerport) Emergency dental service near Østerport station.

Steno Apotek (☑33 14 82 66; www.stenoa potek.dk; Vesterbrogade 6C; ◷24hr; ⬛6A, 26, Ⓢ København H) A 24-hour pharmacy opposite Central Station.

MONEY

ATMs are widely available. Credit cards are accepted in most hotels, restaurants and shops. A small but growing number of businesses accept cards only, not cash.

POST

You'll find a handy **post office** (Map p48; ☑70 70 70 30; www.postnord.dk; Pilestræde 58; ◷8.30am-7pm Mon-Fri, to 2pm Sat; ⬛350S, Ⓜ Kongens Nytorv) just north of the Latin Quarter in the city centre. Most postal services are now from counters within large supermarkets.

TOURIST INFORMATION

Copenhagen Visitors Centre Copenhagen's excellent and informative information centre has a cafe and lounge with free wi-fi; it also sells the **Copenhagen Card** (www.copenhagen card.com; adult/child 10-15yr 24hr 389/199kr, 48hr 549/279kr, 72hr 659/329kr, 120hr 889/449kr).

USEFUL WEBSITES

Visit Copenhagen (www.visitcopenhagen.com) Useful, thematic information on everything from accommodation and sightseeing to dining, shopping and events.

CPH Post (cphpost.dk) Online edition of the *Copenhagen Post,* with plenty of news and cultural insight. In English.

AOK (www.aok.dk) Danish-language guide to all that's new and hot in Copenhagen, including restaurants and retail.

Kopenhagen (http://kopenhagen.dk) Top website for Copenhagen's art scene, with exhibition listings, news and interviews. In Danish.

ⓘ Getting There & Away

AIR

Copenhagen Airport (Map p93; ☏ 32 31 32 31; www.cph.dk; Lufthavnsboulevarden, Kastrup; Ⓜ Lufthavnen, Ⓢ Københavns Lufthavn), Scandinavia's busiest air hub, is in Kastrup, 9km southeast of the city centre. It's user-friendly, with quality eating, retail and information facilities, albeit 'silent' (ie without boarding calls).

BOAT

DFDS Seaways (Map p60; ☏ 33 42 30 00; www.dfdsseaways.com; Dampfærgevej 30; Ⓢ Nordhavn) One daily service to/from Oslo (one way from 675kr, 17¼ hours). Ferries depart from Søndre Frihavn, just north of Kastellet.

Polferries (www.polferries.com) Two daily bus-ferry combos to/from Poland (one way from 400kr). Bus 866 connects Copenhagen to Ystad in Sweden (1¼ hours), from where ferries travel to/from Świnoujście, Poland. Ferry crossings take between six and 7½ hours.

BUS

Copenhagen is well connected to the rest of Europe by daily (or near-daily) buses.

Flixbus (www.flixbus.com; Ⓢ København H) runs services throughout Europe (limited services into Norway and Sweden, however). Destinations, timetables and prices are all online.

TRAIN

All long-distance trains arrive at and depart from København H (Central Station), an imposing 19th-century, wooden-beamed hall with numerous facilities, including currency exchange, a police station, lockers, left-luggage facilities and food outlets. **DSB Billetsalg** (DSB Ticket Office; ☏ 70 13 14 15; www.dsb.dk; Central Station, Bernstorffsgade 16-22; ⊙7am-8pm Mon-Fri, 8am-6pm Sat & Sun; Ⓢ København H) is best for reservations and for purchasing international train tickets.

Destinations include the following:

➡ Roskilde (84kr, 20 to 35 minutes, three to nine hourly)

➡ Helsingør (108kr, 45 minutes, around every 20 minutes)

➡ Odense (308kr, 1¼ to two hours, at least twice hourly)

➡ Aarhus (418kr, 2¾ to 3½ hours, one to three hourly)

➡ Aalborg (468kr, 4½ to five hours, one to two hourly)

DB (www.bahn.com) runs direct Inter-City Express (ICE) trains from København H (Central Station) to Hamburg (from 298kr, 4¾ hours including ferry) several times daily including ferry crossing.

ⓘ Getting Around

We can't stress enough that by far the best way to see Copenhagen is on foot. There are few main sights or shopping quarters more than a 20-minute walk from the city centre.

Copenhagen's bus, metro, S-train and Harbour Bus network has an integrated ticket system based on seven geographical zones. Most of your travel within the city will be within two zones. Travel between the city and airport covers three zones.

➡ The cheapest ticket (*billet*) covers two zones, offers unlimited transfers and is valid for one hour (adult/12 to 15 years 24/12kr). An adult with a valid ticket can take two children under the age of 12 free of charge.

➡ If you plan on exploring sights outside the city, including Helsingør, the north coast of Zealand and Roskilde, you're better off buying a 24-hour ticket (all zones adult/12 to 15 years 130/65kr) or a seven-day FlexCard (all zones 675kr).

➡ Alternatively, you can purchase a **Rejsekort** (www.rejsekort.dk), a touch-on, touch-off smart card valid for all zones and all public transport across Denmark. Available from the Rejsekort machines at metro stations, Central Station or the airport, the card costs 180kr (80kr for the card and 100kr in credit). To use, tap the Rejsekort against the dedicated sensors at train and metro stations or when boarding buses and commuter ferries, then tap off when exiting. Only tap off at the very end of your journey – if your journey involves a metro ride followed immediately by a bus ride, tap on at the metro station and again on the bus, but only tap off once you exit the bus.

➡ The **Copenhagen Card** gives you unlimited public transport throughout the greater region of Copenhagen (including the airport). In addition, you get free entrance to 79 attractions and museums as well as discounts on several restaurants, sights, rentals and more.

➡ Another option is the **City Pass** (www.citypass.dk), which covers all bus, train, metro and Harbour Buses in zones 1 to 4 (adult 24/72 hours 80/200kr, children travel half-price).

AROUND COPENHAGEN

Whether you're hankering for sandy beaches, modern art collections or an alfresco museum showcasing the more bucolic side of Danish history, Copenhagen's city fringes have you covered. Internationalists can even head abroad for the day: Sweden's third largest city, Malmö, is an effortless 35-minute train from Copenhagen Central Station via the majestic Øresund Fixed Link bridge and tunnel. (Just don't forget your passport!)

Lyngby

The main sight of interest in the Lyngby area is **Frilandsmuseet** (Map p93; ☑41 20 64 55; www.natmus.dk; Kongevejen 100, Lyngby; ☺10am–5pm Tue-Sun late Jun–mid-Aug, shorter hours rest of year; ☐184, 194, ⑤Sorgenfri) **FREE** a sprawling open-air museum of old countryside dwellings that have been gathered from sites around Denmark. Its 100-plus historic buildings are arranged in groupings that provide a sense of Danish rural life as it was in various regions and across different social strata.

Rungsted & Humlebæk

★**Louisiana**   MUSEUM
(Map p93; www.louisiana.dk; Gammel Strandvej 13, Humlebæk; adult/student/child 125/110kr/free; ☺11am-10pm Tue-Fri, to 6pm Sat & Sun) This extraordinary museum of modern and contemporary art should be high on your 'to do' list even if you're not normally a gallery-goer. Along with its ever-changing, cutting-edge exhibitions, much of the thrill here is the glorious presentation. A maze-like web of halls and glass corridors weave through rolling gardens such that magnificent trees, lawns, a lake and a beach view set off monumental abstract sculptures (Henry Moore, Jean Arp, Max Ernst, Barbara Hepworth etc), making them feel like discovered totems.

It's hard to predict exactly which pieces from the gallery's huge, stellar collection

will be on display. Such is the quality and breadth that even works by Pablo Picasso and Francis Bacon stay in storage much of the time. There's a better chance of seeing pieces by Alberto Giacometti and prominent Danish artist Asger Jorn, but rotations every two months or so mean that there's always more to discover. Kids are spoilt with an entire section of their own, where they can create masterpieces inspired by the gallery's exhibitions, using everything from crayons to interactive computers.

Louisiana is in the pretty coastal town of **Humlebæk**, 30km north of Copenhagen. From Humlebæk train station, the museum is a 1.5km signposted walk northeast. Trains to Humlebæk run at least twice hourly from Copenhagen (92kr, 35 minutes) but if you're day-tripping, the 24-hour Copenhagen ticket (adult/child 130/65kr) is much better value. Hourly bus 388 from Helsingør stops right outside Louisiana (36kr, 17 minutes) and continues in half an hour to Rungsted, where it passes the Blixen museum.

Karen Blixen Museet   MUSEUM
(Map p93; http://blixen.dk; Rungsted Strandvej 111; adult/child 75kr/free; ☺10am-5pm Tue-Sun May-Sep, 1-4pm Wed-Fri, 11am-4pm Sat & Sun Oct-Apr) Best known as the writer of (and Meryl Streep character in) *Out of Africa,* Karen Blixen grew up in a 400-year-old coaching inn at Rungsted. She returned here from Africa in 1931 bankrupt, heartbroken and suffering heavy-metal poisoning…then started to write. The house remains much as she left it, full of period furniture but also photographs, personal mementos and two rooms of her remarkably impressive paintings.

Charlottenlund & Klampenborg

Charlottenlund is a salubrious coastal suburb with a sandy beach, around 8km north of central Copenhagen. Access is via S-train line C to Klampenborg, which itself has a handy beach (Bellevue) that gets packed with summer sunbathers.

◉ Sights & Activities

Ordrupgaard   MUSEUM
(Map p93; ☑39 64 11 83; www.ordrupgaard.dk; Vilvordevej 110, Charlottenlund; adult/child 110kr/free; ☺1-5pm Tue-Fri, from 11am Sat & Sun; ⑤Klampenborg, then ☐388) An extension by the late architect Zaha Hadid put Ordrup-

Around Copenhagen

Around Copenhagen

◉ **Top Sights**
1 Louisiana...A1

◉ **Sights**
2 Arken Museum of Modern Art...........A4
3 Cykelslangen....................................B4
4 Den Blå Planet.................................B4
5 Frilandsmuseet.................................A2
6 Karen Blixen Museet.......................A2
7 Ordrupgaard....................................B3

🔵 **Activities, Courses & Tours**
8 Amager Strandpark..........................B4
9 Bakken...B3
 Dyrehaven.....................................(see 9)
10 Havnebadet Sluseholmen................B4
11 Helgoland Badeanstalt....................B4

🔴 **Eating**
12 Søllerød Kro..................................A2

Kastrup

Designed to look like a whirlpool from above, **Den Blå Planet** (Map p93; ☎44 22 22 44; www.denblaaplanet.dk; Jacob Fortlingsvej 1, Kastrup; adult/child 3-11yr 170/95kr; ◔10am-9pm Mon, to 5pm Tue-Sun; 🚇5C, Ⓜ Kastrup) is an aluminium-clad aquarium and is the largest in northern Europe. The space is divided into climatic and geographic sections, the most spectacular of which is 'Ocean/Coral Reef'. Home to swarms of tropical fish, the exhibition features a massive 4-million-litre tank brimming with sharks, stingrays and other majestic creatures.

Ishøj

Modern art fans wanting a quick escape from town should consider a trip to the **Arken Museum of Modern Art** (Ark; Map p93; ☎43 54 02 22; www.arken.dk; Skovvej 100, Ishøj; adult/child 115kr/free; ◔10am-5pm Tue & Thu-Sun, to 9pm Wed; Ⓢ Ishøj). It's best known for its temporary exhibitions, spanning the usual modern art spectrum of site-specific installations, sculpture, painting and mixed-media works. The museum's permanent cache of post-1945 works include creations by Warhol, Damien Hirst and Ai Weiwei, as well as art by heavyweight Danes like Per Kirkeby, Asger Jorn and Olafur Eliasson. There's plenty to keep children intrigued too, including the wonderful sandy beach outside.

gaard on the international map, but this petite art museum, housed in an early-20th-century manor house north of Copenhagen, has always had an enviable collection of 19th- and 20th-century art. The museum will be closed for two years from December 2017 as it builds an underground extension by prolific Norwegian architects Snöhetta.

Dyrehaven   WALKING, CYCLING
(Map p93; http://eng.naturstyrelsen.dk; Dyrehaven, Klampenborg; Ⓢ Klampenborg) Formally called Jægersborg Dyrehave, Dyrehaven is a 1000-hectare sweep of beech trees and meadows crisscrossed by an alluring network of walking and cycling trails. Now the capital's most popular picnicking area, the grounds were established as a royal hunting ground in 1669. There are still about 2000 deer in the park, mostly fallow but also some red and Japanese sika deer. Among the red deer are a few rare white specimens.

Zealand

Best Places to Eat

➡ Dragsholm Slot (p123)

➡ Babette (p124)

➡ Skipperhuset (p105)

➡ Restaurant Arken (p119)

➡ Little Cafe (p109)

➡ Vallø Slotskro (p119)

Best Places to Stay

➡ Kyhns Gæstehus (p100)

➡ Rødvig Kro (p122)

➡ Øbjerggaard Bed & Breakfast (p121)

➡ Hotel Bretagne (p105)

➡ Beringgaard B&B (p107)

➡ Bed & Breakfast Hårlandsgård (p109)

Why Go?

Denmark's largest island offers much more than the dazzle of Copenhagen. North of the city lie some of the country's finest beaches and most impressive castles. Here you'll find dazzlingly ornate Frederiksborg Slot in Hillerød and the hulking Kronborg Slot at Helsingør, Shakespeare's Elsinore. Helsingør also features the excellent Maritime Museum of Denmark. En route don't miss Louisiana, the superb modern/contemporary art gallery, not the US state.

West of Copenhagen awaits history-steeped Roskilde, home to a World Heritage–listed cathedral, Scandinavia's classic rock music festival and a tremendous Viking Ship Museum. History also comes to life at nearby Sagnlandet Lejre, an engrossing, hands-on archaeology site.

Further west stands the millennia-old Trelleborg ring fortress, while Zealand's southern assets include medieval charm in Køge and the World Heritage–listed cliff geology of Stevns Klint, plus a nearby Cold War fortress-museum.

When to Go

In July and August the weather is at its warmest, the countryside is a luxuriant green, and the region's beach-strung north coast is at its most enticing. Tourist offices and attractions are in full swing, and world-class cultural events such as the Roskilde Festival attract some of the world's top performers. The downside is that you won't be the only one soaking up the sun, sea and culture. Most Danes take their holiday in July, making coastal towns particularly crowded and accommodation scarce. Book ahead.

June is a great bet, but so too are May and September with mild weather, smaller crowds, and most attractions open at reasonable if not full capacity. In winter, however, the days are cold and short and the region's beach towns feel virtually dormant, with limited opening times at some attractions and others closed outright.

NORTHEAST ZEALAND

Northeastern Zealand's coast has been nicknamed the Danish Riviera, thanks to the indulgent private mansions scattered through the seaside settlements north of Copenhagen. But it's only when you get around to Hornbæk and Tisvildeleje on the northern (Kattegat) coast that you'll find the really gorgeous white sands lapped by gentle waves – or surfable breakers, depending on the day. Beyond the coastal delights, this region's biggest draws are the great historic castles, especially the absurdly ornate interiors of Frederiksborg (p102) in Hillerød and the contrastingly moody Kronborg Slot, setting for Shakespeare's *Hamlet.* The latter is in historic Helsingør (Elsinore), one of Zealand's most compulsively interesting towns.

Helsingør

POP 46,830

Fascinating Helsingør commands the narrowest point of the Øresund, the sound that separates Denmark from today's Sweden. In the 15th and 16th centuries the city became immensely wealthy by taxing shipping that had to pass this way between the Baltic Sea and the open ocean. For a sizeable town, Helsingør has done a pretty good job of maintaining mementoes of its medieval character, best appreciated by strolling through the grid of narrow cobbled streets between the harbour and the bustling shopping core. Here, half-timbered back-alley houses lean precariously behind towering hollyhocks and creeping ivy. The main sight, however, is the gigantic Kronborg Slot, made famous as Elsinore Castle in Shakespeare's *Hamlet,* although the intimate psychological nature of the play is a far cry from the real-life military colossus.

Very frequent ferries shuttle to Helsingborg (Sweden), generally filled with Swedes on a mission to buy 'cheap' Danish alcohol (it's all relative).

◎ Sights

★ **M/S Museet for Søfart** MUSEUM
(Maritime Museum of Denmark; www.mfs.dk; Ny Kronborgvej 1; adult/child 110kr/free; ⏱10am-6pm Jul & Aug, 11am-5pm Sep, closed Mon rest of year) Ingeniously built into a dry dock beside Kronborg Slot, this subterranean museum merits a visit as much for its design as for its informative multimedia galleries. These explore Denmark's maritime history and culture in dynamic, contemporary ways. Alongside nautical instruments, sea charts and wartime objects, exhibitions explore themes including the representation of sailors in popular culture, trade and exploitation in Denmark's overseas colonies, and globe-crossing journeys of modern shipping containers.

Interactive displays can have you inking a sailor's tattoo, testing your navigational skills and even running your own trade company. The museum also houses a contemporary cafe and an excellent gift shop of maritime-themed gifts.

★ **Kronborg Slot** CASTLE
(www.kronborg.dk; Kronborgvej; interior adult/student 140/130kr; ⏱10am-5.30pm Jun-Sep, 11am-4pm Apr & May, 11am-4pm Tue-Sun Oct-Mar) Best known as the Elsinore Castle of Shakespeare's *Hamlet,* this Unesco World Heritage Site is a vast Renaissance masterpiece topped by baroque green-copper spires. It's ringed by moats, fortifications and powerful Vaubanesque star bastions that you can discover without a ticket. But it's well worth the entry fee to explore the inner palace's rooms, tapestries, ceiling paintings and viewpoints and, best of all, to delve into the spooky maze of casemates – subterranean dungeon passages barely lit by flickering paraffin lamps.

The castle began life as Krogen, a formidable tollhouse built by Danish king Erik of Pomerania in the 1420s to command the 4km Øresund strait between Denmark and today's Sweden. Passing ships heading to or from the Baltic had to pay transit fees, which created enormous tax revenues that made the city very wealthy and allowed Frederik II to vastly expand the castle in 1585. A major fire in 1629 destroyed most of the interior, bar the chapel, but Kronborg came back to life under tireless builder-king Christian IV, who preserved the castle's earlier Renaissance style while adding his own baroque touches. During the Danish-Swedish wars, the Swedes occupied the castle from 1658 to 1660, looting everything of value, including its then-famous fountain. Thereafter, Christian V bulked up Kronborg's defences, but the Danish royals gave up trying to make the castle a home. The building was used as a barracks from 1785 until 1924, when it became a museum (the Swedish government sportingly returned some previously looted items).

The site is extensive, and to do it justice you'll need a couple of hours. Around half

Zealand Highlights

1 Frederiksborg Slot (p102) Gawping at lavish furnishings and abundant artworks in one of Denmark's most opulent historic buildings.

2 Hornbæk Surf Beach (p105) Windsurfing from a wide, golden beach that feels more Mediterranean than Danish.

3 Kronborg Slot (p95) Snooping around the immense castle that was the setting for Shakespeare's *Hamlet*.

4 Maritime Culture (p95) Exploring nautical themes at Helsingør's show-stopping M/S Museet for Søfart.

5 Sagnlandet Lejre (p116) Letting your children run free with an axe at an Iron Age settlement near Lejre.

6 Rocking Roskilde (p110) Partying at northern Europe's largest music festival or catching the vibe year-round at Ragnarock's experience-rich pop-music museum.

7 Køge (p119) Cafe-bar-hopping between courtyards and pretty streets of attractive old half-timbered houses.

8 Trelleborg (p125) Puzzling over the enigmatic remains of a perfectly circular Viking ring fortress.

Helsingør

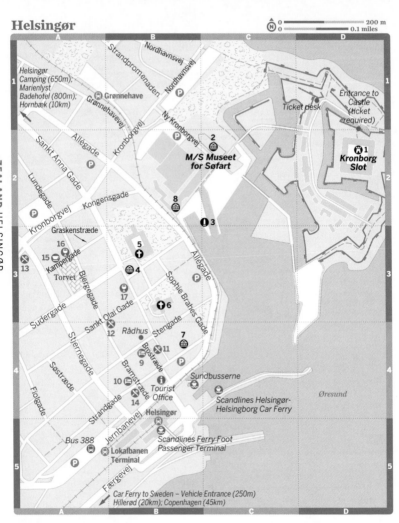

of that will be spent wandering in areas that are open sunrise to sunset without fee, but for the payable area, note that ticket sales (and entries to the 145-step Cannon Tower) stop half an hour before official closing time. Free wi-fi and several QR-coded information points allow you to download commentaries and a Kronborg visitor app for your mobile phone. From mid-June to August before 4pm there are interactive moments where you might encounter actors playing *Hamlet* characters. Tickets include optional guided tours, with English versions typically at noon and 3pm, plus casemates only at 1pm and (possibly) 4pm.

The accessible **Royal Apartments** section covers two floors of the castle with several huge spaces in which the royal ladies would promenade – going outside was too much for their delicate shoes. See the king's desk, his-and-hers royal bedrooms, and what was, in 1585, the longest ballroom in Scandinavia. Banquets held here consisted of 65 courses, with each guest equipped with their own vomiting bucket. You arrive back into the central courtyard via an extensive gift shop, behind which is an easily missed push-screen historical timeline.

Don't give up yet. Across the courtyard, separate doorways lead to the **Cannon**

Helsingør

Tower (great views, sweaty climb), the well-explained **tapestry collection**, the 1582 **chapel** (with original interior fully restored since 1843) and the **casemates**. Though essentially empty apart from nesting bats and a foreboding statue of Viking chief Holger Danske (Ogier the Dane), this very extensive series of low-ceilinged dungeons, storerooms and soldiers' quarters stretches a surprisingly long way beneath the castle. It's suitably dark and creepy, but just follow the dimly lit arrows and you'll emerge... eventually. One extra perk of the paid ticket is the right to walk up to the **Flag Bastion** for views towards Sweden.

Han   STATUE
(Allégade 2) A humorous dig at the Little Mermaid, Han is a 2012 male version of that statue in a similar pose to the Copenhagen original but made in gleamingly reflective polished metal.

It's at the waterfront on a jetty outside Kulturværftet.

Skibsklarerergaarden   MUSEUM
(🖉 49 28 18 36; www.helsingormuseer.dk; Strandgade 91; tour adult/child 35kr/free; ⊘noon-4pm Tue, Thu, Fri & Sun, noon-8pm Wed, 10am-2pm Sat)

Meaning 'Shipwreck Garden', this 1580 terraced building has a feel that has remained virtually unchanged for centuries. The ground floor 'Boutik' (admission free) is maintained as a delightful 1820s chandlery/beer shop. Upstairs, the 1780 house interior (ticket required) can be perused by joining a group tour that teaches you masses about the city's role as a customs and ship-provisioning centre pre-1856.

Tours supposedly run hourly but in fact you'd do best to call ahead. Keep the ticket as it is also valid for the **Helsingør Bymuseum** (www.helsingormuseer.dk; Sankt Anna Gade 36; adult/child 35kr/free; ⊘noon-4pm Tue, Thu, Fri & Sun, noon-8pm Wed, 10am-2pm Sat), a 1516 former sailors' hospital containing a hotchpotch of dolls, bottles and pottery.

Værftsmuseet   MUSEUM
(Harbour Museum; 🖉 49 28 18 16; www.helsingor museer.dk; Allégade 2; ⊘noon-4pm Tue, Thu, Fri & Sun, noon-8pm Wed, 10am-2pm Sat) **FREE** This free museum hosts changing exhibitions that highlight the role of shipbuilding in Helsingør's 19th- and 20th-century history. Once the city's main industry, the shipyard employed more than 3000 workers in the 1960s before slumping in the 1970s and closing altogether in 1983. Outside are memorable statues of striding shipworkers.

**Sankt Mariæ Kirke &
Karmeliterklostret**   CHURCH
(www.sctmariae.dk; Sankt Anna Gade 38; ⊘10am-3pm Tue-Sun) Karmeliterklostret is one of Scandinavia's few fully preserved monastic cloisters, its arched brick arcades giving the feel of an Oxford college. The large attached church has some rather eclectic 15th-century frescoes, in which frogs, foxes, bulls and rams spring from bizarre-looking faces, and where pipers and lute players burst from giant flowers.

Other church highlights include an ornate rococo gallery and a 17th-century organ, once played by baroque composer Dieterich Buxtehude (1637–1707) who was so famed in his day that in 1705, the young Johann Sebastian Bach is said to have walked 400km to meet him.

Sankt Olai Domkirke   CATHEDRAL
(⊘10am-4pm May-Aug, 10am-2pm Sep-Apr) The handsome, red-brick Sankt Olai Domkirke is a Gothic cathedral built in 1559 on the site of a 13th-century original. Eclectic features include a remarkable 1579 brass baptismal font

ZEALAND HELSINGØR

TO BE OR NOT TO BE

Shakespeare set *Hamlet* (1602) in Kronborg Slot (p95), the great castle of Helsingør ('Elsinore'). Despite the vividness of the play, the Bard had never set foot in Denmark. It's possible that he gleaned details of the imposing new fortress from a group of English players who performed in Helsingør in 1585, the year that Kronborg was completed. Shakespeare also included as minor characters two actual Danish noblemen who had visited the English court in the 1590s: Frederik Rosenkrantz and Knud Gyldenstierne (Guildenstern). Their fictionalised personas would later resurface at the heart of Tom Stoppard's absurdist anti-Hamlet comedy *Rosencrantz and Guildenstern Are Dead*.

Although the remaining characters in *Hamlet* are based on a story that was already 800 years old in Shakespeare's time, 17th-century audiences were utterly convinced of the play's authenticity. So many English merchants trading in Helsingør wanted to know where the indecisive Dane was buried that a 'Hamlet's grave' was built in the grounds of Marienlyst Slot, a 1588 hunting palace 1km northwest.

Each August, the Kronborg castle plays host to the open-air **Shakespeare Festival** (www.hamletscenen.dk; Kronborg Slot).

and an over-the-top gilded altarpiece which, at 12m tall, is one of Denmark's largest.

Hanging in the ceiling vault above the small organ of the northeastern chancel is a cannonball that was fired at Helsingør by the British fleet as it passed by, three days before the Battle of Copenhagen (1801).

Danmarks Tekniske Museum   MUSEUM
(www.tekniskmuseum.dk; Fabriksvej 25; adult/child 90kr/free; ☉10am-5pm Tue-Sun, plus Mon during holidays; 🚌802) On an industrial estate southwest of Helsingør, Danmarks Tekniske Museum displays innovative technological inventions from the late 19th and early 20th centuries: early gramophones, radios, motor vehicles and aeroplanes. The latter includes a 1906 Danish-built aeroplane that, it's claimed, was the first plane flown in Europe: it stayed airborne for a full 11 seconds.

The museum is a 25-minute ride away on bus 802, in the direction of Espergærde.

Rådhus   NOTABLE BUILDING
(Stengade 59) Restored in 2015, the attractive, brick, Gothic 1852 town hall building is particularly appealing at night when light strained through the stained-glass windows adds a colourful lustre.

🛏 Sleeping

Booking ahead is wise at any time but essential months in advance for the annual Shakespeare Festival (p100). Don't inadvertently select a place in Helsingborg (Sweden); some hotel-booking sites list both cities together.

Central Helsingør

★**Kyhns Gæstehus**   GUESTHOUSE €€
(☎71 70 84 82; www.kyhnsgaetehus.dk; Stengade 58; r incl breakfast from 995kr; ☉reception 10am-6pm; 🖗) 🅿 Salvaged over many years of reconstruction from a derelict 300-year-old house, this super-central luxury guesthouse has immaculate but characterful and spacious rooms above an inviting central courtyard cafe, opposite the historic town hall building. The biggest rooms come with en-suite bathroom and kitchenette. Climbing the brilliantly wobbly old stairway to room 5 can feel rather disorientating.

After the cafe closes (6pm), there's no reception but you can phone for a later check-in: the owners live just behind.

Madam Sprunck   BOUTIQUE HOTEL €€
(☎49 21 05 91; www.madamsprunck.dk; Bramstræde 5; s/d from 665/895kr; ☉reception 9am-4.30pm Mon-Fri, 9am-2pm Sat) Combining hotel, restaurant, cafe and DJ-lounge-bar, this characterful family place manages a clever melange of traditional and modern elements, including flame-style torch-lamps on corridors and antique-effect desks. Small kettles are provided. Some rooms are in the roof gables, with sloping ceilings liable to catch your head should you wake suddenly in the night.

While the reception desk has short hours, there's a 24-hour check-in system and you can ask for assistance at the restaurant.

🏖 Beach Area

Set back from the beach around a kilometre's coastal walk from Kronborg Slot car park (further if driving), the small, rather cramped **Helsingør Camping** (☑49 28 49 50; www. helsingorcamping.dk; Strandalleen 2; campsites per tent/caravan 50/80kr plus per adult/child 75/35kr; cabin with bathroom 615-850kr; ☺year-round) 🛶 is beside Marienlyst halt, the second tiny station on the Helsingør-Gilleleje railway. Directly northwest is a casino at the huge Badehotel. Continue 600m further to the excellent Danhostel.

Danhostel Helsingør   HOSTEL €
(☑49 28 49 49; www.danhostelhelsingor.dk; Nordre Strandvej 24; dm/s/d/tr 225/495/550/650kr; ℗ ☎; 🖳842) Right on its own little sandy beach with fireplace, lawns and kayak hire, this remarkable hostel is based around a count's 1907 summer mansion. Only five of the 40 rooms are within that building, but the restaurant section remains very grand with sea views. Dorm beds are available only in peak summer season. Sheet hire (59kr) obligatory.

Marienlyst Badehotel   HOTEL €€
(☑49 21 40 00; www.marienlyst.dk; Nordre Strandvej 2; s/d from 1095/1295kr; ℗ @ ☎ ⛲) The star attraction of this sprawling 225-room complex is the lawn-fronted waterfront complete with jetty and beach volleyball. The hotel was founded in 1861 but a displayed cube of wooden beam is all that remains of the original. Today's architecture appears drearily functional, but within, unexpected sweeps of older staircases add a semblance of character.

🍴 Eating

Rådmand Davids Hus   DANISH €
(☑49 26 10 43; Strandgade 70; dishes 48-108kr; ☺10am-5pm Mon-Sat; ☎) What better place to gobble down Danish classics than a snug, lopsided 1694 house, complete with cobbled courtyard? Refuel with honest, solid staples or special 'shopping lunches', typically a generous plate of salad, salmon pâté and slices of pork, cheese and homemade rye bread. Leave room for the Grand Marnier pancakes.

Café Hyacinth   DANISH €
(Bjergegade 4; lunch 109kr; ☺noon-5pm Mon-Thu, 11am-6pm Fri & Sat; ☎) Celebrating Hyacinth Bucket, the Patricia Routledge character from a classic British TV sitcom, this terraced cafe sprawls its summer seats onto the joyously buzzing Axeltorv Sq. One particularly

good-value lunch option comprises three classic smørrebrød (open sandwiches), a beer and a shot of *snaps*.

Spisehuset Kulturværftet   INTERNATIONAL €
(www.kulturvaerftet.dk; Allégade 2; meals 45-95kr; ☺10am-3pm Mon-Fri, to 5pm Sat & Sun; ☎) Part of the striking Culture Yard complex, this casual, light-filled eatery peddles a short selection of fresh cafe lunches (vitamin salad, fishcakes, sandwiches, fish and chips) to snack on as you gaze across the boat-filled waterfront towards Hamlet's pad.

Brostræde Fløde Is   ICE CREAM €
(Brostræde 2; cone 30kr; ☺10am-6pm) Possibly the creamiest ice cream you'll ever taste draws throngs of lickers to this tiny takeaway hatch-shop. Displayed photos show celebrity guests, including the UK's Prince Charles, though he probably got to jump the queue.

La Dolce Vita   ITALIAN €€
(☑92 21 18 80; http://la-dolcevita.dk; Kongensgade 6; pasta/mains from 129/189kr, 3-/4-course dinner 349/399kr; ☺5-9.30pm Mon-Sat) Certainly Helsingør has cheaper places if you just want packet pasta, but for genuine spirited Italian food in a beautiful old half-timbered house (and garden), La Dolce Vita is well worth the extra investment. The menu stretches to monkfish gratin in garlic and rosemary, or red wine guinea fowl with truffles.

Don't be put off by the restaurant's website, which distinctly undersells the place.

🍸 Drinking & Nightlife

The liveliest area for cafes and pubs is on and around the central square Axeltorv, with more around pedestrianised Stengade. Madam Sprunck's lounge-bar has live music some Saturdays. Helsingør has a couple of members-only microbrewing clubs. One craft brewer has tentative plans to open a tasting centre in the ancient cellar that forms part of **Galleri 77** (www.peterchristoffersen.dk).

Københavneren   PUB
(Sankt Anna Gade 17; Wiibroe beer 24kr, lunches 55-105kr; ☺10am-midnight Sun-Thu, 10am-2am Fri & Sat) Decked with beer steins and lit with low-hanging copper pan-lamps, this appealing yet inexpensive bar proudly serves Wiibroe, originally Helsingør's 'home' beer before being bought by Carlsberg. There's a good range of open sandwiches and Danish lunch meals from noon to 4pm, and a tempting beer garden.

Cafe André
CAFE

(www.cafeandre.dk; Kampergade 7; coffee without/with cake 30/69kr; ⊙10am-5pm Tue-Sat) Swoon at the astonishing selection of luscious cakes to accompany the excellent coffee at this cosy cafe facing Axeltorv, Helsingør's most buzzing pedestrian square. A three-cake selection for two people costs 210kr.

Gæstgivergaarden
BEER HALL

(www.gaestgivergaarden.dk; Kampergade 11; beer from 30kr; ⊙10am-11pm Mon-Thu, 10am-1am Fri & Sat) Central half-timbered pub with a decent selection of international and local beers, including Esrum Kloster brews.

❶ Information

There's a **tourist office** (☑49 21 13 33; www.visitnordsjaelland.com; Havnepladsen 3; ⊙10am-5pm Mon-Fri, to 2pm Sat & Sun Jul & Aug, reduced hours rest of year) opposite the train station.

❶ Getting There & Away

BOAT

Scandlines car ferries (☑33 15 15 15; www.scandlines.dk; adult/child 40/28kr, car with up to 9 passengers single/day return 380/390kr; ⊙24hr) take 20 minutes to sail to/from Helsingborg in Sweden, with several departures an hour for most of the day, at least hourly boats late at night. Cars should use the ticket barriers approached from **Søndre Strandvej** (☑33 15 15 15; www.scandlines.dk; Færgevej 8). Foot passengers should buy tickets from the **waiting hall** (1st fl, Helsingør train station) upstairs within the train station above platform 1. From there a series of boarding gantries leads directly to the boat. For the same price, foot passengers can alternatively use the smaller **Sundbusserne** (☑53 73 70 10; https://sundbusserne.dk; Færgevej 24; adult/child 40/28kr; ⊙10.30am-6.30pm Mon-Thu, to 8.30pm Fri & Sat, to 5.30pm Sun) boats.

BUS

Hourly **bus 388** (Jernbanevej) runs to Klampenborg (84kr, 1¼ hours) on the outskirts of Copenhagen, the last stop on the C line of the S-train system. It's slower than the train but offers some beautiful sea views and passes right outside Louisiana (p92) in Humlebæk and the Karen Blixen Museum (p92) in Rungsted.

CAR

The most central free, unlimited parking is at the Lundegade Car Park.

TRAIN

Trains run between once and three times an hour (5am to midnight) to

Copenhagen (108kr, 45 minutes) via Rungsted

Gilleleje (68kr, 45 minutes).

Hillerød (68kr, 30 minutes) via Fredensborg (60kr, 20 minutes)

❶ Getting Around

Very convoluted bus route 802 eventually links Helsingør station to the **Danmarks Tekniske Museum** (p100) and the Flynderupgård (farm and fishing museum), but this takes nearly half an hour.

Hillerød

POP 31,900

A vision of copper turrets, lake islands and baroque gardens, Hillerød's glorious Frederiksborg Slot is one of the most impressive attractions in the region. Otherwise largely forgettable, Hillerød is also a handy transport hub for north Zealand, with train connections for the north coast beaches.

⊙ Sights

★**Frederiksborg Slot**
CASTLE

(www.frederiksborgmuseet.dk; adult/child 75/20kr; ⊙10am-5pm Apr-Oct, 11am-3pm Nov-Mar) One of Denmark's most impressive buildings, this gigantic, Dutch Renaissance–styled fortress-palace rises proudly out of photogenic moat-lake Slotsø. Access is free to the impressive central courtyards and huge, beautifully tended park with baroque gardens. To visit the interiors (ticket required) you'll need around three hours to do justice to the 80-plus rooms overloaded with beautiful furniture, tapestries, endless portraiture and gilded decor of astonishingly pompous grandiosity. Copious info-cards, along with free audio guides in nine languages, add plentiful context.

The oldest part of the castle dates from the reign of Frederik II, after whom it is named. His son Christian IV was born here, and most of the present structure was built by Christian in the early 17th century.

Especially dazzling is the **Slotskirken**, where Danish monarchs were crowned between 1671 and 1840. It retains the original interior commissioned by Christian IV, having survived an 1859 fire that ravaged much of the original castle. It's a deliciously ornate confection of curling gold and pink-cheeked cherubs, the altar, font and pulpit crusted with silver detail and overlooked by a priceless 1610 **Compenius organ** (played on Thursdays for half an hour at 1.30pm).

Also fairly intact is the **Audience Chamber**, an eye-boggling room containing trompe l'œil details, a self-indulgent portrait of bignosed Christian V posing as a Roman emperor, and, best of all, a 17th-century elevator chair, which enabled the king to rise regally through the floor!

Other rooms in the castle were restored to their original appearances in the 19th century, notably the richly embellished **Riddershalen**, a vast ballroom complete with minstrels' gallery and vivid ceiling carvings.

The rest of the 1st and 2nd floors contain the **Museum of National History**, a chronologically arranged portrait gallery of kings, noblemen and olden-day celebrities, interspersed with unusual pieces of furniture. It's a lot to digest in one go – you might be better off concentrating on the time periods that interest you.

North of the castle is an extensive park, **Slotshaven**. The formal **baroque garden** (open from 10am till sunset), made up of perfect terraces and immaculately manicured yew and box, demonstrates that even nature was forced to bend to a king's will. In the Romantic garden, **Indelukket**, 18th-century rigidity melts into a wilder 19th-century notion of gardening. North again is the oak wood of **Lille Dyrehave**, which was planted to provide material for boat-building after the Danish fleet was confiscated by England in 1807. You could easily spend a pleasant hour strolling through the three sections, perhaps combining the walk with a ride on the little **Frederiksborg ferry** (http://partre deriet.dk; Torvet; adult/child 30/10kr; ⊙11am-5pm Mon-Sat, 1-5pm Sun mid-May–mid-Sep).

⌂ Sleeping & Eating

Well out of the centre there's a semi-rural **hostel** (⌨48 26 19 86; www.hillerodhostel.dk; Lejrskolevej 4; dm/s/d 200/585/620kr; Ⓟ⌨; ⌨302, 301) 2.5km east, a functional **business hotel** (⌨48 24 08 00; www.hotelhillerod.dk; Milnersvej 41; s 905-1100kr, d 1150-1370kr; Ⓟ✳@⌨; ⌨305) on a light industrial estate, and a beautifully kept two-star **camping ground** (⌨48 26 48 54; www.hillerodcamping.dk; Blytækkervej 18; campsite per adult/child 100/50kr; ⊙mid-Apr–Sep; Ⓟ) 20 minutes' walk south of the castle.

Spiesestedet Leonora   DANISH €€
(⌨48 26 75 16; www.leonora.dk; Frederiksborg Slot; mains 72-155kr, weekend buffet 159kr; ⊙10am-5pm) In a historic cottage that's semi-hidden among Frederiksborg Slot's outer bastions, Leonora is a fine place for top-quality smørrebrød lunches, a luxury burger or a few more interesting hot dishes, including fruit-stuffed pork loin with cranberries and cream sauce.

Booking ahead is virtually essential for the superb-value Saturday and Sunday brunch buffet.

Café København   CAFE
(www.cafe-koebenhavn.dk; Torvet 4; beer/coffee from 30/25kr, 1/2/3-scoop ice cream 25/30/35kr, mains 69-150kr; ⊙10am-10pm Mon-Thu, to 2am Fri & Sat, to 5pm Sun) There are several cafes, bars and an Irish pub on the central square but Café København is the pick of the crop for its views across the lake towards the castle and for serving luscious scoops of Hansens ice cream.

ⓘ Getting There & Away

Direct S-train services link Hillerød to Copenhagen (adult/pensioner/child 92/69/46kr). On weekdays, line E services (42 minutes) do the run every 10 minutes, continuing all the way to Køge (100kr, 80 minutes). However, after 7.45pm (till around midnight) or on weekends, use the B train (50 minutes). Friday and Saturday nights the B train runs half-hourly all night. On other nights, the nocturnal option is bus 94N running hourly from Copenhagen's Rådhuspladsen.

Other trains from Hillerød run at least hourly to the following places:

Fredensborg (24kr, 10 minutes)

Gilleleje (60kr, 30 minutes)

Helsingør (72kr, 30 minutes)

Tisvildeleje (60kr, 30 minutes)

To/from Gilleleje or Tisvildeleje, using Hillerød's Slotspavillionen station might prove more convenient than the main station as it's closer to the Frederiksborg baroque gardens.

Near the castle there's a sizeable **car park** (per hour 10kr 8am-8pm Mon-Fri, 8am-5pm Sat, Sun free) behind the **tourist office** (⌨48 24 26 26; www.visitnordsjaelland.com; Frederiksværksgade 2A; ⊙10am-4pm Thu-Sat Jun, Mon-Sat Jul–mid-Sep).

ⓘ Getting Around

Buses 301 and 302 depart frequently from the train station and can drop you near the castle gate (24kr).

Fredensborg

POP 8420

Fredensborg *is* its royal palace...with parkland gardens stretching along Denmark's second-largest lake and the town tucked inconspicuously away like an afterthought. The palace is only open to the public in July and early August, but it's well worth a day out here anyway for peaceful greenery, swimming, boating and fishing opportunities.

◉ Sights & Activities

Fredensborg Slot
PALACE

(☑ 33 95 42 00; http://kongeligeslotte.dk; Slotsgade 1; tours adult/child 75/30kr; ⊙ tours Jul–early Aug) Supposedly the Queen of Denmark's favourite abode, the 1720 Fredensborg Slot is a grand palace in Italian baroque style. Getting inside is only possible by tour in midsummer, but you can admire the gracious facade from the forecourt or from behind if you walk anticlockwise through the park, which is a major part of the site's attraction. When the royals are in residence, guards in white-striped uniforms and bearskin hats perform a **changing of the guard** ceremony at noon.

The name Fredensborg – meaning 'Peace Palace' – commemorates the truce that Denmark had just achieved with its Scandinavian neighbours when the palace was commissioned. Indeed, the building's unfortified architectural elegance – which sees it nicknamed 'Denmark's Versailles' – reflects the more tranquil mood of that era, an abrupt contrast with the far more formidable moat-encircled fortresses of Kronborg and Frederiksborg that preceded it.

The palace is well signposted, about 1km north of Fredensborg train station.

Fredensborg Slotshave
GARDENS

(private garden tours incl in palace entry fee adult/child 75/30kr; ⊙ palace park 24hr year-round, private gardens 9am-5pm Jul–early Aug) Fredensborg Slot has around 120 soothing hectares of parkland crossed by an arc of long riding avenues that radiate from the palace. The majority of the park is open year-round without charge, apart from **private gardens** immediately west of the palace, which are only accessible through daily palace tours in July (tours in English 2.30pm). The park is dotted with commemorative rocks, obelisks and statues, notably in a double circle called **Normandsdalen** (Slotshave) FREE featuring 70 life-sized statues of Norwegian and Faroese folk characters.

These are based upon small wooden dolls of fishermen, farmers, soldiers and servants that were carved by an 18th-century postman. He sent them to King Frederik V, who liked them so much that he had them remade far larger in sandstone.

Bådfarten Esrum Sø
BOATING

(☑ 48 48 01 07; www.baadfarten.com; Skipper Allé 6; return adult/child 100/60kr; ⊙ by appointment May-Sep) One-hour boat tours around southern Esrum Sø (p106) depart according to weather and demand from beside the Skipperhuset restaurant, but you'll have to prebook or be lucky enough to hit upon another group's departure with available spaces.

🛏 Sleeping & Eating

Both main accommodation options are around a 200m walk heading south from the palace gates. For simple dining, there are Chinese, Indian, sushi, pizza and sandwich options on the uninspiring pedestrianised section of Jernbanegade that links the palace to the train station.

Danhostel Fredensborg
HOSTEL €

(☑ 48 48 03 15, 60 54 97 00; http://danhostelfredensborg.dk; Østrupvej 3; s/d/tr/q 550/595/655/695kr, without bathroom s/d/tr from 295/395/495kr; ⊙ Jan–mid-Dec; P 🛜) Fredensborg's attractive and thoroughly welcoming hostel is just a short stroll south then west from the main entrance of Fredensborg Slot. In the garden, you can look through foliage towards the royal orangery while sitting on a swing.

Fredensborg Store Kro
HOTEL €€

(☑ 36 44 80 20; www.storekro.com; Slotsgade 6; r/ste from 1195/2095kr; P 🛜) Oozing a jazzy elegance and with exemplary service, the Store Kro is based around an inn that was created in 1723 to host supplicants visiting King Christian IX's court. Cheaper rooms are in an annexe wing behind, with design-book sinks but 140cm queen beds. For bigger mattresses, newer showers and more antique-style furniture, pay more for the main historic building.

Beds are super-comfy, and better rooms have balconies overlooking the hotel lawns. Unwind in the glass-ceilinged, black-walled library and dine in the light-suffused verandah-bistro with its upscale but not unaffordable menu.

★ **Skipperhuset** DANISH €€
(☑ 48 48 10 12; www.skipperhuset.dk; Skipper Allé 6; lunch 95-235kr, 1-/3-/5-course dinner 175/275/400kr; ☺ noon-5pm Tue-Sun mid-Apr–Sep, plus 6-9pm Thu-Sun May-Aug) It's hard to imagine a more idyllic setting for a lazy lunch than this twisted, part-timbered 1754 boathouse perched right beside the jetty on Esrum Sø (p106). Small but beautifully presented lunch plates include fried plaice with Béarnaise sauce or a selection of cold open sandwiches, including daily-changing herring-of-the-day, all served with superb rye bread and seasonal vegetables.

Consider booking ahead for dinner. Between 3pm and 5pm it's drinks or coffee and cake only. Walking here is a delight, 1km downhill on a pedestrian avenue from Fredensborg Slot.

ℹ Information

There's a seasonal **tourist office** (www.visit nordsjaelland.com; Slotsgade; ☺ noon-4pm Mon-Fri mid-Aug–mid-Jun, from 10am mid-Jun–mid-Aug plus 10am-2pm Sat & Sun Jul) in the hotel foyer of **Fredensborg Store Kro**.

ℹ Getting There & Away

Trains stop at Fredensborg about twice hourly between Hillerød (24kr, 10 minutes) and Helsingør (60kr, 25 minutes).

Hornbæk

POP 5260

'Denmark's St Tropez!', shout the tourist brochures. Hornbæk's vast expanses of soft white sand attract their fair share of young socialites, but you'll also find a wind- and kitesurfing crowd here. And then there are the painters. Danish artists first discovered the attractions of what was then a little-known fishing village in the 19th century, with early tourists following hot on their heels.

🏃 Activities

Hornbæk Strand SWIMMING
With beautiful white sand and air scented with salt and wild roses, the beach to the direct west of the harbour is Hornbæk's best for swimming. There's a lifeguard in season, and lots of little picnic spots raised amid partly grassed dunes with views out across the waves.

The easiest access is from the path that is essentially the northern continuation of A R Frilsvej from Cafe Hornbæk Strand.

Hornbæk Surf Beach BEACH
(Lochersvej) For kitesurfing, stick to Hornbæk's eastern beach, easily accessed from behind Fiskehuset (p106) at the marina.

Hornbæk Surf Shop KITESURFING
(☑ 30 24 38 38; www.facebook.com/hornbaek surfshop; Havnevej 20; ☺ 10am-6pm Jun-Aug, to 5pm Sep-May) A few doors down Havnevej from the harbour, this new gear shop caters to wind- and kitesurfers, with rental services and lessons available.

Hornbæk Plantage WALKING
(Nordre Strandvej) Originally planted with trees in the 1790s to prevent erosion, this public woodland extends 3.5km east from Hornbæk, with numerous interconnecting walking trails marked on the tourist office's free map *Vandreture i Statsskovene, Hornbæk Plantage*.

Hikers can easily combine a forest walk with the **coastal path** (Lochersvej), or a bus 342 ride (to/from the further eastern end of the plantation). For drivers, there are several parking areas along Nordre Strandvej (Rte 237) from where you can conveniently start hiking.

🛏 Sleeping

Hotel Bretagne BOUTIQUE HOTEL €€
(☑ 26 23 79 39; www.hotelbretagne.dk; Sauntevej 18; d/deluxe r/ste from 895/1295/1495kr; ☺ reception closes 8pm, closed Jan; ⓟ ⓢ) Looking every bit as French as its name, the Bretagne dates from 1871 and has been a hotel since 1936. But the distinctive shutters and luxuriously calm, soothing cream-and-blue interiors date from a 2017 total rework. Pricier rooms are very spacious and many have inspiring views over lake, trees and mid-distance seascapes: the higher the better. Yes, there's a lift.

Hotel Hornbækhus HOTEL €€
(☑ 49 70 01 69; www.hornbaekhus.com; Skovvej 7; s/d incl breakfast 895/995kr, without bathroom 725/825kr; ⓟ @ ⓢ) Down a lane full of flowers and birds, Hornbækhus is based on a 1904 house that was very much expanded in the 1920s and '30s. Though undermined by a half-hearted reception that is only fully manned till 3pm (waiters help check-ins till 8pm), there are beautifully maintained upstairs lounges that, like many of the 26 rooms, exude a classical-style grandeur.

Some rooms have balconies overlooking the extensive lawns, though certain upper-floor rooms share a very basic WC-shower

ESRUM SØ

At 17 sq km, Esrum Sø is Denmark's second-largest lake. The most popular access point is beside the charming waterside restaurant, Skipperhuset (p105), about 1km west of the Fredensborg Slot (p104) main gate (via Skipper Allé). Here, with advance booking, you can rent **canoes and kayaks** (☑ 20 33 00 33; www.kanoudlejningen.dk; Skipper Allé 6; 2hr/8hr/3-day kayak hire 275/350/950kr, canoe/paddleboard hire from 375/185kr; ⊙ 10am-6pm late Jun-Aug) or take open-boat tours (p104) across to the Unesco-protected former hunting forest of **Gribskov**, on weekends having coffee and cake at the idyllic if nonsensically isolated thatched cottage-cafe **Fændrikhus** (☑ 48 48 01 07; Søvejen 8, Græsted; coffee 25kr; ⊙ 11am-3pm Sat & Sun year-round, plus Fri May-Sep). Around a kilometre beyond the lake's northern bank, the former monastery **Esrum Kloster** (www.esrum.dk; Klostergade 11-12, Esrum; adult/child 75kr/free; ⊙ 11am-5pm Tue-Sun Apr-Oct, Sat & Sun Nov-Mar), while only a shadow of its vast, pre-Reformation self, really comes into its own during the various medieval fairs held in the grounds.

room. The hotel was a noted retreat for poets and artists before and after WWII. While staying in 1956, cartoonist Hergé sketched a special Tintin scene as a Hornbækhus thank you. From June to August, the former Hotel Villa Strand is used as an annexe; it's set back from the coastal dunes, a block further north at Kystvej 12.

Hotelpension Ewaldsgården

GUESTHOUSE €€

(☑ 49 70 00 82; www.ewaldsgaarden.dk; Johannes Ewalds Vej 5; s/d incl breakfast 580/895kr; ⊙ late-Jun–mid-Aug; P @ 🛜) Set in a picture-perfect garden with vine-shaded terrace, this 17th-century farmhouse pension is a delightfully cosy mix of antiques and cottage-style furnishings, but it only operates as a pay-per-room guesthouse by advance reservation and only during the summer holiday season. All 12 rooms have washbasins, but showers and toilets are off the hall. There's a simple guest kitchen.

✖ Eating & Drinking

Fiskehuset Hornbæk

SEAFOOD €

(Havnevej 32; dishes 60-85kr, mixed plate without/with lobster 149/249kr; ⊙ 11am-8pm Jul & Aug, shorter hours rest of year) Sitting right beside Hornbæk's harbourside, this fishmonger-turned-cafe bangs out a range of mostly fried-fish meals that you pick from a large picture menu. Queue to order, collect when called and sit to eat at picnic tables dotted around the waterfront.

Hansens Café

DANISH €€

(☑ 49 70 04 79; www.hansenscafe.dk; Havnevej 19; lunch 69-149kr, dinner mains 209-275kr; ⊙ 5.30-8.30pm Mon, Thu & Fri, 1-4pm & 6-9pm Sat, 1-4pm Sun) Highly photogenic in its old half-timbered thatched cottage, Hansens has tables that spill out into front and rear gardens for sunny alfresco lunches, perhaps Danish beef and capers, fishcakes or caesar salad. Evening menus kick off with imaginative starters that often include Asian elements before Euro-Danish main courses like veal fricassee in red wine sauce.

The little bar is redolent of an old English country pub.

Sunspot Cafe

CAFE

(Hornbæk Strand; beer 20kr; ⊙ 10am-sunset Jun–mid-Sep, Sat & Sun only May) Though ultra-basic and serving very ordinary canned beers, the Sunspot's chairs offer a lovely yet inexpensive spot from which to watch the sun setting into the sea. Simple veggie burgers cost 50kr, pesto-pasta salad 40kr.

❶ Information

Inside the library, just behind the northern side of Nordre Strandvej, the **tourist office** (☑ 49 70 47 47; www.hornbaek.dk; Vestre Stejlebakke 2A; ⊙ 1-5pm Mon & Thu, 10am-3pm Tue, Wed & Fri, 10am-2pm Sat) offers free internet access.

❶ Getting There & Away

Trains connect Hornbæk with Helsingør (36kr, 25 minutes) and Gilleleje (48kr, 20 minutes) once or twice hourly.

❶ Getting Around

Hornbæk is walkably small. From the train station it's a five-minute stroll to the harbour and surf beach heading 400m directly north along Havnevej. Just before you reach the harbour, turn left (after Hansens Café) onto Øresundsvej, then right at Cafe Hornbæk Strand to reach the swimming beach.

Gilleleje

POP 6570

Summer visitors flood to Gilleleje (gi-le-*lai*-ye), mostly to eat at unpretentious seafood restaurants serving fish that's still unloaded fresh each morning from the harbour. The bobbing boats are backed by a triangular arc of lawn, a big 1750 anchor and a pretty mix of tiled and thatched old houses stretching east from the port area. Other low-key charms include a string of beaches, and coastal walks in the woodlands that rise behind them.

◉ Sights & Activities

Fyrhistorik Museum på Nakkehoved
MUSEUM

(www.museumns.dk; Fyrvejen 25A; adult/child 40kr/free; ⊙11am-4pm Thu-Sun plus holidays May-Sep, Sat & Sun Oct, Nov & mid-Feb–Apr) Strolling east from Gilleleje along the coastal footpath, you'll come to a pair of lighthouses. The western one (Vestre Fyr) contains a small museum, but it's worth continuing around 300m further to the second one, if only to grab a drink at the associated restaurant **Fyrkroen 1772** (☑48 30 02 25; www.fyrkroen.dk; Fyrvejen 29; beer/coffee from 30/30kr; ⊙noon-9pm Tue-Sun May-Aug), which has idyllic views from its terrace.

Kierkegaard Memorial
MONUMENT

(Søren Kierkegaard Stenen; www.gribskovinfo.dk/kierkegaard.htm; Gilbjerghoved) On the clifftop path between the Badehotel and the Gilbjerghoved birdwatching area is a simply inscribed boulder that commemorates the visits to this coastline of the philosopher Søren Kierkegaard (1813–55).

The quotation is his 1835 musing, meaning 'What is truth other than an idea given life?'

Gilleleje Strand
BEACH

(Alfavej) It's not as long and golden as those at Hornbæk or Tisvildeleje, but Gilleleje's central beach, directly west of the harbour, has a decent stretch of stony sand.

Stick to the eastern section for swimming, as further west, sea access is impeded by large rocks. Lifeguards keep watch in high summer.

🛏 Sleeping

Beringgaard B&B
B&B **€**

(☑22 71 46 50; www.beringgaardbnb.com; Toftvej 70; s/d without bathroom 500/650kr) If you're mobile, this stylishly upgraded 1850s thatched homestead, 7km south of Gilleleje, makes a wonderful getaway serenaded by crowing

cocks and ethereal birdsong. The two best rooms occupy what is essentially a private wing with big-windowed sunset-view sitting space, loads of candles and full kitchen.

Above the family kitchen, two smaller rooms with a shared balcony are available as doubles (600kr) but are more suitable for one. Pre-arrange arrival times. Cash only.

Hotel Gilleleje Strand
HOTEL **€€**

(☑48 30 05 12; www.gillelejestrand.dk; Vesterbrogade 4B; s 900kr, d 950-1250kr; ⊛) Handily central but not actually on the beach ('strand'), this neat little hotel has 25 rooms entirely rebuilt during 2017 to create whiter-than-white havens of subtle luxury. Bigger doubles have balconies.

Gilleleje Badehotel
HOTEL **€€€**

(☑48 30 13 47; www.gillelejebadehotel.dk; Hulsøvej 15; r incl breakfast from 1590kr; P⊛) This gently luxurious hotel, around 1km west of town, sits amid wooded gardens beside the clifftop path, with a direct passage down to the wild seashore below. Floors of sanded wood and burlap carpet lead up to spacious rooms, many with balconies that enjoy enviable sea views.

Built in 1895, and a hotel since 1905, it has been so heavily restored that from outside it looks essentially new, flanked by a spa in which guests get free use of sauna, hammam and steam room.

🍴 Eating

Adamsens Fisk
SEAFOOD **€**

(☑48 30 09 27; www.adamsensfisk.dk; Havnen 2; mains 60-89kr, meals without/with lobster minimum 2 diners 145/269kr; ⊙9am-5.30pm Mon-Fri, 10am-4pm Sat & Sun) Behind a series of shaded outdoor picnic tables by the harbour, Adamsens combines three sections. The *fiskbutik* (fish shop) sells fresh fish plus ready-to-eat fried fillets, fishcakes and seafood salads. Queue at the window next door for fuller garnished lunch plates. Or walk around the corner to the 'deli' (April to September only) for overloaded savoury crepes.

These are served on disposable but fully 'organic' palm-leaf plates. In midsummer and on weekends, the deli also offers sushi and sashimi.

Gilleleje Havn
DANISH **€€**

(www.gillelejehavn.dk; Havnevej 14; mains 115-245kr; ⊙11.30am-10pm) Set back behind the harbour-facing lawn, Gilleleje Havn occupies two connected historic buildings, and three

DON'T MISS

RUDOLPH TEGNER'S STATUEPARK

Zealand's north coast was once predominantly untamed moorland heath. A small intact patch of this environment between Gilleleje and Hornbæk is curiously dotted with 14 classically styled monumental bronze sculptures, appearing as though by magic on hillocks and in clearings. These are the work of Rudolph Tegner (1873–1950) whose lonely **museum-mausoleum** (www.rudolphtegner.dk; Museumsvej 19, Rusland; museum/park 50kr/free; ☉ park 24hr, museum noon-5pm Tue-Sun mid-Apr–mid-Oct, to 6pm Jun-Aug; 🚌 362) displays over 250 more of his pieces in a discordant concrete building beside the car park.

Two buses get you reasonably close. From Gilleleje take the 362 to the Museumsvej (Villingerødvej) stop, then walk around 1km east . The last 362 returns from Museumsvej at 6.08pm weekdays, 5.07pm weekends. Bus 342 from Hornbæk passes nearly 2km from the museum; the nearest stops outbound/return are Tangvej/Bentsensvej. Last return services from Bentsensvej are 6.54pm, 8.54pm and 10.57pm daily.

dining rooms with distinctly differing decors – the Krostuen room feels the most traditional. On top of typical seafood options and traditional Danish fishcakes, there's a burger menu and small selection of other turf options, including spare ribs.

Restaurant Brasseriet　　　　SEAFOOD €€
(www.brasseriet-gilleleje.dk; Nordre Havnevej 3; lunch 75-158kr, dinner mains 185-325kr; ☉11.30am-4pm & 5.30-9pm) Facing the grassy harbour lawns, this modernised cottage restaurant is most popular for its small, hidden rear garden where tight-packed tables lure lunchers for steaming bowls of mussels, seasonal asparagus and a wide range of salad and seafood options.

The more limited dinner menu usually includes tuna steak, half lobsters and a ribeye steak if you want blood.

☆ Entertainment

Kulturhavn　　　　CONCERT VENUE
(www.kulturhavngilleleje.dk; Peter Fjelstrupsvej 12; ☉7am-10pm; 🛜) Between the station and the harbour, this splendid new culture centre combines theatre-cinema, library, bar and tourist info and is a great central place to unwind if the weather turns nasty.

ℹ Information

The **tourist office** (www.visitnordsjaelland.dk; Peter Fjelstrupsvej 12, Kulturhavn; ☉10am-4pm Mon-Fri Jun-Aug) is a desk in the library that's only (wo)manned on summer weekdays, but its helpful selection of maps and brochures is available throughout the opening times of the **Kulturhavn** building that contains it, usually 7am to 10pm.

ℹ Getting There & Away

Trains run once or twice hourly from Gilleleje to Hillerød (60kr, 30 minutes) and to Helsingør (72kr, 45 minutes) via Hornbæk (48kr, 17 minutes). For Tisvildeleje (36kr, around 50 minutes), start with bus 360R and change to the train in Helsinge.

ℹ Getting Around

Nordkystens Cykeludlejning (☑ 51 29 29 43; www.nordkystenscykeludlejning.dk; Svend Henriksensvej 14; per day/week 125/475kr; ☉10am-2pm or call) Bicycle hire, with bikes delivered to your accommodation within a reasonable distance. Baskets, helmets, kids' bikes and theft insurance (per day 2kr) also available. Call ahead.

Tisvildeleje

POP 1490

Tisvildeleje is a glorious sweep of golden-sand beach backed by hills, forests, nature trails and a ribbon of inconspicuous township. You could easily spend several relaxing days here, sunbathing, swimming, strolling through the woods, poking around the scattering of boutiques, and generally taking things very, very easy.

◉ Sights & Activities

Troldeskoven　　　　FOREST
(Witches' Wood) Troldeskoven is an area of ancient trees that have been sculpted into haunting shapes by the wind. Walking there (about 3km south) from Tisvildeleje car park is possible along the beach or on a dirt path through the woods.

Tisvildeleje Beach   BEACH

(🚽) A kilometre-long stretch of pure sand at the foot of the village is the primary reason many people flock to Tisvildeleje. A shallow-sloping shore and lifeguards at the height of summer make it a favourite with families. There are toilets and an ice-cream kiosk at the edge of the large car park.

Tisvilde Hegn   WALKING

Tisvilde Hegn is an enchanting forest of twisted trees and heather-covered hills that extends southwest of Tisvildeleje for more than 8km, crisscrossed by various walking trails.

One route links to **Asserbo Slotsruin** (Bisp Absalonsvej, Frederiksværk), the fairly minimal ruins of a small, moat-encircled 12th-century manor house and monastery, near the southern boundary of the forest. Free walking maps are available from the Tisvildeleje tourist office.

🛏 Sleeping

★ Bed & Breakfast

Hårlandsgård   GUESTHOUSE €

(📋 48 70 83 96; www.haarlandsgaard.dk; Harlands Allé 12; s 425kr, d 550-600kr, apt per week summer 4500kr, winter-only long lets per month 5500-7000kr; 🅿) Inspiring septuagenarian host Annie offers three rooms in her art-packed 18th-century farmhouse with a barn section that sometimes plays gallery. The two spacious double rooms (one with a modern four-poster bed) share a kitchen and bathroom, and each has direct access to lovely rear lawns. There's also a smaller single, plus, for long-stay guests, a splendid self-contained apartment.

It's around 1km east of the town centre, 150m east of Godhavn station – the house that's straight ahead where Harlands Allé swerves 90 degrees north.

Tisvildeleje Strand Hotel   HOTEL €€

(📋 48 70 71 19; www.strand-hotel.dk; Hovedgaden 75; s/d 1100/1450kr, d without bathroom 950kr; 🗓 Jun-Aug; 🅿🛜) Neutral tones, art books and weathered 'antiques' give this little town-centre hotel a chic 'Hamptons' vibe. Rooms are a soothing combo of coconut rug carpets, woollen throws and contemporary bathrooms – all but three being en suite.

Helenekilde Badehotel   BOUTIQUE HOTEL €€€

(📋 48 70 70 01; www.helenekilde.com; Strandvejen 25; r without/with sea view incl breakfast from 1395/1695kr; 🅿🛜) On raised lawns high above a long, divided beach, this genteel boutique hotel was originally a silver wedding present from a wealthy 19th-century merchant to his (ungrateful) wife. Cosy communal areas feature beautiful furnishings, art and the odd vintage suitcase-turned-coffee table, while the rooms themselves have a low-key elegance, 16 of the 28 looking out across the waves.

Dreamy sea views are also on tap at its casually elegant **restaurant** (Strandvejen 25; lunch 275kr, 3-course dinner 450kr; 🗓 noon-2pm & 6-8.30pm Jun-Aug, closed Sun Sep-May), which serves up a regularly changing menu of classic Danish fare. The hotel is a five-minute walk along a leafy lane (signposted from the station), and there's steep access down to the beach. Parking can get difficult at lunchtime.

🍴 Eating

★ Little Cafe   VEGETARIAN €

(www.facebook.com/thelittlecafetisvildeleje; Hovedgaden 57; panini/salad/dinners 65/95/145kr; 🗓 10am-9pm Thu-Mon Jul & Aug, 10am-5pm Wed-Sun & some dinners Sep-Jun; 🛜🍴) 🌿 Using eclectic music, junk-shop furniture, mismatched crockery, old lamps, pot plants and fresh flowers to fine effect, this fabulously quirky American-run cafe is signed with nothing more than a painted cup. At lunch there are delicious meat-free garlic-spiked paninis and large, flavour-packed fresh salads. Multidish vegetarian dinners might include eggplant with pomegranate dressing, leek salad and apricot quinoa.

Tisvildeleje Brød & Vin   BAKERY €

(Hovedgaden 60; roll/croissant/bread from 10/ 17/38kr, coffee 15kr, ice cream 1/2/3 scoops 25/33/40kr; 🗓 7am-5pm) This family-style bakery has a big old kitchen table for those wishing to eat in. Wine and Kastbergs gourmet ice cream also available.

Tinggården   NEW NORDIC €€€

(📋 48 71 22 35; www.tinggarden.dk; Frederiks værkvej 182; 2-/3-/4-/5-/6-course dinner 420/ 495/570/645/720kr; 🗓 5.30-9pm Wed-Sun May-Oct, Thu-Sun Nov-Apr, daily mid-summer) Jan Friis-Mikkelsen and Charlotte Vendorf create culinary magic with locally sourced fresh produce in a 1702 thatched cottage restaurant on the south side of Tisvilde Hegn. It's beside the main road, 1.3km from Asserbo Slotsruin.

By car it's a convoluted but very pretty 8km drive from Tisvildeleje. Bus 320R stops almost outside at Chr E Bartholdys Allé.

❶ Getting There & Away

Trains run between Tisvildeleje and Hillerød (60kr, 30 minutes) every 30 to 60 minutes. Getting round the coast from Gilleleje by public transport isn't as simple: combine bus 360R Gilleleje-Helsinge with the Helsinge-Tisvildeleje. The whole trip costs 36kr and takes 50 minutes Monday to Saturday, but 80 minutes on Sunday.

ROSKILDE & AROUND

Roskilde

POP 50,390

For decades, Roskilde has been known in musical circles for its rock festival (p113), which vies with Glastonbury for the title of Europe's biggest. This reputation has now been cleverly parlayed into a year-round attraction: the excellent new Ragnarock experiential museum of modern music. That's set in rapidly developing Musicon, a post-industrial area of container-box studios, skateparks and arts-related workshop businesses.

But the historic, cultured city has plenty of other strings to its bow, most notably a Unesco-listed cathedral that peers imperiously down a steep parkland slope towards a fjordland harbour where seaworthy replicas of several Viking ships moor beside a museum containing the real things. Little wonder that Roskilde makes such a popular day trip from Copenhagen, a mere 30km away.

History

Roskilde came to prominence in the Viking Age, when Viking-King Harald Bluetooth built Zealand's first wooden-stave Christian church here in AD 980. That was replaced by a stone building in 1026 on the instructions of a woman named Estrid, whose husband had been assassinated in the stave church after a heated chess match (only in Scandinavia!). The foundations of the 11th-century stone church lie beneath the floor of the present-day cathedral, Denmark's grandest and the pre-Reformation powerhouse of Danish Catholicism. Around that grew royal Roskilde, for centuries capital of Denmark (or co-capital along with Nyborg; p171).

Fortunes began to change when the capital moved to Copenhagen and in 1443 when a terrible fire swept north from the cathedral, destroying a whole swath of the city. That created what is now the beautiful open space of the Byparken fields: although the area is so central, habitations were never rebuilt here since the population was already declining, a situation that was made worse after 1536 by the Reformation.

In the 1730s, the site of the former Bishops' Palace was rebuilt as a baroque-style royal residence, but the northern Provstevænget area remained as a field for grazing cattle and was later preserved as an oasis of open space by the bequest of a 19th-century textile baron.

◉ Sights

★ **Ragnarock** MUSEUM
(www.museumragnarock.dk; Rabalderstræde 16; adult/child 90kr/free; ⊙10am-5pm Tue & Fri-Sun, to 10pm Wed & Thu; ℗; ☐202A) Within a startling architectural statement of a building, this spirit-lifting, highly interactive museum delivers a multisensory, experiential and often humorous journey through the evolution of rock music and youth culture from the 1950s to the present. Walls of headphones let you listen to music time capsules, spin-to-hear turntables explain about gramophones. Play with interactive musical lights, learn why toilets were integral to Danish music production and practise various dance steps on the hot-spot stage beside the 'world's biggest mirror ball'.

There's a powerful start as a sound-blasted Tardis of an elevator deposits you in a disorientating kaleidoscope of mirrors. Turn left and pop your head through a hole to further the experience that tries to suggest what an acid trip might feel like. While a lot is about Danish pop-rock and the star exhibit is Gasolin's 1961 Plymouth in the garage, non-Danes will find ample that's resonant, and much of the info is in English or comes with subtitles. The museum's setting is interesting in itself, within the increasingly arty post-industrial Musicon district south of central Roskilde.

★ **Viking Ship Museum** MUSEUM
(Vikingskibsmuseet; ☑46 30 02 00; www.viking eskibsmuseet.dk; Vindeboder 12; adult/child May–mid-Oct 130kr/free, mid-Oct–Apr 85kr/free; ⊙10am-5pm late Jun–mid-Aug, to 4pm mid-Aug– late Jun, boat trips daily mid-May–Sep; ℗⊞) Five original Viking ships, discovered at the bottom of Roskilde Fjord, are displayed in the main hall of this must-see museum. A short walk away, the same ticket gives access to the workshops of **Museumsø** (incl in Viking Ship Museum ticket adult/child May–mid-Oct 130kr/ free, mid-Oct–Apr 85kr/free), where archaeological and reconstruction work takes place,

and Nordic longboats (p113) depart. There are free 45-minute guided tours in English at noon and 3pm daily from late June to the end of August and at noon on weekends from May to late June and in September.

Roskilde's Viking-era inhabitants were expecting trouble in the mid-11th century. Five clinker-built ships, all made between 1030 and 1042, were deliberately scuttled in a narrow channel 20km north of Roskilde, presumably to block an attacking army. Once they had been holed and sunk, a mass of stones was piled on top to create an underwater barrier.

In 1962, a coffer dam was built around them and sea water was pumped out. Within four months, archaeologists were able to remove the mound of stones and excavate the ships, whose wooden hulks were in thousands of pieces. These ship fragments were painstakingly reassembled onto skeleton frames in the purpose-built **Viking Ship Hall**. This brutal-looking minimalist construction becomes something magical inside, where the ghostly boats seem to float once more on the waters of the fjord.

The ships show off the range of the Viking shipwright skills: there's an ocean-going trading vessel, a 30m warship for international raiding, a coastal trader, a 17m warship probably used around the Baltic, and a fishing boat. Carbon dating and dendrochronology have uncovered further secrets, including the fact that one ship was made in Norway, and another came from Dublin.

Interesting displays about the Viking Age put the boats into a historical context, and the basement cinema runs a 14-minute film (available in Danish, English, French, German, Italian and Spanish) about the 1962 excavation. There's also a fascinating exhibition and film documenting the nail-biting 2007 voyage of the *Havhingsten fra Glendalough* from Roskilde to Dublin and back. Based on the original 60-oared warship *Skuldelev* 2, it's the largest Viking ship reconstruction to date: 340 trees went into its creation.

Along with reconstructions of the other original Viking boats and typical of later Scandinavian wooden vessels, it is moored at nearby Museumsø, a 'museum island' of workshops where, from April to mid-October, those with Ship Museum tickets can watch demonstrations by, perhaps, a blacksmith, tar-burner, weaver, rope-maker and/or fletcher. Children can join in the fun by striking coins and painting their own shields.

★ **Roskilde Domkirke** CATHEDRAL
(www.roskildedomkirke.dk; Domkirkestræde 10; adult/pensioner/child 60/40kr/free; ⊙10am-6pm Mon-Sat, 1-6pm Sun Apr-Sep, to 4pm Oct-Mar) The crème de la crème of Danish cathedrals, this twin-spired giant was started by Bishop Absalon in 1170, but has been rebuilt and tweaked so many times that it's now a superb showcase of 850 years' worth of Danish architecture. As the royal mausoleum, it contains the crypts of 37 Danish kings and queens. Now a Unesco World Heritage Site, the entry fee includes a comprehensive, full-colour 48-page guidebook.

No fewer than 11 spectacular chapels and crypts sprout from the main body of the cathedral. The **chapel of King Christian IV**, off the northern side of the building, contains the builder-king himself. His ocean-green coffin, surrounded by angels, is quite low-key for such an extravagant monarch. But its setting includes overly dramatic paintings of Christian's life surrounded by trompe l'œil details, all dating from a 19th-century rebuild except for the chapel gates, so ornate that they were said to have been created by the devil himself (in conjunction with Christian's favourite metalsmith, Caspar Fincke).

The **chapel of the Magi** has fantastic 15th-century frescoes (the largest in Denmark) and features the Royal Column, showing the heights of visiting princes – from the towering Christian I down to titchy Christian VII (164.1cm). The ornate Renaissance sepulchres of Christian III and Frederik II look like antique temples, guarded by halberd-bearing soldiers.

The neoclassical **chapel of Frederik V** whispers 'death' like no other part of the cathedral. You'll find 12 members of the royal family here, all interred in white alabaster sepulchres, surrounded by skulls, angels and weeping women.

A great highlight in the **nave** is Christian IV's private box, plus an intricate 17th-century pulpit (1610) made of marble, alabaster and sandstone by Copenhagen sculptor Hans Brokman. A killjoy dean disconnected the mechanism of the wonderful **clock** in the 18th century, annoyed that his parishioners paid more attention to it than to him, but today's church-people have relented. St George slays the dragon on the hour, the poor beast lets out a pitiful wheeze and two ballad characters ting the bells.

In the **choir**, Margrethe I's elegant sarcophagus and the shining golden altarpiece

ZEALAND ROSKILDE

Roskilde

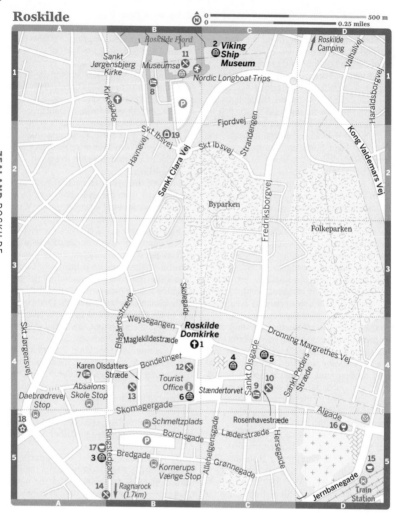

ZEALAND ROSKILDE

attract most attention, but don't miss the wonderfully graphic 15th-century choir-stall carvings.

Free concerts on the 16th-century baroque pipe organ are usually held at 8pm on summer Thursdays. See the website for timetables and for upcoming closures – it's not unusual for the cathedral to shut for special events, especially on Saturdays for weddings.

Sankt Laurentius
MUSEUM
(http://sanktlaurentius.dk; Skomagergade 2, Stændertorvet; adult/child 25kr/free; ⊘11am-3pm Tue-Sat Jun-Aug, Sat only Sep-May) Squeezing up a narrow spiral stairway takes you past two

19th-century jail cells to the clock at the top of this AD 1500 bell tower for peeped views across Roskilde's main square. After you come down from the tower, descend into the basement where you can see the excavated ruins of a much older 12th-century church and a whole series of medieval graves – skeletons and all.

The church was demolished in the 1530s after the Reformation, but the still-new tower was spared and desanctified. Two hundred years later it was incorporated into a new town hall that was built next door, hence its partial historical use as a prison.

Roskilde

ZEALAND ROSKILDE

Lützhøfts Købmandsgård & Håndværksmuseet
MUSEUM
(http://xn--hndvrkermuseet-libt.dk; Ringstedgade 6-8; ⊙11am-5pm Mon-Fri, 10am-2pm Sat) FREE Preserved much as it looked in the 1920s but still functioning as a grocery-hardware shop, Lützhøfts Købmandsgård fronts an enclosed courtyard of old barrows and carriages, plus a lovable tea shop. Upstairs in the green-shuttered mill to the right, a collection of century-old turners' and carpenters' workshops has been preserved complete with old tools.

Insp!
ARTS CENTRE
(www.insp.dk; Køgevej 4-6; lunch 50kr; ⊙10am-6pm or later Mon-Fri, lunch noon-12.30pm) FREE While it's not exactly Christiania (p56), since 2011 Roskilde has had its own tiny, self-organising alternative community in a graffiti-covered area of semi-derelict buildings southwest of the train station.

Drop a coin in the cup and grab a coffee, chat to folks who use the place as a very low-key social centre, or come at noon for the bargain lunches and free wi-fi. There are board games, occasional wandering guitarists and impromptu events. Just ask.

Sankt Jørgensbjerg Kirke
CHURCH
(☏23 34 59 88; www.sjk.dk; Kirkegade 26; ⊙10am-2pm Mon-Fri) Strolling up past a remarkable collection of thatched cottages along Kirkegade and Skt Ibsvej is the highlight of visiting this small 11th-century church.

Museum for Samtidskunst
MUSEUM
(http://samtidskunst.dk; Stændertorvet 3D; adult/student/child 50/40kr/free; ⊙noon-5pm Tue, Thu & Fri, to 8pm Wed, 11am-4pm Sat & Sun) Though

it's housed in Roskilde's elegant 18th-century royal palace, this museum focuses on Fluxus art, often perplexing sound, video or performance installations by Danish and international artists. In most of the eight rooms, exhibits change periodically, but one permanent feature is Morgans Jacobsen's 'Soundbar,' where you select bottles from shelves and imbibe their auditory stimuli.

Roskilde Museum
MUSEUM
(www.roskildemuseum.dk; Sankt Olsgade 18) The city's main historical museum explores Roskilde from the Stone Age through Harald Bluetooth's legacy to the first railway in Denmark.

🏃 Activities

Nordic Longboat Trips
BOATING
(☏46 30 02 00; www.vikingeskibsmuseet.dk; Museumsø, Vindeboder 12; per person 100kr; ⊙May-Sep) Want to leap aboard a longboat? The Viking Ship Museum's (p110) highly amusing 50-minute trips provide the chance to propel a reconstructed traditional Nordic boat across the water by a mixture of sailing, rowing and ducking overhead ropes. Getting a place is first-come, first-served from the Museumsø (p110) ticket office. Departures (one to 10 daily depending on expected demand) are weather-dependent.

🎉 Festivals & Events

Roskilde Festival
MUSIC
(www.roskilde-festival.dk; Darupvej; tickets from 1995kr; ⊙early Jul) Denmark's answer to Glastonbury, Roskilde Festival is northern Europe's largest music festival, a week-long summer binge of bands and booze.

Since 1971 it has attracted the biggest and best international performers – more than 160 rock, techno and world-music bands play on six stages. Line-ups have included countless established acts from Neil Young to Iggy Pop, the Foo Fighters to Arcade Fire. But the promoters are also astute at trend-spotting, so expect to catch hot new acts that haven't yet come into the spotlight.

While the music is the main attraction, there are plenty of other diversions, including a swimming lake, food workshops, art events and a naked run! Many people camp from the Sunday before the festival starts, spending four days 'warming up' for the festival proper. Stalls sell everything from tattoos to produce-driven food, but you may want to bring some food supplies as prices are high.

Full festival tickets start at 1995kr including camping access, or you can pay 1020kr for day tickets for each of the four main days. Pre-purchase online through the official festival website: sales start around October. By June all 75,000-plus tickets are usually sold out. Or consider working at the event – more than 30,000 volunteers are recruited every year. Details, along with a range of accommodation and transport alternatives, are clearly outlined on the website.

🛏 Sleeping

Roskilde has limited accommodation for its size; being so close to Copenhagen, it's a popular day-trip destination and what hotels there are tend to be especially full Monday through Wednesday nights. If you're stuck for a bed for the night, ask at the extremely helpful tourist office, whose staff are happy to call B&Bs for you, though only three or four of the options (500kr to 600kr) are truly central.

B&B Roskilde City   B&B €
(✏ 25 11 10 55; www.bbroskildecity.dk; Lille Højbrøndsstræde 14; s/d/tr 550/650/900kr) On a quiet, super-central lane, this B&B offers three rooms in a family home, the big selling point of which is the glorious layered garden. Very handy for the cathedral area; there's no sign on the door and you'll need to call ahead to make arrival arrangements.

Shared kitchen and bathrooms. Closed during Roskilde Festival. It's up a small alley running north off Lille Højbrøndsstræde.

Roskilde Camping   CAMPGROUND €
(✏ 46 75 79 96; www.roskildecamping.dk; Baunehøjvej 7, Veddelev; camp site 45kr plus per adult/

child 90/45kr, s/d/apt 400/600/950kr, cabins 450-1200kr; ☺ Apr-Sep) Beautifully situated on the fjord-side, 4km north of the Viking Ship Museum (p110), this very extensive, three-star camping ground has many family facilities and is set back from a wide grassy foreshore distantly overlooking Roskilde across a stone-and-sand beach.

Danhostel Roskilde   HOSTEL €
(✏ 46 35 21 84; www.danhostel.dk/roskilde; Vindeboder 7; dm/s/d/q Sep-Jun 225/475/525/580kr, Jul & Aug 250/575/700/750kr; P ⓟ ⓦ; ☐ 203) Roskilde's swish, five-star hostel has a superb position on the waterfront right next door to the Viking Ship Museum (p110). Decorated with funky black-and-white murals, each of the 40 large rooms has its own shower and toilet, and beds are proper doubles.

Laundry costs 30kr plus 15kr for the drier. Sheets/towels are 50/20kr.

Zleep Hotel Roskilde   HOTEL €€€
(Hotel Prindsen; ✏ 70 23 56 35; www.zleephotels.com; Algade 13; r weekday/weekend from 1795/1095kr; P ⓦ) Formerly Hotel Prindsen, this central hotel first opened in 1695, and previous guests have included King Frederik VII and Hans Christian Andersen. Rooms are comfortable if relatively standard business affairs, with a full renovation planned by 2018. The suite maintains a more classic historical look.

Rates vary day by day but generally drop significantly on weekends and public holidays.

🍴 Eating

Cafe Satchmo   CAFE €
(Rosenhavestræde; salads from 79kr; ☺ 10am-5pm Mon-Wed & Sat, to 9pm Thu & Fri; ⓦ) Behind flower boxes and a rack of vintage clothes, this charming central cafe serves a good range of salads and a 125kr vegetarian brunch (till 5pm), along with locally roasted Fairtrade coffee and local Herslev beers.

There's summer seating in a peaceful cobbled courtyard.

CafeKnarr   VIKING €€
(Museumsø, Vindeboder 12; sandwich/sausages/lunch plate 75/95/155kr; ☺ 11.30am-3.30pm) The Viking Ship Museum's (p110) outwardly functional cafe makes sandwiches and huge plates of sausage-and-salad partly using Viking recipes, with ingredients like ramson (wild garlic), sea buckthorn and dried rosehips.

Raadhuskælderen   DANISH, INTERNATIONAL €€
(www.raadhuskaelderen.dk; Stændertorvet; smørrebrød 72-138kr, dinner mains 188-358kr; ☻ 11am-9pm Mon-Sat; 🐾) Dine in a pretty garden with orchard views of the cathedral (p111), or inside within the modernised ancient cellar of what was once the town hall/hospital. Herring platters, shrimps, salads and open sandwiches feature at lunch. Dinner offerings are predominantly barbecued steaks, but there's also a daily fish option and a tempting rack of lamb with tzatziki and rosemary sauce. Vegetarians should look elsewhere.

Why Food & Cocktails   FUSION €€€
(☑ 88 34 19 00; www.whyfoodandcocktails.com; Ringstedgade 28B; green/meat/side dishes 65/85/35kr, meal set without/with dessert 300/350kr; ☻ noon-9.30pm Tue-Sun) For gourmet-quality food with a bar-like buzz and none of the stuffiness of starched tablecloths, this Nordic-Asian fusion concept might appeal. Fizzing with flavour, small taster dishes are assembled into composite shared meals by choosing selections of 'green' and meat/fish plates with sides of rice or potatoes. The open kitchen feels like a showground, and the cocktails flow.

Restaurant Mumm   NEW NORDIC €€€
(☑ 46 37 22 01; www.mummroskilde.com; Karen Olsdatters Stræde 9; dishes 130kr; ☻ 5.30-11pm Mon-Sat, kitchen to 9.30pm, closed Jul) Mumm's unfussy white-tablecloth elegance acts as a neutral backdrop for its exclusive, ever-imaginative Nordic dining experience that plays with gastronomic artistry through a selection of small, contemporary tasting dishes.

🍷 Drinking & Nightlife

★**Kaffe Kilden**   COFFEE
(www.kaffekilden.net; Htorvet; ☻ 7.30am-9pm Mon-Fri, 9am-9pm Sat, 10am-7pm Sun) This marvellous coffee shop looks tiny from the outside but actually links together a series of bare-brick, walled corners full of relaxed, junkshop charm.

Kloster Kælderen   CRAFT BEER
(www.klosterkaelderen.beer; Store Gråbrødrestræde; draft beers 55kr; ☻ 2pm-midnight Mon-Thu, to 2am Fri & Sat) Cosy, candlelit yet unpretentious, this beer cellar, with walls made of giant boulders, has 10 regularly changing craft beers on tap, sometimes including Hornbeer Strong Porter, a remarkably smoky stout. There's also an astounding selection of bottled beers, including every Trappist brew – even the very rarest.

Crowds squeeze in for the live jazz/blues at 8pm on Thursday nights.

Te Salonen   TEAHOUSE
(www.tesalonen-roskilde.dk; Ringstedgade 6A; tea/coffee from 30/25kr; ☻ 10am-6pm Mon-Fri, to 3pm Sat; 🐾) Trying to be British in a very Danish fashion, this is the place for a scone-and-cake high tea (250kr for two) seated at antique chairs on whitewashed old floorboards.

There's loose-leaf tea for sale too, as well as Skarø ice cream, luscious cakes, toasted pesto-rich sandwiches and very good coffee.

☆ Entertainment

Gimle   LIVE MUSIC
(www.gimle.dk; Helligkorsvej 2; beers 30-55kr, meals 49-99kr; ☻ pub noon-midnight Tue & Wed, to 2am Thu, to 5am Fri & Sat, 10am-5pm Sun; 🐾) Gimle's circular former water-tank building is Roskilde's top venue for live music from folk to clubsounds, somehow squeezing in as many as 500 people on a busy night.

Most of the action is from September to May, but in summer there are still a few smaller gigs at the convivial pub-cafe in front, which also serves international snack meals.

🛍 Shopping

Roskilde Gasværk   ARTS & CRAFTS
(http://roskildegasværk.dk; Skt Ibsvej 12; ☻ 10am-5pm Tue-Sat, noon-4.30pm Sun) In the 1894 former gasworks building down by the harbour, a modern art gallery is joined by five commercial artists' workshops, including Skat Snitker's fascinating glass-blowing 'Glasgallery' (also open on Monday), where there are often demonstrations (Monday to Wednesday, not in summer). Unique creations for sale.

ℹ Information

The helpful **tourist office** (☑ 46 31 65 65; www.visitroskilde.com; Stændertorvet 1; ☻ 10am-4pm or 5pm Mon-Fri, to 1pm Sat) provides information, has a 3D map-model of the city and can assist with booking B&Bs. There's even free coffee and left luggage (same day during opening hours only).

There's a **Post Office** (Algade 51; ☻ 10am-5.30pm Mon-Fri) in Kvickly supermarket.

ℹ Getting There & Away

Useful trains from Roskilde:
Copenhagen (84kr, 21 to 30 minutes)
Køge (48kr, 23 minutes)
Odense (232kr, 73 minutes)
Vordingborg (100kr, 45-55 minutes).

For northeastern Zealand, change trains in Copenhagen or use 600S to **Hillerød** (76kr, 70 minutes), which is only marginally faster.

If driving, there's free parking without time limit beside the Viking Ship Museum. Closer to the cathedral, **Schmeltzplads** (Borchsgade) off Bredgade has two-hour free disc parking.

❶ Getting Around

Central Roskilde is compact enough to visit the main sights on foot, or by bicycle, which you can rent from **RosCykler** (☑ 46 32 26 66; Hestetorvet 5; per day 100kr; ☉ 9am-6pm Mon-Fri, 9.30am-3pm Sat). A very pleasant downhill walk from the cathedral through Byparken takes around 15 minutes to the Viking Ship Museum (p110)/harbour area.

Bus 203 from the train station (half-hourly weekdays, hourly weekends) picks up passengers at **Daebrødrevej stop** (Byvolden; ☐ 203), passes close to the hostel (p114) and Viking Ship Museum (five minutes) and continues passing close to the camping ground (p114) (20 minutes).

Musicon-bound bus 202A helpfully picks up at **Kornerups Vænge stop** (Bredgade; ☐ 202A) and on Jernbangade near the train station: for Ragnarock (p110), get off at Teknik Skole and walk 350m north. On return using the Margrethehåb-bound service, you could alight at **Schmeltzplads** (Schmeltzplads, Borchsgade; ☐ 202A) or the **Absalons Skole stop** (Støden; ☐ 202A) for the centre. There's a short-cut route by bicycle.

During the Roskilde Festival (p113), a special train station comes into operation near the festival grounds to cope with the crowds.

Lejre

POP 2400

In rural settings west of Lejre are two great family-oriented attractions, and if you're mobile the area has plenty more to explore. Gammel Lejre village is postcard-pretty.

◎ Sights & Activities

Sagnlandet Lejre   MUSEUM
(Land of Legends; www.sagnlandet.dk; Slangealleen 2, Lejre; adult/child 150/95kr; ☉ 10am-5pm late Jun–mid-Aug, reduced hours rest of year) In this fascinating experimental archaeology centre, enthusiastic re-enactors use ancient technology to test out various theories: how many people does it take to build a dolmen? What plants might have been used to dye clothing? And how do you stop the goats eating your reed roof?

KNUDSKOV

If you have your own transport, walking the meadows, forests and coastline of the narrow 18km-long **Knudshoved Odde** peninsula is given added interest by the numerous Bronze Age stones that litter the area. The main starting point, around 12km west of Vordingborg, is **Knudskov** (www.rosenfeldt. dk; Knudskovvej; parking 15kr; ☉ 24hr), a parking area with a long barrow and tunnel-grave that you can crawl inside. Wander further to among blackthorn, honeysuckle and wild roses, possibly encountering bison which were brought here from America by the Rosenfeldt family, which owns Knudshoved Odde.

A 3km-long path takes you through beautiful rolling landscapes past a Viking Age marketplace, prehistoric burial mounds, a dancing labyrinth and the Iron Age village 'Lethra', through fields of ancient crops, and down to a sacrificial pool and over precarious staked-wood bridges.

Kids can paddle dug-out canoes, attempt to work a fire drill and chop up logs using primitive axes. On weekends and holidays there are many more folks in costume than midweek out of season. Allow around three hours, or more. Note that tickets are valid for unlimited visits throughout the same calendar year.

Fly-High   ADVENTURE SPORTS
(Ledreborg Palace Zip Lines; ☑ 46 48 00 38; www. ledreborg.dk; Ledreborg Allé 2D, Lejre; zip line adult/ child 245/200kr; ☉ 10am-2pm Sat May-Sep) On summer Saturdays you can fly on zip lines through the woodlands, surveying the beautifully laid out grounds of Ledreborg's 18th-century palace. The most exciting 370m run is for adults and taller adolescents only. Pre-booking is usually essential; available time slots are shown on the website.

The grounds are open daily for walkers (20kr), but visiting the palace buildings is for only pre-booked groups.

❶ Getting There & Away

Trains from Roskilde depart at six minutes to the hour to Lejre station, where (on weekdays) they are met by bus 233, connecting to both Ledreborg Palace and Sagnlandet Lejre (eight minutes, last at 4.05pm).

SOUTHERN ZEALAND

While the northeast claims most of Zealand's must-see sites, the south is not without its drawcards. Old half-timbered houses give Køge plenty of charm, and the Unesco–listed cliffs at Stevns Klint seem to confirm the popular dinosaur die-out theory thanks to a thin layer of rather special 'fish clay'.

Køge

POP 36,830

Pretty Køge (*koo*-e) is well worth a look if you're taking the ferry to Bornholm or driving via Stevns Klint towards Denmark's southern islands. The one-time medieval trading centre retains a photogenic core of cobbled streets flanked by some well-preserved 17th- and 18th-century buildings. At its heart, Torvet is claimed to be Denmark's largest square.

Around 7km south, Vallø's moat-encircled Renaissance castle (p119) makes a great destination for a cycle ride along quiet, tree-lined avenues and country lanes. Either side of Køge bay there are passable beaches, though the semi-industrial backdrop of the modern commercial harbour detracts a little from some of the coastal scenery. Further beaches at Solrød and Greve (8km and 17km north of Køge, respectively) are popular S-train escapes for Copenhagen city-dwellers.

⊙ Sights & Activities

Sankt Nicolai Kirke CHURCH
(http://koegekirke.dk; Kirkestræde 31; tower adult/child 10kr/free; ⊙10am-4pm Mon-Fri, noon-4pm Sun, tower from noon Jul & early Aug) Honouring the patron saint of mariners, this powerful brick church features a 14th-century tower. In 1450 a little window-like brick projection (called Lygten) was added to the tower's upper eastern end to hang a burning lantern for guiding ships into harbour. It was from the top of this tower that Christian IV kept watch on his naval fleet as it successfully defended the town from Swedish invaders during the Battle of Køge Bay.

In July and early August visitors can climb the tower for similar, hopefully battle-free, views. Within the church other notable features include the ornately gilded 17th-century altar and multistage pulpit, plus the crest-emblazoned wooden gallery that raised Køge's nobility above the hoi polloi.

Køge Museum MUSEUM
(☑56 63 42 42; www.koegemuseum.dk; Nørregade 4; adult/child 90/40kr; ⊙10am-5pm Jul & Aug, 11am-4pm Tue-Sun Sep-Jun) Occupying a half-timbered 17th-century abode, the revamped Køge Museum uses state-of-the-art technology to bring to life its local-history artefacts. One exhibition examines the ill-fated 17th-century battleship *Dannebroge*, while another explores the 4000 BC Strøby Egede multiple-grave site. The museum is also home to Denmark's biggest coin hoard, a 32kg pile of 17th-century silver unearthed in the courtyard at Brogade 17 by two electricians in 1987.

KØS MUSEUM
(Køge Skitsesamling; www.koes.dk; Nørregade 29; adult/child 60kr/free; ⊙11am-5pm Tue-Sun, to 9pm Thu) Køge's Museum of Art in Public Spaces is a unique entity, displaying not the artists' finished work, but the notes and scribblings, sketches, models and mock-ups that built up into the final piece. It's fascinating to see the creative process deconstructed.

Rådhus HISTORIC BUILDING
(Torvet 1) Though essentially rebuilt in 1903, Køge's original town hall was once a 1550s Renaissance-style palace of a place that was partly built with materials scavenged from an abandoned monastery.

Today, even that building is mostly a facade for a modern complex hidden away behind.

Værftsvej Beach BEACH
Directly north of the marina is a decent strip of white sand made crunchy with lots of shell fragments. The remarkably clear water takes on a sparkling green-blue allure due to shallow sandbanks, but these mean a long stride out for swimming at low tide. At high tide there's a swim-jetty for easier access but no other facilities, bar a toilet.

From town, access is somewhat awkward on foot.

🛏 Sleeping

The town has two central hotels, two camping grounds, an awkwardly situated **Danhostel** (☑61 18 12 03; www.danhostel-koege.dk; Vamdrupvej 1; d/q 500/600kr, dm/d/q without bathroom 200/380/500kr; ⊙reception 4-6pm; [P] [🛜]) 💪 2km northwest and more than a dozen B&Bs in the surrounding area.

Køge

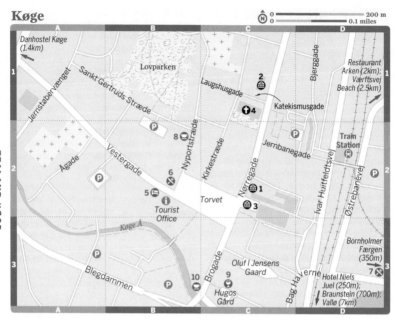

Danhostel Køge
(1.4km)

Lovparken

Sankt Gertruds Stræde

Jerristøbervænget

Sankt Gertruds Stræde

Laugshusgade

2

Katekismusgade

Bjerggade

Restaurant
Arken (2km);
Værftsvej
Beach (2.5km)

4

Nyportstræde

8

Ågade

Vestergade

Kirkestræde

Jernbanegade

Nørregade

Train
Station

Ivar Huitfeldtsvej

Østrebanevej

6

5

Tourist
Office

Torvet

1

3

Køge Å

Blegdammen

Brogade

Oluf I Jensens
Gaard

10

9

Hugos
Gård

Bag Haverne

Bornholmer
Færgen
(350m)

Hotel Niels
Juel (250m);
Braunstein (700m);
Vallø (7km)

7

Troldegården
B&B €€

(☎ 23 32 57 67; www.troldgaarden.dk; Egøjevej 146, Egøje; apt 850-1050kr; ⊙check in after 4.30pm; P 🛜) Less a B&B, more a rural retreat, with four luxurious apartments that feel like a home away from home, with kitchen and lots of tastefully chosen elements. One comes in charcoal grey modernist tones, others with old timbers and fireplace.

There are some lovely outdoor sitting areas, and animal lovers can admire the field of

Highland cattle, yet it's only a 4km drive from town. Cash only; pre-arrange arrival times.

Hotel Niels Juel
HOTEL €€

(☑ 56 63 18 00; www.hotelnielsjuel.dk; Toldbodvej 20; s/d/tr incl breakfast Mon-Thu 1245/1545/1895kr, Fri-Sun & holidays 825/1095/1295kr; ⊙reception 24hr; P 🛜) Close to the harbour, this pleasant hotel-restaurant combo has 51 compact but renovated en-suite rooms with unusual carpet designs that give the impression of walking on a boardwalk across a stony beach. Above the beds are zoological prints that seem torn from old textbooks. Beneath the bar-restaurant is a basement sauna (free for guests) and billiards room.

It's named for the heroic Danish commander who resoundingly defeated the attacking Swedish navy in the 1677 Battle of Køge Bay, widely reckoned to be Denmark's most significant ever naval victory.

Centralhotellet
HOTEL €€

(☑ 56 65 06 96; www.centralhotellet.dk; Vestergade 3; s/d 860/1135kr, s/d/tr/q without bathroom 705/860/1450/1600kr; P 🛜) A black-and-white colour scheme, picked out with abstract art, brings life to this perfectly central hotel's rooms, whose sizes vary radically from a tiny single (560kr) to family rooms with a shared roof terrace (access via spiral stairs).

Three more rooms are tucked behind, facing the four-space car park, whose access through a tunnel is a narrow squeeze for mid-sized cars. Don't miss sitting in the lovely little riverside garden, further back. Beware that the cafe, which doubles as reception, closes at 4pm. If planning to arrive after that, you'll need to phone ahead.

✖ Eating

Havnepladsen, the restored port area just east of the train station, hosts a tempting string of eight very varied restaurants. Wednesday and Saturday mornings see a produce market on Torvet, the main square where otherwise the alfresco eating contest is between vibrant cafes **Vivaldi** (☑ 56 63 53 66; www.cafevivaldi.dk; Torvet 30; brunch 129kr, mains 109-199kr, steak 259kr; ⊗ 10am-10pm Sun-Thu, to 11pm Fri & Sat) and Vanilla. A pedestrian passageway leads south to other options, including a modern brasserie and (just across the river) a reliable Indian restaurant.

★ **Restaurant Arken**   SEAFOOD €€
(☑ 56 66 05 05; www.restaurant-arken.dk; Bådehavnen 21; lunch 70-240kr, dinner mains 158-288kr; ⊗ 11.30am-8.30pm; �📶) Overlooking the marina, 2.5km north of Torvet, Arken has a sterling reputation for seafood, well cooked with top-quality ingredients. The daily changing 175kr lunch plate includes four flavour-packed mini-dishes and a cheese-and-fruit dessert. Even the chips are superb, triple fried with creamy garlic dip. And there's a scallop shell for a side plate on which to rest delicious home-baked rolls.

As well as a well-chosen wine list, there are house-made liquors and a range of beers from Skagen.

Skipperkroen   DANISH €€
(☑ 56 65 02 64; www.skipperkroen.dk; Havnen 25; lunch mains 49-175kr, dinner mains 155-255kr; ⊗ 11am-3pm & 5-10pm) With hanging beer steins and glass buoys, countless sailing-ship prints and gingham cloths on sturdy wooden tables, Skipperkroen is an archetypal harbourside inn, full of old-world character. At lunchtime, local pensioners wolf down a wide range of classic, unsophisticated Danish home cooking like *leverpostej* (hot potted liver pâté with mushrooms and bacon) and *salt-stegt sild* (fried smoked herring and onions).

🍷 Drinking & Nightlife

If you want to go alfresco on the main square, your choice is a V-themed play-off between vibrant cafes Vivaldi and Vanilla. However, tiny Kaffekælderen wins hands down for quaint historical atmosphere and for its cute river terrace, while Hugos Kælder fills its medieval cellar with a truly world-class beer selection.

★ **Kaffekælderen**   CAFE
(www.kaffekaelderen.dk; Brogade 26; coffee 25-42kr, cakes 35-45kr; ⊗ 9.30am-5.30pm Mon-Fri, 9.30am-4pm Sat, 11am-4pm Sun) The coffee is excellent and the dreamily soft forest-fruit meringue cake floats on pillows of flavour. But the greatest attraction here is the time-twisted little building that contains the cafe along with its *brocante* furniture, mini riverside terrace and cobbled courtyard drawn straight from an artist's canvas.

ZEALAND KØGE

WORTH A TRIP

BUCOLIC VALLØ

In a tiny hamlet just 7km from Køge, **Vallø Slot** (www.valloe-stift.dk; Slotsgade; ⊗ gardens 8am-sunset), ticks all the 'proper castle' boxes, with pointed metal-capped turrets and a moat filled with lily pads and croaking frogs. The building has retained its original 16th-century style, although much of it was rebuilt following a fire in 1893. While the castle itself is not open to the public, visitors are free to amble into the central courtyard area and right through the beautiful woods and gardens that extend all the way to the sea. On her birthday in 1737 Queen Sophie Magdalene, who owned the estate, established a foundation that turned the castle into a home for 'spinsters of noble birth'. Unmarried daughters of Danish royalty unable to live in their own castles were allowed to live at Vallø, supported by the foundation and government social programs. The last new residents arrived in the 1970s, with the castle-estate's remit broadened since 1976 to one of a more general public charity. But a handful of ageing blue-blooded *stiftsdamer* women remain in residence. Facing the driveway, **Vallø Slotskro** (☑ 56 26 62 66; www. valloeslotskro.dk; Slotsgade 1; menu without/with wines 600/1200kr; ⊗ 6-9pm Wed-Sat; 🅿) offers gourmet dining that's particularly strong on using forage-based produce.

STROLLING OLD KØGE

Storybook buildings pepper Køge's central streets, recalling centuries of history in a few hundred metres' stroll. To enjoy a selection, start at the bridge, beside which is wobbly **Brogade 26**, a 1721 house that started life as the customs house and is now a delightfully ramshackle cafe (p119). Within its floral, cobbled courtyard lies a wonderfully old-fashioned barber's shop facing the river. **Brogade 23**, now the ClauDine boutique, has carved floral and cherub motifs in its exterior beamwork, created by famed 17th-century artist Abel Schrøder. Beneath **Brogade 19**, entered from another 17th-century courtyard, is the magical beer-bar Hugos Kælder (p120), contained within a medieval brick-built cellar dating back to around 1300. **Brogade 17** is less visually enticing, but in 1987 workers in the courtyard here unearthed an old wooden trunk filled with more than 2000 17th-century silver coins, the largest coin hoard ever found in Denmark. Some of these are now on display at the Køge Museum. Dating from 1636, **Brogade 16** is central Køge's longest timber-framed courtyard building. Behind green-painted timbers and mustard-coloured walls, it houses an optician, as is vividly apparent from the visually descriptive metal sign hanging in front.

As Brogade crosses the old town square, Torvet, it becomes Nørregade after the neoclassical Rådhus (p117), topped by a clock-face pediment featuring the reclining allegorical figures of justice and education. Just beyond is the beautiful half-timbered Køge Museum (p117) building. Across the road, built into the wall of what is now the Rokkjær clothing store, is a simple marble plaque marked *Kiøge Huskors* (Kiøge and Kjøge are old spellings of Køge). This honours the victims of a 17th-century witch-hunt that caused 16 people to be burned at the stake, including two residents of an earlier house on the site.

Walk halfway across Torvet and look north from outside the 1638 house at **Kirkestræde 3** for one of the most photogenic views in Køge. The street is a gem, with the church in middle distance and houses at Kirkestræde 6, 10 and 15 all generously timbered. Notice the twisting chimney on **Kirkestræde 13**, which acted as an advert to passers-by seeking a blacksmith. And just in front of the library at **Kirkestræde 20**, you'll find the quaintest house of all, a steeply roofed building from 1527 that's reputedly Denmark's oldest half-timbered house. Though only a diminutive 4m by 5m, records show that during the late 19th century it managed to house a tanner, his wife and 10 children.

★**Hugos Kælder**   CRAFT BEER
(http://hugos.dk; Brogade 19; beer 30-200kr; ⊗noon-11pm Mon-Thu, noon-2am Fri, 10am-2am Sat, 1-6pm Sun) In a brick-walled 14th-century cellar entered from one of Køge's secret central courtyards, Hugos is a beer-lover's paradise, with three of its own brews among 20 on tap, plus well over 200 further beers available by the bottle.

That includes 50-plus Danish regionals, numerous US craft beers and a menu of Belgian beauties that features all the Trappists brews, including ultra-rare Westvleteren 12, often rated the 'world's best beer'. In summer, live blues, jazz and rock bands play in the courtyard around noon on Saturdays.

Braunstein   DISTILLERY
(☑70 20 44 68; www.braunstein.dk; Carlsensvej 5; beer to go 15kr; ⊗shop 10am-4pm Mon-Fri) Breathe the yeasty smells and catch glimpses of the apparatus as you visit the little shop of the Braunstein brothers' craft brewery and adventurous whisky distillery. Or, on the first Saturday of each month, come for the 'open house' when full tours run two or three times an hour (175kr including tastings).

Café T   CAFE
(www.facebook.com/Cafe.T.4600; Nyportstræde 17; ⊗10am-4pm Tue-Sat) Just off the main square, this oversized doll's house with its mix-and-match furniture is a super-friendly, quietly feminine place for excellent coffee, loose-leaf teas and freshly made quality cakes and cheesecake.

❶ Information

Just off the town's main square, the **tourist office** (☑56 67 60 01; www.visitkoege.com; Vestergade 1; ⊗9.30am-5pm Mon-Fri, 10am-1pm Sat Sep-Jun, closes 1hr later Jul & Aug; 🛜) offers free wi-fi and a remarkable range of brochures for virtually anywhere in Denmark.

Getting There & Away

Køge is the southernmost station on the E-line of greater Copenhagen's S-train network. Trains to København H (100kr, 37 minutes) run three to six times an hour, continuing all the way to Hillerød (100kr, 80 minutes). Due to start as of 2018, the new high-speed Ringsted line should cut the Copenhagen-Køge journey time to 30 minutes, but will stop at a new Køge Nord station, somewhat more distant from the centre than the present station.

Bornholmer Færgen (☎70 23 15 15; www.faergen.dk; Østre Kajgade; adult/child 12-15yr/under 11yr 283/141kr/free, low season 232/116kr/free, car incl 5 passengers return 850-1064kr, sleeping berths dm/d/q 225/450/900kr) Daily, year-round ferries to Bornholm depart from Køge at 12.30am, arriving in Rønne at 6am. From Rønne, the return ferry leaves at 5pm, reaching Køge at 10.30pm. Prices vary according to availability and advance purchase. Book online.

Getting Around

Both **Garant Cykler** (☎56 65 84 85; www.garant-cykler.dk; Vestergade 41; ⏲10am-5pm Mon-Fri, to 2pm Sat) and the **hostel** (p117) rent bicycles (100kr per day). The **tourist office** (p120) sells a pack of eight cycle-tour guide pamphlets (25kr).

Næstved & Around

POP 42,980

The largest city in the region, Næstved has a thousand years of history, but despite a scattering of medieval buildings, including two splendid 13th-century churches, the attractions are too diffuse to create a memorable impression. On the western edge of town there's a decent **zoo** (www.naestvedzoo.dk) and the impressive island estate house of **Gavnø Slot** (www.gavnoe.dk). In nearby Fenmark is the famous glassworks, **Holmegaard Glasværker** (www.holmegaard.dk), and beside Rte 54 east of town you'll find the major theme park, **BonBon Land** (http://bonbonland.dk). More sedate types can explore the lakes and forests to the south and west, or join the happy throngs at seaside **Karrebæksminde**.

If you're looking for a place to stay in Næstved, **Hotel Kirstine** (☎55 77 47 00; www.hotelkirstine.dk; Købmagergade 20; d 1195kr; 🅿📶) is a central option. Vermilion half-timber frames give this delightful old hotel a very distinctive look that's reflected inside with appealingly restored rooms decorated in a soothing floral style.

OFF THE BEATEN TRACK

ØBJERGGAARD BED & BREAKFAST

Flanked by half-timbered outbuildings, this historic three-story **estate-mansion** (www.objerggaard.com; Øbjerggårds Allé 20, Køng; d 545-895kr, without bathroom from 445kr; 🅿📶) oozes atmosphere, especially in the two-floor library full of leather-bound books, entered via the billiards room. Guest rooms are tastefully appointed with creaky, painted floorboards and classical furniture. The communal kitchen is fully equipped but there can be a queue for the single shared bathroom.

It's 16km south of Næstved in the village of Køng, up a splendid tree-lined avenue from Køng Museum, a pediment-fronted building that was once the estate's little flax factory.

Getting There & Away

Trains run once or twice hourly to:

Copenhagen (100kr, one hour)

Køge (68kr, 33 minutes)

Ringsted (36kr, 18 minutes)

Roskilde (76kr, fast/slow 30 minutes/one hour)

Vordingborg (60kr, 14 to 18 minutes)

Stevns Klint

A Unesco World Heritage Site since June 2014, Stevns Klint is a fossil-rich cliff at the south end of Køge Bugt (Køge Bay) where a very narrow layer of grey clay between the chalk and limestone deposits presents important geological evidence supporting a popular dinosaur die-out theory. The best way to see this stratification is to climb down the cliff-side stairway beside the perilously perched old church in Højerup village.

The scenery is an attraction in itself, especially if you walk the clifftop path from Stevns Fyr lighthouse. A couple of kilometres south there's a fascinating Cold War experience before you reach the yacht and fishing harbour of **Rødvig**, which is a pleasant place to dine.

Sights & Activities

Højerup Gamle Kirke CHURCH
(Højerup Bygade 30; ⏲9am-5pm Jun-Sep, shorter hours rest of year) This 13th-century church with faded ochre murals stands so near to

the cliff edge that a small balcony where the altar should be looks out directly across the sea and Stevns Klint.

Indeed, where you're standing was once the church chancel, but on 16 March 1928 this, along with part of the church's cemetery, tumbled into the sea.

Bråten   VIEWPOINT
(Stevns Klint clifftop path) Less than 10 minutes' walk north of Højerup car park along the footpath towards Stevns Fyr (☑ 56 51 06 01; www.facebook.com/StevnsFyr; Fyrvej 2, Tommestrup; ⊗ lighthouse 11am-3pm Mon-Fri, noon-3pm Sat & Sun, gallery 11am-4pm Mon-Fri, noon-4pm Sat & Sun), photographers will adore Bråten, a clifftop perch with the best view down onto the Stevns Klint site.

But tread carefully as there's no fence to stop you falling off the top. It's just north of the Klintgården farmstead B&B.

Koldkrigsmuseum Stevnsfort   MUSEUM
(Cold War Museum; ☑ 56 50 28 06; www.kalklandet. dk; Korsnæbsvej 60, Rødvig; underground fortress guided tour adult/student/child 120/100/70kr, above-ground only 60/50kr/free; ⊗ site 10am-5pm Apr-Oct) This fascinating museum was a secret subterranean fortress used in the 20th-century Cold War era, when nuclear war was a feared possibility in the bellicose stand-off between NATO and the USSR. Visits are by 90-minute guided tours (in Danish, but with a few audio guides available in English and German). You don't need to join a guided tour to explore the above-ground area, which displays a selection of rocket launchers, mobile radar stations and container-box control rooms.

If doing the full 1.7km Stevnsfort tour, it's worth bringing warm clothes as you'll be 18m underground, where the temperature hovers around 10°C. Booking ahead is wise as groups are limited to 30 people and some days there are only one or two departures (most commonly 11am, 1pm and/or 3pm). Click KØB BILLET on the website to see a calendar of available tour times.

The site is 3km south of Stevns Klint, halfway between Højerup and Rødvig, and a pleasant coastal walk from Gamle Kirke.

GeoMuseum Faxe   FOSSIL HUNTING
(www.kalklandet.dk; Østervej 2, Faxe; axe rental 20kr, museum adult/child 60kr/free; ⊗ 10am-5pm) Around 20km west of Stevns Klint, dramatically overlooking a vast limestone quarry, is a new GeoMuseum explaining the hard-to-imagine fact that coral reefs once covered this part of Denmark. More interesting still, you can rent fossil-hunters' axes and walk into the quarry to find prehistoric souvenirs of your own...at your own risk – the quarry is still an active workplace.

🛏 Sleeping

Klintgården   B&B €
(☑ 56 51 00 51; www.stevnsklintegaard.dk; Hærvejen 24, Store Heddinge; s/d incl breakfast 300-500kr; ⊗ mid-May–mid-Sep; 🐾) Just 100m from Stevns Klint's best clifftop viewpoint along the Højerup-Stevns Fyr footpath, this excellent farmhouse B&B has three bedrooms sharing a bathroom and second toilet, plus access to an art-packed sitting/dining room. There's also garden seating.

★ Rødvig Kro   HISTORIC HOTEL €€
(☑ 56 50 60 98; www.roedvigkro.dk; Østersøvej 8, Rødvig; d without/with view 1295/1395kr, without bathroom 950kr) Perfectly pitched between a boutique hotel and an inviting family home, this 1844 building offers 19 well-equipped rooms, many with delightful views across a lawn and ocean bay towards the start of the cliffs. The breakfast room and lounge feel cosy yet historically authentic, and there's an excellent restaurant.

🍴 Eating

In tiny Højerup, Traktørstedet Højeruplund (☑ 56 50 29 11; https://hojeruplund.dk; Højerup Bygade 39; lunch 98-185kr, 1-/2-/3-course dinner 179/198/235kr; ⊗ noon-8pm Jul & Aug, Sat & Sun Nov-Mar, closed Mon & some evenings Apr-Jun, Sep & Oct) serves competent classic Danish grub, and if you spend 50kr (eg its coffee-cake set, available till 6.30pm) you get free parking, which otherwise costs 40kr. Next door, tourists queue for ice cream at Ishuset Højeruplund (2 scoops 30kr; ⊗ 10am-8pm Apr-Aug). Rødvig has more choice, including a supermarket, posh restaurant and five unpretentious eateries, including one serving excellent Thai food.

Aqua Marina   THAI €
(☑ 56 59 90 60; www.aquq-marina.dk; Havenpladsen 2, Rødvig; mains incl rice 89-119kr; ⊗ noon-9pm Easter-Sep) Sitting across the road from the yacht-bobbing harbour in Rødvig, Aqua Marina has a personality crisis. A semi-comical *Jaws*-themed interior sees a shark crashing through a wall towards a scallop-bra hula girl. And there's a sideline in Italian ice cream and moped rental. But the real reason to come is for the well-priced, authentic Thai food.

DRAGSHOLM SLOT
....

Staying at this 800-year-old **castle** (☑59 65 33 00; www.dragsholm-slot.dk; Dragsholm Allé, Hørve; d bistro/gourmet half-board 2700/3990kr; ℗⚹), or in its well-appointed outbuildings, adds to the thrill of tasting some of Denmark's most lauded if deceptively simple New Nordic cuisine, created by ex-Noma chef Claus Henriksen. Accommodation packages typically include double room, breakfast and dinner at either the casually-styled **Spisehuset bistro** (Lammefjordens Spisehus; 2-course lunch 295kr, 3-course dinner 375kr; ⚹noon-3pm & 6-10pm) or Michelin-starred **Slotskøkkenet** (5/7 courses 800/1000kr; ⚹6-10pm Wed-Sat Jun, 6-10pm Tue-Sat Jul-early Sep, reduced days rest of year, Fri & Sat only winter), a whitewashed cellar-like dining room with paintings of vaguely tortured fish. If you didn't book ahead, there's always the low-key **MadBar** (snacks 35-75kr, coffee/wine/beer 35/65/70kr; ⚹11am-9pm Jul & Aug, Fri-Sun Jun & Sep), which has solid tables on the castle's rear terrace where you can get a small selection of drinks and light seasonal snacks – perhaps cabbage rolls stuffed with lamb and dried gooseberries or asparagus on toast. Ideal if you're passing by – though that's somewhat unlikely given the castle's completely out-of-the-way location. No public transport.

ℹ Information

The very informative website and phone app www.kalklandet.dk has masses of useful information.

ℹ Getting There & Away

Stevns Klint lies 29km southeast of Køge via Rte 261. Car parking costs 40kr in Højerup but is free at Stevns Fyr (p122), Koldkrigsmuseum (p122) and Rødvig.

Trains run Køge–Rødvig (60kr, 35 minutes) twice an hour on weekdays, hourly on weekends via Klippinge and Store Heddinge. From Rødvig and Store Heddinge stations, hourly bus 252 connects to Højerup, from where Stevns Klint is just a 500m walk east along Højerup Bygade.

In July and August only, a free shuttle bus route operates five times daily from Klippinge Station via Stevns Fyr, Stevns Klint and the Koldkrigsmuseum to Rødvig, then back again. Once in the morning there's an extra loop via Vallø (p119). See www.stevnsbussen.dk for times and details.

ℹ Getting Around

There is a clear walking trail along the clifftop. Mopeds (per hour/day 75/400kr) and quads (per hour 100kr) are available for rent from Aqua Marina (p122) in Rødvig. Co-owned **Cafe Marina**, 200m further west, rents bicycles (per day 100kr to 150kr).

Vordingborg

POP 11,910

Many Møn-bound visitors will need to change transport in Vordingborg. If you're doing that, it's worth stopping briefly to visit the site of the town's central, once-formidable castle that played a starring role in early Danish history. Today, all that remains are a few moated bastion ruins plus a single round tower (p124), but the site forms an appealing park with views down across a pretty harbour. Danmarks Borgcenter brings the site's history vividly to life using an imaginative self-led tour guided by tablet-computer.

History

Vordingborg's ancient history is synonymous with that of its castle site – the royal residence and Baltic power base of Valdemar I (Valdemar the Great), who reunited the Danish kingdom in 1157 after a period of civil war. It was here in 1241 that Valdemar II (Valdemar the Victorious) signed the Law of Jutland, a civil code spelling out the need for legal legitimacy and objective sovereign justice. The code would become the forerunner to Danish national law. The castle remained of great importance into the 17th century but was left in tatters after the 1660 Swedish war, and Vordingborg never fully recovered its status thereafter.

◉ Sights

Danmarks Borgcenter   MUSEUM
(Danish Castle Centre; www.danmarksborgcenter. dk; Slotsruinen 1; adult/child 125/75kr; ⚹10am-5pm Jul & Aug, Tue-Sun Sep-Jun) Set within the grass ruins of Valdemar's castle, this high-tech museum examines the site's history, as well as that of medieval Danish power, politics and castle life. Using interactive iPads, visitors can explore themes such as the tactics used by kings to gain and retain power, as well as learn about the museum's historical artefacts.

Vor Frue Kirke   CHURCH

(Kirketorvet; ☉8am-4pm) Tucked behind the western pedestrianised side of Algade on central Vordingborg's prettiest square, the brick-built Vor Frue Kirke contains elegant frescoes in its mid-15th-century nave, and there's a 1642 baroque altarpiece by master-carver Abel Schrøder.

Gåsetårnet   TOWER

(Goose Tower; www.danmarksborgcenter.dk; Slots-ruinen) Round, red-brick and 36m tall, the Gåsetårnet gained its name when, in 1365, King Valdemar IV placed a golden goose on top of it. The goose was meant to mock a dec-laration of war made by leaders of the Ger-man Hanseatic League, who Valdemar had branded as mere 'cackling geese'. The original model was later removed (and lost) by Valde-mar's less heroic son, and the current version is an 1871 replacement perched on the tower's 19th-century bronze spire.

🛏 Sleeping & Eating

Business hotel **Kong Valdemar** (☑55 34 30 95; www.hotelkongvaldemar.dk; Algade 101; s/d/tr/ste incl breakfast 595/795/995/1195kr; [P][⋚]) is central but forgettable. There's also a **Dan-hostel** (☑55 36 08 00; http://danhostel-vording borg.dk; Præstegårdsvej 16; s/d/tr/q from 350/500/550/600kr; ☉reception 4-6pm; [P]) 2km north, and a few private homes in the Vordingborg area offer rooms for rent: click 'menu' on www.babette.dk for a short listing. Two-night minimum stay usually required.

The harbour area restaurants are gener-ally better for eating than popular but so-so cafes on Algade facing the castle-ruins park. Within that site, **Cafe Borgen** (www.musee rne.dk; Slotsruinen 1; coffee/beer from 25/30kr, lunch mains 85-110kr; ☉10am-5pm) is a good bet for coffee.

Bed-Bike-Breakfast   B&B €€

(☑28 95 03 65; http://bedbikebreakfast.dk; Kir-ketorvet 16; d without/with bathroom 750/850kr, s 675kr) On the pretty square fronting Vording-borg's historic church, this central B&B offers unexpectedly modern rooms within a histor-ic brick house.

Marina Fisk   SEAFOOD €

(☑35 13 21 40; www.facebook.com/vordingborgfisk; Nordhavnsvej 12; mains 65-95kr; ☉9.30am-8pm Tue-Sat, 10am-3pm Sun) At this great-value, unpretentious place for quick seafood dish-es, you order at the counter and eat on a (hopefully) sunny terrace watching the boats

bobbing in the harbour. It does a great take on the classic *stjerneskud* ('shooting star'), a stack of fried fish, salad, boiled fish, shrimps and roe.

★ Babette   DANISH, INTERNATIONAL €€€

(☑55 34 30 30; www.babette.dk; Kildemarksvej 5; lunch from 295kr, 3-/5-/7-course dinner 575/725/875kr, grand menu with wine 2100kr; ☉noon-3pm & 6-9pm Wed-Fri, 6-9pm Sat) Orchids, white roses, starched tablecloths, abstract art and picture windows set the visual canvas for a full-on gastronomic experience, a showcase of New Nordic cuisine with classic French undercurrents. Bookings are highly advised. Wednesdays and Thursdays out of season you might find more affordable two-course din-ners available (without/with wine 295/325kr).

ℹ Information

The container box that acts as ticket counter and shop for the Danmarks Borgcenter (p123) also doubles as a small **tourist office** (☑70 70 12 36; www.sydkystdanmark.dk; Slotsruinen 1; ☉10am-5pm Jul & Aug, Tue-Sun Sep-Jun).

ℹ Getting There & Away

Vordingborg-Copenhagen trains (142kr) take 68 to 80 minutes via Roskilde, with departures once or twice hourly till late evening. Trains arriving before midnight are met by connecting bus 660R (or 664) to Møn.

WESTERN ZEALAND

Most visitors dash through western Zealand between Funen and Roskilde, but it's easy to stop briefly en route to see the remarkable churches in **Ringsted** and **Sorø**. With more effort you can also visit lonely but signifi-cant Viking sites at Trelleborg (p125) and beside bird-rich **Lake Tissø**. The latter is part way to Kalundborg, an industrial port city with an unusual five-spired church. Well off the beaten track is Michelin-rated Drag-sholm Slot (p123), a medieval castle turned hotel-restaurant.

Ringsted

POP 22,500

Justifying a visit to historic yet otherwise forgettable Ringsted, **Sankt Bendts Kirke** (www.ringstedsogn.dk; Sankt Bendtsgade, Ringsted; ☉10am-4pm May-Aug, to 1pm Sep-Apr) is a huge church packed with fascinating features, which the remarkably knowledgeable care-taker is very keen to explain. Most notable

TRELLEBORG

One of Zealand's most important **Viking Age sites** (www.vikingeborgen-trelleborg.dk; Trelleborg Alle 4; ⊙24hr) FREE, this large ring fortress dates to AD 980. It is essentially a perfectly circular raised earthwork, 300m beyond a **museum** (Trelleborg Alle 4; ⊙10am-5pm Tue-Sun Jun-Aug, to 4pm Tue-Sat Apr, May, Sep & Oct) FREE that explains the context, though if you arrive outside the museum's opening hours, you can still visit the main site. Between the two you'll pass a very atmospheric, full-sized Viking wooden longhouse reconstruction.

On the circular rampart itself, you can readily grasp the strikingly precise geometric design of the fortress. Its grassy banks are 17m wide and 6m high, and were originally topped by a long-gone wooden palisade. The banks protect a central space where two streets once divided the circle into quarters. Each quarter contained a courtyard with four wooden longhouses. They long-ago decayed away, but the post holes and gable ends have been identified and filled with cement to show the outlines of their foundations.

Walking back towards the entrance, look to the left of the museum to find a mini 'village' of six thatch- and turf-roofed Viking building mock-ups. In mid-July, a week-long **festival** (www.vikingeborgen-trelleborg.dk; adult/child 110/30kr) brings this area to life with costumed characters, craftsmen at work and various activities for kids.

are the 14th-century ceiling frescoes, the royal graves and a museum section in the south transept where, if you push the black slider, you can peep in to see the skull-cast of Queen Berengard. There's also a lock of hair from King Valdemar I, whose bronze statue stands out front.

Sorø

POP 7870

With a fair sprinkling of old timber-framed houses and soothing walks beside peaceful lakes, Sorø is a pleasant, off-the-radar spot. It owes its existence to Sorø Akademi, a monastery turned prestigious school that still operates in a new form to this day.

⊙ Sights

Sorø's **Akademi** was once one of Denmark's richest monasteries, founded in 1142 and much expanded after 1161. Post-Reformation it became a school, then from 1623 developed under King Christian IV as the elite Sorø Academy of Knights, educating sons of the nobility in the arts of hunting, behaviour and manners. Although it remains a prominent Danish school, visitors are welcome to stroll through the extensive lakeside grounds.

Shaded with tall oaks, the Akademi area is entered via **Klosterporten** (Storgade), the former monastery's medieval gatehouse. Other than the church, most buildings were entirely rebuilt in the mid-18th century and again after an 1813 fire, but 17th-century Renaissance structures include the **Boldhuset** (today's

library) and the **Ridehuset** (Sorø Akademi grounds), originally built to stable horses and hunting dogs. Many newer buildings are contrastingly banal. Picturesque walking trails follow lakefront lawns. One route passes a **statue of Ludvig Holberg** (Sorø Akademi grounds), the school's great 18th-century playwright-benefactor. Return to central Sorø via the town's prettiest lanes **Søgade** or **Vestergade** – both with good concentrations of old, mustard-yellow houses.

Sorø Kirke   CHURCH

(⊙9am-4pm) Interring several Danish royals, this church within the Sorø Akademi grounds has a simple, harmonious interior brightened by **medieval frescoes** and lightened by a 13th-century Gothic ceiling. It was originally built as part of the 12th-century monastery Sorø Kloster, in part to act as the mausoleum of the Hvide clan, the family of Bishop Absalon who, as one of Denmark's most significant medieval statesmen, had established the Cistercian order here in 1161. Absalon himself is buried behind the main altar.

Sorø Kunstmuseum   MUSEUM

(www.sorokunstmuseum.dk; Storgade 9; adult/child 70kr/free; ⊙11am-5pm Tue, Wed & Fri-Sun, to 6pm Thu) Flaunting an award-winning extension by Copenhagen-based architects Lundgaard & Tranberg, Sorø Kunstmuseum has regularly changing exhibitions of art both modern and classic, but what you will reliably be able to see is part of Denmark's largest collection of Russian icons, and usually a selection of 19th-century Danish 'Golden Age' paintings.

Søro

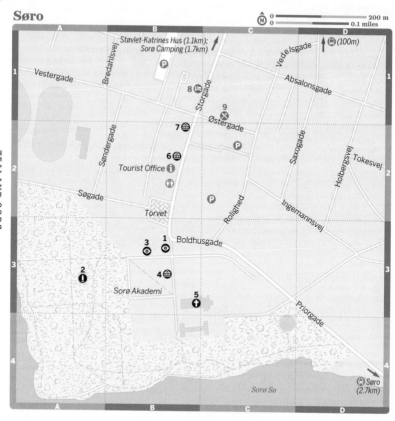

Sorø Museum   MUSEUM
(www.vestmuseum.dk; Storgade 17; adult/child 25kr/
free; ⊙ 11am-4pm Tue-Sun Jul & Aug, 1-4pm Tue-Thu
& Sun, 11am-2pm Sat Sep-Jun) Housed in a handsome half-timbered former inn dating from

1625, Sorø Museum showcases an eclectic
booty of regional artefacts, including ancient
pottery and the partial reconstruction of a
5500-year-old Bornholm longhouse. Several
rooms are adorned with period furnishings,
including the fetching living room of an aris-
tocrat and the personal belongings of the
19th-century poet BS Ingemann, who taught
at Sorø Akademi (p125).

🎇 Festivals & Events

Sorø Jazz   MUSIC
(www.soroejazz.dk; ⊙ Jul) Sorø's ever-growing
jazz festival takes place over a week in late
July, with around 25 concerts performed in
various venues across the municipality, including museums, churches and cafes.

Every year there's a degree of imaginative
cross-fertilisation between the jazz and **classical festival** (www.soroemusik.dk; ⊙ Jul & Aug)
musicians who are in town at the same time.

🛏 Sleeping

Sorø Sø Camping — CAMPGROUND €
(☑ 57 83 02 02; www.soroecamping.dk; Udbyhøjvej 10; campsite per adult/child 79/40kr, caravan site extra 30kr, cabins 500-850kr; 🅿 🛜; 🖳 422) Three-star Sorø Sø camping ground is layered gently up from the lake of the same name. Guests get an electronic entry card to open the private gate for access to the western lakeside footpath that winds 1km into town.

Hotel Postgaarden — HOTEL €€
(☑ 57 83 22 22; www.hotelpostgaarden.dk; Storgade 25; s/d/tr from 700/800/1300kr, s/d without bathroom 600/700kr; 🅿 🛜) With creaking, uneven floors, rooms vary considerably in size and style within this partially refurbished inn-style hotel in a 300-year-old half-timbered building. Five redecorated 2nd-floor rooms share one bathroom; three others have private but non-attached toilets. There's an inviting cafe and summer courtyard terrace. Breakfast included.

✗ Eating

Café Tre Konger — INTERNATIONAL €€
(Østergade 3; lunch 98-130kr, dinner mains 98-278kr; ⊘11am-10pm Mon-Sat, to 9pm Sun) In a stylishly converted movie theatre adorned with mini-chandeliers and rattan chairs, this relaxed cafe is particularly impressive for its Three King salad plates (available lunch and dinner) made with house-smoked duck breast, rocket, walnuts and pickled green tomato. Gourmet burgers are also popular, along with dinner plates of salmon pasta and veal steak.

★ Støvlet-Katrines Hus — DANISH €€€
(☑ 57 83 50 80; www.stovletkatrineshus.dk; Slagelsevej 63; lunch mains 138-175kr, dinner mains 245kr, 7-course dinner 745kr, with wine/beer 1295/1095kr; ⊘noon-4pm & 5.30-9.30pm Mon-Sat, 11am-1pm first Sun of month) Suited-and-tied waiters usher discerning diners to white-clothed tables in this suave, thatch-roofed farmstead that was once home to Christian VII's mistress. These days, lust comes in the form of delicious, seasonal dishes incorporating home-steeped floral and berry syrups.

❶ Information

Tourist Office (☑ 57 82 10 12; www.soroe-turistbureau.dk; Storgade 7; ⊘10am-5pm Mon, Tue & Thu, 10am-3pm Fri, 10am-1pm Sat) Located within the library. Walk through the arched passage opposite Nordea bank and turn left to find the entrance.

❶ Getting There & Away

Sorø is on the railway between Odense (184kr, 46 minutes) and Copenhagen (132kr, 48 minutes via Roskilde, 76kr, 24 minutes). However, as the train station is actually in Frederiksberg, 3km southwest of town, bus 234 can prove more convenient for reaching Ringsted (36kr, 20 minutes) or Slagelse (36kr, 25 minutes), as it uses Sorø's much more central bus terminal. Buses 421, 422 and 425 run from central Sorø to the train station.

Lake Tissø

On the banks of Denmark's fourth largest lake, the new **Fugledegård Visitor Centre** (http://naturparkaamosen.dk; Bakkendrupvej 28, Store Fuglede; adult/child 40kr/free; ⊘9am-3pm Mon-Fri) provides access to what is believed to have been an important ritual centre a millennium ago. The Viking-era wooden buildings are long gone, but their outlines are marked by granite slabs, and the visitor centre has a beautiful reconstruction of the 1.8kg Tissø woven-gold neck-ring, the world's richest Viking gold find that was amongst 12,000 artefact fragments discovered hereabouts. Kids can play paint-and-sacrifice or dress up as Vikings, while an English guide-text gives context to the era's religious beliefs. Reaching the site, a detour from the Korsør–Trelleborg–Kalundborg route, you'll need your own wheels. En route consider stopping in **Løve**, whether to visit the working 1881 **windmill** (www.loevemoelle.dk; Knudstrupvej 6A, Løve; adult/child 25/10kr; ⊘1-4pm Tue & Thu mid-Jun–Aug; 🖳430R) or just for Valentine selfies beside the town sign.

Korsør

POP 14,700

Some 18km long and incorporating a suspension bridge that's arguably as elegant as the Golden Gate, the **Storebælts-forbindelsen** (Great Belt Fixed Link; www.storebaelt.dk; E20 Hwy; one-way toll motorcycle/car/caravan 125/240/365kr) is a remarkable piece of engineering linking Funen and Zealand by road and rail on what has been dubbed Denmark's greatest man-made structure. Few people now stop in Korsør, the port town whose ferries and winter ice-breakers were rendered obsolete by the link's construction. Yet arguably the most photogenic views of the bridge are from near Korsør's **Isbådsmuseet** (Ice Boat Museum; www.byogoverfartsmuseet.dk; Søbatteriet 3; ⊘10am-6pm mid-Apr–mid-Oct) FREE, a one-room ice-breaking museum.

ZEALAND LAKE TISSØ

127

Møn, Falster & Lolland

Best Places to Eat

➡ Bandholm Hotel Restaurant (p142)

➡ Oreby Kro (p142)

➡ Lollesgaard (p134)

➡ Cafe V'sit (p132)

➡ Dhaba (p138)

Best Places to Stay

➡ Skelby Gammel Praestegaard (p140)

➡ Bandholm Hotel (p142)

➡ Hotel Stege Nor (p132)

➡ Liselund Ny Slot (p136)

➡ PilgrimsHuset (p142)

Why Go?

Welcome to Denmark's 'South Sea Islands'. OK, you won't get coconut palms and hula skirts...but do expect a fine glimpse of rural Scandinavian island life amid rolling fields of wheat and sugar beet dotted with occasional neolithic tombs.

Møn deserves the most attention, artistically spirited and home to something very unusual for Denmark: cliffs! Several medieval churches feature memorable frescoes, from masterpieces to primitive daubs. Add evocative beaches, enchanted forests and cosy guesthouses, and you've got a gem of an island escape.

Less discovered, the twin isles of Lolland-Falster are most famous for the extraordinarily long, sandy beach at Marielyst. Patchworks of farms, lakes and woods make for great cycling; agricultural estates are developing local products; Knuthenborg Safari Park is a national drawcard; and the Dodekalitten make Lolland Denmark's Easter Island. Well, almost.

Rail and/or road bridges mean that connections to southern Zealand don't require a ferry trip.

When to Go

➡ To catch a glimpse of Møn's rare orchids, May and June are best.

➡ Falster's famous beaches get crowded in July and early August, but if you don't mind a reduced bar buzz, the shoulder seasons of mid-June and late August are arguably better, with acres of empty sand yet relatively good weather.

➡ By autumn and throughout the winter, many coastal businesses shut for the season. At this time the landscape takes on a brooding, melancholy air, which might appeal to more poetic souls.

➡ April and May are great for watching migratory birds in southern Lolland and Falster, while in autumn there are numerous geese, swans and waders on the Nyord meadows.

Møn, Falster & Lolland Highlights

1 Møns Klint (p134)
Searching for prehistoric fossils at the foot of Denmark's tallest cliffs.

2 Middelaldercentret (p137) Channelling your inner knight or maiden at this medieval-themed museum-village, just outside Nykøbing F.

3 Frescoed Churches of Møn (p135) Deciphering the naive daubs and stick figures on vaulted medieval church ceilings at Keldby, Fanefjord and Elmelunde.

4 Dodekalitten (p143) Contemplating Denmark's answer to Easter Island's *moai*.

5 Marielyst Strand (p139) Finding your own sweep of sand at Falster's longest beach.

6 Klekkende Høj (p137) Blinking in disbelief as your eyes and claustrophobic reactions adjust to being inside a 5000-year-old tunnel grave.

7 Knuthenborg Safari Park (p141) Monkeying around in a world of wildlife imported into the grounds of a great country estate.

MØN

POP 9380

One of Denmark's most magical islands, Møn's best-known drawcard is its sweeping stretch of white cliffs, Møns Klint (p134). Crowned by deep-green forest, they're a popular inspiration for landscape paintings, possibly explaining the island's healthy artist headcount. But the inspiration doesn't end there. Beautiful beaches span sandy expanses and small secret coves, there are haunting Neolithic graves, and several rural churches are adorned with whimsical medieval frescoes. Every year more stargazers come for what are said to be Denmark's darkest night skies, and now they're joined by hikers flooding in to walk the well-organised network of trails known as **Camønoen** (www.camoenoen.dk), named with a punning nod to the classic Camino pilgrim trail.

Stege

POP 3850

Møn's main town and gateway, Stege has an excellent tourist office and a decent selection of accommodation, shops, cafes and supermarkets. There are also a couple of great museums, several galleries and fine church with historic murals.

◉ Sights

Funded by a lucrative herring industry, Stege was once one of Denmark's wealthiest provincial towns, protected (from the 1430s onwards) by a city wall and eastern moat-trench. Fortifications were partly torn down in 1534 by citizens who supported a mutinous attacking army. Today, you can still see remnant sections of now-dry moat close to Møns Museum. Beside that, the layered brick and stone **Mølleporten** (Map p132; Storegade) is Stege's last surviving city gate, narrowly rescued from planned demolition in 1873.

Møn

★Thorsvang MUSEUM

(Map p130; www.thorsvangsamlermuseum.dk; Thorsvangsallé 7; adult/child 60/30kr; ⏲10am-5pm Apr–mid-Oct, Thu-Sun mid-Oct–Mar) Fastidiously detailed and highly atmospheric, this delightful collectors' museum nostalgically recreates 30 mid-20th-century shops and workshops, including a barber, butcher and cinema lobby and an easily missed schoolroom. Behind is a collection of tools, bikes and half a dozen cars, from a 1914 Baker Coupe to a 1971 Fiat 500. Even the ticket office is a marvel, dressed up like an antique grocery shop.

At 11am, 1pm and 3pm there's a chance to go inside the WWII air-defence bunker, but the audio presentation of wartime reminiscences is all in Danish. Thorsvang is 800m west of the bus station, just off Rte 59.

Møns Museum MUSEUM

(Map p132; www.moensmuseum.dk; Storegade 75; adult/child 40kr/free; ⏲10am-4pm Tue-Sun Apr-Oct, to 2pm off season, closed Jan & Feb) Put on the headphones and let the audio guide (English, German or Danish) weave themed historical tales from Stone Age life to local 'smells' that give context to the carefully chosen exhibits.

Møn

Top Sights

1	Fanefjord Kirke	A4
2	Keldby Kirke	C2
3	Klekkende Høj	A3
4	Thorsvang	B3

Sights

5	Elmelunde Kirke	C2
	GeoCenter Møns Klint	(see 7)
6	Liselund	D2
7	Møns Klint	D3
8	Museumsgården	C3

Activities, Courses & Tours

9	Bird-Watching Tower	B1
10	Møns Fyr Cliff Hike	D3

Sleeping

11	Bakkegaard Gæstgiveri	D3
12	Birkely B&B	B3
13	Hotel Stege Nor	B2
	Liselund Ny Slot	(see 6)
14	Møn Hostel & Vandrehjem	D3
15	Møns Klint Resort	D3
	Pension Elmehøj	(see 5)

Eating

	Liselund Ny Slot Cafe & Restaurant	(see 6)

Each room in the fine 1813 building has comfy chairs to relax in while you soak it all in, watched by the odd stuffed bird or animal peeping from between exhibits.

Stege Kirke CHURCH

(Map p132; Provstestræde; ⏲9am-5pm) Stege's central feature, this 13th-century brick church is most notable for endearingly naive aspects of the 14th- and 15th-century frescoes in red and black paint (less extensive than the equivalents at Fanefjord (p137) and Elmelunde (p135). Some look like they were painted by a demented nine-year-old: there are monkey-like faces sprouting from branches, a hunter chasing unidentifiable animals and a sorrowful man covered in big blobs (measles?).

The murals had been painted over until rediscovered in 1892, though a 1998 retouch makes them look almost modern. A 20kr booklet in English explains many other interior features, including the splendidly carved 1630 pulpit. Growing in **Middelalder Have**, the churchyard's small orchard garden, is a fascinating labelled selection of medieval herb and food plants.

Liza's Gallery GALLERY

(Map p132; www.lizasgallery.com; Farverstræde 6; ⏲10am-6pm Jul & Aug, 10am-6pm Wed-Sat, to 4pm Sun Sep-Jun) FREE Liza Krügermeier's bright, striking art, along with works in similar styles by other artists, is displayed in one of central Stege's most beautiful half-timbered buildings, tucked behind the church.

Sleeping

In and around Stege you'll find a handful of B&Bs, two mini-hotels, a camping ground and a golf hotel. The nearest thing to a hostel is **Elmehøj** (Map p130; ☎55 81 35 35; www.elmehoj.dk; Kirkebakken 39; s/d/tr/q without bathroom 350/425/575/690kr; ⏲closed Nov-Mar; P@; 667) in Elmelunde.

Birkely B&B B&B €

(Map p130; ☎93 84 26 10; www.sleep.perhave.dk; Rødkildvej 23; s/d 375/525kr) Hospitable host Per Have's retirement project, this two-room B&B has hotel-quality beds, covered garage space for bicycles and a lovely orchard garden to admire from the verandah breakfast room (breakfast 60kr). The shared bathroom is top-notch, and there's a small room with table, fridge and small kettle but no real kitchen.

Stege

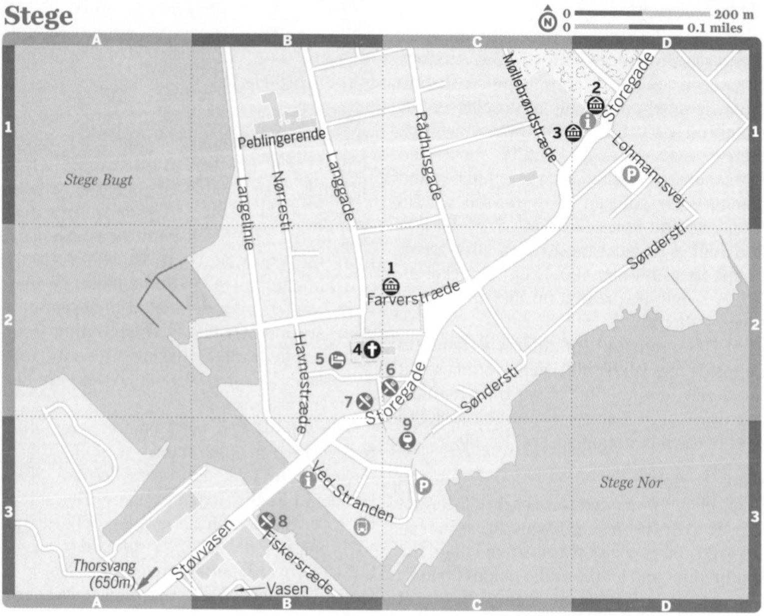

Stege

Sights

1 Liza's Gallery C2
2 Mølleporten D1
3 Møns Museum D1
4 Stege Kirke B2

Sleeping

5 Motel Stege B2

Eating

6 Cafe V'sit C2
7 David's B2
8 Hoffmanns B3

Drinking & Nightlife

9 Det Gamle Bryghus C3

It's Stege's last house as you head towards Bissinge, around 1km southwest of town on the right-hand side of the road.

★Hotel Stege Nor BOUTIQUE HOTEL €€
(Map p130; ☎40 30 45 75; www.hotelstegenor.dk; Klintevej 24; s/d/q from 550/600/1000kr; P 📶; 🚌667) Converted with incredible vision from an 1824 shingle-fronted mill, Stege Nor has enviable views across fields and the marshy Stege Inlet from the orchid-dotted breakfast room, wide front terrace and in-demand rooms 11 and 12 (double 750kr). Decorated with unfussy elegance, rooms are all en suite with excellent beds, and some furniture is antique. It's 1km east of town.

Free kayak rental for guests. Breakfast costs 55kr.

Motel Stege MOTEL €€
(Map p132; ☎55 81 35 35; www.motel-stege.dk; Provstestræde 4; s/d/tr/q 600/750/900/1150kr; P 📶) Motel Stege offers 12 simple yet smart rooms, tucked away on a quiet lane directly behind the church (p131). Leading off the homely communal kitchen-dining area, the six rooms in the main building sleep up to four people, with extra beds on a mezzanine level accessible by a disconcertingly steep ladder. Rooms in the annexe have their own kitchenette.

There's no reception: contact the obliging owners to pre-arrange key collection through a safety deposit box facing the little lawn in the rear yard.

Eating & Drinking

Cafe V'sit INTERNATIONAL €
(Map p132; www.facebook.com/cafevsit; Storgade 17A; mains 75kr, brunch/tapas 145/155kr, coffee 25-40kr; ⏰6am-8pm Mon-Fri, 9.30am-8pm Sat & Sun Jun-Sep, 6am-3pm Mon-Sat Oct-May; 📶) 🍃 This super-friendly cafe is excellent for coffee,

and sublime for organic, pasta-based salads and giant, light bagels buttered with avocado paste and stuffed with assorted fillings. There's a short breakfast menu with fresh rolls, a weekend brunch and a 99kr packed lunch aimed at hikers and cyclists.

Hoffmanns
SEAFOOD €€

(Map p132; ☑ 27 50 70 70; www.facebook.com/ Hoffmannsspisehus; Støvvasen 1; lunch mains 95-135kr, dinner mains 135-245kr; ☺ 11am-4pm & 5.30-10pm) Stark white interiors set off by the black uniforms of the (not particularly efficient) staff create a classy yet low-key feel. The place comes into its own when you're sitting right at the waterside dining on beautifully prepared fresh fish with views across to Stege.

David's
INTERNATIONAL €€

(Map p132; www.davids.nu; Storegade 11A; dishes 96-165kr, brunch 140kr; ☺ 10am-5pm Mon-Fri, to 4pm Sat & Sun; 🐾) David's open kitchen prepares contemporary cafe fare served in an airy modern environment or small garden area behind. Tuck into the celebrated 'tapas' platter or opt for gems like the roll of smoked salmon and apples with trout mousse and green salad. There are also excellent salads, house-made cakes and a range of gourmet sandwiches.

Det Gamle Bryghus
BAR

(Map p132; ☑ 30 74 04 00; http://detgamlebryghus. dk; Luffes Gård, Søndersti 3; small/medium/large beer 40/60/80kr, lunch 99-199kr, dinner mains 219-259kr; ☺ noon-4pm & 5.30-8pm) Tucked into the pretty, cobbled Luffes Gård yard, this is the main outlet shop and unofficial bar-restaurant of the popular Møn Brewery, which was originally situated right here. Beers to take away/drink in cost 25/40kr, or order the four-glass taster (65kr). Particularly interesting is the lemony unfiltered Hvede brew.

There's an extensive lunch menu with luxury open sandwiches and upmarket burgers. Dinners are more refined but with usually just one meat and one fish main-course option, plus steak at extra cost.

ℹ️ Information

The main **tourist office** (Map p132; ☑ 55 86 04 00; Storegade 75; ☺ 10am-4pm Tue-Sun Apr-Oct, to 2pm low season, closed Jan & Feb) is within the museum (p131). There's also a mini-office beside the bus station within the espresso bar **Coffee Connection** (Map p132; www.visitmoen.dk; Storegade 2; coffee from 18kr; ☺ 9am-5pm).

ℹ️ Getting There & Away

Buses depart from a **bus station** (Map p132; Storegade 2) on Ved Stranden. For Vordingborg use bus 660R. For Elmelunde, Keldby and Magleby take bus 667 to Klintholm Havn, where you can switch to the 678 for Møns Klint.

Fri BikeShop (☑ 55 81 42 49; www.fribikeshop. dk/cykler-stege; Storegade 91; per day 70kr; ☺ 7.30am-5pm Mon-Fri, 9am-1pm Sat) rents bicycles. It's east of the centre, just beyond the Fakta supermarket.

Nyord
POP 40

From northern Møn's **Ulvshale Peninsula** a single-lane bridge crosses to the marshy 5 sq km island of Nyord, all a-twitter with birdlife that you can observe from a free roadside **birdwatching tower** (Map p130; Ulvshalevej, Nyord; ☺ dawn-dusk) FREE. The sole village, also called Nyord, sports an octagonal chapel and a cluster of 19th-century tiled and thatched cottages but it's so tiny that you can walk across it in five minutes. Or jump in a kayak from **NyordKajak** (http://nyordkajak.nu) and see it from the water. A handful of other low-key businesses open mostly at weekends for day-trippers. Along with other parts of Møn, Nyord is certified as a 'Dark Sky' community (www.darksky-moen.dk) – one of Denmark's top stargazing spots.

🛌 Sleeping

Bent's Gæstehus
RENTAL HOUSE €

(☑ 28 18 50 76; yrsa.bent@gmail.com; Nordgade 9, Nyord; s/d 500/600kr; ☺ year-round) In a quaint little thatched mini-cottage, this homely hideaway has two single beds and a sitting area tucked into the eaves above a fully equipped kitchen. Bent's collection of Ugandan carved heads downstairs contrasts with the gnome in the upper window.

On warm days, unwind with a book on lawn seats under the apple tree.

Nyord B&B
GUESTHOUSE €

(☑ 55 86 32 57; www.nyord-bb.dk; Aksvej 8, Nyord; s with bathroom 450kr, d 600-775kr, s/d without bathroom 400/500kr; ☺ Apr-Sep; 🐾) With three attractive little outside seating areas, an octagonal summerhouse and a fair-sized shared kitchen, this eight-room B&B offers a couple of ensuite options with tiled floors. There are also airy upper rooms in the eaves (watch your head!) with Indian fabrics and smooth timber floors. Cash payments only. Breakfast costs 75kr.

✕ Eating & Drinking

Lollesgaard   DANISH €€
(☑31 39 99 82; www.lolles.dk; Hyldevej 1, Nyord;
sandwiches/lunch plate from 45/135kr, dinner mains
99-219kr; ☺11am-8pm Jun-Aug, to 4pm Sun-Thu, to
8pm Fri & Sat May, Sep & Oct; ℗) Behind a delightful shady triangle of white garden tables,
Lollesgaard is a very traditional village-style
cottage eatery full of blue-glaze ceramics.
Before 4pm there's a lunchtime choice of
smørrebrød, sandwiches and *frokostplatte*
(cheese, herring, salad and meats). From
5pm, dinner mains are mostly meat-based,
plus a fish of the day. Starters include a vegetarian tart.

Noorbo Handelen   CAFE
(www.noorbohandelen.dk; Nyord Bygade 1, Nyord;
coffee 20-35kr, beer/cocktails 35/65kr, sandwich/
lunch plate 85/125kr; ☺11am-5pm Fri & Sat, to 4pm
Sun) Part gallery, part booze shop with a remarkable plethora of dangling *snaps* bottles,
this converted old barn lies just metres from
the village car park and is a great place to
sample local beers and flavoured shots, or to
simply sit and idle over a lazy lunch. Outdoor
and indoor seating.

ℹ Getting There & Away

Nyord is 12km from Stege. There's no public
transport. Cars should be left at the **car park**
(Nyordvej, Nyord) 100m north of the village
centre.

Central Møn

Between Stege and Møns Klint, don't miss
quick stops at the fresco-rich medieval
churches in Keldby and Elmelunde. With
more time, follow the back lanes to **Muse-
umsgården** (Map p130; www.museumsgaarden.
dk; Skullebjergvej 15, Keldbylille; adult/child 40kr/
free; ☺10am-4pm Tue-Sun mid-May–early Sep; ℗),
one of Denmark's best-preserved thatched
farmstead-museums.

Møns Klint

In comparison with so much of Denmark's
often flat landscape, the woodland-topped
white cliffs of Møns Klint feel like breathtaking geographical wonders. They are so
popular that on midsummer weekends, it's
a wonder that the whole island doesn't tilt
eastwards with the sheer weight of visitors.
Fortunately the glorious rolling patchwork of
surrounding fields and forests is big enough

BUTTERFLIES & WILD ORCHIDS

Strewn throughout **Klinteskoven**, the
woods behind **Møns Klint**, are 18 species of wild orchids, the greatest variety
anywhere in Denmark. Thriving on the
soil's high chalk content, many are rare
and all are protected. Particularly beautiful is pyramidal *Anacamptis pyramidalis*
with mounded, multiblossomed pink
heads. Dark red helleborine (*Epipactis
atrorubens*) is also notable, with oval
leaves, tall stems and numerous crimson
flowers. Peak blooming season is late
May and early June. A good place to seek
them out is just west of Busene village
at **Høvblege** (Map p130; Busene), a
shrubby area that's also home to the last
known population of *Sortplettet Blåfugl*
(Large Blue) butterflies in Denmark.

---

to absorb countless hikers, cyclists and horse
riders. Meanwhile, kayakers paddle past the
cliff bases and paragliders throw themselves
off the top.

◉ Sights & Activities

The main sights are the cliffs themselves.
Most people visit via Store Klint (parking
35kr), where there's an impressive Geo-
Center, a museum that interprets the geological process for folks of all ages. Behind
that a long stairway leads to the foot of the
cliffs. You can also walk here in an hour from
Møns Fyr or visit by **tour boat** (☑21 40 41
81; www.sejlkutteren-discovery.dk; Klintholm Havn;
adult/child 175/90kr; ☺Apr-Oct; ☎667) from
Klintholm Havn, where there are also **sandy
beaches** (Thyravej, Klintholm Havn).

GeoCenter Møns Klint   MUSEUM
(Map p130; www.moensklint.dk; Stengårdsvej
8, Borre; adult/child 120/80kr; ☺10am-6pm
late Jun-early Aug, shorter hours rest of year; ☛)
The chalk cliffs at Møns Klint were created
around 5000 years ago when calcareous deposits from aeons worth of seashells were
lifted from the ocean floor. On the clifftop
at Store Klint, the high-tech GeoCenter
helps make sense of the geological processes
through engrossingly imaginative displays
(trilingual Danish/German/English), bringing other-worldly cretaceous sea creatures to
life for kids, who'll love the inventive hands-
on nature centre and artificial 'ice cave'.

Liselund

GARDENS

(Map p130; ☏ 55 81 21 78; http://en.natmus.dk/museums/liselund; Langebjergvej 4) FREE The enchanting gardens of Liselund were laid out in 1792 by Antoine de la Calmette as the ultimate romantic gift for his wife – the name means 'Lise's Grove'. Paths wind their way between rolling lawns, under chestnut and oak trees, and idyllic lakes. A wooden 'Kissing Bridge' crosses a trickling stream in the woodland and trails continue to a viewpoint on the sea cliffs. Unusual buildings overlooking the estate lawns include a chateau hotel (p136) and thatched manor house.

The latter, with its unusual spire, is open for tours (50kr) at 10.30am, 11am, 1.30pm and 2pm (Wednesday to Sunday, May to September only).

Møns Fyr Cliff Hike

WALKING

(Map p130; Fyrvej, Hampeland; parking free) A fine 75-minute round-trip hike along the base and tops of Møns Klint's southerly cliffs starts from the car park in front of Møns Fyr, an 1845 lighthouse at the southeastern corner of the island.

Walk around three minutes north from Møns Fyr, take the descending footpath then follow the rocky beach for nearly half an hour – but only when the tide is going out. When you reach the next stairway, climb it and return along the clifftop path. Or, with an extra 45 minutes or so, you could extend the loop to Store Klint and the GeoCenter.

🛏 Sleeping & Eating

The patchwork fields and forests behind the cliffs are part of the **Klintholm Estate** (www.klintholm.dk), with a large, well-developed **camping ground** (Camping Møns Klint; Map p130; ☏ 55 81 20 25; www.moensklintresort.dk; Klintevej 544, Børre; adult/child 104/74kr plus per tent 20-60kr, per caravan 30-80kr, power hook-up 40kr; ☺ early Apr-Oct; @ 🛜 🖳; 🚌 678) and a series of **rental cottages** (www.moensklintresort.dk). There's a **hostel** (Map p130; ☏ 20 81 60 30; https://moenhostel.dk; Klintholm Havnevej 17A, Magleby; dm/s/d/q from 225/350/395/560kr; ☺ mid-Apr–mid-Sep while sunny Easter, reception 4-6pm, to 7pm Jul; P 🛜; 🚌 667) in Magleby, and the little 19th-century castle (p136) at Liselund operates as a comfortable mini-hotel.

A cafe serving coffee, cakes and fast food sprawls out onto the wide open terrace behind the GeoCenter. Otherwise, the nearest restaurant selection is around the port at Klintholm Havn, where there are two fish restaurants, an **Italian restaurant** (☏ 55 85 51 81; www.restaurantportofino.dk; Thyravej 4A, Klintholm Havn; pizza 65-99kr, pasta 65-118kr, mains 138-188kr; ☺ 5-8.30pm Wed-Fri, 2-8.30pm Sat & Sun May-Sep, 5-8.30pm Thu-Sun Oct-Apr; 🚌 667, 678), a snack bar and a **supermarket** (Thyravej 6, Klintholm Havn; ☺ 8am-6pm). Castle-hotel **Liselund Ny Slot** (Map p130; ☏ 55 81 20 81; www.liselundslot.dk; Langebjergvej 6; coffee/cake 40kr, lunch sandwich 169kr, 2-/3-course dinner 350/450kr; ☺ 1-5pm & 7-9pm late Jun-early Aug, shorter hours rest of year) has an upmarket dinner-restaurant (booking essential) but also opens as a cafe in the afternoon.

Bakkegaard Gæstgiveri

GUESTHOUSE €

(Map p130; ☏ 55 81 93 01; www.bakkegaarden64.dk; Busenevej 64, Busene; s/d without bathroom from 480/690kr; ☺ check-in 3-5pm or by arrangement; P @; 🚌 678) In a tiny rural hamlet around 3km west of GeoCenter Møns Klint, this large, part-thatched guesthouse sits on a grassy rise with marvellous views down across a wide fieldscape towards the sea. Rooms are decorated with paintings and have

---

THE ELMELUNDE FRESCOES

Memorably naive murals turn the medieval vaulted ceilings of several Møn churches into veritable art galleries, notably at **Keldby** (Map p130; Rte 287; ☺ 8am-4.45pm), **Fanefjord** (p137) and cosier **Elmelunde** (Map p130; www.keldbyelmelundekirke.dk; Kirkebakken 41; ☺ 8am-4.45pm Apr-Sep, to 3.45pm Oct-Mar; 🚌 667) for which the genre is now named. With cartoon-like clarity these frescoes presented illiterate peasants with Bible stories, from light-hearted frolics in the Garden of Eden to depictions of grotesque demons and the yawning mouth of hell. Calm emotionless faces are rendered in distinctive warm earth tones, originally painted with watercolours on new, still-wet plaster. Among the best-preserved in Denmark, the murals' survival was a lucky fluke. Lutheran ministers thought the frescoes too Catholic and whitewashed over them in the 17th century. Ironically, this preserved the medieval artwork from soiling and fading. Yet thanks to a protective layer of dust that separated the frescoes from the whitewash, the latter could be successfully removed again in the 20th century.

sinks, but bathrooms are shared and there's an extra fee for sheets (60kr) and breakfast (free coffee).

It's run by a couple of local artists who organise occasional art classes. The in-house cafe-restaurant serves a mostly organic dinner using local produce (pre-booking required). From the 678-route bus stop Stengårdsvej, walk around 700m northwest along a pretty country lane.

★ **Liselund Ny Slot**   HOTEL €€
(Map p130; ☑ 55 81 20 81; www.liselundslot. dk; Langebjergvej 6; s/d/tr/ste incl breakfast 800/1200/1600/1600kr; P 🖥 ; 🚌 678) For sheer romance, the idea of slumbering in a 19th-century chateau is hard to beat, and waking up to glimpses of Liselund's (p135) majestic park is a delight. But beyond the elegant restaurant (p135), don't expect too much indulgence. The 17 rooms are pleasant but relatively simple, with wooden floor-boards, inserted toilet-shower booths and neither kettle nor fridge.

Small but unique room 226 is tucked into the spired tower. Half-timbered rooms 227 and 228 are contrastingly bright and spacious. Communal delights include a 'secret' library/sitting room, enchanting lawn seating and a panel-walled lounge area attached to the restaurant.

ℹ Getting There & Away

Bus 667 from Stege (departing hourly between 8.37am and 4.37pm) runs via Keldby and Elmelunde, stops at Magleby (22 minutes) then swings south to Klintholm Havn (30 minutes total). From there you can take boat rides (p134) to see the cliffs from the sea, or switch to the 678 bus, departing almost as soon as the 667 arrives. The 678 takes 12 minutes to the GeoCenter (p134; last return 5.56pm), 20 minutes to the camping ground (p135) and 25 minutes to Liselund (p135) (last return 5.32pm).

ℹ Getting Around

You can hire bicycles from the Min Købmand (p135) supermarket in Klintholm Havn (70kr per day). Guests can also get them from the hostel (p135) in Magleby (70kr per day) and from the camping ground (p135; 100kr per day).

A novel way to experience the white cliffs of Møns Klint is on a pre-booked two-hour boat trip (p134) from Klintholm Havn. There are departures two to six times daily between April and October, most regularly at 2pm and 4pm. Bookings are usually essential, and payment is cash only. Full times listed on the website.

Western Møn

You'll see more pheasants than people on the rolling country lanes at the western end of Møn. Public transport isn't conducive to exploring the area, but with a vehicle it's easy to see the two little-visited main sights in a couple of hours while in transit between Stege and Falster via the **Stubbekøbing–Bogø** (☑ 30 53 24 28; www.bogoe-stubbekoebing. dk; Havnsgade; one way adult/child 25/15kr, car/motorbike/bicycle 65/25/20kr; ☺ May-Sep) car ferry. For fans of half-forgotten megalithic *jættestuer* (passage-graves) and long-barrows dating from before 1800BC, there is plenty more to explore.

WORTH A TRIP

ART AT FUGLSANG KUNSTMUSEUM

This beautifully arranged, purpose-built **gallery** (www.fuglsangkunstmuseum.dk; Nystedvej 71; adult/under 26yr 75kr/free; ☺ 11am-5pm Jul & Aug, closed Mon May & Jun, 11am-4pm Wed-Sun Sep-Apr; 🚌) is set on a rural agricultural estate and culminates in a trio of seats surveying a sheep-nibbled bucolic scene that echoes some of the landscape paintings displayed. The collection, originally started in 1887 by brewer Carl Jacobsen, is an impressively comprehensive walk-through of Danish art's development from the 1830s to today.

Highlights are mostly early 20th century works, including Jais Nielsen's striking futurist painting *Afgang!* (1918) and Ejnar Nielsen's 1930 mourning scene that appears to insert Soviet–realist-style figures into a church-like iconographic setting. You'll also find changing temporary exhibitions, a cafe and a small, savvy gift shop. The estate's moated 19th-century mansion offers four B&B rooms (http://fuglsangherregaard.dk).

The site is just off the Nykøbing–Nysted road (Rte 297). Take bus route 730 (24kr, 15 minutes from Nykøbing F station) to Fuglsang (Nystedvej) then walk 400m.

⊙ Sights

★**Klekkende Høj** ARCHAEOLOGICAL SITE
(Map p130; Klekkendevej, Røddinge; ⊘24hr)
Viewed from the car park, this neolithic tumulus looks little more than a grassy knoll on a contoured field. But walk 300m through the cornfield and you'll find that there's a double-holed entry into two passageways. They're barely 1m high but if you can overcome claustrophobia and crawl through the northern one, you'll be rewarded with a thrilling sight: faintly lit behind a glass screen within is a burial chamber complete with grave-goods and several skulls dating back 5000-plus years.

★**Fanefjord Kirke** CHURCH
(Map p130; Fanefjordvej; ⊘8am-6pm) In a rural setting overlooking a pretty inlet, this splendid whitewashed church dates from around 1250, but is most famous for the remarkable frescoes on interior ceiling vaults that were added around 1500. Painted by the 'Elmelunde master', they form a cartoon-like 'paupers' Bible' that you can partially decipher with the help of a laminated guide-sheet, available in English.

Unique images include a gruesome image of Judas with two devils pulling out his soul; Mary on doomsday, tipping the judgment scales in humanity's favour; and a gleeful horny-kneed demon listening to two women gossiping. Views from outside might appeal to watercolourists.

FALSTER & LOLLAND

POP 102,700

Clinging to each other through a series of bridges, Lolland and Falster are mostly peaceful, green patchworks of woodlands and gently undulating farmland. Falster's main draw is the lovely, pristine beach (p139) that traces the island's southeastern coast down to Gedser, a port that competes with Rødby in southwest Lolland as Denmark's main ferry departure point to Germany.

Nykøbing F

POP 16,620

Although Nykøbing's 'F' stands for Falster, this regional hub town actually straddles the Falster–Lolland divide. Falster-side central Nykøbing has a forgettable waterfront dominated by a sugar refinery that sweetens the air when becoming briefly active each

October. Amid the predominantly newer buildings are a handful of medieval houses, notably on very pretty cottage-lined **Baste-brostræde**, which leads up from the main car park to commercial street Langgade with its lovely old pipe shop, museum and intriguing Rolink barbershop. Langgade's northern extension, Slotsgade, is good for drinking and dining. However, the town's main attractions, Middelaldercentret and Fuglsang Kunstmuseum, are across the sound on the more rural Lolland side.

⊙ Sights

★**Middelaldercentret** AMUSEMENT PARK
(Medieval Centre; www.middelaldercentret.dk; Ved Hamborgskoven 2, Sundby L; adult/child/family 130/85/400kr; ⊘10am-5pm Jul–mid-Aug, to 4pm May, Jun & mid-Aug–Sep, closed Mon May & Sep; ⊕; 🚌702) Time-travel to the days of damsels and knights at this recreated early-15th-century medieval village populated by numerous costumed craftspeople at work. There's a daily roster of demonstrations, typically archery, a 1.30pm jousting tournament and the firing at noon of a brutal-looking *trebuchet* (siege engine). The most picturesque spot is an old merchant's house with its own harbour and boats. Many hands-on play experiences add fun for kids, and the Gæstgiveri (p138) allows you to feast on food from the same era.

The centre is across the bridge on Lolland. Bus 702 from Brovejen/Nykøbing F train station (24kr, 18 minutes) runs roughly half-hourly on weekdays and hourly on weekends. From Hotel Liselund (p138) you can walk to the museum centre along a very pretty waterside path in around 20 minutes (1.2km).

Vandtårnet GALLERY
(http://vandtaarnet.multicentersyd.dk; Hollandsgård 20; 10kr; ⊘10am-4pm Mon-Fri) Nykøbing's unexotic skyline icon is a century-old water tower now containing a **cafe** (coffee 15-30kr, sandwiches 50kr; ⊘10am-4pm Mon-Fri), studio spaces for young artists and galleries on four higher levels. However, the greatest incentive to climb the 151 steps is for the 360-degree views from the uppermost windows.

Falsters Minder MUSEUM
(http://aabne-samlinger.dk/falsters-minder/falsters-minder-en; Færgestræde 1A; 50kr; ⊘10am-5pm Mon-Fri, to 4pm Sat mid-Jun–Aug, 10am-4pm Tue-Fri, 10am-2pm Sat Sep–mid-Jun) Above Czarens Hus (p138), but entered from the tourist office, this nicely presented local-history museum

occupies one of Nykøbing F's oldest houses. It displays costumes, toys, glass, ceramics and reconstructed 19th- and early-20th-century rooms and shops – look for the elegant, Pompeiian-themed goldsmith shop. Labelling is in Danish.

🛏 Sleeping

Hotel Liselund is across the sound within walking distance of the Middelaldercentret (p137), but most other accommodation is on the Falster side with both a **camping ground** (☑ 54 85 45 45; www.fc-camp.dk; Østre Alle 112; sites per adult/child 80/40kr, small/large huts 300/440kr; ☺ Easter-Sep; 🅿 🛜) and likeable **Danhostel** (☑ 54 85 66 99; www.danhostel. dk/nykoebingfalster; Østre Alle 110; dm/s/d/tr/q 300/420/580/660/768kr; ☺ reception 4-6pm; 🅿 🛜; 🚌 742) 1km east of the train station near the zoo (bus 742).

Hotel Liselund   HOTEL **€**
(☑ 54 85 15 66; www.hotelliselund.dk; Lundevej 22, Sundby; s/d May-Sep 560/710kr, Oct-Apr 460/610kr; ☺ 🛜) This well-maintained low-rise hotel has a soothingly peaceful vibe and is just moments from an idyllic waterfront pathway that leads in under 20 minutes to the Middelaldercentret (p137). The 24 rooms are compact but squeeze in a desk and small table behind a big picture window; all but four (rooms 28 to 31) look out onto a lovely central tree-shaded lawn.

Bold art and big mirrors make rooms feel bigger, and the verandah-corridor has appeal, but no kettle, fridge or extras are provided. Bike rental available. Breakfast 85kr.

Avant Garden   B&B **€**
(☑ 20 10 40 30; www.avant-garden.dk; Nørre Blvd 72; s/tw incl breakfast 495/695kr; 🛜) Characterful Avant Garden is a 1940s home filled to the brim with the artwork and collections of gregarious Patricia Satchwell, the spiritually minded Irish owner. The three lower-ground-floor guest rooms are small and somewhat dark but have a separate entrance and shared lounge, toilet and excellent walk-in shower. In good weather, breakfast is taken on the garden terrace.

🍴 Eating

The majority of places to eat are on or close to Slotsgade, including gourmet-inclined **Vinkælderen** (☑ 54 85 09 10; www.restaurant vinkaelderen.dk; Slotsgade 22; mains 215-260kr, 2-/3-/6-course dinner 275/365/495kr; ☺ 5.30-9pm

Tue-Sat) and the imaginative yet affordable Indian restaurant **Dhaba** (www.dhaba.dk; Slotsgade 36; mains 69-129kr, multidish feast 199kr; ☺ noon-10pm Mon-Fri, to 11pm Sat & Sun).

Flamez   DANISH **€€**
(www.flamez.dk; Torvet 7; lunch mains 119-210kr, dinner mains 150-265kr, 2-/3-course menu 299/365kr; ☺ noon-10pm Mon-Sat, bar to 2am Fri & Sat) Tuck into steaming bowls of mussels or deliciously generous smørrebrød lunches on Flamez' sunny floral terrace, then return to sip late-night weekend cocktails. Or dine on plaice, roast capon or Hereford beef with onion marmalade in the stylish semi-underground main dining space with its filament-globe lamps.

Vegetarian options are available on request; desserts include elderflower mousse. Leffe and Grimbergen beers are on tap.

Czarens Hus   DANISH **€€**
(☑ 41 90 43 00; www.czarenshus.dk; Langgade 2; lunch mains 138-198kr, 2-/3-/4-course dinner 269/329/379kr; ☺ noon-9pm Wed-Sat, 10am-3pm Sun) Decked with engraved portraiture, historic fittings and fireplaces, this superb old house is supposedly where Russian tsar Peter the Great dined in 1716 and is probably Denmark's longest-running restaurant. Dinner menus change seasonally but you might find scallops with grilled asparagus followed by gooseberry halibut on grilled pak choi and a dessert of baked rhubarb.

Gæstgiveri Den Gyldne Svane   MEDIEVAL **€€**
(☑ 53 81 65 55; www.dengyldnesvane.dk; Middelaldercentret; adult/child 155/70kr; ☺ 12.30-3pm May-Sep, closed Mon May & Sep) Once your eyes and ears have experienced the 15th century at the Middelaldercentret (p137), give your taste buds their turn at this attached candle-lit tavern-restaurant where you sit at wooden benches and dine on authentic period foods using wooden utensils. It's wise to book a place in advance.

ℹ Information

The **tourist office** (☑ 51 21 25 08; www.visit lolland-falster.com; Færgestræde 1A; ☺ 10am-4pm Mon-Fri, to 2pm Sat, 1hr later summer; 🛜) doubles as ticket office for the Falsters Minder (p137) museum. Free wi-fi.

Danske Bank (☑ 45 12 53 00; https:// danskebank.dk; Langgade 13; ☺ 10am-4pm Mon, Tue, Wed & Fri, to 5pm Thu) changes foreign currencies with buy-sell split around 5%, 40kr commission.

ℹ Getting There & Away

Trains run at least hourly to Maribo (60kr, 23 minutes) and to Vordingborg (60kr, 28 minutes), where you'd change for Møn. Buses 741 or 742 to Marielyst (24kr, 22 minutes) leave approximately hourly from the Brovejen stop (p137), near the train station's west exit.

Marielyst

POP 725

Marielyst is one of Denmark's prime beach-vacation areas, yet visiting outside the busy midsummer holiday weeks you'd never know it. Standing on the glorious multi-kilometre strip of white sand, all that's visible is apparently unspoiled coastline, separated from any development by a wide reed-grass dune-sward and backed by what appears to be an unbroken barrier of forest. Behind that lurk the town's 6000-plus well-spaced holiday homes stretching all the way to Gedser. But even in summer, the beach is long enough that you should be able to find a relatively private patch of your own.

◎ Sights & Activities

The town centre is a partly pedestrianised strip of bars, pizza places and ice-cream kiosks running west, ie perpendicularly back from the main beach access point. At the big roundabout where traffic from Nykøbing arrives is **Strandpark**, a large 'Welcome' complex with bowling centre, volleyball, fitness and wellness facilities. A couple of kilometres south of Strandpark are the golf and 'adventure' golf courses. South then west from there is the main camping ground and waterpark (3km) then 600m further west, a centre for paintball and **go-karting** (www.gokart.dk). Some of the quietest beaches are several kilometres south.

★**Marielyst Strand**   BEACH
Stretching around 14km along Falster's southeast coast, this paradise strip of dazzling white sand seems to be backed by nothing more than forest and a wide dune area topped by reed-grasses. In fact, amid the trees are thousands of holiday homes, but tight building regulations keep them out of sight and well-spaced so that even in summer, despite considerable crowds, you should be able to find a patch of sand for yourself.

Surfcenter Falster   KITESURFING
(☑23 60 30 26; www.surfcenterfalster.dk; Marielyst Strandvej 30) Timo Sander's wind- and kite-

surfing school is based in a small shop-shack beside Dr Emil's Nightclub, around 600m back from the beach. Courses for adults and children are available in Danish, English and German. Call to make arrangements.

Golf & Fun Park   MINIGOLF
(http://golffunpark.dk; Bøtø Ringvej 2E; per round adult/child 75/55kr, driving range club/30 balls 10/20kr; ⊙mid-Apr–Oct, see online calendar; ▣742) The main attraction of this appealing funpark, 1.8km south of Strandpark, is an 18-hole 'golf' course where instead of using clubs you kick/throw a football/frisbee into target baskets at the end of each grassy fairway.

There's also a baseball cage, driving range, toddler-sized bumper balls and a contact-football game played wearing mini zorbing-style spheres that turn the wearers into walking dodgems. And there's a real golf course 600m north, too.

🛏 Sleeping & Eating

Hundreds of Marielyst houses are rented out by the week through one of three main agencies (www.dansommer.dk, www.novasol.dk and www.sologstrand.dk), all with offices in the **Strandpark Velkomstcenter** (www.dansommer.dk; Strandpark 3; per week low/high season from 1500/3500kr), where you collect keys. Changeover day is Saturday. Though the vast majority of rentals are pre-booked, drop-in bookings are possible (three-day minimum). For shorter sleeps, the tourist office (p140) has a daily updated list of available rooms (from around 800kr per double). The nearest approximation to a hostel is Bed & Beach.

Marielyst Familiecamping   CAMPGROUND €
(http://marielystfamiliecamping.dk; Godthåbs Allé, Marielyst Feriepark; site 35kr plus adult/child 75/40kr, cabin 695-835kr plus cleaning 500kr; ⊙early Apr-Sep; P ≋; ▣742) Arranged around two lakes, this sizeable camping ground lies within a large park with various attractions (water slide, climbing adventure, pool and themed islands); these had essentially been abandoned for several years but are slowly being restored by the new owners. The site is 700m south of Golf & Fun Park, 1km east of the go-kart course.

Bed & Beach   GUESTHOUSE €
(☑29 60 45 57; Holmevej 11; s/d/q 350/450/600kr) Cheaper than a hostel yet just two minutes' stroll from a gorgeous stretch of beach, relatively isolated Bed & Beach is a work in

MØN, FALSTER & LOLLAND MARIELYST

SKELBY GAMMEL PRAESTEGAARD

It's hard to imagine a more delightful B&B, especially in this modest price range, than this lovingly upgraded historic **priests' house** (☑29 60 45 57; Gammel Landevej 59, Skelby; d/tr/q 550/700/850kr; ☐740), located 10 minutes' drive from Marielyst beside the old church in tiny Skelby hamlet. Reservations are only possible through www.booking.com, and you should pre-arrange an arrival time as the charming owners don't live close.

The seven bright-white guest rooms with wood or brick floors and teak furniture are in three apartment-like arrangements, each with a shower-toilet, two with well-equipped kitchen. Each such apartment is private to a booked group, offering great value for families. The excellent breakfast (75kr) is served in a period dining room with splendid chandelier.

progress, taking a 1960s children's camp building and creating unfussy but well-appointed new budget rooms. So far eight doubles and four bunk-equipped quads are ready.

There's a lawn area but the communal lounge is not slated for completion until 2019. You must book through www.booking.com and contact the manager to arrange arrival details as there's neither sign nor reception. From the Gedser–Nykøbing road turn right at photogenic Gedesby Mølle windmill, drive about 2km and turn left, taking Holmevej to the end. The property is on your left. If you have a good map there's a short-cut walking route from Gedser.

Oldfruen B&B De Luxe   GUESTHOUSE €€

(☑54 13 13 80; www.oldfruen.dk; Marielyst Strandvej 25A; s/d/tr/q 600/800/900/1000kr; ☺cafe 10am-8pm Jun-Aug, reduced hours Sep-May) Handily central, almost opposite Hotel Nørrevang, this selection of neat, new guest rooms, tucked behind the revamped Oldfruen Cafe, represent the best-value short-stay accommodation available on Marielyst's main drag. You get an ensuite unit with kitchenette plus a trio of extra beds up ladder-stairs on a half-floor in the eaves overlooking the main sleeping space.

Hotel Nørrevang   HOTEL €€

(☑54 13 62 62; www.norrevang.dk; Marielyst Strandvej 32; s/d with breakfast from 559/845kr, cottages from 1150kr; Ⓟ🗑🏊) Seen from the roadside, Hotel Nørrevang is a photo-perfect delight of a 19th-century thatched farmstead. However, only the restaurant and rooms 52 to 56 are actually in that building, with most others in a soulless 1970s extension behind or in similarly aged cottages.

Larsen på Torvet   INTERNATIONAL €€

(Larsens Plads; ☑54 13 21 70; www.larsens-plads.dk; Marielyst Strandvej 53; pizzas 49-85kr, mains 149-169kr, brunch/dinner buffet 119/169kr; ☺10am-9pm) This large, idiosyncratic bar-restaurant in a much-extended 1919 cottage commands the top location on Marielyst's central pedestrianised area. It's packed full of model ships, dangling lanterns, gramophones and cheeky signage, while upstairs, museum-like sub-rooms create a 1940s feel. Dine on classic pub grub including pizza, fish or steak.

ℹ Information

The small, central **tourist office** (☑54 13 62 98; www.visitmarielyst.com; Marielyst Strandvej 54; ☺10am-3pm Jun & Aug, to 5pm Jul, 10am-3pm Sat & Sun Sep-May; 🤙) is on the main pedestrianised square beside the pointed tower.

ℹ Getting There & Away

Buses 741 and 742 run approximately hourly from Nykøbing F (24kr, 22 minutes). Bus 741 terminates at **Marielyst Torv bus stop** (Bøtøvej), beside the tourist office in a short block south of the town centre, and runs 24 hours on summer Saturday nights. Bus 742 continues further south.

ℹ Getting Around

Dansommer at the Strandpark Velkomstcenter (p139) rents bicycles in a wide variety of types and sizes for 60kr to 75kr per day (250kr to 300kr per week). You can arrange to have one waiting at your rental property, or collect from the tourist office. Tandems and baby carts are also available.

Maribo & Bandholm

POP 5890 & 560

Set on the shores of a large inland lake, Maribo's modest charms include its historic cathedral, thick beech woods, waterside walking paths and a few small museums. A few times weekly in summer, it's linked by a steam railway called **Museumsbanen** (☑54 78 85 45; www.museumsbanen.dk; Maribo Station; single/return adult 50/80kr, child 25/40kr;

⊙ 10.05am, 1.05pm & 3.05pm Sun or Tue &/or Thu mid-Apr–mid-Oct) to gently attractive Bandholm (8km north), a small port where you'll find a great hotel & restaurant close to the exit from Denmark's foremost safari park (the entry is via Maglemer village).

⊙ Sights & Activities

Knuthenborg Safari Park ZOO

(☑ 54 78 80 89; www.knuthenborg.dk; Knuthenborg Allé; adult/child under 11yr 220/130kr; ⊙ 10am-5pm May–mid-Sep, to 6pm Jul, to 4pm mid-Sep–early Oct; ⊕) Drive-through Knuthenborg Safari Park is northern Europe's biggest safari park and one of Denmark's top attractions. Its collection of more than 1000 wild animals includes free-roaming zebras, antelopes, giraffes, rhinoceroses, tigers, camels and other exotic creatures. The park occupies one of Denmark's largest private estates and has an arboretum, aviary and a big adventure playground for your own little monkeys. There are 23km of roads within the park.

Several areas, including the savannah, are off-limits to anyone not inside a vehicle, so coming by bicycle (or on foot) is a bad idea.

Maribo Domkirke CATHEDRAL

(Klostergade; ⊙ 9am-5pm) Set amid mature trees overlooking the lake, Maribo's large brick cathedral has an imposing west-facing nave divided in three by hefty, octagonal columns. The 1641 gilt altarpiece and 1606 pulpit contrast beautifully with the echoing whitewashed interior.

The building was originally conceived as the church of a 1416 Bridgettine monastery.

This became a Protestant convent after the 16th-century Reformation, and it was there that Countess Leonora Christina, now buried in the crypt, retired to compose her astonishing 17th-century autobiography *Jammers Minde*, having finally been released from two decades in a royal prison whose rats, fleas and randy jailer her book so vividly describes.

Frilandsmuseet Maribo MUSEUM

(http://aabne-samlinger.dk/frilandsmuseet/frilands museet; Meinckesvej 5; adult/child 50kr/free; ⊙ 10am-4pm Jul & Aug, Tue-Sun May, Jun & Sep) Frilandsmuseet is a collection of around a dozen mostly thatched buildings and a wooden post-mill, plucked from elsewhere in Denmark to form a mini-village. It's an attractive site even when closed as you can peep in between the beech hedges and mature oaks. To get there walk for about four minutes along the lakeside from the camping ground (p142).

Stiftsmuseum Maribo MUSEUM

(www.aabne-samlinger.dk; Banegårdspladsen 11; adult/child 50kr/free; ⊙ 10am-6pm Mon-Fri, to 2pm Sat) Beside Maribo's train station, this excellent little museum is most notable for its moodily lit room featuring nine 13th-century figures of the 'suffering Christ', rescued from Lolland's medieval churches.

Anemonen BOATING

(☑ 54 78 04 96; http://uk.naturparkmaribo.dk; Maribo Kirkegaard; adult/child return ticket to Borgø 80/30kr) The good ship *Anemonen* sails on Maribo's island-dotted lake in summer, starting from the jetty outside the cathedral. Trips

MØN, FALSTER & LOLLAND MARIBO & BANDHOLM

THE CLOISTERED COUNTESS

Buried in Maribo Domkirke is Countess Leonora Christina, a feisty and talented daughter of King Christian IV, remembered for her vivid autobiography *Jammers Minde*. She had been wife of the scheming Lord Corfits Ulfeld, whose numerous acts of treachery against Christian's successor Frederick III ultimately caused Denmark to incur considerable territorial losses to Sweden. Ulfeld and Leonora fled to avoid his prosecution, but Ulfeld continued to attempt a comeback by stirring up trouble against Denmark. Finally exiled in Bruges (Flanders), Leonora set off to England in an audacious attempt to reclaim debts owed by England's King Charles II to her once wealthy husband. Instead she was arrested and sent back to Denmark in 1663, where she was held as a bargaining chip to leverage Ulfeld's capture.

Despite Ulfeld's death the following year, Leonora Christina remained imprisoned in the 'Blue Tower' of Copenhagen Castle for 22 years, due largely to the vindictiveness of Frederick III's queen, Sophia Amelia (Ulfeld had once been accused – probably unfairly – of attempting to poison her). After Leonora's tardy release, she moved to Maribo, where she spent her final years editing her journals. Though not actually published for another 200 years, the collected tales of her adventures have since become regarded as a literary classic of the genre.

are typically either 50-minute loops or two hours with a stop on Borgø, an island that hides the ruins of an 11th-century fortress destroyed by a medieval peasants' uprising.

🛌 Sleeping

Close to Maribo's lake there's a busy **camping ground** (☑54 78 00 71; www.maribo-camping. dk; Bangshavevej 25; sites per adult/child 78/42kr, cabins 500-900kr; ☺Apr–mid-Oct; 🛜) 500m southwest of the Domkirke and a very functional **hostel** (☑54 78 33 14; www.maribo-vandrerhjem.dk; Søndre Blvd 82B; s/d/tr/q 350/400/500/550kr; ☺reception 4-6pm Jun-Aug or by appointment; 🅿🛜) 1.5km southeast facing the hospital. More central PilgrimsHuset is tiny but far more charming. If you're on wheels, unsophisticated but pleasantly rural good-value options include **Otel Våbensted B&B** (☑54 70 63 63; http://otelvaabensted.dk; Krårup Møllevej 6, Våbensted; s/d 415/660kr, without bathroom s/d/tr 375/575/825kr; ☺check-in 3-10pm; 🅿🛜) (5km west) and **Hotel Femern** (☑50 59 88 08; http://hotel-femern.com/en; Møllevej 3, Fuglse; d 599kr, s/d/tr/q without bathroom 349/499/649/799kr; ☺reception 4-10pm; 🅿🛜; 🖥730) (8km south). The region's most appealing accommodation is the more indulgent four-star Bandholm Hotel.

★ PilgrimsHuset
HOSTEL €

(☑30 63 66 20; www.pilgrimshus.dk; Klostergade 18; per person 200kr) This cute, historic building right by the cathedral (p141) is a very friendly mini-hostel with four small, neat, whiter-than-white rooms around a shared kitchen. The idea is to offer value accommodation to those hiking two classic long-distance pilgrims' ways that cross in Maribo: the Camino of St James and the Danish monastery route. Call ahead to make sure someone's there.

★ Bandholm Hotel
HERITAGE HOTEL €€€

(☑54 75 54 76; www.bandholmhotel.dk; Havnegade 37, Bandholm; s/d incl breakfast from 1095/1195kr; ☺reception 7am-11pm; 🅿🛜) Indulgently classy with modernised facilities, this excellent 40-room hotel is Lolland's top option. It's based around a proud 1886 whitewashed brick building, but also incorporates a courtyard annexe and two neighbouring historic cottages, and is brilliantly located across lawns from Bandholm's grain and fishing port.

Of the 15 standard (annexe) rooms, 111 to 115 are the best bet, with lovely little garden patios. Rooms in the main building (from 1800kr) come with chandeliers and free minibar. The **restaurant** (☑54 75 54 76; www.

bandholmhotel.dk; mains 165-225kr, 7-course meal incl wine 1495kr; ☺11am-5pm & 5.30-9pm Mon-Sat, to 7.30pm Sun; 🅿🛜) is inventive, and shaded tables spill out onto the grounds with sea views.

🍽 Eating & Drinking

Maribo has several restaurants, including Thai, Chinese, steakhouse and pizza options plus a pleasant bakery-cafe. Meal-sized salads are served at Café Victoria. For something more special consider pre-booking for the Bandholm Hotel's spectacular gourmet dinner (Thursday to Saturday before 7.30pm), or driving around 8km to Oreby Kro.

★ Oreby Kro
DANISH €€

(☑54 17 44 66; www.orebykro.dk; Orebygaard 2, Oreby; lunch dishes 150kr, 2-/3-course dinner 275/350kr, coffee-cake set 60kr; ☺noon-9pm Thu-Sat, to 3pm Sun, hours vary seasonally) Peacefully remote, 3km northwest of Sakskøbing, this restored 1847 estate-mill has three wooden-floored dining rooms partly adorned with 19th-century furniture and the odd mounted deer. Food is locally sourced and lovingly cooked, though choice is limited. With beautiful views across the reed-banked fjord, the cafe-style terrace is also a delight for coffee and cake or local Krenkerup beers.

Café Victoria
CAFE

(http://victoriamaribo.dk; Lollands Centret 26; beer 35-65kr, coffee 25-35kr; ☺11am-10pm Mon-Sat, noon-10pm Sun, kitchen to 9pm) With barista coffee from 25kr and four beers on tap including Belgian Grimbergen Double, this spacious, convivial modern brasserie is a delight that you'd never expect from its surroundings deep within a miserable shopping centre.

ℹ Information

Maribo's phenomenally helpful and obliging **tourist office** (☑54 78 04 96; www.visitlolland-falster.com; Banegårdspladsen 11; ☺10am-6pm Mon-Fri, to 2pm Sat) doubles as a mini-cafe and the ticket office for the Stiftsmuseum (p141).

Lollands Bank (www.lollandsbank.dk; Vestergade 3; ☺1-4pm Mon-Fri) changes money but the exchange desk only opens after 1pm.

ℹ Getting There & Away

Maribo–Nykøbing F trains (60kr, 25 minutes) run once or twice an hour until around midnight. Bicycle rental costs 90/375kr per day/week from very central **Larsson Cykler** (☑42 64 20 24; Torvet 11; standard/child/electric bicycle per day 90/60/200kr; ☺8am-5pm Mon-Thu, to 6pm Fri, 9am-1pm Sat).

Rødby

POP 2080

Not really quaint enough to linger in, Rødby's vaguely pleasant main street is 700m west of the terminal for Germany-bound ferries and 1.5km east of pleasure-park Lalandia Rødby. This child-centred **play-village** (www.lalandia.dk; Lalandia Centret 1, Rødby; ⊙most activities 8am-10pm, water park 10am-7pm, see website for opening dates; ⏏) is primarily designed as a residential family experience, but when it's not packed with live-in guests, day visitors can take advantage of the facilities, most notably a **skating rink** (adult/child 60/50kr), the soft-play area **'Monky Tonky Land'** (child 70kr) and especially the **Aquadome** (adult/child 220/170kr), a complex of indoor and outdoor pools, water slides, Jacuzzis and wave machine.

ⓘ Getting There & Away

Car ferries (www.scandlines.com) bound for Puttgarden, Germany (45 minutes) depart twice hourly. Pedestrian gantries connect boats to Rødby Færge train station, where a machine sells ferry tickets for foot passengers (adult/child 90/45kr) and cyclists. Use the underpass to find bus 720R to Maribo (24kr, 40 minutes). That runs once/twice hourly on weekends/weekdays, passing Lalandia after nine minutes.

Western Lolland

Driving to or from **Tårs-Spodsbjerg (Langeland) Ferry** (⏲70 23 15 15; www.faergen.dk; Spodsbjergvej, Tårs; adult/child/bicycle 80/40/10kr, motorbike/car incl passengers 130/265kr), consider detours to some of Lolland's great agricultural estates: taste cherry wines at **Frederiksdal** (Frederiksdalvej 30, Harpelunde; ⊙10am-4pm Jun-Aug, Fri-Sun May) **FREE**, nibble organic cheeses at Knuthenlund or visit the engrossing Reventlow museum. And don't miss the eerie Dodekalitten.

★**Dodekalitten** SCULPTURE
(www.dodekalit.dk; Glentehøjvej, Ravnsby; ⏱725, 719) Melding the ideas of contemporary installation art with those of ancient standing stones, this modern henge features six 7m-tall megaliths, each weighing more than 25 tonnes. The stone-tops are being carved into staring human faces (three had been completed at the time of research), and an underground sound system makes them hum as though they were singing to each other. The mystical vibe is compounded by a lonely set-

KRENKERUP BRYGGERI

A lordly estate southeast of Sakskøbing with a private, picture-perfect 1631 moated castle is home to celebrated local brewery **Krenkerup Bryggeri** (⏲54 70 54 85; http://krenkerupbryggeri.dk; Krenkerupvej 33, Sakskøbing; beer from 30kr, three-glass taster 60kr, sandwiches 120kr; ⊙noon-6pm Jun-Aug, to 4pm Fri Sep-May). Its German-style beers include the excellent 1367 Premium and prize-winning honeyed bock, though some other brews are far less successful. Taste eight varieties on tap at the oddly hard-to-spot Traktørstedet (beer-garden pub) on a courtyard of red half-timbered outbuildings.

Although open each summer afternoon, from September to May it's only accessible four hours a week (on Fridays).

ting with sweeping views across fields of waving wheat towards a mid-distance seascape.

From Maribo station take bus 725 to Rævegade stop in Kragenæs (48kr, 36 minutes) and walk 1km south through Klinkesov Forest. Bus 719 from Nakskov also works.

Reventlow-Museet MUSEUM
(www.museumlollandfalster.dk; Pederstrup Park, Saltov; park free, museum adult/child 50kr/free; ⊙park sunrise-sunset, museum 11am-4pm Tue-Sun Jun-Aug, Sat & Sun May & Sep) If you're driving through rural northwest Lolland, the attractive Pederstrup Park is worth a brief detour. Annually changing sculptures front a 200-year-old mansion whose heavily restored, plain facade belies an impressive interior now forming a museum explaining the life and times of CDF Reventlow, a major force in the liberation of Denmark's peasantry from essential serfdom.

Knuthenlund Organic Farm CHEESE €
(⏲54 71 13 80; http://knuthenlund.dk/en; Knuthenlundvej 7B, Stokkemarke; lunch 149kr; ⊙10am-4pm Jun-Aug, Thu-Sun Sep-May) This large, modern farm shop offers 99kr taster plates selecting four of its excellent homemade cheeses, including a brie that has won international prizes. Meanwhile, look through the big glass panels and watch sheep being milked to produce the next batch. The rural estate setting is idyllic, and there are bikes to rent (25kr) if you want to explore further.

Bornholm

Best Places to Eat

➡ Kadeau (p149)

➡ Nordbornholms Røgeri (p158)

➡ Hallegaard (p152)

➡ Kalas-Kalas (p158)

➡ Fru Petersens Café (p158)

➡ Torvehal Bornholm (p148)

Best Places to Stay

➡ Stammershalle Badehotel (p156)

➡ Nordlandet (p158)

➡ Nordly (p157)

➡ Hotel GSH (p147)

➡ Allinge Badehotel (p158)

➡ Christiansø Gæstgiveri (p159)

Why Go?

The sunniest part of Denmark, Bornholm lies way out in the Baltic Sea, 200km east of Copenhagen (and closer to Sweden and Poland than to mainland Denmark). But it's not just (relatively) sunny skies that draw the hordes each year. Mother Nature was in a particularly good mood when creating this Baltic beauty, bestowing on it rocky cliffs, leafy forests, bleach-white beaches and a pure, ethereal light that painters do their best to capture.

Humankind added the beguiling details, from medieval fortress ruins and thatched fishing villages, to the iconic *rundekirke* (round churches) and contemporary Bornholms Kunstmuseum (p156). The island's ceramic and glassware artisans are famed throughout Denmark, as are its historic smokehouses and ever-expanding league of food artisans, doing brilliant things with local harvests. It's no wonder that 600,000 people visit annually – and expect that number to increase as word continues to spread.

When to Go

➡ Bornholm blooms from June to mid-September, with attractions, tourist offices, transport and cultural events operating at full steam. Needless to say, pre-book accommodation in the summer, especially in the most crowded month, July.

➡ Long days and warmer weather during the peak months are ideal for hiking, cycling and getting wet on Bornholm's beautiful beaches.

➡ On the food front, June plays host to Denmark's most famous one-day cook-off, Sol over Gudhjem.

➡ Outside the warmer months, the island slows down, with many attractions, restaurants and accommodation options reducing their hours or closing down for the season (do your homework on what's open at www.bornholm.info).

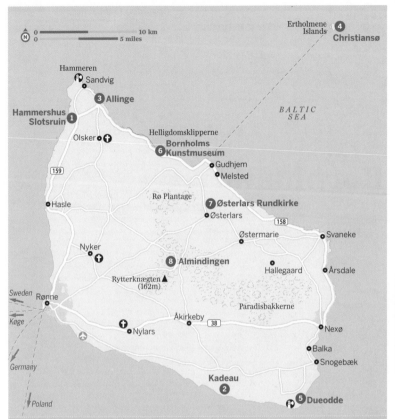

Bornholm Highlights

1 Hammershus Slotsruin (p157) Snooping around commanding clifftop ruins.

2 Kadeau (p149) Feasting on extraordinary New Nordic cuisine at the island's Michelin-recognised hotspot.

3 Smokehouses (p158) Tucking into smoked fish at a traditional *røgeri*, like Nordbornholms Røgeri in Allinge.

4 Christiansø (p159) Time-travelling to a far-flung island fortress for a taste of cosy village life.

5 Dueodde (p150) Wiggling the finest white sand between your toes on this sweeping beach.

6 Bornholms Kunstmuseum (p156) Admiring art indoors, and nature's handiwork outdoors.

7 Østerlars Rundkirke (p155) Hitting the bike trail from Gudhjem to one of the island's iconic round churches.

8 Almindingen (p149) Cycling through storybook woods, scouting for wild deer and possibly bison.

Rønne

POP 13.600

Rønne is Bornholm's largest settlement and its main transport hub with the ferry port and airport. The town has been the island's commercial centre since the Middle Ages, and while the place has expanded and taken on a more suburban look over the years, a handful of well-preserved quarters still provide pleasant strolling. Especially appealing is the old neighbourhood west of Store Torv, with its period buildings and cobblestone streets, among them Laksegade and Storegade.

Rønne

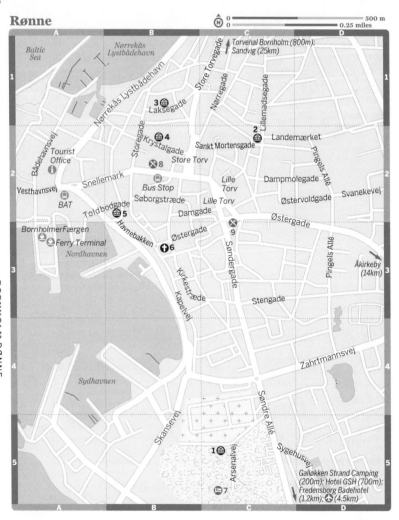

BORNHOLM RØNNE

Rønne

⊙ Sights

Mølgaard & Marcussen   GALLERY
(☎ 81 75 48 67; www.mølgaard-marcussen.dk; Raadhusstræde 1A; ⊙ 10am-4pm Mon-Fri, to 1pm Sat)
Bornholm overflows with creative types and has a long tradition of ceramics. The two friendly owners of this studio gallery and store are great proponents of the art, and their pastel-hued creations are truly covetable.

Erichsens Gård   MUSEUM
(☎ 56 95 07 35; www.bornholmsmuseum.dk; Laksegade 7; adult/child 50kr/free; ⊙ 10am-4pm Fri & Sat mid-May–mid-Oct) Pretty in pink, this

merchant's house from 1806 is a photogenic half-timbered idyll on a cobbled lane. There are short opening hours, when you can view the rooms and lovely garden.

Bornholms Forsvarsmuseum MUSEUM
(Defence Museum; ☑ 51 33 00 33; www.bornholms forsvarsmuseum.dk; Arsenalvej 8; adult/child 55/ 35kr; ☉10am-4pm Mon-Fri mid-May–late Oct) A 17th-century citadel called Kastellet houses part of the Defence Museum, south of the town centre. There are extensive displays of guns, blades, bombs and military uniforms, but the historical context they are given is somewhat scant. Some brief explanatory notes in English are available from the ticket desk. There are especially large displays on the Nazi occupation of the island and on the bombing of Rønne and Nexø by the Soviets at the end of WWII.

Bornholms Museum MUSEUM
(☑ 56 95 07 35; www.bornholmsmuseum.dk; Sankt Mortensgade 29; adult/child 70kr/free; ☉10am-5pm Jul–mid-Aug, closed Sun mid-May–Jun & mid-Aug–late Oct, shorter hours rest of year) Prehistoric finds including weapons, tools and jewellery are on show at Bornholm's museum of cultural history, which has a surprisingly large and varied collection of local exhibits, including some interesting Viking finds. A good maritime section is decked out like the interior of a ship, and there's a hotchpotch of nature displays, antique toys, Roman coins, pottery and paintings.

Hjorths Fabrik MUSEUM
(☑ 56 95 07 35; www.bornholmsmuseum.dk; Krystalgade 5; adult/child 70kr/free; ☉10am-5pm Mon-Sat mid-May–late Oct, shorter hours rest of year) This ceramics museum features a working studio, and watching the master artisans turn clay into beautifully moulded works of art is the real highlight. You'll find some fetching locally made wares for sale in the shop in front (which is free to enter).

Sankt Nicolai Kirke CHURCH
(Kirkepladsen 20) The town's elevated landmark has a distinctive witch's-hat tower. Its present form dates from 1918, though it sits on the site of a 13th-century chapel.

🛏 Sleeping

The holiday action lies outside Rønne, and many visitors stay by the beach rather than in the main town – some good options lie along Strandvej, south of town.

It's not a great idea to turn up on the island without a booking in July. Generally, though, the tourist office (p148) can advise you on accommodation options and make a call.

Danhostel Rønne HOSTEL €
(☑ 56 95 13 40; www.danhostel-roenne.dk; Arsenalvej 12; dm/s/d/q without bathroom 200/ 375/475/575kr; ☉Apr-late Oct; P ⊠ ☎) This immaculately kept 26-room hostel is a secluded building with a neatly tended garden. Expect small, tidy, if somewhat soulless dorms, all with shared bathroom; common areas are cosy. The garden is full of kid-friendly diversions, and there are cycling paths on the doorstep (and on-site bike hire). Breakfast/ linen costs 60/80kr.

Galløkken Strand Camping CAMPGROUND €
(☑ 56 95 23 20; www.gallokken.dk; Strandvejen 4; adult/child/site 79/40/35kr; ☉May-Aug; ☎) Around 2km south of the ferry dock, this well-equipped, family-orientated beachside camping ground has basic but attractive wooden cabins (from 550kr per day) and bikes for rent.

★Hotel GSH HOTEL €€
(☑ 56 95 19 13; www.greensolutionhouse.dk; Strandvejen 79; s/d incl breakfast 1100/1300kr; ☎) 🌱 The 'Green Solution House' is easily one of Denmark's most innovative places to stay, and gives detailed insight into the possible future of construction. Every aspect of sustainability has been considered, and an exhibit on the ground level explains the decisions made and materials used in the award-winning overhaul and extension of an old hotel on this site.

It has been transformed into a hotel, conference centre and quality restaurant. The rooms are simple, comfy and slightly retro – in keeping with the spirit of recycling, functional older furniture has been reupholstered and repurposed. The light-filled lobby is a treat, as is the wall of plant life.

Fredensborg Badehotel HOTEL €€
(☑ 56 90 44 44; www.bornholmhotels.dk; Strandvejen 116; s/d/f incl breakfast 1100/1350/1565kr; P ☎) Perched on a knoll overlooking wave-pounded rocks at the southern end of Rønne, the newly renovated Fredensborg has been transformed into a bathing hotel with on-trend rooms, all with sea views. There's also a fine restaurant renowned for its fish buffets. To cover the 2.5km into Rønne's centre, cycle or walk a delightful forested trail.

✕ Eating & Drinking

There's a reasonable variety of restaurants and cafes in and around the main square of Store Torv, though no standout venues. Consider a walk to the hotel restaurants on Strandvej, at GSH (p147) and Fredensborg (p147) hotels.

The closest traditional smokehouse to Rønne, **Hasle Røgeri** (☑56 96 20 02; www.hasleroegeri.dk; Søndre Bæk 20, Hasle; dishes 58-115kr; ⊙10am-9pm Jul-late Aug, to 5pm May, Jun & late Aug-Oct), is by the water in Hasle, about 11km north of town. This century-old place has iconic square chimneys, lots of outdoor seating and a super spread of smoked-fish goodness (herring, salmon, mackerel, eel, prawns) in a 149kr lunch buffet.

Self-Catering

In a former slaughterhouse, **Torvehal Bornholm** (☑31 43 72 00; www.torvehalbornholm.dk; Gartnervangen 6; mains from grill 145-190kr; ⊙10am-5pm Wed & Thu, to 8pm Fri-Sun Jun-Aug, shorter hours rest of year) is an excellent food hall where you can find the output of some of Bornholm's finest producers, nibble on snacks from a food truck, sample beer brewed on-site and dine on meat fresh off the grill. **Jensens Bageri** (☑56 91 10 67; www.jensensbageribornholm.dk; Snellemark 41; ⊙6.30am-5.30pm Mon-Fri, to 2pm Sat) is a petite central bakery and **Oste-Hjørnet** (☑56 95 05 99; Østergade 40B; lunchtime rolls 35kr; ⊙9am-5.30pm Mon-Thu, to 6pm Fri, to 1pm Sat) a superb little deli.

ℹ Information

Tourist Office (Bornholms Velkomstcenter; ☑56 95 95 00; www.bornholm.info; Nordre Kystvej 3; ⊙9am-5pm Jul–mid-Aug, to 4pm Mon-Fri rest of year, hours vary Sat) A few minutes' walk from the harbour, this large, friendly office has masses of information on all of Bornholm and Christiansø.

ℹ Getting There & Away

Bornholm can be reached by plane, ferry or a combination ticket that couples a ferry with a bus or train via Sweden.

AIR

The island's airport, **Bornholms Lufthavn** (www.bornholms-lufthavn.dk; Søndre Landevej 2, Rønne), is 5km southeast of Rønne using bus 5. **DAT** (www.dat.dk) operates several daily flights to/from Copenhagen.

COMBINATION TICKETS

By land from Copenhagen via Ystad (Sweden) plus ferry to Rønne there are three major combination tickets each taking three to four hours total:

DSB (www.dsb.dk) train (adult/pensioner/child/bicycle 262/185/130/93kr)

Bornholmerbus 866 (adult/pensioner/child 260kr/160kr/130kr)

Bus 700 (www.rute700.dk) daily from Copenhagen airport (300/225/150/80kr)

SEA

BornholmerFærgen (☑70 23 15 15; www.faergen.dk; Dampskibskajen 3, Rønne) operates ferries connecting Rønne to the following destinations:

Køge 40km south of Copenhagen (adult/car 284/1631kr, 5½ hours). Sails daily year-round, overnight eastbound. Sleeping berth 276kr extra.

Ystad, Sweden (adult/car 91/119kr, 80 minutes, two to nine daily)

Sassnitz, Germany (adult/car 238/1190kr to 1823kr, 3½ to four hours) Operates April to October, daily in July and August.

Fares quoted are standard one-way in high season, with car prices including up to five passengers. Low-season fares and online deals can be significantly reduced. Children aged 11 and under travel free. Those aged 12 to 15 pay half the adult fare.

TT-Line (www.ttline.com) has a weekly ferry service in summer connecting Świnoujście (Poland) and Rønne.

ℹ Getting Around

BICYCLE

Some 235km of bike trails crisscross Bornholm, mapped out on the free brochure *Welcome to Our Bike Island* (in Danish, English or German). Find bike-rental outlets in most major towns, including **Bornholms Cykeludlejning** (☑56 95 13 59; www.bornholms-cykeludlejning.dk; Nordre Kystvej 5; bike rental per day/week 75/450kr; ⊙9am-noon & 2-6pm Mon-Fri, 9.30am-6pm Sat & Sun Jul & Aug, shorter hours rest of year) handily close to the Rønne ferry terminal and main tourist office. Taking your bike on public buses adds 24kr to the fare.

BUS

BAT (☑56 95 21 21; www.bat.dk; Munch Petersensvej 2, Rønne) operates bus services on the island. Fares are based on a zone system, with the maximum fare being for five zones. Tickets cost 13kr per zone, and are valid for unlimited trips within one zone for 30 minutes. Another 15 minutes' validity is added for each added zone.

The multiride 'klippekort' ticket is good for 10 rides and can be used by more than one person. Day/week passes cost 150/500kr and cover all zones. Children travel for half-price. Buses operate all year, but schedules are less frequent from October to April. Most ticket types can be purchased on board (but not the week pass).

Buses 7 and 8 circumnavigate the island, stopping at all major towns and settlements. Other buses make direct runs from Rønne to Nexø, Svaneke, Gudhjem and Sandvig. There are bus stops near the cycle shop and on Snellemark, close to Store Tov.

CAR & TAXI

Close to the ferry terminal, **Europcar** (☑ 56 95 43 00; www.europcar.com; Finlandsvej 2, Rønne) rents cars from around 600kr per day. For taxis call ☑ 70 25 25 25.

Around Rønne

Buses 5 and 6 pass through Nylars and Åkirkeby between Rønne and Nexø.

★**Nylars Rundkirke**   CHURCH
(www.nylarskirke.dk; Kirkevej 10K, Nylars; ☺ 7am-6pm Apr-Sep, 8am-3.30pm Oct-Mar) Built around 1150, Nylars Rundkirke is the most well-preserved and easily accessible round church in the Rønne area. Its central pillar is adorned with wonderful 13th-century frescoes, the oldest in Bornholm. The works depict scenes from the creation myth, including Adam and Eve's expulsion from the Garden of Eden. The cylindrical nave has three storeys, the top one a watchman's gallery that served as a defence lookout in medieval times.

Inside the church, the front door is flanked by two of Bornholm's 40 Viking rune stones.

From Nylars bus stop, the church is 350m north on Kirkevej.

★**NaturBornholm**   MUSEUM
(☑ 56 94 04 00; www.naturbornholm.dk; Grønningen 30; adult/child 120/60kr; ☺ 10am-5pm Apr-Oct; 🔊) NaturBornholm offers a terrific geological and biological narrative of the island spanning back to its fledgling days as a cooling slab of magma. The museum is packed with interesting facts and impressive interactive displays, making it especially popular with families. Aptly, the centre is perched atop the ancient fault line where Bornholm's sandstone south is fused with its gneiss and granite north. The building itself was designed by Henning Larsen, whose claims to fame also include the Copenhagen Opera House.

WORTH A TRIP

GOURMET EXCURSION

Book ahead to experience one of Denmark's most exciting and innovative destination restaurants, **Kadeau** (☑ 56 97 82 50; www.kadeau.dk; Baunevej 18, Vestre Sømark; lunch 550-700kr, 5-/8-course dinner 800/1100kr; ☺ noon-4pm & 5.30pm-midnight Jul–mid-Aug, shorter hours rest of year, closed Oct–mid-Apr). The menu is a confident, creative celebration of Nordic produce and foraged ingredients, including wild herbs from the adjacent beach and woods. Lunch options are limited but inspired; the *tour de force* is dinner, where exquisite dishes celebrate Bornholm's nature and harvest and will leave you swooning.

Now with a Michelin star, the nature-surrounded restaurant is right on the beach (off Søndre Landevej), 8km southeast of Åkirkeby.

It's in Åkirkeby, 200m south of 12th-century **Aa Kirke** (www.aa-kirke.dk; Storegade 2; ☺ 8am-5pm), Bornholm's largest church.

Interior Woodlands

A fifth of Bornholm is wooded, making it the most forested county in Denmark. Beech, fir, spruce, hemlock and oak are dominant. There are three main areas, each laid out with walking trails (pick up free maps at tourist offices). Bicycle trails connect them all; the beautiful route 22 takes you through Almindingen and Paradisbakkerne.

Almindingen, the largest forest (6000 hectares), is in the centre of the island and can be reached by heading north from Åkirkeby. It's the site of Bornholm's highest point, the 162m hill **Rytterknægten**, which has a lookout tower called Kongemindet from where you can view the surrounding countryside.

A small herd of European **bison** have successfully been introduced to a fenced enclosure within Almindingen, by Svinemose bog. You can visit the area and try some bison-spotting off Chr X Vej, north of Åkirkeby.

Paradisbakkerne (Paradise Hills) contains wild **deer** and a trail that passes an ancient monolithic gravestone. It's 2km northwest of Nexø.

Rø Plantage, about 5km southwest of Gudhjem, has a terrain of heather-covered hills and woodlands.

Dueodde

At Bornholm's southernmost point, vast, breathtaking **Dueodde Beach** (🏖) is backed by deep-green pine trees and expansive dunes. Its soft sand is so fine-grained that it was once used in hourglasses and ink blotters. The only beachside 'sight' is a climbable **lighthouse** on the western side of the dunes with seemingly endless sand and sea views. There's no real village, but buses 7/8 from/to Nexø drive down the dead-end access road. A boardwalk leads to the beach across marshland from the bus stop where there are a couple of food kiosks, a steakhouse and the apartment-style **Dueodde Badehotel** (📞56 95 85 66; www.dueodde-badehotel.dk; Sirenevej 2; d per 3 nights incl breakfast 2262-3744kr, self-catering apt per 3 nights 1454-4159kr; 🅿🛜). Upbeat **Dueodde Camping & Hostel** (📞20 14 68 49; www.dueodde.dk; Skrokkegårdsvejen 17; s/d/q from 375/425/580kr, campsites per adult/child 75/45kr, per site 30-45kr; ⊙May-Sep; 🅿🛜🏊) is a 10-minute walk east.

At the main road junction, 1km north, **Bornholmertårnet** (📞40 20 52 40; www.bornholmertaarnet.dk; Strandmarksvejen 2; adult/child 75/50kr; ⊙10am-5pm May-Oct) is a 70m-tall viewing tower with exhibits that detail the site's history as NATO's easternmost listening post during the Cold War.

En route to Nexø you'll pass through **Snogebæk** (population 700), a quaint seaside village famed for sweet treats, organic seasonal ice creams from **Boisen Iscafé** (📞28 30 96 67; www.boisen-iscafe.dk; Hovedgade 4; 1/2 scoops 22/32kr; ⊙noon-5pm late Jun–mid-Sep, Sat & Sun Easter–late Jun) and *flødeboller* (Danish chocolate snowballs) from **Kjærstrup Chokolade** (📞56 48 80 89; www.kjaerstrup.dk; Hovedgade 9; flødeboller 22kr; ⊙11am-5.30pm).

Nexø

POP 3640

◎ Sights & Activities

Bustling Nexø (also spelt Neksø) is Bornholm's second-largest town, with a large modern harbour where fishing vessels unload their catch. To see how the place looked before being bombed to bits in WWII, visit modest **Nexø Museum** (📞56 49 25 56; www.nexoemuseum.dk; Havnen 3; adult/child 40kr/free; ⊙10am-4pm Mon-Fri, to 1pm Sat Jul & Aug, 1-4pm Mon-Fri mid-May–Jun & Sep–mid-Oct) in one of the few historic buildings that survived. Although Nexø's central waterfront is industrial, **Balka Strand** 2km south of town is a popular, gently curving white-sand beach with good opportunities for windsurfing, kitesurfing and stand-up paddleboarding through **Eastwind** (📞29 33 09 91; www.eastwind.dk; Vestre Strandvej; intro windsurfing course 575kr; ⊙10am-5.30pm late Jun-early Sep).

Bornholms Sommerfuglepark　　　NATURE RESERVE
(📞56 49 25 75; www.sommerfuglerparken.dk; Gammel Rønnevej 14B; adult/child 90/60kr; ⊙10am-5pm May-Sep; 🏖) Just outside of Nexø is Sommerfuglepark, offering jungle climates and more than 1000 butterflies in its plant-filled butterfly house.

Martin Andersen Nexø Huset　　　MUSEUM
(📞56 49 45 42; www.andersennexoe.dk; Ferskesøstræde 36; adult/child 40kr/free; ⊙1-4pm Tue-Fri, 10am-1pm Sat mid-May–mid-Oct) Snoop around the childhood home of the author of *Pelle the Conqueror* (the book that inspired the 1988 Oscar-winning film). The house is in the southern part of town and displays photos of the author, along with some of his letters and other memorabilia.

🛏 Sleeping

Strand Hotel Balka Søbad　　　HOTEL €€
(📞56 49 22 25; www.hotel-balkasoebad.dk; Vestre Strandvej 25; s/d incl breakfast from 950/1175kr; ⊙May-Sep; 🅿@🛜🏊) Boasting its own

---

bathing beach, this hotel has 106 rooms in two-storey buildings scattered around forest-ed grounds. Rooms might recall the late '70s, but they're pleasant and clean, and have at least two twin beds, a sofa bed, balcony and kitchenette. The lobby's decor is something out of *Mad Men*. Facilities include a tennis court, swimming pool, bar and restaurant.

Hotel Balka Strand HOTEL €€
(☑56 49 49 49; www.hotelbalkastrand.dk; Boulevarden 9; s/d/f incl breakfast 890/1090/1595kr; ☺mid-Apr–mid-Oct; 🅿🛜🐕) Only 150m from Balka's sandy beach, this friendly hotel has double rooms and cheery apartments, all with outdoor terraces and functional but dated decor. On-site, family-oriented pluses include a pool, games room, large garden, bike hire, bar and restaurant.

Eating

A supermarket and a couple of simple eateries are at the eastern side of the church on Torvet (just off Jernbanegade).

★Restaurant Molen DANISH €€
(☑88 87 67 33; www.restaurantmolen.dk; Havnen 6; lunch dishes 95kr; 4-course lunch/dinner 325/425kr; ☺noon-3pm & 6-8.30pm) Right on the harbour's pier, this is Nexø's most interesting eating option, and home to a chef (Daniel Kruse) of fine local pedigree. It's an unassuming spot for clever, creative cooking that showcases local produce, and worth going out of your way for. Kruse's desserts are particularly memorable.

ℹ Information

Tourist Office (☑56 95 95 00; Havnen 4; ☺11am-5pm Mon-Fri, 10am-4pm Sat & Sun late Jun–mid-Aug, shorter hours rest of year) At the harbour, this helpful office has information on Nexø, Snogebæk, Svaneke and Dueodde.

ℹ Getting There & Away

Bus 6 runs between Rønne and Nexø. Buses 3, 5, 7 and 8 also pass through town.

Svaneke

POP 1060

Svaneke is a super-cute harbour town of red-tiled 19th-century buildings that has won international recognition for maintaining its historic character. Popular with yachters and landlubbing holidaymakers, its pretty

harbourfront is lined with mustard-yellow half-timbered former merchants' houses, some of which have been turned into hotels and restaurants.

Svaneke is also home to plenty of fab island flavours: a renowned smokehouse (p152), a notable microbrewery (p153), and beloved makers of gourmet liquorice, caramels and chocolates – all of which are highly recommended.

◉ Sights

The easternmost town in Denmark, Svaneke is quite breezy and has a number of windmills. To the northwest of town, around Møllebakken, you'll find an old **post mill** (a type of mill that turns in its entirety to face the wind) and a **Dutch mill**, as well as an unusual three-sided **water tower** designed in the 1950s by architect Jørn Utzon (of Sydney's Opera House fame).

On the main road 3km south of Svaneke in the hamlet of **Årsdale**, there's a working windmill where grains are ground and sold.

Glastorvet SQUARE
If you're interested in crafts, there are a number of ceramics and handicraft shops dotted around town, and at Glastorvet in the town centre there's a workshop of renowned local designer Pernille Bülow, where you can watch glass being melted into orange glowing lumps and then blown into clear, elegant glassware. This is a lovely spot to explore local flavours and artisans.

Svaneke Kirke CHURCH
(Kirkepladsen 2; ☺8am-3pm Mon-Fri) You'll find some interesting period buildings near the elevated landmark of Svaneke Kirke, a few minutes' walk south of Svaneke Torv. The watermelon-hued church, home to a rune stone, dates from 1350, although it was largely rebuilt during the 1880s.

🛏 Sleeping

Hullehavn Camping CAMPGROUND €
(☑56 49 63 63; www.hullehavn.dk; Sydskovvej 9; adult/child/site 78/40/35kr; ☺May–mid-Sep; 🛜) Hullehavn has the more natural setting of Svaneke's two camping grounds, including its own sandy beach. If you don't have your own gear, hire a caravan or on-site tent. You're just a short walk to the old lighthouse – check out the fab kiosk here too, called Syd-Øst for Paradis.

Danhostel Svaneke
HOSTEL €

(📞 56 49 62 42; www.danhostel-svaneke.dk; Reberbanevej 9; d/q 520/570kr; ☺ Apr-late Oct; P 🛜) A popular budget option, 600m southeast of the town centre and nicely positioned close to the waterfront and woods. Simple, bunk-filled rooms all have bathrooms.

Hotel Siemsens Gaard
HOTEL €€

(📞 56 49 61 49; www.siemsens.dk; Havnebryggen 9; s/d incl breakfast from 875/1325kr; ☺ closed Jan & Feb; P @ 🛜) 🅿 Although the straightforward rooms at this prime-position harbourfront hotel are a little dowdy, they are comfortable and generally well equipped (some doubles have kitchenettes). Request a room in the old wing, a beautiful half-timbered building that dates from the mid-17th century.

🍴 Eating

★ Røgeriet i Svaneke
SEAFOOD €

(📞 56 49 63 24; www.roegerietsvaneke.dk; Fiskergade 12; snacks & meals 40-120kr; ☺ from 10am Apr-Oct) You'll find a fine selection of excellent smoked fare at the long counter here, including smørrebrød (Danish open sandwiches), mackerel, trout, salmon, herring, shrimp and *fiskefrikadeller* (fish cakes). Sit inside with a view of the massive, blackened doors of the smoking ovens or at the outdoor picnic tables overlooking the old cannons, with a view of the five iconic chimneys.

You'll find the smokehouse by the water at the end of Fiskergade, just north of the town centre. Closing time varies: 8pm in July, 5pm in cooler months.

Svanereden
INTERNATIONAL €

(📞 50 50 72 35; www.svanereden.dk; Gruset 4; mains 75-120kr; ☺ 10am-9pm mid-May–mid-Sep; 🍴) When the weather gods are smiling, this casual outdoor restaurant positioned above the harbour is a great spot to dine and unwind. The choices are simple and good (from champagne brunch to tapas platters to wok-fried dishes and stews cooked over an open fire). Kids are actively welcomed, and the views and atmosphere are tops.

Opening hours, naturally, are weather-dependent.

Lakrids by Johan Bülow
SWEETS €

(www.liquorice.nu; Glastorvet 1; ☺ 9am-5.30pm Mon-Fri, to 2pm Sat) Scandis are mad for *lakrids* (liquorice; the saltier the better, it often seems). Svaneke is where this brand began, and you can now find its gorgeously

HIDDEN HAMS

Artisanal charcuterie Hallegaard (📞 56 47 02 47; www.hallegaard.dk; Aspevej 3, Østermarie; tapas plate 200kr; ☺ cafe noon-3pm, shop 10am-5pm late Jun–mid-Sep, shorter hours rest of year) is a darling of Danish locavores, and many of Copenhagen's top chefs procure their meats from this bucolic farmhouse, hidden away down a country lane 8km southwest of Svaneke. In all, Hallegaard produces around 30 types of charcuterie, some of which is smoked in traditional brick ovens.

The cold smoked ham (a Bornholm 'prosciutto' of sorts) spends months in former WWII bunkers! Try some as a part of a tapas plate paired with ale from Hallegaard's small-batch brewery.

To find Hallegaard, follow the 'Gårdbutik' (farm shop) sign off Svanekevej, at Lyrsbyvej just east of Østermarie.

packaged goods in gourmet stores across Denmark and the world. Drop by for a taste and pick up a great souvenir.

Svaneke Chokoladeri
SWEETS €

(📞 56 49 70 21; www.svanekechokoladeri.dk; Svaneke Torv 5; flødeboller from 20kr; ☺ 10.30am-5.30pm Mon-Fri, to 5pm Sat, 11am-5pm Sun; 🍴) Located at the entrance to Bryghuset is one of Bornholm's top chocolatiers. Made on the premises, the seductive concoctions include a very Bornholm *havtorn* (sea buckthorn) dark-choc truffle, and gourmet *flødeboller* (try the raspberry and liquorice combo).

There's also a store on Rønne's Store Torv.

Dagli'Brugsen
SUPERMARKET €

(Nansensgade 11; ☺ 8am-8pm Jun-Aug, to 6pm Sep-May) For self-catering and picnic supplies, just off Svaneke Torv.

Hotel Siemsens Gaard Restaurant
DANISH €€

(📞 56 49 61 49; www.siemsens.dk; Havnebryggen 9; lunch 72-168kr, dinner mains 208-268kr; ☺ 11.30am-9pm) With terrace dining overlooking the harbour, this hotel's restaurant makes an ideal lunch choice on a sunny day. There is a focus on local produce, and it does good light lunches such as daintily presented smørrebrød, and smoked and marinated salmon. A two-course dinner option is decent value at 298kr.

🍸 Drinking

★ **Bryghuset** MICROBREWERY
(☑ 56 49 73 21; www.bryghuset-svaneke.dk; Svaneke Torv 5; lunch 79-139kr, dinner mains 169-299kr; ⏰ 11am-midnight, kitchen closes 8.30pm; 🚻) This is one of the most popular year-round dining and drinking hotspots on the island, known throughout Denmark for its excellent beers brewed on the premises. It also serves decent, hearty pub grub that pairs well with its brews. Danish lunch classics include smørrebrød, *fiskefrikadeller* and a fine burger. Dinner mains are mostly juicy, fleshy affairs.

ℹ️ Information

Tourist Office (☑ 56 95 95 00; Peter F Heerings Gade 7; ⏰ 10am-4pm Tue-Sat mid-Jun–late Sep) By the harbour.

ℹ️ Getting There & Away

There are bike-rental places in town. Buses 3, 5, 7 and 8 pass through.

Gudhjem & Melsted

POP 715

Gudhjem is the best-looking of Bornholm's harbour towns. Its rambling high street is crowned by a squat windmill standing over half-timbered houses and sloping streets that roll down to the picture-perfect harbour. The town is a good base for exploring the rest of Bornholm, with cycling and walking trails, convenient bus connections, plenty of places to eat and stay, and a boat service (p155) to Christiansø.

Gudhjem's shoreline is rocky, though sunbathers will find a small sandy beach at Melsted, 1km southeast.

👁 Sights

★ **Oluf Høst Museet** MUSEUM
(☑ 56 48 50 38; www.ohmus.dk; Løkkegade 35; adult/child 75kr/free; ⏰ 11am-5pm Jun-Aug, Wed-Sun Sep & Oct; 🚻) This wonderful museum contains the workshops and paintings of Oluf Høst (1884–1966), one of Bornholm's best-known artists. The museum occupies the home where Høst lived from 1929 until his death. The beautiful back garden is home to a little hut with paper, paints and pencils for kids with a creative itch.

Melstedgård MUSEUM
(☑ 56 95 07 35; www.gaarden.nu; Melstedvej 25; adult/child 70kr/free; ⏰ 10am-4pm Sun-Fri late Jun–mid-Aug, shorter hours mid-May–late Jun & mid-Aug–mid-Oct; 🚻) This folk/farm museum has a new addition, and a second name: 'Gaarden – Bornholms Madkulturhus'. It's a mouthful when translated (Bornholm's House of Food Culture), but it's an engaging place. You can visit the old farmhouse, see the sweet farm animals kept here, and admire the modern new building that hosts events like farmers markets and cooking courses.

Gudhjem Glasrøgeri GALLERY
(☑ 56 48 54 68; www.gudhjem-glasroegeri.dk; Ejnar Mikkelsensvej 13A; ⏰ 10am-5.30pm Mon-Fri, 11am-5pm Sat & Sun Easter-Nov) Watch top-quality Bornholm glass being hand-blown at Gudhjem Glasrøgeri at the dockside.

🏃 Activities

M/S Thor BOATING
(☑ 56 48 51 65; www.ms-thor.dk; Gudhjem Havn; one-way/return 100/125kr; ⏰ from Gudhjem 11.30am May-Sep) Take a cruise along the coastline west of Gudhjem to view the rugged rock formations of **Helligdomsklipperne**. You can stay on the boat and return to Gudhjem, or disembark at the landing place by the cliffs and walk up to visit Bornholms Kunstmuseum (p156).

There are additional sailings in July and August.

Walking

A short five-minute climb up the heather-covered hill, **Bokul** (Bokulvej) provides a fine view of the town's red-tiled rooftops and out to sea.

From the hill at the southeastern end of Gudhjem harbour you'll be rewarded with a harbour view. You can continue along this path that runs above the shoreline 1.5km southeast to Melsted, where there's a little sandy beach. It's a delightful **nature trail**, with swallows, nightingales and wildflowers.

Heading west for around 6km takes you along the scenic elevated coastline of Helligdomsklipperne and to the excellent Bornholms Kunstmuseum. The path *(sti)* heads along the coast from Nørresand.

🎉 Festivals & Events

Sol over Gudhjem FOOD & DRINK
(Sun over Gudhjem; www.solovergudhjemkonkurrence.dk; ⏰ Jun) Taking place on a Saturday afternoon in late June, Gudhjem's famous harbourside cook-off sees four of Denmark's hottest chefs battle it out as they use Bornholm produce to create a tantalising

Gudhjem & Melsted

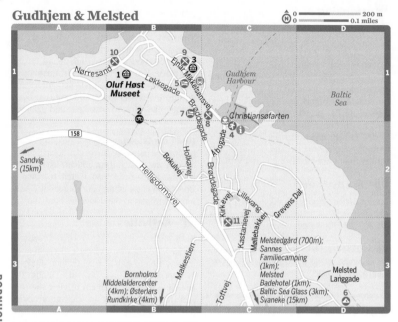

Gudhjem & Melsted

◎ Top Sights
1 Oluf Høst Museet B1

◎ Sights
2 Bokul..B1
3 Gudhjem Glasrøgeri.............................B1

✪ Activities, Courses & Tours
4 M/S Thor..C2

🛏 Sleeping
5 Danhostel Gudhjem.............................B1
6 Gudhjem Camping D3
7 Jantzens Hotel......................................B1

✕ Eating
8 Cafe Klint...C1
9 Gudhjem Røgeri B1
10 Norresan...B1
11 Spar..C3

two-course menu. The event also features an appetising food market, with 50 stalls showcasing the best of Danish produce and specialities, from herring to honey and cheeses.

The official cook-off usually starts at 1pm. Head in early to get a good seat: the event can draw an astonishing 10,000 spectators.

🛏 Sleeping

The town has a few midrange hotels, a very central **hostel** (✆56 48 50 35; www.danhostel-gudhjem.dk; Ejnar Mikkelsensvej 14; dm/s/d from 260/400/500kr; ☏) and a couple of camping grounds: **Gudhjem Camping** (✆56 48 50 71; www.gudhjemcamping.dk; Melsted Langgade 45; per adult/child 78/40kr, per site 35-55kr; ☉mid-May–mid-Sep; P☏) is just 15 minutes' walk southeast from the harbour, but beachside **Sannes Familiecamping** (✆56 48 52 11; www.familiecamping.dk; Melstedvej 39; per adult/child 90/60kr, per site 30-90kr, 4-person cabin per week 3150-11,050kr; ☉Apr-Oct; P☏🛏), 1km further, is a four-star delight with sauna and wellness centre.

There are seaside hotels beyond town, and a few places renting out rooms/apartments can be found through www.gudhjem.nu.

Jantzens Hotel　　　　　BOUTIQUE HOTEL €€
(✆56 48 50 17; www.jantzenshotel.dk; Brøddegade 33; s/d incl breakfast from 875/1225kr; ☉late Apr–mid-Sep; ☏) One of the island's true charmers, Jantzens offers smallish but supremely cosy, stylish rooms in a handsome period building. Some rooms have sea views, and the breakfast is one of Bornholm's best.

Melsted Badehotel   BOUTIQUE HOTEL €€€

(☑56 48 51 00; www.melsted-badehotel.dk; Melstedvej 27; d incl breakfast 1510-1975kr; ☺May-Sep) The gorgeous green grounds are a feature of this boutique seaside complex, complete with croquet lawn, putting green and Adirondack chairs that lend a refined air. Rooms are bright, fresh and full of good taste.

✖ Eating

Good eating options are found in the waterfront area and on Brøddegade, where there's also a **Spar supermarket** (Brøddegade 14; ☺8am-6pm). For something special, book well ahead at the Stammershalle Badehotel restaurant (p156), north of town.

★**Norresan**   CAFE €

(☑20 33 52 85; www.facebook.com/norresand; Nørresand 10; cake/sandwich 35/70kr; ☺11am-9pm Jul, shorter hours Apr-Jun & Aug-Oct) In a beautiful old smokehouse by the water (close to Oluf Høst Museet; p153), this whitewashed cafe wins over visitors with views, home-baked cakes and cookies, tasty ice cream and a sweet ambience. Check its Facebook page for opening hours, and for details of visiting food trucks for sunset-watchers.

Gudhjem Røgeri   SEAFOOD €

(☑56 48 57 08; www.smokedfish.dk; Ejnar Mikkelsensvej 9; dishes 64-115kr, buffet 130-185kr; ☺from 10am Apr-Oct) Gudhjem's popular smokehouse serves deli-style fish and salads, including the classic smørrebrød topping known as Sol over Gudhjem (Sun over Gudhjem; smoked herring topped with a raw egg yolk, chives and radish on rye bread). There's indoor and outdoor seating, and live music most nights in July and August. Usually closes at 9pm, or 10pm in peak season.

Cafe Klint   INTERNATIONAL €€

(☑56 48 56 26; www.cafeklint.dk; Ejnar Mikkelsensvej 20; snacks & mains 60-199kr; ☺from 10am Apr-Oct; 🛜) On a sunny day the patio here is the spot to kick back with a beer and a harbour view. Tasty edibles include salads, sandwiches, tapas and flavourful steaks. It's a popular evening hang-out, with free live music most nights in peak summer. Closing times vary widely: 2am in July, 9pm the rest of summer, 5pm in the cooler months.

❶ Information

Tourist Office (☑56 95 95 00; Ejnar Mikkelsensvej 27; ☺10am-3.30pm Mon-Fri Jun-Aug) Small tourist office right by the harbour.

It's staffed in summer, and open for self-service (brochures etc) for a few hours in the morning daily from mid-April to mid-October.

❶ Getting There & Away

BOAT

Christiansøfarten (☑56 48 51 76; www.christiansoefarten.dk; Ejnar Mikkelsensvej 25; Christiansø return adult/child 250/125kr; ☺hours vary) operates passenger ferries to Christiansø from Gudhjem. From July to late August, ferries depart Gudhjem daily at 10am, 12.30pm and 3pm; return ferries depart Christiansø at 2pm, 4.15pm and 7.30pm. Sailing time is around an hour. Note that there are fewer sailings outside peak summer.

In a gorgeous gesture, 10am sailings in summer are serenaded from Gudhjem's harbour by the local choir.

From November to mid-April, there is a weekday service with the post-boat – check the website for details.

BUS

The main **bus stop** (Ejnar Mikkelsensvej) in Gudhjem is near the harbour. There are good bus links to other parts of the island.

Around Gudhjem & Melsted

South of Gudhjem

Inland, around 5km from Gudhjem, just north of **Østerlars** village is a medieval centre and Bornholm's most impressive round church. Come by bicycle, bus 1 or 9 from Gudhjem or bus 4 from Rønne.

Around 3km southeast of central Gudhjem on the coast road, large, modern **Baltic Sea Glass** (☑56 48 56 41; www.balticseaglass.com; Melstedvej 47; ☺10am-5pm) is one of Bornholm's best independent workshop-galleries for ceramics and glass-blowing.

Near Østermarie, Fru Petersens (p158) is a worthy pilgrimage for cake lovers.

Opening hours are reduced (as are prices and activities) outside the summer peak.

◉ Sights

★**Østerlars Rundkirke**   CHURCH

(www.oesterlarskirke.dk; Vietsvej 25, Østerlars; 10kr; ☺10am-5pm Mon-Sat Apr-Oct, to 2.45pm Tue-Sat Nov-Mar) The largest and most impressive of Bornholm's round churches dates to at least 1150, and its seven buttresses and upper-level shooting positions give away its former role as a fortress. The roof was originally constructed with a flat top to serve as a battle platform, but the excessive weight this exerted on the walls saw it eventually replaced with its present conical one. The interior is largely whitewashed, although a swath of medieval frescoes has been uncovered and restored.

Bornholms Middelaldercenter   MUSEUM
(☑56 49 83 19; www.bornholmsmiddelaldercenter. dk; Stangevej 1, Østerlars; adult/child 140/70kr; ☉hours vary Easter–Oct; ⓓ) This 'Medieval Centre' re-creates a medieval fort and village, and gives the Danes another chance to do what they love best: dressing up in period costume and hitting each other with rubber swords. They also operate a smithy, tend fields, grind wheat in a water mill and perform other chores of yore throughout the summer months. In July the activity schedule is beefed up to include archery demonstrations and hands-on activities for children.

North of Gudhjem

◎ Sights

★**Bornholms Kunstmuseum**   MUSEUM
(☑56 48 43 86; www.bornholms-kunstmuseum. dk; Otto Bruuns Plads 1; adult/child 70kr/free; ☉10am-5pm Jun-Aug, closed Mon Apr, May, Sep & Oct, shorter hours rest of year) Occupying a svelte, modern building and overlooking sea, fields and (weather permitting) the distant isle of Christiansø, Bornholms Kunstmuseum echoes Copenhagen's Louisiana. Among its exhibits, the museum displays paintings by artists from the Bornholm School, including Olaf Rude, Oluf Høst and Edvard Weie, who painted during the first half of the 20th century.

The grounds are a delight – take a walk past grazing highland cows to reach the photogenic Helligdomsklipperne (p153), high and rugged rock formations by the sea.

A walking path leads along the top of the cliffs to Gudhjem, some 6km away, and there is a boat (p153) that travels between Gudhjem and the museum (stairs lead up from the landing place).

There's a cafe on-site. A number of bus routes stop in front of the museum (including bus 2 from Rønne, and buses 4 and 8 from Gudhjem).

🛏 Sleeping & Eating

★**Stammershalle Badehotel**   BOUTIQUE HOTEL €€
(☑56 48 42 10; www.stammershalle-badehotel.dk; Søndre Strandvej 128, Stammershalle; s/d incl breakfast from 700/900kr; ☉May-Oct, Wed-Sat Mar, Apr & Nov; ⓟⓢⓟ) One of Bornholm's top slumber spots occupies an imposing, early-20th-century bathing hotel overlooking a rocky part of the coast a few kilometres north of Gudhjem. It's a calming blend of white-washed timber and understated Cape Cod–esque chic, not to mention the home of an excellent restaurant. Book well ahead, especially in the summer high season.

Stammershalle Badehotel   DANISH €€€
(Lassens; ☑56 48 42 10; www.stammershalle-badehotel.dk; Søndre Strandvej 128, Stammershalle; small/large tasting menu 450/595kr; ☉6-10pm May-Oct, Wed-Sat Mar & Apr) An ode to relaxed Scandi elegance, the restaurant at Stammershalle Badehotel is a foodie hotspot. Service is knowledgeable and personable, and the sea-and-sunset panorama as inspired as the kitchen's creations. Bookings are essential.

BORNHOLM'S ROUND CHURCHES

As the windmills are to Mykonos or the stone heads are to Easter Island, so are the four 12th-century round churches *(rundekirke)* to Bornholm. The churches are symbols of the island, immediately familiar to every Dane. Each was built with 2m-thick whitewashed walls and a black conical roof at a time when pirating Wends from eastern Germany were ravaging coastal areas throughout the Baltic Sea. They were designed not only as places of worship but also as refuges against enemy attacks – their upper storeys doubled as places to fire arrows from. They were also used as storehouses to protect valuable possessions and trading goods from being carried off by the pirates.

Each church was built about 2km inland, and all four are sited high enough on knolls to offer a lookout to the sea. These striking and utterly distinctive churches have a stern, ponderous appearance, more typical of a fortress than of a place of worship. All four churches are still used for Sunday services. You'll find them at Østerlars (p155), Olsker (p157), Nyker and Nylars (p149).

Sandvig & Allinge

POP 1600

Sandvig is a genteel seaside hamlet with storybook older homes, many fringed by rose bushes and flower gardens. It's fronted by a gorgeous sandy bay and borders a network of walking trails throughout the Hammeren area and southwest to Hammershus.

Most commercial facilities, including banks, grocery shops and the area's tourist office (p158), are 2km southeast in larger, less quaint Allinge.

◎ Sights

★**Hammershus Slotsruin**   RUINS
(Slotslyngvej) FREE The impressive ruins of Hammershus Slot, dramatically perched on top of a cliff 74m above the sea, are the largest in Scandinavia. The castle was thought to have been built in the early 1300s, and a walk through the evocative site, enjoying the views, is a must for Bornholm visitors. The grounds are always open and admission is free. A smart new **visitor centre** is being built, sympathetic to the surrounds (opening 2018; likely with an admission fee for exhibits).

Construction of the castle probably began around 1250 under the archbishop of Lund, who wanted a fortress to protect his diocese against the Crown, engaged at the time in a power struggle with the Church. In the centuries that followed, the castle was enlarged, with the upper levels of the square tower added on during the mid-16th century.

Eventually, improvements in naval artillery left the fortress walls vulnerable to attack and in 1645 the castle temporarily fell to Swedish troops after a brief bombardment. Hammershus served as both military garrison and prison – King Christian IV's daughter, Leonora Christina, was imprisoned here on treason charges from 1660 to 1661.

In 1743 the Danish military abandoned Hammershus and many of the stones were carried away to be used as building materials elsewhere. Still, there's much to see.

There's an hourly bus (2 and 8) from Sandvig to Hammershus, but the most enjoyable access is via footpaths through the hills of Hammeren – a wonderful hour's hike. The well-trodden trail begins by the Sandvig Familie (p158) camping ground and the route is signposted.

If you're coming from Rønne, take (infrequent) bus 7.

Hammeren   NATURE RESERVE
Hammeren, the hammerhead-shaped crag of granite at the northern tip of Bornholm, is criss-crossed by **walking trails** leading through hillsides thick with purple heather. Some of the trails are inland, while others run along the coast. The whole area is a delight for people who enjoy nature walks.

For something a little more challenging, follow the trails between Sandvig and Hammershus Slot. The shortest route travels along the inland side of Hammeren and passes **Hammersøen**, Bornholm's largest lake, and **Opalsøen**, a deep pond in an old rock quarry (a very cool **zip line** sets up here from late June to mid-July; see www.tovbanen.dk). A longer, more windswept route goes along the rocky outer rim of Hammeren, passes a **lighthouse** at Bornholm's northernmost point and continues south along the coast to the delightful small harbour at **Hammerhavn**.

From Hammershus Slot there are walking trails heading south through another heather-clad landscape in a nature area called **Slotslyngen**, and east through public woodlands to **Moseløkken granite quarry**. Moseløkken is also the site of the Moseløkken Stenbrudsmuseum.

Olsker Rundkirke   CHURCH
(Sankt Ols Kirke; Rønnevej 51, Olsker; 10kr; ◎10am-5pm Mon-Fri May-Oct) Five kilometres south of central Allinge, on the southern outskirts of the small village of **Olsker**, is the highest (26m) and most slender of the island's four round churches.

Moseløkken Stenbrudsmuseum   MUSEUM
(☏56 48 04 68; www.moseloekken.dk; Moseløkkevej 9; adult/child 80/70kr; ◎9am-4pm Mon-Fri late Apr-Sep) Situated at the Moseløkken granite quarry, this small museum showcases the work of local stonemasons and sculptors, with occasional demonstrations of traditional rock-cutting techniques.

⌂ Sleeping

★**Nordly**   HOSTEL €
(☏56 48 03 62; www.nordlybornholm.dk; Hammershusvej 94; d/q without bathroom from 475/610kr; ⓟⓢ) A young couple have taken over this old Danhostel not far from Hammershus, and transformed it into cosy, stylish budget digs. Double and family rooms surround a courtyard out back, while the main building has some fun retro stylings and inviting common areas. All rooms have shared bathrooms.

Sandvig Familiecamping CAMPGROUND €
(☑ 56 48 04 47; www.sandvigcamping.dk; Sandlinien 5, Sandvig; per adult/child 75/40kr, per site 15-40kr; ⊙ late Mar-Oct; 🛜) This shady camping ground occupies a great spot near Sandvig's fine beach and is handy for the walking tracks at Hammeren (p157). There are good hut options, including family-sized ones (rented by the week in peak summer) and tiny, overnight 'Gotiske hytter' (budget Gothic huts, a little touch of glamping on Bornholm).

★ **Nordlandet** BOUTIQUE HOTEL €€
(☑ 56 48 03 44; www.hotelnordlandet.com; Strandvejen 68, Sandvig; r incl breakfast from 1190kr; P 🛜) Wowsers, talk about a makeover. The folks behind the first-class Kadeau (p149) restaurant in southern Bornholm have turned their attention to this hotel, with similarly stellar results. The coast-hugging complex offers minimalist, on-trend rooms; most have sea views, some have terraces and/or kitchens. Also on-site: a beautifully appointed restaurant (book ahead) and cool bar serving local beer and snacks.

Allinge Badehotel GUESTHOUSE €€
(Byskrivergården; ☑ 56 48 08 86; www.byskriver gaarden.dk; Løsebækegade 3, Allinge; s/d incl breakfast 780/1050kr; ⊙ mid-May–mid-Sep; P 🛜) This enchanting, white-walled, black-beamed converted farmhouse sits right on the water a short walk from Nordbornholms Røgeri restaurant. The rooms are simple and comfortable (try to get the sea-facing, not the road-facing, ones). There's a flower-filled garden, a large, cheerful breakfast room and rock pools nearby if you fancy taking a dip.

✖ Eating

Allinge has prominent waterfront eateries and supermarkets at the southern end of the harbour. There are beachside options in Sandvig, plus some tucked-away gems.

★ **Kalas-Kalas** CAFE €
(☑ 60 19 13 84; www.kalasbornholm.dk; Strandpromenaden 14, Sandvig; 2/3 ice-cream scoops 34/44kr, coffee 30-40kr; ⊙ 11am-10pm late Jun–mid-Aug, shorter hours rest of year) The best island combination: great coffee, handmade ice cream the locals queue for, picture-perfect rocky coastline out the windows, and beanbags on the terrace for sunset cocktails. Ice-cream flavours come courtesy of local gardens and fields: elderflower, rhubarb, redcurrant, various berries. Ask here about boat trips and snorkelling tours run by the owners' sons (www.boatingbornholm.dk).

CAKE CRUSADER

Cake lovers, come hungry! **Fru Petersens Café** (☑ 21 78 78 95; www. frupetersenscafe.dk; Almindingensvej 31, Østermarie; cake buffet incl drinks 145kr; ⊙ noon-6pm Jun-Aug, to 5pm Wed-Sun Apr, May, Sep, Thu-Sun Oct) is a cute-as-a-button cafe that lies about 1km west of Østermarie, and draws sweet tooths from all over the island with its exceptional *kagebord* (cake buffet). Its Insta-worthy table groans under the weight of home-baked cakes, tarts, cookies, pastries and more. The rooms are a *hyggelig* (cosy) haven of antiques and trinkets, and there's garden seating.

★ **Nordbornholms Røgeri** SEAFOOD €
(☑ 56 48 07 30; www.nbr.dk; Kæmpestranden 2, Allinge; dishes 60-115kr, buffet 189kr; ⊙ 11am-10pm; 🛜) Several of Bornholm's top chefs praise this smokehouse as the island's best. Not only does it serve a bumper buffet of locally smoked fish, salads and soup (ice-cream dessert included), but its waterside setting makes it the perfect spot to savour Bornholm's Baltic flavours.

Café Sommer INTERNATIONAL €€
(☑ 56 48 48 49; www.timos.dk; Havnegade 19, Allinge; lunch 125-175kr, dinner 2/3 courses 245/295kr; ⊙ 11.30am-9pm late May-Aug) Sporting a popular harbour-facing terrace and urbane interiors, Café Sommer is a sound (albeit pricey) spot for tasty lunchtime salads, burgers and smørrebrød, or heartier dinner options.

☆ Entertainment

Gæsten LIVE MUSIC
(www.gaestgiveren.dk; Theaterstræde 2, Allinge; ticket prices vary; ⊙ bar from 5pm, concerts from 8pm Mon-Sat Jul-early Aug) This summertime institution offers live music six nights a week in peak summer; see the program and buy tickets online, or tickets are generally also available at the door. There's usually a party atmosphere in the courtyard, and also a fine vegetarian buffet from 6pm (160kr; meat and fish dishes available too).

ℹ Information

Tourist Office (☑ 56 95 95 00; Sverigesvej 11, Allinge; ⊙ 11am-5pm Mon-Fri, 10am-4pm Sat & Sun Jul & Aug, shorter hours rest of year) Helpful office by the harbour in Allinge.

ⓘ Getting There & Away

Bus 1 runs frequently from Rønne, bus 4 from Gudhjem.

Christiansø

POP 95

If you think Bornholm is as remote as Denmark gets, you'd be wrong. Even further east, way out in the Baltic, is tiny Christiansø, an intensely atmospheric 17th-century island fortress about 500m long. It's an hour's sail northeast of Bornholm (departing from Gudhjem), and makes an idyllic day-trip destination.

There is something of the Faroe Islands about Christiansø's landscape (on a much less epic scale), with its rugged, moss-covered rocks, historic stone buildings and even hardier people. There is a real sense, too, that you are travelling back in time when you visit here, particularly if you stay overnight at the charming Christiansø Gæstgiveri and get to experience the island once most of the day-trippers have gone.

History

A seasonal fishing hamlet since the Middle Ages, Christiansø fell briefly into Swedish hands in 1658, after which Christian V turned it into an invincible naval fortress. Bastions and barracks were built; a church, school and prison followed.

Christiansø became the Danish Navy's forward position in the Baltic, serving to monitor Swedish trade routes, and in less congenial days as a base for attacks on Sweden. By the 1850s, though, the island was no longer needed as a forward base against Sweden, and the navy withdrew. Those who wanted to stay on as fishermen were allowed to live in the old cottages as free tenants. Their offspring, and a few latter-day fisher-

WILD ERTHOLMENE

Christiansø, Frederiksø and Græsholm are collectively known as the Ertholmene Islands. They attract a colony of seals and serve as spring breeding grounds for up to 2000 eider ducks. As the ducks nest near coastal paths, visitors should take care not to scare mothers away, leaving unattended eggs prey to predator gulls. Græsholm, a wildlife refuge, is also important for guillemots, razorbills and other seabirds.

folk and artists, currently make up Christiansø's circa 100 residents. The entire island is an unspoiled reserve – there are no cats or dogs, no cars and no modern buildings – allowing the rich birdlife to prosper.

◉ Sights

Lille Tårn   LANDMARK, MUSEUM

(Little Tower; adult/child 20/5kr; ⊙11.30am-4pm Mon-Fri, to 2pm Sat & Sun May-Sep) Lille Tårn on Frederiksø dates from 1685 and is now the local history museum. The ground floor features fishing supplies, hand tools and ironworks; upstairs there are cannons, vintage furniture pieces, models and a display of local flora and fauna.

Store Tårn   LANDMARK

(Great Tower; adult/child 40/20kr; ⊙11am-6pm Tue-Thu, to 4pm Fri-Mon mid-Jun–mid-Aug, 11am-4pm Tue-Sun Easter–mid-Jun & mid-Aug–mid-Oct) Built in 1684, Christiansø's Store Tårn is an impressive structure measuring a full 25m in diameter, and the tower's 100-year-old lighthouse offers a sweeping 360-degree view of the island. After major restoration work, the tower reopened in June 2017 with new exhibits on local history and birdlife.

⬛ Sleeping

Christiansø Teltplads   CAMPGROUND €

(☑20 31 29 13; www.christiansoe.dk; per site 75-100kr, plus per person 40kr; ⊙May–mid-Sep) Tent camping is allowed in summer in a small field at the northern end of Christiansø, but limited space means it can be difficult to book a site. There's a small kitchen for guests.

Christiansø Gæstgiveri   GUESTHOUSE €€

(☑56 46 20 15; www.christiansoekro.dk; s/d 1150/1250kr; ⊙closed late Dec-Jan) Built in 1703 as the naval commander's residence, this is the island's only inn, with six simple (pricey) rooms with bathroom. There's a traditional Danish restaurant open for lunch and dinner daily, with a sunny, view-blessed terrace.

ⓘ Information

Information is online at www.christiansoe.dk.

ⓘ Getting There & Away

Access is by boat from Gudhjem. **Christiansøfarten** (☑56 48 51 76; www.christiansoefarten. dk; return ticket adult/child 250/125kr; ⊙mid-Apr–late Oct) ferries run three times daily July to late August, less frequently outside midsummer. November to mid-April, there is a weekday post-boat.

Funen

Best Places to Eat

➜ Falsled Kro (p178)

➜ Vester Skerninge Kro (p179)

➜ Restaurant Generalen (p186)

➜ Oluf Bagers Gård (p167)

➜ Restaurant No 61 (p169)

➜ Fiske Restaurant Rudolf Mathis (p173)

Best Places to Stay

➜ Broholm Castle (p179)

➜ Pension Vestergade 44 (p189)

➜ Bjørnegården (p174)

➜ Stella Maris Hotel (p182)

➜ Bed & Breakfast Juelsberg Slot (p172)

Why Go?

Funen (Fyn in Danish) is Denmark's proverbial middle child. Lacking Zealand's capital-city pull or Jutland's geographic dominance, it's often overlooked by visitors, who rarely do more than make a whistle-stop visit to Hans Christian Andersen's birthplace, Odense.

Certainly the master of fairy tales makes a worthy favourite son and Odense is a lively cultural and commercial centre. But there is much more to Funen. Thatched farmhouses, picture-book coastal towns and grand Renaissance castles dot the island's patchwork of fields and woodlands. There's a remarkable Viking-era ship grave near Kerteminde. Rolling southern pastures and orchards grow some of the country's best produce. Curiously minimalist shelters are set up for cyclists and kayakers. And handsome harbour towns give access to a yacht-filled archipelago of idyllic seafaring islands. All in all, if you take the trouble to explore, you'll find Funen is a microcosm of the very best of Denmark.

When to Go

➜ As with elsewhere in Denmark, Funen really comes alive in the school holiday period of July and early August, with special events and an influx of yachties to Funen's southern harbours.

➜ While the peak of summer feels especially festive, if you come in mid-June or late August you'll still find most places open but you'll miss the worst of the crowds and save on ferry fares.

➜ Odense's excellent museums and quality dining have year-round appeal; festivals peak in August, but the lead-up to Christmas is also sparkly and sweet.

Funen Highlights

1 **Ærø** (p187) Sailing to Denmark's 'wedding island' of undulating country lanes.

2 **Egeskov Slot** (p178) Exploring a splendid castle with its park full of mazes, museums and marvels.

3 **Hindsholm Peninsula** (p174) Seeking out ultra-quaint villages of thatched, half-timbered houses north of Kerteminde.

4 **Odense** (p162) Immersing yourself in the fairy-tale world of Hans Christian Andersen.

5 **Vikingemuseet Ladby** (p173) Discovering Denmark's only Viking-era ship grave, the last resting place of a 10th-century chieftain.

6 **Langelandsfort** (p186) Pondering the intricacies of

Cold War manoeuvrings from 20th-century gunners' bunkers.

7 **Svendborg** (p179) Reflecting on hard times in the former poorhouse before inspecting wooden ships on the waterfront.

8 **Tickon** (p185) Squinting to differentiate art from nature in this vast sculpture park behind Tranekær's grand fortress.

ODENSE

POP 175,245

Pronounced *o*-thn-se (or *ohn*-se if you're local), Funen's millennium-old hub is Denmark's third-biggest city, a buzzing place undergoing a very major revamp. The birthplace of fairy-tale writer extraordinaire Hans Christian Andersen, there's a profusion of Andersen-related attractions, including museums, a children's centre and sculptures interpreting his most famous stories. Even the lights at pedestrian crossings feature Andersen in silhouette.

Yet there's much more to Odense than top-hatted storytellers, including several great museums, imaginative art galleries, Denmark's best zoo (p165), a superb 'village' museum (p163) of historic houses, and a fizzing bar and cafe scene. With dozens of parks, the city is also a family-friendly destination that lives by its motto: *at leger er at leve* (to play is to live).

Odense is Funen's transport hub and has a small but impressive choice of budget accommodation.

History

Meaning 'Odin's shrine', Odense was named after the Viking god of war, poetry and wisdom, who was said to have had his home here. As the era changed, so too did Odense's religious associations: after the murder of King Knud II in what would later become the cathedral, the bones of the rapidly canonised monarch soon became the object of a popular pilgrimage, bringing considerable wealth to the town. Thus, despite having no harbour, Odense was already Denmark's largest provincial town, even before it was finally linked to the sea by a large canal (from 1800). With a new harbour and an important textile industry, it went from strength to strength until the late 20th century.

21st-century Reinvention

Facing a changing world, the city has been reorienting itself towards education, tourism and high-tech medical and robotics industries. It's investing very heavily in new infrastructure, including a new 14km light railway and a totally reinvented central core. While building continues (due for completion in around 2020), crossing the reconstruction zone of the city centre is only possible on one small footpath at the western end of Hans Jensens Stræde. Old maps of the city will be almost useless. To see the future plans, visit the red Infoboksen (p171) hut.

◉ Sights

If you want to follow in the footsteps of Hans Christian Andersen you can do just that – following the boot-shaped trail marked on the city's pavements that links a series of sights related to his life. The app and brochure at http://andersensodense.dk help to make sense of what you see en route.

◉ Central Odense

★ **Jernbanemuseet**　　　　MUSEUM
(www.jernbanemuseet.dk; Dannebrogsgade 24; adult/child late Jun-late Aug & holidays 95/50kr, off season 65kr/free; ◷10am-4pm; ⊕) For train buffs, this fabulous video-rich museum is almost reason enough to come to Denmark. The core collection of over 30 engines and wagons, ranging from 1868 to 1981, includes an 1869 snow plough, a double-decker carriage and Christian IX's plush 1900 royal saloon car. There are also model trains and ships, and, upstairs, extensive exhibitions on signalling, tunnels and disasters. The 1970s InterRail exhibit is likely to be gushingly nostalgic for any 50-something visitor.

Prices increase somewhat in summer and at holiday periods, when there are numerous extra activities including mini-train rides, a turntable demonstration at 11.45am and 2pm, vintage bus rides (Wednesdays, several between 11am and 2pm) and occasional short steam-train rides.

★ **HC Andersens Hus**　　　　MUSEUM
(www.museum.odense.dk; Bangs Boder 29; adult/child 95kr/free; ◷10am-5pm Jul & Aug, to 4pm Tue-Sun Sep-Jun; ⊕) Lying amid the seemingly miniaturised streets of the former poor quarter is the sparse little cottage where Hans Christian Andersen was born. Visiting it is a small part of a much bigger, modern museum experience that gives a thorough, lively account of Andersen's extraordinary life. His

---

ⓘ ODENSE SIGHT SAVINGS

If you are visiting several museums in a day, the tourist office's 24-hour City Pass (169kr) might save you money – it gives free admission to most sights plus 50% off zoo entry and free bus travel. Alternatively, you can save 30% on some museums by showing the entry ticket to another (within one week), and a few are free on Thursday evenings. Most museums are closed on Mondays from September to May.

achievements are put into interesting historical context and leavened by some engaging audiovisual material and quirky exhibits.

There's also a reconstruction of his Copenhagen study, displays of his pen-and-ink sketches and paper cuttings, and a voluminous selection of his books, which have been translated into some 140 languages. The ticket gets you same-day entry to HC Andersens Barndomshjem, his childhood home.

Brandts 13   MUSEUM
(www.brandts.dk; Jernbanegade 13; combined same-day ticket with Brandts adult/child 95kr/free; ☉10am-5pm Wed & Fri-Sun, noon-9pm Thu) In a stately, porticoed building from 1884, this airy gallery presents regularly changing contemporary art exhibitions, a lot of them multimedia which juxtapose interestingly with the neoclassical architecture.

Møntergården   MUSEUM
(www.museum.odense.dk; Mønterstræde 1; adult/child 50kr/free; ☉10am-5pm Jun-Aug, to 4pm Tue-Sun Sep-May) The new, stylishly designed main section of this city-history museum takes visitors on a thematic walk through humorously named 'Funen – Centre of the Universe', looking at world events and cultural currents through a Funen lens. Different areas cover pre-Viking gods, the Industrial Revolution's effect on villages, WWII occupation, the Cold War and how Funen came to be known as 'Denmark's garden' (the gigantic apple dominating the entry-level hall is a bit of a hint).

Separate buildings include exhibits on Odense in the Middle Ages and Renaissance period, and reveal the inside of a restored 1646 townhouse. Anyone strolling up quaint little Mønterstræde is invited to open the three doors of a 17th-century almshouse. Look inside and love the knitted food.

Brandts   MUSEUM
(www.brandts.dk; Brandts Torv 1; adult/child 95kr/free, after 5pm Thu free; ☉10am-5pm Tue, Wed & Fri-Sun, noon-9pm Thu) This sprawling arts centre occupies a beautifully converted 1887 textile mill. Most of the gallery space is used for well-curated, frequently changing modern art exhibitions, but at least two rooms display highlights of the Brandts Samling permanent collection, tracing 250 years of Danish art.

Highlights from the classical period include HA Brendekilde's powerful *Udslidt* (Worn Out; 1889), depicting a collapsed farm worker. The excellent Dansk Modernisme section includes Olaf Rude's take on Cubism, Karl Isakson's impressionism and

Vilhelm Bjerke Petersen apparently aping Miró. On the 3rd floor, the fascinating if very Denmark-specific **Mediemuseum** (http://museum.odense.dk/mediemuseet; 3rd fl, Brandts, Brandts Torv 1; adult/child 35kr/free; ☉10am-5pm Tue, Wed & Fri-Sun, to 9pm Thu), which requires a separate ticket, traces the development of the press.

Odense Domkirke   CHURCH
(Canute's Cathedral; www.odense-domkirke.dk; Klosterbakken; ☉10am-5pm Apr-Oct, to 4pm Nov-Mar) A feast of whitewashed Gothic arches and vaulting, Odense's imposing cathedral took 200 years to build (1300–1499) with the tower added in the 1580s.

Its most intriguing attraction lies in the chilly crypt, down an inconspicuous staircase to the right of the altar. Here you'll find a glass case containing the 900-year-old skeleton of Denmark's patron saint, King Knud (Canute) II, alongside the bones of his younger brother Benedikt. Both were killed by Jutland peasants during a revolt against taxes; legend holds that Knud was murdered while kneeling to pray in a wooden church that was the cathedral's forebear. Although Knud was less than saintly, the pope canonised him in 1101 in a move that helped secure the Catholic Church in Denmark as well as Odense's status as a medieval pilgrim magnet.

Børnekulturhuset Fyrtøjet   CULTURAL CENTRE
(Tinderbox Children's Culturehouse; www.museum.odense.dk; Hans Jensens Stræde 21; 80-95kr; ☉10am-4pm Fri-Sun Feb–mid-Dec, daily school holidays; ⏵) In the charming Fyrtøjet, children are encouraged to explore the world of Hans Christian Andersen through music and storytelling.

HC Andersens Barndomshjem   MUSEUM
(www.museum.odense.dk; Munkemøllestræde 3-5; adult/child 30kr/free; ☉11am-6pm Jul & Aug, to 3pm or 4pm Tue-Sun Sep-Jun) The small childhood home of Hans Christian Andersen paints a picture of the writer's poverty-stricken childhood. He lived here from 1807 to 1819, aged two to 14. If you visit the HC Andersens Hus on the same day, that ticket will get you in here for free.

◉ Greater Odense

★**Den Fynske Landsby**   MUSEUM
(www.museum.odense.dk; Sejerskovvej 20; adult summer/off season 85/60kr, child free; ☉10am-6pm Jul & Aug, to 5pm Tue-Sun Apr-Jun, Sep & Oct; 🚌110, 111) Wind back the clock to the 1850s

FUNEN ODENSE

Odense

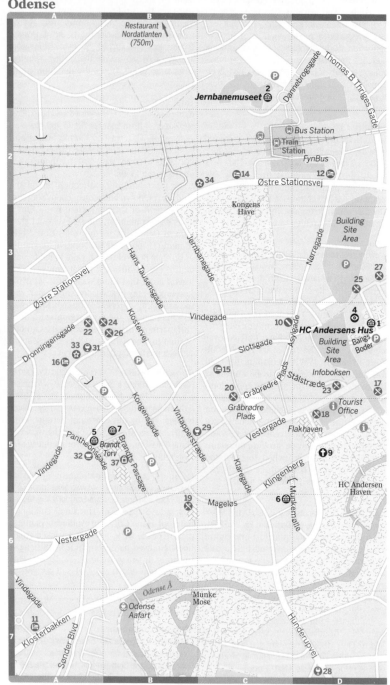

Restaurant Nordatlanten (750m)

Thomas B Thriges Gade

Dannebrogsgade

Jernbanemuseet 2

Bus Station

Train Station

FynBus

Østre Stationsvej

34 14 12

Kongens Have

Norregade

Building Site Area

P 27

25

Østre Stationsvej

Hans Tausensgade

Jernbanegade

Klostervej

Vindegade

10 4 1

HC Andersens Hus

Building Site Area Bangs Boder

22 24 26

33 31

Dronningensgade

16

Slotsgade

Asylgade

Infoboksen

15

23

17

20 Gråbrødre Plads

Stålstræde

Gråbrødre Plads

Tourist Office

Vestergade

18

Flakhaven

Kongensgade

5 7

Brandt Torv

Vindegade Pantheonsgade

32 37

Vintapperstræde

29

9

Klaregade

Klingenberg

HC Andersen Haven

6 Munkemølle

19

Mageløs

Vestergade

P

Vindegade

Odense Å

Munke Mose

Odense Aafart

11

Klosterbakken

Sønder Blvd

Hunderupvej

28

at this delightful open-air museum, a landscaped 'village' of over two dozen furnished old buildings transplanted from around Funen. The scene comes complete with farmyard animals, a duck pond and a windmill, while daily in summer (plus on some other weekends) costumed 'peasants' tend to the geese, while children in knickerbockers play with hoops and sticks.

For context, start the visit with a 15-minute film (English subtitles) and use one of the two guide pamphlets; the less comprehensive one links the sights you see to a Hans Christian Andersen theme.

The museum is in a green zone 4km south of the city centre; buses 110 and 111 (24kr) stop outside at least hourly. Or, May to August, come by boat – the **Odense Aafart** (🕿66 10 70 80; www.aafart.dk; Klosterbakken; adult/child return 90/60kr; ⊙10am-6pm Jul, to 5pm May, Jun, Aug & Sep; 🚢) from Munke Mose sails via Odense Zoo to Fruens Bøge, from where it's a 15-minute woodland walk to the museum.

Odense Zoo   ZOO
(🕿66 11 13 60; www.odensezoo.dk; Søndre Blvd 306; adult/child under 11yr 195/95kr; ⊙10am-4pm or later, see website; 🚢) Denmark's showpiece zoo, 2km south of the city centre, is an active supporter of conservation and education programs. There's an 'oceanium' with penguins and manatees, and a 'Kiwara' open space that aims to mimic the African savannah. Its residents include tigers, lions, zebras and chimpanzees.

✿ Festivals & Events

Tinderbox   MUSIC
(www.tinderbox.dk; Falen; 1-/3-day ticket 1030/1530kr; ⊙3rd weekend Jun) This big, multigenre music festival celebrates the best in pop, indie, electronic and urban music on four stages. Though relatively new, it already draws very big names. The packed line-up in 2017 included Sean Paul, The Killers, Mar+in Garri×, Gogol Bordello, Pet Shop Boys, Martin Solveig and Run-DMC.

Unlike most big rock fests, there's no on-site camping, so Odense's accommodation gets completely packed during the festival and you might be forced to stay miles away in other cities.

Odense Blomsterfestival   FLOWERS
(www.blomsterfestival.dk; ⊙mid-Aug) The Flower Festival turns central Odense into a riot of colour and perfume over a long weekend in mid-August.

FUNEN ODENSE

Odense

◉ Top Sights
1 HC Andersens Hus	D4
2 Jernbanemuseet	C1

◉ Sights
3 Albani Brewery	E5
4 Børnekulturhuset Fyrtøjet	D4
Brandts	(see 7)
5 Brandts 13	A5
6 HC Andersens Barndomshjem	C6
7 Mediemuseum	B5
8 Møntergården	E3
9 Odense Domkirke	D5

⊙ Activities, Courses & Tours
10 Diving 2000	C4

⊜ Sleeping
11 Ansgarhus Motel	A7
12 Cabinn Odense Hotel	D2
13 City Hotel	E3
14 Danhostel Odense City	C2
15 First Hotel Grand	C4
16 Odense City B&B	A4

⊗ Eating
17 Ben Thanh Cafe	D4
18 Bryggeriet Flakhaven	D5
19 Cafe Kosmos	B6
20 Cafe Skt Gertrud	C4
21 Den Gamle Kro	E4
22 Goma	A4
23 Lagkagehuset	D4
24 Mmoks	B4
25 Oluf Bagers Gård	D3
26 Restaurant No 61	B4
27 Under Lindetræt	D3

◉ Drinking & Nightlife
Cafe Biografen	(see 5)
28 Carlsens Kvarter	D7
29 Christian Firtal	B5
30 Den Lille Kro	F6
31 Den Smagløse Café	A4
32 Nelle's Coffee & Wine	A5

◉ Entertainment
Cafe Biografen	(see 5)
33 Dexter	A4
34 Musikhuset Posten	C2
35 Odense Koncerthus	E3
36 Odeon	E3

◉ Shopping
37 Dina Vejling Crafts	B5
38 Kramboden	E4
MRA	(see 38)

Odense Film Festival   FILM
(OFF; www.filmfestival.dk; Brandts Klædefabrik; ⊙ late Aug) Popular festival in late August celebrating short films, with most screenings free.

HC Andersen Festivals   CULTURAL
(http://hcafestivals.com; ⊙ late Aug) Are you at all surprised that the city celebrates its famous native son? This week-long program in the fourth week of August features plenty of HCA performances and lectures, plus concerts, comedy and various family friendly events at a wide range of venues.

⊨ Sleeping

★ **Odense City B&B**   B&B €
(☑ 71 78 71 77; www.odensecitybb.dk; Vindegade 73B; s/d without bathroom from 250/450kr; ⊛) Well-travelled hosts provide seven immaculate modern rooms that must rate as the best value in Odense. Super central, it's entered through a tunnelway between two appealing little restaurants. Deposit your shoes in the box and head upstairs past a small kitchenette on the landing where there's free coffee, tea and fruit. The two shared bathrooms are on the 1st floor.

Billesgade   B&B €
(☑ 20 76 42 63; www.billesgade.dk; Billesgade 9; d/apt from 575/900kr; ℙ ⊛) This spotless B&B has six hotel-standard rooms, each trio sharing a bathroom. There's a communal kitchenette with free coffee and tea, or you can opt for an agreeable breakfast (60kr) made with eggs laid by the hosts' own chickens.

Cabinn Odense Hotel   HOTEL €
(☑ 63 14 57 00; www.cabinn.com; Østre Stationsvej 7; s/d from 495/625kr; @ ⊛) Right at the train station, this functional budget-bed chain has four categories of compact en-suite rooms, all with wet-room and mini-kettle; mint-green linens and towels are provided. In the cheapest economy category, find the ladder to reach the rather claustrophobic upper bed. Standard rooms (double/triple 690/820kr) have a pull-out third bed.

Danhostel Odense City   HOSTEL €
(☑ 63 11 04 25; www.odensedanhostel.dk; Østre Stationsvej 31; dm/s/d/tr/q from 319/435/570/655/690kr; ⊙ reception 4-8pm; @ ⊛) Built in 1914 as the then-grand Park Hotel, this hostel is handily located for the train station, with Kongens Have (park) directly opposite.

Rooms have been modernised with en-suite bathrooms, and there's a guest kitchen, laundry and a basement TV room. Sheets cost 60kr. The 24-hour check-in system uses your bankcard as a room key. No cash accepted.

DCU-Odense City Camp
CAMPGROUND €

(☑ 66 11 47 02; www.camping-odense.dk; Odensevej 102; sites 55kr plus per adult/child 96/51kr, cabins without/with bathroom 560/815kr; 🔊🍴; 🚐 61, 62) This camping ground with hedge-divided plots lies near a wooded area with walking and cycling paths, 4km south of central Odense.

First Hotel Grand
HOTEL €€

(☑ 66 11 71 71; www.firsthotels.dk; Jernbanegade 18; s/tw/d from 995/1045/1095kr; 🅿🔊) Odense's grand dame dates from 1897 and its exterior is still a head-turner. Skilful makeovers have given her rooms an up-to-date feel with dark wooden floors and black furniture setting off white walls and magenta fabrics. The brasserie-restaurant has gilt-capitals on its pillars and many a chandelier, but don't miss the smaller, cosier bar with its classic mini-library wall.

Ansgarhus Motel
HOTEL €€

(☑ 66 12 88 00; www.ansgarhus.dk; Kirkegårds Allé 17; s/d incl breakfast 595/795kr; 🅿🔊) Though there are several free-parking spaces, the term 'motel' undersells this 15-room family guesthouse in a quiet residential area near the river and parkland. Room sizes vary considerably from very compact singles to some impressively spacious doubles. There's an inviting, plant-filled courtyard-garden behind.

City Hotel
HOTEL €€

(☑ 66 12 14 33; www.city-hotel-odense.dk; Hans Mules Gade 5; incl breakfast s 600-950kr, d 750-1200kr; 🅿🔊) Very handy for the HCA Quarter, this light, bright 43-room hotel has comfortable, very clean if unremarkable rooms with slightly faded art prints off corridors that feel like an upmarket hospital. While there's no in-room kettle, guests can help themselves from a coffee machine beside the hostel-style breakfast room.

✖️ Eating

Ben Thanh Cafe
VIETNAMESE €

(Torvegade 1; mains 45-72kr, sandwiches 39kr; ⊗ 11am-8pm Mon-Sat, to 7pm Sun) You'd easily walk right past its unfussy frontage, but for 100% authentic Vietnamese flavours and recipes, Ben Thanh is a superb discovery. Its short menu includes classic *pho* (noodle soup), French-bread sandwiches and delicious *bún thit nuóng* (pork slices, salad and peanuts on noodles), but the star choice is light, minty *goi cuon tôm thit* (shrimp-and-herb roll with soy-peanut dip).

Cafe Kosmos
VEGAN €

(☑ 25 11 31 23; www.facebook.com/cafekosmosvegan organic; Lottrupgård 1; meals 50-99kr; ⊗ 11am-8pm Tue-Fri, to 4pm Sat; 🍴) Positively smelling of good health, this pure vegan cafe serves wraps, veggie burgers, pesto veg bowls and a daily changing special. Organic beers and good coffee also available.

It's hidden just south of Vestergade, guarding the alleyway that leads into the hidden, half-timbered courtyard of Lottrupsgård.

Lagkagehuset
BAKERY €

(http://lagkagehuset.dk; Vestergade 1; ⊗ 6.30am-7pm Mon-Fri, to 6pm Sat & Sun) With big communal tables and a push-button-ticket queuing system, this early-opening bakery-cafe chain has three Odense branches. It's ideal for breakfast, and also does a good range of lunchtime salads and sandwiches plus freshly squeezed juices. Outdoor seating available.

Bazar Fyn
INTERNATIONAL €

(www.bazarfyn.dk; Thriges Plads 3; ⊗ shops 10am-6pm, restaurants noon-9pm Tue-Sun) This roofed market-mall is far from attractive, but it's a great place to get inexpensive fruit and veg or Turkish bread and pastries. After noon, graze at a series of cheap restaurants that give a culinary insight into Odense's multiculturalism: Lebanese *shawarma* (doner kebab), Greek souvlaki, Indian curries, Vietnamese *pho*, Persian *chelo kebab*.

Cafe Skt Gertrud
FRENCH €€

(www.gertruds.dk; Jernbanegade 8; mains 136-298kr; ⊗ 9am-1am Mon-Sat, 10am-midnight Sun; 🔊) Affecting the attitude of a Parisian brasserie complete with Bar-Tabac sign, this very inviting street cafe serves French favourites like mussels in white wine or *ris-de-veau* (fried sweetbreads with apple), as well as steak, salads, fish and scallops with asparagus and blackberry mayo.

★ Oluf Bagers Gård
DANISH €€€

(☑ 64 44 11 00; http://olufbagersgaard.dk; Nørregade 29; cold/hot lunch dishes from 50/125kr, dinner 325kr; ⊗ noon-5pm & 5.30-9.30pm Mon-Sat) This charming mixture of old beams, yellow-brick floors and big low-wattage ball lights offers lunchtime smørrebrød dishes that are works of art. But it's best known for fixed-menu

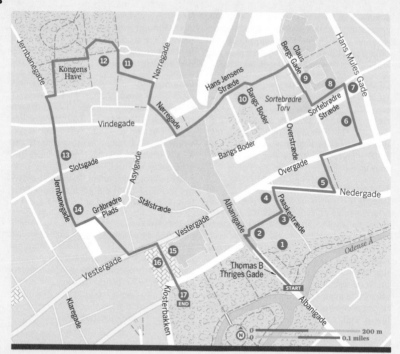

City Walk
Old Odense

START ALBANIGADE BRIDGE
END ODENSE DOMKIRKE
LENGTH 1.5KM; ONE TO TWO HOURS

Walk north past the recently salvaged medieval bishop's house that's now the **1 SDU Office** to the soaringly spired 1867 Catholic church, **2 Sankt Albani Kirke**. Then turn east on Adelgade to **3 Paaskestræde**, whose picturesque houses descend towards pretty riverside gardens. The quaint building at **4 Paaskestræde 1** was once the poorhouse school where Hans Christian Andersen studied. Turn right onto cobbled Nedergade, whose northern side is lined with crooked old houses, galleries and eclectic stores. Beside delightful **5 Kramboden** (p170), a half-timbered courtyard-alley cuts through to Overgade. On another pretty alley, **6 Mønterstræde**, don't miss opening the doors marked Kig Ind ('look inside') to see the furnished interiors of 17th-century almshouses. After the interesting museum **7 Møntergården** (p163), turn left passing

a **8 Hans Christian Andersen statue** that seems to be popping up through a puddle to look at a 1631 house. Around the corner, another **9 HCA statue** sits awaiting selfies on a hotel seat. Storybook streetscapes along Ramsherred and Hans Jensens Stræde take you past the back of the **10 HC Andersens Hus** (p162). Cross the 'reconstruction zone' then some car parks to find triple transepted **11 Sankt Hans Kirke**, linked by an archway to **12 Odense Slot** – a former monastery rebuilt as a palace in 1723, but now used as city offices. Return south on Jernbanegade passing portico-fronted gallery **13 Brandts 13** (p163). Beyond, **14 Gråbrødre Kloster** was once another monastery, then a madhouse in which Andersen's grandad once languished. Now it's a home for the elderly. The surrounding area has great cafes, bars and even a microbrewery within the grand 1881 **15 Rådhus** (town hall) building. Outside, used by toddlers as an unlikely slide, is **16 Oceania**, a muscular reclining nude facing **17 Odense Domkirke** (p163).

dinners that give you nine small dishes presented in three trios, all offering seasonal flavours garnished with love.

The historic building is currently rather easy to miss on a quaint courtyard accessed off the pedestrian lane that links the east and west sections of this split city. However, by late 2018 expansion plans should see it extended onto Nørregade.

Restaurant Nordatlanten DANISH €€€

(☑ 22397600, 66137085; www.restaurantnordatlanten.dk; Nordatlantisk Promenade 1, Finlandkaj; lunch 120-175kr, weekend brunch 225kr, dinner buffet without/with wine 249/499kr; ☺ 11.30am-11pm Mon-Fri, 10am-11pm Sat, 10am-4pm Sun) At the waterfront, in one of the sternly rectilinear modernist buildings of the newly revamped harbour area, is the **North Atlantic House** (www.nordatlantiskhus.dk), celebrating sub-Arctic culture through art, activities and this high-quality fish-based restaurant. Gourmet buffets are good value and can be washed down with Icelandic and Faroese beers.

Under Lindetræt INTERNATIONAL €€€

(☑ 66 12 92 86; https://underlindetraet.dk; Ramsherred 2; brunch/dinner 225/495kr; ☺ noon-2.30pm Thu-Sun, 6-9.30pm Tue-Sat) Right opposite the Andersen House's (p162) most attractive north windows, Under Lindetræt is a dollhouse-quaint 1771 cottage serving celebrated weekend brunches and a fixed-menu gourmet dinner with a regularly changing seasonal line-up. Bookings are essential.

Mmoks NEW NORDIC €€€

(☑ 28 26 29 23; www.mmoks.dk; Kongensgade 65; meals from 300kr; ☺ 5.30-9pm Mon-Sat; 🐾) Combine three or four starter-size dishes (each 100kr) to create an inspired melee of contemporary flavour combinations. The menu changes regularly but might include chicken wings and fennel with rhubarb and broccoli sauce, or cauliflower with mussels and roast almonds.

★ Restaurant No 61 EUROPEAN €€€

(☑ 61 69 10 35; www.no61.dk; Kongensgade 61; 1/2/3 courses 195/275/325kr; ☺ 5-10pm Mon-Sat; 🐾🍴) Family-friendly yet gastronomically oriented, this farmhouse-chic bistro has a short, simple, monthly changing menu of seasonal dishes using produce plucked straight from the Funen fields: white asparagus with truffle-infused hollandaise sauce perhaps, or a confection of strawberry, rhubarb, white chocolate and crème anglaise. Reservations recommended.

Goma JAPANESE €€€

(☑ 66 14 45 00; www.goma.nu; Kongensgade 66-68; set menus 300-500kr; ☺ 5.30pm-late Tue-Sat) Goma is a curious combination. There's a suavely contemporary gin lounge on the ground floor. Then stairs lead down past a titanium-surfaced open kitchen to a basement restaurant with a great reputation for artistically prepared sushi and Japanese-Danish fusion dishes.

Den Gamle Kro DANISH €€€

(☑ 66 12 14 33; www.dengamlekro.eu; Overgade 23; smørrebrød 80-155kr, dinner mains 225-362kr, 2-/3-/4-/5-course meals 298/385/428/449kr; ☺ 11am-10pm Mon-Sat, to 9pm Sun) Combining several half-timbered 17th-century houses around a film-set-worthy roofed courtyard, this place is so romantic that you might find tourists snapping photos of you as you dine.

🍷 Drinking & Nightlife

★ Carlsens Kvarter PUB

(www.carlsens.dk; Hunderupvej 19; beer from 32kr, craft beers 55-225kr; ☺ noon-1am Mon-Sat, 1-7pm Sun; 🐾) From outside it looks entirely forgettable, but within, Carlsens offers Odense's best selection of beers (20 on tap, over 130 in bottles), including such hard-to-find delights as Amager's sublimely hopped miracle Batch 1000, and, if you're lucky, Midtfyns Bryghus' fabulous Imperial Stout.

★ Den Smagløse Café BAR

(www.facebook.com/densmagloesecafe; Vindegade 57; beer 25-58kr, cocktails 70kr, coffee 25-50kr; ☺ noon-midnight or later; 🐾) This friendly, utterly offbeat place uses old radios, caged lamps, yellowing newspaper and junk-shop furniture to create an eccentric atmosphere. But it's the collages of dolls' body parts that get your head spinning – until you stumble into the *'pølseūm'*, a museum display of bottled sausages. Yes. Honestly. There's a cosy garden area if all of the above becomes too much.

Christian Firtal CRAFT BEER

(www.facebook.com/Firtallet; Vintapperstræde 31; ☺ 11am-midnight Mon-Wed, to 2am Thu-Sat) One of central Odense's best places for finding an excellent range of tap beers and whiskies, served at bench seats inside or on a merry street terrace.

Nelle's Coffee & Wine COFFEE

(www.nellesbar.dk; Pantheonsgade; coffee 24-45kr, tea 36kr; ☺ 9am-10pm Mon-Thu, to midnight Fri & Sat, to 5.30pm Sun; 🐾) Many locals rate Nelle's Fairtrade Ugandan coffee as the best in town.

FUNEN ODENSE

BREWED IN ODENSE

Right in the city centre beside the tourist office, **Bryggeriet Flakhaven** (☑66 12 02 99; www.flakhaven.dk; Flakhaven 2; mains 198-298kr, 2-/3-course meal 255/325kr, with beer 313/413kr; ☺11am-11pm Mon-Sat, kitchen noon-2.45pm & 5-9pm) is a combination of micro-brewery, bar and fine restaurant. Four of the staff are qualified 'beer sommeliers' and the monthly changing menu revolves around the planned beer pairing. Downstairs is a tasting room where the 21-beer selection includes not only the restaurant's own brews, many with Hans Christian Andersen–related names, but also Ghost-brewed Coisbo beers, including the remarkably balanced barley wine 'Seven', a great stout and a gluten-free IPA. If you want to drink by the litre, you can choose a half-yard, designed like a Belgian Kwak glass, but you'll need to leave a shoe as deposit...

More mainstream, the various Odense beers served in local pubs come from the city-centre **Albani Brewery** (Tværgade 2), which takes its name from a local saint. First brewed in 1859, its easy-drinking ale was reputedly once a favourite beverage of Hans Christian Andersen. Though it's now part of a big multinational, the brewery is still active and you can peep through big windows in the west wall on Albanigade to admire the brewing stills and, from round the corner on Tværgade, watch part of the bottling line.

Around 10km south in Årslev, modern microbrewery **Midtfyns Bryghus** (☑63 90 88 80; http://midtfyns-bryghus.dk; Industrivej 11-13) produces some of the island's most imaginative beers, including an absolutely glorious 9.5% imperial stout, with smooth notes of gently burnt cocoa. Its chilli beers are exciting discoveries and Eddie the irrepressible US-born boss does occasional standup beer-comedy shows. The brewery has its own shop, or save the journey and taste a selection at Carlsens Kvarter (p169) in Odense.

There are three locations to choose from, all airy, bright places in which you might want to linger.

Den Lille Kro PUB

(Benediktsgade 40; beer 22kr; ☺11am-6pm Mon-Thu & Sat, to 8pm Fri, to 4pm Sun) Smokily unpretentious, this clutter-filled gem dates from 1932 and is very much a locals' local, serving a small range of inexpensive Odense beers.

☆ Entertainment

Odeon CONCERT VENUE

(https://odeonodense.dk; Claus Bergs Gade) Built in 2014, Odeon is Odense's sparkling-new centre for theatre, concerts, musicals, ballet and conference-style events. There's a packed calendar in spring and autumn.

Musikhuset Posten LIVE MUSIC

(www.postenlive.dk; Østre Stationsvej 35) In a former postal warehouse close to the train station, Posten presents live music across widely varying genres (rock, pop, hip hop etc) from both established and upcoming artists.

Odense Koncerthus CONCERT VENUE

(www.odensesymfoni.dk; Claus Bergs Gade 9; ☺Sep-May) Specialising in classical music, the Koncerthus is home to Odense Symphony Orchestra.

Dexter LIVE MUSIC

(www.dexter.dk; Vindegade 65; ☺Sep-Jun) Run mostly by volunteers, this intimate live-performance venue focuses primarily (but not exclusively) on jazz, blues, folk and world music, from Danish and international artists. There are jam sessions every Monday (free entry), but like many of the city's venues, it closes for most of the summer, except during the Jam Days music festival in early August.

Cafe Biografen CINEMA

(www.cafebio.dk; Brandt Torv) Cafe Biografen's cinema shows first-run movies and art-house flicks, and is the stalwart venue for the Odense Film Festival (p166).

🛍 Shopping

★ Kramboden HOMEWARES

(☑66 11 45 22; www.kramboden.net; Nedergade 24; ☺10am-5.30pm Mon-Fri, to 2pm Sat) In a late-16th-century merchant's house with neither heating nor running water, this superb place sells everything from brooms to locks to bottles to Danish flags. It is more museum than shop, yet survives entirely on sales along with metal repairs in the dinky workshop behind. Visitors are free to take photos.

MRA   ART

(www.gallery-mra.com; Nedergade 22; ⊙11am-5pm Tue-Fri, 10am-1pm Sat) This small gallery on the quaintest stretch of Nedergade exhibits Malgorzata Ravn's paintings and, most relevantly, her *papirklip* works (silhouette paper cuts; 350kr to 400kr including frame) in the style of Hans Christian Andersen, who once survived by making similar art.

ℹ Information

INTERNET ACCESS

Virtually every cafe and hotel has free wi-fi.
Galaxy Net Café (Østre Stationsvej; per hour 15-17kr; ⊙9am-12.30am), a space station of a web cafe that's half lit with blue-globe lamps, is on the 2nd floor of the Banegård Center/train station.

MONEY

The main shopping street, Vestergade, has several ATMs.
Forex (✆66 11 66 18; www.forexbank.dk; 2nd fl, Odense Banegård Center; ⊙9.30am-5.30pm Mon-Fri, 10am-3pm Sat) exchanges a wide range of currencies. Good rates; commission (45kr) payable when buying kroner but not for selling.

TOURIST INFORMATION

In the town hall, the **tourist office** (✆63 75 75 20; www.visitodense.com; Vestergade 2; ⊙9.30am-6pm Mon-Fri, 10am-3pm Sat, 11am-2pm Sun Jul & Aug, 10am-4.30pm Mon-Fri, to 1pm Sat Sep-Jun; ☞) and its website are very useful resources.
Infoboksen (Albani Torv; ⊙noon-5.30pm Mon-Fri, 10am-2pm Sat) has updated exhibitions on Odense's city regeneration projects.

ℹ Getting There & Away

BUS

FynBus (✆63 11 22 00; www.fynbus.dk; Dannebrogsgade 10; ⊙ticket office 9am-5pm Mon, to 3.45pm Tue-Fri) runs most of the bus services within Funen and Odense City. These and other longer-distance buses *(rutebiler)* currently depart from various points north of the rail tracks, an area loosely described as a **bus station** (Dannebrogsgade; ⊙info desk 9.30am-4pm Mon-Fri).

Services run at least hourly to numerous destinations including Faaborg (bus 141; 72kr, one hour) and Kerteminde (bus 150; 42kr, 43 minutes).

TRAIN

The train station is within the **Odense Banegård Center** (OBC), a complex containing cafes, shops, the public library and travel facilities including luggage lockers and the train **ticket office** (⊙7am-6pm Mon-Fri, 9am-4pm Sat, 10am-6pm Sun) on the 2nd floor. Note that the concourse

closes 1.15am to 5am, so for night services use the tunnel between platforms 7 and 8.

Direct trains run at least hourly to:
Aarhus (244kr, 1¾ hours)
Copenhagen (278kr, 75 to 95 minutes)
Esbjerg (222kr, 80 minutes)
Nyborg (53kr, 15 minutes)
Svendborg (78kr, 42 minutes, twice hourly)

ℹ Getting Around

At the time of writing, construction of a new light train/tram system (www.odenseletbane.dk) was due for completion by 2020.

NORTHEAST FUNEN

Nyborg

POP 16,500

Attractive Nyborg vies with Roskilde in seeing itself as Denmark's 'first capital'. In its favour, Nyborg's centrepiece castle hosted the Danehof (Danish parliament) before 1413 and was the venue for the signing of the country's first constitution in 1282. The old town surrounds the partially preserved castle's moat with pretty older houses and contoured park areas that reveal remnants of once-vast 16th-century bastions.

Around 1km east, the coastline has a narrow beach fronted by a trio of resort-style hotels with views towards the Storebælts-forbindelsen (p127) bridges, whose construction put Nyborg's ferries out of business. The port has since been redeveloped as a marina and residential area.

⊙ Sights

Nyborg Slot   CASTLE

(www.nyborgslot.dk; Slotsgade 34; museum adult/student/child 70/60kr/free; ⊙10am-4pm Jun-Aug, to 3pm Tue-Sun Apr, May, Sep & Oct) The castle in the heart of Nyborg town was an important royal palace from the 13th century up until 1560, and it was here that Denmark's first constitution was signed in 1282. Though only a part of the structure survives, the castle is fairly impressive seen from certain angles, and houses banqueting halls and a **museum**. It's photogenically set behind earthwork bastions and a partial moat amid a loop of pretty medieval buildings.

Borgmestergården   MUSEUM

(Slotsgade 11; adult/student/child 40/35kr/free; ⊙10am-4pm Jun-Aug, 10am-3pm Tue-Sun Apr, May, Sep & Oct, Thu-Sun Jan–mid-Feb) Combining the

1601 mayor's house with two 1630s merchant buildings, the town museum is still being reworked but will eventually walk visitors through a series of interactive exhibits designed to give the feeling of Renaissance Denmark. The visit starts with an old-world shop.

🛏 Sleeping & Eating

★ Bed & Breakfast

Juelsberg Slot HISTORIC HOTEL **€€**
(☑ 65 31 00 99; www.juelsbergslot.dk; Juelsbergvej 11; s/d incl breakfast without bathroom 500/800kr) Beautifully decorated museum-like rooms are full of antiques, and several sport canopy beds. They fill one wing of a 1776 estate-palace, 5km northwest of Nyborg. Breakfast is included in a similarly period-style dining room downstairs, and the attached park is a delight to wander. There's no reception per se and you'll need your own wheels to get here.

Hotel Hesselet HOTEL **€€**
(☑ 65 31 30 29; http://hotel-hesselet.dk; Christianslundsvej 119; s/d from 1095/1195kr; P 🛜 ⛵) The most alluring of Nyborg's three main beach hotels, the soothingly calm Hesselet offers unusually obliging service and has several star features, including lawn views of the Storebælts-forbindelsen (p127) bridge, a mid-sized indoor swimming pool with sauna and Jacuzzi, and an evocative bar that feels like a gentleman's club.

Built in 1967, it maintains a certain retro feel, albeit more '80s than '60s, and is dotted with east-Asian Buddha statues. Most rooms have views, while a few newer versions have big balconies. Upmarket restaurant on-site.

Central Caféen DANISH **€€**
(Nørregade 6; lunch mains 58-165kr, dinner mains 165-248kr; ⊙ noon-9pm Mon-Sat; 🛜) Wallowing in over 160 years of history, Central Caféen is the archetype of a lovably old-fashioned cafe. A covered courtyard supplements its slightly chintzy dining rooms, where fresh posies of hedgerow flowers sit on gingham tabletops.

Café Apostrof CAFE
(www.cafeapostrof.dk; Havnegade 2A; coffee/beer/wine from 35/30/46kr, mains 75-159kr; ⊙ 10am-10pm or later) This great little cafe-restaurant serves a tasty range of international favourites (spare ribs, tapas, burgers), but is also a relaxing, jazzy-toned place to wind down with a coffee or glass of wine facing Nyborg's yacht harbour.

ℹ Information

There's a **tourist office** (☑ 63 33 80 90; www.visitnyborg.dk; Torvet 2; ⊙ 10am-4pm Mon-Fri, 11am-2pm Sat) on the main square, where the town's medieval fair, **Danehof** (www.danehof.dk; Torvet; ⊙ 1st weekend Jul), holds its highlight jousting competition.

ℹ Getting There & Away

Nyborg is on the main Kolding–Odense–Copenhagen railway line, 30 minutes from Sorø and 15 minutes from Odense (52kr). Bus 195 also goes to Odense but takes an hour. Bus 920 runs hourly from Kerteminde (42kr, 35 minutes); alight at the **Skolegade bus stop** (Nørrevoldgade) for central Nyborg.

Kerteminde & Around

POP 5900

Bridging the almost-closed mouth of a fjord, small, sleepy Kerteminde has a lovable old heart with streetscapes of irregular tiled-roof houses and half-timbered historical courtyards. There are a few museums and several great B&Bs, and the town makes a handy base for visiting the superb Viking-era ship grave at Ladby or for exploring the quiet, rural Hindsholm Peninsula (p174), with two of Denmark's most photogenic villages, Viby and Måle.

⊙ Sights

There's a popular aquarium (www.fjord-baelt.dk; Margrethes Plads 1; adult/child 140/60kr; ⊙ 10am-5pm mid-Jun–Aug, to 4pm Tue-Sun Feb–mid-Jun & Sep-Nov; 🚻) in town and the 1881 **Lundsgaard Gods** (☑ 60 77 60 31; www.anexet.dk; Lundsgaardsvej 15) farm estate, has an impressive gallery space plus a weekend cafe.

Farvergården MUSEUM
(Langegade 8; ⊙ 10am-4pm Tue-Sun) **FREE**
One of the town's oldest and most crooked wooden-framed shop-houses now doubles as a cute little museum celebrating Kerteminde through the ages.

Johannes Larsen Museet MUSEUM
(www.johanneslarsenmuseet.dk; Møllebakken 14; adult/child 80kr/free; ⊙ 10am-5pm Jun-Aug, 11am-4pm Tue-Sun Sep-May) Set around a charming hilltop garden, the centrepiece of this calming museum is the former home of Johannes Larsen, painter of vivid, naturalistic wildlife canvases and provincial Danish scenes. There's also a collection by some 50 other

VIKINGEMUSEET LADBY
....

Vikingemuseet Ladby (www.vikingemuseetladby.dk; Vikingevej 123, Ladby; adult/child 70kr/free; ☉10am-5pm Jun-Aug, 10am-4pm Tue-Sun Sep-May), 6km southwest of Kerteminde, preserves the site of the only known Viking-era ship grave in Denmark. The key site is hidden within a grassy burial mound. Press a knob and electronic doors swing open, allowing you to enter a spooky chamber. Here, complete with bones of 11 sacrificed cattle, the ship's ghostly remnants are preserved in a low-lit, airtight display. Outside, a lawn leads 100m down to the fjordside where a sea worthy reconstruction of the boat is moored.

But before walking 300m to reach the mound, peruse the child-friendly museum, which shows some discovered grave goods and tries to imagine the context of the era (AD 900 to 930). On Wednesdays local women embroider a Bayeux-inspired **Ladby Tapestry**. In the basement there's a reconstructed mock-up of the boat before it was interred. Above that, on the hour and half hour, a wordless, impressionistic six-minute cartoon-video plays out.

The museum is 1.2km north of Ladby village, to which bus 482 (24kr, six minutes) runs from Kerteminde five times on school days only – it's better to cycle. Many visitors bring a picnic to enjoy on the waterside lawns.

---

artists from the Fyn school, along with impressive temporary exhibitions that change around three times annually. Don't miss peeping into the artist's studio with attached greenhouse where Larsen's wife and fellow artist, Alhed, captured lush blooms.

Beside the studio, with views down across the beach, the museum's appealing cafe (open 11am to 4pm) serves light lunches till 1.30pm as well as filter coffee and home-baked cakes. There's a photogenic **windmill** across the street.

🛏 Sleeping

The **Danhostel Kerteminde** (☎65 32 39 29; www.dkhostel.dk; Skovvej 46; s/d/tr/q 560/595/620/640kr; 🛜) is unusually classy for a hostel, there's a **camping ground** (☎65 32 19 71; www.kertemindecamping.dk; Hindsholmvej 80; camping per adult/child 89/49kr; ☉Mar-Sep) at the north end of the beach and the partly 19th-century **Tornøes Hotel** (☎65 32 16 05; www.tornoeshotel.dk; Strandgade 2; s/d/ste incl breakfast 845/1045/1745kr, Jul & Aug 945/1145/1845kr; 🛜) is helpfully central. But the best choices are B&Bs, with lovely options both in town and on the idyllic Hindsholm Peninsula (p174).

Købmandsgårdens B&B   GUESTHOUSE €
(☎65 32 46 51; www.bnb-kerteminde.dk; Andresens Købmandsgård 4; s/d without bathroom 450/550kr; 🛜) Within a very photogenic, half-timbered ensemble of 16th- to 19th-century merchants' houses set around a cobbled courtyard, this great-value B&B has four attractive rooms and a sizeable common area right in

the heart of town. Call a little before arrival as the owners don't live on site.

⭐**Kerteminde Bed & Breakfast**   B&B €€
(☎20 20 78 43; www.kertemindebedbreakfast.dk; Strandvejen 2; small/medium/large d without bathroom 499/649/749kr) A stone's throw from the waterfront and bus station, this lovable, century-old former fisherman's house is furnished with pipes, old violins and countless fine paintings. Even the smaller rooms have a kettle and sink, the shared bathrooms are well equipped and there's a small communal kitchen accessible in the evenings.

🍴 Eating

The town has three pizza joints plus pleasant dining alternatives beside the church, on the marina and in the Tornøes Hotel. For cheap, unsophisticated fish fry-ups there's harbour-front **Cafe Boris** (☎27 12 26 56; Jollehavnen; mains 69-95kr, takeaway snacks 15kr, beer 30-45kr; ☉11am-8pm late Jun-Aug).

⭐**Fiske Restaurant Rudolf Mathis**   SEAFOOD €€€
(☎65 32 32 33; www.rudolf-mathis.dk; Dosseringen 13; mains 345kr, 3-course lunch/dinner 495/595kr; ☉noon-1.45pm & 6-9.30pm Tue-Sat Mar-Dec) Frequently rated as one of Funen's best restaurants, this is a place where classic fish and seafood dishes are served in innovative ways and paired with locally grown produce and floral-herb flourishes to create artistic culinary magic. The harbourside setting is a plus, though the large verandah-style interior feels a little staid.

🍷 Drinking & Nightlife

Though Kerteminde's only a tiny town, there are a couple of very authentic local pubs, **Skænkestuen** (Muusgården 9; beer 17-22kr; ☺10am-7pm Mon-Fri, to 6pm Sat & Sun) and **Varmestuen** (Dosseringen 8A; beer 20kr, meals 75kr; ☺9am-7pm, kitchen till 4pm or 5pm), the latter with live music on Tuesdays from 5pm.

Lulu's Cafe   CAFE
(http://luluscafe.dk; Langegade 2A; coffee 25-35kr; ☺10am-5.30pm Wed-Mon) At the south end of Kerteminde's pretty main street, Lulu's serves good coffee at a street terrace shaded by gigantic parasols, or indoors beneath lampshades. The cafe doubles as an interior-design boutique.

🛍 Shopping

Høkeren   HOMEWARES
(Trollegade; ☺10am-5.30pm Mon-Fri, to 1pm Sat Jun-Aug plus holidays) Høkeren feels more like a museum than a shop, with a nostalgic range of old-world wares from baskets to rope to woven shoes to liquorice sticks. There's a good commercial art gallery next door too.

ℹ Information

Kerteminde Turistbureau (☏65 32 11 21; www.visitkerteminde.com; Strandvejen 6; ☺10am-6pm Mon-Fri, to 3pm Sat & Sun Jun-Aug, 11am-5pm Mon-Fri, 10am-noon Sat Sep-May) shares a building with the post office. Rents bikes (per day 100kr).

ℹ Getting There & Away

Buses 151 and 885 connect Kerteminde with Odense (48kr, 40 minutes). Bus 920 takes a convoluted route to Faaborg via Nyborg (42kr, 35 minutes) and Egeskov Slot (60kr, one hour), but for Faaborg itself it's quicker to change in Odense.

Driving or riding a bike (rental available through the tourist office are the best ways to reach Ladby or the Hindsholm Peninsula, to which bus services are limited to a few per week.

Hindsholm Peninsula

For pretty, undulating contours and countless glimpses of inspiring seascapes, head to the sparsely populated Hindsholm Peninsula by bike or small car (narrow roads don't suit bigger vehicles). Particularly memorable are the picture-perfect thatch-and-timber villages of **Viby** and **Måle**, there are galleries at **Langø** and **Nordskov**, and for excellent **sea-trout fishing** visit **Måle Strand**. For lunch, the inn at **Mesinge** is essentially the only restaurant, though there is a seasonal bakery in Måle. And to stay, it's hard to beat nine-room **Bjørnegården** (☏26 83 33 00; Bjørnegårdsvej 140, Hersnap; s/d 350/600kr, breakfast 50kr), an idyllically peaceful 1638 farmstead B&B with low beams and cosy public spaces full of splendid art and classic Danish designer furniture. It's set in a field-sized garden around 500m from a stony east-coast beach, 12km north of Kerteminde via Dalby.

SOUTHERN FUNEN

The island's southern towns, Faaborg and Svendborg, are delights in themselves, as well as the main access points for the 55-island South Funen Archipelago. Shaped by glaciation around 18,000 years ago, these geological bumps were initially hills and ridges but became islands when sea levels rose and water eventually burst through the Langeland Gap, partly drowning a Stone Age culture and creating what a recent Faaborg exhibition dubbed 'Funen's Atlantis'.

Above water, the islands are some of Denmark's true gems for those with a little time to explore. Most offer summertime bike rental and overnighting opportunities. While **Tåsinge** and Langeland (p184) are connected to Funen by road, for most of the islands you'll need to take a ferry. Delightful Ærø is the best known as a holiday destination, but several others are easy to reach by scheduled summertime boat services, whether from Faaborg (**Lyø**, **Avernakø** and **Bjørnø**), Svendborg (**Drejø**, **Skarø** and **Hjortø**), Marstal (**Birkholm**) or Rudkøbing (**Styrnø**).

With the Ø-hop ticket, midsummer visitors also have a way to island-hop using the Sea Hawk (p177), which links Avernakø, Drejø and Skarø four times daily, starting and ending its run in Svendborg. Further connections have been mooted, of which the most advanced is the reintroduction of a Marstal–Rudkøbing service, tentatively planned for 2019.

For a vast range of activity ideas throughout South Funen and the islands, refer to **Archipelago Map** (www.archipelagomap.dk), **VisitFyn** (www.visitfyn.com) and **Danish Archipelago** (www.detsydfynskeoehav.dk). Sea kayaking, windsurfing, angling, sailing, scuba diving and cycling are all well represented. And for hikers there's the week-long Øhavssti trail. Dotted throughout the area, ultrabasic **Booken Shelter huts** (http://booken

shelter.dk) are available for cyclists, kayakers and walkers with their own bedding. Some have a modest booking charge (usually 30kr per person), while others are free but first-come, first-served. The website's 'Find a Shelter' map gives locations and contact details.

Faaborg

Faaborg first appears in Danish historical documents in 1229, but its heyday was the 17th century when the town claimed one of the country's largest commercial fishing fleets. While sleepier these days, the port still has island-hopping ferries, and vestiges of Faaborg's former golden years live on in cobblestone streets lined with crooked cottages, as on Adelgade, Tårngade, Feltens Rist and dog-legged Holkegade. You'll also find galleries, statues and museums (including a free one in the bus station), plus one of the oddest public sculptures for miles around.

⊙ Sights

Ymerbrønden   STATUE
(Torvet) Over a century after its unveiling in 1912, Kai Nielsen's astonishing statue is still likely to raise eyebrows. Yes, that is indeed a naked man lying beneath a cow and sucking from its bronze udders. Well, not exactly a man, but the frost giant Ymir, from whose body the sky and earth were made according to a Norse creation myth. This prominent version on the main old-town square outside Sydbank is, in fact, a copy. The granite original is within the Faaborg Museum.

Faaborg Arrest   MUSEUM
(https://ohavsmuseet.dk; Torvet 19; adult/student/child 50/40kr/free; ⊙10am-4pm Jul & Aug, 11am-3pm Tue-Sun mid-Feb–Jun, Sep & Oct) Faaborg's 12-cell former jail remained in service until 1989. Now it's a fascinating museum examining the changing justice system since the 18th century, with some very imaginative interactive exhibits mostly focused on the early 20th century.

Klokketårnet   TOWER
(Bell Tower; www.klokketaarnet.dk; Tårnstræde; adult/child 20kr/free; ⊙11am-4pm mid-Jun–mid-Aug, 10.30am-1pm mid-Aug–late Aug) This 16th-century bell tower had been under construction as part of a new church when the Reformation swept through Denmark. The never-finished church building was demolished in 1550 but the tower survived, its rococo spire added in 1778. It's now a Faaborg icon and in summer visitors can climb 108 steps within, though the best views are actually from the penultimate floor.

Faaborg Museum   GALLERY
(www.faaborgmuseum.dk; Grønnegade 75; adult/student/child 80/50kr/free; ⊙10am-4pm Jun-Aug, closed Mon Sep-May) In a tailor-made 1915 townhouse building with a flower-filled garden, this impressive gallery's 700-plus permanent collection focuses on the healthily realist, light-infused paintings of the early-20th-century pre-Impressionist Fynboerne artists, notably Johannes and Alhed Larsen, Peter Hansen, Jens Birkholm and Anna Syberg.

Vesterport   HISTORIC BUILDING
(West Gate; Vestergade) One of the most attractive glimpses of Vestergade's half-timbered houses is from where the street tunnels through this step-gabled brick gatehouse, which dates back to the 15th century.

Den Gamle Gaard   HISTORIC BUILDING
(https://ohavsmuseet.dk; Holkegade 1; ⊙11am-3pm daily Jul, 11am-3pm Sat & Sun Jun & Aug-late Oct) FREE Den Gamle Gaard is a beautiful 1720s timber-framed house arranged to show how a wealthy merchant lived in the early 19th century. If you can get inside (opening times are limited and change each year), you can peruse 22 rooms full of antique furniture, porcelain, toys and maritime objects.

FUNEN FAABORG

WALKING THE ØHAVSSTI

The 220km **Øhavssti (Archipelago Trail)** is a series of long-distance walking routes that snake across southern Funen, northern Langeland and Ærø. It's divided into seven 25km to 35km sections, each covered by a free map-guide. These are available in Danish, German and English-language versions from local tourist offices or to download at www.visitodense.com/ln-int/funen/natural-areas/south-funen-archipelago-trail. You can also buy a more detailed 180-page guidebook covering the whole lot.

Vagabond Tours (www.vagabondtours.dk) offers six-night, seven-day packaged walk programs ferrying your luggage to the next accommodation as you hike the route (5050kr per person, minimum two people).

Faaborg

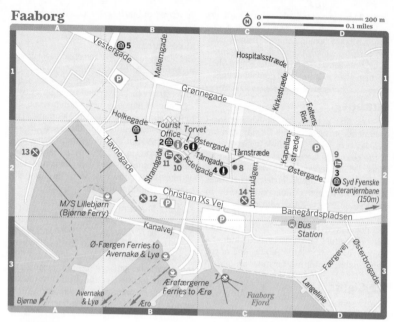

Faaborg

🏃 Activities

Sea-Bathing Pool
SWIMMING

(Langelinie) One of the harbourfront's most curious modern constructions is a wave-like wooden structure with steps up to two viewing platforms. Beneath is a kayak storeroom and changing area with toilets and sauna. A floating boardwalk leads out to a diving place and an enclosed wooden area that forms a sea-water swimming pool.

Syd Fyenske Veteranjernbane
RAIL

(☑ 62 61 17 09; www.veteranbanen-faaborg.dk; one way/return 50/90kr) This antique (but usually not steam-powered) train makes half-hour summer runs to Korinth on Sundays, Tuesdays and/or Thursdays in late June, July and early August, departing at 11am and 2pm and returning an hour later (ie the whole trip lasts 90 minutes).

On Thursdays in July there's also a 7pm train. In Faaborg the departure point is east of the Lidl supermarket, on Østebrogade. If you want to continue from Korinth, bus 920 takes you to Ringe (42kr, 25 minutes) on the Odense–Svendborg main line.

👉 Tours

Vaegterne
WALKING

(The Watchmen; Torvet; ⊗ from 9pm early Jul-late Aug) FREE An intriguing way to get into the spirit of old Faaborg is to follow the costumed nightwatchman, who begins his rounds from Klokketårnet (p175) at 9pm on summer evenings.

🛏 Sleeping

Danhostel Faaborg HOSTEL €

(☑ 62 61 12 03; www.danhostelfaaborg.dk; Grønne-gade 71-72; s/d/tr/q 375/450/550/600kr; ⊙ Apr-Sep; 🐾) This oh-so-cosy, city-centre hostel has 20 bright-white rooms in its two historic buildings. Most are twins with two further fold-down wall-bunks and rather-too-few in-room electric sockets. Sheets cost 70kr.

Fresh new toilets incorporate swing-door showers. These lead off the kitchen, which has stools at two long tables plus modest cooking equipment (microwave, kettle, sink and fridge). The hostel is right beside the Faaborg Museum (p175). Prices increase around 10% at peak holiday periods.

Magazin Gaarden Hotel Faaborg HOTEL €€

(☑ 62 61 02 45; http://hotelfaaborg.dk; Torvet 13-15; s/d/ste incl breakfast 750/950/1200kr; 🐾🐾) Above a fairy-tale restaurant and a more urban-style cafe, this hotel's 13 rooms are modestly fashion-conscious with wet-room bathrooms, a chocolate on your pillow and the odd Klee print to add colour to the monochrome decor. Room 15 has a particularly good view across the main square.

Dogs are permitted to stay for 150kr per night extra. Check in through the restaurant or (Sundays and Mondays) via the cafe. Prearrange a key pick-up if arriving late.

🍴 Eating

Faaborg Røgeri SEAFOOD €

(www.faaborgroegericafe.com; Vestkaj 3; fish dishes 34-82kr; ⊙ 10am-9pm late Jun–mid-Aug, reduced hours rest of year) This smokehouse fish-shop right at the harbourside sells takeaway fish cakes and fish fillets (by weight), but also doubles as a cafe with the same items made into lunch plates with basic salads or bread.

Dangved Brønden THAI €€

(☑ 62 61 11 35; www.dangvedbronden.dk; Torvet 5; mains incl rice 165-195kr; ⊙ 5-9pm Mar-Nov) Enchanting lanterns, flickering flower-candles and glittering Buddhas add an inviting east-Asian twist to this historic main-square house, serenaded by mellow jazz. Follow silky smooth *tom kha kai* (chicken-coconut soup) with sinus-blasting green curries that are as authentic as any beyond Bangkok.

Hotel Færgaarden DANISH €€

(http://hotelfg.dk; Christian IXs Vej 31; mains 85-185kr, 2-/3-/4-course dinner 295/356/425kr) Hotel Færgaarden's unique feature is the smaller of its dining rooms with original 1919 cabinets,

1929 glass ceiling and a menu that comes with optional beer pairings, all from Funen's foremost local microbreweries.

Det Hvide Pakhus DANISH €€

(☑ 62 61 09 00; www.dethvidepakhus.dk; Christian IXs Vej 2; lunch 88-155kr, dinner mains 155-265kr; ⊙ 11.30am-10pm Jul & Aug, reduced hours rest of year) Set in a light-infused harbourside warehouse, Det Hvide Pakhus wins on location, obliging service and light-touch fashionable decor. Lunches are Danish standards plus salads and burgers, while dinner menus add steaks and grills.

ℹ Information

On the 1st floor of the former courthouse, the helpful **tourist office** (☑ 63 75 94 44; www.visitfaaborg.com; Torvet 19; ⊙ 9am-5pm Mon-Fri, to 2pm Sat Jun-Aug, 10am-4pm Mon-Fri Sep-May) has cycling and hiking maps, sells a 20kr city walking guide and organises fishing licences. Downstairs, open longer hours (9am to 9pm), is an unmanned information room full of free leaflets and with a touchscreen computer.

ℹ Getting There & Away

BOAT

The little **M/S Lillebjørn** (☑ 20 29 80 50; www.bjoernoe-faergen.dk; return adult/child/bicycle late Jun–mid-Aug 59/30/18kr, off season 20/10/10kr) passenger ferry to Bjørnø takes 17 minutes each way.

For Ærø, use the **Ærøfærgerne car ferries** (☑ 62 52 40 00; www.aeroe-ferry.dk; Kanalvej) to Søby (one hour), departing at 5.10am (weekdays only), 11.40am and 5pm. With a car, book a week or more ahead in summer. Pedestrians can generally buy tickets on board without fuss.

Ø-Færgen (☑ 72 53 18 00; http://islandferry.fmk.dk; return adult/child/bicycle 120/85/30kr, off season 45/30/10kr) car ferries operate triangular routes to the small islands of Lyø and Avernakø, five to eight times daily. Tickets are valid for a return trip including stops on one or both islands (overnight stop allowed).

In midsummer, foot or cycle passengers can also use the **Sea Hawk** (www.sea-service-express.dk) to island-hop onward from Avernakø via Drejø and Skarø (with a few hours in each) to reach Svendborg the same evening using the same ticket.

BUS

Destinations from Faaborg's **bus station** (Banegårdspladsen) include the following:

Egeskov Slot (42kr, 26 minutes) bus 920

Odense (60kr), bus 141 (one hour) or bus 111 (95 minutes)

Svendborg (52kr, one hour) bus 931

ℹ️ Getting Around

Faaborg Cyceludlejning (☎ 25 13 06 60; www.faaborgcyceludlejning.dk; Svendborgvej 270; per day/week 100/440kr) at the appealing Askeris B&B, around 4km east of Faaborg, rents various types of bicycle, delivered by arrangement to any local address for a small fee (25kr for up to four bikes).

There's **free parking** (Christian IXs Vej) near the harbour. A smaller **car park** (Grønnegade) near the Danhostel (p177) has three-hour free disc parking.

Around Faaborg

Those with their own wheels can enjoy several special eating and accommodation options just outside Faaborg, notably in pretty port-village Fasled (9km northwest via Millinge) and at Horne (4km west), famed for its distinctive if not-so-round 'round' church.

Horne

With its spired tower and indulgently ornate dining rooms and lounges, **Hvedholm Slotshotel** (☎ 63 60 10 20; www.slotshotel.dk; Hvedholm 1; s 650-850kr, d 900-1100kr, ste 2000-2200kr) is a castle-hotel where you feel like you've entered an 18th-century costume drama. Guest rooms are all different, most with canopy-style beds, and while a few suffer slightly from chipped paint and musty Laura Ashley–esque fittings, all are great value and many are spacious. Breakfast is included.

Fasled & Millinge

Steensgaard   DELI €€
(☎ 62 61 94 52; Steensgaard 7, Millinge; charcuterie plate 165kr; ☺ noon-9pm Fri-Sun mid-Jun–Aug; 🛜) Vegetarians beware: this farm estate's unique shop-cafe is all about top-quality meat, with a large window through which you can often watch a carcass being butchered as you dine. The cuts come from thoroughly loved animals, grass-fed and managed with as much humanity as possible, making Steensgaard a great place for animal-loving carnivores.

⭐ **Falsled Kro**   DANISH €€€
(☎ 62 68 11 11; www.falsledkro.dk; Assensvej 513, Falsled; 6-/8-course dinner menu 1075/1795kr, with wine 2150/3290kr) Book well ahead for a full-on gourmet experience, but with bigger portions and far warmer service than in so many upmarket places. Falsled Kro's cuisine focuses on prime, locally harvested ingredients cooked using French techniques with

Nordic twists. Dine on a lawn-front verandah or within the picture-perfect thatched inn (rebuilt 1851). It's 10km west of Faaborg.

No 517 Falsled   CAFE
(☎ 40 33 71 03; www.tallerkengalleriet.dk; Assensvej 517, Falsled; coffee/beer/wine 20/35/40kr; ☺ 12.30-5pm Wed-Sat & holidays) If you're strolling through the pretty village of Falsled, this shop-cafe is a great place for house-roasted coffee, ground for you using 100-year-old machines. Also available are Icelandic beers, Greenlandic gin and Hansens ice cream.

Egeskov Slot

Complete with moat and drawbridge, **Egeskov Slot** (www.egeskov.dk; Egeskov Gade 18, Kværndrup; adult/child castle & grounds 210/130kr, grounds only 180/110kr; ☺ 10am-7pm Jul–mid-Aug, to 5pm mid-Apr–Jun & mid-Aug–mid-Oct; ♿) is a magnificent example of the lavish castles that sprang up during Denmark's 'Golden Age'. Though still lived in, you can look inside many of the furnished rooms and/or explore the beautiful 15 hectares of garden, sections of which have a vast range of family-friendly activities, a treetop walk of shaky bridges with push-button birdsong and several museums displaying a remarkable collection of antique vehicles. Plus a fun if cheesy Dracula Crypt.

The castle was built in 1554, requiring a foundation of thousands of upright oak trunks. Accessible rooms display antique furniture, grand period paintings and an abundance of macabre hunting trophies. But most intriguing is the 'never-moved' figure in the toy-filled attic, plus Titania's Palace, a superb room-sized dollhouse built as a miniature fantasy palace for a 19th-century version of Shakespeare's Queen of the Fairies.

Check the website for 'Open by Night' events (usually Wednesdays in peak summer), when the grounds stay open until 11pm, with a program of evening concerts and fireworks. There's also pre-Christmas activity, a midsummer bonfire and **Heartland** (2-day ticket 1290kr; ☺ 1st weekend Jun), an international rock festival.

Within the castle park is an Italian-leaning cafeteria and a couple of hot-dog/ice-cream kiosks. Just outside the gates there's a basic, tent-only camping ground. It's free but shower tokens cost 5kr from the castle ticket office. If you want grander accommodation, fairy-tale Broholm Castle is around 20 minutes' drive away.

ℹ Getting There & Away

Hourly bus 920 costs 52kr from Faaborg (25 minutes), 60kr from Nyborg (one hour) or 60kr from Kerteminde (95 minutes). It stops 400m south of the castle entrance gate at Egeskov Gade on Rte 8. That's around 2km west of Kværndrup, which has a station on the Odense–Svendborg railway line.

Faaborg to Svendborg

If you have your own transport, there is a selection of off-beat attractions that lie not too far from the pleasant Faaborg–Svendborg main road.

◉ Sights

Egebjerg Mølle   VIEWPOINT
(www.egebjergmollenaturrum.dk; Alpevej 36, Stenstrup; ⊘24hr) **FREE** North of Otterup, this former windmill has lost its sails and had its crown replaced by faceted-glass viewing windows, creating an observation point to admire the surrounding countryside and distant seascapes. Inside, a fascinating series of maps shows the region's changing topography during and after the ice ages. There's also a gallery section and a series of nature-based activity ideas.

Gorilla Park Svendborg   BUNGEE JUMPING
(🗹29 16 74 75; http://gorillapark.dk; Rødmevej 45, Stenstrup; adult/child 305/255kr; ⊘daily late Jun–mid-Aug, other dates vary, closed Nov-Mar) Spend half a day walking, climbing and flying through the forest on a remarkable network of ropeways and zip lines, as well as base jumps and a pair of 'Tarzan swings'.

Book ahead online and don't be late: your four-hour experience has to start with a set-time 45-minute training session. The entrance booth has a cafe and lovely view, but is in the middle of nowhere, 4km from Sendstrup Syd station.

M/F Ærøsund   DIVING
(www.dyk-sydfyn.dk/16-home.html; Ballen) Deliberately scuttled in 2014 to create a pollution-free wreck dive, this former ferry is already developing into a mini-reef and makes for one of Denmark's most intriguing scuba adventures at depths between 6m and 19m.

The site is some 7km west of Svendborg, offshore from the charmingly simple, 'organic' **Syltemae Camping** (www.syltemae-camping.dk), near Ballen village. The website gives plenty of practical details, while Diving 2000 (p181) in Odense is a useful contact for arranging equipment and can combine

OFF THE BEATEN TRACK

BROHOLM CASTLE

Set behind a double moat, **Broholm** (http://broholm.dk; Broholmsvej 32, Gudme; d/ste 1795/2195kr, mill house s/d without bathroom 695/895kr; 🚍930, 931) is one of Denmark's most historic castles and much of it remains packed museum-like with antiques, paintings and heirlooms. Indeed, it has a 19th-century archaeological museum of its own as well as antique dolls, a well-stoked fireplace and classy restaurant, and yet the atmosphere here is less stuffy than at many other upmarket castle hotels.

The 19 rooms are all different, but are photographed in detail on the website. Four in the oldest wing share two huge bathrooms. Most others are period-elegant en suites within the castle's late-18th-century west wing, while three significantly cheaper options (sharing two bathrooms) are in a beautifully appointed thatched watermill-cottage across the road (with communal kitchen and lounge, but guests can still use the castle lounges). If you want to dine more cheaply than at the in-house restaurant (starters/mains 165/265kr, breakfast 145kr), drive 5km east to Lundeborg, which has four harbour cafes.

a weekend's diving here with gaining your PADI wreck-diving certification.

✗ Eating

★ Vester Skerninge Kro   DANISH €€
(🗹62 24 10 04; www.vesterskerningekro.dk; Krovej 9, Vester Skerninge; lunch mains 95-168kr, dinner mains 158-225kr, 3-/4-/5-course menu 370/420/470kr; ⊘noon-3pm & 6-9pm Wed-Sun) Beside Vester Skerninge church on the main Svendborg–Faaborg road, this photogenic thatched inn is an absolute classic. The traditional Danish fare is excellent quality, and if you don't fancy accompanying it with wine or one of the fine craft beers try sipping its subtly flavoured homemade rhubarb or elderflower cordials.

Svendborg

POP 27,070

Gateway to Funen's beautiful southern archipelago, Svendborg is the darling of the Danish yachting fraternity, with a harbour packed with yachts and older wooden boats

Svendborg

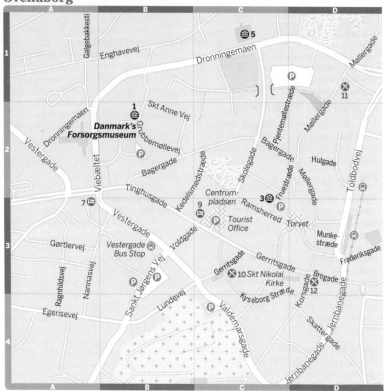

and schooners. Although it has its modern light-industrial sectors, Svendborg has wooded cycling areas, popular beaches, cafe-dotted streets and a summer ferry service that putters south through the island-dotted estuary to Valdemars Slot (p183).

⊙ Sights

As well as its museums, harbour and boat-lined waterfront, the town has a few pretty back alleys and an impressive central church. Svendborg's oldest house, the 1560 **Anne Hvides Gård** (www.svendborgmuseum.dk; Fruestræde 3), leans tipsily to one side in stark contrast to the modernist cafe next door.

★**Sejlskibsbroen**   WATERFRONT
Sejlskibsbroen is a jetty lined with splendidly preserved wooden sailing ships, including some multimasted schooners, all seaworthy and making regular sorties, along with a plethora of yachts from the adjoining marina.

★**Danmark's Forsorgsmuseum**   MUSEUM
(www.forsorgsmuseet.dk; Grubbemøllevej 13; adult/student/child 50/40kr/free; ⊙10am-4pm Tue-Sun mid-Feb–mid-Dec) This highly thought-provoking 'welfare museum' is housed in Svendborg's old poorhouse, within which paupers lived segregated by sex, as virtual prisoners during its century of operation (from 1872). They became forced labourers making rope-matting or doing mindless chores like packing bundles of ice-lolly sticks.

There were two ways to be admitted to this institution – the 'worthy' poor (the elderly or those with disabilities, for example), or the 'unworthy poor' (capable of work but unemployed, alcoholics, vagrants or 'women of easy virtue'). It's hard to reconcile this with today's equitable Danish society, but the museum does an excellent job in explaining the times and extending the debate to ponder today's attitude to the destitute.

FUNEN SVENDBORG

designed to give a very visual introduction to wildlife, with children a target audience. But while there are plenty of films to watch and some fun hands-on games (can you tap faster than a woodpecker?), the main attractions are countless stuffed animals and birds, so if you're not a fan of taxidermy this might be a place to avoid.

🏃 Activities

The Svendborg area is tailored for those who love the sea. Yachts are attracted like magnets to Sejlskibsbroen and to pretty Troense across the sound. A range of boats, including the elegant schooner Meta, take visitors to lonely islands. Summer **sea kayaking** is easy to arrange through NicusNature (p184). And, with a little more planning, there are a selection of offshore **dive-sites** mapped on www.dyk-sydfyn.dk. These include shallow-water Stone Age sites accessible even to snorkellers, while for experienced green-water scuba divers there's wreck-diving on the M/F Ærøsund (p179), a scuttled former ferry. Odense's **Diving 2000** (Diveresort Fyn; ☑ 66 13 00 49; http://diveresortfyn.dk; Asylgade 16; ⊙ 10am-5pm Mon-Fri, to 1pm Sat) rents gear and organises occasional group trips.

Danmarks Museum for Lystsejlads MUSEUM
(National Yachting Museum; www.lystsejlads.dk; Frederiksø 2; adult/child under 15yr 65kr/free; ⊙ 10am-4pm or later Jul & Aug, 10am-2pm Tue-Fri, 10am-6pm Sat & Sun Sep) In a large harbourside warehouse you can peruse over 30 out-of-water sailboats, along with a collection of outboard motors and a workshop where, when volunteers are on hand, you can learn various knot-making techniques.

Interesting boats include *Stormy II*, in which adventurer Sven Billesbøll sailed around the world between 1988 and 1994, and *Meteor IV*, the 1892 steam pinnace of Germany's Kaiser Wilhelm II.

Naturama MUSEUM
(www.naturama.dk; Dronningemaen 30; adult/child 140kr/free; ⊙ 10am-5pm late Jun-Aug, to 4pm Tue-Sun Sep, Oct & Feb-late Jun; 🚼) Impressive for its sweeping three-storey modern layout and multisensory approach, Naturama is

Meta BOATING

(☎63 75 94 92; www.billet.dk/skonnerten-meta; Havnepladsen 2; Skarø cruise adult/child 300/200kr, sunset cruise 200/150kr; ⊙late Jun-late Aug) During the summer holiday period twin-masted schooner *Meta* makes four-hour sailing tours to Skarø, departing 10am on Sundays, Mondays and Tuesdays, plus two-hour sunset jollies on the same days at 7pm.

On other days it departs from Rudkøbing (Wednesday, Friday) or Marstal (Thursday). Pre-book online or through the tourist office.

Festivals & Events

Organ Festival MUSIC

(www.sct-nicolai-kirke.dk; Sankt Nikolai Kirke, Kyseborg Stræde 1; ⊙early Aug) A series of organ concerts in Svendborg's central Sankt Nikolai church.

Sleeping

Central Svendborg has a **Danhostel** (☎62 21 66 99; www.danhostel-svendborg.dk; Vestergade 45; s/d/tr/q 575/600/630/660kr, with linen & breakfast 600/750/850/900kr; P@) that's more like a hotel and several good but tiny B&Bs. Many more options including a superb castle-hotel lie further afield, with two camping grounds and several 'Svendborg' B&Bs across the sound on Tåsinge.

Hotel Ærø HOTEL €€

(☎62 21 07 60; www.hotel-aeroe.dk; Brogade 1; s/d incl breakfast 850/1025kr;) This brilliantly located hotel extends through four buildings with over 60 rooms in varying styles, with 1930s- to '40s-style mock antique furniture in many. Harbour views cost 100kr extra. The main section is near the Ærø ferry dock, with an atmospheric pub-reception and a wood-panelled old-world restaurant.

Hotel Svendborg HOTEL €€

(☎62 21 17 00; www.hotel-svendborg.dk; Centrumpladsen 1; s 800-1225kr, d 900-1325kr; @) This pleasant, unsurprising business hotel is handily central.

★**Stella Maris Hotel** HOTEL €€€

(☎62 21 25 25; www.stellamaris.dk; Kogtvedvænget 3; d incl breakfast from 1495kr) The epitome of light-touch luxury, the Stella Maris has as its core a 19th-century villa, revamped with oodles of gently contemporary flair. For the full effect book room 8, the Romantic Suite (2895kr), with double-aspect views of the bay, private balcony-terrace and a Jacuzzi.

Eating & Drinking

Børsen GASTROPUB €€

(www.borsenbar.dk; Gerritsgade 31; mains 95-165kr, brunch buffet 155kr, beer from 35kr; ⊙10am-11pm or later) Serving a mixture of international and Danish classics from nachos and burgers to salads and herring, this large but lovable multi-roomed pub is especially notable for its daily brunch (before 2pm).

The central copper brewing vessel is only decorative, but don't miss peeping upstairs in the 'Martha' room, a pseudo ship's cabin evoking the Danish cult comedy movie from 1967, which is replayed amid hearty carousing every 'Martha Day', the first Friday of May.

Vintapperiet FRENCH €€

(☎62 22 34 48; Brogade 37; lunch 85-145kr; ⊙11am-6pm Mon-Fri, to 4pm Sat) Mixing rustic France with merry Denmark, the snacks and salads at this appealing little bistro make a tasty lunch or a good accompaniment to an indulgent glass or three from the extensive wine list. The place is tucked within a half-timbered courtyard house behind Cafe Ø. If you want dinner, stumble down the road to the co-owned Madtapperiet.

Pizzeria La Pupa ITALIAN €€

(www.lapupa.dk; Møllergade 78; pizzas 90-146kr, mains 200-250kr; ⊙5.30-10pm Tue-Sun) Run by a real-deal Sicilian family, this archetypal old-style Italian restaurant is unafraid to flaunt its chianti bottles at all comers.

Kammerateriet BAR

(www.kammerateriet.com; Frederiksø; Albani/craft beers from 35/55kr; ⊙2-11pm or later) With black cushions on black benches, warehouse-style Kammerateriet's main bar area feels like you're camping in a cinema foyer, but there's a chance of live music or DJ nights from 9pm on summer weekends. When the sun's shining, you can take your booze and tapas across the road onto what approximates as an artificial sandy 'beach'.

Shopping

Bente Sonne Glasblæseriet GLASSWARE

(www.glasblaeseriet.dk; 1st fl, Brogade 37; ⊙10am-5.30pm Tue-Fri, to 1pm Sat) Hand-blown glassware that you can see being made (early mornings best).

Information

The **tourist office** (☎63 75 94 80; www.visitsvendborg.dk; Maritime Centre, Havnepladsen 2; ⊙9am-5pm Mon-Fri, 9am-1pm Sat Jul &

Aug, 9am-4pm Mon-Fri Sep-Jun) is within the 19th-century maritime centre building, cohabiting with the **Pakshusbutikken**, a store selling souvenirs and local produce from across the South Funen area.

❶ Getting There & Away

Trains leave Odense for Svendborg twice an hour (78kr, 42 minutes). Bus 931 stops in Svendborg between Faaborg (52kr, 50 minutes) and Nyborg (72kr, 50 minutes). Both train and main bus stations are north of the Ærø ferry terminal, on Toldboldvej, but for Langeland, it's better to pick up bus services at the Vestergade stop.

BOAT

Ærø car ferries to Ærøskøbing (p187) cross up to 12 times daily (75 minutes).

To five other small islands, any one-day combination of rides from Svendborg costs only 100/60/20kr per adult/child/bicycle, or 120/85/30kr if you use the Ø-Færgen (p177) ferry between Avenakø and Faaborg.

The deal is valid on the following:

Sea Hawk (p177) high-speed passenger boat, with a complex mid-summer only multi-route flitting between Svendborg, Lyø, Avenakø, Skarø and Drejø (with some double-backs).

Højestene (⏹ 62 21 02 62; www.hoejestene. dk; adult/child 4-12yr return 100/60kr, bicycle/ motorbike/car 20/100/200kr), a year-round car ferry from Svendborg to Drejø (80 minutes) via Skarø (35 minutes, four or more daily).

Hjortøboen (www.hjorto.dk/faergen.html; adult/child/bicycle summer 100/60/20kr, off season 40/24/8kr) ferry to Hjortø (one to three daily), stopping at Skarø on one return leg but only in the summer holidays.

❶ Getting Around

The town centre is walkably small but bicycle rental is available from **Fri BikeShop** (⏹ 44 22 10 16; www.fribikeshop.dk/cykler-svendborg; Johannes Jørgensens Vej; bicycle per day/ week 100/250kr, mountain bike 300/650kr; ⏱ 8am-5.30pm Mon-Fri, to 2pm Sat), opposite the Danhostel, and from social-charity outfit **Cykeltutten** (Svendborg Cykeludlejning; ⏹ 52 24 58 66; www.svendborgcykeludlejning.dk; Frederiksø 18F; first/subsequent day 90/60kr). The tourist office (p182) has maps and brochures outlining scenic bike paths.

BOAT

From mid-May to early September, the vintage vessel **M/S Helge** (www.mshelge.dk) sails between Svendborg and Valdemars Slot (60kr, 55 minutes). En route it makes four intermediate stops. First is Vindebyøre (Svendborg Sund camping ground; 30kr, 10 minutes), then the popular beach area of Christiansminde (30kr, 15 minutes), pretty Troense (60kr, 30 minutes) and Grasten on Thurø island. It departs Svendborg harbour at 10am, 12.30pm and 2.30pm with extra July departures at 4.30pm, 6.30pm and 8.30pm. You can use it as a sightseeing tour (60kr one way) or a short-hop transport option riding two stops for 30kr.

Around Svendborg

Northern Tåsinge

Across the forest-edged sound from Svendborg, **Troense** is a very pretty village crammed with thatched, half-timbered cottages (especially along streets Grønnegade and Badstuen), and spiked with a series of picturesque yacht jetties. It's best known for 'Denmark's biggest private house', the historic palace-castle of Valdemars Slot, 1km southeast. If you come by road, consider a quick stop en route in **Bregninge** village, where a quaint **museum** (www.taasinge-museum.dk; Kirkebakken 1; adult/child 40kr/free; ⏱10am-4pm Tue-Sun Jun-Aug, Thu-Sun early–mid-Sep) and lovely picnic spot lie across the road from a brick church with panoramic views from its **tower** (www.bregningekirke.dk; Kirkebakken 2A; tower adult/child 5/2kr).

◉ Sights & Activities

Valdemars Slot   CASTLE
(www.valdemarsslot.dk; Slotsalleen 100; adult/child 105/55kr; ⏱10am-5pm Jun-Aug, closed Mon May & Sep) Ideal as a boat-trip excursion from Svendborg, this lavish palace is crammed with antique furniture, Venetian glass, 17th-century Gobelin tapestries and little eccentricities like a toilet hidden in a window frame, a secret ammo store and Niels Juel's sea chest pasted with engravings. In the attic, the **Jagt & Trofæmuseet** (www.bhfnaturskole.dk) displays a grisly horde of hunting trophies.

Not to be confused with the much older fortress (p125) at Vordingborg, this Valdemars Slot was originally built in 1644 by King Christian IV for his son Valdemar Christian, who died on a Polish battlefield before the place was completed. Badly damaged in the Danish-Swedish wars, the castle was gifted to naval hero Niels Juel, who transformed it into the baroque mansion you see today.

Sailing to Valdemars Slot from Svendborg on the M/S *Helge* passenger ferry is a pleasure in itself, and you don't need a castle ticket to walk around the eastern decorative pond, to stand on the narrow strip of beach near the jetty, to buy ice cream in the sparse

FUNEN AROUND SVENDBORG

baroque pavilion-cafe or to lunch at the semi-smart **restaurant** (☑62 22 59 00; www. valdemarsslot.dk; Slotsalleen 100; lunch 99-149kr, 2-/3-course dinner 235/298kr, coffee and cake 65kr; ☉11am-5pm Feb-Oct, plus 5-8.30pm Jul & Aug) in the castle's vaulted cellars. However, there's a 25kr admission charge to enter the western **ornamental park**.

To return to Svendborg a different way, you could walk 1km to pretty Troense village and catch the half-hourly bus back from **Mærskgården/Lodsvej** (bus 250 stop; 24kr, 28 minutes; Eghavevej).

NicusNature KAYAKING
(☑30 30 13 33; www.nicusnature.com; Kullinggade 29; kayaks per 3hr/day from 200/350kr) Kayaks and paddleboards to rent plus spear-fishing trips by arrangement. The small hut-store is at the entrance to Svendborg Sund Camping. Call ahead for opening hours.

🛏 Sleeping

Svendborg Sund Camping CAMPGROUND €
(☑21 72 09 13; www.svendborgsund-camping.dk; Vindebyørevej 52, Vindeby; per adult/child/dog/ site 85/60/20/30kr, Jul–mid-Aug 90/65/20/70kr, small/large hut 450/800kr, Jul–mid-Aug 600/975kr; ☉Apr-Sep; 🛜) Arrive by ferry (p183) from Svendborg at this well-kept facility that tops a field slope leading up from the M/S *Helge* jetty. As well as cottages and camping grounds, there are glamping arrangements where you rent a pre-erected, bedded tent. Bicycle and kayak rental available.

B&B Teglgaarden B&B €€
(☑28 11 71 82; www.teglgaarden.dk; Jydevej 3, Gammel Nyby; d incl breakfast 700kr, without bathroom 650kr) Around 1.2km east of Bregninge, Pia welcomes guests into a rural courtyard farm where you can sit and gaze across fields, pet horses and enjoy partly organic breakfasts including eggs from the house chickens. Four of five rooms share bathrooms between pairs but are appointed with antique furniture and attractive art. All have doors to private terrace or garden areas.

Langeland

Great for cycling or bird-watching, Langeland is a long, mainly agricultural island dotted with windmills and farming villages, and fringed by the odd beach. Apart from sometimes frenetic traffic on the main spine road, everything moves at an unhurried pace.

Langeland & SE Funen

Connected by bridge to Svendborg via Tåsinge, Langeland's major town is gently attractive Rudkøbing. Greater attractions lie north at Tranekær with its castle and sculpture park, and around Bagenkop on the south tip, where the former NATO military stronghold of Langelandsfort (p186) gives intriguing insights into the paranoia of the 20th-century Cold War era.

ⓘ Information

A free, 142-page tri-lingual Langeland guidebook is available from the Rudkøbing tourist office.

ⓘ Getting There & Away

Bridges link Langeland to Funen. Buses 930 and less frequent 810 shuttle between Svendborg and Rudkøbing (42kr, 30 minutes). For Lolland, the 45-minute Spodsbjerg–Tårs **car ferry** (www. faergen.dk; Spodsbjerg; car/motorbike incl passengers 265/130kr, pedestrians adult/child 80/40kr) runs hourly from 5.15am to 10.15pm in each direction.

ℹ Getting Around

Island transport starts from Rudkøbing, bus 912 running south and 913 going north. Both start from the **main bus stand** (Ringvejen), but if you're in the town centre, the Rudkøbing Rådhus **stop** (Fredensvej) is more convenient.

Rudkøbing

POP 4590

Viewed from the high bridge as you arrive on the island, Langeland's main town offers a pleasing mass of red-tiled roofs, punctuated by a church spire and windmill, and looking onto a yacht marina. Several Rudkøbing streets are lined with low, tilting houses fronted by hollyhocks and roses – **Ramsherred** and **Smedegade** are especially pretty.

It's worth strolling on past the church to the main square, Torvet, where the tourist office gives away a free tri-lingual guidebook covering the attractions of Langeland. Then continue along partly pedestrianised Østergade, which has several cafes, the fabulous everything-shop **Tingstedet** (www.tingstedet-langeland.dk; Østergade 16; ⊙11am-5pm Mon-Thu, to 6pm Fri, 10am-1pm Sat) and a **museum** (langelandsmuseum.com; Østergade 25; ⊙11am-4pm Wed-Fri, 10am-2pm Sat May-Dec) [FREE]. There are several art galleries around town too.

Rudkøbing has two hotels, a **hostel** (Rudkøbing Camping; http://rudkobing-camping.dk; Engdraget 11; d/tr/q 450/500/550kr, without bathroom 375/425/475kr; ⊙Feb-Sep; P🛇🏕) with camping ground and a selection of private rooms that you can book via the **tourist office** (📞62 51 35 05; www.langeland.dk; Torvet 5; ⊙9.30am-4.30pm Mon-Fri Jan-Dec & 9.30am-2.30pm Sat Jul & Aug).

There's a series of cafes along Østergade, including a popular branch of Skovsgaard's organic-oriented **MadMarked** (www.skovsgaard madmarked.dk/cafe; Østergade 6; lunch 85kr; ⊙11am-5pm Mon-Sat, daily midsummer; 🛇) 🍴.

WATERFOWL WILDERNESS

Encompassing marshy shallows and several coastal lakes, **Tryggelev Nor** (www.fuglevaernsfonden.dk/fuglereserva ter/tryggelev-nor; Stenbækvej) is a hotspot for wading birds and waterfowl. The beautiful area has a couple of somewhat worn observation hides, and is accessed from a driveable track that approaches along a beachside causeway from the south.

Tranekær

POP 250

Little Tranekær is Langeland's most appealing village. Forming a kink in the Langeland highway, it's flanked by 19th-century houses, a few galleries and the cerise-red castle Tranekær Slot with its magical park full of outdoor art installations. Nearby there's a garden of medicinal herbs.

◉ Sights

Tranekær Slot CASTLE
(☑stays 62 59 10 12, tours 60 96 80 90; www.tranekaergods.dk; Slotsgade 86; per person 150kr; ⊙tours mid-Jul only, generally 11am & 3pm Tue-Sat mid-Jul only; 🚌913) Site of fortifications since the 13th century, Tranekær Slot has been in the hands of one noble family since 1659. The spired castle is mostly used for exclusive business meetings and pheasant-hunting stays, and the interior is only accessible to the general public for two or three weeks in July, limited to those prebooking a tour.

Tickon GARDENS
(Tranekær International Centre for Art & Nature; Botofte Strandvej; adult/child 25kr/free; ⊙sunrise-sunset; 🚌913) A unicorn's horn sprouts in a glade. A river of tree trunks floods down a hillside. A giant basket disgorges a flood of boulders. These and 15 more naturalistic, outdoor art installations are set in over 200 acres of Tranekær Slot's lakeside grounds. The fun is finding them in the beautiful mature woodlands, in which 70 of the trees are also identifiable through the entry pamphlet or using QR-coded pillars. Populations of red deer seem quite oblivious to onlookers. When the gate is unmanned, pay using coins in the honesty box.

Tranekær Slotsmølle WINDMILL
(http://slotsmoelle.dk; Lejbøllevej 3; ⊙11am-5pm daily Jul & Aug, Tue & Thu May, Jun & Sep; 🚌913) One of the island's many impressive old windmills, the 1834 Slotsmølle contains a little museum and has a simple cafe with coffee and cake for just 25kr.

It's 1.5km north of the castle, just off the main Rte 305, though it's easy to miss driving northbound due to the masking trees.

🛏 Sleeping & Eating

By special arrangement groups can stay in the castle itself. In the village, Sukkerfabrikken is a summer-only option, Tranekær Slotskro has 14 guest rooms and Restaurant

Generalen operates a handful of converted apartments. In the surrounding countryside there are several more B&Bs, plus there's upmarket camping by the pleasant if seaweed-plagued beach at **Emmerbølle Strand** (Feriepark Langeland; ☑ 62 59 12 26; http://ferie park-langeland.dk/en/emmerboelle; Emmerbøllevej 24; adult/child 99/78kr plus site peak periods only 69-139kr; ⊙ Easter–mid-Sep).

Æblegaarden   B&B €

(☑ 59 64 02 44; www.aeblegaarden.dk; Fæbækvej 25; per adult/child incl breakfast 385/185kr; 🛜; 🚌 913) Part farm, part orchard garden, this rural B&B 8km north of Tranekær Slot (p185) offers two stylish, light-filled rooms with shared kitchenette and bathroom. An excellent breakfast is included, but do arrange arrival times in advance.

Sukkerfabrikken   GUESTHOUSE €€

(www.sukkerfabrikken.dk; Slotsgade 76; s/d 470/780kr; ⊙ Jul–mid-Aug; 🅿🛜; 🚌 913) 🥾 This large, 1804 building has been a kindergarten and a brewery, having failed as Denmark's first sugar refinery – it could only ever manage syrup. It's now a residential learning centre packed with works by local artists, but in summer the attractively furnished if simple oak-floored rooms are for rent, hotel style. Prices include sheets, towels, wi-fi and breakfast in the organic cafe.

★ Restaurant Generalen   DANISH €€

(☑ 62 53 33 03; http://housepichardt.dk; Slotsgade 82; lunch mains 89-135kr, dinner mains 215-245kr; ⊙ 11.30am-9pm daily Jun-Aug, 6-9pm Thu, 11.30am-9pm Fri & Sat, noon-4pm Sun Feb-May & Sep-Nov; 🅿; 🚌 913) At the western base of Tranekær Slot (p185), Generalen has converted classic 1800 stables into a stylish restaurant, maintaining the horse-box divisions between tables, though there is also cafe seating outside. Menus are typical Danish, concentrating on locally sourced produce and often reworking recipes from the castle's 1815 cookbook.

Tranekær Slotskro   AFRICAN, DANISH €€€

(Tranekjær Gæstgivergaard; ☑ 62 59 12 04; Slotsgade 74; lunch mains 80-200kr, dinner mains 225-275kr; ⊙ 10am-9pm; 🅿) This 1802 village inn, 200m south of the castle (p185), is run by a Tanzanian family who offer Indo-African cuisine (lunch sets include samosas, fried banana, couscous) alongside more typical Danish fare in a dining room with scarlet ribbons on white chairs.

The hotel section has 14 guest rooms (double/suite 600/1000kr), most of which are in a 1970s annexe behind.

❶ Getting There & Away

Every two hours, bus 913 heads north from Rudkøbing's Plads A stop, reaching Tranekær (32kr) in around 20 minutes.

Bagenkop

POP 468

Langeland's southernmost settlement, Bagenkop has a busy marina with restaurants and a tower to survey the area. Finds from a 5000-year-old tunnel-grave burial mound south of town revealed evidence of Europe's oldest known dentistry, while more interesting underground visits take you into gunners' bunkers at the late-20th-century Langelandsfort museum. At the island's rural tip, semi-wild Exmoor ponies keep the coastal meadows cropped near the very modest earthen cliff at **Dovnsklint**.

◉ Sights

★ Langelandsfort   HISTORIC SITE

(www.langelandsfort.dk; Vognsbjergvej 4B; adult/child 95kr/free; ⊙ 10am-4pm May-Sep, to 3pm Apr & Oct) Built in 1952–53, this complex of gun emplacements dug into the Langeland fields was designed to delay an assumed Warsaw Pact invasion if the Cold War turned hot. Exhibitions within bunkers add context: those on spying and shell-loading are especially gripping. Adding to the experience, you can board Denmark's last submarine (decommissioned in 2004 and now sitting in a field), explore a minesweeper and peep inside fighter planes, comparing a Soviet MiG-23 with a NATO Draken A-005.

Exhibits are predominantly in Danish but with English and German summaries and plenty of video footage that is self-explanatory. To see everything involves a walk of about 2km, so you'll need at least a couple of hours to do the place justice, plus an umbrella on rainy days.

Hulbjerg Jættestuen   ARCHAEOLOGICAL SITE

(Søgårdsvej) Dating back to around 3200 BC, this tunnel-grave mound 2km south of Bagenkop is so well-enough preserved that you can confront your claustrophobic demons and crawl inside. It's a slightly disquieting experience, but don't expect to bump into the skeletons of its original 53 corpses.

They were removed in 1960, when one of the skulls was found to have had its teeth drilled in what's the oldest-known evidence of dental work in Europe.

🛏 Sleeping

Bagenkop Kro INN €€

(☑ 62 56 13 04; www.bagenkopkro.dk; Østergade 15; s/d 500/800kr, breakfast 89kr; 🛜) This revamped old inn is mother ship to 44 guest rooms dotted about in half a dozen buildings around Bagenkop village. What draws the constant crowds is its remarkable half-board deal offering double rooms with seafood buffet dinner, including beer, wine, coffee and cake, all for just 1195kr per couple (or 995kr midweek, off season).

❶ Getting There & Away

Every couple of hours, bus 912 connects Rudkøbing to Bagenkop (52kr, 35 minutes) passing within 700m of Langelandsfort.

Ærø

POP 6290

Just 30km long and 9km wide, Ærø (pronounced 'with difficulty' – or *air*-rue) is the front runner for the title of Denmark's loveliest – and friendliest – island.

Country roads roll through gentle countryside peppered with thatched-roofed, half-timbered houses and old windmills. There's a rich maritime history, beaches with photogenic bathing huts and the little town of Ærøskøbing is a picture-book beauty. The island is famed as Europe's up-and-coming wedding capital, thanks to both its romantic setting and its 'can-do' attitude towards hitching foreigners with awkward paperwork issues. Accommodation is mostly in family-run guesthouses and B&Bs. There's a **Jazz Festival** (www.aeroejazzfestival.dk) in early August.

❶ Information

The useful Ærø Guide is available at tourist offices or via www.aeroe.dk.

❶ Getting There & Away

Ærøfærgerne (☑ 62 52 40 00; www.aeroeferry.dk; Søby Havn; return adult/child/car late Jun–mid-Aug 212/106/463kr, mid-Aug–late Jun 80/40/166kr) runs year-round car ferries on three routes:

Svendborg–Ærøskøbing The main service, running up to 12 times daily (75 minutes).

Faaborg–Søby Twice/three times daily weekends/weekdays (one hour).

SKOVSGAARD

Spired and moated but more modest than many other publically accessible rural manor houses, **Skovsgaard** (☑ 62 57 26 66; www.skovsgaard.dn.dk; Kågårdsvej 12, Hennetved; adult/child 60kr/free; ☺ 10am-5pm Apr-Oct) is part organic farm, part museum-gallery. Most fascinating in the main building is the well-preserved series of 'below stairs' rooms, furnished with dummies and models to give an insight into 1930s servant life with kitchen cellar, pheasant hanging room, vegetable stack and staff dining room. The stables hold a collection of carriages and tractors, and an excellent, hands-on nature-education centre called **Kiss the Frog** (www.kys-froen.dk; Skovsgaard Gods; ☺ 24hr; 🖼) 🖉 . Wonderful for kids. Near the entrance, deli-cafe **MadMarked** (www.danmarksnaturfond.dk; lunch plate 85kr, Thu dinner 120kr; ☺ 10am-5pm Apr-Sep, Thu-Sun Oct-Mar, to 9pm Thu) brims with fresh, organic local produce – some balcony seats are raised above the castle's moat.

Fynshav–Søby From Fynshav on the island of Als (southern Jutland). Three times daily, 70 minutes.

Prices are the same on all three routes. All tickets are return fares that can be combinations of any two routes. For most of the year the return fare is 80/40/166kr per adult/child/car, but it increases steeply between late June and mid-August when you'll pay 212/106/463kr. Bicycles cost 29kr at any time. If you have a car, it's wise to reserve a few days ahead, further ahead for summer weekends.

The former ferry link between Marstal and Rudkøbing (on Langeland) has not operated since 2013, but at the time of writing, there were tentative plans to restore it in 2019.

❶ Getting Around

The free, local Jesper bus (www.jesperbus.dk) runs the length of the island, approximately hourly each way. Well-signed cycle routes offer a 60km, three-day circuit. Bikes can be rented in Ærøskøbing, Marstal and Søby, or get them delivered to you through **Bike Erria** (☑ 32 14 60 74; www.bike-erria.dk; Pilebækken 5, Ærøskøbing), who can also transport your bags between destinations. If you're tired, you can take your bike on the bus after 9am.

Ærø

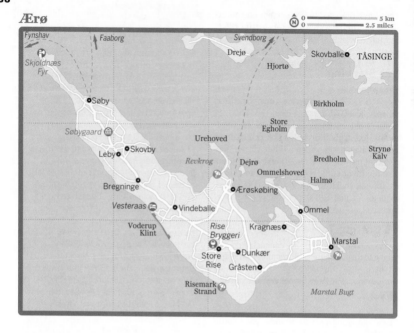

Ærøskøbing

POP 940

The utterly delightful little 17th-century merchants' town of Ærøskøbing has bucket loads of character. Its core is a triangular web of gently curving cobblestoned streets where crooked houses are cheerfully painted, gently skewed and gaily fronted with roses and hollyhocks. In half-hidden courtyards, hand-blown glass windows and low doorways offer tantalising glimpses into snug, private worlds. Outstanding accommodation, great cafes and alluring dining options, plus several little museums and a whisky distillery, all add to the magic. And with regular direct ferries to Svendborg, it's also the easiest town on Ærø for transport access.

◉ Sights

★ Det Gamle Værft   MUSEUM

(www.detgamlevaerft.dk; Havn 2; ◔11am-4pm Mon-Fri Jun-Sep, to 3pm Mon-Thu Oct-May) In a still-active mini ship-repair yard with century-old boats on the rear slipways, this memorable hands-on activities experience lets you hammer your name in runes into recycled copper, weave rope, catch crabs by hand and learn how to work a blacksmith's forge.

Hammerichs Hus   MUSEUM

(www.arremus.dk; Gyden 22; adult/child 40kr/free; ◔noon-3pm Mon-Fri Jul & Aug, by appointment rest of year) Our favourite of Ærøskøbing's lovable trio of little museums, half-timbered Hammerichs Hus is a gnarled, old hobbit-hole of a cottage, packed with antiques collected by sculptor Gunnar Hammerich. The walls upstairs are lined with around 3000 beautiful 17th- and 18th-century Dutch tiles.

Ærø Museum   MUSEUM

(www.arremus.dk; Brogade 3-5; adult/child 30kr/free; ◔11am-4pm Mon-Fri, to 3pm Sat & Sun Jul & Aug, 11am-3pm Mon-Sat May, Jun & Sep or by appointment) For now, this little museum is a classic clutter of domestic ethnographic items, ship paintings, furniture and glass cases that rattle as you walk by on the creaky floors. But room 10 has a more modern approach with its town model and QR-coded 'tour' of Ærøskøbing in its 1863 heyday. The whole place expects a major revamp by 2018.

Don't miss the pretty rear garden, planted to look as it did in the 1920s.

Flaske Peters Samling   MUSEUM

(Smedegade 22; adult/child 40kr/free; ◔10am-4pm Jul & Aug, 11am-3pm Mon-Sat mid-Apr–Jun & Sep–mid-Oct, by appointment rest of year) In what was once the poorhouse, peruse over

500 ships-in-bottles representing the amazing life's work of Peter Jacobsen, nicknamed 'Bottle Peter'.

⚡ Activities

Vesterstrand   BEACH
(Vestre Strandvej) For a swim, or for sunset-watching amid two dozen brightly painted bathing huts, walk or cycle to this beach, a few minutes north of town via Strandvejen or Sygehusvejen. The beach is a mix of sand and pebbles, with a jetty to get you over the worst of the accumulating seaweed.

☞ Tours

Nightwatchman Tour   WALKING
(Torvet; adult/child 30kr/free; ⊙9pm Jul, 8pm Aug) Dressed up in costume and cap, the nightwatch man or woman walks visitors around on pre-sunset tours of the old town for around an hour. On Wednesdays and Saturdays the tour is in English.

🛏 Sleeping

Ærøskøbing Camping   CAMPGROUND €
(☑62 52 18 54; www.aeroecamp.dk; Sygehusvejen 40; per site adult/child 78/48kr) A kilometre north of the town centre, and two minutes' walk via a footpath from Vesterstrand, this gently sloping camping ground has a very attractive aspect, hedge-sheltered plots, playground and pool-room/kitchen.

★ Pension Vestergade 44   B&B €€
(☑62 52 22 98; www.vestergade44.com; Vestergade 44; s/d without bathroom incl breakfast 990/1090kr; ⊛) Surrey-born Susanna and her laid-back Gordon setter Tillie are perfect hosts at this large, beautifully appointed 1784 house originally built by a sea captain for his daughter. Full of books, framed etchings and period furniture, most rooms are named after their colour scheme, and there's also a self-contained unit in the extensive, tree-shaded garden, itself an oasis of delight.

Det Lille Hotel   BOUTIQUE HOTEL €€
(☑62 52 23 00; www.det-lille-hotel.dk; Smedegade 33; s/d 650/950kr; ℙ⊛) Above a well-regarded restaurant, charming bright-white rooms share three little bathrooms, plus there's an apartment in the upper eaves. While the entrance is on Smedegade, there's alternative access through the garden and a small parking area that backs onto the grassy harbour foreground.

På Torvet   APARTMENT €€
(☑62 52 40 50; www.paatorvet.dk; Torvet 7; d/ste 1190/1690kr; ⊙closed Jan–mid-Mar; ⊛) Above and behind an excellent, light-filled cafe-bar on the idyllic main square is a series of beautifully conceived studio-rooms each with sitting area, kettle and fridge (downstairs bigger than up). However, the best options are up creaky 170-year-old stairs above the cafe.

Andelen Guesthouse   GUESTHOUSE €€
(☑61 26 75 11; www.andelenguesthouse.com; Søndergade 28A; d/tr without bathroom 895/1095kr, ste 2295kr) Adventurous British overland traveller Adam has converted an 1898 granary warehouse into a stylishly characterful guesthouse, maintaining wooden floors, many low beams and even the original grain-hoist in the split-level suite (sleeps four). The other five rooms share two large, well-designed bathrooms.

🍴 Eating

Den Gamle Købmandsgaard   DELI €
(The Old Merchant's Court; https://dgkshop.com; Torvet 5; ⊙10am-5.30pm Mon-Fri, 10am-4pm Sat) This picturesque outlet shop for local produce was originally set up by volunteers at a time when the old square seemed set to lose its last surviving shop. Now something of an attraction in itself, DGK sells fine local produce (bread, beer, salami, ice cream, honey and chocolate), and has a charming cafe section and a whisky distillery in the yard.

Ristorante Pizzeria
Badehotel Harmonien   PIZZA €
(☑42 50 00 05; Brogade 1; pizza 70-120kr; ⊙5-10pm May-Sep, 5.30-9pm Thu-Tue Oct-Apr) Italian-owned and -run, the restaurant of the Badehotel has lots of character, with views to the waterfront and plenty of alfresco seating.

Mumm Restaurant   INTERNATIONAL €€
(http://mumm.restaurant; Søndergade 12; lunch mains 75-115kr, dinner mains 140-185kr, steak 230-270kr; ⊙noon-9pm Jun–mid-Sep, 6-9pm Wed-Sat mid-Sep–May; ⊛🍴) With flickering candles, dark-painted beams and old-fashioned chairs, Mumm is a perennial favourite with relatively informal mini-wedding parties (Prosecco/Champagne per bottle 295/495kr). But it's warmly welcoming to all comers, including vegetarians: it's hard to beat its lunchtime bean tartare with hummus and watermelon carpaccio.

FARMSTAY RETREAT

For a very special middle-of-nowhere experience, stay at **Vesteraas Bed & Nature** (☑ 61 28 62 52; www.vesteraas. dk; Voderup 41; cottage 750-1250kr; ☺ May-Sep), a family-friendly, sustainable farm where cows and chickens roam. Two atmospheric, self-contained units, each sleeping up to six, are well equipped if rambling and very rustic. One is a converted old stable, its facade drowning in wild roses, the rear door opening out to fabulous sweeping views.

Café Aroma   INTERNATIONAL **€€**
(☑ 62 52 40 02; www.cafe-aroma.dk; Gilleballetofte 2A; mains 82-158kr, steak 248kr; ☺ 10am-9pm mid-Jun–mid-Aug, 11am-7pm Apr–mid-Jun, Sep & Oct) Half of this terraced, harbour-area institution is given over to selling its delicious homemade ice cream. The other half is an informal cafe cosily plastered with film posters and sporting old cinema seats, a battered sofa and a barber's chair. The all-day menu includes fish, salads and vegetarian burgers.

☆ Entertainment

Bio Andelen   CINEMA
(☑ 62 52 17 11; www.bio-andelen.dk; Søndergade 29A; adult/child 70/50kr; ☺ 7.30pm Tue-Sat, 3pm Sun, closed Jul–mid-Aug) Claiming to be Denmark's smallest cinema, this sweet little 50-seater is beneath the Andelen Guesthouse (p189), whose guests get complimentary tickets. It is also a venue for many gigs during the annual Jazz Festival (p187).

❶ Information

There's a **Tourist Office** (☑ 62 52 13 00; www. visitaeroe.dk; Havn 4; ☺ 9am-4pm Mon-Fri) directly south of the ferry terminal. If you're here to get married, **Danish Island Weddings** (☑ 25 56 64 42; www.getmarriedindenmark.com; Torvet 5) can provide tailored support services.

❶ Getting There & Away

The **Ærøfærgerne** (☑ 62 52 40 00; www.aeroe-ferry.com) car **ferry to Svendborg** (☑ 62 52 40 00; www.aeroe-ferry.com; return adult/child/car late Jun–mid-Aug 212/106/463kr, mid-Aug–late Jun 80/40/166kr) departs three times every four hours between 5.35am and 8.35pm. The ticket you bought to get to Ærø will be valid so there's no need to buy another one, but for vehicles, pre-booking the departure slot can be wise at busy periods.

Hourly free buses to both Marstal (25 minutes) and Søby (25 minutes) pick up passengers from a **stop** (Vestergade) opposite the tourist office, around 100m southwest of the harbour.

❶ Getting Around

Tiny Ærøskøbing is easily walkable. A mixed-bag assortment of different bicycles is available for hire from **Pilebækken Cycles** (Pilebækken 5; per day/week 75/400kr; ☺ 9am-4.30pm Mon-Fri year-round plus 9am-1pm Sat & Sun Jun–mid-Sep), or choose the newer ones from **Andelen Guesthouse** (p189; per day 100kr).

If driving, note that the narrow lanes of the triangular old town area have two-hour parking limits, so set your disk (there are few signs to remind you). It's much wiser and almost as easy to use 12-hour or unlimited-time car parks just outside the centre.

Marstal

POP 2230

At Ærø's eastern end, Marstal is larger and more workaday than Ærøskøbing but still has several charming, narrow streets descending gently from the old church. In its 1890s heyday, more than 300 merchant ships pulled into port annually and eight shipyards were operating. At time of writing, the last of these was due to close by the end of 2017, but the traditions are still celebrated in a superb maritime history museum. Meanwhile, on nearby **Erikshale Strand** (Kalkovnsstien), a much-photographed 1930s thatched beach hut has become an icon of Æro and, indeed, of the whole southern archipelago.

◉ Sights & Activities

Marstal Søfartsmuseum   MUSEUM
(www.marmus.dk; Prinsensgade 1; adult/child 60kr/free; ☺ 9am-5pm daily Jun-Aug, 10am-4pm mid-Apr–May, Sep & Oct, 11am-3pm Mon-Sat Nov–mid-Apr) You'll need an hour or two to do justice to this packed-full maritime museum with countless model ships, paintings, sea chests and grippingly realistic boat interiors, some complete with sound effects and shifting horizons that can create the illusion of seasickness.

Ærø Kajak Udlejningen   KAYAKING
(☑ 29 40 96 56; http://kajakudlejningen.dk; kayak per day/week 500/2000kr, paddleboard 400/1200kr, deposit 500kr; ☺ May-Sep, call ahead) Kayaks and paddleboards available for rent; prices include wetsuit, drybag and delivery. Call owner Thea well ahead to arrange a collection spot and time.

🛏 Sleeping & Eating

The town has several B&Bs and three hotels, one acting partly as a hostel. There's a low-key camping ground close to the beach directly west of Erikshale Strand.

Femmasteren Hotel & Hostel HOSTEL €
(🖉53 60 48 21; http://femmasteren.dk; Færgestræde 29; d 995kr, s/d without bathroom 495/750kr, 2-/3-/4-/5-bed hostel room 470/600/800/1000kr; ⊙early Apr-Oct; 🛜) This basic but feel-good place has a stylish dining area with wood fire, and for 200kr you can use the sauna and hot tub. About half the rooms are organised hostel-style, with fold-down bunks and extra charge for sheets (or BYO). Twelve more come with sheets and breakfast; four are en suite. No dorms; only one single room.

Restaurant Fru Berg DANISH, INTERNATIONAL €€
(🖉24 63 56 57; www.bergsrestauranter.dk; Havnepladsen 6; lunch mains 119-198kr, dinner mains 198-249kr; ⊙noon-9.30pm Apr-Oct) Ideally placed at the port-side where tall-masted boats dock, this restaurant has enviable terrace views and an inviting, clean-lined nautical interior.

Den Gamle Vingaard INTERNATIONAL €€
(www.den-gamle-vingaard.com; Skolegade 17; dinner mains 99-170kr, steaks 172-450kr; ⊙noon-3pm & 5-9.30pm) Walls and ceilings dangling with pulleys, axes, bells and old lanterns add character to the pub-like interior here, while yard seating out the back is partly shaded by spreading vines. Pasta, pork fillet, lamb curry and king-crab legs join a long list of high-quality steaks.

Ø-Bolcher CAFE
(🖉25 73 36 09; Kongensgade 31A; coffee 20-35kr, wine 45kr, lunch 75-125kr; ⊙10am-5.30pm Mon-Fri, to 1pm Sat) This bare-brick shop-cafe plays Sinatra-esque music and serves excellent espresso that comes with a wrapped toffee – one of the numerous, locally famous candies made in the open kitchen behind the cafe's ice-cream section.

ℹ Information

Marstal Tourist Office (Prinsensgade 21A; ⊙1-6pm Mon, Wed & Thu, 10am-1pm Tue & Fri) is inside the library at the south end of the pedestrianised shopping street Kirkestræde. To steep yourself in Marstal's seafaring history, a great starting point is reading *We, the Drowned*, Carsten Jensen's bestselling maritime epic set during the 1848–51 Treårskrigen (First Schleswig War).

ℹ Getting There & Away

Free buses to Søby via Ærøskøbing depart on the hour most hours from a **stop** (Havnepladsen) in the harbour parking area. From 2019, **ÆrøXpressen** (www.facebook.com/aero xpressen) plans a new ferry service to Rudkøbing on Langeland, subject to funding.

ℹ Getting Around

Bicycle rental is available from sail-maker/yachting supplies shop **Stean Møller** (🖉62 53 12 71; www.steanmøller.watski.dk; Sejlmagervej 2; per day/week 70/350kr; ⊙9am-5pm Apr-Oct) near the marina, and less conveniently from **Nørremarks Cykeludlejning** (🖉62 53 14 77; Møllevejen 77; per day/week 75/300kr; ⊙8am-5pm Mon-Fri, 8am-2pm Sat) at the Thygesen petrol station near the western edge of town.

Søby

POP 450

Søby port, due for a large expansion, is a useful alternative arrival/departure point for linking Ærø to Faaborg or Als (for Jutland/Germany-bound drivers), and there's some beautiful countryside between here and Ærøskøbing. However, the town lacks the tourist charm of Ærøskøbing or Marstal.

You might drive or cycle 5km northwest to **Skjoldnæs Fyr** (adult/child 20/10kr; ⊙sunrise-sunset), a climbable lighthouse on the island's western tip. Or wend your way east via **Søbygaard** (www.arremus.dk; adult/child 60/25kr; ⊙10am-4pm May-late Oct, by appointment rest of year; 🅿), a small, historic manor house turned exhibition centre. Halfway to Ærøskøbing, the grassy, eroded moraine cliffs of **Voderup Klint** are geologically interesting and make for lovely sunset viewing spots.

ℹ Getting There & Away

Hourly free buses link Søby to Marstal via Ærøskøbing from a **stop** (Søby Havn) beside the harbour.

Ærøfærgerne (p187) operates year-round car ferries from Søby to:

Faaborg (one hour) at 4am, weekdays only, 10.15am and 3.15pm.

Fynshav (70 minutes) at 6.20am, 12.55pm and 6.10pm, 70 minutes.

ℹ Getting Around

Combined with an ultra-basic camping ground (per person 25kr) and the local mini-golf course, **Søby Cykeludlejning** (🖉40 33 91 14; Havnevejen 2, Pedersminde; per day/week 70/300kr; ⊙8am-8pm May-Sep) is a family outfit that rents bicycles from a barn on Søby's main road.

Southern Jutland

Best Places to Eat

➜ Sønderho Kro (p212)

➜ Hattesgaard (p202)

➜ Restaurant Ros (p199)

➜ Industrien (p210)

➜ Kolvig (p208)

➜ Kislings (p197)

Best Places to Stay

➜ Hotel Koldingfjord (p195)

➜ Sønderho Kro (p212)

➜ Schackenborg Slotskro (p200)

➜ Danhostel Ribe (p207)

➜ Kolding Hotel Apartments (p195)

➜ Hjerting Badehotel (p212)

Why Go?

Southern Jutland gets its inspiration from a few sources – from the North Sea, naturally, but also from the south. This is the only part of Denmark connected to mainland Europe (by a 68km-long border), and in some places you can feel the historic ties with Germany.

This is a region of salty offshore islands, understated royal palaces and character-filled historic towns, with unexpectedly modern treats in the form of edgy art and architecture, and offbeat design museums. The jewel in the crown is Ribe, the country's oldest town and historic Denmark at its most photogenic. The islands of Als, Fanø and Rømø have clear-cut appeal for beach-going holidaymakers, and bird-watchers also love this region. The tidal rhythms of the Wadden Sea bring an abundance of feathered friends (and their fanciers). An eclectic mix of royal-watchers, castle-collectors and design enthusiasts may also be ticking must-sees off their list.

When to Go

➜ If it's sunshine and beaches you're after, June to August is the obvious time to join the crowds on islands such as Rømø, Fanø and Als – early June or late August are less crowded.

➜ The region's biggest festival (Tønder Festival) farewells summer in style in late August.

➜ Ribe charms at any time of year – December is delightful, with a Christmas market and festivities that make the atmosphere extra *hygge* (cosy).

➜ The attractions of larger towns (Kolding, Esbjerg, Sønderborg, Tønder) are also year-round.

➜ Note that in spring (March to April) and autumn (mid-September to October) there's some unique bird-watching by the Wadden Sea; for oyster-harvesting you're best to visit between October and April.

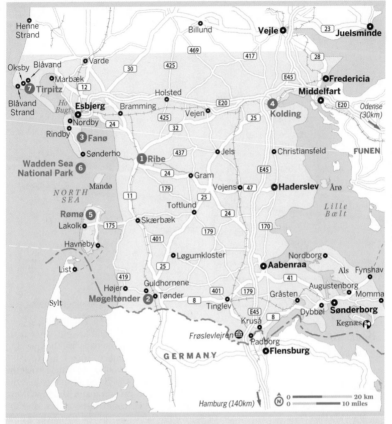

Southern Jutland Highlights

❶ **Ribe** (p203) Joining the nightwatchman on an evening walk through Ribe's historic neighbourhoods.

❷ **Møgeltønder** (p200) Dialling the cuteness factor up to 11 in a fairy-tale setting.

❸ **Fanø** (p211) Sailing from modern, industrial Esbjerg to this island charmer in only 12 minutes.

❹ **Kolding** (p193) Envying this town's appealing mix of the old and the new.

❺ **Sønderstrand** (p201) Checking out the wind-driven blokarts and kite buggies at Rømø's Sønderstrand.

❻ **Wadden Sea National Park** (p202) Seeing birds dance across the sky during the 'Sort Sol', or sampling freshly shucked oysters.

❼ **Tirpitz** (p209) Investigating wartime stories and west-coast wilderness at this remarkable new museum.

Kolding

POP 58,000

Kolding is an eminently likeable mid-sized town with a crowd-pleasing mix of old and new, encapsulated in its major drawcard, the hilltop castle Koldinghus.

◉ Sights & Activities

Stroll around the central lake spotting the town's oldest houses – 1595 **Borchs Gård** (Akseltorv 2A), and the wonky 1589 **Helligkorsgade 18** on an unassuming shopping strip. Then head to Trapholt (p194) to admire the modern furniture design for which Denmark is renowned.

Kolding

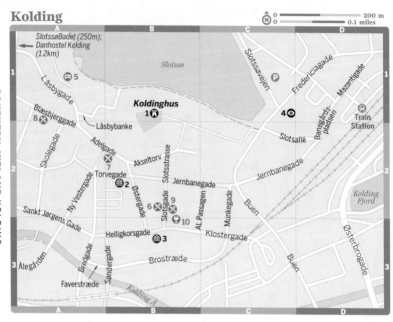

Kolding

◉ Top Sights
1 Koldinghus B1

◉ Sights
2 Borchs Gård..B2
3 Helligkorsgade 18.................................B3
4 Kolding Bibliotek C1

🛏 Sleeping
5 Kolding Hotel Apartments A1

🍴 Eating
6 Den Blå Café B2
7 Hyggefabrikken B2
8 Nicolai Biograf & Café..........................A1
9 Rafaels B2

🍷 Drinking & Nightlife
10 You'll Never Walk Alone Pub..............B3

The low-key religious settlement of **Christiansfeld**, an austere Unesco World Heritage Site, lies about 16km south.

★ Koldinghus
CASTLE, MUSEUM

(☏76 33 81 00; www.koldinghus.dk; Koldinghus 1; adult/child 90kr/free; ⊙10am-5pm; ♿) Koldinghus is Kolding's extravagant showpiece, with the requisite turbulent history. A for-tress occupied the land in 1268, while parts of the castle you see today can be traced to the mid-15th century. After a fire in 1808, the prevailing school of thought was that the castle would be left in ruins (at the time, the Danish state was at war and bankrupt). Now, however, the reborn castle shines, and the interplay between old and new architectural styles is a highlight.

There are very good displays, including collections of art and silverware, and changing contemporary exhibits – grab a floor plan to help find your way around. It's a climb to the top of the tower but you'll be rewarded with a panoramic view of the town.

★ Trapholt
MUSEUM

(☏76 30 05 30; www.trapholt.dk; Æblehaven 23; adult/child 110kr/free; ⊙10am-5pm Tue & Thu-Sun, to 8pm Wed; ♿) Design buffs should get out of town to the Trapholt modern art and design museum, housed in an architectural wonder in Kolding's residential northeastern outskirts. There are a couple of classic artworks from the Skagen artists, vibrant modern pieces and a **sculpture garden**. Downstairs, the ace **furniture collection** has examples of covetable Danish chairs, with many fine examples by the likes of iconic designers Hans Wegner, Verner Panton and Arne Jacobsen.

One of Trapholt's more intriguing exhibits is Jacobsen's prototype summerhouse, **Kubeflex** (the only one of its kind). It was designed by Jacobsen in 1969–70 and involves cubic modules designed to be added to as the need arose. The house is open at 1pm and 3pm daily (also at 11am weekends).

All up, Trapholt is one of the most impressive museums in Jutland – and the view-enriched cafe and gift shop are also top-notch. Take bus 7 or 9 to get here.

Kolding Bibliotek   LIBRARY
(☑79 79 11 00; www.koldingbib.dk; Slotssøvejen 4; ☺8am-9pm Mon-Thu, to 6pm Fri, 10am-2pm Sat) Another example of how good Denmark's public spaces are. This modern library is home to inviting chill-out spaces, events, information desks and installations from Danish-Icelandic artist Olafur Eliasson (the man behind the rainbow walkway atop Aarhus' ARoS art museum).

SlotssøBadet   SWIMMING
(☑75 50 01 50; www.ssbad.dk; Hospitalsgade 16; adult/child 68/43kr; ☺5.30am-9pm Mon & Wed, 6am-10pm Tue & Thu, 6am-6pm Fri, 9am-6pm Sat & Sun; ⊞) By the lake, this is a popular indoor swimming pool and waterpark. There's an attached spa and wellness centre.

🛏 Sleeping

★**Danhostel Kolding**   HOSTEL €
(☑75 50 91 40; www.danhostelkolding.dk; Ørnsborgvej 10; dm 215kr, d without/with bathroom 475/635kr; ☎) This top-notch option is above a park about 1.5km north of the city centre (a 20-minute walk from the station). There are pleasant rooms in the older-style main building, and a newer annexe with private bathrooms and modern kitchen-dining area. It's deservedly popular with families and backpackers; bus 2 stops nearby.

★**Hotel Koldingfjord**   HOTEL €€
(☑75 51 00 00; www.koldingfjord.dk; Fjordvej 154; r from 1195kr; @☎⊠) Play lord of the manor at this grand, castle-like estate (a former sanatorium) 7km east of the city, amid forest on Kolding Fjord (2km past Trapholt museum). It's a gorgeously restful spot, with first-class facilities (indoor pool, free bikes, cafe, terrace and restaurant), and the rooms are an ode to Scandi minimalism and design.

★**Kolding Hotel Apartments**   APARTMENT €€
(☑75 54 18 00; www.koldinghotelapartments.dk; Kedelsmedgangen 2; d/f apt from 805/1185kr; ☎)

This central, well-run lakeside complex does family holidays in style. On offer are stylishly furnished apartments of various sizes (sleeping up to six) in funky three-storey buildings – triangular, circular, octagonal and star-shaped (great when admired from the Koldinghus tower). It's a prime location, and real effort has gone into design and service. Parking and breakfast cost extra (packages available).

🍴 Eating & Drinking

Hyggefabrikken   EUROPEAN €€
(☑42 92 04 77; www.hyggefabrikken.dk; Adelgade 7; 4-course menu 299kr; ☺5-10pm Mon-Sat) The name (which means 'The Hygge Factory') may be the first thing that catches your eye here, but the set menu deserves attention: four courses including a welcome drink for 299kr. Begin with soup, followed by a tapas board, and end with dessert. The main dish is usually a choice of meat, fish or vegetarian. BYO wine, too.

Rafaels   ITALIAN €€
(☑88 82 32 32; www.rafaelspizzeria.com; Slotsgade 17; pizza & pasta 120-160kr; ☺5-9.30pm, plus noon-3pm Sat) A buzzing, beloved local pizza joint, with pasta and risotto dishes too. Rustic interior and plenty of alfresco tables (or takeaway available).

Nicolai Biograf & Café   ITALIAN €€
(☑75 50 03 02; www.nicolai-cafe.dk; Skolegade 2, entry on Blæsbjerggade; pizzas 88-138kr; ☺3-9pm Mon-Fri, 10am-9pm Sat & Sun; ⊞) Inside a renovated old school, the Nicolai cultural centre houses an art-house cinema alongside a relaxed cafe serving gourmet pizza. The weekend brunch buffet (168kr) is a hit with in-the-know locals – kids can visit the cinema while adults eat. There's also a great-value evening pizza and pasta buffet (118kr to 148kr, cheaper earlier in the week).

Den Blå Café   FRENCH €€
(☑75 50 65 12; www.denblaacafe.dk; Slotsgade 4; lunch 100-150kr, dinner mains 145-250kr; ☺10am-10pm Mon-Wed, to midnight Thu, to 2am Fri & Sat, to 8pm Sun) The Blue Cafe has a decided French accent and a large alfresco area for people-watching. The menu draws from easy-pleasing bistro favourites (caesar salad, croque-monsieur, *moules-frites* etc). You can also drop by for coffee or late-night drinks.

You'll Never Walk Alone Pub   PUB
(☑75 50 80 44; www.denengelskepub.dk; AL Passagen 2; ☺2-10pm Mon, noon-midnight Tue-Thu,

SOUTHERN JUTLAND CHRISTIANSFELD

GRÅSTEN ROYAL PALACE GARDENS

For three weeks each summer the sleepy town of **Gråsten** (population 4200) is abuzz as Queen Margrethe and Prince Henrik (and usually the extended family) head for some R&R at their summer residence, **Gråsten Slot**. The lake-side palace itself is private but when the royals aren't visiting, its lovely **garden** (www.royalpalaces.dk/en; Slotsgade; ⏰ from 7.30am) FREE is open to the public (till 4.30pm in winter, as late as 8pm in summer). For a few hours a week, the richly adorned **chapel** (⚒ 74 65 14 54; Slotsbakken 1; ⏰ 11am-2pm Mon, 10am-noon Sat, 2-4pm Sun Apr-Oct) is also accessible. Built between 1699 and 1702, that's the only section of the originally 16th-century castle to survive a 1757 fire – today's main palace building dates mostly from 1842. Signs on the garden gates indicate dates that the site is closed to the public, or check online for royal family activity at http://kongehuset.dk/en. From Sønderborg (42kr) take bus 223 (30 minutes) or Flensburg-bound route 110 (22 minutes).

11am-late Fri & Sat, 2-8pm Sun) Known in town simply as 'the English pub', this traditional boozer lies in a passage between Jernbanegade and Klostergade. Outdoor seating, meals, weekend live music and big-screen football matches give it an appeal beyond the 300-plus beers on the menu (including Danish microbrews).

ℹ Information

Find online info at www.visitkolding.dk or snag brochures and maps from inside Kolding Bibliotek (p195).

ℹ Getting There & Away

Regular train services link to Esbjerg (101kr, 50 minutes) and most places in Jutland along with Odense (122kr, 40 minutes) and on to Copenhagen; some travel east may involve a change of train in Fredericia.

If you're driving to/from Germany (82km), Rte 170 is a pleasant, if slower, alternative to the E45.

Christiansfeld

POP 2950

The small town of Christiansfeld is an under-the-radar place that in 2015 was awarded Unesco World Heritage status for its unique history and homogenous if soberly unadorned yellow-brick architecture.

Founded in 1773 by the Moravian Church, a non-conformist Lutheran congregation, the town was designed to put their pioneering egalitarian philosophy into practice by creating a Protestant urban ideal. Across the road from the central church, **Christiansfeld Centret** (⚒ 79 79 17 73; www. christiansfeldcentret.dk; Nørregade 14, Christiansfeld; ⏰ 10am-5pm Apr-Oct, to 4pm Nov-Mar) is a

visitor centre that provides an overview of what makes this design so special. Pick up a walking map here, outlining the town's buildings and their functions. And be sure to sample Christiansfeld's other claim to fame: its delicious honey cake (*honningkage*), sold from central bakeries.

From Kolding, take hourly bus 134 (32kr, 20 minutes).

Sønderborg

POP 27,400

Sønderborg spreads along both sides of the Als Sund, joined by two bridges. Despite the mid-12th-century origins of its fortress, erected by Valdemar I (the Great), the place has a fundamentally modern feel.

Historically, Sønderborg's role as a battleground in two 19th-century wars against Germany has fundamentally shaped Denmark. In 1864, during the battle of Dybbøl, Danish forces gathered here while a bombardment of 80,000 German shells paved the way for the German occupation of southern Jutland that lasted some 60 years. Only after WWI did the region once again become Danish soil.

Bombardment of another kind continues today – the annual descent of German and Danish holidaymakers. Understandably, German is the second language in these parts with more limited English spoken.

◉ Sights

The town centre and Sønderborg Slot are on the east (Als) side of the Sund. The Dybbøl area and the train station are on the western (Jutland) side. Services can be found on the pedestrian street Perlegade, immediately north of Rådhustorvet.

Sønderborg Slot
CASTLE, MUSEUM

(📞 74 42 25 39; www.museum-sonderjylland.dk; Sønderbro 1; adult/child 80kr/free; ⊙10am-5pm Jun-Sep, to 4pm Tue-Sun Apr, May & Oct, 1-4pm Tue-Sun Nov-Mar) Sønderborg Castle dates from the mid-12th century, when a stronghold was built on the site; later bastions were added for further fortification. It's rich in lore, and nowadays it houses a **museum** of regional history with exhibits on the wars of 1848 and 1864 as well as paintings from the Danish 'Golden Age' and insight into the political history of the region.

Between 1532 and 1549 the castle was used to hold the deposed king, Christian II. In the late 16th century the fortified castle was turned into a royal residence (the 1568 **chapel** rates as one of Europe's oldest preserved royal chapels). It took on its baroque appearance during further restorations in 1718. During the German occupation it was used as a German barracks.

Historiecenter Dybbøl Banke
MUSEUM

(📞 74 48 90 00; www.museum-sonderjylland.dk; Dybbøl Banke 16; adult/child 120/70kr; ⊙10am-5pm Apr-Oct; 👶) On 18 April 1864 the German army steamrolled the Danes and took control of southern Jutland until the end of WWI. On the western edge of town, this history centre gives an informative glimpse into the bloody war of 1864, with demonstrations and storytelling. Although it offers typically high-quality displays of a very important time, if you're not Danish, German or have no interest in military history, it can probably be skipped. Bus 1 runs out here from town.

Twice bombed, the nearby **Dybbøl Mølle** (📞 74 48 90 00; www.museum-sonderjylland.dk; Dybbøl Banke 7; adult/child 45/30kr; ⊙11am-4pm mid-Apr–mid-Oct) is as much a national symbol as a windmill and contains exhibits that explain the site's symbolism.

EXPLORING ALS

For a snapshot of a laid-back Danish country life, take lazy drives or cycle rides out of Sønderborg around the island of Als, perhaps to the sheltered southern beach at **Kegnæs**, or to engaging little villages on the east coast. More conveniently, hop just 10km along Rte 8 to **Augustenborg** where you can wander the gardens and sculpture park of the grand yellow-and-white Augustenborg Slot.

🛏 Sleeping

The city has a good assortment of accommodation, including business-minded hotels, an idyllically located **camping ground** (📞 74 42 41 89; www.sonderborgcamping.dk; Ringgade 7; per adult/child/site 80/35/45kr; ⊙Apr-Sep; 🎈) close to the yacht marina and a **Danhostel** (📞 74 42 31 12; www.sonderborgdanhostel.dk; Kærvej 70; dm 175kr, s/d/f 435/450/540kr; @🎈) that's 15 minutes' walk north of the town centre (or a hop by bus 3).

★Hotel Bella Italia
BOUTIQUE HOTEL €€

(📞 74 42 54 00; www.bella-it.dk; Lille Rådhusgade 29-33; s/d incl breakfast 998/1198kr; 🎈) Newly opened, this hotel is a smart, fresh option attached to a popular Italian **restaurant** (📞 74 42 54 00; www.bella-it.dk; Lille Rådhusgade 33; pizza & pasta 89-150kr, mains 199-329kr; ⊙5-9.30pm). Stylish, well-equipped rooms are crisply decorated in whites and charcoals.

Hotel Sønderborg Garni
HOTEL €€

(📞 74 42 34 33; www.hotelsoenderborg.dk; Kongevej 96; s/d incl breakfast from 650/875kr; 🎈) Friendly service and a prime location in an upmarket residential neighbourhood sweeten the gloomy appearance of this small hotel (complete with turret). The 1904 building has 18 rooms, all different (the cheapest singles are tiny) and with a homely, relaxed feel.

🍴 Eating

You'll find a selection of eateries down by the harbour (on Havnegade) and a bunch of all-day cafe-bars on Rådhustorvet. Stairs link the two areas.

★Kislings
CAFE €

(www.kislings.dk; Perlegade 49; snacks & meals 20-89kr; ⊙8am-6pm Mon-Thu, to 9pm Fri, to 3pm Sat) Get caffeinated here, on what may just be southern Jutland's best coffee. This stylish main-street cafe boasts a lovely garden area, eclectic decor, and a short menu of high-quality local produce and tasty breads.

Café Ib Rehne Cairo
INTERNATIONAL €€

(📞 74 42 04 00; www.ibrehnecairo.dk; Rådhustorvet 4; meals 79-225kr; ⊙10am-11pm Mon-Wed, to midnight Thu, to 2.30am Fri & Sat, to 9pm Sun) Named after the sign-off of a veteran Danish correspondent, this all-day cafe-bar sports fresh decor and a classic-hits menu (smørrebrød, burgers, salads). The alfresco tables on the square get a workout from brunchtime, but there's also a loungey area inside, perfect for evening cocktails.

ℹ Information

On the main street, the **tourist office** (☑74 42 35 55; www.visitsonderborg.com; Perlegade 50; ☺10am-5pm Mon-Fri, 10am-1pm Sat) shares space with a cafe specialising in local food.

ℹ Getting There & Away

Trains depart every two hours to Kolding (162kr, 80 minutes) via Gråsten (p196) and eventually to Copenhagen (388kr, 3½ hours).

The bus station is more central, a block east of Perlegade. Bus 225 runs to Fynshav (32kr, 25 minutes) on the east coast of Als, from where car ferries leave thrice daily to Søby on Ærø and seven to 12 times daily to Bøjden (near Faaborg on Funen). Bus 110 connects to Flensburg (Germany) via Gråsten.

ℹ Getting Around

Town buses 1 and 2 connect the Jutland-side train station to the town centre.

Padborg

POP 4390

Right by the German border, Padborg is best known for its **motor-racing circuit** (padborg park.dk). But also intriguing, 4km northwest of town, is the site of WWII internment camp **Frøslevlejren** (☑74 67 65 57; www.natmus.dk; Lejrvej 83, Padborg; adult/child 50kr/free; ☺10am-5pm mid-Jun–mid-Aug, shorter hours rest of year, closed Dec & Jan). It was used first by Germans to 'weed out' Danish patriots for deportation, then after the war ended and power dynamics changed, to house new inmates suspected as Nazi collaborators. A museum here tells fascinating stories of the Danish Resistance movement. No public transport.

Tønder

POP 7600

Tønder is an appealing place that's had a rocky journey through serious flooding to German annexation; strong German links remain (not surprising, given Tønder's proximity to the border, just 4km south).

During the 16th century, a series of dikes were erected to prevent the imminent threat of flooding. In doing so, the town isolated itself from its sea-port connection and turned elsewhere for economic prosperity. Lace-making was introduced – an economic windfall that employed up to 12,000 workers during its peak in the 18th century.

◉ Sights

Tønder Museum   MUSEUM
(☑74 72 89 89; www.museum-sonderjylland.dk; Wegners Plads 1; adult/child 70kr/free; ☺10am-5pm Jun-Aug, closed Mon Sep-May) Three-in-one Tønder Museum houses **Kulturhistorie Tønder**, a collection of delicate Tønder lace and decoratively painted furniture. In the adjacent wing is **Kunstmuseet i Tønder**, home to changing art exhibitions. Our favourite feature is the 1902 **Vandtårnet** (water tower), with panoramic views. Take the lift up and walk down – on each of the tower's eight floors are the fabulous chair designs of locally born Hans Wegner, one of the most innovative and prolific of all Danish furniture designers.

You will no doubt have seen Wegner's designs on your travels through Denmark – check out the Ox Chair on the 5th floor, the quirky Valet Chair on the 4th floor, and the Peacock and Wishbone chairs on the 2nd floor.

Uldgade   STREET
For a glimpse of the past, head south from Torvet along Søndergade and turn right into Uldgade. The cobbled street has Tønder's best collection of unique gabled houses. It ends in a sweet square that has a couple of interesting dining options.

Drøhses Hus   MUSEUM
(☑74 72 49 90; www.museum-sonderjylland.dk; Storegade 14; adult/child 50kr/free; ☺11am-5pm Tue-Fri, 10am-2pm Sat Apr-Dec, plus open Mon Jun-Aug) On the main pedestrian street, Drøhses Hus dates from 1672; it's been meticulously restored and is open to the public, exhibiting lace and arts and crafts. For 80kr, you can buy a combination ticket that includes admission to Tønder Museum. The building is also home to a lovely craft and design store (free to enter).

Kristkirken   CHURCH
(www.toender-kristkirke.dk; Kirkepladsen 4; ☺10am-4pm Mon-Sat) The grand Kristkirken on the northeastern side of Torvet dates back to 1592. Its opulent interior came courtesy of the town's rich cattle and lace merchants, who invested heavily between the late 17th and 18th centuries.

Det Gamle Apotek   HISTORIC BUILDING
(The Old Pharmacy; ☑74 72 51 11; www.det-gamle-apotek.dk; Østergade 1; ☺10am-5.30pm Mon-Fri, to 4pm Sat & Sun) Det Gamle Apotek, beside Torvet, has an elaborate 1671 baroque doorway

flanked by two lions that stand guard over the old-fashioned interior and extensive gift-shop collection inside (everything you never thought you'd need, and then some).

✦ Festivals & Events

Tønder Festival MUSIC
(www.tf.dk; ☺Aug) Growing in reputation and scale each year, the four-day Tønder Festival takes place in the last week of August and draws some 20,000 attendees from all corners of the globe. It's regarded as one of the best folk music festivals in Europe, with top-quality international folk and roots music.

🛏 Sleeping

B&Bs in the area can be found online at www.toenderbb.dk. For something special, head to the old *kro* (inn; p200) in Møgeltønder.

Motel Apartments HOTEL €
(☑23 21 37 60; www.motel-apartments.dk; Vestergade 87; s/d/apt 520/625/1300kr; ☎) A solid, well-priced and well-placed option, this hotel is behind a plain facade that does it no favours. On offer are comfy rooms with kitchenette (some with garden terrace). There are also apartments for those after more space. Breakfast is 70kr.

Danhostel Tønder HOSTEL €
(☑74 92 80 00; www.tsfc.dk; Sønderport 4; dm 220kr, s & d with bathroom 500kr; @☎) Cut from the same cloth as other southern Jutland Danhostels, this is a plain, low-slung brick building with plentiful rooms (all with bathroom), friendly staff, appealing communal areas and fresh, clean facilities. It's a few minutes' walk southeast of the town centre. The next-door camping ground shares the reception; guests have access to the affiliated sports centre and swimming pool.

✕ Eating & Drinking

Torvet is home to a market selling fruit, vegetables and cheese on Tuesday and Friday mornings.

Eating spots are around Torvet and the pedestrianised Storegade. Take a detour up Lillegade to reach some sweet options on a cobbled square.

Frigrunden has a cocktail bar open Friday and Saturday nights, and there are a few watering holes along Storegade.

Victoria INTERNATIONAL €
(☑74 72 00 89; www.victoriatoender.dk; Storegade 9; mains 79-259kr; ☺11am-10pm Sun-Thu, to 2am Fri

& Sat) At the turn of the 19th century Tønder had one bar for every 49 inhabitants. Only the Victoria kicks on as a jack-of-all-trades pub/cafe/restaurant. It's a winner, with an all-ages crowd, old-world timber-rich decor and a good range of beers. The menu is long, varied (burgers, burritos, pasta, sandwiches) and well priced (most items under 120kr). Kitchen closes around 9pm.

Café Engel CAFE €
(☑74 72 70 80; www.cafe-engel.dk; Frigrunden 3; sandwiches around 80kr; ☺11am-5pm Tue-Sat) At the end of Uldgade, this cafe has a cosy interior, pretty outdoor seating, good coffee and a small but tempting offer of sandwiches and cakes. Hours are somewhat flexible – if the small flagpole is out, the cafe is open.

★ Restaurant Ros DANISH €€
(☑27 19 31 93; www.restaurantros.dk; Spikergade 21; 3-/5-course menu 298/398kr; ☺5.30-11pm Wed-Sat, plus noon-3pm Sat) Earning a deserved reputation as the town's gourmet hot spot, Ros is owned by two young chefs busy opening a handful of new venues in town (including a neighbouring cocktail bar open weekends, and a casual burger joint). Ros showcases the excellent regional produce in an intimate and elegant setting; the prices are top value. Bookings advised.

Marcel's Brasserie INTERNATIONAL €€
(☑74 72 20 22; www.marcelsbrasserie.dk; Storegade 12; meals 89-229kr; ☺11am-10pm Mon-Thu, to 11pm Fri & Sat, to 9pm Sun) Newly opened, this main-street bistro charms with chandeliers and a streamlined aesthetic. The menu courses from light (omelette, bouillabaisse, chicken sandwich) to more substantial (steak or spare ribs). Also: cocktails, good coffee and a super Sunday brunch spread.

Klostercaféen CAFE €€
(☑73 72 41 04; www.klostercafeen-toender.dk; Torvet 11; mains 70-150kr; ☺10am-5pm) Options around Torvet include photogenic Klostercaféen, inside Tønder's oldest house (from 1520 and boasting beautiful old tiles). The menu is a highly traditional one, featuring sandwiches, salads and meals such as fish fillets and schnitzel.

❶ Information

Tourist Office (☑74 75 51 30; www.visittonder.dk; Storegade 2-4; ☺10am-5.30pm Mon-Fri, to 2pm Sat) Helpful office with information on the town and Møgeltønder, plus Rømø.

ℹ️ Getting There & Away

Tønder is on Rte 11, 4km north of the border with Germany and 78km south of Esbjerg.

The train station is on the western side of town, about 1km from Torvet via Vestergade. Trains run regularly to/from Ribe (78kr, 50 minutes) and Esbjerg (112kr, 80 minutes).

Bus 266 runs regularly to Møgeltønder (22kr, 15 minutes).

Møgeltønder

POP 850

This little village is impossibly cute – if you could, you'd wrap it up and take it home for your grandmother. A royal castle, one of the most beautiful main streets in Denmark, and a church rich in frescoes are some of the gems to be found here.

◉ Sights

★ **Møgeltønder Kirke** CHURCH

(www.mogeltonderkirke.dk; Sønderbyvej 2; ⊙8am-4pm May-Sep, 9am-4pm Oct-Apr) At the western end of Slotsgade is Møgeltønder Kirke, its lavish interior a feast for the senses. The Romanesque nave dates back to 1180 and the baptismal font is from 1200. The church has had many additions, however, as the Gothic choir vaults were built during the 13th century, the tower dates from about 1500 and the chapel on the northern side was added in 1763. The interior is rich in frescoes, gallery paintings and ceiling drawings.

You'll also find the oldest functioning church organ in Denmark, dating from 1679. The elaborately detailed gilt altar dates from the 16th century. Note the 'countess' bower', a balcony with private seating for the Schack family, who owned the church from 1661 until 1970.

Schackenborg Slot PALACE

(☎79 30 69 00; www.schackenborg.dk; Schackenborgvej; guided palace/garden tour 100/50kr; ⊙tours Jul & Aug) On the village's eastern edge is Schackenborg, a small castle from the late 17th century that was home to Queen Margrethe's youngest son, Prince Joachim, from 1995 to 2014 (when he moved to Copenhagen with his family).

There are public events (concerts etc) held at the palace and its lovely grounds; there are also popular guided tours once or twice weekly in summer (in Danish and German; enquire about English tours). Timetables and ticket-purchasing options are outlined on the website.

☞ Tours

Sort Safari TOURS

(☎73 72 64 00; www.sortsafari.dk; Slotsgade 19; Sort Sol tour adult/child from 145/95kr) This expert local company can help you explore the Wadden Sea area, with tours arranged for bird-watching, including the Sort Sol (p203) phenomenon, plus oyster collecting and seal-spotting by boat.

🛏️ Sleeping & Eating

Møgeltønder Camping CAMPGROUND €

(☎74 73 84 60; www.mogeltondercamping.dk; Sønderstrengvej 2; per adult/child/site 72/42/45kr; 🛜🏊) Spacious, family-friendly camping ground on the western edge of town. Cabins and on-site caravans available.

★ **Schackenborg Slotskro** HOTEL €€€

(☎74 73 83 83; www.slotskro.dk; Slotsgade 42; s/d incl breakfast from 1199/1449kr; 🛜) This classy inn dates from the 1680s and has high-pedigree history and the palace as its neighbour. There are 25 elegant, well-equipped rooms, at the inn and in nearby houses.

The *slotskro* has a fine reputation for traditional Danish cooking and makes a lovely spot for lunch (109kr to 279kr) or the full-blown evening treatment (three-/four-course menu 398/458kr).

★ **Mormors Lille Café** CAFE €

(☎73 72 14 18; Slotsgade 9; cakes 40-60kr; ⊙noon-6pm May-Sep, Fri-Sun Oct-Apr) 'Grandma's little cafe' is perfectly in keeping with the village's character, cute as a button under its low, thatched roof, surrounded by outdoor tables and flowerbeds. Old-school *lagkage* (layer cake) or *kiksekage* (biscuit cake, with chocolate) are the order of the day. *Hygge* factor: sky-high.

ℹ️ Getting There & Away

Møgeltønder is 5km west of Tønder via Rte 419. Bus 266 connects the towns (22kr, 15 minutes).

Rømø

POP 650

Summer sees the large island of Rømø fill with tourists (predominantly from Germany). This is hardly surprising given the entire west coast is one long, sandy beach that's prime happy-holiday turf, perfect for sun-bathing and sunset-watching or something more active.

Rømø is connected to the mainland by a 10km causeway (with cycle lane). During the colder months it's a windswept sleeper with get-away-from-it-all charm that couldn't be more removed from its busy summer incarnation.

ⓘ Orientation

As you cross the causeway to Rømø from the mainland, you continue straight to reach **Lakolk**, a large camping-ground-turned-village on the central west coast. It's also where you'll find the most popular beach – **Lakolk Strand**.

Heading left (south) immediately after reaching Rømø takes you to **Kongsmark**, **Havneby** and the activity-rich **Sønderstrand** beach.

If you head right (north) as you reach the island, you'll arrive at the historic centre, **Toftum** and **Juvre**. The far northern end of the island is a military zone (access prohibited).

⊙ Sights

Naturcenter Tønnisgaard   VISITOR CENTRE
(✆74 75 52 57; www.tonnisgaard.dk; Havnebyvej 30, Tvismark; exhibits adult/child 22/11kr; ⊘10am-4pm Mon-Fri mid-Mar–Oct, Mon-Wed Nov–mid-Mar; ⊞) This Rømø-based information and activity centre for the Wadden Sea National Park has exhibitions, plus family-friendly tour offerings depending on the season (eg bird-watching, and shrimp, oyster or herb collecting). Tours are in Danish and German, but English can be arranged with notice.

Kommandørgården   HISTORIC BUILDING
(✆74 75 52 76; www.natmus.dk; Juvrevej 60, Toftum; adult/child 50kr/free; ⊘10am-5pm Tue-Sun May-Sep, to 3pm Oct) The handsome thatched Kommandørgården, 1.5km north of the causeway, is the preserved home of one of Rømø's 18th-century whaling captains. It stands as testimony to the prosperity that such men brought to the island through their whaling expeditions. It has Dutch tiles lining many walls and woodwork painted in rococo style (there is minimal labelling in English, however). In the barn is the skeleton of a 13m-long sperm whale that was stranded on Rømø in 1996.

🏃 Activities

★**Sønderstrand**   BEACH
At the southwest corner of the island is Sønderstrand, a remarkable sight – full of cars, colour and land-based activities making great use of the air that blows in fresh from the North Sea. There's a small area for parking your car where the sealed road reaches the sand, or you can continue driving on the beach itself.

As the sealed road reaches Sønderstrand, to your left is an area dedicated to *strandsejlads*, aka land-yachts or blokarts (a three-wheeled go-kart that utilises a sail to capture the wind). To the right, it's all about *kitebuggykørsel* – buggies with attached parachute-like kites. Great speeds are reached, and it's quite a spectacle. If you want a crack at either, there are companies that can help with lessons and/or gear rental (usually open from about late April to early October, if weather and conditions are agreeable).

Rømø Adventures   ADVENTURE SPORTS
(✆20 21 03 06; www.romo-adventures.dk; Sønderstrand; 1hr blokart lesson 375kr) For these guys, it's all about harnessing the power of the wind. They offer instruction in blokarting, kitesurfing, kite buggies and more (plus rental of equipment). Based at Sønderstrand beach when the weather is kind.

Kommandørgårdens Islændercenter   HORSE RIDING
(✆74 75 51 22; http://islander.kommandoergaarden.dk; Borrebjergvej 15; ⊞) Affiliated with Hotel Kommandørgården (p202), this centre has a stable full of Icelandic horses and a range of rides to appeal to kids, beginners and more-experienced horse-folk, through forest and along the beach. A three-hour sunset tour costs 385kr; a full-day tour to the north of Rømø 895kr; and a day tour to Mandø (4½ hours of riding) is 1145kr.

Enjoy Resorts Rømø   SPA, ACTIVITY CENTRE
(✆74 75 56 55; www.enjoyresorts.dk; Vestergade 31, Havneby; ⊞) This resort en route to Sønderstrand is home to a relaxation-inducing wellness spa (250kr for nonguests); indoor swimming pool and fitness centre (adult/child 75/35kr); bowling alley (one hour 120kr); and a challenging links golf course (18 holes 350kr). Club and buggy hire are available.

🛏 Sleeping

Scattered around the island are some 1600 summer houses and apartments, mostly rented by the week in high season, or with three-night minimum at other times. The tourist office has a catalogue and handles bookings.

★**Danhostel Rømø**   HOSTEL €
(✆74 75 51 88; www.danhostel.dk/romo; Lyngvejen 7, Østerby; dm 260kr, d without/with bathroom 420/520kr; ⊘Apr-Sep; ⊚) A picturesque red, thatched-roof complex (an old sea-captain's

house) that's well hidden off the main road and set among pines, but walking distance to a supermarket and bakery. The rooms (a few with bathroom) are basic but spick and span, and the flower-filled outdoor areas beckon.

First Camp Lakolk Strand   CAMPGROUND €

(📞 74 75 52 28; http://en.firstcamp.se/lakolk-strand; Vesterhavsvej, Lakolk; site per adult/child 105/60kr; ⊙ Apr-Oct; 🐾) In high summer, the huge beachside camping ground and shopping centre at Lakolk is holiday heaven or hell, depending on your outlook. It's bursting at the seams with families praying for good weather and is wall-to-wall with campervans and all the requisite facilities, including cabins for rent (from 755kr).

Hotel

Kommandørgården   HOTEL, CAMPGROUND €€

(📞 74 75 51 22; www.kommandoergaarden.dk; Havnebyvej, Østerby; campsite per adult/child/site 82/45/75kr; hotel s/d from 995/1195kr; @ 🐾 🛒) This large complex has everything from camping and cabins to hotel rooms and apartments, and a restaurant and bar – but it's looking a little dated in parts. There are activities laid on thick, including a wellness centre, bike hire, kayaking, horse riding, kids' play centre, and indoor and outdoor swimming pools.

⭐ **Enjoy Resorts Rømø**   RESORT €€€

(📞 74 75 56 55; www.enjoyresorts.dk; Vestergade 31, Havneby; 2 nights 4 people from 2500kr; 🐾 🛒) A luxury-leaning, activity-rich playground for families enjoying the golf course, wellness centre, restaurant and large complex of two-bedroom, fully equipped houses (sleeping up to eight). There's a two-night minimum, plus plenty of weekly deals and golf/wellness packages.

✖ Eating

Havneby is the island's culinary hot spot, with a large supermarket and good array of mostly family-oriented eateries. At Lakolk there's a small supermarket and some casual refuelling spots including a bistro, summer nightclub, pizzeria, ice creamery and cafes.

On menus, keep an eye out for Rømø produce, particularly *marsklam* (marsh-grazing lamb) and *rejer* (shrimps).

⭐ **Hattesgaard**   CAFE €

(📞 73 75 52 11; www.hattesgaard.dk; Hattesvej 17, Tvismark; cake 45-50kr; ⊙ 11am-6pm) Well worth the detour (turn off the main road at Naturcenter Tønnisgaard; p201) is this old sea

captain's house, converted into a pretty-as-a-picture antique and homewares store. The cafe side of the business serves up delectable homemade cakes, and the grounds are dotted with tables.

Otto & Ani's Fisk   SEAFOOD €

(📞 74 75 53 06; Havnespladsen, Havneby; meals 60-195kr; ⊙ 11am-5pm; 🚤) This no-frills cafeteria is right on the harbourside at Havneby, so the fish are as fresh as they come. Pull up a pew outside and feast on fish and chips or a bread roll filled with Rømø shrimp. You can also buy fresh uncooked fish and seafood, and smoked fishy delicacies. Longer hours of an evening in peak summer.

ℹ Information

Tourist Office (📞 74 75 51 30; www.romo.dk; Nørre Frankel 1, Havneby; ⊙ 9am-5pm Mon-Sat, to 3pm Sun Jul & Aug, 9am-4.30pm Mon-Sat, to noon Sun Sep-Jun) In central Havneby; can arrange cottage rental through the booking agency **Feriepartner Rømø** (www.feriepartner.com/roemoe).

ℹ Getting There & Away

Rømø is on Rte 175, 14km west of Skærbæk. Bus 285 runs from Skærbæk to Havneby (32kr, 40 minutes) a handful of times daily. Hourly trains link Skærbæk with Ribe, Tønder and Esbjerg.

The **Sylt Ferry** (📞 73 75 53 03; www.syltferry.com) operates between Havneby and the nearby German island of Sylt several times a day (one-way car ticket including passengers 363kr, adult return 88kr); journey time is 40 minutes.

ℹ Getting Around

Roads allow cars to access the beaches at Lakolk and Sønderstrand (p201), and you can drive up and down the west coast along the sand.

The Havneby–Skærbæk bus (route 285) isn't especially useful for local travel; your best option is to rent a bike from **Rømø Cykler** (📞 88 93 50 40; www.romocykler.dk; Nørre Frankel 1B, Havneby; bike hire per day/week from 60/300kr; ⊙ 10am-5pm Apr-Jun, Sep & Oct, to 6pm Jul & Aug), as Rømø is as flat as a pancake and perfect for cycling.

Wadden Sea National Park

Mudflats and salt marshes don't sound as sexy as alpine peaks, but Denmark's west-coast national park demonstrates how appealing they can be, with tractor-bus rides to salty offshore islands, fat harbour seals

DON'T MISS

SORT SOL

One of the most popular ways to get close to Wadden Sea National Park's natural wonders is to experience the 'Sort Sol' (Black Sun) in spring (approximate dates March to April) and autumn (mid-September to late October). This describes the phenomenon of large numbers of migrating starlings (up to a million) gathering in the marshes outside Ribe and Tønder. 'Sort Sol' takes place in the hours just after sunset, when the birds gather in large flocks and form huge formations in the sky before they decide on a location to roost for the night. The movements of the formations have been likened to a balletic dance and the birds are so numerous they seem to obliterate the sunset.

lolling on sandbanks, and the chance to put on waders and pluck and shuck oysters. Plus birds – so many birds!

In the Wadden Sea National Park (in Danish, Nationalpark Vadehavet), the seabed meets the horizon twice daily, when low tide exposes tidal flats of sand and mud, and birds swoop to hoover up the buffet on offer (tasty morsels like worms, cockles, crabs, shrimp and snails). Annually, some 12 million feathered friends use this region as a feeding place, or to rest, on their migrations.

The history of humans in the region is also on show, with dikes and polders as evidence of the struggle to master the watery landscapes.

◉ Sights

★ **VadehavsCentret**   VISITOR CENTRE
(Wadden Sea Centre; ☎ 75 44 61 61; www.vadehavs centret.dk; Okholmvej 5, Vester Vedsted; adult/child 100/50kr; ⊙10am-5pm May-Sep, to 4pm Oct-Apr; ⛟) About 10km southwest of Ribe, VadehavsCentret is a top-notch information and activity centre and the best source of information about the park. Inside a beautiful new extension (built from reed thatch), there are **exhibitions** on the tides, flora and fauna of the national park. The information on migratory birds is superb.

The centre runs a calendar of seasonal **tours** that range from bird-watching and seal-spotting to mudflat walks and food foraging; some are designed for kids and families.

A five-hour oyster safari is 280kr (runs October to April); Sort Sol viewing is 75kr. Details and departure points are outlined on the website.

Mandø   ISLAND
(www.visitmandoe.dk) At low tide, tractors haul buses 11km from VadehavsCentret, driving over the mudflats to deliver visitors to the small outlying island of Mandø. This peaceful place (8 sq km; population approximately 35) is a microcosm of the national park. Hire a bike to get the full experience, and set off on the 10km trail around the flat island to discover oyster banks, dikes, birdlife, sunbaking seals and cosy inns.

There are overnighting opportunities, including camping and B&Bs.

Two companies run tractor-buses (return fare adult/child 60/40kr) daily from about Easter until October. For timetables and package deals on tours and accommodation, see www.mandoebussen.dk and www.mandoekro.dk/mandoe-traktorbusser.

ⓘ Information

VadehavsCentret is the perfect place to get a park overview, and there is also information online at www.nationalparkvadehavet.dk.

ⓘ Getting There & Away

You can access the park from a base anywhere along Jutland's southwest coast – from towns such as Esbjerg, Ribe and Tønder, or from the islands Fanø and Rømø.

There are buses and trains linking major towns and smaller settlements, and tour operators visiting areas of the park. Your own wheels are useful – in summer, a bike is a good option.

Ribe

POP 8200

The crooked cobblestone streets of Ribe (*ree-buh*) date from the late 9th century, making it Denmark's oldest town. It's easily one of the country's loveliest spots at which to stop and soak up some history.

It's a delightfully compact chocolate-box confection of crooked half-timbered 16th-century houses, a sweetly meandering river and lush water meadows, all overseen by the nation's oldest cathedral. Such is the sense of living history that the entire 'old town' has been designated a preservation zone, with more than 100 buildings registered by the National Trust. Don't miss it.

History

Founded around AD 700, Ribe evolved into a key post of the hailed Viking era. It began when the Apostle of the North, Ansgar, was given a parcel of land by the Danish king around 860 and permission to erect a church. It's not known when the church was built, but the earliest record of the existence of a bishop in Ribe is 948 – and bishops have cathedrals. During the Viking era, Ribe, linked to the sea by its river, flourished as a centre of trade between the Frankish empire and the Scandinavian states to the north.

In the 12th century the Valdemar dynasty fortified the town, building a castle and establishing Ribe as one of the king's Jutland residences.

The end of the medieval period saw Ribe enter its most torrid time. Two factors combined to send the town into 250 years of decline. A fire ripped through in 1580, and the relocation of the royal family to Copenhagen saw royal money leave the town. In turn the population diminished, and the bustling trade port turned into a struggling town with little regional importance or influence.

This economic downturn was something of a blessing – there was no finance available for building bigger and better houses, so the old town remained virtually untouched. In 1899 a tourist and conservation organisation (showing remarkable foresight) was established, and in 1963 the town council issued a preservation order covering the core of the old town. Their good sense has been well rewarded, with tourists flocking to soak up Ribe's old-world charm.

◉ Sights

★Ribe Domkirke   CHURCH
(☑24 66 07 37; www.ribe-domkirke.dk; Torvet; tower adult/child 20/10kr; ◷10am-5pm Mon-Sat, noon-5pm Sun May-Sep, shorter hours Oct-Apr) Dominating Ribe's skyline is the impressive

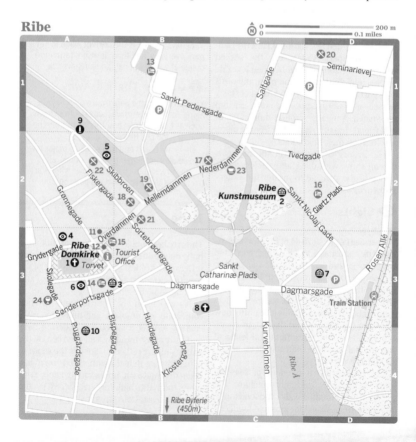

Ribe

Ribe Cathedral, which dates back to at least 948 (the earliest record of the existence of a bishop in Ribe) – making it the oldest in Denmark. The cathedral was largely rebuilt in 1150 when Ribe was at the heart of royal and government money, which in turn paved the way for some fine architectural structures.

The new cathedral was constructed primarily from tufa, a soft porous rock quarried near Cologne and shipped north along the Rhine. It took a century for the work to reach completion. Later additions included several Gothic features, but the core of the cathedral is decidedly Romanesque, a fine example of medieval Rhineland influences in architecture.

The interior decor is a hotchpotch of later influences. There's an organ with a facade designed by renowned 17th-century sculptor Jens Olufsen, a baptismal font from 1375, and an ornate pulpit created in 1597 (a mark on the pillar behind the pulpit shows where the flood of 1634 reached). You can find remains of paintings from the 16th century on the last two pillars on the northern side of the cathedral, while in the apse are modern-day frescoes, stained-glass windows and seven **mosaics** created in the 1980s by artist Carl-Henning Pedersen. The funky mosaics enliven the church and add a fascinating contrast to the more sombre features.

For a view over the countryside, climb the 248 steps (52m) up the cathedral **tower**, which dates from 1333. A survey of the surrounding marshland makes it easy to understand why the tower once doubled as a lookout station for floods. **Museum exhibits** in the tower cover the cathedral's history.

For added atmosphere, look out for summer classical-music concerts held in the cathedral.

⭐ **Ribe VikingeCenter**　　MUSEUM

(☑ 75 41 16 11; www.ribevikingecenter.dk; Lustrupvej 4; adult/child 120/60kr; ⊙ 11am-5pm late Jun-late Aug, 10am-3.30pm Mon-Fri early May-late Jun & late Aug–mid-Oct; ⓘ) Embrace your inner Viking (ignore any pillaging tendencies, OK?) at this fun, hands-on, open-air museum. It re-creates a slice of life in Viking-era Ribe using various reconstructions, including a 34m longhouse. The staff, dressed in period clothing, bake bread over open fires, demonstrate archery and Viking-era crafts such as pottery and leatherwork, and offer falconry shows and 'warrior training' (for kids, using a sword and shield). You'll undoubtedly learn more about Viking life than you could from a textbook.

⭐ **Ribe Kunstmuseum**　　MUSEUM

(☑ 75 42 03 62; www.ribekunstmuseum.dk; Sankt Nicolaj Gade 10; adult/child 75kr/free; ⊙ 11am-5pm Jul & Aug, to 4pm Tue-Sun Sep-Jun) An undeniable benefit of being the oldest town in the land is the opportunity to amass an impressive art collection. Ribe's beautifully restored art museum has been able to acquire some of Denmark's best works, including those by 19th-century 'Golden Age' painters.

The gallery's riverside garden presents a glorious backdrop to collection pieces by big-name Danish artists. It's worth exploring the delightfully verdant area behind the art gallery (open to all), where paths pass over the river and lead either to Sankt Catharinæ Kirke or Nederdammen.

Historic Ribe
AREA

For a leisurely stroll that takes in some of Ribe's handsome half-timbered homes and idyllic cobbled lanes, head along any of the streets radiating out from Torvet (note that the night-watchman walks cover much of this ground).

To help you appreciate the surrounds, drop by the tourist office (p208) and pick up a copy of the free *Town Walk in Old Ribe* brochure; it's available in Danish, English, German, Dutch, Italian, Spanish and French.

On Puggårdsgade is a 16th-century manor house, the charmingly skew-whiff **Taarnborg** (Puggårdsgade 3), where no corner is 90 degrees. Next door at No 5 is a half-timbered house from 1550.

From Grønnegade, narrow alleys lead down and across pretty Fiskergade to Skibbroen and the picturesque riverfront.

Sankt Catharinæ Kirke
CHURCH

(www.sct-catharinae.dk; Sankt Catharinæ Plads; ⊙10am-4pm Tue-Sun) Founded by Spanish Blackfriars in 1228, St Catharine's Church was originally built on reclaimed marshland, but it eventually collapsed. The present structure dates from the 15th century. Of the 13 churches built during the pre-Reformation period in Ribe, Sankt Catharinæ Kirke and Ribe Domkirke (p204) are the only survivors.

In 1536 the Reformation forced the friars to abandon Sankt Catharinæ Kirke and, in the years that followed, the compound served as an asylum for the mentally ill and a wartime field hospital, to name a couple of its incarnations. These days the abbey provides housing for the elderly.

In the 1920s Sankt Catharinæ Kirke was restored at tremendous cost (due to its still-faulty foundations) and was reconsecrated in 1934. The interior boasts a delicately carved pulpit dating to 1591 and an ornate altarpiece created in 1650.

For a 5kr fee you can enter the tranquil cloister garden and enjoy a few minutes of contemplative silence.

Den Gamle Rådhus
HISTORIC BUILDING

(⚡76 16 88 10; www.detgamleraadhusiribe.dk; Von Støckens Plads; adult/child 20kr/free; ⊙1-3.30pm Mon-Fri mid-May–mid-Sep, plus Sat & Sun Jun-Aug) This is the oldest town hall (1496) in Denmark and was used as a courthouse until 2006 – these days it's a popular spot for civil weddings. As well as ceremonial artefacts, there's an exhibit on local law and order (including a collection of medieval weapons and the executioner's axe).

Museet Ribes Vikinger
MUSEUM

(⚡76 16 39 60; www.ribesvikinger.dk; Odins Plads 1; adult/child 75kr/free; ⊙10am-6pm Jul & Aug, to 4pm Sep-Jun, closed Mon Nov-Mar; 📖) To better come to grips with Ribe's Viking and medieval history, visit the informative displays of the Museum of Ribe's Vikings. Two rooms provide snapshots of the town in 800 and during medieval times in 1500. These portrayals are complemented by rare archaeological finds and good explanations, which add real substance to the tales.

Johanne Dan
LANDMARK

(moored on Skibbroen) *Johanne Dan* is an old sailing ship designed with a flat bottom, which allowed it to navigate through the shallow waters of the Ribe Å; an onboard visit is usually only possible in conjunction with a guided tour (enquire at the tourist office; p208).

Kannikegården
NOTABLE BUILDING

(Torvet 15) This award-winning building on the main square houses the church office. Through windows you can see the results of excavations in the area; these found evidence of Christianity arriving in Ribe a century earlier than historians had previously believed.

Stormflodssøjlen
MONUMENT

(Skibbroen) Along the riverfront is Stormflodssøjlen, a wooden flood column commemorating the numerous floods that have swept over Ribe. The ring at the top indicates the water's depth during the record flood of 1634 (6m above normal!), which claimed hundreds of lives. Although these days a system of dikes affords low-lying Ribe somewhat more protection, residents are still subject to periodic flood evacuations.

Tours

Ghost Walks
WALKING

(⚡75 42 15 00; www.ribesvikinger.dk; adult/child 50kr/free; ⊙9pm Wed Jul & Aug; 📖) The weekly summertime ghost walks operated by (and departing from) Museet Ribes Vikinger show the town in a whole new light – listen out for tales of Maren Spliid, who was burned at the stake in 1641, the last victim of Denmark's witch-hunt persecutions. Tours are in Danish and English.

NIGHT-WATCHMAN TOUR

One of the best free activities in Denmark is Ribe's 45-minute night-watchman tour, which departs nightly in the warmer months. Interesting factual titbits, singing and colourful stories of memorable Ribe citizens (in Danish and English) are part of the act. Throw in narrow streets, pretty-as-a-picture houses and a late sundown and it's a great way to end a history-soaked day.

Nowadays, it's a stroll through the town's historic streets, designed to entertain and educate visitors to Ribe, but the night-watchman's walk was originally born of necessity. As early as the 14th century these watchmen made their nightly rounds in Ribe, making sure the streets were safe for locals to walk. They were also charged with being on the lookout for fires or floods threatening the town. The job was abolished in Ribe in 1902, but reinstated in 1932 as a tourist attraction. Bookings aren't required.

Town Walks WALKING
(adult/child 85kr/free; ⏰ 11.30am Mon-Fri Jul & Aug, Mon Apr-Jun, Sep & Oct) The tourist office (p208) stages guided 90-minute town walks in the high season. At the time of research these were being conducted in Danish and German only. Tours in other languages can be arranged by request (see www.visitribe.dk).

🛏 Sleeping

★ **Danhostel Ribe** HOSTEL €
(📞 75 42 06 20; www.danhostel-ribe.dk; Sankt Pedersgade 16; dm 240kr, s/d/q from 455/500/760kr; P ◉ 🛜) 🍃 Knowledgeable staff, sparkling rooms (all with bathroom) and impressive facilities make this a top option for both backpackers and families. It rents bikes and is a stone's throw from Ribe's historic centre; equally impressive is its commitment to the environment, from the Good Origin coffee in its vending machines to its promotion of sustainable travel in the Wadden Sea region.

Breakfast costs 75kr; linen hire is 70kr.

Ribo B&B GUESTHOUSE €
(www.ribobandb.dk; Giørtz Plads 3; s/d 475/550kr; 🛜) One of a new breed of Danish 'self-service' sleeping options, where the guesthouse is unstaffed, you book online and a security code is given so you can access your room. It's impersonal, but the prices are often excellent – as they are at Ribo, a central, modern, three-room guesthouse, with spick-and-span facilities plus access to a kitchen. Breakfast is 75kr.

Ribe Camping CAMPGROUND €
(📞 75 41 07 77; www.ribecamping.dk; Farupvej 2; per adult/child/site 84/60/90kr; ◉ 🛜 🏊) Just 2km north of the train station lies this busy, well-equipped camping ground bursting with good cheer and excellent amenities; a summertime outdoor heated swimming pool and playgrounds are at your disposal. There are also some pretty swanky cabins for hire (some with spa) from 600kr.

Weis Stue GUESTHOUSE €
(📞 75 42 07 00; www.weisstue.dk; Torvet 2; s/d without bathroom 395/495kr; 🛜) An ancient wooden-beamed house from 1600, Weis Stue has eight small, crooked rooms (with shared bathrooms) above its restaurant (p208). Rooms have lashings of character: creaking boards, sloping walls and low overhead beams.

Den Gamle Arrest GUESTHOUSE €€
(📞 75 42 37 00; www.dengamlearrest.dk; Torvet 11; d incl breakfast 740-1090kr) You need to be creative when turning jail cells into guest rooms, and Annitha, the lovely owner of this place, can take a bow. This superbly positioned building served as a jail until 1989; now it holds cells converted into bright, simple rooms that maximise space (a mezzanine level holds table and chairs above a petite roll-away bed).

Most former cells have a washbasin but share bathroom facilities; there are also wardens' rooms with full bathroom.

Ribe Byferie APARTMENT €€
(📞 79 88 79 88; www.ribe-byferie.dk; Damvej 34; apt for 4 people 915-1400kr; P ◉ 🛜) This is a well-run 'village' of modern apartments in a quiet part of town, a 10-minute walk south of Torvet. Roomy self-catering apartments sleep from two to seven; families are catered for with a wellness centre, games room, bike and canoe hire, kids' club, playground and barbecue area. Prices fluctuate with the season; you pay extra for linen and breakfast.

Hotel Dagmar HOTEL €€
(📞 75 42 00 33; www.hoteldagmar.dk; Torvet; s/d incl breakfast from 1125/1325kr; ◉ 🛜) Classy, central Hotel Dagmar is Denmark's oldest hotel (1581) and exudes all the charm you'd expect. There's a golden hue to the hallways and rooms, with old-world decor alongside tiling, artworks and antiques.

Eating

Empanadas
INTERNATIONAL €

(Nederdammen 31; empanadas 25kr; ⊙11.30am-5pm Mon-Fri) This is a simple, heart-warming place, where Iran-born Ali creates delicious South American–style empanadas filled with spinach, beef or chicken. He also serves good-value meals like meatballs or pasta for 55kr to 60kr, plus smoothies and milkshakes.

Kvickly
SUPERMARKET €

(Seminarievej 1; ⊙8am-8pm Mon-Fri, to 6pm Sat & Sun) Well placed for self-caterers staying at the hostel (p207); the post office is inside.

Isvaflen
ICE CREAM €

(☑75 41 06 88; Overdammen 11; 2/3 scoops 26/32kr; ⊙10am-10pm Jul & Aug, shorter hours Sep-Jun; ⊕) Pizza places and ice-cream sellers aren't hard to find along the main drag. On a warm day, Isvaflen is swamped with holidaymakers devouring the great ice-cream flavours.

★Kolvig
DANISH €€

(☑75 41 04 88; www.kolvig.dk; Mellemdammen 13; lunch 88-189kr, dinner mains 230-250kr; ⊙11am-midnight Mon-Sat) Kolvig's alfresco terrace overlooks the river, offering prime Ribe-watching. The menu is the most ambitious in town, showcasing local produce; most interesting is the delicious tapas plate of Wadden Sea flavours, including shrimp, ham, smoked lamb and local cheese. It makes for a good drinking spot, too; the kitchen closes at 9.30pm.

★Sælhunden
DANISH €€

(☑75 42 09 46; www.saelhunden.dk; Skibbroen 13; lunch 69-169kr, dinner mains 129-289kr; ⊙11am-10pm) This handsome old black-and-white inn is by the riverfront, with outdoor seating by the Johanne Dan (p206) boat. *Sælhund* means seal, so it's no surprise there's quality seafood in traditional Danish guises, including lunchtime smørrebrød (Danish open sandwiches). Try the delicious house speciality *stjerneskud* (one fried and one steamed fillet of fish served on bread with prawns and dressing).

Weis Stue
DANISH €€

(☑75 42 07 00; www.weisstue.dk; Torvet 2; lunch 94-134kr, dinner mains 169-265kr; ⊙11.30am-10pm) Don't come here looking for modern, could-be-anywhere cuisine. As befits the setting (one of Denmark's oldest inns (p207), wonky and charming), the menu is a traditionalist's dream. The large meat-and-potatoes portions are full of northern European flavour (pepper pork medallions, Wiener schnitzel), best washed down with locally brewed beer. There's bags of atmosphere, but little joy for vegetarians.

Quedens Gaard
CAFE €€

(☑75 41 10 50; www.quedensgaard.dk; Overdammen 10; mains 59-169kr; ⊙10am-6pm) This bright and cheerful, history-packed place makes a perfect main-street pit stop for a morning coffee or lunchtime panini or burger. It dates from 1583; the best feature is the sweet, cobbled courtyard.

Hotel Dagmar
INTERNATIONAL €€

(☑75 42 00 33; www.hoteldagmar.dk; Torvet 1; ⊙Dagmar noon-10pm, Vægterkælderen 5-10pm) The town's main hotel, in plum position by the cathedral (p204), has two main restaurants: the more refined Restaurant Dagmar (three courses for 385kr), plus Vægterkælderen, the 'night-watchman's cellar', which makes for a *hyggelig* (cosy) winter spot. In summer, the best option is the all-day outdoor area on Torvet, where you can choose from a casual menu of salads and burgers.

🍷 Drinking & Nightlife

Ribe Bryghus
BREWERY

(☑40 43 17 16; www.ribebryghus.dk; Skolegade 4B; ⊙10am-2pm Sat) Look out for this label's locally brewed beers at restaurants and bars around town, or pop into the brewery (in the courtyard) during its limited opening hours. Note it's also 'open' whenever the brewers are inside working their hoppy magic. Groups of eight or more can arrange a tour.

Postgaarden
CAFE

(☑75 41 01 12; www.postgaarden-ribe.dk; Nederdammen 36; ⊙10am-5.30pm Mon-Fri, to 4pm Sat) Postgaarden has a range of Danish and international microbrews for sale in its gourmet food and wine store, and a changing selection of boutique (and sometimes obscure) brews on tap to accompany its cafe-style menu, best enjoyed in the photogenic 1668 courtyard.

ℹ Information

Tourist Office (☑75 42 15 00; www.visitribe. dk; Torvet 3; ⊙9am-6pm Mon-Fri, 10am-4pm Sat Jul & Aug, 9am-4pm Mon-Fri Sep-Jun plus 10am-1pm Sat Sep-Dec & Apr-Jun; ☎) Has an abundance of information on the town and surrounding areas. There is an unstaffed brochure area open 9am to 10pm every day.

ℹ️ Getting There & Away

Trains from Ribe run hourly on weekdays and less frequently at weekends to:

Esbjerg (60kr, 35 minutes)
Skærbæk For Rømø (31kr, 20 minutes)
Tønder (78kr, 50 minutes).

ℹ️ Getting Around

Ribe is a tightly clustered town, so it's easy to explore. Everything, including the hostel (p207) and the train station, is within a 10-minute walk of Torvet, the central square that's dominated by the huge cathedral (p204).

Central parking is free but generally has a two-hour daytime limit; there is four-hour parking by the hostel, and just north of the hostel on Saltgade is 48-hour parking. North of the train station (on Rosen Allé) is another area of 48-hour parking.

Bicycles can be hired from Danhostel Ribe (p207) and cost 80/140kr for one/two days.

Esbjerg

POP 72,300

Esbjerg (roughly pronounced *ess*-be-air) has a touch of the 'wild frontier' about it – a new city (by Danish standards) that's grown big and affluent from oil, fishing and trading. Its business focus lies to the west, to the oilfields of the North Sea, but its ferry link with the UK ceased in 2014.

Esbjerg fails to pull heartstrings on first impressions – its silos and smokestacks hardly compete with the crooked, storybook streets of nearby Ribe. In the harbour you may see offshore drilling rigs being repaired. Away from the industrial grit, however, Esbjerg redeems itself with some quirky attractions and its easy access to the beautiful, time-warped island of Fanø, just a 12-minute ferry ride away.

⊙ Sights

★ **Mennesket ved Havet** MONUMENT
(Sædding Strandvej) On the waterfront opposite Fiskeri- og Søfartsmuseet is Esbjerg's most interesting landmark, *Mennesket ved Havet* ('Man Meets the Sea'): four stark-white, 9m-high, stylised human figures, sitting rigid and staring out to sea. They were created by Danish sculptor Svend Wiig Hansen to commemorate the city's centennial in 1995; they make a striking backdrop to holiday snaps.

Fiskeri- og Søfartsmuseet AQUARIUM
(☑76 12 20 00; www.fimus.dk; Tarphagevej 2; adult 115-140kr, child free; ⊙from 10am daily; 🚻) For an

OFF THE BEATEN TRACK

TIRPITZ BUNKER

Tirpitz (☑75 22 08 77; www.vardemuseerne.dk; Tirpitzvej 1, Blåvand; adult/child 125kr/free; ⊙9am-7pm Jul & Aug, 10am-5pm Sep-Jun) is a large, menacing-looking bunker built in the coastal dunes during WWII as part of Hitler's Atlantic Wall defence. Abandoned since 1944, it was reopened in 2017 as part of a clever, tunnel-like museum designed by the starchitect Bjarke Ingels Group (BIG). This showcases the effects of war on Jutland's wild west coast, while also incorporating a beautiful collection of amber – Jutland's coast is one of the best places to hunt for it.

Tirpitz is near the west-coast resort town of Blåvand, 38km northwest of Esbjerg by Rtes 463 and 431. If you're continuing north, it's another 30km to reach the standout restaurant Henne Kirkeby Kro (p217).

up-close look at North Sea marine life, head to the saltwater aquarium at the Fisheries & Maritime Museum (take bus 3 or 6). Here you can see assorted local fish species getting along swimmingly, plus seals being fed at 11am and 2.30pm daily. The newest exhibitions concentrate on life on an offshore rig in the North Sea. Closing time varies (from 4pm to 6pm).

Musikhuset Esbjerg ARCHITECTURE
(☑76 10 90 00; www.mhe.dk; Havnegade 18) Famed Danish architect Jørn Utzon (he of the Sydney Opera House) designed Esbjerg's Music House together with his son, Jan. The performing arts centre opened in 1997 and is the city's main venue for cultural events including concerts, opera and ballet.

🛏️ Sleeping

Danhostel Esbjerg HOSTEL €
(☑75 12 42 58; www.esbjerg-danhostel.dk; Gammel Vardevej 80; dm 240kr, d without/with bathroom 570/720kr; @🛜) An excellent choice if you don't mind being out of the city centre. It's in a spiffy location, neighbouring a sports stadium, swimming pool, park and cinema. The old building is lovely and the communal facilities top-notch; rooms in the new wing all have private bathrooms. It's 3km northwest of the city centre on bus 11.

Esbjerg

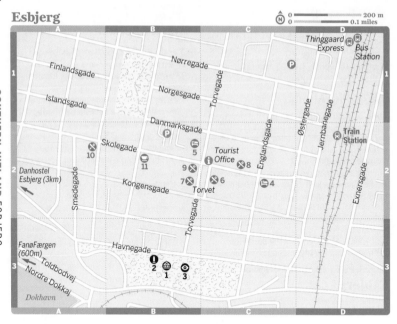

Esbjerg

⊙ Sights

1 Esbjerg Kunstmuseum	B3
2 Esbjerg Vandtårn	B3
3 Musikhuset Esbjerg	B3

🛏 Sleeping

4 CabInn Esbjerg	C2
5 Hotel Britannia	B2

🍴 Eating

6 Dronning Louise	C2
7 Guldægget Cafe	B2
8 Industrien	C2
9 Posthuset	B2
10 Sand's Restauration	A2

🍸 Drinking & Nightlife

11 Portlands	B2

CabInn Esbjerg
HOTEL €

(📞 75 18 16 00; www.cabinn.com; Skolegade14; s/d from 495/625kr; 🅿 @ 🛜) Esbjerg's best central value is found in this century-old building that's been thoroughly renovated and sits in a prime inner-city location. It's a hit with international and local visitors, who enjoy its reasonable rates and petite, light-filled rooms, all with bathroom, kettle and TV. You pay extra for more space (and for parking, and breakfast).

Hotel Britannia
HOTEL €€

(📞 75 13 01 11; www.britannia.dk; Torvegade 24; s/d incl breakfast 1295/1495kr; 🅿 @ 🛜) This super-central, business-oriented hotel has professional service, smart rooms, a well-regarded restaurant and an English pub, but its rack rates seem pitched at expense-account business travellers.

🍴 Eating

Guldægget Cafe
BAKERY, CAFE €

(📞 92 44 07 79; www.cafeguldaegget.dk; Torvet 16; sandwiches & salads 45-59kr; ⊙8am-7pm Mon-Fri, 9.30am-5pm Sat & Sun) There are loads of nooks inside this huge bakery-cafe on the main square, plus a big outdoor terrace. Carb up with pastries and an assortment of sandwiches, or go healthier with salads and smoothies.

⭐ Industrien
INTERNATIONAL €€

(📞 75 13 61 66; www.indubar.dk; Skolegade 27; meals 100-179kr; ⊙ kitchen 5.30-9pm Mon-Thu, noon-9pm Fri & Sat) This cool 'rock gastro bar' is a local darling for its live music, vinyl selection, late hours (till 3am Friday and Saturday) and excellent kitchen. Build a super-tasty dinner from the selection of gourmet sliders (mini-burgers; 50kr a pop, veg options too) and creative side dishes, then sit back and enjoy the house gin cocktails and good times.

Posthuset
INTERNATIONAL €€

(📞 69 13 60 13; www.posthuset.dk; Torvet 20; burgers 139-229kr; ⊙restaurant & burgers 11am-9pm) A stylish multipurpose venue on the main square, the brand-new Posthuset has taken shape inside the distinctive old post office, and offers something for most appetites and budgets. Options range from a casual burger joint on the ground level to weekend fine dining in the 'loft'. In between are a mainstream restaurant, coffee bar and weekend nightclub, plus outdoor terrace.

Dronning Louise
INTERNATIONAL €€

(📞 75 13 13 44; www.dr-louise.dk; Torvet 19; mains 125-295kr; ⊙kitchen 10am-10pm Mon-Sat, to 9pm Sun, bar to midnight or later) Jack of all trades, the Queen Louise commands a great central position on Torvet: she's a restaurant, pub and even a nightclub (Friday and Saturday), with occasional live music too. You can dine from the broad, classic-hits menu (sandwiches, burgers, steak) on the square, inside or in the rear courtyard. Brunch is served until 4pm.

Sand's Restauration
DANISH €€

(📞 75 12 02 07; www.sands.dk; Skolegade 60; lunch 59-189kr, dinner mains 119-249kr; ⊙11.30am-9.30pm Mon-Sat) One for the traditionalists. The menu at this classy, century-old restaurant is an ode to old-school Danish favourites: lunchtime smørrebrød and herring platters (accompanied by *snaps*), evening fish (try the *bakskuld*, salted and smoked flatfish) and plenty of classic *bøf* (beef).

🍷 Drinking & Nightlife

Daytime venues morph into evening venues, while Torvet and Skolegade are thick with options. Industrien does great cocktails and music; Dronning Louise has a nightclub for weekends.

Portlands
CAFE, BAR

(📞 79 30 18 00; www.portlands.dk; Skolegade 48; ⊙9am-11pm Mon-Wed, to midnight Thu, to 2am Fri & Sat, 11am-8pm Sun) A welcoming, all-day cafe-bar, ideal for daytime smoothies or good coffee, or evening wine, cocktails or microbrews. There's limited food (cheese or charcuterie platters, plus a few cakes), but there are plenty of couches, tables and outdoor seating. Plus: board games. It's the kind of place you could easily spend hours at.

ℹ️ Information

Tourist Office (📞 75 12 55 99; www.visit esbjerg.dk; Skolegade 33; ⊙10am-8pm Sun-

Wed, to 6pm Thu-Sat) Unstaffed central office, on the corner of Torvet. Offers info screens, plus self-service racks of brochures and maps.

ℹ️ Getting There & Away

AIR

Esbjerg Airport (www.esbjerg-lufthavn.dk) is 10km northeast of the city centre, with daily connections to two other North Sea oil bases: Stavanger (Norway) and Aberdeen (Scotland).

BOAT

FanøFærgen (📞 70 23 15 15; www.faergen. com; Dockvej) runs boats to Fanø (p212) at least hourly (12 minutes).

BUS

From the **bus station** (Jernbanegade), buses 915X (32 minutes) and far slower 8C (55 minutes) connect Esbjerg with Ribe (60kr). **Thinggaard Express** (📞 98 11 66 00; www.expressbus.dk) bus 980 departs daily to Frederikshavn (340kr, 5¼ hours), calling at Viborg and Aalborg en route.

TRAIN

Regular train connections include:
Aarhus (270kr, 2½ hours)
Kolding (101kr, 45 minutes)
Ribe (60kr, 30 minutes)
Tønder (112kr, 1½ hours)

ℹ️ Getting Around

Torvet, the city square, can be found where Skolegade and Torvegade intersect. The train and bus stations are about 300m east of Torvet; the Fanø ferry terminal (p211) is 1km southwest.

Most city buses can be boarded at the train station; it's 22kr for a local ticket (available from the driver).

City buses 11, 12 and 13 run to the harbour (for the ferry to Fanø).

Parking in the city centre is free but has a time limit (usually two or four hours) and a parking disc *(P-skive)* is required, to show the time you arrived.

Rent bikes from **PJ Ferie** (📞 75 45 62 33; www. pjferie.dk; Hjertingvej 21; bike rental per day/week 50/250kr; ⊙noon-5pm).

Fanø
POP 3200

Just 12 minutes' ferry ride from Esbjerg, the island of Fanø appeals with two traditional seafaring settlements full of idyllic thatch-roofed houses, blooming gardens and cafe-lined cobblestone streets. The exposed west coast is blessed with wide strips of sand that welcome summer beach-goers and host a world-famous and super-photogenic

WORTH A TRIP

BATHING BEAUTY

If Esbjerg's industrial grit has you yearning for a little trademark Danish *hygge* (cosiness), make your way 10km northwest of town to **Hjerting Badehotel** (☑ 75 11 70 00; www.hjertingbadehotel.dk; Strandpromenaden 1; s/d incl breakfast from 1195/1395kr; 🛜), a delightful, century-old 'bathing hotel' right on the beach. Accommodation is in fresh, pastel-hued rooms or stylish beach houses sleeping four. There's a wellness centre, kayaks and bikes for hire and a choice of fine dining options: book ahead for the gourmet sea-view restaurant **Strandpavillonen** (3/5 courses 439/619kr; ⏱ 6-11pm Mon-Sat; 🛜), or choose more the casual all-day Ship Inn.

gathering for **kite-fliers** (www.kitefliersmeeting fanoe.de; ⏱ Jun). In the island's centre, **Klitplantage** is a 1421-hectare nature reserve attracting walkers and wildlife-watchers.

🛏 Sleeping

Møllesti B&B   GUESTHOUSE €
(☑ 75 16 29 49; www.mollesti.dk; Møllesti 3, Nordby; s/d without bathroom from 300/450kr; ⏱ May-Aug; 🛜) This well-priced B&B is hidden away in the atmospheric lanes of Nordby. It's home to four simple, comfy guest rooms sharing two bathrooms and a kitchenette/lounge, in a restored sea-captain's house from 1892. Breakfast costs an additional 50kr; there's a two-night minimum stay.

★ Sønderho Kro   INN €€€
(☑ 75 16 40 09; www.sonderhokro.dk; Kropladsen 11, Sønderho; s/d incl breakfast from 1300/1650kr; ⏱ May-Oct, Fri & Sat Nov-Apr) The loveliest place to stay on the island (and renowned around the country) is this thatched-roof slice of *hyggelig* (cosy) heaven. It dates from 1722, and its 13 individually decorated rooms feature local antiques.

🍴 Eating & Drinking

Slagter Christiansen   DELI €
(☑ 75 16 20 67; www.fanoeslagteren.dk; Hovedgaden 17, Nordby; ⏱ 8am-5.30pm Mon-Thu, to 6pm Fri, to 1pm Sat) The Nordby butcher, Slagter Christiansen, is known throughout Denmark for his *Fanø skinke* (Fanø ham), a ham in the style of Italian parma. The store is a delicatessen full of local gourmet produce.

★ Rudbecks Ost & Deli   CAFE €€
(☑ 24 93 85 05; www.rudbecks.dk; Hovedgaden 90, Nordby; mains 89-189kr; ⏱ 10am-5.30pm Mon-Fri, to 4pm Sat) This fab family-run deli-cafe gives a great snapshot of island flavours: house-made bread, butter and ice cream, salmon smoked on Fanø, burgers made from local marsh-grazing lamb and beef. Grab picnic supplies (there's a great cheese cabinet) or linger over brunch, lunch or delicious cake.

Sønderho Kro   DANISH €€€
(☑ 75 16 40 09; www.sonderhokro.dk; Kropladsen 11, Sønderho; lunch 149kr, 2-/3-/5-course dinner 439/539/650kr; ⏱ noon-8.30pm Apr-Oct, by appointment Sat & Sun rest of year) Renowned throughout Denmark, delightful Sønderho Kro has an acclaimed gourmet restaurant, which showcases local and seasonal specialities in a steeped-in-time dining room. Bookings advised.

Fanø Bryghus   MICROBREWERY
(☑ 76 66 01 12; www.fanoebryghus.dk; Strandvejen 5, Nordby; ⏱ 11am-6pm Jun-Aug, shorter hours Sep-May) Thirsty? Stop by this excellent brewery on the outskirts of Nordby. BYO food to eat in the beer garden (there's no food served), and settle in to sample as many as 40 beers.

ℹ Information

ATMs are found on Nordby's main street, Hovedgaden, a block west of the ferry terminal.

ℹ Getting There & Away

If you're doing a day trip or overnight stay from Esbjerg, you're better off leaving your car on the mainland and hiring a bike or taking the bus once you reach the island.

FanøFærgen (☑ 70 23 15 15; www.fanoe faergen.dk; Langelinie, Nordby) shuttles car ferries between Esbjerg and Nordby one to three times hourly from 5am to 2am. Sailing time is 12 minutes. A return ticket for a foot passenger is 45/25kr per adult/child; bikes travel free. It costs 195/415kr in the low/high season to transport a car (return trip, including passengers).

ℹ Getting Around

Bus 431 from the ferry dock runs the length of the island 12 times daily connecting Nordby with Sønderho (32kr, 20 minutes) via Fanø Bad (22kr) and Rindby Strand (22kr).

Bicycles can be hired from a number of places, including **Fri BikeShop** (☑ 75 16 24 60; Mellemgaden 12, Nordby; bike rental per day 100-145kr; ⏱ 10am-5.30pm Mon-Fri, to 2pm Sat & Sun). Taxis can be reached on ☑ 75 16 62 00.

Central Jutland

Best Places to Eat

➡ Molskroen (p242)

➡ Hotel Julsø (p227)

➡ Henne Kirkeby Kro (p217)

➡ Aarhus Street Food (p236)

➡ Langhoff & Juul (p237)

➡ Frederikshøj (p237)

Best Places to Stay

➡ Niels Bugges Hotel (p247)

➡ Hotel Guldsmeden (p235)

➡ Hotel Legoland (p219)

➡ Legoland Holiday Village (p219)

➡ Villa Provence (p235)

➡ Danhostel Silkeborg (p225)

Why Go?

Easily the largest and most varied of all Danish regions, central Jutland encompasses dramatically different features, from the calm beaches of the sheltered east coast to the wild west coast, battered by North Sea winds. Lying in between, offering visual stimulation among the flatness, are the rolling hills and forests of the Lake District.

The real beauty of this region is that you can skip between themes depending on your mood. Fancy world-class art and top-notch restaurants? Aarhus, Jutland's main city and Denmark's second-largest metropolis, can provide. How about Viking history? Set sail for Hobro. Religious history? Off to Jelling. Want to explore the great outdoors? Head for Rold Skov or Silkeborg. Care to tackle nature's forces? Explore the waters of Hvide Sande. And OK, you've suppressed that inner child long enough – make a beeline for Billund and all things Lego (but beware the accompanying pangs of childhood nostalgia).

When to Go

➡ Warm weather is the key to enjoying much of this region (the beaches, theme parks, festivals, activities), but Aarhus holds year-round appeal. Its museums, cafes and boutiques entertain in all weather, but the city's bars are quieter in summer, when Aarhus University has its break.

➡ If visiting in the shoulder season (May, June, September), it's worth checking when the various safari and amusement parks are open. LEGOLAND Billund, central Jutland's star attraction, is open daily May to August and most days April, September and October (it's closed from early November to March).

➡ Big-ticket family attractions close in winter, but cultural life steps up, with plenty of live theatre and music. December is rich with Christmas markets, festive *hygge* (cosiness) and good cheer.

Central Jutland Highlights

1 ARoS Aarhus Kunstmuseum
(p230) Viewing Aarhus rooftops through rainbow-tinted glass.

2 Aarhus (p227)
Exploring the top-class sights, then eating superbly and drinking plentifully.

3 Lake District
(p222) Revelling in the great outdoors on a canoe trip.

4 Billund (p217)
Marvelling at plastic-fantastic detail at both LEGOLAND Billund and the awesome new Lego House.

5 Hvide Sande
(p216) Enjoying the wind in your hair – and sails – while learning to windsurf.

6 Jelling (p220)
Feeling the weight of history at the spiritual home of the Danish royal family.

7 Djursland
(p241) Hopping between beaches, theme parks and animal parks in prime family holiday turf.

8 Henne Kirkeby Kro (p217)
Escaping to this acclaimed inn to savour fine local flavours.

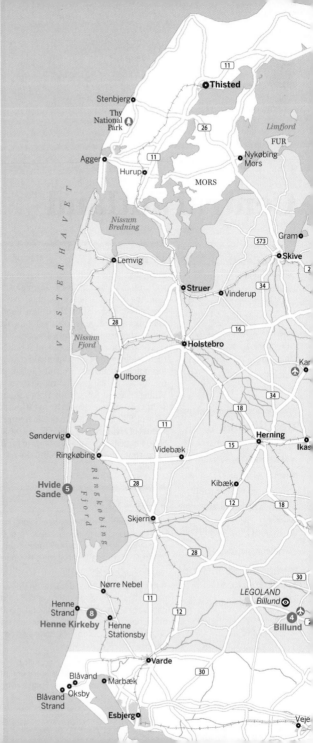

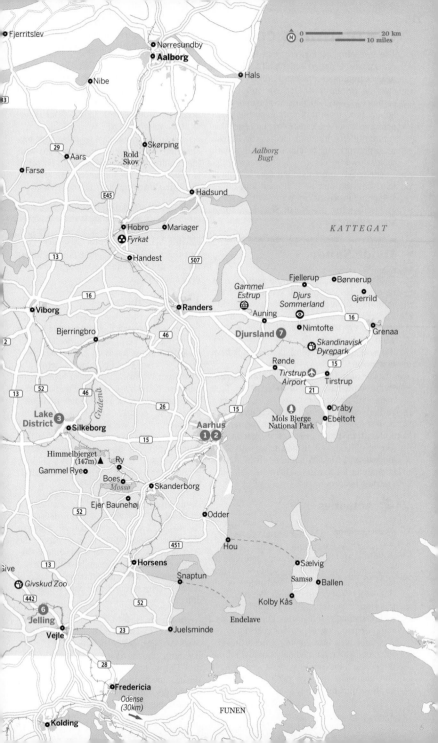

CENTRAL WEST COAST

The sweeping, windswept coastline of the central west is dotted with small settlements full of camping grounds and holiday houses, catering primarily to German and Danish summer tourists. The fjordside town of Ringkøbing is a pleasant, if unremarkable, place acting as a service centre for the beachside communities – it's connected to the Danish train network and regular buses link it with towns down the coast.

The coast's most flaunted area is Holmsland Klit, the thin neck of sand and dunes stretching nearly 35km from north to south and separating the North Sea from Ringkøbing Fjord.

Hvide Sande

POP 3050

Hvide Sande (meaning 'white sands') owes its existence to the wind. Wind caused the sand migration that forced the construction of a lock here in 1931 to assure a North Sea passage for the port of Ringkøbing. And wind continues to be the big drawcard for the large number of tourists who come here to windsurf.

Aside from the wind, it's all about the fish. Hvide Sande has a busy deep-sea fishing harbour, with trawlers, fish-processing factories and an early morning **fish auction**. There's also a small **fishing museum/aquarium** adjacent to the tourist office. Ask at the tourist office about fishing trips with local anglers, and the fish auctions (held weekly in summer for tourists). There are also summertime boat tours.

🏃 Activities

Westwind   WINDSURFING
(☑97 31 25 99; www.westwind.dk; Gytjevej 15; ⊙May-Oct) A consistent, howling westerly coupled with both an invitingly safe lake in Ringkøbing Fjord and the wild North Sea make this area ideal for windsurfers of all skill levels. Just north of town, Westwind offers instruction (in English, German or Danish) in surfing, windsurfing, kitesurfing and stand-up paddling (SUP), plus gear rental.

A three-hour introductory windsurfing lesson costs 400kr; a nine-hour course (in three three-hour blocks) costs 995kr – and staff here guarantee you'll be able to windsurf after those nine hours.

Westwind has a second base just south of town, opposite the camping ground.

Kabel Park   WATER SPORTS
(☑28 72 80 00; www.kabelpark.dk; Gytjevej 15B; 1/2hr 180/225kr; ⊙Apr-Oct) Next to the northern branch of Westwind (in what's labelled the 'Aqua Sports Zone') is this entertaining waterpark, where water-skiers and wake-boarders are pulled by cable rope-tow along an 800m-long course, complete with jump-ramps for the experienced. There's a two-hour intro class for novices (375kr). BYO skis/wake-board and wetsuit, or hire here.

Vinterlejegaard Ridecenter   HORSE RIDING
(☑75 28 22 77; www.vinterlejegaard.dk; Vesterledvej 9; 1hr ride 230kr) Hvide Sande is perfect for viewing a coastal sunset on horseback. Contact this riding centre for details; it's about 10km south of Hvide Sande and offers one-hour beach rides.

🛏 Sleeping

It is a summer-holiday hot spot with plentiful camping grounds including **Hvide Sande Camping** (☑97 31 12 18; www.hvidesande camping.dk; Karen Brands Vej 70; per adult/child/ site 85/45/45kr; ⊙Apr-Oct) handily across the road from Westwind's southern base. **Feriepartner** (☑96 59 35 93; www.feriepartner.dk/ hvide-sande; Nørregade 2B) handles numerous apartment, cottage and houseboat rentals, mostly on a weekly basis. The nearest transport hub-town, Ringkøbing (population 10,000), has its own excellent **hostel** (ROFI-Centret; ☑97 32 24 55; www.rofi.dk; Kirkevej 28; dm 210kr; d without/with bathroom 410/510kr; 🛜) and a central old hotel.

Danhostel Hvide Sande   HOSTEL €
(☑97 31 21 05; www.danhostel-hvidesande.dk; Numitvej 5; dm 210kr, d without/with bathroom 425/490kr; @🛜) Tucked away from the crowds in a side street on the northern side of the channel, this homely hostel offers no-frills rooms (many with bathroom) and access to the nearby sports centre with which it is affiliated.

Hvide Sande Hotel   HOTEL €€
(☑97 31 10 33; www.hssh.dk; Bredgade 5; s/d/f from 745/945/1245kr; @🛜) The only hotel in town has fresh, simple rooms (all with bathroom and TV) in an old seamen's home down at the bustling harbour. Online bookings obtain decent discounts (as low as 645/745kr per single/double).

DANISH DELIGHTS

Tucked away in a scenic, off-the-radar part of west Jutland, about halfway between Esbjerg (40km south) and Hvide Sande (36km north) is **Henne Kirkeby**, a hamlet that includes the kind of historic countryside inn, **Henne Kirkeby Kro** (📋 75 25 54 00; www.henne kirkebykro.dk; Strandvejen 234, Henne; lunch/dinner menu 595/1250kr; ☺ noon-3pm Thu-Sat, 6-9.30pm Wed-Sat Apr-Nov), that Copenhagen gourmands will happily travel hours to reach (now joined by global food lovers, especially after the *kro* (inn) was awarded a Michelin star in 2016).

The accomplished kitchen team is led by Paul Cunningham, a British-born chef who has worked in many of Denmark's best kitchens. Deluxe, design-driven suites here befit the status of destination inn (rooms including breakfast from 1650kr); the menu is a thing of beauty, drawing on the enormous kitchen garden and first-rate local produce.

If you're looking for more accommodation options, the beachside resort town of Henne Strand is 4km west of the *kro*.

Eating

At the harbour (on the south side of the bridge) there's a supermarket and no shortage of cafes, ice creameries and bakeries competing for holidaymakers' appetites. A few more options are on Troldbjergsvej, north of the bridge.

★ Nordsø Fisk   SEAFOOD €

(📋 28 58 75 05; www.facebook.com/nordsofisk; Metheasvej 11; sandwiches 35-45kr; ☺ 9am-7pm Mon-Fri, to 6pm Sat & Sun Jul & Aug, shorter hours rest of year) A proud purveyor of all things fishy, at the harbour. Build your own picnic – bread rolls deliciously stuffed with shrimp, salmon or *fiskefrikadeller* (fish balls) sell for a bargain 35kr. You can also order fish and chips and sit at outside picnic tables.

Restaurant Under Broen   SEAFOOD €€

(📋 97 31 30 40; www.underbroen.dk; 1st fl, Toldbodgade 20; lunch 94-199kr, dinner mains 124-228kr; ☺ 11.30am-8.30pm) Given the prime harbourside location of this elegant dining room and the fishing boats moored just metres away, it doesn't take a brainiac to know the menu will feature super-fresh seafood options (including prawns, mussels and flounder). The downstairs Cafe Marina has simpler fare at cheaper prices.

ℹ Information

Tourist Office (📋 70 22 70 01; www.hvide sande.dk; Nørregade 2; ☺ 8.30am-4pm Mon-Fri) On the northern side of the channel.

ℹ Getting There & Away

Bus 580 runs between Hvide Sande and Ringkøbing station (40kr, 30 minutes) several times daily. From Ringkøbing buses 15 and 952X link to Herning (90kr, 55 minutes), the 952X continuing 11 times daily to Aarhus (200kr, 2½ hours). For Esbjerg (112kr, 1¾ hours) use trains changing in Skjern.

SOUTH-CENTRAL JUTLAND

The landscape of Jutland's interior ranges from hilly woodland up the middle to rolling fields in the east. Industry is prominent throughout, and there are plenty of medium-sized towns that are pleasant enough places to while away a day, but are not particularly worth going out of your way for (no offence to the towns themselves, but we're talking about the likes of Fredericia, Vejle and Horsens).

Billund & Legoland

POP 6200

The attractions of the 'company town' of Billund (built around a little Danish product you might know: Lego) are so geared to families you might feel a little, well, underdressed if you visit without your own set of excited offspring. But don't let that stop you from embracing your inner child and allocating the wondrous LEGOLAND Billund (p218) and awesome new Lego House some generous time in your itinerary.

◉ Sights & Activities

★ Lego House   CULTURAL CENTRE

(📋 82 82 04 00; www.legohouse.com; Ole Kirks Plads 1; Experience Zones ticket 199kr; ☺ 9.30am-8.30pm most days) Newly opened in 2017 in the heart of Billund, Lego House is a hands-on 'experience centre' with a thoroughly brilliant design that resembles a stack of 21 gigantic Lego bricks. It is marketed as the 'Home of the Brick' and incorporates top-quality **museum** displays of the company's history, plus exhibition areas and rooftop terraces. The ground level (home to eateries and a Lego store) has free public access; access to the **Experience Zones** requires a prebooked ticket.

The building is divided into four colour-coded Experience Zones that emphasise Lego's philosophy of learning through play – much planning has gone into these, and the technology is impressive (and super-fun). You can join 20-minute **Creative Labs** (facilitated by teachers) and build a stop-motion movie, for example. As you explore the zones, note the building's standout central feature: the **Tree of Creativity**, 15m high and built of 6.3 million Lego bricks.

The building was seven years in the making and is a design from Danish starchitect Bjarke Ingels. It offers a stellar year-round reason to visit Billund (even in winter, when LEGO-LAND Billund is closed). Check times and buy tickets online.

★ **LEGOLAND Billund**　　　AMUSEMENT PARK
(☑75 33 13 33; www.legoland.dk; Nordmarksvej; adult/child 379/359kr; ☺10am-8pm or 9pm Jul-mid-Aug, shorter hours Apr-Jun & mid-Aug-early Nov, closed early Nov-Mar; P ☀) Mind-blowing Lego models, fun rides and the happy-family magic associated with great theme parks have transformed LEGOLAND Billund into Denmark's most visited tourist attraction outside of Copenhagen. It's a great day outing (you'll need a day to do it justice) and it sits smack-bang in the middle of Jutland, 1km north of Billund.

The heart of LEGOLAND Billund is **Miniland** – 20 million plastic Lego blocks snapped together to create miniature cities and replicate global icons (and re-create scenes from *Star Wars* movies).

You can't help but marvel at the brilliant Lilliputian models of the Kennedy Space Center, Amsterdam, Bergen or a Scottish castle and you'll no doubt vow to head home and drag your Lego out of storage to see what masterpiece you can create (surely it's not that hard?). In Miniland you can also do some advance sightseeing of Danish landmarks including Copenhagen's Nyhavn, Ribe, Skagen or various royal palaces. You can take a trip in miniboats past landmarks such as the Statue of Liberty, the Acropolis and an

Egyptian temple. The reconstructions are on a scale of 1:20 to 1:40 and the attention to detail is incredible. The park's largest piece, a model of Indian chief Sitting Bull, was built with 1.4 million Lego bricks.

Pick up a map to assist with further exploration. The park is divided into themed areas, including **Legoredo Town**, a Wild West area that's home to a haunted house; **Knights' Kingdom**, where a medieval castle awaits; **Pirate Land**, which hosts ships, sword-play and a swimming area; **Adventure Land**, a strange hybrid of Indiana Jones meets Egypt; **Polar Land**, with a roller coaster and a penguin habitat; and **Duplo Land**, with plenty of safe, simple rides and activities for littlies.

For some downtime stop by **Atlantis**, an aquarium built around Lego models of divers and submersibles. For the chilled park-goer there are placid rides, from merry-go-rounds to a tranquil train ride; adrenaline junkies should seek out the roller coasters. Once the entrance fee is paid, all rides are free – the only exception is the **SEAT Driving School** (99kr), for kids aged seven to 13.

Note that the admission price is slightly cheaper if you buy your tickets in advance online. Family passes are also available online (two adults and two kids 1176kr).

Lalandia Billund　　　ACTIVITY CENTRE
(☑76 14 94 70; www.lalandia.dk; Ellehammers Allé; Aquadome adult/child 220/220kr, Monky Tonky Land 60kr; ☀) Adding to the extreme family-friendly focus of Billund is Lalandia, a showy entertainment complex that's like Vegas for kids. This huge roofed complex (where the sky is always blue and the temperature warm) is free to enter – once inside, you pay for activities.

These include the huge Aquadome water-park, Monky Tonky playland, mini-golf, tenpin bowling, ice-skating rink and a smorgasbord of sports activities. There are free kids' concerts, too.

There's also an associated estate of holiday houses for rent ('residents' access the Aquadome and Monky Tonky for free) – see the website for more.

🛏 Sleeping

Billund hotels are pricey, but they're all busy catering to a market focused firmly on family fun (colourful decor, playrooms, peak-summer activities etc). Advance bookings are highly recommended. Official agency **Legoland Holidays** (☑96 23 47 92; www.legolandholidays.dk) organises packages.

ℹ️ LEGOLAND PRACTICALITIES

LEGOLAND Billund is no doubt the reason you're in Billund. To maximise your time, consider buying your tickets online to avoid the queues (you can also buy tickets at most accommodation providers in the area). Note that adult tickets are for those aged 13 and over; infants under two years are free. Seniors over 65 pay the child's price. To enable a cheaper second day at the park, visit a ticket booth with your ticket and pay an additional 129kr. Car parks in the area charge 50kr.

Closing times vary – from 6pm to 9pm. Also worth knowing (and not well publicised) is that the park opens its gates a half-hour before the rides open and no ticket is necessary to enter. Rides normally close one or two hours before the park itself (check the website), so with a bit of luck you could end up with 2½ hours to browse and check out Miniland for free.

Less costly are a handful of B&Bs and guesthouses and a no-frills **Zleep chain hotel** (✉ 70 23 56 35; www.zleephotels.com; Billund Airport, Passagerterminalen; d 720-1280kr; @ 🛜) beside the airport terminal. There are affordable Danhostels 23km away in Givskud (p222) and 13km west in **Grinsted** (✉ 75 21 19 19; www.danhostel-grinsted.dk; Banegårdsvej 34, Grinsted; s/d/f 595/645/795kr; @ 🛜), with easy bus connections.

★ Legoland

Holiday Village   CAMPGROUND, MOTEL **€€**
(✉ 79 51 13 50; www.legoland-village.dk; Ellehammers Allé; camping ground 295kr, motel r/cabin from 1595/1175kr; ☺ Apr-early Nov; @ 🛜) Taking everything up a notch with marvellous Lego detail, this outstanding 'village' incorporates the Pirates' Inn Motel and a huge camping ground. In the motel, pirate-themed rooms sleep up to five and include bathroom, wifi, TV and linen, plus kitchen access. Self-contained, family-sized cabins are available (choose fun Wild West or Ninjago themes), plus tepees or small glamping barrels.

The camping ground is enormous, and well equipped. Families will love the minigolf, playgrounds and petting zoo. There's also a restaurant on-site (breakfast buffet adult/child 99/69kr; motel rates include breakfast).

Refborg   BOUTIQUE HOTEL **€€**
(✉ 75 33 26 33; www.refborg.dk; Buen 6; s/d/f incl breakfast 1195/1395/1795kr; 🛜) An old *kro* (inn) in the town centre has been stylishly renovated into this classy midrange hotel, with popular on-site restaurant (dinner mains 185kr to 295kr) and lovely gourmet shop. It makes a refreshing change from the large hotels and Lego-focused activity elsewhere in town.

Hotel Propellen   HOTEL **€€**
(✉ 75 33 81 33; www.propellen.dk; Nordmarksvej 3; s/d/f incl breakfast from 1248/1348/1748kr; @ 🛜 🏊) Compared to other places in town, Propellen has a grown-up feel, but still caters to families with its indoor pool, playroom and playground. Adults will enjoy the sauna, Jacuzzis, fitness centre and restaurant.

★ Hotel Legoland   HOTEL **€€€**
(✉ 79 51 13 50; www.hotellegoland.dk; Aastvej 10; r standard/themed incl breakfast from 1820/2170kr; @ 🛜) Lego is *everywhere* here, alongside spectacular kid-friendly detail – but there's also plenty of appeal for grown-ups at this 223-room hotel. Standard (business-oriented) rooms are unremarkable, though good quality. Where this place shines is in the family rooms, and the fabulous themed rooms (choose from knight, princess, pirate and Ninjago themes, and more) – but these come at a sizeable premium.

Packages usually include parking, buffet breakfast and two days' park admission.

🍴 Eating

There are offerings within LEGOLAND Billund and Lego House (p217), inside Lalandia Billund, and at hotel restaurants. You can also head into Billund itself, which has a supermarket, good bakery-cafe, pizzerias and a few other well-priced options, primarily clustered around Lego House.

Within LEGOLAND Billund there are picnic spots, plus buffet and pizza restaurants and outlets selling the usual theme-park fare. From the park you can also access the buffet restaurant at Hotel Legoland (p220).

Pirates' Inn   BUFFET **€€**
(✉ 79 51 13 50; Ellehammers Allé 2; buffet adult/child 225/99kr; ☺ 5.30-9pm; 🍴) At the Legoland

PLASTIC FANTASTIC

A carpenter by trade, Ole Kirk Christiansen turned his tools to making wooden toys in Billund when business was slow during a Depression-era slump in 1932. Christiansen came up with the business name Lego, a contraction of *leg godt*, meaning 'play well' in Danish (in a beautiful piece of symmetry, *lego* can mean 'I put together' in Latin). By the late 1940s Lego became the first Danish company to acquire a plastics-injection mould-ing machine for toy production and began making interlocking plastic blocks called 'binding bricks' – the forerunner of today's Lego blocks.

In 1960 the wooden-toy warehouse went up in flames, and Lego decided to focus pro-duction on its plastic toys instead. Lego blocks soon became the most popular children's toy in Europe – in 2000 *Fortune* magazine named the Lego brick 'toy of the century'.

The statistics are incredible: enough Lego has been produced to supply 102 bricks to every person on the planet.

The company (but not the theme park) is still owned by Ole Kirk's descendants; pri-mary concept and development work takes place at the Billund headquarters, and the small town is growing thanks to the influx of international workers.

In 2017, Lego House (p217) was built by the company to showcase the 'Home of the Brick'. There is a museum here tracing the company's rise.

Holiday Village is this economical option, serving a family-friendly buffet every evening. It also offers takeaway options.

Panorama Restaurant –
Hotel Legoland   BUFFET €€€
(☑ 75 33 12 44; Aastvej 10; ☺ noon-3pm & 5.30-9pm; ⊕) A large, light-filled place with a compre-hensive kids menu. The buffet lunch (adult/child 198/99kr) and dinner (265/125kr) rep-resent reasonable value, and kids (adults, too) will love the potatoes shaped like Lego bricks. The hotel is also home to a separate à la carte steakhouse (mains 225kr to 325kr), if you're after a less crowded (or later) dinner. Reser-vations recommended.

ℹ Information

Tourist Office (☑ 79 72 72 99; www.visit billund.dk; Hans Jensensvej 6; ☺ 9am-3pm Mon-Thu, to 1pm Fri) In Billund township, 1km southwest of LEGOLAND Billund.

ℹ Getting There & Away

AIR
Sitting almost right outside LEGOLAND Billund's gate, **Billund Airport** (www.billundairport.dk; Passagerterminalen 10) is Denmark's second-busiest. Numerous direct flights to Scandinavian and European cities are provided by SAS and British Airways. Budget carrier Ryanair connects to London (Stansted), Berlin, Milan, Rome, Barcelona and more.

BUS
From the nearest train station at Vejle, express bus 43 and slower bus 143 drive to LEGOLAND

Billund (p218), Billund town centre and **Bil-lund Airport** (60kr), taking 30 or 45 minutes, respectively. Bus 166 runs from Kolding (70kr, 50 minutes). Bus 912X connects Aarhus with Billund Airport (160kr, 1½ hours).

ℹ Getting Around

Most local buses stop at Billund **town centre** (Hans Jensensvej), on Hans Jensensvej, near the tourist office, LEGOLAND Billund (p218) and the airport.

A free summertime shuttle bus (late June to mid-August) connects the accommodation and attractions of Billund with the town centre and airport (and makes good sense to save on parking fees).

Rent bikes from **Jupiter Cykler** (☑ 75 33 12 03; www.jupitercykler.dk; Granvej 2A; per day 75-120kr; ☺ 9am-5.30pm Mon-Fri, to 1pm Sat) in the centre of town.

Jelling
POP 3400

A sleepy town with a big history, Jelling is revered as the birthplace of Christianity in Denmark, the monarchy and all that is truly Danish. The town served as the royal seat of King Gorm during the Vikings' most dom-inant era; Gorm the Old was the first in a millennium-long chain of Danish monarchs that continues unbroken to this day. The site of Gorm's ancient castle remains a mystery, but other vestiges of his reign can still be found at Jelling Kirke.

The town is a kind of spiritual touchstone for the Danes. Virtually all of them will visit at some point, to pay homage at the church, inspect the two rune stones and climb the burial mounds. The area became a Unesco World Heritage Site in 1994.

⊙ Sights

★ Jelling Kirke   CHURCH
(☑75 87 11 17; www.jellingkirke.dk; Thyrasvej 1; ⊙8am-8pm May-Aug, to 6pm Mar, Apr, Sep & Oct, to 5pm Nov-Feb, opens 12.30pm Sun) Inside this small whitewashed church, erected around 1100, are some vividly restored 12th-century **frescoes**; the main attractions, however, are the two well-preserved **rune stones** just outside the church door.

The smaller stone was erected in the early 10th century by King Gorm the Old in honour of his wife. The larger one, raised by Gorm's son, Harald Bluetooth, is adorned with the oldest representation of Christ found in Scandinavia and is commonly dubbed 'Denmark's birth certificate'.

The stone reads: 'King Harald ordered this monument to be made in memory of Gorm his father and Thyra his mother, the Harald who won for himself all Denmark and Norway and made the Danes Christians.' A replica of the stone (in full colour, as the original would once have appeared) is at **Kongernes Jelling** (☑41 20 63 31; www.natmus. dk; Gormsgade 23; ⊙10am-5pm May-Oct, closed Mon Nov-Apr) FREE, a large interactive museum opposite the church that provides enthralling insight into the town's monuments and burial mounds.

Harald Bluetooth did, in fact, succeed in routing the Swedes from Denmark and began the peaceful conversion of the Danish people from the pagan religion celebrated by his father to Christianity.

☷ Sleeping & Eating

Jelling Kro has rooms, and there's a camping ground on the outskirts of town with alternatives in nearby Givskud or Billund (about 20km west). There's a supermarket and a bakery for picnic supplies, and a few dining options.

★ Cafe Sejd   CAFE €
(☑29 61 54 16; www.cafesejd.dk; Gormsstorv 7A; lunch 45-79kr; ⊙11am-5pm) Bjarne and Ole, the guys behind this stylish, mythologically inspired cafe, are storytellers up for a chat (about Viking times or current affairs). There's good coffee on offer, plus local microbrews, and tasty fare such as platters of bread and dips.

BLUETOOTH TRIVIA

Today the term 'Bluetooth' is used to describe the wireless transportation of electronic data between computers, mobile phones etc. It is named after 10th-century Harald Bluetooth, who was known for his unification of previously warring tribes from Denmark and Norway (including the then-Danish territory of Skåne in Sweden, which is where Bluetooth technology was developed by Swedish company Ericsson). Bluetooth was likewise intended to unify different technologies. The Bluetooth logo merges the Nordic rune symbols H and B.

Jelling Kro   DANISH €€
(☑75 87 10 06; www.jellingkro.dk; Gormsgade 16; lunch 79-129kr, dinner mains 95-215kr; ⊙11am-9.30pm Wed-Mon) In a 1780 bright-yellow building bristling with character, this country inn serves up traditional, meat-heavy Danish fare. It also has a couple of guest rooms (with shared bathroom; double including breakfast 595kr to 750kr).

Byens Café   CAFE €€
(☑76 80 19 90; www.byenshus.com; Møllegade 10; mains 100-160kr; ⊙noon-9pm Tue-Sat, to 5pm Sun) Byens Hus (The Town's House) is home to the local library, cinema, gallery and a spacious cafe serving simple all-day dishes (sandwiches, salads, burgers). Inside you'll see the big copper vats of the local microbrewery, Jelling Bryggeri, and can also sample the wares.

ⓘ Information

Tourist information is offered at Kongernes Jelling, and there are brochures and maps at Byens Hus, which is home to the library.

There is online information at www.visitvejle.com.

ⓘ Getting There & Away

Jelling is on the Fredericia–Herning–Struer railway line. Trains run at least hourly on weekdays, less frequently on weekends. Change in Vejle (32kr, 15 minutes) for bus 43 to Billund.

ⓘ Getting Around

Jelling Kirke is in the centre of town, a five-minute walk due north from the train station along Stationsvej.

Givskud

POP 620

The prime (only?) reason to visit Givskud is its safari park, though its excellent **Danhostel** (☑75 73 05 00; www.givskudzoo.dk; Løveparkvej 2B; dm/s/d/f 200/600/700/770kr; ☎) is useful as the nearest hostel to LEGOLAND Billund (23km). Bus 211 connects to Vejle, via Jelling.

Givskud Zoo (Zootopia; ☑75 73 02 22; www.givskudzoo.dk; Løveparkvej 3; adult/child 200/110kr; ☉from 10am mid-Apr–Oct; ☎) is an entertaining safari park with plenty of African animals, and you can explore certain areas from the comfort of your own car or in the park-run safari buses (40kr). Walking trails will take you past elephant and gorilla enclosures. There's also a petting zoo.

Check the website for closed days; note that closing times vary (from 4pm to 8pm). Bus 211 runs regularly to the zoo from Vejle, via Jelling.

Herning

POP 49,200

If you're a fan of modern art, chances are you've heard of Italian conceptual artist Piero Manzoni (1933–63). What you may not know is that the biggest public collection of his work is not in Milan, but on the eastern fringe of Herning, a regional textile centre 40km west of Silkeborg. You'll find Manzoni's work, and that of other visionaries, at **HEART** (☑97 12 10 33; www.heartmus.dk; Birk Centerpark 8; adult/child 75kr/free; ☉10am-4pm Tue-Sun), Herning's striking museum of contemporary art. Designed by US architect Steven Holl, the museum's cloth-like crumpled walls and sleeve-inspired roof honour the collection's founder, Danish shirt manufacturer and passionate art collector Aage Damgaard (1917–91). In the summers of 1960 and 1961, Damgaard invited Manzoni to indulge his creative spirit in Herning. The result was a string of masterpieces and the forging of Herning's Manzoni legacy. But HEART doesn't stop at 20th-century conceptual art, with several world-class exhibitions of contemporary art staged annually.

Across the street, the **CHPEA Museum** (☑96 28 86 50; www.chpeamuseum.dk; Birk Centerpark 1, Herning; adult/child 100kr/free; ☉10am-4pm Tue-Sun) showcases the riotously colourful paintings, watercolours, mosaics, ceramics and sculptures of artists Carl-Henning Pedersen (1913–2007) and Else Alfelt (1910–74); there's a large sculpture park beyond the museum.

Herning's other claim to fame is **Boxen** (www.mch.dk; Kaj Zartows Vej 7), a slick indoor sporting arena and concert venue hosting big-name international touring acts. It's south of the city, off Hwy 15.

❶ Getting There & Away

For HEART, get off the train from Silkeborg at Birk Centerpark station (65kr, 32 minutes), not at Herning St. For Boxen, continue to Herning Messecenter Station. Jelling-Herning trains (92kr, 40 minutes) run hourly. Buses 15 and 952X link to Ringkøbing for Hvide Sande.

THE LAKE DISTRICT

Søhøjlandet (the 'Lakelands' region) gently dazzles with hills, forests and lakes. It's home to Denmark's longest river (the 160km Gudenå), Jutland's biggest lake (Mossø) and Denmark's highest point, Møllehøj at a smidge under 171m, bless its cotton socks. It's unlikely to induce nosebleeds, but it's a delightful area for rambling in superbly pretty scenery. Hugely popular as a summer destination, the area is thick with camping grounds (most offering cabins too), plus hotels in the towns, a smattering of hostels, and some B&Bs and traditional *kro* (inns).

Silkeborg

POP 43,200

In a flat country, the modern town of Silkeborg is something of a black sheep, surrounded as it is by hills, sitting on an expansive lake and spaciously laid out. Modern-art lovers and history boffins will find cause to stop here, but nature lovers have the most to celebrate. It's Silkeborg's surrounding landscapes that draw tourists – not thrill-seekers but rather families and outdoorsy folk drawn to the lush forests and waterways that are perfect for cycling, rambling and, especially, canoeing.

◉ Sights

★ **Indelukket** PARK
(Åhave Allé; ☎) Don't miss a stroll through this riverside park – follow Åhavevej south to reach it. There's a snack bar here, as well as mini-golf, a playground, a marina and an open-air stage. If you're on foot, it's the desired route to get to Museum Jorn, the camping ground (p225) and points further south.

★ **Museum Silkeborg**   MUSEUM

(☎ 86 82 14 99; www.museumsilkeborg.dk; Hovedgårdsvej 7; adult/child 65kr/free; ⊘ 10am-5pm May-Oct, noon-4pm Tue-Sun Nov-Apr) Here you can check out the amazingly well-preserved body of the 2400-year-old **Tollund Man**, the central (albeit leathery) star in an otherwise smart but predictable collection. The well-preserved face of the Tollund Man is hypnotic in its detail, right down to the stubble on his chin. Like the Grauballe Man at Aarhus' Moesgaard Museum (p233), the life (and death) of the Tollund Man remains a mystery.

His intact remains were found on the outskirts of Silkeborg in 1950, and have been radiocarbon dated to around the 4th century BC. The autopsy suggests he had been hanged, yet he was placed as though lying asleep with only a leather hat over his face and a thin leather noose around his neck. Was he an executed prisoner, or a sacrifice to the gods? That's the big unanswered question, but the accompanying displays aren't as engrossing as those at Moesgaard.

KunstCentret Silkeborg Bad   MUSEUM

(☎ 86 81 63 29; www.silkeborgbad.dk; Gjessøvej 40; adult/child 75kr/free; ⊘ 10am-5pm Tue-Sun May-Sep, noon-4pm Mon-Fri, 11am-5pm Sat & Sun Oct-Apr) This former spa dates from 1883 and is now a beautiful, modern art space, with permanent works and changing exhibitions of art, sculpture, ceramics, glassware, design and architecture. It's surrounded by parkland (always open) featuring contemporary sculpture.

Museum Jorn   MUSEUM

(☎ 86 82 53 88; www.museumjorn.dk; Gudenåvej 7-9; adult/child 100kr/free; ⊘ 10am-5pm Tue-Sun) This wonderful art space contains some striking pieces. It displays many of the works of native son Asger Jorn and other modern artists, including Max Ernst, Le Corbusier and Danish artists from the influential CoBrA group. It's 1km south of the town centre.

Aqua   AQUARIUM

(☎ 89 21 21 87; www.visitaqua.dk; Vejlsøvej 55; adult/child 160/90kr; ⊘ from 10am; ⊕) Aqua, 2km south of the town centre, is an entertaining aquarium, zoo and exhibition centre built into several outdoor lakes. It explores the ecosystems of the area, with lots of touch-tanks and fishy creatures, cute otters and birds among the imaginative displays. Closing times vary, from 4pm in winter to 8pm in July.

Local bus 4 runs down this way, but a nicer option in summer is to take a boat with Hjejlen Boat Company.

🏃 Activities

The website www.silkeborg.com has information on canoeing, kayaking, hiking, cycling, swimming and more (including options such as golf, horse riding and fishing).

★ **Østre Søbad**   SWIMMING

(Horsensvej) For idyllic swimming, head to the lakeshore of Almindsø. Head south of town on Frederiksberggade and take a left at the roundabout in the direction of Horsens. The swimming area is signposted on your right after 1km; there are bathing jetties, change rooms and a kiosk here.

Silkeborg Kanocenter   CANOEING

(☎ 86 80 30 03; www.silkeborgkanocenter.dk; Østergade 36; canoes per hr/day 100/400kr; ⊘ 9am-8pm Jun–mid-Aug, to 5pm May & late Aug; ⊕) Silkeborg Kanocenter hires out canoes and can help plan a range of tour options (adaptable from two to five days). You can also hire motorboats (per hour/day 200/900kr) if the exertion of canoeing doesn't appeal.

Hjejlen Boat Company   BOATING

(☎ 86 82 07 66; www.hjejlen.com; Sejsvej 2; one way/return 100/150kr; ⊘ May-Sep; ⊕) The *Hjejlen*, the world's oldest operating paddle steamer, has been plying the waters of the Lake District since it was first launched in 1861. These days the boat shuttles tourists from Silkeborg to Himmelbjerget during the summer season, along with a fleet of other boats (departures 10am, 11am, 1.30pm and 2.30pm on operating days; additional sailings in peak summer).

The route takes in a wealth of river and lake scenery and is one of the most popular outings in the Lake District. Boats also stop at the hostel (p225), Indelukket park and Aqua aquarium. There is also an option for a one-hour nonstop sightseeing cruise on the lakes (adult/child 100/50kr).

Silkeborg Kayak og SUP Center   KAYAKING

(☎ 22 37 70 07; www.skcu.dk; Åhave Allé 7; kayaks per hr/day 100/300kr; ⊘ noon-4pm Mon-Thu, 10am-6pm Fri & Sat Jun, 10am-6pm Jul–mid-Aug, by arrangement rest of year; ⊕) At the northern end of Indelukket (p222) park, this centre has single and family kayaks available for short and multiday rental, plus stand-up paddleboards (SUPs) and motorboats.

Silkeborg

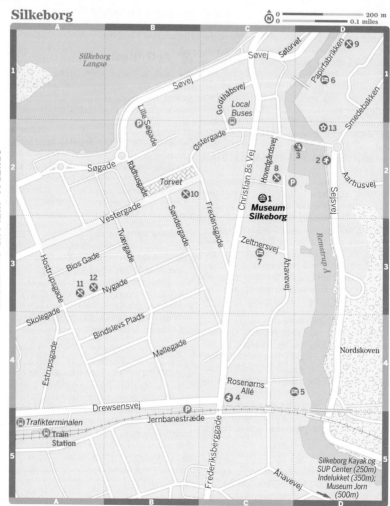

Hiking & Cycling

There are various maps and brochures on hiking and cycling routes – look out for *12 Beautiful Bicycle Tours* or *12 Lovely Walks in the Lakelands.*

Silkeborg Mountainbike Center (☎24 60 37 12; www.silkeborgmtbcenter.dk; Christian 8s Vej 2A; mountain-bike rental per day 350kr) has mountain bikes for hire; for a taster, consider taking a bike on the boat to Himmelbjerget and cycling back (15km). If you're after a regular (cheaper) bike, head to **Silkeborg Sø Camping** (☎86 82 28 24; www.seacamp.dk; Aarhusvej 51; bike rental per day/week 125/600kr; ☺Apr-Oct).

The beech forest of **Nordskoven** is criss-crossed with hiking and biking trails. To reach Nordskoven head south down Åhavevej, then go left over the old railway bridge near the hostel.

The track of the old railway from Silkeborg to Horsens is now an excellent walking and cycling trail of about 50km or so.

Hærvejen (www.haervej.com) is an ancient trackway that passes through the Lake District west of Silkeborg. This is a 250km historic route from the German border north to Viborg along the backbone of Denmark; it's been converted into a cycling, hiking and horse-riding trail.

Silkeborg

✷ Festivals & Events

Riverboat Jazz Festival   MUSIC
(www.riverboat.dk; ☺ Jun) Scandis love jazz, and Silkeborg has embraced it with the five-day Riverboat Jazz Festival, held in late June. It's not quite New Orleans, but you can buy a ticket and take a cruise down the river, or stroll the streets and take advantage of the free performances.

⌂ Sleeping

★ **Danhostel Silkeborg**   HOSTEL €
(☑ 86 82 36 42; www.danhostel-silkeborg.dk; Åhavevej 55; dm 275kr, d without/with bathroom 520/750kr; ☺ Mar-Nov; @ 🛜) The truly lovely riverbank location, good facilities and lack of budget alternatives in town make this hostel popular, so book ahead. Once here, enjoy the outdoor tables and communal areas alongside cyclists, families, school groups and Euro-backpackers. Dorm beds are available July to mid-September; breakfast costs 80kr.

★ **Villa Zeltner**   B&B €
(☑ 29 82 58 58; www.villa-zeltner.dk; Zeltnersvej 4; s/d/apt from 400/550/700kr; 🛜) Super-central and with loads of style, this great-value B&B houses a handful of rooms with shared bathroom and kitchen access, plus a couple of small apartments with private kitchen and bathroom. There's garden access and a grill, too. Breakfast can be arranged at additional cost.

Gudenåens Camping   CAMPGROUND €
(☑ 86 82 22 01; www.gudenaaenscamping.dk; Vejlsøvej 7; per adult/child/site 88/54/72kr; ☺ Apr-Oct; @ 🛜) Follow the signs for Aqua (p223) to find this tree-filled riverside park, about 2km south of the town centre (just south of Indelukket; p222). Cabins and caravans are available for hire, and facilities are family focused. Local bus 4 runs down this way.

Radisson BLU Hotel   HOTEL €€
(☑ 88 82 22 22; www.radissonblu.com/hotel-silkeborg; Papirfabrikken 12; d incl breakfast from 1275kr; @ 🛜) This polished performer lives in the redeveloped paper factory that was once the backbone of the local economy. It's right on the river, among a clutch of restaurants, and the designer rooms are petite but comfy and well equipped. Weekend rates are cheaper than midweek.

✕ Eating

There are two areas to investigate when scouting for eating (and drinking) options: the reinvigorated Papirfabrikken (the old paper factory), and Nygade, with its fast food and international cuisines.

Landmad   DELI, CAFE €
(☑ 20 20 88 32; www.landmad.dk/silkeborg; Nygade 32A; sandwiches & salads 59-69kr; ☺ 9am-5.30pm Mon-Thu, to 6pm Fri, 10am-3pm Sat) A kind of small, indoors farmers market, Landmad showcases local produce and offers excellent take-home meals, plus sells coffee, drinks and cracker sandwiches and salads.

Okkels Is   ICE CREAM €
(☑ 86 81 83 99; www.okkelsis.dk; Nygade 26E; 2/3 scoops 30/40kr; ☺ 11am-10pm May–mid-Aug, shorter hours rest of year; 🖟) Excellent home-made Italian-style ice cream.

Føtex   SUPERMARKET €
(Torvet; ☺ 8am-9pm) Central supermarket with on-site bakery and cafe (bakery opens at 7am).

Evald Brasserie & Cafe   INTERNATIONAL €€
(☑ 86 80 33 66; www.evald.nu; Papirfabrikken 10B; lunch 85-190kr, dinner mains 140-290kr; ☺ 11am-11pm Mon-Thu, to midnight Fri, 10am-midnight Sat, 10am-10pm Sun; 🖟) Among the family restaurants, cinema and cafe-bars of Papirfabrikken is bustling Evald, wooing patrons with a crowd-pleasing menu. Sit at a riverside table, order a beer from the local Grauballe Bryghus (brewery), and try the bumper Evald burger or three-course set dinner menu.

Classique Fiske Restaurant SEAFOOD €€€
(☑86 20 12 15; www.classiquefiskerestaurant.dk; Åhavevej 2A; lunch 79-235kr, dinner mains 229-259kr; ☺noon-10pm) From its cheerful yellow exterior to its designer-clad interior, this grand old villa bids a warm welcome. Eat inside, among the owner's great art and furniture collection, or outside in the garden. There's a high-class, fish-focused menu, but guests are equally welcome to stop in for a coffee or glass of wine.

☆ Entertainment

Jysk Musikteater THEATRE
(www.jmts.dk; Papirfabrikken 80) This large modern theatre hosts regular concerts and stage shows.

ℹ Information

Website www.silkeborg.com is full of helpful information. There's no tourist office but an assortment of touchscreens and info-brochure stands are found around town, including in the foyer of the Jysk Musikteater.

ℹ Getting There & Away

Silkeborg is 44km west of Aarhus on Rte 15.

Half-hourly trains connect Silkeborg with Aarhus (90kr, 45 minutes) via Ry (40kr, 15 minutes).

Long-distance buses stop at **Trafikterminalen** (Drewsensvej), next door to the train station.

ℹ Getting Around

Local buses stop at Trafikterminalen and at a central **stop** (Godthåbsvej) close to Torvet.

Ry

POP 5700

Mellow, rural Ry lies in the heart of the Lake District. It has a pretty duck-filled marina, where you'll find canoe hire and tourist boats to Himmelbjerget. It's surrounded by lovely landscapes and quaint villages perfect for exploring.

🏃 Activities

Hjejlen Boat Company BOATING
(☑86 82 07 66; www.hjejlen.com; one way/return 70/100kr) Schedules three boats daily from Ry to Himmelbjerget, operating most days June to August (and weekends in May and September; see the website to confirm sail dates). Boats leave Ry at 10.30am, 12.45pm and 3pm, and sail from Himmelbjerget one hour later. It's good to book a day in advance.

Ry Kanofart CANOEING
(☑86 89 11 67; www.kanoferie.dk; Kyhnsvej 20; canoes per hr/day 100/400kr; ☺9am-6pm Jun-Aug, 9am-6pm Sat & Sun May & Sep, or by appointment) Ry Kanofart has canoes for hire. As with the operators in Silkeborg, staff here can help you plan a day or multiday trip paddling on the Gudenå and lakes.

Ry Cykler CYCLING
(☑86 89 14 91; www.rycykler.dk; Parallelvej 9B; regular/mountain-bike rental per day 75/200kr; ☺9.30am-5.30pm Mon-Fri, to noon Sat) Rents bikes.

🛏 Sleeping

Knudhule Badehotel HOTEL €€
(☑86 89 14 07; www.knudhule.dk; Randersvej 88; s/d from 585/770kr; ☎) About 2km outside Ry, this hotel is in a pretty locale, across the road from the bathing jetties of Knudsø lake. On offer is a collection of freshly renovated rooms and cabins – the cheapest rooms are petite but well-equipped. There are also four family-sized cabins with kitchen. On-site is the excellent Restaurant Gastronomisk Institut.

Hotel Ry HOTEL €€
(☑86 89 19 11; www.hotelry.dk; Kyhnsvej 2; s/d from 840/1000kr; ☎) New owners have taken over the town's big main-street hotel. When we visited they were in the process of giving the place a major makeover, and when they're done there will be 55 fresh, colourful and individually styled rooms, plus a raft of new eateries (including a restaurant, gastropub and takeaway). Stop by to check it out.

🍴 Eating

There are sushi and Italian restaurants on Skanderborgvej plus a few takeaways. Opposite Ry train station **Le Gâteau** (☑86 89 03 37; www.legateau.dk; Klostervej 12; sandwiches from 45kr; ☺7am-5.30pm Mon-Fri, to 2pm Sat, to noon Sun) is a smart bakery with good coffee. **Kvickly Supermarket** (Siimtoften 2; ☺8am-8pm) is just back from the marina.

Lakeside INTERNATIONAL €€
(☑70 70 71 13; www.lakesidery.dk; Skimminghøj 2; mains 75-200kr; ☺5.30-9pm Tue, 11.30am-9pm Wed-Sun Jul & Aug, shorter hours rest of year) The couple behind the popular Hotel Julsø at Himmelbjerget are also responsible for this appealing new option down by the marina. It's an idyllic spot for their relaxed decor and crowd-pleasing menu of pasta, burgers, steak

and a couple of French classics like *moules-frites*. Plus, attached is a kiosk selling home-made Italian ice cream, panini and fish and chips.

Restaurant Gastronomisk Institut EUROPEAN €€
(📞 86 89 14 07; www.knudhule.dk; Knudhule Bade-hotel, Randersvej 88; lunch 89-199kr, dinner mains 125-299kr; ⏱ noon-2pm & from 6pm Mon-Sat) The ambitious name creates high expectations and this high-end restaurant delivers, with changing menus showcasing regional, sea-sonal produce (and good-value set menus, including four dinner courses for 365kr). Leisurely lunchers enjoy classic smørrebrød (open sandwiches); dinner ranges from pan-fried plaice to veal tenderloin. The restaurant is outside town at the lakeside Knudhule Ba-dehotel; bookings recommended.

ⓘ Information

Tourist Office (📞 86 69 66 00; www.visit skanderborg.com; Klostervej 3; ⏱ 10am-4pm Mon-Fri, to noon Sat Jul & Aug, 10am-3pm Mon-Fri Apr-Jun & Sep) At the train station. Par-ticularly helpful given that there is no longer a staffed tourist office in Silkeborg. From October to March you can call in on weekdays (11am to 2pm) to help yourself to brochures.

ⓘ Getting There & Away

Half-hourly trains connect Ry with Aarhus (70kr, 30 minutes) and Silkeborg (40kr, 15 minutes).

The two-hour, 7km walk northwest to Him-melbjerget starts along Munkedalsvej, which branches off Rodelundvej just south of the Ry bridge. The signposted path leads to the Him-melbjerget boat dock before climbing the hill to the tower. A nice option is to hike out and catch a boat back to Ry or on to Silkeborg.

Himmelbjerget

There's something quite endearing about a country that names one of its highest points Himmelbjerget (meaning 'sky mountain'), es-pecially when that peak only hits 147m. It's a mere hillock to non-Danes, but it does af-ford charming vistas of the surrounding for-ests and lakes and is a popular tourist spot, complete with ice-cream kiosks and souvenir stalls ringing the car park.

It costs 10kr to park your vehicle. Once you've completed the brief pilgrimage from the car park to the mountaintop, you could climb the elegant 25m **tower** (10kr; ⏱ 10am-5pm May–mid-Sep) built in 1875, but the view from outside the tower is just as panoramic.

There are a number of memorials in the vicinity, plus kids' play areas and marked hik-ing trails.

A trail leads 1km from the mountaintop of Himmelbjerget down to the lakeshore where boats from Ry and Silkeborg dock. At the dock you'll find **Hotel Julsø** (📞 86 89 80 40; www.hotel-julso.dk; Julsøvej 14, Ry; lunch 110-245kr, 2-/3-course dinner 325/385kr; ⏱ 11.30am-10pm Mon & Thu-Sat, to 5pm Tue, Wed & Sun Jun-Aug, shorter hours Apr, May, Sep & Oct), a photogenic timber *kro* (inn) with a watery panorama and a gourmet menu that highlights the talents of the Italian-born chef. The *kro* can also be reached by road off Rte 445.

Events are held here during the summer peak; it's worth calling ahead to reserve a table – and to ensure it's open, as it has a complex schedule of closing days from April to mid-October.

ⓘ Getting There & Away

From Ry, Himmelbjerget is a 10-minute drive west on Rte 445 (no bus), a pleasant 7km hike/ bike ride or a scenic Hjejlen (p223) boat ride, thrice daily on operating days (one-way/return 70/100kr, 50 minutes, see website calendar). A boat also links to Silkeborg four to six times each operating day (100/150kr, 75 minutes).

AARHUS

POP 269,000

Aarhus (*oar*-hus) has long laboured in the shadow of consummate capital Copenha-gen, but transformation is afoot. Denmark's second-largest city is busy staking a claim for visitor attention, and building a reputa-tion as an emerging European destination for savvy city-breakers, festival-goers, art and food fans, and those looking beyond the capital-city conga.

This Viking-founded, student-filled hub has accrued some weighty accolades to shore up its appeal, too: in 2017 its titles included European Capital of Culture and European Region of Gastronomy (the latter was awarded to Aarhus and the larger cen-tral Denmark region). The ever-expanding menu of architectural landmarks, lauded restaurants, bars, festivals and boutiques is a mark of a vibrant city on the rise. It's a great place to explore – compact, photogenic and friendly (its local nickname is 'the city of smiles'). Here you'll be left in little doubt why Denmark scores so highly in those live-ability lists.

Aarhus

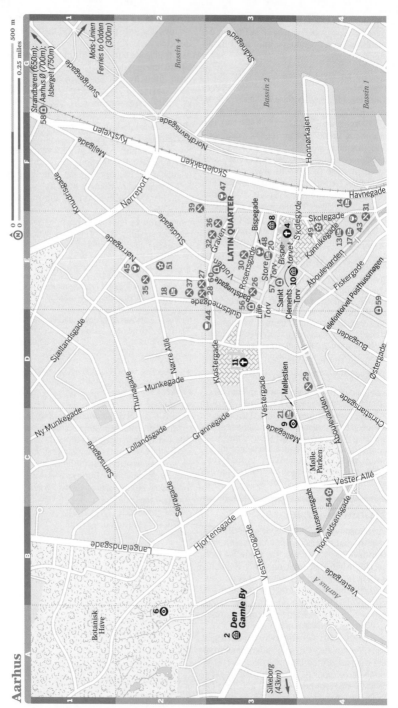

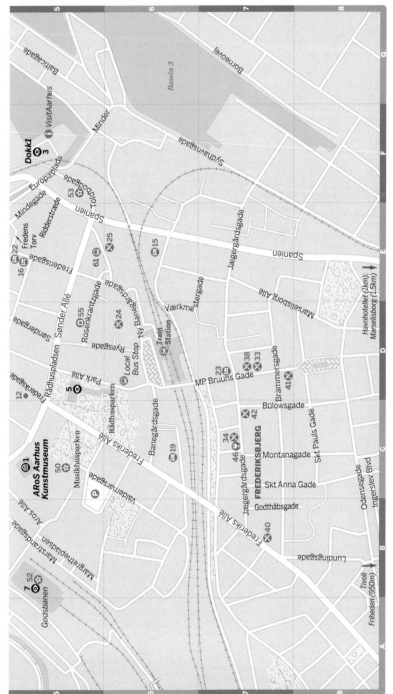

Aarhus

◉ Sights

The train station marks the south side of the city centre. A pedestrian shopping street extends 850m from here to Aarhus Domkirke (the cathedral) in the heart of the old quarter.

The best neighbourhoods for exploring, shopping and eating are the **Latin Quarter**, north of the cathedral; and **Frederiksbjerg**, south of the train station.

Don't miss idyllic **Møllestien**, easily Aarhus' prettiest street with its cobblestones, roses and pastel-coloured cottages.

If you're planning to tick off city sights, the **AarhusCard** is worth considering. Dokk1 (p231), the bus station (p240) and most accommodation providers sell the pass (24/48/72 hours 299/449/599kr), which allows unlimited transport on local buses as well as free admission to most sights. See www.visitaarhus.com for more info.

★ **ARoS Aarhus Kunstmuseum**   MUSEUM
(☑ 87 30 66 00; www.aros.dk; Aros Allé 2; adult/child 130kr/free; ☉ 10am-5pm Tue & Thu-Sun, to 10pm Wed; ⚑) Inside the cubist, red-brick walls of Aarhus' showpiece art museum are nine floors of sweeping curves, soaring spaces and white walls showcasing a wonderful selection of Golden Age works, Danish modernism and an abundance of arresting and vivid contemporary art. The museum's cherry-on-top is the spectacular **Your Rainbow**

Panorama, a 360-degree rooftop walkway offering technicolor views of the city through its glass panes in all shades of the rainbow.

Intriguingly, ARoS' main theme is Dante's *The Divine Comedy;* the entrance is on level 4 and from there you either descend into **Hell** or climb towards **Heaven**. Hell is **De 9 Rum** (The 9 Spaces) on the bottom floor, painted black and home to moody installation pieces; Heaven is the rooftop rainbow halo, the brainchild of Olafur Eliasson, a Danish-Icelandic artist famed for big, conceptual pieces.

Another iconic piece is Ron Mueck's **Boy**, an astoundingly lifelike, oversized (5m-high) sculpture of a crouching boy.

The museum stages varied special exhibitions – check what's on when you're in town. ARoS also houses a great gift shop and light-filled cafe on level 4 (free entry) and a restaurant on level 8.

★**Dokk1**   CULTURAL CENTRE
(☑89 40 92 00; www.dokk1.dk; Hack Kampmanns Plads 2; ⊙8am-10pm Mon-Fri, 10am-4pm Sat & Sun; ⊞) Opened in 2015 as part of Aarhus' large-scale waterfront regeneration, Dokk1 is the kind of public space Danes excel at, and houses Scandinavia's largest library. It's a great building, home to countless reading nooks, a cafe, kids' play area and an information desk for visitors to the city.

★**Den Gamle By**   MUSEUM
(The Old Town; ☑86 12 31 88; www.dengamleby.dk; Viborgvej 2; adult/child 135kr/free; ⊙10am-5pm, hours vary by season; ⊞) The Danes' seemingly limitless enthusiasm for dressing up and re-creating history reaches its zenith at Den Gamle By. It's an engaging, picturesque open-air museum of 75 half-timbered houses brought here from all corners of Denmark and reconstructed as a provincial market town from the era of Hans Christian Andersen. Re-created neighbourhoods from 1927 and 1974 are the newest additions.

You can take a **horse-drawn wagon ride** around the site and then visit each building, store and workshop to see craftspeople practising their trade. Small museums cater to different interests – the **Danish Poster Museum** has some fabulous retro pieces, the **Toy Museum** showcases antique playthings and the **Gallery of Decorative Arts** displays silverware, porcelain and clocks. Don't miss the **apartment block from 1974** for a peek into past lives or the TV and hi-fi store stocking authentic 1970s gear. The museum is

constantly evolving, too: the latest additions are **Aarhus Story**, a great journey back in the city's history, plus a beloved local jazz bar that closed in 2008, and a home of Somali migrants from 2016.

Den Gamle By is 1.5km west of the city centre (a 20-minute walk from the train station); buses 3A, 19 and 111 stop nearby. There's a detailed schedule of opening hours and admission prices (set according to the museum's activities) outlined on the website. Outside of opening hours you can stroll the cobbled streets for free; access is via the **Botanisk Have** (http://sciencemuseerne.dk/botanisk-have; Vesterbrogade; ⊙24hr; ⊞) **FREE**.

Aarhus Domkirke   CHURCH
(www.aarhus-domkirke.dk; Store Torv; ⊙9.30am-4pm Mon-Sat May-Sep, 10am-3pm Mon-Sat Oct-Apr) With a lofty nave spanning nearly 100m in length, Aarhus Domkirke is Denmark's longest church. The original Romanesque chapel at the eastern end dates from the 12th century, while most of the rest of the church is 15th-century Gothic.

Like other Danish churches, the cathedral was once richly decorated with frescoes that served to convey biblical parables to unschooled peasants. After the Reformation in 1536, church authorities, who felt the frescoes smacked too much of Roman Catholicism, had them all whitewashed, but many have now been uncovered and restored. They range from fairy-tale paintings of St George slaying a dragon to scenes of hellfire.

A highlight of the cathedral is the ornate, five-panel, gilt altarpiece made in Lübeck by the renowned woodcarver Bernt Notke in the 15th century.

Aarhus Ø   AREA
Aarhus' docklands is a new neighbourhood that's home to some head-turning residential developments – the brilliantly spiky **Isberget** (Iceberg) has won architecture awards and lots of Instagram fans. The district is worth a

---

AARHUS IN...

Two Days

Start by mixing the old with the new at two of Aarhus' big-ticket attractions – **ARoS** (p230) for cutting-edge art and architecture, **Den Gamle By** (p231) for a taste of yesteryear – with lunch at one of the city's fun **food halls** in between. Finish with dinner at one of Aarhus' new breed of award-winning eateries like **Restaurant Hærværk** (p237). Next day, visit the remarkable **Moesgaard Museum** (p233), then return to town to visit the **cathedral** (p231) and poke around the boutiques and bistros of the **Latin Quarter**, where you'll have no trouble finding a cool spot to refuel or hear live music.

Four Days

On the third day, take a cycling tour or do your own two-wheeled investigating: venture south to **Marselisborg** (p233), or north to **Risskov** via **Aarhus Ø** (p231). Later, check out the boutiques and restaurants of the **Frederiksbjerg** neighbourhood. On day four, consider some out-of-town options: **LEGOLAND Billund** (p218), the pretty waterways of the **Lake District** (p222), or the beaches or funparks of **Djursland** (p241).

---

wander for some cool sea and city views and excellent architecture. The popular summertime Strandbaren (p238) is here.

Godsbanen   CULTURAL CENTRE
(www.godsbanen.dk; Skovgaardsgade 3) The renovated Godsbanen freight yard is an alternative cultural hub for the city; it's home to theatre stages, workshops and cafes, and hosts exhibitions, markets and events – it's well worth a look. Live music venue Radar (p239) is here.

Aarhus Rådhus   ARCHITECTURE
(Rådhuspladsen; ⊙8am-4pm Mon-Fri) Aarhus' controversial town hall was co-designed by renowned architect Arne Jacobsen, a pioneer of Danish modernism, and completed in 1942. It's clad in Norwegian marble and has a distinctive grey appearance. Jacobsen also designed many of the interiors (along with Hans Wegner) – for design buffs, it's well worth a look inside.

Anyone can pop into the building during working hours to see the lobby. Check the website of Aarhus Guiderne (p233); the organisation generally leads a weekly guided tour of the building (usually Saturday mornings; 80kr). No booking is required, but it is worth confirming the meeting time.

Kvindemuseet   MUSEUM
(✆25 45 45 10; www.kvindemuseet.dk; Domkirkeplads 5; adult/child 65kr/free; ⊙10am-5pm Tue & Thu-Sat, to 4pm Sun, to 8pm Wed; ☻) Denmark is a model for equality, but this hasn't always been the case. In a fresh, engaging exhibition inside the old town hall, the Women's Museum charts women's lives in Denmark and

their hard-won achievements. It's inspiring stuff, but it's not just one for the ladies – families will love the hands-on kids' exhibits in the 'History of Childhood' section. There's also a pretty cafe here.

Vor Frue Kirke   CHURCH
(www.aarhusvorfrue.dk; Frue Kirkeplads; ⊙10am-4pm Mon-Fri, to 2pm Sat) Set back from Vestergade, the Church of Our Lady is like a Russian *matryoshka* (nesting doll), opening to reveal multiple layers. It was here that the original Aarhus cathedral was erected shortly after 1060. That cathedral stood until about 1240, when it was replaced by the current red-brick church, whose main treasure lies in its basement: the vaulted **crypt** of the original cathedral (enter via the stairs beneath the chancel), uncovered by chance in 1955 during a restoration.

Vikingemuseet   MUSEUM
(www.moesgaardmuseum.dk; Sankt Clements Torv 6; ⊙10.15am-4pm Mon-Fri) **FREE** There's more than the expected vaults in the basement of Nordea bank, a stone's throw from the city's cathedral. In the mid-1960s this site was excavated and artefacts from the Viking era were unearthed. Concise exhibits include a skeleton, a reconstructed pithouse, 1000-year-old carpentry tools and pottery.

⊙ Marselisborg & Moesgård

A green belt begins 2km south of the centre hugging the coast for nearly 10km south through the Marselisborg, Moesgård and Fløjstrup areas, names taken from the former estates of which they were once part. It's a great place for hiking and cycling. In **Marselisborg** are a royal palace, an amusement park and a Jysk Væddeløbsbane (horse-trotting track). **Moesgård** is famed for its museum from which an enjoyable walking trail, dubbed the 'Prehistoric Trackway' (Oldtidsstien) leads 2km across fields of wildflowers, past grazing sheep and through beech woods down to Moesgård Strand, one of Aarhus's best sandy beaches (return by summer bus 31).

★ **Moesgaard Museum**   MUSEUM
(⌕87 39 40 00; www.moesgaardmuseum.dk; Moesgård Allé; adult/child 140kr/free; ⊙10am-5pm Tue & Thu-Sun, to 9pm Wed; ⊞) Don't miss the reinvented Moesgaard Museum, 10km south of the city, housed in a spectacularly designed, award-winning modern space. The star attraction is the 2000-year-old **Grauballe Man**, whose astonishingly well-preserved body was found in 1952 in the village of Grauballe, 35km west of Aarhus. Aside from the Grauballe Man, the museum brings various eras (from the Stone Age to the Viking era) to life with cutting-edge archaeological and ethnographic displays.

The superb display on the Grauballe Man is part history lesson, part *CSI: Crime Scene Investigation* episode. Was he a sacrifice to Iron Age fertility gods, an executed prisoner or simply a victim of murder? Either way, the broken leg and the gaping neck wound suggest his death, sometime around 290 BC (give or take 50 years), was a violent one. His body and skin, tanned and preserved by the unique chemical and biological qualities of the peat bog in which he was found, are remarkably intact, right down to his hair and fingernails.

Bus 18 runs here frequently. With your own wheels, it's a nice drive – take Strandvejen south, then Oddervej and follow the signs.

Tivoli Friheden   AMUSEMENT PARK
(⌕86 14 73 00; www.friheden.dk; Skovbrynet 5; adult/child 120kr/free; ⊙mid-Apr–mid-Sep; ⊞) Neither as big nor as fabulous as Copenhagen's major drawcard, Aarhus' Tivoli is still a fun, wholesome family attraction, full of childhood favourites (dodgem cars and a Ferris wheel) as well as newer, faster rides. You can buy a multi-ride pass (245kr, including admission), or pay for each ride individually. The park is at the northern edge of Marselisborg woods, reached on bus 16.

Marselisborg Palace & Park   PALACE
(Kongevejen 100; ⊙park 8am-9pm Apr-Sep, 9am-4pm Oct-Mar) Marselisborg Palace is a summer home of the royal family, and when they're not in residence the public can explore the English-style grounds and rose garden (free admission). When the blue-bloods are here, watch the changing of the guard at noon from a vantage point on the road. The palace is reached on bus 19.

Check online for royal family activity (http://kongehuset.dk/en).

🏃 Activities

Den Permanente   BEACH
(Salonvejen; ⊙6am-7pm Mon-Sat, 7am-7pm Sun Jun-Aug) FREE North of town is this much-loved beach spot, with changing facilities, lifeguards and sunbathing platforms. It's backed by woodlands at Risskov and is close to the Danhostel (p235).

👉 Tours

★ **Cycling Aarhus**   CYCLING
(⌕27 29 06 90; www.cycling-aarhus.dk; Frederiksgade 78; 2/3hr tour 199/299kr; ⊙bike rental 9am-1pm May-Oct, other times by arrangement) Helping you join the cycling locals, this company offers two-wheeled tours from April/May to October. The Must See Tour takes in Aarhus' highlights over 12km and three hours, departing at 10.30am daily from the company's central base (where bike rental is also available). Tours also run according to themes, including harbour exploration and architectural appreciation. Schedules and bookings are online.

Aarhus Guiderne   TOURS
(⌕25 88 88 17; www.aarhusguiderne.dk) The website of Aarhus Guides outlines its offerings, which range from a weekly tour of the Rådhus to guided city wanderings (in English) on weekends in the summer. Tour details are outlined on the site. Tours generally cost 80/40kr per adult/child.

ⓘ STUDENT SAVINGS

In a city full of students, an ISIC or ID card from your home university is an asset. If you have one, flaunt it. From pubs to restaurants to museums, students are given favourable prices.

✦⁂ Festivals & Events

NorthSide Festival   MUSIC
(www.northside.dk; ⊘ Jun) A three-day music festival in mid-June that's building a big reputation – line-ups rival the legendary Roskilde Festival.

Viking Moot   CULTURAL
(www.moesgaardmuseum.dk; ⊘ Jul) The 'moot' is a meet, where the Viking era springs to life at Moesgård Strand over a weekend in late July. Costumed folks? Check. Craftsmanship and authentic food such as spit-roasted meats and mead? Absolutely. Warrior and cavalry displays? Oh yes!

Spot Festival   MUSIC
(www.spotfestival.dk; ⊘ May) This annual event, held in May, showcases up-and-coming Danish and Nordic musical talent, in and around Musikhuset (p239).

Aarhus Jazz Festival   MUSIC
(www.jazzfest.dk; ⊘ Jul) This week-long jazz celebration in mid-July sees big-name local and international acts doing their thing in various theatres, cafes and squares.

Aarhus Festival   CULTURAL
(www.aarhusfestuge.dk; ⊘ Aug) The city dons its shiniest party gear at the end of August, when this festival transforms the town for 10 days, celebrating music, food, short film, theatre, visual arts and outdoor events (many of which are free) for all ages. It culminates in early September with a **foodie weekend** (www.foodfestival.dk).

ARoS Triennial   ART
(www.aros.dk) Inaugurated in summer 2017, this is a new international contemporary art exhibition to be presented every three years. It is curated by ARoS Aarhus Kunstmuseum (p230) and staged in various parts of the city.

🛌 Sleeping

Wakeup Aarhus   HOTEL €
(📞 44 80 00 00; www.wakeupcopenhagen.dk; MP Bruuns Gade 27; d from 500kr; 🛜) A new arrival in mid-2017, this budget hotel offers 315 fresh, functional rooms in a prime location, close to the train station. There are few frills, but there is dependable Scandi style and smart design. Best deals come with advance online booking. You pay extra for a little more space, a view or a flexible reservation.

FOREST FEST
If music festivals are your thing, you need to know about **Smukfest** (www.smukfest.dk; ⊘ Aug), a huge annual music fest held on the second weekend in August and billed as 'Denmark's most beautiful festival'. The title is due to its gorgeous location among beech forest near the Lake District's Skanderborg, which is about 28km southwest of Aarhus, and roughly the same distance from Silkeborg.

CabInn Aarhus Hotel   HOTEL €
(📞 86 75 70 00; www.cabinn.com; Kannikegade 14; s/d/tr/f from 495/625/805/950kr; 🅿@🛜) 'Best location, best price' is the CabInn chain's motto and, given that this huge branch overlooks the river and is in the centre of town, it's pretty spot on. The 400 functional rooms are based on ships' cabins (hence the name) – the cheapest is *tiny*, but all come with bathroom, kettle and TV.

Havnhotellet   HOTEL €
(BB Hotel; www.bbhotels.dk; Marselisborg Havnevej 20; d/tr incl breakfast 670/920kr; 🅿🛜) These fresh, good-value rooms at the marina are straight off the Ikea production line. All booking is done online (hence no phone number), and check-in is via a computer. The hotel is 1.5km south of the centre (off Strandvejen; catch bus 19) and walking distance to Marselisborg (p233); at your doorstep is a handful of restaurants (and free parking).

Tip: choose a room on the 1st floor as ground-floor rooms lack privacy.

City Sleep-In   HOSTEL €
(📞 86 19 20 55; www.citysleep-in.dk; Havnegade 20; dm 190kr, d without/with bathroom 460/520kr; @🛜) This central hostel used to house seamen and is a real one-off with its rambling layout of sitting rooms, terraces, rooms and dorms. There is a large communal kitchen and a bar-cafe with regular live music. Colourful murals cover the walls and the furnishings are an eclectic and comfortable mishmash of styles and eras.

The doubles are pricey for what you get – if you need to rent bed linen (50kr) and a towel (20kr), it might pay to look at a budget hotel.

Danhostel Aarhus
HOSTEL €

(☑86 21 21 20; www.aarhusdanhostel.dk; Marienlundsvej 10; dm 275kr, d without/with bathroom 550/720kr; ⊙early Jan–mid-Dec; P 🛜) The main building here is as pretty as a picture: it's a large octagonal room that was once a dancehall. Accommodation is bright and basic; some rooms have private bathrooms. Linen costs extra; breakfast costs 69kr. The hostel is 3km north of the city centre, in pretty woods close to the beach; take bus 5A, 17, 18 or 20.

DCU-Camping Blommehaven
CAMPGROUND €

(☑86 27 02 07; www.camping-blommehaven.dk; Ørneredevej 35; adult/child 96/51kr, site 55-70kr; ⊙late Mar-late Oct; P 🛜) This big beachside camping ground 6km south of the city centre lies in the scenic Marselisborg (p233) woods en route to Moesgård. It's got loads of family-oriented facilities, plus simple four-/six-berth huts (500/650kr). If you're driving, follow Strandvejen south; otherwise, take bus 18 or (in summer) 31.

★Hotel Guldsmeden
BOUTIQUE HOTEL €€

(☑86 13 45 50; https://guldsmedenhotels.com/aarhus; Guldsmedgade 40; d with/without bathroom from 1075/895kr; 🛜) 🔊 A top pick for its excellent location, warm staff, French Colonial-style rooms with Persian rugs, pretty garden oasis and relaxed, stylish ambience. Bumper breakfasts (mainly organic) are included, as is Guldsmeden's own organic toiletries range. *Guldsmed* means both goldsmith and dragonfly in Danish – look for sweet use of the dragonfly motif in the decor.

Originally a family home, this was the first of a small chain of hotels located throughout Denmark.

Møllestien Cottages
COTTAGE €€

(☑86 13 06 32; www.house-in-aarhus.com; Møllestien 49 & 51; d 800-900kr) On Aarhus' prettiest street (p230), a ceramicist rents out two neighbouring cottages – small, homely places each with courtyard, kitchen, lounge and bathroom (the cheaper of the two is more rustic). Be warned that the staircases to the upstairs bedrooms are steep. One-night stays cost an extra 300kr. Book early.

Comwell Aarhus
HOTEL €€

(☑86 72 80 00; www.comwellaarhus.dk; Værkmestergade 2; d from 1200kr; P 🛜) A new addition to the Comwell chain, this large, modern hotel stylishly showcases Danish design courtesy of furnishings by local company HAY (p240). Higher rooms have sweeping views,

the breakfast spread is top-notch and the location is central.

Hotel Oasia
HOTEL €€

(☑87 32 37 15; www.hoteloasia.com; Kriegersvej 27; d incl breakfast 895-1695kr; P 🛜) Clearly a subscriber to the minimalist school of design, Oasia offers bright modern rooms full of clean lines and the best of Scandinavian fittings (Hästens beds, Bang & Olufsen TVs, designer chairs). It's well placed for the train station and for Frederiksbjerg dining treats.

Hotel Aarhus City Apartments
APARTMENT €€

(☑86 27 51 30; www.hotelaca.dk; Fredensgade 18; d from 799kr, studio/apt from 989/1189kr; P 🛜) Good for families and long-stayers, this three-storey apartment block is home to modern rooms, studios and apartments. All have kitchens (kitchenettes in the rooms) and cable TV. There's no reception, so you need to book ahead and arrange to be met.

Hotel Ferdinand
BOUTIQUE HOTEL €€

(☑87 32 14 44; www.hotelferdinand.dk; Åboulevarden 28; s/d studio from 950/1150kr, ste from 1100/1300kr; 🛜) Ferdinand is in the centre of the Åboulevarden action, with a swank French brasserie (p237) downstairs. There are eight suites above the restaurant (large and luxurious); in the neighbouring building are 11 studio apartments, well equipped with kitchen, washing machine and balconies.

★Villa Provence
BOUTIQUE HOTEL €€€

(☑86 18 24 00; www.villaprovence.dk; Fredens Torv 12; d incl breakfast 1395-1900kr; P 🛜) Elegant rooms (individually decorated in Provençal country style) for a mature, well-heeled crowd. The superior rooms are large and lovely; standard rooms are smaller but with the same attention to detail – all have TVs, minibar, French linen and original French movie posters. Besides the gourmet breakfast, our favourite feature is the courtyard, with flowering pot plants and fairy-lit trees.

Hotel Royal
HOTEL €€€

(☑86 12 00 11; www.hotelroyal.dk; Store Torv 4; s/d from 1295/1445kr; P 🛜) If you've come to expect restrained Scandi style in your top-end Danish hotels, prepare to be surprised. From the over-the-top entrance portico to the chandelier-lit reception area and incredible murals, the Royal seems a little, well, gaudy in parts. But fun, too – we love the fish-tank reception desk and the rich colour schemes.

✗ Eating

There's a food revolution sweeping Aarhus, with new restaurants, cafes, microbreweries and provedores springing up regularly and giving diners plenty to hunger over, including two new food halls and a handful of Michelin-starred restaurants. The Latin Quarter is good for international cuisine and pretty bistro-style cafes. South of the train station, the area centred on MP Bruuns Gade and Jægergårdsgade is a hunting ground for good eats.

★ Social Foodies   SWEETS €

(☑ 22 10 01 35; www.socialfoodies.dk; MP Bruuns Gade 60; ice cream 25-39kr; ☉10am-10pm) Social Foodies should be applauded for its ethos (it's involved in a number of socially minded programs in Africa), but it also receives loud local plaudits for its beloved ice cream and chocolates, including the most quintessential of Danish sugar hits, *flødeboller* (marshmallowy cream puffs coated in chocolate). Our favourite feature: sign up for a fun *flødeboller*-making course.

★ La Cabra   CAFE €

(www.lacabra.dk; Graven 20; ☉8am-6pm Mon-Fri, 9am-6pm Sat, 10am-5pm Sun) First-rate bean sourcing and roasting combine with fine barista skills to make La Cabra one of the city's best coffee spots, and the queue for a takeaway brew attests to that. An airy interior, alfresco seats, and delectable pastries and sandwiches help to round out its appeal.

★ Aarhus Street Food   FOOD HALL €

(www.aarhusstreetfood.com; Ny Banegårdsgade 46; mains 50-150kr; ☉11.30am-9pm Sun-Thu, to 10pm Fri & Sat; 🛜🍴) 🍴 A former garage at the back of the bus station (p240) now houses a buzzing street-food venue serving everything from pizza slices to bumper burgers, by way of Thai curries and Vietnamese *banh mi*. The place has fast become one of *the* places to meet, greet and graze in town – on-site bars stay open until midnight Friday and Saturday.

★ OliNico   INTERNATIONAL €

(☑ 86 25 05 70; www.olinico.dk; Mejlgade 35; mains 60-165kr; ☉11.30am-2pm Mon-Sat, 5.30-9pm daily) You may need to fight for one of the sought-after tables at OliNico, a small deli-restaurant with a menu of classic dishes at excellent prices (*moules frites* for 65kr, fish and chips for 60kr). The daily-changing, three-course dinner menu (for a bargain

130kr) may be Aarhus' best-kept food secret. No reservations; takeaway available.

Arla Unika   DELI €

(☑ 91 31 46 66; www.arlaunika.dk; Klostergade 20; toasted sandwich 45kr; ☉10am-5.30pm Mon-Thu, to 7pm Fri, to 4pm Sat) Drop by this sophisticated deli (primarily selling cheese and high-end booze) to see how design permeates all aspects of Danish life. Taste-test local flavours (*gammel knas* and *havgus* are the best-selling cheeses), pick up picnic supplies, or sit in the back room and enjoy a coffee and top-notch toastie.

Aarhus Central Food Market   FOOD HALL €

(www.aarhuscentralfoodmarket.dk; Sankt Knuds Torv; mains 50-150kr; ☉11.30am-8pm Mon-Thu, to 9pm Fri & Sat, to 6pm Sun) Nicely placed on the town's pedestrianised high street is this new foodie temple, inspired by Copenhagen's Torvehallerne KBH (p71). A collection of stalls serving snacks, meals and drinks, with plenty of seating, it's a more refined version of the more grungy Aarhus Street Food, which opened around the same time. Some local restaurants have mini-outlets here – it's a great place to graze.

F-Høj   CAFE €

(www.fhoj.dk; Grønnegade 2; smørrebrød 65-75kr; ☉11am-4pm Tue-Sat) This cool little deli-cafe overlooks the river and has a polished menu of smørrebrød (open sandwiches). It's the 'everyman' lunchtime outpost of the Michelin-starred Frederikshøj restaurant, so you know kitchen standards are stellar. There are also wonderful cakes, hot and cold drinks, and wines by the glass.

Emmerys   BAKERY, CAFE €

(☑ 51 85 76 97; www.emmerys.dk; Guldsmedgade 24; sandwiches & salads 60-70kr; ☉7am-7pm Mon-Fri, to 6pm Sat, to 5pm Sun) A fine flag-waver for the Danish preoccupation with baked goods. Stop by for morning coffee and pastry, or lunchtime sandwiches. Emmerys was the city's first modern-style cafe-bakery-deli and it now has various branches.

Haute Friture   FAST FOOD €

(☑ 32 14 00 95; www.facebook.com/hautefrituredk; Graven 16; hot dogs 45kr; ☉noon-8pm Sun-Thu, to 9pm Fri & Sat) The traditional Danish hot dog (*pølse*) is ripe for a gourmet makeover, and the guys here have done just that. Their Asian-inspired 'hot duck' is a revelation: confit duck fried in pastry (spring-roll style), then served on bread with chilli mayo and wakame salad. The menu is small; there are also a few sandwich options.

★ Langhoff & Juul
DANISH €€

(☑30 30 00 18; www.langhoffogjuul.dk; Gulds-medgade 30; lunch 98-175kr, 1-/2-/3-course dinner 198/258/338kr; ☺9am-10pm Mon-Sat, 10am-4pm Sun) Ticking all the right boxes, Langhoff & Juul is a rustic, informal space in the Latin Quarter, where the casual setting belies the accomplished food coming out of the kitchen, especially of an evening. There's a super brunch spread every day (148kr), and smør-rebrød and salads at lunch. Plus: polished service, great aesthetics, and a relaxed and enjoyable atmosphere.

★ Kähler Spisesalon
DANISH €€

(☑86 12 20 53; www.spisesalon.dk; MP Bruuns Gade 33; 1/3 pieces smørrebrød 79/200kr; ☺9am-10pm Mon-Sat, 10am-10pm Sun) This elegant 'salon' charms with plants, lamps, vintage photos and covetable ceramics (made by Kähler, a 175-year-old ceramic company with its flagship store down the road, at No 41). It's a great choice at any time of day: for its weekday breakfast buffet (80kr), weekend brunch (159kr) and excellent coffee, but especially for its artful reinterpretation of classic smørrebrød.

Restaurant Hærværk
DANISH €€

(☑50 51 26 51; www.restaurant-haervaerk.dk; Frederiks Allé 105; 5-course menu 450kr; ☺5.30-11pm Wed-Sat) The name means 'vandalism', and this is one of Aarhus' new breed of restaurants challenging the established order with bold new ideas. To wit: the set menu changes from day to day, sometimes from table to table; unique ingredients are sourced locally (preferably from small producers). Add the wine menu (four glasses 350kr) and you've got a top-flight, fair-priced option.

Klassisk 65 Bistro & Vinbar
FRENCH, DANISH €€

(☑86 13 12 21; www.klassiskbistro.dk; Jægergårds-gade 65; mains 165-295kr; ☺5.30-10pm daily, plus noon-4pm Fri & Sat, 10am-2pm Sun) Heavy on rustic, shabby-chic charm, this tightly packed place is all about carefully mismatched furniture and crockery, and shelves laden with wine. Locals flock here for the much-prized *hyggelig* (cosy) atmosphere and value for money. The kitchen puts a Danish spin on French country cooking, and the three-course menu of the day is perfect at 295kr.

Ferdinand
FRENCH €€

(☑87 32 14 44; www.hotelferdinand.dk; Åboulevarden 28; small dishes 95-185kr; ☺11am-10pm) Enjoying an ace position overlooking the river, this bistro delivers on atmosphere (which is humming), and its sound menu of modern and classic, French-leaning dishes utilising fine local produce. Of an evening, choose between a collection of small dishes, or a set four-course menu for 445kr.

AC Perch's Thehandel
TEAHOUSE €€

(☑33 15 35 62; www.perchstearoom.dk; Volden 3; meals 120-200kr; ☺10am-5.30pm Mon-Thu, to 6pm Fri, to 5pm Sat) This timeless tearoom makes a most civilised pit stop. There is enough choice here to satisfy the most discerning cuppa lover; consider indulging in the popular high tea (known as the tea ceremony; 200kr) with finger sandwiches, petits fours, scones with jam and clotted cream, and a bottomless pot of tea.

Jams, honeys, handmade biscuits and fudge are sold in the adjacent shop, as are the beautifully packaged teas.

Klassisk Fisk
SEAFOOD €€

(☑28 71 99 95; www.klassiskfisk.dk; Nørregade 38; lunch 68-165kr, dinner mains 195-250kr; ☺12.30-4pm & 5.30-10pm) Elegant decor, a relaxed feel and a menu of fresh fishy treats – it's as simple, and as delicious, as that. The crew behind bistro Klassisk 65 turn their attention to seafood here: oysters naturel, lobster, tuna carpaccio, soft-shell crab and bouillabaisse vie for menu attention, or opt for the three-course menu of the day for 325kr.

Globen Flakket
INTERNATIONAL €€

(☑87 31 03 33; www.globen-flakket.dk; Åboulevarden 18; dinner mains 112-198kr; ☺8.30am-10.30pm Sun-Thu, to 1am Fri & Sat; 🖼) Pitching to a broad demographic, this upbeat riverside venue is a decent option at any hour. As well as a classic-hits menu of burgers, pasta etc, plenty of good-value buffet options draw in the punters (including the weekday breakfast buffet for 42kr, weekend brunch for 129kr and afternoon cake buffet for 42kr).

★ Frederikshøj
DANISH €€€

(☑86 14 22 80; www.frederikshoj.com; Oddervej 19-21; 6-course menu 995kr; ☺6pm-midnight Wed-Sat) Bookings are essential to experience this Michelin-starred restaurant's forested setting just south of the centre, and to savour the gastronomic wizardry of Beirut-born owner-chef Wassim Hallal. A variety of menus are offered, from three courses of long-established favourites to a 10-course 'deluxe' extravaganza. Hallal's kitchen has a penchant for high-end headliners like lobster, caviar, oysters and foie gras.

Kähler Villa Dining
DANISH €€€

(☑86 17 70 88; www.villadining.dk; Grenåvej 127; 5-course dinner incl wine 599-699kr; ☺6.30-9.30pm Mon-Sat) This local favourite lies about 5km north of the centre in a gracious villa where gustatory magic happens, at an accessible price. It's a clever concept: for a flat rate of 699kr (599kr Monday to Thursday), and at a set time, diners enjoy a set menu of snacks, appetiser, starter, main and dessert, plus as much wine as they fancy.

Take Skovvejen north past Risskov, and the road becomes Grenåvej. Plenty of local buses serve this route, including 13, 18 and 100.

Note: kids under 12 are half-price. There's also a cheaper offer Monday to Thursday: four courses (no dessert, no drinks) for 299kr.

St Pauls Apothek
DANISH €€€

(☑86 12 08 33; www.stpaulsapothek.dk; Jægergårdsgade 76; 2-/3-course menu 265/345kr; ☺5.30pm-midnight Tue-Thu, to 2am Fri & Sat) What was once a pharmacy is now one of Aarhus' hottest dining destinations: a Brooklyn-esque combo of hipster mixologists, vintage architectural detailing and slinky mood lighting. The menu is small on choice but big on Nordic produce and confident food pairings – and for 645kr, you can enjoy three courses matched with inspired, delicious cocktails. Book ahead.

The Apothek is also in hot demand as a luxe drinking den – visit in the wee hours to sample a few of the killer cocktails.

Nordisk Spisehus
INTERNATIONAL €€€

(☑86 17 70 99; www.nordiskspisehus.dk; MP Bruuns Gade 31; lunch dishes 89kr, 3-/5-/8-course dinner 499/699/899kr; ☺noon-3pm & 5.30pm-midnight Mon-Sat) A clever concept restaurant, where the menu is usually geographically themed ('Rome', for example, or 'New York Meets Paris') and dishes are borrowed from (consenting) Michelin-starred restaurants around the globe, then given a Nordic twist. Menus change every two months – it's no doubt a huge challenge, but the kitchen handles it with aplomb. Lunch is good value.

Gastromé
DANISH €€€

(☑28 78 16 17; www.gastrome.dk; Rosensgade 28; menus from 598kr; ☺from 6pm Tue-Sat) Gas-tromé is the essence of Nordic elegance, all pale timber and sheepskins. It's a calming setting that allows the food to hog the spotlight – and well it should, as it's Michelin-star-winning stuff. Select between three menu options: half-throttle (598kr) gives you a wallet-friendly introduction to the kitchen's prowess, while full throttle (898kr) goes harder, and the signature menu sings.

🍷 Drinking & Nightlife

Aarhus has a sizeable student population, which enlivens the city's parks and cobblestone streets (and fills its drinking holes). Jægergårdsgade and surroundings in Frederiksbjerg are home to plenty of bars and cafes. The north side of Åboulevarden is full of chic restaurant-bars, the south side has big drinking dens and nearby Skolegade has intimate boozers and dive bars. On Frederiksgade, boisterous English and Irish pubs often have live music and jam sessions. In the Latin Quarter, Mejlgade is a good spot to seek out quality bistros and wine bars.

Plenty of eating options are also primed for a drink, like St Pauls Apothek for great cocktails, and Aarhus Street Food (p236) for chilled-out grazing and boozing.

★ Strandbaren
BAR

(www.facebook.com/strandbarenaarhus; Pier 4, Havnebassin 7; ☺May-Sep) Plonk shipping containers and sand on a harbourfront spot and voila: beach bar. This chilled hang-out at Aarhus Ø (p231) offers food, drink, flirting and weather-dependent activities and events. Check hours and location on the Facebook page (harbour redevelopment may require an annual location change; opening hours are 'when the sun is shining'). Bus 33 comes here, but cycling is best.

★ Mikkeller Bar
BAR

(☑32 16 01 92; www.mikkeller.dk; Jægergårdsgade 61; ☺2pm-midnight Sun-Wed, to 1am Thu, to 2am Fri, 1pm-2am Sat) Copenhagen's renowned nomad brewer has a popular outpost in Frederiksbjerg, and it's a bright, Scandi-streamlined place in which to sample one (or many) of the uniquely crafted beers. Let knowledgeable staff help you narrow down the 20 options on tap.

★ Løve's Bog- & VinCafé
BAR

(☑27 83 16 33; www.loeves.dk; Nørregade 32; ☺9am-midnight Mon-Fri, 10am-midnight Sat, 10am-6pm Sun) This snug 'book and wine cafe' is full of book-lined shelves and old furniture, and reading/laptopping regulars. Occasional poetry readings and live music add to the cultured air, while the short, simple tapas menu nicely fills in any writer's-block moments.

Under Masken   BAR

(Bispegade 3; ⊘ noon-2am Mon-Wed, to 3am Thu-Sat, 1-11pm Sun) Artist-run Under Masken keeps things kooky with its jumble of gilded mirrors, African tribal masks, sailor pictures and glowing fish tanks. Slide in for a loud, smoky and fun night on the tiles. Note: no food served.

Ris Ras Filliongongong   BAR

(🖉 86 18 50 06; Mejlgade 24; ⊘ noon-2am Mon-Thu, to 3am Fri & Sat, 2-7pm Sun) The vintage furniture and quirky titbits make Ris Ras (named after a children's nursery rhyme) feel like the living room of a cool local friend. This place is small, intimate and friendly – the essence of *hygge*. Note: you can smoke inside (which may be a buzzkill for nonsmokers).

Great Coffee   CAFE

(www.greatcoffee.dk; Klostergade 32H; ⊘ 9am-5.30pm Mon-Fri, 10am-4pm Sat) Doing exactly as its name suggests, this industrial-cool space makes top-notch, award-winning brews (limited food). Head through to the courtyard to find it.

GBar   GAY & LESBIAN

(🖉 21 35 35 61; www.gbar.dk; Skolegade 28; ⊘ 9pm-3am Thu, 10pm-5am Fri & Sat) Aarhus' main gay bar and club, open and welcoming to all. See its Facebook page for events and parties.

☆ Entertainment

★ Øst for Paradis   CINEMA

(🖉 86 19 31 22; www.paradisbio.dk; Paradisgade 7-9) Art-house cinema in the northern reaches of the Latin Quarter. Shows films in their original language, with Danish subtitles.

Aarhus Teater   THEATRE

(🖉 89 33 23 00; www.aarhusteater.dk; Teatergaden) This is a suitably theatrical building dating from 1900, embellished with gargoyles and other extravagant decor. Performances are largely in Danish, but musical and dance productions are also staged.

VoxHall & Atlas   LIVE MUSIC

(🖉 87 30 97 97; www.fondenvoxhall.dk; Vester Allé 15) VoxHall is a well-established live-music locale hosting an eclectic range of acts. Attached is the more-intimate Atlas (capacity 300), specialising in jazz and world-music performers.

Radar   LIVE MUSIC

(🖉 86 76 03 44; www.radarlive.dk; Skovgaardsgade 3) Radar offers a glimpse into Aarhus' indie scene with a wide range of live music (including rock, techno, punk and folk) from its home inside the cool Godsbanen (p232) cultural centre.

Train   LIVE MUSIC

(🖉 86 13 47 22; www.train.dk; Toldbodgade 6) Aarhus' premier club, Train is first and foremost a concert venue, with shows a couple of nights a week and some big international acts on the program. Train opens as a late-night club as well as on Friday and Saturday nights, with room for up to 1300 party-people and top-notch DJ talent. The complex also incorporates Kupé, a funky lounge club.

Musikhuset Aarhus   LIVE MUSIC

(🖉 89 40 90 00; www.musikhusetaarhus.dk; Thomas Jensens Allé) Aarhus' concert hall is a large, glass-fronted venue that hosts a range of musical events, from Rod Stewart to *Rigoletto*, performances from Den Kongelige Ballet (the Royal Danish Ballet) or the Aarhus Symphony Orchestra.

🛍 Shopping

★ Illums Bolighus   DESIGN

(🖉 87 41 50 00; www.illumsbolighusaarhus.dk; Lille Torv 2; ⊘ 10am-7pm Mon-Fri, to 6pm Sat, 11am-4pm Sun) Copenhagen's shrine to good taste has a branch in Aarhus, and it's every bit as lovely. Furniture, homewares and clothing are among the temptations.

Salling   DEPARTMENT STORE

(🖉 87 78 60 00; www.salling.dk; Søndergade 27; ⊘ 10am-8pm Mon-Fri, to 6pm Sat & Sun) Central department store on the pedestrian street, with a good gourmet section and all the big local brands. Its newest addition: a rooftop garden with city views plus scheduled events (from Christmas markets to live music).

ARoS Aarhus Kunstmuseum Store   BOOKS, GIFTS & SOUVENIRS

(Aros Allé 2; ⊘ 10am-5pm Tue & Thu-Sun, to 10pm Wed) The gift shop at ARoS (p230) art museum has an extensive range of art books, homewares, accessories and nifty knick-knacks.

Paustian   DESIGN

(🖉 86 20 89 89; www.paustian.dk; Skovvejen 2; ⊘ 10am-6pm Mon-Fri, to 3pm Sat) A shrine to the best of Danish (and international) design. Prepare to desire everything that couldn't possibly fit in your suitcase...

ⓘ AARHUS SHOPPING AREAS

Søndergade This 850m-long pedestrian street (known as Ryesgade at its starting point opposite the train station) is home to mainstream shopping and chain stores. The strip is also referred to as Strøget.

Latin Quarter A cobblestone, largely pedestrianised area offering cool fashion and design boutiques. Check out Badstuegade, Volden and west along Vestergade.

Frederiksbjerg This neighbourhood has boutiques and eclectic finds, including some retro stores and artisan studios.

Summerbird Chocolaterie   CHOCOLATE
(☑86 19 00 50; www.summerbird.dk; Volden 31; ⊙11am-5.30pm Mon-Thu, to 6pm Fri, 10am-3pm Sat) Exquisite choc-shop in the Latin Quarter. The pretty packaging makes these a classy souvenir for someone back home.

HAY   DESIGN
(☑42 82 08 20; www.hay.dk; Rosenkrantzgade 24; ⊙10am-6pm Mon-Fri, to 4pm Sat) Excellent examples of the latest Danish furniture as well as designer homewares, textiles and rugs.

ⓘ Information

VisitAarhus (☑87 31 50 10; www.visitaarhus.com; Hack Kampmanns Plads 2; ⊙10am-4pm Mon-Sat, 11am-2pm Sun) has a good website, touchscreens around town and a free app. Its social media pages are useful for up-to-date info. The main staffed information desk is a small one inside Dokk1 (p231); there's another info point inside the **bus station** (Rutebilstation; Fredensgade 45).

LEFT-LUGGAGE
Coin-operated lockers are available at the train and bus stations; a small/large locker costs 20/40kr for a 24-hour period.

MONEY
Forex Bank (Banegårdspladsen 20; ⊙10am-6pm Mon-Fri, to 3pm Sat) Foreign exchange close to the train station.

ⓘ Getting There & Away

AIR
Aarhus Airport (AAR; www.aar.dk; Ny Lufthavnsvej 24, Kolind), also known as Tirstrup Airport, is 45km northeast of the city.

Scandinavian Airlines (SAS) has frequent daily flights to/from Copenhagen; Sun-Air (affiliated with British Airways) operates direct connections to Stockholm, Gothenburg and Oslo. Ryanair has daily connections to/from London (Stansted).

Bus 925X connects Aarhus train station with the airport (115kr, 50 minutes, www.midttrafik.dk) on a schedule geared to meet all incoming and outgoing flights. Or pay 650kr for a taxi.

Note that Billund Airport (p220), 95km southwest of Aarhus, is a busier flight hub. Bus 912X gets you there (160kr, 1½ hours) from Aarhus bus station, and from a stop on Banegårdspladsen outside the train station.

BOAT
Mols-Linien (☑70 10 14 18; www.molslinien.dk; Hveensgade 4; 🐾) Operates high-speed ferries between Aarhus and Odden in north Zealand (standard one-way fare adult/car 349/699kr, 1¼ hours), with multiple sailings daily. Rates for car passage include passengers; low-price options available online.

BUS
From Aarhus bus station, 300m northeast of the train station, the blue X-bus network covers most of Jutland.

Book ahead online for Copenhagen services on **Abildskou** (☑32 72 93 86; www.abildskou.dk) Express bus 888 (149kr to 249kr, 3½ to 4½ hours, up to 10 times daily via Funen) and **Kombardo Expressen** (www.kombardoexpressen.dk; 99kr to 299kr, 3½ hours, via the Odden ferry).

TRAIN
Trains leave frequently to:
Aalborg (197kr, 1½ hours)
Copenhagen (388kr, three to 3½ hours), via Odense (244kr, 1½ hours)
Frederikshavn (256kr, 2½ hours)
Silkeborg (90kr, 45 minutes)

ⓘ Getting Around

BICYCLE
Free **Aarhusbycykel** (www.aarhusbycykel.dk) city bikes are available from locations around the city from April to October (download a map from the website). You need to put a 20kr coin into the slot to obtain the bike (refunded when you return it). Some of the bikes are not in great shape.

If you want a better-quality bike, Cycling Aarhus (p233) is your best bet. The company offers tours from a central location, plus bike rental (one day/week 110/595kr). See its website for details of its free city app with suggestions for cycling destinations.

BUS
Aarhus has an extensive, efficient local bus network. Most in-town (yellow) buses stop (Park Allé) close to the train station on Park Allé. Buy your ticket from the on-board machine (single ticket 20kr).

Information on tickets, passes, routes and schedules is available from the bus station on Fredensgade or through **Midttrafik** (☑ 70 21 02 30; www.midttrafik.dk). Doubtless when the Letbane opens, bus routes will be significantly affected.

LETBANE LIGHT RAIL

A new light-rail line (known as the Aarhus Letbane) is opening in stages from late 2017 into 2018.

The first phase includes a 12km tramway from Aarhus train station via the harbour (stopping at Dokk1; p231) to Nørreport, where the line divides into two tracks to the north, including one that runs via the university and main hospital. Eventually, the Letbane will reach Grenaa in Djursland.

DJURSLAND

Djursland, the large peninsula northeast of Aarhus (Jutland's 'nose'), is prime summer-holiday territory for hordes of beach-going Danish, Swedish and German families. The area's standout towns are Ebeltoft and Grenaa. Sprawling Grenaa (connected by ferry to Varberg in Sweden) is the larger of the two and the surrounding beaches are better, but Ebeltoft has more charm.

There are some top-notch sandy beaches all over the peninsula (particularly in the north, at Fjellerup, Bønnerup and Gjerrild, and just south of Grenaa), while family-focused, land-based activities range from historic manor houses to animal parks, shark pools and a hugely popular funpark.

Ebeltoft

POP 7500

Ebeltoft has all the ingredients you need for a summer getaway. Cobblestone streets lined with half-timbered houses, white-sand beaches and a classic warship attract large numbers of holidaymakers, and the pretty surrounds are now a national park.

Fregatten Jylland and the harbour are along Strandvejen. From the harbour walk a block east on Jernbanegade or Toldbodvej to reach Adelgade, the main shopping street. Torvet, the town square, is at the southern end of Adelgade.

◉ Sights & Activities

★**Adelgade**   STREET

Cobbled Adelgade is one of the loveliest main streets in Jutland, lined with pastel-coloured cafes and stores, and pretty courtyards. At its southern end is the diminutive old **town hall**, built in 1789. It has a half-timbered, chocolate-box appearance (it's a popular spot for weddings) and is now home to local history exhibits (free admission).

Glasmuseet Ebeltoft   MUSEUM

(☑ 86 34 17 99; www.glasmuseet.dk; Strandvejen 8; adult/child 100/30kr; ☺ 10am-6pm Jul & Aug, to 5pm Apr-Jun, Sep & Oct, 10am-4pm Wed-Sun Nov-Mar) Contemporary glass art is beautifully showcased at sleek Glasmuseet, with stunning permanent pieces plus changing exhibitions gracing its light-filled interior. You can also watch glass-blowers working their magic on-site.

Fregatten Jylland   SHIP

(☑ 86 34 10 99; www.fregatten-jylland.dk; SA Jensen Vej 4; adult/child 125/80kr; ☺ from 10am mid-Feb–Dec; ﹙﹚) The frigate *Jylland* has quite a presence. From bow to stern it measures 71m, making it the world's longest wooden ship. It was launched in 1860 and played an instrumental role in Denmark's navy in the 19th century; today it's been restored for visitors – step inside and experience the life of a crew member.

Ree Park Safari   ZOO

(☑ 86 33 61 50; www.reepark.dk; Stubbe Søvej 15, Ebeltoft; adult/child 185/95kr; ☺ from 10am mid-Apr–Oct; ﹙﹚) Ree Park houses an impressive collection of animals from all corners of the

---

MOLS BJERGE NATIONAL PARK

Covering 180 sq km of Djursland forests, moors and open grasslands as well as lakes, coastal areas and the sea, **Mols Bjerge National Park** (http://eng.nationalparkmols bjerge.dk) even encompasses the town of Ebeltoft and nearby villages. It's named after the region's best-known natural feature, the rolling, heather-covered Mols Hills that rise to all of 137m. The park's most-visited attraction is **Kalø Slotsruin** (Molsvej 31, Rønde), atmospheric ruins of a 1313 castle built by Danish king Erik Menved. They sit atop a small island in an inlet of Kalø Bay south of Rønde. A 500m causeway leads there from a parking area and restaurant.

globe, with Africa taking more than the lion's share (pun intended). Visitors can pay extra to take a Land Rover tour through the 'African savannah' (45kr) or a train across the 'North American prairie' (55kr). There are plenty of animal feedings throughout the day, and camel rides too.

Ebeltoft Beach
BEACH

(Nordre Strandvej) Ebeltoft sits on a calm, protected bay, fringed with white-sand beaches; you'll find a nice stretch right along Nordre Strandvej, the coastal road that leads north from the town centre.

🛏 Sleeping

★ Danhostel Ebeltoft
HOSTEL €

(☑86 34 20 53; www.ebeltoft-danhostel.dk; Egedalsvej 5; s/d/tr/q 500/530/585/630kr; @ 🛜) A map/GPS is almost compulsory to find this hostel, perched high above the town (3km by road, or about a 25-minute walk). But it's worth the trip, with hotel-standard accommodation (all rooms with bathroom and TV) and some cool design features. Linen costs 55kr; breakfast is 70kr.

Ebeltoft Strand Camping
CAMPGROUND €

(☑86 34 12 14; www.ebeltoftstrandcamping.dk; Nordre Strandvej 23; site/adult/child 100/95/60kr; 🛜 🏊) The first camping ground you'll see, on your right as you drive into town, has plenty of good sites and cabins backing onto the beach. It's well geared for family fun, with pool, playgrounds and mini-golf. Bikes and kayaks can be hired.

Hotel Ebeltoft Strand
HOTEL €€

(☑86 34 33 00; www.ebeltoftstrand.dk; Nordre Strandvej 3; s/d incl breakfast from 1195/1395kr; 🛜) In a plum position on the beachfront and close to Fregatten Jylland (p241), this sprawling hotel offers good facilities and a range of price options, including rooms (all with sea view) plus an assortment of stylish, family-sized apartments.

🍴 Eating

★ Restaurant Kampmann
CAFE €€

(☑86 34 18 18; www.restaurantkampmann.dk; Strandvejen 8; mains 95-185kr; ⊙ 11am-5pm Apr-Oct, to 4pm Feb, Mar, Nov & Dec) Behind Glasmuseet Ebeltoft (p241), this small, sleek cafe has a sunny deck overlooking the water. There's a short, flavourful menu of gourmet smørrebrød, salads and home-baked cakes, plus locally brewed beer and soft drinks. Check hours online.

Brasseriet
FRENCH €€

(☑86 36 22 00; www.molskroen.dk; Hovedgaden 31A, Femmøller Strand; mains 98-288kr; ⊙ 11.30am-9pm) Molskroen's owners have rejuvenated Femmøller's beach hotel (now known as Molskroen Strandhotel), with high-quality dining choices found here. The all-day Brasseriet has a menu of Gallic classics (foie gras, steak tartare) and easy favourites including *moules-frites* and lobster naturel. A second restaurant is the high-quality steakhouse A Hereford Beefstouw.

★ Molskroen
DANISH €€€

(☑86 36 22 00; www.molskroen.dk; Hovedgaden 16, Femmøller Strand; lunch 150-450kr, dinner mains 250-550kr; ⊙ noon-3pm & 6-9pm Mon-Sat) For something special, make your way to this beautiful *kro* (inn), renowned throughout Denmark and a popular gourmet destination. Outside, it's all half-timbered charm in idyllic grounds; inside is sleekly contemporary with copper lights and elegant furnishings. Of an evening, the set menus shine with culinary prowess and beautifully presented local fare (three/five courses 550/800kr). Book ahead.

ℹ Information

Tourist Office (☑87 52 18 00; www.visit djursland.com; SA Jensen Vej 4; ⊙ from 10am mid-Feb–Dec) Inside the ticket office of *Fregatten Jylland*, and open the same hours as the attraction.

ℹ Getting There & Away

BOAT

Mols-Linien (☑70 10 14 18; www.mols-linien. dk; Færgevejen 60) operates a high-speed car ferry between Ebeltoft and Odden in north Zealand (standard one-way fare adult/car 349/699kr, 55 minutes). Rates for car passage include passengers; low-price options available online. Note that there are far fewer crossings on this route compared with Aarhus–Odden.

BUS

Useful links from Ebeltoft:
Aarhus (90kr, 1¼ hours), bus 123
Grenaa (60kr, one hour), bus 351
Randers (90kr, 1½ hours), bus 212

ℹ Getting Around

Bikes can be hired from **LP Cykler** (☑86 34 47 77; lpcyklerogmaskiner@mail.dk; Nørrealle 5; bike hire per day/week 80/40kr; ⊙ 8am-5.30pm Mon-Fri, to noon Sat).

Grenaa

POP 14,600

A purpose-built harbour complete with (captive) sharks, a historic old town and 7km of sandy beaches are the defining attractions of Grenaa. The old town, radiating out from Torvet, is the economic and shopping hub of the district. It's about 4km west of the harbour, where the waterfront is peopled by shark-fanciers and Sweden-bound ferry-goers.

⊙ Sights & Activities

Kattegatcentret
AQUARIUM

(☑ 86 32 52 00; www.kattegatcentret.dk; Færgevej 4; adult/child 165/90kr; ⊙ 10am-4pm or 5pm; ⊕) If you fancy being just inches from a shark and in total control, you'll love the glass tunnel at Kattegatcentret, where the focus is on surrounding sealife. At 2pm you can watch the shark-feeding session – a good way to see just why sharks are at the top of the food chain. There is also a seal pool (and feeding sessions), and a kid-friendly touchpool.

Museum Østjylland Grenaa
MUSEUM

(☑ 87 12 26 00; www.museumoj.dk; Søndergade 1; ⊙ 10am-4pm Tue-Sun) FREE You can't miss this eye-catching regional museum: it's housed in a large, green-and-gold merchant's house south of Torvet.

Grenaa Beach
BEACH

(accessed from Kystvej; ⊕) Grenaa's 7km of Blue Flag–winning beach runs south of town and is where it's at on hot days; this area is known for its child-friendly shallow waters. To get here, follow the coast south from the harbour. The northern end of the beach is a hive of activity, but as you run south it becomes a little more private.

🛏 Sleeping & Eating

Grenaa Strand Camping
CAMPGROUND €

(☑ 86 32 17 18; www.grenaastrandcamping.dk; Fuglsangvej 58; site/adult/child from 100/84/62kr; ⊙ Apr–mid-Sep; @ 🤶 🌊) A super family option if your visit to Grenaa is all about the beach, this site is in pole beachside position a few kilometres south of town. A pirate theme (aarghh!), high-season activities for kids, plus mini-golf and a swimming pool will keep families happy. Cabins and on-site caravans are well priced; there's also a minimarket and summertime cafe.

Hotel Grenaa Havlund
HOTEL €€

(☑ 86 32 26 77; www.hotelgrenaahavlund.dk; Kystvej 1; s/d incl breakfast 695/895kr; 🤶) This sunny little hotel offers no-frills rooms about 1km south of the Grenaa harbour area, just steps from the beach.

MundGodt
CAFE €€

(☑ 53 62 32 10; www.mundgodt.com; Storegade 6; lunch 72-128kr, 2-/3-course dinner 268/298kr; ⊙ 11am-10pm Wed-Sat) A lovely multipurpose place: cafe and wine store by day, restaurant and wine bar by night, with an appealing outdoor area. Daytime smørrebrød gives way to a small evening menu; the kitchen's output is polished and the wine choices are top-notch.

Restaurant Skakkes Holm
SEAFOOD €€

(☑ 86 30 09 89; www.skakkesholm.dk; Skakkes Holm 56, Lystbådehavn; dinner buffet incl drinks adult/child from 229/88kr; ⊙ 11.30am-2pm & 5-10pm; ⊕) Over a footbridge by Kattegatcentret is the marina, a pleasant little place to explore. In evenings, you'll find hungry folks loading their plates from the impressive buffet at Restaurant Skakkes Holm. Given the surroundings, it's only fitting that the emphasis here is on fish. The buffet's also held at lunchtime on weekends.

ℹ Information

Tourist Office (☑ 87 58 12 00; www.visit djursland.com; Torvet 1; ⊙ 10am-4pm Mon-Fri, to 1pm Sat) Close to the cathedral, in the main square.

ℹ Getting There & Away

BOAT

Stena Line (www.stenaline.com; Færgevej 1) has frequent ferries connecting Grenaa with Varberg in Sweden.

BUS

From **Trafikterminalen** (Stationsplads), a short walk from Torvet, take bus 83, 120 or 123 to Aarhus (110kr, 80 minutes), bus 351 to Ebeltoft (60kr, 50 minutes).

TRAIN

By late 2018, you should be able to reach Grenaa on the new Letbane light railway from Aarhus.

Around Djursland

Theme park, zoo, manor-museum and safari park – they're all within day-tripping distance of Djursland's nicest coastal towns, Ebeltoft and Grenaa – especially if you're driving.

👁 Sights

Djurs Sommerland   AMUSEMENT PARK

(☑86 39 84 00; www.djurssommerland.dk; Rand-ersvej 17, Nimtofte; 260-280kr; ⊘season May-Oct, daily mid-Jun–mid-Aug; 🚼) One of Djursland's biggest drawcards is this much-hyped amuse-ment park with arguably the best outdoor rides in Jutland (more than 60, including Denmark's longest roller coaster) and a waterpark, with pools and water slides for all ages.

Skandinavisk Dyrepark   ZOO

(☑86 39 13 33; www.skandinaviskdyrepark.dk; Nød-agervej 67B, Nødager; adult/child 180/95kr; ⊘from 10am mid-Apr–mid-Oct; 🚼) Nordic species are top of the food chain here, where the biggest attraction is the impressive polar-bear facility. Other star performers: brown bears, moose, musk ox and wolves. Fallow deer and rein-deer, and goats can be fed by hand.

Gammel Estrup   MUSEUM

(☑86 48 30 01; www.gammelestrup.dk; Randersvej 2, Auning; manor & museums adult/child 100kr/free; ⊘10am-5pm mid-Apr–mid-Oct, shorter hours rest of year) On the outskirts of Auning, 33km west of Grenaa, lies this grand manor house, home to two museums, splendid gardens and an aura of Danish gentility.

The moat-encircled manor that is home to Herregårdsmuseet (Manor Museum) has been preserved and presented in much the same way as it was in the 17th century, with an-tique furniture, elaborate tapestries, historic portraits and glorious views.

Also on the estate is Det Grønne Muse-um (The Green Museum; www.gl-estrup.dk), whose high-quality exhibits tell the story of Danish farming, food and food culture.

NORTH-CENTRAL JUTLAND

Randers

POP 62,300

Randers' appeal lies predominantly in its most flaunted attraction – a triple-domed zoo that mesmerises families and wildlife-enthusiasts alike. Industrial and commercial pursuits are still the heartbeat of the city, but there's history and culture if you know where to look.

👁 Sights

Central Randers is an architectural hotch-potch with some antique gems alongside more-modern eyesores. Hunt down the pearls, and the stories behind them, with the *Star Route* brochure, free from the tourist office. It outlines a 2.5km, self-guided tour around town, highlighting the likes of 1434 Helligåndshuset (Erik Menveds Plads), once part of a medieval monastery, and the im-posing 15th-century red-brick church, Sankt Mortens Kirke (Vester Kirkestræde 7).

⭐ Randers Regnskov   ZOO

(www.regnskoven.dk; Tørvebryggen 11; adult/child 190/110kr; ⊘from 10am; 🚼) Randers' most-visited attraction is this dome-enclosed trop-ical zoo ('*regnskov*' means rainforest), where the temperature is always a humid 20°C to 30°C (dress accordingly). Trails within the sultry domes pass through impressive en-closures housing crocodiles, monkeys, man-atees, pythons, iguanas, orchids, hibiscus and other rainforest flora and fauna. The South American dome is a standout (the others rep-resent Africa and Asia), as waterfalls and an abundance of wildlife engulf you.

Memphis Mansion   MUSEUM

(Graceland Randers; ☑86 42 96 96; www.memphis mansion.dk; Graceland Randers Vej 3; museum adult/child 99/69kr; ⊘10am-9pm) Four kilo-metres southeast of Randers' town centre is the Elvis Presley Museum, housed in a replica Graceland mansion (double the size of the original). True, you don't expect to find a shrine to the King in regional Denmark, but one mad-keen local fan has proved his dedi-cation in building this showcase for his per-sonal collection of memorabilia. Inside the kitschy complex there's also a well-stocked Elvis shop, American diner and mini movie theatre. Thankyouverymuch.

🛏 Sleeping

Hotel Randers   HOTEL €€

(☑86 42 34 22; www.hotel-randers.dk; Torvegade 11; d/ste from 1255/1525kr; 🛜) This is an old-world, art-deco treasure. It was built in 1856 and refurbished in the 1920s; a fire in 2015 ne-cessitated a widespread renovation, but the hotel's unique style has been retained. The decor is rich and elegant – if you can afford to upgrade to a suite you can live the high life for a night. Online deals available.

**Stephansen Hotel
& Restaurant** BOUTIQUE HOTEL €€
(☑86 44 27 77; www.stephansenshotel.dk; Møll-
estræde 4; s/d incl breakfast 750/1075kr) Just
200m north of the tourist office is this petite,
family-owned gem, with 10 fresh, pristine-
white rooms. A sweet courtyard garden and
small restaurant are attached.

✖ Eating

Café Borgen CAFE €
(☑86 43 47 00; Houmeden 10; light meals 40-75kr;
⊙10am-10pm Mon-Thu, to 2am Fri & Sat, 11am-6pm
Sun) Borgen offers a little slice of Euro life,
with Parisian-style outdoor seating and a
low-lit interior. Home to rich coffee and lazy
lunches, it morphs into an inviting spot for
evening drinks.

Bistroteket FRENCH €€
(☑88 97 27 37; www.bistroteket.dk; Rosengade 2;
lunch 85-145kr, dinner mains 205-275kr; ⊙11.30am-
3pm & 5.30-10pm Tue-Sat) Winning hearts and
palates, this central bistro successfully marries French flavours with Danish classics. The
three-course dinner menu is excellent value
at 350kr, and the option of matching it with
a 'nice wine menu' or a 'great wine menu'
shows there's humour here too.

Café Mathisen INTERNATIONAL €€
(☑87 11 30 68; www.cafemathisen.dk; Torvegade
11; lunch 99-149kr, dinner mains 129-270kr; ⊙11am-
11pm Mon-Sat) Part of the delightful Hotel
Randers, the Mathisen has elegant black-
and-white decor that brings to mind the art
deco era. Its lunch offerings are light and
simple (club sandwiches, caesar salad), and
it's not too fancy to put a burger next to guinea fowl on the evening menu.

☕ Drinking & Nightlife

Storegade is wall-to-wall bars, cafes and
pubs, with a few nightclubs and burger joints
thrown in.

ℹ Information

Tourist Office (☑86 42 44 77; www.visit
randers.com; Rådhustorvet 4; ⊙10am-5pm
Mon-Fri, 9am-1pm Sat Jun-Aug, 10am-4pm
Mon-Fri Sep-May) Plenty of local information
and helpful staff.

ℹ Getting There & Away

Randers is 81km south of Aalborg and 42km
north of Aarhus on the E45. Rte 16 leads 44km
west to Viborg, and 58km east to Grenaa.

All trains between Aarhus (80kr, 30 minutes)
and Aalborg (112kr, 55 minutes) stop here, at the
station on Jernbanegade, west of the city centre.

Bus links with central Jutland towns are also
strong. The **bus station** (Dytmærsken) is central.

ℹ Getting Around

It's a 15-minute walk from the train station via
Vestergade to Rådhustorvet, the central square.

Rebild Bakker
& Rold Skov

The heart-warming story of Rebild Bakker
(the Rebild Hills) dates back to 1912, when
a group of Danish-Americans presented 200
hectares of (previously privately owned) forest to the Danish government on the provi-
so that it would remain in a natural state,
be open to all, and be accessible to Danish-
Americans for celebration of US holidays.

This act of goodwill inspired the Danish
forest service to acquire adjacent woodland
and collectively the 80-sq-km area is known
as Rold Skov (Rold Forest; Denmark's largest).
The area has good walking and mountain-
biking trails that take you through rolling
heather-covered hills, while its woods contain European aspen, beech and oak trees.

Rebild Bakker is a sleepy place (more a
day-trip destination), but it's now position-
ing itself as an outdoor-activity centre for
cross-country runners and mountain-bikers.
The tourist office has info on all activities in
the area, including canoeing, fishing, horse
riding and golf.

◎ Sights & Activities

RebildPorten VISITOR CENTRE
(☑99 88 90 00; www.rebildporten.dk; Rebildvej 25A;
⊙10am-5pm Tue-Sun) This striking new building houses the tourist office (and its helpful
staff, maps and brochures) and some nicely
done local exhibits, including ones on the nature and folklore of the forest.

Walking

There are numerous walking trails criss-
crossing the park. One 4km route begins
in a sheep meadow west of the car park. It
goes past **Tophuset**, a small century-old
thatched house (now a cafe) that was built
by the first caretakers; the neighbouring
Blokhusmuseet, modelled on the log cabin
that US president Abraham Lincoln grew up
in; a large glacial boulder called **Cimbres-
tenen**, sculpted in the form of a Cimbrian

FYRKAT VIKING RING FORTRESS

Fundamentally similar to larger, better-known Trelleborg (p127) in Zealand, the 1000-year-old **Fyrkat ring fortress** (☑ 98 51 19 27; www.nordmus.dk; Fyrkatvej 45; adult/child incl entry to Vikingecenter Fyrkat 75kr/free; ◷ 10am-4pm May, to 5pm Jun-Aug, to 3pm Sep) is presumed to have been built by the Viking king Harald Bluetooth around 980. Grass-covered 3m-high circular ramparts are divided into four quadrants, each with a central 'courtyard' area surrounded by four symmetrical buildings. Although no structures whatever remain within the ramparts, just outside is a replica Viking longhouse, and a kilometre north, **Vikingecenter Fyrkat** (☑ 99 82 41 75; www.nordmus.dk; Fyrkatvej 37; adult/child incl entry to Fyrkat 75kr/free; ◷ 10am-4pm May, to 5pm Jun-Aug, to 3pm Sep; ◼) is an archaeologically accurate reconstruction of the type of farmstead that would have supplied the fortress with fresh produce. Its 33m longhouse is particularly impressive and costumed interpreters here provide demonstrations of silverwork, archery, bread-making, music and other Viking crafts.

Fyrkat is in a lovely rural setting but without bus service. The nearest public transport is to Hobro, 3km northeast, a town on the Aarhus-Randers–Aalborg railway line.

bull's head by Anders Bundgaard; a hollow where 4th of July celebrations are held; and **Sønderland**, the park's highest hill (102m). It's a particularly lovely stroll in summer and autumn, when the heather adds a purple tinge to the hillsides.

Mountain Biking

The park is a magnet for mountain-bikers, and there are loads of bike trails. The popular 25km 'Blue Route' journeys past lakes and through forested hills.

Skørping Cykler   CYCLING
(☑ 98 39 13 05; www.skørpingcykler.dk; Møldrupvej 10, Skørping; mountain bikes per half/full day 200/275kr) Bike hire and route info is available from this operator in Skørping.

🛏 Sleeping & Eating

Danhostel Rebild   HOSTEL €
(☑ 98 39 13 40; www.danhostelrebild.dk; Rebildvej 23; s/d/f 405/460/510kr; @ 🛜) Sitting pretty under its thatched roof, this hostel is of a typically high standard. Rooms are in an annexe behind the main building and all have their own bathroom.

Comwell Hotel Rebild Bakker   HOTEL €€
(☑ 98 39 12 22; www.comwellrebildbakker.dk; Rebildvej 36; d incl breakfast from 1098kr; 🛜 ⛱) Marketing itself as a 'sports hotel', this sprawling complex promotes active holidays and backs it up with an indoor pool, sauna, gym, healthy options in its restaurant, free mountain bikes for guest use, and daily training sessions (yoga, boxing, water aerobics, running, cycling). Rooms are modern and comfy.

Rold StorKro   DANISH €€
(☑ 98 37 51 00; www.rold.dk; Vælderskoven 13; lunch 68-139kr, dinner mains 188-308kr; ◷ noon-9.30pm) Some 2km past the park entrance, off Rte 180 to Hobro, is this classic, old-school inn whose best feature is its Panorama Restaurant, which offers a forested outlook and a traditional menu. Lunchtime smørrebrød classics give way to fish, pork and beef; venison (farmed on the property) is the house speciality. The three-course dinner menu is good value at 325kr.

❶ Information

The helpful tourist office is inside the striking RebildPorten (p245).

❶ Getting There & Away

Rte 180 runs through the Rold Skov forest, connecting Rebild Bakker with Hobro, 23km to the south.

Trains running between Aalborg (50kr, 25 minutes) and Aarhus (162kr, 70 minutes) stop in Skørping, from where it's 3km west to Rebild Bakker. Bus 104 runs a few times between Skørping and Rebild Bakker (22kr) on weekdays only.

Viborg

POP 39,000

Rich in religious history and bordering two idyllic lakes, Viborg is a sweetly romantic getaway. During its holiest period (just prior to the Reformation), 25 churches lined the streets. Nowadays, only two can be found in the town centre.

◉ Sights & Activities

Viborg Domkirke   CHURCH
(☑ 87 25 52 55; www.viborgdomkirke.dk; Sankt Mogens Gade 4; adult/child 10kr/free; ⊙ 11am-5pm Mon-Sat, noon-5pm Sun May-Sep, to 3pm Oct-Apr) The striking, twin-towered cathedral is equally impressive inside and out, with **frescoes**, painted over five years (1908–13) by artist Joakim Skovgaard, evocatively portraying the story of the Protestant bible. In 1876 the cathedral was almost entirely rebuilt, becoming the largest granite church in Scandinavia (an enduring claim to fame). The crypt is all that survives from its birth date, 1100.

Sankt Mogens Gade   STREET
The old part of town lies just to the north and west of the cathedral. Sankt Mogens Gade has a charming pocket of homes from the mid-16th century, including Den Hauchske Gård at No 7, Villadsens Gård at No 9A and Den Gamle Præstegård at No 11. B&Bs can also be found here.

Skovgaard Museet   MUSEUM
(☑ 86 62 39 75; www.skovgaardmuseet.dk; Domkirkestræde 2-4; adult/child 60kr/free; ⊙ 10am-5pm Tue-Sun Jun-Aug, 11am-4pm Tue-Sun Sep-May) Just outside the cathedral, this museum highlights further work of cathedral artist Joakim Skovgaard, among other works by his family and his contemporaries, plus changing exhibitions.

Margrethe I   BOATING
(☑ 87 87 88 88; www.visitviborg.dk; Randersvej 1; adult/child 60/40kr; ⊙ 2pm & 3.30pm mid-May–Aug) Jump onboard the *Margrethe I* for a one-hour cruise of the town lakes. The boat departs from outside Golf Salonen on Randersvej. The surrounding park is lovely; from mid-May to September you can rent canoes and rowboats from the park kiosk for lake exploration.

⏚ Sleeping

There's a well-run **Danhostel** (☑ 86 67 17 81; www.danhostelviborg.dk; Vinkelvej 36; dm/s/d 210/415/515kr; @ 🛜) and waterfront camping ground across the lake east of town (3km, no bus).

★ **Niels Bugges Hotel**   BOUTIQUE HOTEL €€
(☑ 86 63 80 11; www.nielsbuggeskro.dk; Egeskovvej 26, Hald Ege; d incl breakfast without/with bathroom 850/1350kr; 🛜) This old inn, set amid forest on the outskirts of town, is a destination hotel where design and gastronomy are taken seriously and the result is something special. Rooms epitomise farmhouse chic, all florals, patchworks and antiques. Add a library, romantic grounds and wonderful New Nordic–inspired restaurant, Skov (meaning 'forest'), and you too will be dreading checkout.

Oasen   B&B €€
(☑ 86 62 14 25; www.oasenviborg.dk; Nørregade 9; s/d 395/650kr, with bathroom 650/795kr, all incl breakfast; 🛜) Oasen is an inviting complex of central rooms and apartments, nicely bridging the gap between hostels and business hotels. Some rooms have shared bathroom; all have cable TV plus kitchen access (or private kitchen). Breakfast is taken in a sweet little 'cafe' in the garden.

✖ Eating

Café Morville   EUROPEAN €€
(☑ 86 60 22 11; www.cafemorville.dk; Hjultorvet 4; lunch 69-139kr, dinner mains 149-185kr; ⊙ 10am-10pm Mon & Tue, to 11pm Wed & Thu, to midnight Fri & Sat, 11am-5pm Sun; 🛜) One of those chic all-day cafes that seem compulsory in Danish towns. You can park yourself on the leather banquettes for a mid-morning coffee or late-night drink and everything in between.

Niels Bugges Kro   DANISH, FRENCH €€€
(☑ 86 63 80 11; www.nielsbuggeskro.dk; Ravnsbjergvej 69, Dollerup; lunch 168-238kr, dinner mains 265-365kr; ⊙ noon-9pm Mon-Sat, to 5pm Sun) The owners of the lovely Niels Bugges Hotel also have this nearby *kro* (inn) in lakeside Dollerup. The atmospheric *kro* houses a traditional restaurant that turns the spotlight to French gastronomy of an evening.

ⓘ Information

Banks and other services can be found on Sankt Mathias Gade.

Tourist Office (☑ 87 87 88 88; www.visitviborg.dk; Tingvej 2A; ⊙ 10am-4pm Mon-Fri, to 1pm Sat Jul & Aug, 10am-3pm Mon-Fri Sep-Jun) Clued up on the area, with good brochures and maps, plus bike hire (100kr per day). This office is a little out of the centre.

ⓘ Getting There & Away

Viborg is 66km northwest of Aarhus on Rte 26 and 44km west of Randers on Rte 16.

Regular trains run to/from Aarhus (140kr, 65 minutes). The train station is 1km southwest of the cathedral; walk via Jernbanegade and Sankt Mathias Gade.

Northern Jutland

Best Places to Eat

➡ Applaus (p254)

➡ Museumscaféen (p260)

➡ Penny Lane (p253)

➡ Ruths Gourmet (p260)

➡ Jacobs Fiskerestaurant (p257)

Best Places to Stay

➡ Villa Vendel (p263)

➡ Aahøj (p257)

➡ Badepension Marienlund (p259)

➡ Ruths Hotel (p260)

➡ Strandgaarden Badehotel (p256)

Why Go?

Northern Jutland, split from the rest of Jutland by the Lim-fjord, wows visitors with its magnificent light and beautiful barren landscapes of shifting sands. The region is promoted as 'Lysets Land', or the Land of Light, and if you witness the soft blue nuances by the water as day turns into night, you'll understand how the name came about (and begin to com-prehend the region's appeal to artists).

But it's not just painters who flock here. Surfers and beach-goers make a beeline for the north the minute the weather turns kind. Families head off to the zoos, aquariums and funparks, and seafood lovers rejoice in the fresh-off-the-boat catches.

The area's most coveted tourist destination is Skagen, at Denmark's northern tip. It's both a civilised haven of chichi restaurants and art museums, and a wild place where nature calls the shots – which sums up the entire region, really.

When to Go

➡ Summer is prime time to visit the north. The beaches, theme parks, festivals and activities are in full swing in July and August, when accommodation prices hit their peak.

➡ The shoulder season (May, June and September) usually offers decent weather and smaller crowds.

➡ Aalborg has year-round attractions and events, including its popular Carnival celebrations in May, and plenty of performances in its arresting new concert hall.

➡ There's also some appeal to the notion of rugging up and braving the cooler weather someplace such as Skagen, where you can admire the turbulent tides and shifting sands without the summer crowds and high-season prices. Winter is better for the Danish art of *hygge* (cosiness), after all.

Northern Jutland Highlights

1 Grenen (p258) Surveying two seas at Denmark's northernmost point.

2 Skagens Museum (p258) Finding inspiration in treasured artworks with a real sense of place.

3 Aalborg (p250) Discovering the new, improved appeal of this waterfront city.

4 Klitmøller (p263) Surfing 'Cold Hawaii'.

5 Gammel Skagen (p260) Watching a glorious sunset over a memorable meal.

6 Løkken Beach (p262) Snapping beach huts and learning to surf from this lovely stretch of sand.

7 Rubjerg Knude (p263) Losing a lighthouse amid endless sand dunes.

8 Thy National Park (p264) Finding your favourite spot along this 55km stretch of coastline, dunes and moors.

9 Læsø (p255) Taking a salt bath on a low-key time-warp island.

Aalborg

POP 112,200

Things are on the way up for Aalborg, Denmark's fourth-largest city. It sits at the narrowest point of the Limfjord (the long body of water that slices Jutland in two), and recent developments have seen the waterfront become the focal point of the town. A concerted effort is being made to rejuvenate the central industrial areas and turn neglected spaces into something far more appealing.

Traditionally, Aalborg has flown under the traveller's radar, but that could easily change. There are enough low-key diversions here to occupy a few days for most visitors, from architecture fans to families, and party animals to history boffins.

◎ Sights

★Waterfront
LANDMARK

(Jomfru Ane Parken) The Aalborg waterfront promenade, extending east from Limfjordsbroen, is a great example of urban regeneration, taking what was a scruffy dockside area and opening it up to locals. Here you'll find restaurants, a park, playground, basketball courts and moored boats (including an old ice-breaker, now a restaurant-bar). One of the best features is the **Aalborg Havnebad** (Jomfru Ane Parken 6; ⊙10am-7pm Jul–mid-Aug, noon-6pm Jun & late Aug) FREE, a summertime outdoor pool that lets you take a dip in the Limfjord.

East of the Utzon Center there's more new development, including university buildings and smart, low-cost housing for the city's growing student population. The latest addition is the shiny new Musikkens Hus (p254), a first-class, futuristic-looking concert hall.

★Kunsten
MUSEUM

(☑99 82 41 00; www.kunsten.dk; Kong Christians Allé 50; adult/child 95kr/free; ⊙10am-5pm Tue & Thu-Sun, to 9pm Wed) Housed in a stunning white-marble building designed by the great Finnish architect Alvar Aalto, Kunsten is Aalborg's high-quality museum of modern art. The building's light-filled interior complements a fine collection of predominantly Danish works and changing exhibitions. Lovely grounds and a smart cafe make it an easy place to spend some time.

To get to Kunsten, take the tunnel beneath the train station, which emerges into **Kildeparken**, a green space with statues and water fountains. Go directly through the park, cross Vesterbro and continue through a wooded area to the museum, about a 12-minute walk in all. Alternatively, take bus 15.

★Utzon Center
ARCHITECTURE, MUSEUM

(☑76 90 50 00; www.utzoncenter.dk; Slotspladsen 4; adult/child 80kr/free; ⊙11am-5pm Tue, Wed & Fri, to 9pm Thu, 10am-5pm Sat & Sun) This impressive 700-sq-metre design and architecture space, with its distinctive silver roofscape, sits pretty on the waterfront. It's the last building designed by celebrated Danish architect, Jørn Utzon (1918–2008), who famously designed the Sydney Opera House. Utzon grew up in Aalborg and died shortly after the eponymous centre was finished.

The centre hosts a changing program of exhibitions on architecture and design – if you're not a huge design buff, you might consider the admission price a little steep.

★Lindholm Høje
ARCHAEOLOGICAL SITE

(Vendilavej, Nørresundby; ⊙dawn-dusk) FREE The Limfjord was a kind of Viking motorway providing easy, speedy access to the Atlantic for longboat raiding parties. It's not surprising, then, that the most important piece of Aalborg's historical heritage is a predominantly Viking one.

The atmospheric Lindholm Høje is a Viking burial ground where nearly 700 graves from the Iron Age and Viking Age are strewn around a hilltop pasture ringed by a wall of beech trees.

Many of the Viking graves are marked by stones placed in the oval outline of a Viking ship, with two larger end stones as stem and stern. At the end of the Viking era the whole area was buried under drifting sand and thus preserved until modern times.

Lindholm Høje Museet (☑99 31 74 40; www.nordmus.dk; Vendilavej 11, Nørresundby; adult/child 75kr/free; ⊙10am-5pm Tue-Sun Apr-Oct, to 4pm Nov-Mar) adjoins the site and explains its history, and has displays on finds made during its excavation. Murals behind the exhibits speculate on how the people of Lindholm lived.

Aalborg Zoo
ZOO

(☑96 31 29 29; www.aalborgzoo.dk; Mølleparkvej 63; adult/child 185/115kr; ⊙10am-7pm Jun-Aug, shorter hours rest of year; ▣) Teeming with feathered, furry and four-legged friends, it's no surprise this zoo is one of Denmark's most popular. Some 1200 animals call it home, including tigers, zebras, elephants, giraffes, chimpanzees, penguins, and brown and polar bears.

Aalborg

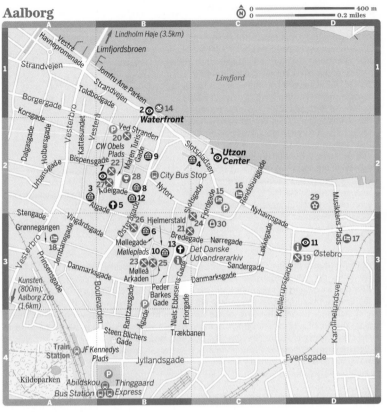

Aalborg

HISTORIC AALBORG

Aalborg has lost chunks of its historical quaintness to industrial and commercial development, but the centre contains enough ancient half-timbered buildings to give you an idea of the kind of affluence its Renaissance merchants enjoyed.

East of Budolfi Domkirke are three noteworthy buildings: the baroque-style **old town hall** (c 1762; Gammel Torv), at the corner of Østerågade and Gammel Torv; the five-storey **Jens Bangs Stenhus** (c 1624) at Østerågade 9; and **Jørgen Olufsens House** (c 1616) at Østerågade 25. The latter two are lovely Renaissance buildings. Jens Bang's house was built by a well-heeled merchant; today there's a jewellery store at ground level. Jørgen Olufsen's house was built by a wealthy mayor and now operates as a cosy Irish pub.

In addition, the neighbourhood around **Vor Frue Kirke** (Peder Barkes Gade; ◎10am-2pm Mon-Fri, to noon Sat) is worth a wander, particularly the cobbled L-shaped street of **Hjelmerstald**. Halfway down the street is **Langes Gård** (☑98 13 82 68; www.lange keramik.dk; Hjelmerstald 15; ◎showroom 10.30am-5.30pm Mon-Fri, 10am-2pm Sat), a courtyard full of fun sculptures and ceramics, with a showroom and workshop too.

Ask at the tourist office (p255) for the English-language *Good Old Aalborg* booklet, which maps out walking tours and provides details of buildings and sights along the way.

Gråbrødrekloster Museet   MUSEUM

(☑99 31 74 00; www.nordmus.dk; Algade 19; ◎10am-5pm Tue-Sat Apr-Oct, to 4pm Nov-Mar) This underground museum allows you to step off one of Aalborg's busiest shopping streets to explore the life of a Franciscan friary in medieval times. Entry is via an elevator outside Salling department store on Algade; the museum is free to enter, but you pay to ride the elevator (40kr per group).

Helligåndsklostret   MONASTERY

(☑98 12 02 05; www.aalborgkloster.dk; Klosterjordet 1; adult/child 50kr/free; ◎tours 2pm Tue & Thu Jul & Aug) An alley off CW Obels Plads leads to the rambling Monastery of the Holy Ghost, which dates from 1431 and is home to some fascinating frescoes. The interior can only be visited on a guided tour (conducted in Danish and English).

Budolfi Domkirke   CHURCH

(☑98 12 46 70; www.aalborgdomkirke.dk; Algade 40; ◎9am-4pm Mon-Fri, to 2pm Sat Jun-Aug, 9am-3pm Mon-Fri, to noon Sat Sep-May) This 12th-century cathedral marks the centre of the old town and its elegant carillon can be heard every hour, on the hour. Its whitewashed interior creates an almost Mediterranean ambience.

As you enter the cathedral from Algade, look up at the foyer ceiling to see colourful frescoes from around 1500. The interior boasts some beautifully carved items, including a gilded baroque altar and a richly detailed pulpit.

Aalborg Historiske Museum   MUSEUM

(☑99 31 74 00; www.nordmus.dk; Algade 48; adult/child 40kr/free; ◎10am-5pm Tue-Sat Apr-Dec, to 4pm Jan-Mar) Just west of Budolfi Domkirke is the town's history museum, with artefacts from prehistory to the present, and furnishings and interiors that hint at the wealth Aalborg's merchants enjoyed during the Renaissance.

Aalborghus Slot   HISTORIC BUILDING

(Slotspladsen; ◎dungeon 8am-3pm Mon-Fri May-Oct) **FREE** An anachronism among all the waterfront development, the mid-16th-century, half-timbered Aalborghus Slot is more an administrative office than a castle, but there's a small dungeon *(fangehul)* you can visit.

★ Festivals & Events

Aalborg Carnival   CULTURAL

(www.aalborgkarneval.dk; ◎May) Each year in late May, Aalborg kicks up its heels hosting this week-long festival (the biggest Carnival celebrations in northern Europe), when up to 100,000 participants and spectators shake their maracas and paint the town red.

⌂ Sleeping

With few exceptions, Aalborg's hotel scene is lacklustre.

CabInn Aalborg   HOTEL €

(☑96 20 30 00; www.cabinn.com; Fjordgade 20; s/d/tr from 495/625/820kr; @ ⊚) The cheap, reliable CabInn chain operates a large, central hotel across the road from the Utzon Center and neighbouring **Friis** (www.friisa alborg.dk; Nytorv 27; ⊙10am-7pm Mon-Fri, to 5pm Sat, 11am-4pm 1st Sun of month) shopping centre. All 239 rooms have TV and bathrooms; the super location may make up for the fact that there's little room for cat-swinging in the cheaper rooms. Breakfast costs 75kr.

BBBB i Aalborg
HOSTEL, CAMPGROUND €

(☎98 11 60 44; www.aalborg-vandrerhjem.dk; Skydebanevej 50; s/d/q 470/580/732kr; [P][@][🖙]) Formerly a Danhostel, this place is handy for boating activities on the fjord but it's hardly central. The surrounds are green and the accommodation is basic (all rooms have bathrooms). It's at the marina area about 3km west of the town centre; take bus 2 (which stops short of the hostel). Linen/breakfast costs 52/62kr; dorm beds are available in summer. There's an adjoining camping ground (adult/child/site 60/30/60kr) with budget cabins.

Villa Rosa
GUESTHOUSE €€

(☎98 12 13 38; www.villarosa.dk; Grønnegangen 4; r & apt incl breakfast 500-800kr; [P][🖙]) Book early to snare one of only six theatrically decorated rooms over three floors (no lift) at this late-19th-century villa. The three small self-contained apartments are the standout bargain – the English Room is especially lovely. Three rooms share a large bathroom and guest kitchen. It's the town's most interesting option, so the reasonable rates and central location are added bonuses.

First Hotel Aalborg
HOTEL €€

(☎98 10 14 00; www.firsthotels.com; Rendsburggade 5; d incl breakfast from 920kr; [P][@][🖙]) Some of the newly renovated rooms at this smart fjordside hotel near the Utzon Center (p250) have water views. Parking is available (95kr per day), and the central location and on-site gym and bar are a bonus. Best rates are found online.

Hotel Aalborg
HOTEL €€

(Sømandshjemmet; ☎98 12 19 00; www.hotel-aalborg.com; Østerbro 27; s/d from 795/945kr; [P][🖙]) This old seamen's hotel was once oddly placed, but encroaching harbourside redevelopment now sees it in the heart of the action, with Nordkraft (p254) and Musikkens Hus (p254) as neighbours. Comfortable, no-frills rooms are on offer, but there are plans for extension and makeover (including the addition of high-end rooms). Free parking, bike hire and friendly staff, too.

Eating

Good areas for dining include CW Obels Plads, Ved Stranden and Østerbro, around Nordkraft (p254).

★Penny Lane
CAFE, DELI €

(☎98 12 58 00; www.pennylanecafe.dk; Boulevarden 1; meals 89-135kr; ⊙8am-6pm Mon-Fri, to 5pm Sat, 10am-5pm Sun) This ace cafe-delicatessen (now with petite attached creperie) has an in-house bakery, so its freshly baked bread, local cheeses and cured meats are extremely picnic-worthy. There's a buzzing cafe offering a brunch platter or lunchtime sandwiches, salads and tapas plates.

Aurum 79
CAFE, DELI €

(☎93 89 79 14; www.aurum79.dk; Slotsgade 4; snacks & meals 35-95kr; ⊙10am-5.30pm Mon-Thu, to 6pm Fri, to 4pm Sat) An appealing pit stop, this on-trend deli-cafe has a short menu of toasties, sandwiches and platters utilising the fine hams, salamis and cheeses on sale.

Café KlosterTorvet
CAFE €

(☎98 16 86 11; www.klostertorvet.dk; CW Obels Plads 14; meals 39-91kr; ⊙10am-11pm Mon-Wed, to 1am Thu, to 3am Fri & Sat, to 10pm Sun) On a square full of great choices, KlosterTorvet is a cosy, laid-back cafe-bar with a studenty feel, thanks largely to its budget-friendly meals (baguettes, salads, pasta etc; kitchen closes 9pm), strong coffee and well-priced beer.

Føtex
SUPERMARKET €

(Slotsgade 8; ⊙8am-9pm) Central supermarket. Bakery opens from 7am.

Abbey Road
CAFE €€

(☎98 11 42 43; www.abbeyroadcafe.dk; Kjellerupsgade 1A; meals 89-175kr; ⊙8am-10pm Mon-Sat, 10am-5pm Sun) Opposite Nordkraft (p254) is this near-perfect all-day cafe-bar: quality coffee, tea and wines by the glass, mishmashed furniture and plentiful *hygge*. A little sister to the long-established Penny Lane, Abbey Road dispenses salads, sandwiches and tapas plates, plus some seriously tasty baked goods.

Caféministeriet
CAFE €€

(☎98 19 40 50; www.cafeministeriet.dk; Møllegade 19; dinner mains 105-189kr; ⊙9am-midnight Mon-Thu, to 2am Fri & Sat, to 11pm Sun) A fashionable crowd enjoys classic cafe fare here, preferably on the summer terrace in the centre of the traffic-free square, Mølleplads. The menu courses from fruity breakfasts to burgers by way of smørrebrød and tapas selections.

Pingvin
INTERNATIONAL €€

(☑98 11 11 66; www.cafepingvin.dk; Adelgade 12; dinner 4/6/8 tapas 218/258/288kr; ⊙noon-11pm Mon-Sat) This chic restaurant-bar offers a selection of up to 30 'tapas' (not so much shared dishes, but more of an individual tasting-plate approach). Enjoy small portions of Asian-style fish soup, coq au vin or beef carpaccio (with good vegetarian options).

★ Applaus
DANISH €€€

(☑71 72 81 81; www.restaurantapplaus.dk; Ved Stranden 9A; 10-course menu 395kr; ⊙5.30pm-12.30am Tue-Sat) Much effort goes into this kitchen's accomplished output – the results are fab, and the prices incredible value. You can order from the short menu, but the treat here is to put yourself in the staff's capable hands and enjoy the 10-course 'social menu' that runs from snacks to dessert.

Mortens Kro
DANISH €€€

(☑98 12 48 60; www.mortenskro.dk; Møllea 4-6; 3-course dinner menu from 348kr; ⊙5.30pm-1am Mon, 11am-3pm & 5.30pm-2am Tue-Sat) Among the best in town, sleek Mortens Kro is owned by celebrity chef Morten Nielsen. It's a stylish, well-hidden place where top-quality local, seasonal produce is showcased.

🍷 Drinking & Nightlife

Irish House
PUB

(☑98 14 18 17; www.theirishhouse.dk; Østerågade 25; ⊙1pm-1am Mon-Wed, to 2am Thu, noon-4am Fri & Sat, 2pm-midnight Sun) It's almost too beautiful a setting in which to get sloshed. Inside a 17th-century building loaded with timber carvings and stained glass, this pub offers live music Thursday to Saturday, big-screen sports, cheap pub grub and a range of beers.

Søgaards Bryghus
MICROBREWERY

(☑98 16 11 14; www.soegaardsbryghus.dk; CW Obels Plads 4; ⊙11am-11pm Mon-Wed, to midnight Thu, to late Fri & Sat, 10.30am-10pm Sun) Every Danish town worth its salt has a microbrewery, and Aalborg's is a cracker. With loads of outdoor seating and a long meaty menu of beer accompaniments, you could easily lose an afternoon sampling Søgaard's impressive array of brews. The attached Missing Bell Brewpub has 24 beers on tap.

☆ Entertainment

Inside a former power station, **Nordkraft** (www.nordkraft.dk; Kjellerups Torv; ⊙7am-11pm) is a cultural centre hosting a theatre, concert venue, art-house cinema, gallery and fitness centre and small tourist office, so it's worth popping in to see what's happening.

★ Musikkens Hus
CONCERT VENUE

(☑60 20 30 00; www.musikkenshus.dk; Musikkens Plads 1; ⊙10am-10pm) One of the new additions to the revitalised Aalborg waterfront (p250) is Musikkens Hus, a shiny, futuristic-looking concert hall that opened in 2014. Its ambitious design is by the Austrian firm Coop Himmelb(l)au; stop in to admire the interior and check out what's scheduled during your stay. The venue is home base for the Aalborg Symphony Orchestra.

🛈 Information

Det Danske Udvandrerarkiv (The Danish Emigration Archives; ☑99 31 42 20; www.udvandrerarkivet.dk; Arkivstræde 1; ⊙10am-4pm Mon-Wed, to 5pm Thu, to 3pm Fri) Behind Vor Frue Kirke; keeps records of Danish emigration history and (for a fee) helps foreigners of Danish descent trace their roots.

🛈 BUS & TRAIN TRAVEL

The good-value NT Travel Pass covers 24/72 hours of transport in Northern Jutland (train and bus) for 150/250kr. Buy the pass online (www.nordjyllandstrafikselskab.dk/travelpass) and it's delivered to your phone.

The Danish train system doesn't extend to northwest Jutland. If you're holidaying in the area in summer and don't have your own transport, you may come to rely on the number 99 bus that runs a few times daily from the top tip of Jutland (Grenen) along the northwest coast, taking in Skagen, Gammel Skagen, Hirtshals, Tornby Strand, Hjørring, Lønstrup, Løkken, Fårup Sommerland (where it connects with bus 200 to Aalborg) and Blokhus. Naturally, it also does the route in reverse.

This service runs only for about six weeks (the height of the summer season, when Danish schools are on vacation) from late June to early August. Pick up a timetable or call ☑98 11 11 11. The website for local bus company **Nordjyllands Trafikselskab** (www.nordjyllandstrafikselskab.dk) is primarily in Danish, but timetables should be easy enough to access (just look for 'Sommerbusser').

Forex (Ved Stranden 22; ⊘ 9.30am-5.30pm Mon-Fri, 10am-2pm Sat) Offers foreign exchange. There's a concentration of ATMs around Nytorv.

Tourist Office (☑ 99 31 75 00; www.visit aalborg.com; Nordkraft, Kjellerups Torv 5; ⊘ 10am-5.30pm Mon-Fri, to 2pm Sat) A small but well-stocked office inside **Nordkraft**.

❶ Getting There & Away

AIR

Aalborg Airport (www.aal.dk; Ny Lufthavnsvej 100, Nørresundby) is 6.5km northwest of the city centre. There are plentiful direct connections with Copenhagen, and direct flights to/from Oslo and Amsterdam. **Norwegian** (www.norwegian.com) and **Ryanair** (www.ryanair.com) have connections with London.

BUS

Long-distance buses stop at the **bus station** (John F Kennedys Plads 1) south of John F Kennedys Plads, behind the Kennedy Arkaden shopping centre, and not far from the train station.

From Aalborg you can reach most major Jutland towns on the X-bus network (see www.nordjyllandstrafikselskab.dk). **Abildskou** (☑ 70 21 08 88; www.abildskou.dk) bus 888 operates one to three times daily between Aalborg and Copenhagen (from 209kr, 5½ to 6½ hours), stopping at the capital's train station, bus station or airport. **Thinggaard Express** (☑ 98 11 66 00; www.expressbus.dk) bus 980 from Esbjerg to Frederikshavn runs once or twice daily, calling at Viborg and Aalborg en route.

TRAIN

Trains run hourly north to Frederikshavn (100kr, 1¼ hours), where there are onward connections to Skagen (from Aalborg 120kr, two hours).

About two trains hourly run south to Aarhus (197kr, 1½ hours) and to Copenhagen (438kr, 4½ to five hours).

❶ Getting Around

TO/FROM THE AIRPORT

Town bus 12 runs frequently between the bus station, city centre and airport (22kr). A taxi from the airport to the town centre should cost under 100kr.

BICYCLE

Bikes can be hired from **Munk's Eftf** (☑ 98 12 19 46; www.munk-aalborg.dk; Løkkegade 25; bike rental per day/week 100/500kr; ⊘ 8.30am-5.30pm Mon-Fri, 10am-1pm Sat). Note, however, that the store is closed for most of July.

A good option is to use the **Donkey Bike app** (www.donkey.bike/cities/bike-rental-aalborg) to find and rent bikes in town (100kr per day).

BUS

Almost all city buses (22kr, pay driver) leave from south of JF Kennedys Plads and pass the city-centre stops on Østerågade and Nytorv, near Burger King.

CAR & TAXI

There's free but time-restricted parking along many side streets, metered parking in the city centre and several large commercial car parks costing up to 18/160kr per hour/day. Call ☑ 98 10 10 10 for a taxi.

Frederikshavn

POP 23,500

A transport hub rather than a compelling destination, Frederikshavn's draw is as Jutland's busiest international ferry terminal, with **Stena Line** (☑ 96 20 02 00; www.stenaline.com; Færgehavnsvej 10) connections to Gothenburg (Sweden) and Oslo (Norway) plus frequent local ferries to the island of Læsø.

For arriving foot passengers, an overhead walkway leads from terminals to the **tourist office** (☑ 98 42 32 66; www.visitfrederikshavn.dk; Skandiatorv 1; ⊘ 9am-4pm Mon-Sat, 10am-2pm Sun Jul–mid-Aug, 9.30am-4pm Mon-Fri, 10am-1pm Sat mid-Aug–Jul) and central commercial district. The train station and the adjacent bus station are a 10-minute walk further north. Pedestrian shopping strip Danmarksgade has banks and other services. The city's one feature attraction is **Bangsbo** (☑ 98 42 31 11; www.kystmuseet.dk; Dronning Margrethesvej 6; adult/child 75kr/free; ⊘ 10am-4pm Mon-Fri, 11am-4pm Sat & Sun Jun-Aug, Mon-Fri Sep–May), a country estate-museum with botanical garden and WWII bunker fort. That's 3km south by bus 3.

Trains depart hourly to Aalborg (100kr, 1¼ hours), Aarhus (256kr, 2½ hours) and Skagen (60kr, 35 minutes). Daily **Thinggaard Express** (☑ 98 11 66 00; www.expressbus.dk) buses to Esbjerg call at Viborg and Aalborg en route.

Læsø

POP 1800

Home to small farms, sandy beaches, heathlands, dunes, salty traditions and charming small communities, the island of Læsø is just 28km off the coast of Frederikshavn but feels a hundred years away.

◉ Sights & Activities

The island has a few small towns (Vesterø Havn, Byrum and Østerby Havn), a couple of medieval churches, and a scattering of **museums**, one an old farm roofed with seaweed.

NORTHERN JUTLAND FREDERIKSHAVN

South of the main island is **Rønnerne**, an area of tidal wetlands with extensive seaside meadows and heathland, impressive birdlife and unique flora and fauna.

★ **Læsø Kur**   SPA
(☑98 49 13 22; www.saltkur.dk; Vesterø Havnegade 28, Vesterø Havn; day entry 275kr; ⊙9.30am-9.30pm mid-Jun–mid-Aug, to 5pm or 6pm rest of year) Take a salt bath at this beautifully designed wellness centre, inside a former church a short walk from the ferry port. Massages and body scrubs can be booked; there are steam baths and saunas as well as indoor and outdoor spa baths and various salt baths.

🛏 Sleeping & Eating

Den Gamle Elværk   HOSTEL €
(Læsø Vandrerhjem; ☑98 49 91 95; www.dge-laesoe.dk; Lærkevej 6, Vesterø Havn; d without/with bathroom 550/650kr; 🛜) This simple, cheerful hostel is well placed for the ferry, Læsø Kur and the beach. Half of the 24 rooms have private bathroom.

★ **Strandgaarden Badehotel**   HOTEL €€
(☑98 49 90 35; www.badehotel.eu; Strandvejen 8, Vesterø Havn; d without/with bathroom incl breakfast from 825/1175kr; ⊙Apr-Oct; 🛜) This 'bathing hotel' sits pretty as a picture under its thatched roof, with beds for most budgets plus bike hire, lovely gardens, easy access to the beach and an excellent restaurant.

Thorsen Fisk   SEAFOOD €
(☑23 60 64 55; Industrivej 1, Østerby Havn; meals 60-75kr; ⊙10am-5pm Mon-Sat, to 4pm Sun) There are some good choices at the waterfront main square in Østerby Havn, including this busy fish-seller where you can sample the local speciality, *jomfruhummer* (Norway lobsters, aka langoustine). There's also fresh, tasty fish and chips and *fiskefrikadeller* (fish cakes).

❶ Information

Tourist Office (☑98 49 92 42; www.visit laesoe.dk; Havnepladsen 1, Vesterø Havn; ⊙9am-3.30pm Mon-Fri, to 2pm Sat & Sun mid-Jun–mid-Aug, shorter hours rest of year) At the ferry terminal in Vesterø Havn.

❶ Getting There & Away

Færgeselskabet Læsø (☑98 49 90 22; www.laesoe-line.dk; Havnepladsen 1, Vesterø Havn; return adult/child Jul & Aug 270/130kr, Sep-Jun 210/100kr) sails three to seven times daily year-round between Læsø and Frederikshavn (adult/child/bicycle 55/50/45kr, 1½ hours). Car with passengers costs from 240kr each way.

❶ Getting Around

A free public bus runs between the villages of Vesterø Havn, Byrum and Østerby Havn; it operates in connection with ferry departure and arrival times.

Bicycles can be rented from **Jarvis Cykler** (☑98 49 94 44; www.jarvis-laesoe.dk; Vesterø Havnegade 29, Vesterø Havn; bike rental per day/week 80/400kr; ⊙9am-5.30pm Mon-Fri, to 1.30pm Sat & Sun), close to the ferry terminal. The tourist office has cycling maps outlining various routes.

Sæby

POP 8800

While busier Skagen is the inspiration behind world-renowned Scandinavian artists, Sæby could well be called the spiritual home (or at least the holiday house) of Danish literature.

◉ Sights

The pretty town was the inspiration behind Herman Bang's Sommerglæder *(Summer Pleasure)*. And those disappointed with Copenhagen's Little Mermaid might prefer the stature and presence of Sæby's Lady from the Sea statue. That's based on Henrik Ibsen's play of the same name, which he wrote after a summer spent in and around Sæby. It's at the photogenic, yacht-filled harbour, also home to fish-peddling restaurants and ice-cream kiosks. A path marked 'Kirkestien' leads up behind **Sæby Kirke** (www.saebykirke.dk; Strandgade 5; ⊙9am-4pm), a visually imposing church that is all that remains of a four-winged Carmelite monastery dating from 1470. Peep inside for beautiful medieval frescoes. Then walk along **Algade**, the town's oldest street lined with gardens, half-timbered houses and a handful of artists' studios and craft shops, showcasing ceramics, glass-blowing and amber. Here, the town's small, sweet **museum** (☑98 46 10 77; www.kystmuseet.dk; Algade 1; adult/child 75kr/free; ⊙11am-3pm Mon-Fri Feb-Dec) in a 17th-century timber-frame house displays more amber, a 1920s classroom and a classically furnished Victorian sitting room.

🛏 Sleeping & Eating

Sæby Fritidscenter & Hostel   HOSTEL €
(☑98 46 36 50; www.saebyfritidscenter.dk; Sæbygaardvej 32; d without/with bathroom from 460/600kr; 🖥🛜) This hostel is 1.5km west of the town centre, at a large sports centre and with plenty of open space. Facilities are of a high standard, and there's a choice of rooms

WORTH A TRIP

RÅBJERG MILE
••••••••••••••••••••••••••••••••••

Denmark's largest expanse of drifting sand dunes, **Råbjerg Mile** (off Kandestedvej) is an amazing natural phenomenon. These undulating, 40m-high hills are fun to explore and almost big enough to lose yourself in. The dunes were formed on the west coast during the great sand drift of the 16th century and have purposefully been left in a migratory state (moving towards the forest at a rate of 15m per year). The dunes leave a moist layer of sand behind, stretching westwards to Skagerrak.

Råbjerg Mile is 16km southwest of Skagen, signposted off Rte 40 on the road to Kandestederne. It's about 4km from Hulsig station, on the Frederikshavn–Skagen train line.

– the cheapest have shared bathrooms, while the A++ rooms (805kr) have bathroom, balcony and TV. There are also simple cottages.

★ **Aahøj**   GUESTHOUSE €€
(☑ 98 46 11 27; www.aahoj.dk; Hans Aabelsvej 1; s/d incl breakfast from 695/795kr; 🛜) The top pick in town, for its intimate atmosphere (nine homey rooms in an elegant 1896 villa), central location and idyllic riverside garden.

★ **Jacobs Fiskerestaurant**   SEAFOOD €€
(☑ 98 46 11 56; www.jacobsfiskerestaurant.dk; Havnen 7; buffet lunch/dinner 145/219kr; ⊙11.30am-10.30pm) In the harbour area, restaurants woo you with tables loaded with fresh fish bounty. Upstairs at Jacobs is a smart, light-filled restaurant offering buffet or à la carte choices (buffets are the best value for money); downstairs is Jacobs Fiskebix, a kiosk serving good-value fish and chips (70kr) to a beer-drinking, sun-seeking crowd.

Frøken Madsen's Spisehus   DANISH €€
(☑ 98 40 80 36; www.frk-madsen.dk; Pindborggade 1; mains 179-329kr; ⊙5-9pm Wed-Sat, plus noon-2pm Sat & Sun) Frøken Madsen serves up Danish favourites (and some exotic surprises) in a cosy building a block back from the main street. On warm evenings, tables on the garden terrace above the small river are in demand. Kind to the purse-strings is the weekend lunch buffet (129kr) and the Friday-night dinner buffet (229kr); book ahead.

ℹ️ Information

Tourist Office (☑ 98 46 12 44; www.visitsaeby.dk; Algade 14; ⊙9am-4pm Mon-Sat, 10am-2pm Sun Jul–mid-Aug, 9.30am-4pm Mon-Fri, 10am-1pm Sat mid-Aug–Jun) Sharing space with some galleries on the town's oldest street.

ℹ️ Getting There & Away

Hourly bus 973X stops at Sæby between Frederikshavn (32kr, 18 minutes) and Aalborg (80kr, 45 minutes). Slower bus 73 also goes to Frederikshavn (26 minutes). **Sæby bus station** (Stationspladsen 4) is 300m southwest of the town centre via Stationsvej off Vestergade.

You can rent bicycles from **Cykelgården** (☑ 98 46 14 10; Søndergade 6A; bike hire per day/week 90/390kr; ⊙9am-5.30pm Mon-Fri, to noon Sat).

Skagen
POP 8200

Located at Jutland's northern tip where the Baltic meets the North Sea, Skagen (pronounced 'skain') features a rich art heritage, fresh seafood, photogenic neighbourhoods and classic character that combine to create a delicious slice of Denmark.

In the mid-19th century, artists flocked here, charmed by the radiant light's impact on the ruggedly beautiful landscape. Now tourists come in droves, drawn by an intoxicating combination of the busy working harbour, long sandy beaches and buzzing holiday atmosphere. The town gets packed in summer but maintains its charm, especially in the intimate, older neighbourhoods filled with distinctive yellow houses framed by white-picket fences and red-tiled roofs.

Catering to the tourist influx are numerous museums, art galleries, bike-rental outlets, ice-creameries and harbourside restaurants. Come and see why half the Danish population lights up whenever the town's name is mentioned.

⊙ Sights

The closest **beach** to town is accessed from Østre Strandvej; east-coast beaches are sheltered and good for families, while the west coast is wilder.

Art lovers should consider a combination ticket (180kr) that gives admission to Skagens Museum, Anchers Hus and Drachmanns Hus.

Skagen

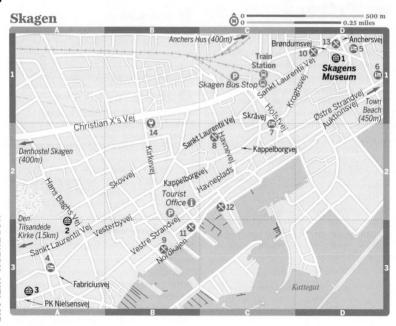

Skagen

◎ Top Sights

◎ Sights

🛏 Sleeping

🍴 Eating

🍷 Drinking & Nightlife

★ **Grenen**   BEACH

Appropriately enough for such a neat and ordered country, Denmark doesn't end untidily at its most northerly point, but on a neat finger of sand just a few metres wide. You can actually paddle at its tip, where the waters of the Kattegat (an arm of the Baltic Sea) and Skagerrak (part of the North Sea) clash, and you can put one foot in each sea – but not too far. Bathing here is forbidden because of the ferocious tidal currents.

The tip is the culmination of a long, curving sweep of sand at Grenen, about 3km northeast of Skagen along Rte 40. Where the road ends there's a car park, an excellent restaurant and a small art gallery. From the car park the 20-minute walk up the long, sweeping stretch of sand passes the grave of writer Holger Drachmann (1846–1908).

The tractor-pulled bus, the **Sandormen** (☑ 40 30 50 42; www.sandormen.dk; Grenen; adult/child return 30/15kr; ☉ Apr-Oct; 🚼), can take you out to the point; it leaves from the car park at Grenen from 10am daily and runs regularly all day, according to demand.

★ **Skagens Museum**   MUSEUM

(☑ 98 44 64 44; www.skagensmuseum.dk; Brøndumsvej 4; adult/child 100kr/free; ☉ 10am-5pm May-Aug, Tue-Sun Mar, Apr, Sep & Oct, Thu-Sun Nov-Feb; 🚼) This wonderful gallery showcases the outstanding art that was produced in Skagen between 1870 and 1930. Artists discovered

Skagen's luminous light and its wind-blasted heath-and-dune landscape in the mid-19th century and fixed eagerly on the romantic imagery of the area's fishing life that had earned the people of Skagen a hard living for centuries. Their work established a vivid figurative style of painting that became known internationally as the 'Skagen School'.

Drachmanns Hus   MUSEUM
(☑ 98 44 64 44; www.skagenskunstmuseer.dk; Hans Baghs Vej 21; adult/child 50kr/free, incl Skagens Museum & Anchers Hus 180kr/free; ☉11am-4pm May-Aug, Tue-Sat Apr & Sep, closed Oct-Mar) West of the town centre, this sweet museum was the home of renowned Skagen painter (and poet) Holger Drachmann.

Anchers Hus   MUSEUM
(☑ 98 44 64 44; www.skagenkunstmuseer.dk; Markvej 2; adult/child 80kr/free, incl Skagens Museum & Drachmanns Hus 180kr/free; ☉11am-5pm May-Aug, reduced hours Sep-Apr, closed Dec & Jan) Visit the atmospheric former home of renowned Skagen painters Anna and Michael Ancher, preserved in time exactly the same as when Anna Ancher died in 1935. You can inspect their personal possessions and more than 280 pieces of art. There is also a cafe, small shop and a separate gallery for temporary exhibitions.

Skagen Kystmuseet   MUSEUM
(Skagen By- og Egnsmuseum; ☑ 98 44 47 60; www.kystmuseet.dk; PK Nielsensvej 8; adult/child 75kr/free; ☉10am-4pm Mon-Fri, 11am-4pm Sat & Sun Jun-Aug, closed Sat & Sun rest of year; ⊞) Evocatively presented, this open-air museum, 200m southwest of the harbour, depicts Skagen's maritime history and gives an insight into the traditional fishing community that so transfixed the Skagen artists (but without the romanticism!).

Skagen Odde Naturcenter   VISITOR CENTRE
(☑ 96 79 06 06; www.skagen-natur.dk; Bøjlevejen 66; adult/child 70/30kr; ☉10am-4pm Mon-Fri, from 11am Sat & Sun May-Oct; ⊞) In a beautiful Utzon-designed building on the northern outskirts of town, this centre gives an insight into the natural elements that surround Skagen and make it unique. It's pricey, but worth a visit if you're into architecture. There are also changing art exhibitions, and family activities.

Den Tilsandede Kirke   RUINS
(Gamle Landevej 63) The 'sand-covered church', built during the late 14th century, was once the region's biggest church. It fell victim to a sand drift that began in the 17th century

and became progressively worse – so much so that churchgoers eventually had to dig their way in. In 1795 the relentless sand drift broke the will of the congregation and the church was closed. The main part of the church was torn down in 1810 but the photogenic whitewashed **tower** (Gamle Landevej 63; adult/child 20kr/free; ☉10am-6pm Jun-Aug, Sat & Sun Apr, May & Sep) still stands. You can enter and climb the stairs for a scenic view.

The tower and the surrounding area comprise part of **Skagen Klitplantage**, a nature reserve. It's about 5km south of Skagen and well signposted from Rte 40. The nicest way to get here is by bike; take Gamle Landevej from Skagen.

🛏 Sleeping

Danhostel Skagen   HOSTEL €
(☑ 98 44 22 00; www.danhostelskagen.dk; Rolighedsvej 2; dm/s/d 180/525/625kr; ☉Mar-Nov; ⓟ🅟) Always a hive of activity, this hostel is modern, functional and clean. It's decent value, particularly for families or groups. Low-season prices drop sharply. It's 1km towards Frederikshavn from the Skagen train station (if you're coming by train, get off at Frederikshavnsvej).

Grenen Strand Camping   CAMPGROUND €
(☑ 63 60 63 61; www.campone.dk/grenen; Fyrvej 16; site 55-110kr, plus per adult/child 87/55kr; ☉Apr-Oct; @🅟) This busy, well-organised place is in a fine seaside location on the outskirts of town towards Grenen. There's plenty of tree cover and good facilities, including wee four-bed cabins.

★Badepension Marienlund   GUESTHOUSE €€
(☑ 28 12 13 20; www.marienlund.dk; Fabriciusvej 8; s/d incl breakfast 680/1190kr; ☉Apr-Oct; ⓟ🅟) A cosy atmosphere, idyllic garden and pretty lounge and breakfast areas make Marienlund a top option. There are only 14 rooms, all light, white and simply furnished (all with bathrooms). You'll find the hotel in a peaceful residential neighbourhood.

Brøndums Hotel   HOTEL €€
(☑ 98 44 15 55; www.broendums-hotel.dk; Anchersvej 3; s/d with shared bathroom incl breakfast from 595/895kr; 🅟) This charming hotel is steeped in history – it had close associations with the Skagen artists in its heyday. There have been renovations to bring the decor up to date, but prices can be very steep given bathrooms are shared. There's a cheaper nearby annexe, Admiralgaarden, with more rooms (some with bathrooms).

Hotel Plesner
BOUTIQUE HOTEL **€€**

(☑98 44 68 44; www.hotelplesner.dk; Holstvej 8; s/d incl breakfast 1395/1495kr; ☜) Candy-striped designer touches run throughout this boutique hotel, home to 17 fresh, petite guest rooms. Highlights include an alluring garden lounge (where afternoon tea is served in summer) and a smart breakfast spread.

Finns B&B
GUESTHOUSE **€€**

(☑98 45 01 55; www.finns.dk; Østre Strandvej 63; s/d incl breakfast from 500/775kr; ☺May–mid-Sep; ☜) Take a 1923-vintage 'log cabin' built for a Norwegian count, fill it with art, antiques and memorabilia, and you have this fabulously quirky slumber spot. Gay-friendly, TV-free and adults-only (no kids under 15), Finns is a stone's throw from the beach and has six individually decorated rooms (a few with shared bathroom). Three-night minimum in peak summer.

✖ Eating

A handful of seafood shacks line the harbour, where prawns/shrimp *(rejer)* are the favourite order. For more salubrious summer dinners it's advisable to make reservations when the town is heaving.

★ Museumscaféen
CAFE **€**

(www.skagensmuseum.dk; Skagens Museum, Brøndumsvej; lunch 90-100kr; ☺10.30am-4.30pm May-Aug, 11.30am-4.30pm Tue-Sun Sep & Oct) For lunch or a cuppa in a magical setting, head to the Garden House cafe at Skagens Museum (p258), serving lunchtime dishes plus a super spread of home-baked cakes and tarts. Note: you don't need to pay the museum's admission to visit the cafe.

Jorgens Spisehus
DANISH **€**

(☑98 44 26 24; www.joergensspisehus.dk; Sardinvej 7; mains 70-199kr; ☺10am-7.30pm Tue-Fri, from 11am Sat & Sun) A down-to-earth place where you can depend on no-fuss traditional dishes and cheerful service. The decor and ambience are nothing to get excited about but the 79kr dish of the day *(dagens ret)* will put a smile on your face. Specialities include *stjerneskud* (one pan-fried and one steamed fish fillet, plus shrimp and asparagus on bread). Kitchen closes 7pm.

Skagen Fiskerestaurant
SEAFOOD **€€**

(☑98 44 35 44; www.skagenfiskerestaurant.dk; Fiskehuskajen 13; mains 120-299kr; ☺11am-10pm Apr-Oct, shorter hours rest of year) This dockside place has a winning sales pitch: fresh, casual cafe fare at lunch and dinner *(fiskefrikadeller,* creamy fish soup, fish and chips), an in-demand outdoor terrace and summertime live music. It's rustic and fun – you know a place doesn't take itself too seriously when the floor is covered in sand.

Pakhuset
SEAFOOD **€€**

(☑98 44 20 00; www.pakhuset-skagen.dk; Rødspættevej 6; cafe mains 95-230kr; ☺cafe 11am-late) Seafood is the star at Pakhuset, from simple *fiskefrikadeller* (fish cakes) with remoulade to swoon-inducing flambéed Norwegian lobster tails. It has long hours and a superb ambience both outdoors (slap bang on the harbour) and indoors (think wooden beams and cheerful ship mastheads). Fine-dine in the restaurant upstairs (three courses 395kr, from 6pm), or keep it cheaper in the downstairs cafe.

DON'T MISS

GAMMEL SKAGEN & OLD RUTH

Refined **Gammel Skagen** ('Old Skagen', also known as Højen), is renowned for its gorgeous sunsets and well-heeled summer residents. It was a fishing hamlet before sandstorms ravaged this windswept area and forced many of its inhabitants to move 4km west to Skagen on the more protected east coast. Coming here makes a pleasant cycle ride. Or, given the funds, stay and/or dine at beautifully positioned **Ruths Hotel** (☑98 44 11 24; www.ruths-hotel.dk; Hans Ruths Vej 1, Gammel Skagen; r incl breakfast from 1750kr; P☜☲), one of Denmark's grand bathing hotels. As well as a wellness centre and stylish modern-meets-traditional decor, there are two acclaimed restaurants. Intimate **Ruths Gourmet** (4/5/8 courses 795/865/1295kr, from 6pm, weekends only off-season) spotlights modern Danish cuisine with an innovative regional focus. Book well ahead to score one of the mere 22 seats. Otherwise, **Ruths Brasserie** (meals 180kr to 345kr) is a très bon backup option with a marvellous terrace and an all-day menu of classic French dishes including *moules-frites, escargot* and duck confit.

Jakobs Café & Bar INTERNATIONAL €€
(☑98 44 16 90; www.jakobscafe.dk; Havnevej 4; lunch 59-159kr, dinner mains 190-280kr; ☺9am-2am Mon-Thu, to 3.30am Fri & Sat, to midnight Sun; 🖥) The terrace of this all-day cafe-bar is primed for people-watching, and the comprehensive menu has favourites such as brunch plates, smørrebrød, burgers, salads and steaks. On summer nights the place is generally heaving with young Danes enjoying warm-up drinks. The kitchen closes at 9pm (10pm Friday and Saturday); DJs or live music kick off at 10.30pm.

Brøndums Hotel
Restaurant FRENCH, DANISH €€€
(☑98 44 10 55; www.broendums-hotel.dk; Anchersvej 3; lunch 135-235kr, dinner mains 235-355kr; ☺11.30am-9pm) French cuisine is the main influence on Brøndums' menu, under the helm of renowned, Michelin-awarded chef Michel Michaud. There's lots of fish and classic Danish smørrebrød at lunchtime. Meals are served in the old-world ambience of the dining room. There's also a picture-perfect garden for alfresco dining.

Self-Catering
★Slagter Munch DELI €
(☑98 44 37 33; www.munch-skagen.dk; Sankt Laurentii Vej 1; ☺9am-5.30pm Mon-Fri, 8am-1pm Sat) The queues out the door attest to this butcher's reputation for award-winning *skinke* (ham) and sausages. There's also a selection of fine, picnic-worthy salads and deli produce for sale.

Krages Bageri BAKERY, CAFE €
(☑98 44 55 20; Sankt Laurentii Vej 104; ☺6am-5.30pm Mon-Fri, to 4pm Sat & Sun) A cracker bakery well placed for museum visits, full of fresh bread, cakes and pastries. Sandwiches, quiches and salads too.

Drinking

Skagen Bryghus MICROBREWERY
(☑98 45 00 50; www.skagenbryghus.dk; Kirkevej 10; ☺10.30am-6pm Mon-Thu, to 7pm Fri & Sat, to 4pm Sun) Lots of summertime live music, a snack-worthy menu and a big beer garden make this microbrewery an ideal spot for a lazy afternoon. Sample your way through the beer varieties, starting with the award-winning Drachmann pilsner.

ℹ Information

Tourist Office (☑98 44 13 77; www.skagen-tourist.dk; Vestre Strandvej 10;

WORTH A TRIP

TORNBY STRAND

If all you're after is a long stretch of white sand, **Tornby Strand** (Strandvej) delivers it in spades (and buckets), 5km south of Hirtshals. As the sand is compact enough to drive on, many park next to the breakers. Hiking is possible among the high mounded dunes and into the coastal woodlands that back the southern side of the beach.

Around 1km inland there's a year-round **camping ground** (☑98 97 78 77; www.tornbystrandcamping.dk; Strandvejen 13; per adult/child/site 85/50/60kr; 🖥🏊) with indoor and outdoor pools, mini-golf and playroom as well as family-size cabins and budget 'transit rooms' (double 250kr to 350kr) – ideal if all you need is a bed before a ferry departure.

☺9am-4pm Mon-Sat, 10am-2pm Sun late Jun–mid-Aug, shorter hours rest of year) In front of the harbour.

ℹ Getting There & Away

In July and August only, 'Skagerakkeren' bus 99 (www.nordjyllandstrafikselskab.dk) runs along the west coast connecting Skagen to Gammel Skagen, Tversted, Hirtshals, Løkken, Fårup Sommerland and Blokhus. **Buses** (Banegårdspladsen, Sankt Laurentii Vej) stop outside the train station, which is on the long main street Sankt Laurentii Vej, 100m north of the pedestrian town centre. Trains run roughly hourly to Frederikshavn (60kr, 35 minutes), where you can change for destinations further south.

ℹ Getting Around

BICYCLE
The best way to get around is by bike and loads of places offer rental. **Skagen CykelUdlejning** (☑98 44 10 70; www.skagencykeludlejning.dk; Banegårdspladsen, Sankt Laurentii Vej; bike hire per day/week 90/375kr; ☺9am-5pm Apr–mid-Sep) is adjacent to the train station and has a range of bikes. It has a second, year-round **outlet** (☑98 44 10 70; www.skagencykeludlejning.dk; Fiskergangen 10) close to the harbour, inside the bike shop at Fiskergangen 10.

BUS
Daily from late June to early August Bybus route 1 (www.nordjyllandstrafikselskab.dk) takes in the major sites, from the Grenen (p258) car park to Gammel Skagen and Den Tilsandede Kirke (p259). Tickets are 22kr, or buy a 50kr day pass from the tourist office.

CAR

Parking is at a premium in summer – there are metered car parks (11kr per hour, from 9am to 6pm) beside and in front of the tourist office (p261) and beside the train station.

TAXI

Taxis are available at the train station or you can call and order one on ☑ 98 44 22 44.

Hirtshals

POP 6000

Frequented by discount-hungry Norwegians and largely inhabited by hardened seamen, this town's appearance won't take your breath away. Despite a standout aquarium, Hirtshals is most useful for its ferry connections to Iceland, the Faroe Islands and Norway.

It's a five-minute walk from Lilleheden station on the Hjørring-Hirtshals train line.

If you've always wondered what lurks beneath, head to the impressive **Nordsøen Oceanarium** (☑ 98 94 44 44; www.nordsoen oceanarium.dk; Willemoesvej 2; adult/child 170/90kr; ☺ 9am-6pm Jul & Aug, 10am-4pm or 5pm rest of year, closed early Jan; ⚙), home to one of the largest aquariums in northern Europe. Here, 4.5 million litres of seawater is home to thousands of elegantly balletic mackerel and herring in a huge, four-storey tank. Check the website for feeding times: in summer, these are 11am and 3pm in the oceanarium (done by a diver with a video camera), and noon and 4pm at the outdoor seal pool.

There's a handful of motels and hotels in town, including **Hotel Hirtshals** (☑ 98 94 20 77; www.hotelhirtshals.dk; Havnegade 2; s/d/f incl breakfast from 845/950/1645kr; 🛜) on the main square above the fishing harbour. But if awaiting boats, you might prefer to stay in bigger, more atmospheric **Hjørring**, 17km south, where attractive, midrange **Hotel Phønix** (☑ 98 92 54 55; www.phoenix-hjoerring.dk; Jernbanegade 6; s/d incl breakfast from 695/895kr; P @ 🛜) is handy for the train station.

For pre-ferry stock-ups, Hirtshals has supermarkets on Jørgen Fibigersgade. There are dining and alfresco drinking choices on the waterfront area and on Hjørringgade where **Slagter Winther** (☑ 98 94 16 11; www. slagterwinther.dk; ☺ 9am-9.30pm) is a quality deli selling discounted meats and booze.

Southwest of the train station and the ferry terminals there are ATMs and a small **Tourist Office** (☑ 98 94 22 20; www.visithirtshals.dk; Jyllandsgade 10; ☺ 9am-4pm Mon-Fri, to 1pm Sat) along Nørregade, the main pedestrian street.

🛈 Getting There & Away

BOAT

International ferry links:

Color Line (www.colorline.com; Norgeskajen 2) To Kristiansand and Larvik (Norway).

Fjord Line (www.fjordline.com; Containerkajen 4) Fast catamaran to Kristiansand (mid-May to mid-September) plus year-round ferry to Stavanger and Bergen, and to Langesund (all in Norway).

Smyril Line (www.smyrilline.com; Containerkajen 4) Weekly departures to the Faroe Islands and Iceland.

For details see the Transport chapter (p301) and individual websites.

BUS

Summer-only bus 99 stops at Nordsøen Oceanarium, beaches Tornby Strand and Løkken, plus at Hirtshals and Hjørring stations.

TRAIN

The train station is on Havnegade, west of the ferry terminals. Private trains run at least hourly to Hjørring (32kr, 22 minutes). From there, regular DSB services include:

Aalborg (80kr, 40 minutes)

Aarhus (232kr, two hours)

Frederikshavn (50kr, 30 minutes)

Skagen (60kr, 1¼ hours) Changing trains at Frederikshavn.

Løkken

POP 1600

A generation of Danish holidaymakers may raise an eyebrow when they read this, but Løkken is now an appealing holiday spot for all ages. It was once the renowned summer habitat of teenage party-animals, but has matured considerably since those heady days and now draws a tamer crowd, with a focus on activities like surfing.

The former fishing town's biggest drawcard is its wide, sandy beach, and the requisite shops, ice creameries and cafes welcome the summer bombardment. Colder months see the town go into hibernation.

🏃 Activities

★ **Løkken Beach**   BEACH

Go looking for your own beachside fun at Løkken's long strand, lined with neat rows of white wooden beach huts and a few stout little fishing vessels (interestingly, the 485 beach huts are stored inland during winter). Check out the kitesurfers taking advantage of west-coast winds (BYO gear), or join a surfing lesson with **North Shore Surf School** (☑20 70 86 43; www.northshoresurf.dk; Sønder Strandvej 18; 2hr surf lesson 350kr; ☺ Jul & Aug; ♿).

🛏 Sleeping & Eating

★**Villa Vendel**   GUESTHOUSE €€
(☑20 65 38 56; www.villavendel.dk; Harald Fischers Vej 12; r & apt 550-950kr; ☎) East of Torvet is this delightful option, a member of the Small Elegant Hotels group (an apt description), with four rooms (all with bathrooms) and two apartments. There's a classy old-world feel with wooden floors and neutral decor, plus a guest kitchen and a large garden.

North Shore Surf Café   CAFE €
(☑20 70 86 43; www.northshoresurf.dk; Sønder Strandvej 18; snacks & meals 40-120kr; ☺from 10am Jul & Aug) Drop by this shack, nestled among the dunes behind Løkken Beach, for a coffee, ice cream or snack (toasties, fish and chips, prawns etc). The outdoor terrace is a little suntrap blocked from onshore winds. Closing time depends on the weather, and the various activities organised by North Shore Surf School.

Restaurant Løkken Badehotel   DANISH €€
(☑98 99 22 00; www.restaurantlb.dk; Torvet 8; lunch 89-159kr, dinner mains 159-239kr; ☺9am-9pm) This sunshine-yellow hotel sits in pole position on Torvet, with a large terrace and a menu of well-prepared, old-school Danish favourites, from lunchtime smørrebrød to *pandestegt rødspætte* (pan-fried plaice).

ⓘ Information

Tourist Office (☑98 99 10 09; www.loekken. dk; Jyllandsgade 15; ☺10am-4pm Mon-Fri, 9am-4pm Sat Jul & Aug, 10am-3pm Mon-Fri, 9am-noon Sat Sep-Jun) Helpful office beside the SuperBrugsen supermarket.

ⓘ Getting There & Away

Frequent bus 71 stops in Løkken between Hjørring (42kr, 30 minutes) and Aalborg (60kr, 70 minutes). Løkken is also on the summertime bus 99 route.

Around Løkken

★**Rubjerg Knude**   LIGHTHOUSE
(www.rubjergknude.dk; Fyrvejen) About 14km north of Løkken (en route to the town of Lønstrup (p263)) is Rubjerg Knude, an area of sand dunes that show just how Mother Nature calls the shots on this wind-whipped coast. **Rubjerg Knude Fyr** (the lighthouse)

stood 200m inland when it opened in 1900, 60m above sea level. Over time the sea moved closer, and by the late 1960s the lighthouse was closed because frequent heavy sand drifts were making its light near-impossible to see from the sea.

In 1980 the lighthouse opened as a museum with exhibitions about the migrating sands, but had to close in 2002 as the sand drift was burying the museum buildings. Today, it attracts tourists as a photogenic landmark and curiosity, partly submerged in sand. It is expected that the lighthouse will fall into the sea in the coming decade, due to coastal erosion.

Lønstrup   VILLAGE
Some 15km north of Løkken (past Rubjerg Knude), this beachside resort has an upmarket feel and streets lined with artist studios, galleries and ceramicists. It's worth a visit for a stroll and to check out the cafes.

Fårup Sommerland   AMUSEMENT PARK
(☑98 88 16 00; www.faarupsommerland.dk; Pirupvejen 147, Blokhus; 240-275kr; ☺from 10am mid-Jun–mid-Aug, also open select days May, Sep & Oct) One of the most-visited Danish attractions, this wholesome (and pricey) amusement park caters to holidaying families in search of distractions – of which there are plenty, from roller coasters to kiddie-safe rides and a huge waterpark. Everyone over the age of three pays the same entrance fee.

Klitmøller

POP 900

Klitmøller's windy ways and curving waves have transformed the small fishing village into one of Europe's premier surfing destinations, known colloquially as 'Cold Hawaii'. It's a small holiday settlement of summer houses and fisherfolk, where wetsuit-clad surfers roam the streets and outdoorsy folk get around on bikes, seemingly oblivious to the cracking wind.

Klitmøller hosts a PWA (Professional Windsurfing Association) world cup event each September.

🏃 Activities

Do not despair if you're not world-championship windsurfing material. In addition to the challenging waves of the North Sea, the calmer waters of the lake Vandet Sø or the Limfjord are close by, so there are conditions suitable for all levels.

DON'T MISS

THY NATIONAL PARK

One of Denmark's handful of newly protected spaces, **Thy National Park** (http://eng. nationalparkthy.dk) stretches 55km south along the North Sea coast, covering an area of 244 sq km of coastline, dunes, lakes, pine forest and moors. There are plenty of windswept, wide-open spaces to access: marked hiking, cycling and horse-riding trails, bird-watching opportunities, big waves, photogenic beaches, plus a good dose of history in fishing hamlets and WWII-era German bunkers.

Local tourist offices can help with information on activities within the park, or check out www.visitthy.dk. A small park information centre lives at **Stenbjerg Landingsplads** (Stenbjergvej; ⊙1-5pm Apr-Oct), an atmospheric cluster of fishermen's huts off Rte 181.

Also worth a stop is the small beach resort of **Nørre Vorupør**, where fishing vessels are winched up onto the sand. There's a *havbad* (sea bath) here, with a concrete pool built in the North Sea shallows to enable safe swimming.

Westwind Klitmøller
SURFING

(☑97 97 56 56; http://klitmoller.westwind.dk; Ørhagevej 150; ⊙mid-Mar–Oct) Long-established Westwind has enthusiastic surfers keen to show you the ropes of surfing, windsurfing, kitesurfing and stand-up paddle boarding (SUP), in English, German or Danish. Multi-day surf camps are also offered.

Cold Hawaii Surf Camp
SURFING

(☑29 10 88 73; www.coldhawaiisurfcamp.com; Ørhagevej 151) There's an excellent backstory to how this young Israeli-Tahitian couple with fine surfing pedigrees ended up in Klitmøller. They run a surf shop, and offer learn-to-surf lessons and multiday surf camps. There's also gear rental.

🛏 Sleeping

Travellers who sign up for surf camps can arrange accommodation with the surf companies. Otherwise, there is a handful of guesthouses and a camping ground all in high demand in summer. More accommodation is available down the road in Nørre Vorupør.

Gaarden Klitmøller
GUESTHOUSE €

(☑97 97 56 80; www.gaardenklitmoller.dk; Kalles Mark 2; r without bathroom 400-550kr; 🛜) Part of this old building has been converted into a colourful guesthouse, with four guest rooms sharing a bathroom, living space, kitchenette and garden terrace. It's lovely and homely.

Nystrup Camping
CAMPGROUND €

(☑97 97 52 49; www.nystrupcamping.dk; Trøjborgvej 22; per adult/child 84/39kr, site 30-80kr; ⊙Mar-Oct; 🛜) Populated by windblown types and littered with surfing kits, this popular, well-run ground has plenty of trees for shelter and decent facilities including cabins, bike hire and a playground.

Guesthouse Klitmøller
GUESTHOUSE €€

(☑41 66 04 77; www.guesthouse-klitmoller.dk; Ørhagevej 84; d without bathroom 650-750kr, with bathroom 950kr; 🛜) Strong evidence of the rebirth of Klitmøller, this guesthouse has big-city style in its smart timber exterior and Nordic simplicity in its white interior. There are 11 rooms, three with private bathroom.

🍴 Eating & Drinking

There's a supermarket and a handful of eateries along the main street, Ørhagevej, plus food trucks in summer. Don't miss tasting local brews from Thisted Bryghus, including the aromatic Cold Hawaii 'New Nordic Beer'.

Kesses Hus
CRÊPES €

(☑61 69 38 16; www.kesseshus.dk; Bavnbak 4; pancakes 40-90kr; ⊙11am-9pm Jul–mid-Aug, shorter hours Apr-Jun & mid-Aug–Oct) Delicious savoury galettes and sweet pancakes are on offer here, with some gourmet fillings. Start with smoked hake with green pea purée or goat's cheese with parsley pesto and tomato compote.

Fiskerestaurant Niels Juel
SEAFOOD €€

(☑69 13 51 88; www.nielsjuel.com; Ørhagevej 150; fish buffet adult/child 189/59kr; ⊙5.30-9pm Tue-Sun May-Sep) The large terrace of this elevated restaurant – whitewashed under a thatched roof – is the best spot to watch the surfing action. The good-value fish buffet heaves with herrings, prawns and salmon.

ⓘ Getting There & Away

Bus 322 runs ten/three times daily on weekdays/weekends, between Klitmøller and Thisted (32kr, 30 minutes). From there, buses 70/970X run to Aalborg (140kr, 2¼/1¾ hours) and you can reach Viborg by either 940X bus (130kr, 1¾ hours, eight daily) or train (184kr, up to three hours, four daily with a change in Struer).

Understand Denmark

Denmark Today

The Danes are, overwhelmingly, a happy bunch. If you believe the contentment surveys and liveability lists, Denmark is among the happiest nations on earth, enjoying some of the best quality of life. It's not hard to see why: it has among the highest per-capita GDPs in the EU and unemployment is relatively low. Education is free, work–life balance is paramount, and Danish social-welfare programs are the envy of many (just ask Bernie Sanders). Plus: Danes know how to *hygge* (be cosy)!

Best on Film

Babette's Feast (1987) Set in a rugged west-coast village in 1871. Setting the gold standard for food films to follow.

Pelle the Conqueror (1987) Award-winning depiction of the life of an immigrant in 19th-century Denmark.

Festen (The Celebration; 1998) The first of the Dogme95 movies, from celebrated writer-director Thomas Vinterberg.

In a Better World (2010) Playground bullying, conflicting moral choices – engineered to question the cosy stereotype of Denmark.

A Royal Affair (2012) A mad king, a young queen, an illicit affair. Period drama based on a true story.

Best in Print

The Complete Fairy Tales (Hans Christian Andersen; 1874) The most famous Danish book in the world.

Either/Or (Søren Kierkegaard; 1843) By the father of existentialism.

Miss Smilla's Feeling for Snow (Peter Høeg; 1992) A worldwide hit set largely in Copenhagen.

The Year of Living Danishly (Helen Russell; 2015) A Brit discovers the secrets of Danish life.

We, the Drowned (Carsten Jensen; 2006) An epic tale of sailors from seafaring Marstal on Ærø.

Happiness & Harmony?

There is more to the Danes' story of contentment. Stroll around almost any Danish town and you'll experience some of the most harmonious civic spaces anywhere. Look a bit closer, however, and (as in a Hans Christian Andersen fable) you'll find a darker side, too. As with other European nations, there's been a gradual shift to the political right in this famously liberal nation. Concern has grown over immigration – particularly from Muslim countries – and an erosion of traditional values.

For all the talk of assimilation and the comprehensive state effort to achieve it, racial, cultural and religious fault lines and prejudices remain. This challenge to tolerance has unnerved many Danes; many of them avoid confronting their underlying resentment towards non-European newcomers. In mid-2015 the issue was highlighted when the anti-immigration, anti-EU Danish People's Party (DPP) won 21% of the vote at the general election, becoming the second-largest party in the parliament. Pollsters had notably underestimated the party's support – possibly due to some voters' reluctance to openly admit their backing of DPP policies.

Politics & Economics

Danish politics is a complex, multiparty beast, and there is a long tradition of minority governments and consensus politics (watch the *Borgen* TV series for a fictional primer). As of the 2015 elections, nine parties are represented in parliament; government is formed by coalition.

The political pendulum swung right in the most recent general election, held in 2015 amid concerns over immigration and the government's tough economic reforms. After one term in power, the left-leaning coalition led by Social Democrat Helle Thorning-Schmidt (Denmark's first female prime minister) was ousted and a centre-right coalition took its place. Denmark's current prime minister is Lars Løkke Rasmussen, who was PM before Thorning-Schmidt won power in 2011. Time will tell if the pendulum swings again at the next election (due by June 2019).

What is not under dispute is that the DPP is a growing force, winning 21% of the vote in 2015 (almost doubling its support from 2011). Many voters in *udkantsdanmark* (the sparsely populated, 'peripheral' areas of the country) feel the answers to their problems lie in the DPP's policies, as opposed to Social Democrat promises. As in other Nordic countries, populist parties like the DPP frame the choice for voters as agreeing to high immigration levels or protecting the welfare system (with the subtext of 'taking care of our own').

Sustainability

As well as their admirable attitudes to civic duties (voter turnout at the last parliamentary election was around 86%; there is relatively low tax evasion), Danes operate with a green conscience.

While some Western governments continue to debate the veracity of climate-change science, Denmark gets on with innovative, sustainable business. Check out State of Green (the country's 'green brand'; www.stateofgreen.com) for insight into how it's doing this.

Wind power generates around 40% of Denmark's total energy consumption, and the country is a market leader in wind-power technology. The long-term goal for Danish energy policy is clear: the entire energy supply is to be independent of fossil fuels by 2050. The city of Copenhagen has pledged to go carbon-neutral by 2025; the capital has already reduced its carbon emissions by more than 40% since 1990 while its population has grown by 50%.

Cycling culture is another example of Denmark's green outlook. Copenhagen has around 400km of continuous, safe cycle paths, and in 2016 the number of bikes actually surpassed the number of cars in the city centre. The cycling infrastructure continues to expand, and more cities are seeking to learn from the bike-friendly master.

Urban versus Rural

Copenhagen's population is expected to increase by 15% in the coming decade, according to Danmarks Statistik, placing pressure on the city's infrastructure and affordability. Meanwhile, there is much marginalising talk about the so-called *udkantsdanmark*. A negative press has portrayed these as *rådne banan* ('rotten banana') regions, home to poor, poorly educated and/or unemployed folks. To prevent a growing geographical class division, the government has started to relocate a number of government agencies (and 4000 jobs since 2015) out of the capital to regional centres.

AREA: **43,094 SQ KM**

GDP: **US$46,600 PER CAPITA**

COASTLINE: **7314KM**

HIGHEST POINT: **MØLLEHØJ 171M**

UNEMPLOYMENT: **4.2%**

POPULATION: **5.761 MILLION**

if Denmark were 100 people

76 would be Lutheran
4 would be Muslim
20 would be other

population urbanisation
(%)

Urban   Rural

population per sq km

DENMARK   UK   NORWAY

≈ 15 people

History

Denmark's size is deceptive: this corner of Scandinavia has played a significant role in shaping the region. By the late 4th century, the Jutes had invaded and settled in England, followed centuries later by the Vikings, whose own presence spanned from Newfoundland to Baghdad. By the beginning of the 19th century, Denmark's colonial power reached four continents. Yet even with the dramatic shrinking of Danish territory, the Danes have continued to inspire, influence and shape the global sphere.

Of Stone, Bronze & Iron

Humans first trod the Danish earth and dug the region's flint tens of thousands of years ago as retreating glaciers let lichen and mosses grow, attracting herds of reindeer. Permanent settlements sprang up in about 12,000 BC.

Stone Age culture relied primarily on hunting, but as the climate gradually warmed, these hunters resettled near the sea, subsisting on fish, sea birds and seals. Small-scale agriculture followed and villages developed around the fields.

Around 1800 BC the first artisans began fashioning weapons, tools, jewellery and finely crafted works of art in the new metal, bronze, traded from as far away as Crete and Mycenae.

Locally available iron led to superior ploughs, permitting larger-scale agricultural communities. Present-day Denmark's linguistic and cultural roots date to the late Iron Age arrival of the Danes, a tribe thought to have migrated south from Sweden about AD 500.

At the dawn of the 9th century, the territory of present-day Denmark was on the perimeter of Europe, but Charlemagne (r 768–814) extended the power of the Franks northward to present-day northern Germany. Hoping to ward off a Frankish invasion, Godfred, king of Jutland, reinforced an impressive earthen rampart called the Danevirke. However, the raiding Franks breached the rampart, bringing Christianity to Denmark at sword point.

Stone Age villagers buried their dead in dolmens, a type of grave monument comprising upright stones topped by a large capstone, features still common to Denmark's meadows.

TIMELINE	c 12,000 BC	c 4000 BC	c 1800 BC
	The first permanent settlements are established on Jutland and the nearby Baltic islands.	People begin to grow more food crops. The advent of agriculture sees woods cleared by slash-and-burn and grain is sown in the resulting ash.	Bronze is introduced to Denmark, giving rise to skilled artisans who fashion weapons, tools, jewellery and works of art. Trade routes to the south bring the supply of bronze.

The Vikings

To the modern imagination, the word 'Viking' commonly conjures images of bearded thugs in horned helmets, jumping from longships and pillaging their way through early Christendom. While some of these Northmen (as they were known in Britain) were partial to a spot of looting and slaughter – not to mention slave trading – the real history of these Scandinavian seafarers is far more complex.

The Viking era spanned several centuries and took on different characteristics throughout that time. Although unrecorded raids had probably been occurring for decades, the start of the Viking Age is generally dated from AD 793, when Nordic Vikings ransacked Lindisfarne Monastery, off the coast of Northumbria in northeastern England. Survivors described the Vikings' sleek square-rigged vessels as 'dragons flying in the air' and the raiders as 'terrifying heathens'.

Early Viking raiders often targeted churches and monasteries for their wealth of gold and jewels. Books and other precious but perishable cultural artefacts were just some of the raids' collateral damage. Roughing up monks – who wrote the history of the age – hardly endeared the Vikings to posterity.

The Vikings were initially adventurous opportunists who took advantage of the region's turmoil and unstable political status quo, but in time their campaigns evolved from piratical forays into organised expeditions that established far-flung colonies overseas.

They were successful traders, extraordinary mariners and insatiable explorers whose exploits took them to Byzantium, Russia and North Africa, and even as far as the Caspian Sea and Baghdad. They also established settlements in Iceland, Greenland and Newfoundland.

The Vikings settled in several places too, including northern France and the British Isles, proving to be able farmers. They were also shrewd political players, establishing their own kingdoms and intermarrying with local nobles or squeezing protection money from local kings. Even the historically pivotal 1066 Battle of Hastings can be thought of not as a battle between England and France, but essentially a fight between two leaders descended from this Nordic stock (William and Harold).

Settlement and assimilation was one reason for a decline in raiding and fighting. The Jelling Stone of Harald I (Bluetooth) that still stands in the churchyard in Jelling is the document of an even more important factor: in the 10th century Scandinavia embraced Christianity and thus a degree (very relatively speaking) of 'civilisation'.

So fearsome were the Vikings that the English introduced a special prayer into church services: 'From the fury of the Northmen, good Lord, deliver us'.

HISTORY THE VIKINGS

Just for the record, Vikings didn't have horned, or winged, helmets (sorry!). Nor did they celebrate slaughter by drinking mead from cups made of skulls, another popular myth. Happily, they did rejoice in some storybook names, including Erik Bloodaxe and Sweyn Forkbeard.

c AD 500	793	950–85	985–1014
Arrival of the Danes in the late Iron Age. This tribe, thought to have migrated south from Sweden, forms present-day Denmark's linguistic and cultural roots.	The first documented raid at Lindisfarne on northeastern England by Danish Vikings.	King Harald I (Bluetooth), son of Gorm the Old, unifies Denmark. He spearheads the conversion of Danes to Christianity from his court at Jelling.	During the reigns of Harald Bluetooth's son Sweyn Forkbeard and grandsons Harald II and Canute the Great, England is conquered and a short-lived Anglo-Danish kingdom formed.

A (Quasi) Unified Denmark

By the early 9th century Jutland (and parts of southern Norway) were more or less united under a single king. In the late 9th century, unification of the territories that make up modern-day Denmark inched forward when warriors, led by the Norwegian chieftain Hardegon, conquered the Jutland peninsula; Hardegon then began to extend his power base across the rest of Denmark's territory.

The current Danish monarchy traces its roots back to Gorm the Old, Hardegon's son, who reigned in the early 10th century from Jelling in central Jutland. His son, Harald Bluetooth, who ruled for 35 years, concluded the conquest of Denmark as well as completing Denmark's adoption of Christianity, partly to appease his powerful Frankish neighbours to the south who, a century earlier, had sent the missionary Ansgar to build churches in the Danish towns of Ribe and Hedeby.

Harald Bluetooth's son Sweyn (Svend) Forkbeard (r 987–1014) and grandsons Harald II (r 1014–18) and Canute the Great (r 1019–35) conquered England, establishing a short-lived Anglo-Danish kingdom over much of the British Isles. Canute the Great was the first true Danish king to sit on the throne of England, reigning in much the same manner as an English king except that he employed Scandinavian soldiers to maintain his command.

When Canute's son Hardecanute died, the balance of power shifted to the English heirs of Alfred the Great, although many of the Danes who had settled in England elected to stay on.

Unsuccessful attempts by the Danes to reclaim England followed and the defeat of the Norwegian Vikings by Harold II of England at the Battle of Stamford Bridge in 1066 heralded the end of the Viking era.

The Bloody Middle Ages

Internal strife, plots, counter-plots and assassinations involving rival nobles, wealthy landowners and corrupt church leaders blighted the early medieval era.

King Valdemar I eventually united a war-weary country and enacted Denmark's first written laws, known as the Jyske Lov (Jutland Code), in Vordingborg, Zealand. His successors enacted other laws that were quite progressive for their time: no imprisonment without just cause, an annual assembly of the *hof* (national council), and the first supreme court.

Margrethe, who had assumed de facto control of the Crown after her young son Oluf died in 1387, became the official head of state and Denmark's first ruling queen. The next year Swedish nobles sought Margrethe's assistance in a rebellion against their unpopular German-born king. The Swedes hailed Margrethe as their regent, and in turn she sent Danish troops to Sweden, securing victory over the king's forces.

Human trafficking was not uncommon among the Vikings, who captured and enslaved women and young men while pillaging Anglo-Saxon, Celtic and Slavic settlements. These captives were subsequently sold in giant slave markets in Europe and the Middle East.

Key Viking Sites

Lindholm Høje (p250)

Viking Ship Museum (p110)

Vikingemuseet Ladby (p173)

Nationalmuseet (p45)

Trelleborg (p125)

1066	1137–57	1219	1363
The defeat of Norwegian Vikings by Harold II of England at the Battle of Stamford Bridge heralds the end of the Viking era.	Civil strife, assassinations, plots and general skulduggery continue until Valdemar I, son of Knud Lavard, takes the throne in 1157, introducing progressive policies in the Jyske Lov (Jutland Code).	The Dannebrog (Danish flag; today the oldest national flag in the world) is raised for the first time, its creation supposedly divinely provided and firing the Danes to victory in Estonia under Valdemar II.	Norway's King Haakon marries Margrethe, daughter of the Danish king Valdemar IV, who is to become an influential and powerful queen.

A decade later Margrethe established a formal alliance between Denmark, Norway and Sweden known as the Kalmar Union, to counter the powerful German-based Hanseatic League that had come to dominate regional trade.

In 1410 King Erik of Pomerania, Margrethe's grandson, staged an unsuccessful attack on the Hanseatic League, which sapped the Kalmar Union's vitality. This, together with Erik's penchant for appointing Danes to public office in Sweden and Norway, soured relations with aristocrats in those countries. In 1438 the Swedish council withdrew from the union, whereupon the Danish nobility deposed Erik in 1439.

Erik's successor, King Christopher III, made amends by pledging to keep the administrations of the three countries separate. However, the union continued to be a rocky one, and in 1523 the Swedes elected their own king, Gustav Vasa. The Kalmar Union was permanently dissolved, but Norway would remain under Danish rule for another three centuries.

> The Danish monarchy can be traced back to Viking king Gorm the Old, who ruled from c 936 to his death in c 958. The monarchy is the oldest in Europe.

The Lutheran Reformation & Civil War

The monarchy and the Catholic Church played out a pivotal power struggle during the Danish Reformation. Caught in the middle of this religious and political foment was King Frederik I, who over the course of 10 years went from promising to fight heresy against Catholicism to inviting Lutheran preachers to Denmark. When Frederik died, the lack of a clear successor left the country in civil war.

The following year (1534) Hanseatic mercenaries from Lübeck (now in Germany) invaded southern Jutland and Zealand. By and large, the Lübeckers were welcomed as liberators by peasants and members of the middle class, who were in revolt against the nobility.

Alarmed by the revolt, a coalition of aristocrats and Catholic bishops crowned the Lutheran Christian III as king. Still, the rebellion raged on. In Jutland, manor houses were set ablaze and the peasants made advances against the armies of the aristocracy.

Christian's general, Rantzau, took control, cutting Lübeck off from the sea and marching northward through Jutland, brutally smashing peasant bands. Rantzau's troops besieged Copenhagen, where merchants supported the uprising and welcomed the prospect of becoming a Hanseatic stronghold. Cut off from the outside world, Copenhagen's citizens suffered starvation and epidemics before surrendering after a year in 1536.

Christian III quickly consolidated his power, offering leniency to the merchants and Copenhagen burghers who had revolted in exchange for their allegiance. Catholic bishops, on the other hand, were arrested, and monasteries, churches and other ecclesiastical estates became the property of the Crown.

> The word 'Denmark' (Danmark in Danish) dates back to the Viking age and its first recorded use is on the famous Jelling Stones from c 900. The larger stone is affectionately known as the nation's birth certificate.

1375–87	1396–1439	1534	1588–1648
Five-year-old Oluf becomes king of Denmark following the death of Valdemar IV, and five years later also becomes king of Norway. His mother assumes de facto control on his death.	Reign of King Erik of Pomerania, Margrethe's grandson. He stages an unsuccessful attack on the Hanseatic League, which exhausts the resources of the Kalmar Union. The Danish nobility depose Erik in 1439.	Following King Frederik I's death, Hanseatic mercenaries from Lübeck (now in Germany) invade southern Jutland and Zealand. Danish peasants and members of the middle class welcome the invaders.	The early prosperous and peaceful years of Christian IV's long reign end in 1625 when Christian attempts to neutralise Swedish expansion by beginning the Thirty Years' War. Denmark suffers crippling losses.

Thus the Danish Lutheran Church became the only state-sanctioned denomination and was placed under the direct control of the king. Buoyed by a treasury enriched by confiscated Church properties, the monarchy emerged from the civil war stronger than ever.

War & Absolute Monarchy

A period of peace marked the early reign of Christian IV, who then spoiled it by embarking on what would become the ruinous Thirty Years' War. The aim of the war was to neutralise Swedish expansion; its outcome for Denmark was morale- and coffer-sapping losses.

Seeing a chance for revenge against Sweden, following its troubled occupation of Poland, Christian IV's successor, Frederik III, once again declared war in 1657. For the Danes, ill-prepared for battle, it was a tremendous miscalculation.

DENMARK'S BOG BODIES

The people of Iron Age Denmark left little evidence and precious little by way of written records of themselves. Thankfully, some extraordinary discoveries in the last couple of centuries offer tantalising insights into this culture.

Drainage and peat cutting in Denmark's bogs has yielded hundreds of often amazingly well-preserved bodies of men, women and children, mostly from the Iron Age (the early centuries BC and AD).

Many of the bodies are also compelling historical who- and why-dunnits. Burial was unusual (cremation was common at the time) and some appear to have been ritually killed, perhaps due to the supernatural power the Iron Age people are thought to have attributed to the bogs.

If it was ritual killing, were these people victims or willing participants? Windeby I, for example, discovered in 1950 in Germany and aged about 16, was found underneath rocks and branches, presumably used to push down the body and suggesting some kind of ritual. Others may have simply been waylaid, murdered and dumped.

The Grauballe Man certainly died a nasty death that suggests a brutal execution. It's a history and forensics conundrum, brilliantly illustrated at his current resting place, the Moesgaard Museum (p233) in Aarhus. In Copenhagen's Nationalmuseet (p45), the Woman from Huldremose met a seemingly horrific end, a vicious cut almost severing her right upper arm. Twenty-two centuries after her death, she remains wrapped in her skirt, scarf and snug-looking capes.

The most famous body of all is that of the Tollund Man. On show at the Museum Silkeborg (p223), his head is extraordinarily preserved, right down to the stubble on his chin. He died, aged in his 30s, naked but for the beautifully plaited leather noose used to strangle him and the leather cap he has worn for 2000 years. It frames an utterly serene face. Was he a holy sacrifice or a punished prisoner? The mystery remains unsolved.

1658	1660–65	1675–1720	1784
Denmark signs the Treaty of Roskilde, the most lamented humiliation in its history, losing a third of its territory, including the island of Bornholm and all territories on the Swedish mainland.	King Frederik III establishes absolute monarchy. He introduces an absolutist constitution called the Kongeloven (Royal Act), which becomes the law of the land for most of the following two centuries.	The monarchy rebuilds the military and fights three more wars with Sweden (1675–79, 1699–1700 and 1709–20), without regaining its lost territories. A period of relative peace follows.	The young Crown Prince Frederik VI assumes control, brings progressive landowners into government and introduces a sweeping series of reforms improving rights for the masses.

Sweden's King Gustave led his troops back from Poland through Germany and into Jutland, plundering his way north. During 1657–58 – the most severe winter in Danish history – King Gustave marched his soldiers across the frozen seas of the Lille Bælt between Fredericia and the island of Funen. King Gustave's uncanny success unnerved the Danes and he proceeded without serious resistance across the Store Bælt to Lolland and then on to Falster.

The Swedish king had barely made it across the frozen waters of the Storstrømmen to Zealand when the thawing ice broke away behind him, precariously separating him and his advance detachment from the rest of his forces. However, the Danes failed to recognise their sudden advantage; instead of capturing the Swedish king, they sued for peace and agreed to yet another disastrous treaty.

In 1658 Denmark signed the humiliating Treaty of Roskilde, ceding a third of its territory, including the island of Bornholm and all territories on the Swedish mainland. Only Bornholm, which eventually staged a bloody revolt against the Swedes, would again fly the Danish flag.

Absolute monarchy returned in 1660, when King Frederik III cunningly convened a gathering of nobles, placed them under siege, and forced them to nullify their powers of council. Frederik declared his right of absolute rule, declaring the king the highest head on earth, above all human laws and inferior to God alone.

In the following decades the now all-powerful monarchy rebuilt the military and continued to pick fruitless fights with Sweden. Peace of a sort eventually descended and for much of the 18th century the Danes and Swedes managed to coexist without serious hostilities.

> Learn everything you ever wanted to know about a millennium of Danish royals at www.danmark skonger.dk.

> A History of Denmark by Palle Lauring is a well-written excursion through the lives and times of the Danish people.

Revolution

By the turn of the 19th century, Denmark's trading prowess was worrying Britain, by now the world's preeminent sea power. When Denmark signed a pact of armed neutrality with Sweden, Prussia and Russia, Britain's navy attacked Copenhagen in 1801, heavily damaging the Danish fleet and forcing Denmark to withdraw from the pact.

Denmark managed to avoid further conflicts and actually profited from the war trade until 1807, when a new treaty between France and Russia once again drew the Danes closer to the conflict.

Wary of Napoleon's growing influence in the Baltic, Britain feared that Denmark might support France. Despite Denmark's neutrality, the British fleet unleashed a devastating surprise bombardment on Copenhagen, setting much of the city ablaze, destroying its naval yards and confiscating the entire Danish fleet.

> Denmark's highest-ranked honour is the Order of the Elephant, officially created in 1693 by King Christian V.

1790s	1800–01	1846–49	1901
Feudal obligations of the peasantry are abolished. Large tracts of land are broken up and redistributed to the landless. Education is made compulsory for all children under the age of 14.	Denmark signs a pact of armed neutrality with Sweden, Prussia and Russia. In response, Britain's navy attacks Copenhagen, battering the Danish fleet and forcing Denmark to leave the pact.	Political ferment sweeps Europe; two growing Danish factions (farmers and liberals) join forces to form a liberal party in 1846. The Danish constitution is enacted in 1849 and absolute monarchy is abolished.	The Venstrereform-parti (Left Reform Party) sweeps to power and embarks on an ambitious social reform program, including amending the constitution to give women the right to vote.

Although the unprovoked attack was unpopular enough back home to have been roundly criticised by the British parliament, Britain nonetheless kept the Danish fleet. The British then offered the Danes an alliance – they unsurprisingly refused the offer and instead joined the continental alliance against Britain, who retaliated by blockading both Danish and Norwegian waters, causing poverty in Denmark and famine in Norway.

Despite the disastrous early years of the 19th century, by the 1830s Denmark was flourishing again, economically and culturally. Philosopher Søren Kierkegaard, theologian Nikolaj Frederik Severin Grundtvig and writer Hans Christian Andersen emerged as prominent figures. Sculptor Bertel Thorvaldsen bestowed his grand neoclassical statues on Copenhagen, and Christoffer Wilhelm Eckersberg introduced the Danish school of art.

> When Napoleon fell in 1814, the Swedes, then allied with Britain, successfully demanded that Denmark, an ally of France, cede Norway to them.

Democracy

When revolution swept Europe in the spring of 1848, Denmark's new political parties, which had arisen from the debating chambers of the new provincial assemblies, waxed with the waning power of the monarchy. The new Danish king, Frederik VII, under pressure from the new liberal party, abolished the absolute monarchy and drew up a democratic constitution, establishing a parliament with two chambers, Folketing and Landsting, whose members were elected by popular vote.

Although the king retained a limited voice, parliament took control of legislative powers. The constitution also established an independent judiciary and guaranteed the rights of free speech, religion and assembly. Denmark had changed overnight from a virtual dictatorship to one of the most democratic countries in Europe.

When Denmark's new constitution threatened to incorporate the border duchy of Schleswig as an integral part of Denmark, the German population in the duchy allied with neighbouring Holstein, sparking years of unrest. In 1864 the Prussian prime minister, Otto von Bismarck, declared war on a militarily weak Denmark and captured Schleswig.

DENMARK'S FINEST HOUR

Soon after taking full control of the country in August 1943, Denmark's Nazi occupiers planned, as they did in the other parts of Europe they occupied, to round up Jewish Danes and deport them to their deaths in concentration camps. The Danish resistance had other ideas and in an extraordinarily well coordinated operation smuggled some 7200 Jews – about 90% of those left in Denmark – into neutral Sweden. In recognition of its actions in saving its Jewish population, Denmark is remembered as one of the Righteous Among the Nations at the Yad Vashem Holocaust Memorial in Jerusalem.

1943	1953	1973	1989
In a hastily planned operation, the Danish resistance successfully smuggles some 7200 Jews into Sweden after hearing of Nazi plans to round them up and transport them to its European concentration camps.	The Danish constitution is amended to allow a female monarch, paving the way for Margrethe II to become queen, Denmark's first female monarch since the 14th century.	Denmark joins the European Community (now the EU).	Denmark passes a bill legalising registered partnerships, becoming the world's first country to legally recognise same-sex unions.

Further eroding Denmark's sovereignty, it raised doubts about Denmark's survival as a nation.

In the wake of that defeat, a conservative government took and retained power until the end of the century. The conservatives oversaw a number of economic advances: extending the railway throughout the country and rapid industrialisation that established large-scale shipbuilding, brewing and sugar-refining industries.

The 20th Century

Denmark declared neutrality at the outbreak of WWII, but Germany, threatened by the growing Allied presence in Norway, coveted coastal bases in northern Jutland and in April 1940 seized key Danish strategic defences and occupied the country.

Managing to retain a degree of autonomy, the Danes trod a thin line, running domestic affairs under close Nazi supervision until August 1943 when the Germans took outright control. A Danish resistance movement quickly mushroomed.

Although the island of Bornholm was heavily bombarded by Soviet forces, the rest of Denmark emerged from WWII relatively unscathed. With the country officially free from German control on 5 May 1945, Danes took to the streets, burning the black shades used to cover their windows during bombing raids.

The Social Democrats led a comprehensive social-welfare state in postwar Denmark and cradle-to-grave medical care, education and public assistance were established. As the economy grew and the labour market increased, women entered the workforce in unprecedented numbers and household incomes reached new heights.

In the 1960s a rebellion by young people, disillusioned with growing materialism, the nuclear arms race and an authoritarian educational system, took hold in the larger cities. The movement came to a head in Copenhagen in 1971, when protesters tore down the fence of an abandoned military base at the east side of Christianshavn and turned the site into the still-thriving commune of Christiania.

Denmark's external relationships were not without their troubles either. It joined the European Community, the predecessor of the EU, in 1973, but has been rather more hesitant about the subsequent expansion of the EU's powers. Denmark rejected the 1992 Maastricht Treaty (which set the terms for much greater economic and political cooperation) as well as the adoption of the euro.

Meanwhile, Denmark maintained its leadership stance for socially liberal policies, including same-sex unions (instituted in 1989) and aggressive implementation of alternative energy sources.

In addition to Denmark itself, the Kingdom of Denmark also comprises Greenland and the Faroe Islands, both of which have autonomous self-rule.

A polar bear was included in the Danish coat of arms in the 1660s to symbolise the country's claim of sovereignty over Greenland.

2000	2000	2004	2005–06
Reaching the limits of their tolerance for the European project, Denmark votes against adopting the new European currency, the euro.	The Øresundsbroen (Øresund Bridge) and adjoining Drogten tunnel are officially opened, providing a direct road and rail link between Denmark and Sweden.	Crown Prince Frederik weds Australian-born Mary Elizabeth Donaldson in a fairy-tale ceremony watched by millions of people around the world.	Denmark becomes a villain to many Muslims and the focus of violent demonstrations following the publication of cartoons depicting the prophet Mohammed in Jyllands-Posten.

In the late 1990s and early 2000s, the government was a coalition of the centre-right Venstre party and the Conservative People's Party, sometimes also calling on the support of the generally nationalist right-wing Danish People's Party (DPP). This new power structure led Denmark to impose some of the toughest immigration laws in Europe in 2002, including restrictions on marriage between Danes and foreigners.

Modern Times

The first decade of the 21st century proved somewhat turbulent by Danish standards. Concerns over immigration – particularly from Muslim countries – saw a resurgence of the political right and increased support for the traditionalist DPP. In practical terms, the DPP's participation contributed to Denmark's joining the USA, UK and other allies in the 2003 Iraq War and Denmark's commitment to maintain its role in Afghanistan.

In 2006 Denmark found itself in the unfamiliar role of villain in the eyes of many Muslims following the publication of cartoons depicting the prophet Mohammed – a deep taboo for many Muslims but an issue of freedom of speech for liberal news editors – in the *Jyllands-Posten* newspaper. The depiction sparked violent demonstrations across the world, and the beamed images of protestors burning Danish flags shocked a nation not accustomed to such intense, widespread vitriol.

By 2010 the political pendulum began swinging to the left again as discontent over the country's stuttering economic performance grew. In 2011 parliamentary elections saw a new, centre-left coalition take over after a closely fought election. At the helm was Denmark's first female prime minister, Helle Thorning-Schmidt.

Thorning-Schmidt's one-term reign was ended when the pendulum swung again at the next general election in mid-2015. A minority government was formed under Lars Løkke Rasmussen, head of the Venstre party. The government later formed a coalition with other conservative parties.

The next general election is scheduled to be held by June 2019.

In 2000 Denmark resoundingly rejected the adoption of the euro by a referendum. In the same year, the Øresundsbroen (Øresund Bridge) was opened, connecting Denmark and Sweden by road and rail.

2011	2015	2016	2017
Helle Thorning-Schmidt, leader of the Social Democrats, defeats incumbent prime minister Lars Løkke Rasmussen in the Danish general election, becoming Denmark's first female prime minister.	The tables turn and the results of the general election see Lars Løkke Rasmussen become prime minister again. His centre-right party later becomes part of a ruling right-wing coalition.	Denmark hits the headlines for its strict asylum policies and active deterrence during Europe's refugee crisis.	Prince Henrik causes a stir by stating he won't be buried alongside his wife, Queen Margrethe, in Roskilde Cathedral. It is later announced that the prince is suffering from dementia.

The Danish Lifestyle

You'd be forgiven for thinking that Danish life is pretty much perfect. Not only are the Danes impossibly good-looking, they're famously civic minded, egalitarian and masters of mood lighting. What makes these Nordic role models tick? Just how perfect are their enlightened Scandinavian lives? What can other nationalities learn from the Danes' attitudes to happiness, cosiness and equality?

How to Hygge

Befriend a Dane or two and chances are you'll be invited to partake in a little *hygge*. Usually it translates as 'cosiness' but in reality, *hygge* (pronounced hoo-gah or hue-guh) means much more than that. Indeed, there really is no equivalent in English. *Hygge* refers to a sense of friendly, warm companionship of a kind fostered when Danes gather together in groups of two or more, although you can actually *hygge* on your own, too. The participants don't have to be friends (indeed, you might only have just met), but if the conversation flows – avoiding potentially divisive topics like politics – the bonhomie blossoms and toasts are raised before an open fire (or, at the very least, lots of candles), you are probably coming close. Atmosphere, harmony and comfort are key.

Most Danes experience *hygge* in the comfort of their own home, but many cafes, bars and restaurants do their utmost to foster a *hyggelig* atmosphere (note: *hyggelig* is the adjectival form of *hygge*). This comes with open fires or tea lights lit no matter what time of day or year, plus free-flowing drinks and comfort food served in a warm, softly lit, attractive setting. Christmas is the most *hyggelig* time of year.

Interestingly, the word's origin is not Danish but Norwegian. Originally meaning something along the lines of 'well-being', *hygge* first appeared in Danish writing in the early 1800s, and it might originate from the word 'hugge' (to embrace). Remarkably, after becoming a hot trend for lifestyle magazines and wellness bloggers around the globe in 2015–16, the term *hygge* was added to the Oxford English Dictionary in 2017.

The international 'discovery' of *hygge* has prompted the publication of a handful of books explaining the concept, plus manuals on how non-Danish *hygge*-seekers can create and experience it. To find out more, don some woollen socks, light a few candles, make a cup of cocoa and get comfy on your sofa (blankets and cushions essential), then take lessons from *The Little Book of Hygge* by Meik Wiking. Wiking is the CEO of the Happiness Research Institute in Copenhagen, so the man knows *hygge*.

Equality

Despite being renowned for its progressiveness, Denmark scored surprisingly low in the 2016 Global Gender Gap Index, compiled by the World Economic Forum. The index ranks more than 140 countries on their gender equality, and Denmark ranked number 19, far below its Nordic neighbours (which took out the top four spots).

According to the 2016 Corruption Perceptions Index released by Transparency International (www.transparency.org), Denmark and New Zealand are the least corrupt countries in the world.

Get the low-down on Danes' happiness and *hygge* in official, scientific form from reports published by the Happiness Research Institute (www.happinessresearchinstitute.com).

Denmark does relatively well, with some impressive results (it topped the ranking for parity in the field of educational attainment), but other statistics are cause for concern, and its neighbours do better overall. You can view some gender comparisons at **Statistics Denmark** (www.dst. dk). Female students outnumber male ones at tertiary level, while figures released by the **OECD** (Organisation for Economic Co-operation and Development) in 2014 showed the average Danish man spends 107 minutes per day on housework, in contrast to the average Danish woman's 145 minutes. These statistics gave Denmark close to top billing in terms of chore equity in the 29 countries surveyed. Danish policies, including mandatory paternal leave and postmaternity re-entry programs, have also helped shaped a society in which women can more easily balance a career and family.

Still, sexism in Denmark has not been fully relegated to the history books. One high-profile Dane all too aware of this is former prime minister Helle Thorning-Schmidt, whose well-documented love of designer labels earned her the nickname 'Gucci Helle' in the media and by some of her political opponents. While Thorning-Schmidt's detractors argued that her passion for expensive fashion undermined the core principles of her party – the Social Democrats – others pointed to the fact that her male counterparts never face the same scrutiny when it comes to their appearance.

> Danes aren't just leaders in happiness, they're also leaders in sustainability. State of Green (www.stateof green.com) is the country's 'green brand' – read all about its eco plans and green solutions.

Happy, Shiny People

There have been five World Happiness Reports published by the UN since 2012, ranking more than 150 countries around the globe by their happiness levels. Denmark came top of the class in that first report, and has scored in the top three happiest countries in each report since (in 2017, Denmark was pipped to first place by Norway).

The rankings are determined by scores in six key variables – namely GDP per capita; healthy years of life expectancy; social support (ie having someone to count on in times of trouble); trust (ie a perceived absence of corruption in government and business); perceived freedom to make life decisions; and generosity (as measured by recent donations).

In 2017 Denmark scored a total of 7.522 on a scale from 0 to 10. Fellow Nordic nations Norway, Iceland and Finland made it into the Top 5, a long way off from the US at 14 and Britain at 19.

So, what's the secret? According to *The Happy Danes,* a report released in 2014 by Denmark's Happiness Research Institute, the nation's high happiness rating is due to a number of factors, including the following:

> Anne and Peter are the most common first names in Denmark today. The most common surname is a tightly fought race between Jensen and Nielsen.

➡ a strong civil society – exemplified by social cohesion and high participation in voluntary work

➡ a well-functioning democracy – as evidenced by high voter turn-out at elections

➡ a high degree of security – in part due to the welfare system

➡ trust – globally, only one in four people feel that they can trust others; in Denmark, that figure is three in four

➡ freedom – most Danes feel genuinely empowered to make changes and improvements, both in their own lives and in the communities in which they live

➡ prosperity – Denmark is among the world's richest countries

➡ good working conditions that allow room for a balanced life

> *The Almost Nearly Perfect People* by Michael Booth is a very readable exploration of the myths and stories behind the 'Nordic miracle'.

WELFARE FOR ALL

When it comes to explaining their enviable lifestyle, most Danes will point proudly to their nation's famous welfare system. It's a system that remains one of the world's most generous: within it, a number of services are available to citizens, free of charge. The Danish health and educational systems, for example, are free.

Even in adulthood, minds are kept active with state-supported access to Denmark's iconic *højskoler* (folk high schools), arts-focused schools offering courses in everything from philosophy, debating and creative writing, to dance, applied arts, cooking and even gardening. One in 10 Danish adults make use of these institutions, either to explore an interest or to simply meet new people.

The origins of the *højskoler* stretch back to the mid-19th century and the revered Danish theologian and political figure Nikolaj Frederik Severin Grundtvig (1783–1872). Arguing that a newly democratic Denmark would only succeed if all its citizens were able to partake in the country's political life, Grundtvig went about establishing liberal arts colleges for the rural poor. These schools would eventually develop into the folk high schools dotted across the country today.

Grundtvig's ideas would play a formidable role in developing modern Denmark's values of egalitarianism and civic responsibility. While class divisions do exist in Denmark, the gap between rich and poor is much narrower than it is in many other developed countries. Income disparity is also relatively narrow, discouraging the snooty judgment of less-profitable jobs.

Civic responsibility is shown in the Danes' attitude to paying taxes. Surveys show that Danes are generally happy to pay their taxes, despite a tax rate considered high by many other nationalities. As Meik Wiking from Copenhagen's Happiness Research Institute wrote for the 'Best Countries' rankings in 2016 (www.usnews.com/news/best-countries), that's due to 'awareness of the fact that the welfare model turns our collective wealth into well-being. We are not paying taxes. We are investing in our society. We are purchasing quality of life.'

Summer Highs, Winter Lows

A friendly shoulder to lean on can come in quite handy as autumn's leaves flutter to the ground and another long, gloomy Danish winter looms. It's in November that Mother Nature usually unfurls her thick winter fog over the country, extinguishing all hope of just one more mild autumnal day.

For roughly 12% of the population, that little sadness is in fact Seasonal Affective Disorder (SAD), a seasonally triggered depression most prolific in the autumn and winter months. Whether affected or not, many Danes combat the winter blues with escapes to warmer climes, from nearby Malaga to the far-flung beaches of Thailand. They are also prolific users of sunbeds, despite health warnings. At home, however, it's *hygge* to the rescue as flickering candles, soft lighting and toasty catch-ups with friends turn the darkness into a celebration of all things snug. It's a Danish tradition that reaches fever pitch at Christmas, when Christmas markets, twinkling lights and hot, flowing *gløgg* (mulled wine) turn cities and towns into winter wonderlands.

Not surprisingly, Denmark's short, sweet summers are embraced with fervent gusto, the long nights of winter replaced by deliciously long, invigorating days. Parks become veritable seas of bronzing flesh, outdoor festivals are in full swing, and those with a *sommerhus* (summer house) or *grill* (barbecue) dust them down for another much-awaited season.

According to the OECD Better Life Index (www.oecd betterlifeindex. org), Danes have a better work–life balance than any other country surveyed.

Want to know more about the World Happiness Report, and where your country ranks? See http:// worldhappiness. report/.

Danish Design

Is there a more design-conscious nation than Denmark, or a more design-obsessed capital than Copenhagen? One of the country's most inspirational qualities is its love and mastery of the applied arts. Along with its Scandinavian neighbours, Denmark has had a massive influence on the way the world builds its public and private spaces, and on the way it designs interiors, furniture and homewares.

Architecture

Denmark's architectural portfolio is rich and eclectic, graced with the millennia-old military precision of Trelleborg, the medieval curves of Bornholm's round churches, the Renaissance whimsy of Helsingør's Kronborg Slot, and the rococo elegance of Copenhagen's Marble Bridge.

On the world stage, Danish architecture has shone especially bright since the mid-20th century, its enlightened, innovative approach to design pushing boundaries and enjoying accolades across the globe.

Among its deities is Arne Jacobsen (1902–71). An innovator in international modernism, the pipe-smoking architect pioneered Danish interpretations of the Bauhaus style. Among his celebrated works are the Radisson Blu Royal Hotel in Copenhagen, the functionalist town hall he designed for Aarhus (with interiors by Hans Wegner), and his Kubeflex prototype summer house at Kolding's Trapholt museum, all of which encapsulate Jacobsen's masterful sense of proportion.

Equally famous is Jørn Utzon (1918–2008), whose work reflected the organic trend within modernism. Creator of the World Heritage–listed Sydney Opera House, constructed in the 1960s, Utzon famously incorporated elements as wide-reaching as Mayan, Japanese and Islamic influences into traditional Danish design. In Jutland you can admire Utzon's work in Esbjerg and Skagen, but the best place to visit is the Utzon Center in Aalborg. This impressive design and architecture space was the last building designed by the celebrated architect before his death in 2008.

Utzon is not the only Dane to design an architectural icon for a foreign city, with Viborg-born architect Johan von Spreckelsen (1929–87) responsible for Paris' cubelike, monument-cum-skyscraper La Grande Arche. Completed in 1989, the building's ability to balance the dramatic and the unorthodox with a sense of purity and harmony epitomises the aesthetic of many contemporary Danish creations. Among these is Henning Larsen's award-winning The Wave, a striking yet soothing housing development in Vejle, Jutland, sculpted like giant white waves.

An even more recent example is Denmark's National Maritime Museum in Helsingør, a concrete and glass complex ingeniously built in and around a former dry dock. The museum is the work of prolific firm BIG (Bjarke Ingels Group), whose groundbreaking creations also include the Copenhagen apartment complex VM Bjerget (Mountain Dwellings), a stepped, pyramidal structure with a clever configuration that gives each apartment a sense of spaciousness and privacy more akin to detached suburban abodes.

The Danish Architecture Centre (www.dac.dk) is a brilliant source of information about new architecture, innovation and urban development in the capital. Its website offers downloadable podwalks for archi-buffs, as well as information about its guided walking tours in Copenhagen.

BIG's latest creations include the whimsical Lego House in Billund, celebrating all things Lego inside a fun edifice designed to resemble stacked bricks, and Tirpitz, an inspired museum inside a WWII-era bunker and tunnel under the sand dunes on the west coast of Jutland. Special mention must go to Amager Bakke, a still-under-construction waste-to-energy plant in Copenhagen that will feature an artificial ski slope and hiking on its roof.

Capital Drama

Copenhagen's most iconic modern buildings include:

Radisson Blu Royal Hotel (1960, Arne Jacobsen) Not content with merely creating a building, Jacobsen designed every item in the hotel, down to the door handles, cutlery and the famous Egg and Swan Chairs. Room 606 remains entirely as it was on opening day in 1960.

The Black Diamond (1999, Schmidt, Hammer & Lassen) Copenhagen's monolithic library extension offers sharp contrast to the original red-brick building. While the latter sits firmly and sombrely, the black granite extension floats on a ribbon of raised glass, leaning towards the harbour as if wanting to detach and jump in.

Operaen (2005, Henning Larsen) While its squat exterior has drawn comparisons to a toaster, the maple-wood and Sicilian marble interior is a triumph.

Royal Danish Playhouse (2008, Lundgaard & Tranberg) Dark, subdued and elegant, the award-winning Skuespilhuset's projected upper floor of coloured glass contrasts playfully with the building's muted-grey, English clay bricks.

Den Blå Planet (2013, 3XN) Denmark's National Aquarium made quite a splash with its spiral, whirlpool-inspired design. Its gleaming silver facade is clad diamond-shaped aluminium plates designed to adapt to the building's organic form.

INDEX: Design to Improve Life (www.design toimprovelife.dk) is a Danish-based nonprofit organisation that works to promote design and design processes that have the capacity to improve the lives of people worldwide.

Furniture & Interiors

As wonderful as Danish design-focused shops, museums, hotels and restaurants are, the very best place to see Danish design is in its natural environment: a Danish home. To the Danes, good design is not just for museums and institutions; they live with it and use it every day.

Visit a Danish home and you'll invariably find a Bang & Olufsen stereo and/or TV in the living room, Poul Henningsen lamps hanging from the ceiling, Arne Jacobsen or Hans Wegner chairs in the dining room, and the table set with Royal Copenhagen dinner sets, Georg Jensen cutlery and Bodum glassware.

Modern Danish furniture focuses on a practical style and the principle that its design should be tailored to the comfort of the user. This smooth, unadorned aesthetic traces its roots to architect Kaare Klint, founder of the furniture design department at the Royal Academy of Fine Arts in Copenhagen.

In 1949 one of Klint's contemporaries, Hans Wegner (1914–2007), created the Round Chair. Its fluid, curving lines made it an instant classic and a model for many furniture designers to follow, and helped establish the first successful overseas export market for Danish furniture. A wonderful array of Wegner-designed chairs is displayed in the Tønder Museum in the designer's home town.

KAARE KLINT

While modern Danish design bloomed in the 1950s, its roots are firmly planted in the 1920s and the work of pioneering Danish modernist Kaare Klint (1888–1954). The architect spent much of his career studying the human form and modified a number of chair designs for added functionality. Klint's obsession with functionality, accessibility and attention to detail would ultimately drive and define Denmark's mid-20th-century design scene and its broader design legacy.

FOUR LEGS GOOD: CLASSIC DANISH CHAIRS

Labouring with an almost fetishistic obsession, the great Danish designers such as Arne Jacobsen could spend long, angst-ridden months, even years, perfecting a single chair. Still, the results made the world sit up straight; in the 1950s *Time* magazine even devoted a cover to the phenomenon. There are dozens to choose from, but some of the classics follow:

The Round Chair (Hans Wegner) In 1950, US *Interiors* magazine put the chair on its cover, calling it 'the world's most beautiful chair'. It became known simply as 'the Chair', and began making high-profile appearances such as the televised 1960 presidential debates between Nixon and Kennedy.

The Ant Chair (Jacobsen) Perhaps the most (in)famous chair in the world, thanks to the 1960s Lewis Morley photograph of call girl Christine Keeler (from the British Profumo Affair) sitting on one.

The Egg Chair (Jacobsen) This represents the essence of jet-setting 1950s modernity. Jacobsen designed the Egg Chair for the Radisson Blu Royal Hotel.

The Panton Chair (Verner Panton) After helping with Jacobsen's Ant Chair, Panton went on to do great things in plastic, the most iconic being his Panton Chair.

Nxt Chair (Peter Karpf) Beech plywood moulded into angular planes is the defining characteristic of this striking design, which took 30 years to reach production. It helped spawn the Voxia line, which is still going strong.

A decade after Wegner's Round Chair, Arne Jacobsen created the Ant, a form of chair designed to be mass-produced, which became the model for the stacking chairs now found in schools and cafeterias worldwide. Jacobsen also designed the Egg and the Swan; both are rounded, uncomplicated upholstered chairs with revolving seats perched on pedestal stands.

Danish design prevails in stylish lamps as well. The country's best-known lamp designer was Poul Henningsen (1894–1967), who emphasised the need for lighting to be soft, for the shade to cast a pleasant shadow and for the light bulb to be blocked from direct view. His PH5 lamp created in 1958 remains one of the most popular hanging lamps sold in Denmark today.

The clean lines of industrial design are also evident in the avant-garde sound systems and TVs produced by Bang & Olufsen; and in Danish silver and cutlery design generally. The father of modern Danish silverwork was the sculptor and silversmith Georg Jensen (1866–1935), who artistically incorporated curvilinear designs; his namesake company is still a leader in the field.

Despite the large shadow cast by the modernists, a new generation of Danish designers are making their mark. While some remain influenced by the heroes of the 1950s, others are challenging their hegemony, with fresh designs that are often bold and irreverent. Among the latter is prolific designer Thomas Bentzen (b 1969), whose whimsical furniture and lighting hum with an almost animated personality.

With stores in major Danish cities (not to mention across the globe), design firm Hay (www.hay.dk) is a well-known showcase for contemporary Danish designers, among them Thomas Bentzen, Hee Welling and Lee Storm.

Food & Drink

In little over a decade beginning in the early 2000s, Denmark raced from dining dowager to culinary darling. The trumpeted arrival of New Nordic cuisine wowed food critics and foodies alike, and in its wake Danish classics enjoyed resurgent popularity and modern interpretations. It's hardly surprising: Denmark has stellar local produce and skilled, ambitious chefs. Old recipes are being rediscovered and interest in traditional and modern food culture continues to soar. The result is an ever-evolving culinary landscape, ripe for delicious exploration.

New Nordic Cuisine

Despite some claims of overexposure, Denmark's New Nordic cuisine continues to garner lots of media attention and praise from food critics, bloggers and general gluttons across the globe. It is evolving, too, which all good trends should do.

A simple, fascinating, 10-point manifesto for the Nordic Kitchen was created in 2004, and it gave birth to New Nordic cuisine. Read it at www.newnordicfood.org.

The movement stems from 2004, when Nordic chefs attending a food symposium in Copenhagen created a 10-point manifesto defining the cuisine's aims. According to the manifesto, New Nordic is defined by seasonality, sustainability, local ingredients and produce, and the use of Nordic cooking methods to create food that originally and distinctly reflects Scandinavian culture, geography and history.

The movement threw the spotlight on Denmark's fantastic raw ingredients, from excellent pork products, beef, game and seafood, to root vegetables, wild berries and herbs. It also serves as a showcase for rarer ingredients from the wider Nordic region, among them Greenlandic musk ox, horse mussels from the Faroe Islands, obscure berries from Finland, and truffles from the Swedish island of Gotland.

The world's most famous New Nordic restaurant was Noma, four times topping the list of the World's 50 Best Restaurants (2010–12 and again in 2014). In its heyday, owner-chef René Redzepi eschewed all nonindigenous produce in his creations, including olive oil and tomatoes. Redzepi is renowned for playing with modest, often-overlooked ingredients and consulting food historians, digging up long-lost traditions. Famously, he also forages in the wilderness for herbs and plants. At Noma, the ingredients were then skilfully prepared using traditional techniques (curing, smoking, pickling and preserving) alongside contemporary experiments that included, among other things, ants.

Apart from Copenhagen, another first-rate destination for foodies is Bornholm – home to excellent fish smokehouses, nationally renowned charcuterie Hallegaard (p152), New Nordic restaurant marvel Kadeau (p149), and scores of local specialities, from caramel to microbrews.

From 2014 to 2017, Noma took to the road and set up in new homes (in Tokyo, Sydney and Tulum in Mexico) for a short spell, embracing indigenous ingredients and methods in each location. At the end of 2016, Noma's Copenhagen restaurant closed. There are plans to reopen in a different format, in a different location in the capital – stay tuned.

In the meantime, a newer wave of Danish chefs (many of whom are Noma alumni) seem to be taking a less dogmatic approach, with their own seasonal, Nordic menus splashed with the odd foreign ingredient. Some are creating more casual restaurants, making New Nordic relatively affordable and more accessible.

A newer trend is super high-quality, contemporary 'non-Danish' food made with the same precision and design savvy that defines New Nordic. While some may argue that this compromises the very concept of New Nordic, others see it as the next step in the evolution of contemporary Danish cooking.

Danish Staples & Specialities

Meat

The Scandinavian Kitchen, by Danish chef and media personality Camilla Plum, outlines over 100 essential pan-Scandi ingredients and 250 recipes. Plum is a household name in Denmark; she runs an organic farm north of Copenhagen that's open to visitors (www.fuglebjerggaard.dk).

Traditional Danish grub has a soft spot for the carnivorous. Pork (*flæsk* or *svinekød*) is ubiquitous, served as *flæskesteg* (roast pork), *mørbradbøf* (pork tenderloin) and comfort-food favourite *frikadeller* – fried minced-pork meatballs commonly served with boiled potatoes and red cabbage. Watch nostalgia wash over Danish eyes at the mere mention of crispy *flæskesvær* (pork crackling or rind), eaten as a salty snack and now back in vogue on some of Copenhagen's trendiest bar menus. Equally wicked is *æbleflæsk,* a heady concoction of fried bacon, onions and apples served on *rugbrød* (rye bread), best paired with dark beer and *snaps*.

Beef (*bøf* or *okse*) is also popular, ranging from cheaper comfort-food dishes using mince to expensive cuts of steak, often served with Béarnaise sauce. *Hakkebøf* is a dish of minced-beef burger, usually covered with fried onions and served with boiled potatoes, brown sauce and beets. Also finding its way back onto menus is *pariserbøf,* a rare-beef patty topped with capers, raw egg yolk, beets, onions and horseradish.

Fish & Seafood

Expansive coastlines mean no shortage of excellent seafood options. Herring (*sild*) is a staple. Often served marinated in numerous ways, including in sherry, mustard, orange or curry, it's also commonly served smoked, fried or charred. Cured or smoked salmon (*laks*) is also prolific, a favourite dish being *gravad laks,* cured or salted salmon marinated in dill and served with a sweet mustard sauce.

Then there's *stegt rødspætte,* fried breaded plaice, often served with parsley potatoes; *kogt torsk,* poached cod married with mustard sauce and boiled potatoes; and the ubiquitous *fiskefrikadeller,* pan-fried fish patties served with thick remoulade or tartar sauce and fresh lemon wedges. Equally iconic is the majestic *stjerneskud.* Literally 'Shooting Star', it's a belt-busting combination of both steamed and fried fish fillets, topped with smoked salmon, shrimp and caviar, and served on buttered bread.

The Danes are great fish smokers, and the wonderfully woody flavour of smoked seafood is one of Scandinavia's most distinctive culinary highs. You'll find smokehouses (called *røgeri*) all around Denmark's coast, preserving herring, eel, shrimp and other fresh seafood. The most renowned are on Bornholm.

Across on the northern tip of Jutland, Skagen is a top spot to feast on fresh shrimp (*rejer*) and lobster (*hummer*).

Denmark is home to two high-calibre food festivals: Copenhagen Cooking & Food Festival (p66), held annually in August, and Denmark's biggest chef competition, Sol over Gudhjem (p153), held on the island of Bornholm in June.

Smørrebrød

Although the earliest recorded mention of smørrebrød is in the 13th-century *Hákonar Saga,* the elaborate Danish open sandwich known today stems back to the late 19th century. As the number of posh-nosh restaurants grew in Copenhagen, the city's modest beer and wine cellars began sprucing up their bread and butter standard with fancy new toppings, in turn creating Denmark's most celebrated culinary export.

The basic smørrebrød is a slice of rye bread topped with any number of ingredients, from roast beef or pork, to juicy shrimps, pickled herring, liver pâté or fried fish fillet. The garnishes are equally variable, with the sculptured final product often looking too good to eat. In the laws of Danish smørrebrød, smoked salmon is served on white bread, and herring on rye bread. Whatever the combination, the iconic dish is best paired with *akvavit* and an invigorating beer.

Smørrebrød is a lunchtime staple in countless restaurants and cafes, the most famous of which is Copenhagen's Schønnemann (p72), a celebrated 19th-century veteran whose offerings span the classical to the modern, with twists like cold-smoked venison leg paired with porcini remoulade and beetroot chips.

Generally speaking, smørrebrød is cheapest in bakeries or specialised smørrebrød takeaway shops found near train stations and office buildings. Try to pronounce smørrebrød as 'smuhr-bruth', but don't feel bad if your pronunciation doesn't match a native Dane's (it never will).

Koldt Bord

Another distinctively Danish presentation is the *koldt bord* (cold table), a buffet-style spread of cold foods – such as cold sliced meats, smoked fish, cheeses, vegetables, salads, condiments, breads and crackers – plus usually a few hot dishes such as *frikadeller* and breaded, fried fish (usually plaice). The cornerstone of the *koldt bord* though is herring, which comes in pickled, marinated and curried versions.

Pastries

Denmark is Valhalla for lovers of all things flaky, sticky and sweet, and its bakeries are a constant source of temptation.

Ironically, what is commonly known as a 'Danish pastry' abroad is known to the Danes as a *wienerbrød* (Viennese bread), and nearly every second street corner has a *bageri* (bakery) with different varieties. As legend has it, the naming of the pastry can be traced to a Danish baker who moved to Austria in the 18th century, where he perfected the treats of flaky, butter-laden pastry. True to their collective sweet tooth, Danes eat them for breakfast.

Not that Denmark's pastry selection ends there. Other famous treats include *kanelsnegle,* a luscious cinnamon scroll sometimes laced with thick, gooey chocolate, and the equally popular *tebirkes,* a flaky, croissant-like pastry filled with a marzipan spread and sprinkled with poppy seeds.

Hot Dogs

Traditionally, the favourite fast food is a *pølse* (hot dog) from one of the wagons dotted around town – all churning out precisely the same frankfurters, buns and dressings. Late at night, after a couple of beers, we have

Claus Meyer (www.meyers mad.dk) is Denmark's food superstar: he's a founder of Noma and the New Nordic food movement, TV chef, food educator, author and, since 2016, has taken on the Agern restaurant in New York's Grand Central Terminal.

FOOD & DRINK DANISH STAPLES & SPECIALITIES

ESSENTIAL DANISH FLAVOURS

New Nordic flavours Sample Nordic produce cooked with groundbreaking creativity at top-shelf hotspots like Copenhagen's Geranium (p78) or Kadeau (p77), or at more affordable Höst (p74) and 108 (p77).

Smørrebrød Rye or white bread topped with anything from beef tartare to egg and shrimp, the open sandwich is Denmark's most famous culinary export.

Sild Smoked, cured, pickled or fried, herring is a local staple, best washed down with generous serves of *akvavit* (an alcoholic spirit commonly made with potatoes and spiced with caraway).

Kanelsnegle A calorific delight, the 'cinnamon snail' is a sweet, buttery pastry, sometimes laced with chocolate.

Koldskål A cold, sweet buttermilk soup eaten in summer, made with vanilla and traditionally served with crunchy biscuits such as *kammerjunkere*.

Beer Carlsberg may dominate, but Denmark's expanding battalion of craft brewers include Mikkeller, Amager Bryghus and Bryghuset Møn.

to admit that a hot dog covered with fake mustard and ketchup can be damned hard to resist.

Look out for places reworking the humble dog into innovative forms, including DØP (p72) in Copenhagen and Haute Friture (p236) in Aarhus.

Where to Eat & Drink

While much of Denmark's culinary ingenuity remains centred in Copenhagen, a number of destination restaurants dot the country, from urban hotspots like Gastromé (p238) in Aarhus, to eat-and-slumber castles and manor houses. Since 2015, Michelin and the **White Guide** (www.whiteguide-nordic.com) have awarded many a star to restaurants outside the capital.

Gourmet markets like Torvehallerne KBH (p71) take self-catering to a new level. Meanwhile, driving along rural lanes you can often buy the freshest local produce from a *gårdbutik* (farm shop) or from roadside stalls, the latter usually working on an honesty-box system in place. *Jordbær* are strawberries, *kirsebær* are cherries, and *nye kartofler* are much vaunted new potatoes.

Cheap Eats

Dining out can be expensive in Denmark, with coveted, high-end nosh spots often more costly than comparable restaurants in Paris and London. Keep in mind that alcohol is also spectacularly costly in fashionable places, and can easily double the price of your meal.

In Copenhagen, a number of top-end restaurants (or their alumni chefs) have launched relatively cheaper, more casual spin-offs serving innovative New Nordic food. Among the best are Höst (p74), Bror (p73) and 108 (p77).

Aside from smokehouses, bakeries and cafes, there are other options for a feed that won't hurt your wallet too much. Torvehallerne KBH has had quite an impact on hungry folks in the capital, and a similar gourmet market hall has opened in Aarhus, plus a smaller version in Rønne on Bornholm. Food halls that are a permanent home to street-food kitchens are also a huge hit in Copenhagen and Aarhus.

Thai and Chinese restaurants are common, though rarely authentic. Pizza is another option, though few serve the wood-fired perfection you may be hoping for, while simple Lebanese and Turkish eateries selling inexpensive *shawarma* (a filling pitta-bread sandwich of shaved meat)

> A couple of important customs: make eye contact with everyone during a toast. And before you leave the table, *always* thank your host or hostess for any food or drink, even if it's just a cup of coffee.

> Danish kitchens close relatively early: aim to eat before 10pm, before 9pm or earlier in smaller towns. Sit down by 7.30pm for opulent multicourse menus.

YULETIDE FEASTING

Not only does the traditional Danish Christmas (*jul*) ooze *hygge* (cosiness), it explodes with festive grub.

The biggest festivities are on Christmas Eve, when gift-giving and songs sung around the Christmas tree are fuelled with *akvavit* and specially brewed Yuletide beers. The culinary centrepiece is roast pork, duck or goose, served with red cabbage and boiled potatoes cooked in butter and sugar. After the meal it's time for warming rice pudding (called *risalamande* and served with cherry sauce). Inside the pudding lies a single whole almond, and the person who finds the almond in his or her bowl gets a prize, such as a sweet made of marzipan. Come 25 December, the leftovers from Christmas Eve make for an excellent *koldt bord* (cold table) lunch.

Of course, the Yuletide treats begin well before Christmas Eve and Day, with common Advent bites including *brunkager* and *pebernødder* (spice cookies), golden *klejner* (deep-fried knotted dough) and *æbleskiver* – small, spherical pancakes traditionally served with *gløgg* (mulled wine).

are another option. Equally common (if not particularly healthy) are the *pølsevogn:* wheeled carts peddling a variety of hot dogs.

Breakfast & Brunch
Danes rarely eat breakfast out. They do, however, embrace brunch with gusto. Many cafes and restaurants put on lavish buffets on weekends, running from about 10am to 2pm and generally priced between 120kr and 200kr (higher prices will include refillable tea or coffee, possibly a glass of champagne).

On weekdays, numerous eateries offer a 'brunch plate' *(brunch tallerken)* on their menu. Served from 10am through lunch, these often consist of samplings of brunch classics, from muesli and yoghurt, to cold cuts, bread, cheese and something sweet (pastry or pancakes), all served on the one plate.

Vegetarians & Vegans
Despite the countrywide adoration of all things pork, vegetarians should be able to get by comfortably throughout Denmark (although in smaller towns the options will be limited). Danish cafes commonly serve a variety of salads, and vegetarians can usually find something suitable at the smørrebrød counter. Most restaurants will have at least one herbivorous dish on the menu, or be able to whip something up on request.

Vegans will face more of a challenge; options for eating out (and kitchens that can accommodate vegan requests) will be more common in bigger cities compared with regional areas.

Drinks
Beer *(øl),* wine *(vin)* and spirits are served in most restaurants and cafes. For many restaurants and cafes, the closure of the kitchen signals a move into 'bar mode', with drinks available until late.

Alcohol is available at grocery shops during normal shopping hours. When buying virtually all soft drink or bottled beer you'll pay a refundable deposit, which you can reclaim later by feeding the empty vessel into a reverse vending machine, found at any supermarket. See www.danskretursystem.dk.

Beer
The Danes are prodigious producers and consumers of beer. The oldest trace of beer in Denmark dates back to 2800 BC, with Copenhagen's first brewing guild established in 1525. The Copenhagen-based Carlsberg Group that markets the Carlsberg and Tuborg labels is one of the world's largest brewery conglomorates and Europe's largest beer exporter.

But while the best-selling beers in Denmark remain *pilsner* lagers (from 20kr in cheap pubs), there are scores of other beers to choose from, notably a growing taste for Belgian imports and microbrewed craft beers (typically costing 50kr-plus). Any Danish town worth its salt now has its own –often innovative – *bryghus* (brewery or brewpub), with more than 170 small breweries around the country, up from just 21 in 2002.

A growing number of bars, pubs and restaurants proudly list their boutique bottled offerings and changing draught ales, and specialist beer bars cater to ever more discerning drinkers. In May, Copenhagen's big beer festival, Ølfestival (p66), showcases over 800 brews.

Wine
Despite its northerly latitude, Denmark is home to a niche winemaking industry. It has its own industry association, Danske Vingårde (Danish Vineyards), and over 50 winegrowers, including Zealand's **Kelleris**

Want to dine in a real Danish home? Three agencies can fix it (around 500kr per head), but book well ahead:
Dine with the Danes *(Facebook DineWithThe Danes)*
Meet Gay Copenhagen *(www.meetgay copenhagen.dk)*
Meet the Danes *(www.meet thedanes.dk)*

Essential beer terms:
øl – beer
pilsner – lager (4.6%)
lyst øl – light beer (1.7%)
lagerøl – dark lager
fadøl – draught
porter – stout

SIP, SUP & SLUMBER: TOP GOURMET RETREATS

These castles and inns combine atmospheric slumber and inspired, seasonal menus for a getaway worth any detour.

Dragsholm Slot (p123) Take an ancient castle, add ex-Noma chef Claus Henriksen, and you have this celebrated culinary retreat in rural northwest Zealand.

Falsled Kro (p178) A former smugglers' inn turned unpretentious pamperer in southern Funen.

Henne Kirkeby Kro (p217) This hip, revamped inn in western Jutland's heathlands presents the clean, contemporary New Nordic flavours of expat Brit, chef Paul Cunningham.

Molskroen (p242) Gallic-inspired, Scandi-refined brilliance in Ebeltoft near Aarhus.

Ruths Hotel (p260) Skagen's light-washed maritime beauty meets New Nordic ingenuity.

Vingaard (www.kellerisvingaard.dk), **Dyrehøj Vingård** (www.dyrehoj-vingaard.dk) and **Ørnberg** (www.oernberg-vin.dk). Jutland's **Skærsøgaard Vin** (http://dansk-vin.dk) has won recognition for its sparkling, white and dessert wines.

Curiously, it's not global warming driving the industry's growth, but the development of grape varieties that bud and mature early, making them ideal for the region's short growing season. Among these are the commonly used hybrid grape Rondo and the Regent, the latter producing richly coloured wines that are vigorous and intense. That said, it's Denmark's white and sparkling wines that show the most promise, with common white grape varieties including the Riesling-like Johanitter.

Even more notable, however, are the apple-based wines made by Jutland's innovative **Cold Hand Winery** (www.coldhandwinery.dk). Among these is the award-winning Malus X – Feminan, a beautifully balanced dessert wine.

Currently, the vast majority of Denmark's home-grown drops are sold on the local market, with a few showcased at modern Danish restaurants in Copenhagen, as well as at Copenhagen's gourmet food market Torvehallerne KBH.

Akvavit

The most popular spirit in Denmark is the Aalborg-produced *akvavit*. There are several dozen types, the most common of which is made from potatoes and spiced with caraway seeds. In Denmark *akvavit* is not sipped but is swallowed straight down as a shot, usually followed by a chaser of beer.

Literature, Film & Television

Like so many Danish forays onto the world stage, Denmark's contribution to Western culture has been in inverse proportion to the country's size. From fairy tales to philosophy, the written word has felt the Danes' impact. In more recent times, minimalist film-making practices and Nordic noir stories on the page and the small screen have caused widespread ripples and garnered legions of fans.

On Page

Dubbed the 'Golden Age', the first half of the 19th century saw Denmark flourish both culturally and economically. Among the writers of the period were two icons of the Danish literary legacy: Hans Christian Andersen (1805–75), whose fairy tales have been translated into more languages than any other book except the Bible; and noted philosopher and theologian Søren Kierkegaard (1813–55), considered the father of existentialism.

Once Upon a Time

As well as single-handedly revolutionising children's literature, Hans Christian Andersen wrote novels, plays and several fascinating travel books. Stories such as *The Little Mermaid*, *The Emperor's New Clothes* and *The Ugly Duckling* have been translated into over 170 languages and are embedded in the global literary consciousness like few others.

Andersen infused his animals, plants and inanimate objects with a magical humanity. His antagonists are not witches or trolls, but human foibles such as indifference and vanity, and it's often his child characters who see the world most clearly. The result is a gentleness that crosses borders and generations. His work is said to have influenced Charles Dickens, Oscar Wilde and innumerable modern-day authors.

Andersen was born in Odense, the son of a cobbler and a washerwoman. In his autobiographies he mythologised his childhood as poor but idyllic. His father died when Andersen was 11, and Andersen left for Copenhagen soon after, an uneducated 14-year-old on a classic fairy-tale mission: to make his fortune in the big city. He tried and failed at various occupations until he eventually found success with his writing, initially with his poems and plays, and then his first volume of short stories.

A neurotic, highly strung hypochondriac, Andersen lived a troubled life. It may go some way to explaining why he was such a restless nomad to the last. Andersen's collected works (156 in all) include poems, novels, travel books, dramatic pieces and three autobiographies. Succumbing to liver cancer, Andersen now rests in Copenhagen's Assistens Kirkegård.

20th-Century Literature

Around 1870, a trend towards realism emerged in Danish literature, dubbed the 'modern breakthrough'. Focused on contemporary issues, the movement's leading figure was Georg Brandes (1842–1927), a writer and social critic who called passionately for a style of literature designed to

How to tackle Kierkegaard's works? Consider starting with *Kierkegaard*, by Michael Watts, which gives a short biography of the philosopher's life and family, plus tips and ideas on how to read and analyse his complex work.

Hans Christian Andersen Sites

Børnekulturhuset Fyrtøjet, Odense

HC Andersens Barndomshjem, Odense

HC Andersens Hus, Odense

Assistens Kirkegård, Copenhagen

spark debate and challenge societal norms. Among those who achieved this was Jens Peter Jacobsen (1847–85), his novel *Marie Grubbe* being the first in Denmark to deal with women's sexuality.

Another realist was Henrik Pontoppidan (1857–1943), who won a Nobel Prize for Literature (shared with compatriot Karl Gjellerup) in 1917 for 'his authentic descriptions of present-day life in Denmark'. The prize would be given to Johannes Vilhelm Jensen in 1944, his historical novel *The Fall of the King* acclaimed as the best Danish novel of the 20th century in 1999.

The most famous Danish writer of the 20th century is Karen Blixen (1885–1962). Starting her career with *Seven Gothic Tales*, published under the pen name Isak Dinesen, she is best known for *Out of Africa*, the memoirs of her farm life in Kenya, penned in 1937. Her Danish estate in Rungsted is now a museum dedicated to her life and work.

One of Denmark's leading contemporary novelists is Peter Høeg, whose works focus on nonconformist characters on the margins of society. In 1992 he published the global hit *Miss Smilla's Feeling for Snow* (published as *Smilla's Sense of Snow* in the USA and made into a movie in 1997), a suspense mystery about a Danish-Greenlandic woman living in Copenhagen.

Recent Trends

Although the hugely popular genre of Scandinavian crime fiction seems dominated by Swedes (most notably Henning Mankell and Stieg Larsson) and Norwegians (Jo Nesbø), noteworthy Danish authors are contributing to the genre.

Among them is Jussi Adler-Olsen, winner of the 2010 Glass Key award, a prestigious literary prize dedicated to Nordic crime/suspense fiction. The first of his series dealing with the intriguing cold-case squad Department Q was published in English in 2011 – in the UK with the title *Mercy*, and in the US as *The Keeper of Lost Causes*. His latest (seventh) instalment in the series is titled *The Scarred Woman* in English.

Another notable contemporary crime writer is Copenhagen-based journalist Erik Valeur, whose debut novel *The Seventh Child* won the 2012 Glass Key prize. Intricately crafted, its plot revolves around the mysterious death of a woman, an orphanage and seven unidentified orphans suspected to be the abandoned children of Denmark's elite.

New names on the scene include Thomas Rydahl, whose book, *The Hermit*, won the Glass Key in 2015. A fellow Dane was also awarded the prize the following year: Ane Riel's novel *Harpiks* won the judges over, but was not yet available in English at the time of research.

Acclaimed for its rich visual textures and innovative use of close-ups, *La Passion de Jeanne d'Arc* (1928), by director Carl Theodor Dreyer (1889–1968), was named the most influential film of all time in a list of the 'Essential 100' published by the Toronto International Film Festival in 2010.

On Screen

Academy Success

Although Danish cinema stretches back to the end of the 19th century, it wasn't until the 1980s that Danish directors attracted a broader international audience, with a swag of trophies to prove it.

Director Gabriel Axel's *Babette's Feast* (1987) won the Academy Award for Best Foreign Film in 1988. An exploration of the impact a French housekeeper has on two pious sisters, the film is an adaptation of a story by Karen Blixen, whose novel *Out of Africa* had been turned into an Oscar-winning Hollywood movie just three years earlier.

Remarkably, just a year later, a Danish film again won Best Foreign Film at the Academy Awards (as well as the Cannes Film Festival's Palme d'Or): *Pelle the Conqueror* was directed by Bille August and adapted from Martin Andersen Nexø's book about the harsh life of an immigrant in 19th-century Denmark.

The award fell into Danish hands one again in 2010 with *In a Better World*. Directed by Susanne Bier, the contemplative drama begins with playground bullying and takes in infidelity, bereavement, evil warlords and revenge – a plot engineered by Bier to question the cosy stereotype of her homeland.

In 2017, Denmark's (unsuccessful) nominee for the Academy Award was the well-received *Land of Mine,* directed by Martin Zandvliet. Its gripping storyline explores the animosity felt by Danes towards Germans after WWII, when young German POWs were forced to defuse the thousands of landmines laid by the occupying German army along the west coast of Jutland.

Directors of Note

Denmark has produced some high-profile directors, many of whom have crossed over from local Danish-language films to Hollywood productions.

Bille August Known for his literary adaptations: *Pelle the Conqueror* (1987); *The House of the Spirits* (1993), based on the novel by Chilean writer Isabel Allende; *Smilla's Sense of Snow* (1997), from the bestseller by Peter Høeg; *Les Misérables* (1998), adapted from Victor Hugo's classic tale; and *Night Train to Lisbon* (2013), based on Pascal Mercier's philosophical novel.

Susanne Bier One of Denmark's leading directors, she has made a name for herself internationally with respected local films *Brothers* (2004; remade into an American production with the same name), *After the Wedding* (2006) and *In a Better World* (2010). In 2016 she moved into TV with the acclaimed British miniseries *The Night Manager,* adapted from the novel by John le Carré.

Lone Scherfig Scherfig's romantic comedy *Italian for Beginners* (2000) dealt with diverse but damaged Danes learning the language of love, and became an international hit. She also directed the dark comedy *Wilbur Wants to Kill Himself* (2002), a Danish-Scottish coproduction, as well as the UK films *An Education* (2009), *The Riot Club* (2014) and *Their Finest* (2016).

Thomas Vinterberg Cofounder of the Dogme95 movement, Vinterberg conceived, wrote and directed the first of the Dogme movies, *Festen* (The Celebration; 1998), to wide acclaim. Although subsequent films flopped, *The Hunt* (2012) won the 2013 Nordic Council Film Prize, and was nominated for Best Foreign Language Film at the 2014 Academy Awards.

Nicholas Winding Refn Famous for writing and directing the gritty and violent *Pusher* trilogy (the first in 1996, with later instalments in 2004 and 2005), which explores the criminal underworld of Copenhagen. His film, the US 'art-house noir' *Drive,* won him the Best Director award at the 2011 Cannes Film Festival.

And then there's Lars von Trier (see p292)...

Top Danish Films
Pelle the Conqueror (1987)
Babette's Feast (1987)
Breaking the Waves (1996)
Festen (1998)
After the Wedding (2006)
In a Better World (2010)
The Hunt (2012)
A Royal Affair (2012)
Land of Mine (2015)

Television

Over the past decade or two, Denmark has cemented its reputation for superlative TV crime drama, characterised by gripping plot twists and a dark, moody atmosphere.

Planting the seed of success was the four-season drama *Unit One*. Based around an elite mobile police task force, the show won an Emmy Award for best non-American television drama series in 2002. On its tail was *The Eagle*, its 24 episodes revolving around a small Danish investigation unit solving everything from terrorist threats to international fraud. The show would also go on to receive an Emmy, in 2005.

Come 2007 audiences were introduced to *The Killing* and its protagonist Sarah Lund, a Copenhagen police detective known for her astute crime-solving abilities and love of Faroese knitwear. During its three seasons, the series became an international cult hit, screening in almost 20 countries, winning a British BAFTA Award and spawning an American remake.

LARS VON TRIER & DOGME95

Whether he's depicting explicit sexual encounters in *Nymphomaniac* (2013), the apocalypse in *Melancholia* (2011), or framing female genital mutilation in the polarising *Antichrist* (2009), there is little doubt that the leading Danish director and screenwriter of the 21st century remains Lars von Trier, who continues to live up to his label as the film world's *enfant terrible*.

Von Trier's better-known films include the melodrama *Breaking the Waves* (1996), which featured Emily Watson and took the Cannes Film Festival's Grand Prix; *Dancer in the Dark* (2000), a musical starring Icelandic pop singer Björk and Catherine Deneuve, which won Cannes' Palme d'Or in 2000; and the frequently difficult and experimental *Dogville* (2003), starring Nicole Kidman.

Von Trier is a cofounder of Dogme95, sometimes dubbed the 'vow of chastity'. This artistic manifesto pledged a minimalist approach to film-making using only hand-held cameras, shooting on location with natural light and rejecting the use of special effects and pre-recorded music. It attracted both ardent fans and widespread dismissal, but its impact and influence on modern cinema cannot be underestimated.

Police tape gave way to spin doctors with the acclaimed political drama *Borgen*. Launched in 2010, the three-season hit stars much-loved Danish actor Sidse Babett Knudsen as Birgitte Nyborg, an idealistic politician suddenly thrown into the oft-challenging position of the country's *statsminister* (prime minister). Praised for its strong female characters, the show's string of awards include a Prix Italia (2010) and a BAFTA (2012).

Debuting in 2011, Danish-Swedish crime thriller *The Bridge* hooked viewers from its very first scene, in which a pair of severed corpses are discovered on the Øresund Bridge, at the very border between Sweden and Denmark. Screened in over 170 countries to date, the series would also spawn American and British-French versions.

More recent productions haven't had the same impact or achieved the same cult status, but if you need a binge of Danish TV, try *Dicte* (2012–16), a procedural crime drama refreshingly set in Aarhus; family drama *The Legacy* (2014–17); or *Follow the Money* (2016–), a glossy but relatively ho-hum story of white-collar crime. *Below the Surface* (2017–) may just hit the jackpot, given that it's a terrorist hostage thriller created by some of the people behind *Borgen* and *The Killing*.

Survival Guide

Directory A–Z

Accommodation

High standards are the norm. It's good to book ahead; in peak summer (late June to mid-August), bookings are essential in popular holiday areas.

Hostels High-quality budget options, country-wide.

B&Bs and private rooms Often quite affordable; from home-style rooms to larger hotel-like guesthouses.

Hotels Budget chains, business-minded options, castles or designer digs – there are plenty of options and price points.

Camping grounds Plenty of full-service, family-focused options. Many are located by the water and offer in-demand cabins and cottages. In high demand in summer.

Self-catering apartments and summer houses Appealing and cost-effective alternatives, especially for families and groups. May have a minimum stay.

The Basics

→ Local tourist offices (and their websites) can provide lists of local accommodation and may help arrange bookings for a small fee.

→ Accommodation prices listed are for peak summer (late June to mid-August), when Danish schools are on vacation and most locals take holidays. Prices at holiday hotspots peak in summer, while business-oriented hotels in cities may drop summer rates to attract guests. Websites list up-to-date prices.

→ Many hotels, hostels and restaurants are members of the Green Key eco accreditation scheme (www. greenkey.global).

→ There is no hard-and-fast rule about the inclusion of breakfast in prices – many hotels include it in their rates, but for others it is an optional extra. It is never included in the price of hostels and budget hotels (but is usually available for around 75kr). Ironically, breakfast is usually *not* included in B&B rates.

Opening Hours & Self-Service

→ Not all hotels and guesthouses have staffed reception desks. At some places you need to prearrange arrival times. Alternatively, you might be asked to phone an hour before arriving. Or there might simply be a phone number stuck to the door to call when you arrive.

→ 'Self-service' (*selvbetjening*) hotels like the BB Hotels chain (www. bbhotels.dk) are essentially unstaffed apart from cleaners. Guests book online and receive a security code that accesses the building and/or room. There may be a 'help-yourself' breakfast from a fridge.

→ Hostels are generally unstaffed for much of the day. Check-in is generally 4pm to 6pm (or to 8pm in summer) and for late arrivals you'll need to be in touch with the hostel manager.

Bed & Breakfasts

Some B&Bs are traditional homestays but an ever-increasing number are private rooms in small guesthouses, where you may share a bathroom and kitchen with other guests, or have a studio-style apartment to yourself. From 350/600kr for a single/double, they're often cheaper than a private room at a hostel and rates generally include linen. Breakfast is usually optional (around 70kr to 90kr extra).

→ Some B&Bs cannot process credit card payments.

→ Tourist offices maintain B&B listings for their areas.

➺ Many are bookable on the usual accommodation booking sites.

➺ Useful online resource: www.bedandbreakfastguide.dk.

Camping

➺ Denmark is very well set up for campers, with nearly 600 camping grounds, Some are open only in the summer months, while others operate from spring to autumn. About 200 stay open year-round (and have low-season rates).

➺ You need a camping card (called Camping Key Europe) for stays at all camping grounds. You can buy a card at the first camping ground you arrive at, at local tourist offices or from the **Danish Camping Board** (see www.danishcampsites.com). The cost for an annual pass for couples is 110kr; it covers all accompanied children aged under 18.

➺ The per-night charge to pitch a tent or park a caravan is typically around 80kr for an adult, and about half that for each child. In summer, some places also tack on a site charge of 50kr to 80kr per tent/caravan; some also have a small eco tax.

➺ Many camping grounds rent cabins (a few offer on-site caravans) sleeping four to six people. Cabins range from simple huts with bunk beds to full cottages with kitchen and bathroom. You generally BYO linen or pay to hire it. In the summer peak (late June to mid-August), many cabins can only be hired by the week (around 3500kr, but it very much depends on the cabin's size and facilities).

➺ The Danish Nature Agency (http://eng.naturstyrelsen.dk) oversees some primitive camping areas and shelters in forested areas. See its website for more details and the rules on wild camping.

➺ Backpackers and cyclists, note: even if a camping

SLEEPING PRICE RANGES

The following price ranges refer to a double room in high season. Unless otherwise noted, rooms have private bathrooms.

€ less than 700kr

€€ 700kr–1500kr

€€€ more than 1500kr

ground is signposted as fully booked, there may be sites for light-travelling campers.

➺ If you're touring around, look for camping grounds offering 'QuickStop', a cheaper rate whereby you arrive after 8pm and leave again by 10am.

➺ Check www.smaapladser.dk for a list of 34 camping grounds that are smaller and more intimate, with a maximum of 145 camping pitches.

➺ Best online resources: www.danishcampsites.com and www.dk-camp.dk.

Farm Stays

➺ A great way to get a feel for rural Denmark is on a farm stay, which can simply mean bed and breakfast accommodation or actually helping out with farm activities.

➺ The website of Landsforeningen for **Landboturisme** (www.visitfarmen.dk) links to 60 farms throughout Denmark that offer accommodation (from farmhouse rooms to family-sized self-contained flats and small rural houses). You book directly with the farm owner.

➺ Although it's best to plan in advance, if you're cycling or driving around Denmark you may well come across farmhouses displaying *værelse* (room) signs.

Hostels

➺ Some 68 hostels make up the **Danhostel association** (☏ 33 31 36 12; www.danhostel.dk), which is affiliated with Hostelling International (HI).

Some are dedicated hostels in holiday areas, while others are attached to sports centres (and hence may be busy with travelling sports teams etc).

➺ If you hold a valid HI card, you receive a 10% discount on Danhostel rates (these can be purchased from hostels and cost 160kr for non-Danes). We list prices for noncardholders.

➺ Note that there are a growing number of private hostels not affiliated with the Danhostel association.

➺ Danish hostels appeal to all ages and are oriented as much towards families and groups as to budget travellers. Hiring a private room is the norm. Outside Copenhagen, only some hostels offer dorm beds in shared rooms (some may only offer these in the summer, from July to mid-September).

➺ Typical costs are 200kr to 300kr for a dorm bed. For private rooms, expect to pay 400kr to 600kr per single, 450kr to 750kr per double, and up to 100kr for each additional person in larger rooms. All hostels offer family rooms; many rooms come with private bathrooms.

➺ Duvets and pillows are provided, but you'll have to bring or hire your own sheets and towel (typically between 50kr and 80kr per stay).

➺ Almost all hostels provide an all-you-can-eat breakfast costing around 75kr, and some also provide dinner. Most hostels have guest kitchens with pots and pans.

EATING PRICE RANGES

The following price ranges refer to a standard main course.

€ less than 125kr

€€ 125kr–250kr

€€€ more than 250kr

➡ Advance reservations are advised, particularly in summer. In a few places, reception closes as early as 6pm. In most hostels the reception office is closed, and the phone not answered, between noon and 4pm.

➡ Between May and September, hostels can get crowded with children on school excursions, or sports groups travelling for tournaments.

➡ A number of Danish hostels close for part of the low season.

➡ A note on costs: if you need to hire linen, the price of a double room plus sheets and towels may become more expensive than a room at a budget hotel. Consider what you're after (kitchen access, for example, which hostels offer but hotels don't) and book accordingly.

Hotels

➡ A few brands tend to dominate in the hotel business. For budget hotels, look for **CabInn** (www.cabinn.dk), Zleep (www.zleephotels.com) and self-service **BB Hotels** (www.bbhotels.dk) across the country, and **Wake Up** (www.wakeupcopenhagen.com) in Copenhagen and Aarhus.

➡ Business-standard hotel chains include **Scandic** (www.scandichotels.com), **Radisson** (www.radisson.com), **Comwell** (www.comwell.dk) and **First Hotels** (www.firsthotels.com).

➡ There's a good range of boutique hotels in larger cities and popular upmarket destinations (Bornholm, for example, and Skagen), but true luxury or design hotels

are not especially common outside Copenhagen and Aarhus. If you're looking for something more memorable than a chain hotel, consider staying in a castle, historic manor house or rural property. Also look out for a *badehotel* or *strandhotel* (an old seaside 'bathing inn') – many of these are now restored. Great resources for something a little special: www.guldsmedenhotels.com, www.slotte-herregaarde.dk and www.smalldanishhotels.com.

➡ Be careful: the inclusion of *kro* in a name usually implies a country inn, but it is also (less commonly) the Danish version of a motel, found along major motorways near the outskirts of town.

➡ Some hotels have set rates published on their websites; others have dynamic rates that fluctuate according to season and demand. Most hotel websites offer good deals and packages, as do the usual booking engines.

➡ Many business hotels offer cheaper rates on Friday and Saturday nights year-round, and during the summer peak (from late June until the start of the school year in early/mid-August), when business folk aren't travelling.

➡ There is no hard-and-fast rule about the inclusion of breakfast in prices – many hotels include it in their price, but for others it is optional. It is never included in the price of budget hotels (you can purchase it for around 75kr to 100kr). Hotel breakfasts are usually pretty decent all-you-can-eat buffets.

Manor Houses

➡ Denmark is stuffed with castles and manor houses, some of them offering atmospheric accommodation in beautiful grounds. The website of the **Danske Slotte & Herregaarde association** (www.slotte-herregaarde.dk) has links to around 15 such places that offer accommodation.

Rental Accommodation

➡ Many seaside resort areas are filled with cottages and apartments. These are generally let out by the week and require reservations. Rates vary greatly, depending on the type of accommodation and the season, but generally they're cheaper than hotels.

➡ **DanCenter** (www.dancenter.com) handles holiday-cottage bookings nationwide. Many tourist offices can also help make reservations. Alternatively, try **Novasol** (www.novasol.dk), which organises self-catering options in cottages and summer houses.

➡ Hundreds of places (summer cottages, inner-city apartments, family-friendly houses) can be rented direct from the owner via the usual online booking engines.

Etiquette

Road Rules If you'll be driving or cycling, brush up on the rules of the road. Cyclists often have the right of way, and for drivers it's particularly important to check cycle lanes before turning right.

Punctuality Trains and tours run on time and aren't a minute late. Danes operate similarly in social situations.

Queuing When you go to a Danish bakery, pharmacy or tourist office – just about any place there can be a queue – there's invariably a machine dispensing numbered tickets. Grab a ticket as you enter.

Toasts As you raise your glass and say 'skål' (cheers!), make eye contact with everyone.

Electricity

Denmark uses the two-pin continental plug like most other European countries – it has two round pins and operates on 230V (volts) and 50Hz (cycles) AC.

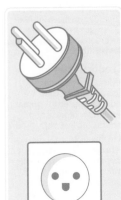

230V/50Hz

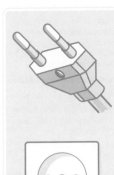

230V/50Hz

Embassies & Consulates

The following embassies and consulates are in and around Copenhagen:

Australian Embassy (☑70 26 36 76; www.denmark.embassy. gov.au; Dampfærgevej 26; ☐26, 27)

Canadian Embassy (☑33 48 32 00; www.denmark.gc.ca; Kristen Bernikows Gade 1; ☐1A, 26, ⓂKongens Nytorv)

French Embassy (☑33 67 01 00; www.ambafrance-dk.org; Kongens Nytorv 4; ☐1A, 26, 350S, ⓂKongens Nytorv)

German Embassy (☑35 45 99 00; www.kopenhagen.diplo. de; Stockholmsgade 57; ☐1A, ⓈØsterport)

Irish Embassy (☑35 47 32 00; www.embassyofireland.dk; Østbanegade 21; ⓈØsterport)

Netherlands Embassy (☑33 70 72 00; www.nederlandwere ldwijd.nl/landen/denemarken; Toldbodgade 33; ☐1A, 66, ⓂKongens Nytorv)

New Zealand Consulate (☑33 37 77 00; www.nzconsulate.dk; Store Strandstræde 21; ☐1A, 66, ⓂKongens Nytorv)

UK Embassy (☑35 44 52 00; http://ukindenmark.fco.gov.uk; Kastelsvej 36-40; ☐37)

US Embassy (☑33 41 71 00; https://dk.usembassy.gov; Dag Hammarskjölds Allé 24; ☐1A, ⓈØsterport)

Gay & Lesbian Travellers

Denmark has a high degree of tolerance for alternative lifestyles of all sorts.

➡ Copenhagen in particular has an active, open gay community with a healthy number of venues, but you'll find LGBT venues in other cities too, as well as mainstream venues that are welcoming to all.

➡ Useful websites: for general info www.lgbt.dk, for traveller listings www.

rainbowbusinessdenmark.dk, for events www.oaonline.dk.

➡ The main LGBTQ events of the year is August's week-long **Copenhagen Pride** (www.copenhagenpride.dk), plus October's film festival **Mix Copenhagen** (www. mixcopenhagen.dk).

Health

Denmark is a relatively healthy place and travellers shouldn't need to take any unusual health precautions.

➡ You can get medical treatment anywhere in the country by contacting a doctor during consultation hours.

➡ If you're in urgent need of medical care outside office hours (evenings and weekends), you can contact an emergency doctor (Lægevagten). Visit the website www.laegevagten. dk/kontakt-laegevagten and click where you are on the map of Denmark to find the telephone number of the doctor in your area.

➡ The Danish National Health Service provides free healthcare to residents but does not cover visitors to Denmark. A doctor's appointment may cost around 350kr to 500kr.

➡ For minor ailments, pharmacists can give advice and sell over-the-counter medication. They can also advise when more specialised help is required and point you in the right direction. Look for the sign *apotek* (pharmacy).

Insurance

➡ Although Denmark is a very safe place to travel, theft does occasionally happen, and illness and accidents are always a possibility. A travel insurance policy to cover theft, loss and medical problems is strongly recommended.

➡ Worldwide travel insurance is available at www.lonelyplanet.com/travel-insurance. You can buy, extend and claim online anytime – even if you're already on the road.

➡ If you're an EU citizen, the European Health Insurance Card (EHIC) covers you for most medical care, but not for nonemergencies or for emergency repatriation home. Apply online via your government's health department website.

➡ Citizens from other countries should find out if there is a reciprocal arrangement for free medical access in Denmark. Make sure your health insurance covers you for the worst possible scenario, such as an accident requiring an emergency flight home.

Internet Access

➡ With the proliferation of wi-fi, and most locals and travellers carrying tablets and/or smartphones, the old-fashioned internet cafe is a dying breed in Denmark. There may be a couple catering to gamers and laptop-less travellers in the major cities, but public libraries are your best bet in mid-sized and small towns for free use of computers with internet access.

➡ Libraries also have free wi-fi (you will generally need a code), as do many cafes and bars, and trains and buses. Wi-fi is ubiquitous in hotels and hostels and is usually free. Some hostels and hotels will offer a computer for guests to use, free or for a small charge.

Legal Matters

➡ Authorities are strict about drink driving, and even a couple of drinks can put you over the legal limit of 0.05% blood-alcohol level. Drivers detected under the influence of alcohol are liable to receive stiff penalties and a possible prison sentence.

➡ Always treat drugs with a great deal of caution. In Denmark all forms of cannabis are officially illegal.

Money

➡ Although Denmark is an EU member nation, Denmark's citizens rejected adopting the euro in a referendum in 2000.

➡ Denmark's currency, the krone, is most often written with the symbol DKK in international money markets, and kr within Denmark.

➡ One krone is divided into 100 øre. There are 50 øre, 1kr, 2kr, 5kr, 10kr and 20kr coins. Notes come in denominations of 50, 100, 200, 500 and 1000 kroner.

➡ Relatively few banks exchange money, and some businesses are entirely non-cash.

ATMS

➡ Most banks in Denmark have 24-hour ATMs that give cash advances on Visa and MasterCard credit cards as well as Cirrus and Plus bank cards.

➡ Typically, you'll get a good rate when withdrawing money directly from a Danish ATM, but keep in mind that your home bank may charge you a fee for international transactions or for using another bank's ATM – check before you leave.

➡ A few banks, especially in Copenhagen, have 24-hour cash machines that change major foreign currencies into Danish kroner.

Credit Cards

➡ Credit cards such as Visa and MasterCard are widely accepted in Denmark (American Express and Diners Club less so).

➡ In many places (hotels, petrol stations, restaurants, shops) a surcharge may be imposed on foreign cards (up to 3.75%). If there is a surcharge, it must be advertised (eg on the menu, at reception).

Tipping

➡ Hotel and restaurant bills and taxi fares include service charges in the quoted prices.

➡ Further tipping is unnecessary, although rounding up the bill is not uncommon when service has been especially good.

Opening Hours

Opening hours vary throughout the year, especially for sights and activities.

Banks 10am–4pm Monday to Friday

Bars & Clubs 4pm–midnight, to 2am or later Friday and Saturday (on weekends clubs may open until 5am)

Cafes 8am–5pm or midnight

Restaurants noon–10pm (maybe earlier on weekends for brunch)

Shops 10am–6pm Monday to Friday, to 4pm Saturday, some larger stores may open Sunday

Supermarkets 8am–9pm (many with in-store bakeries opening around 7am)

Seasonal Variations

Family-friendly attractions (museums, zoos, funparks) in holiday hotspots will generally open from June to August (possibly May to September), and for the spring and autumn school holidays.

The Danish summer vacation, which generally runs from the final week of June through the first week of August, is a six-week period when opening hours of attractions are longest. Hours generally decrease in the shoulder and low seasons.

Post

➡ The Danish postal service (www.postnord.dk) is reliable and efficient, and rates are comparable to other Western European countries.

➡ There are fewer post offices these days – many have moved to counters within large supermarkets.

➡ Full list of rates, branches and opening hours are available online.

Public Holidays

Many Danes take their main work holiday during the first three weeks of July, but there are numerous other holidays as well.

Banks and most businesses close on public holidays and transport schedules are usually reduced.

New Year's Day (Nytårsdag) 1 January

Maundy Thursday (Skærtorsdag) Thursday before Easter

Good Friday (Langfredag) Friday before Easter

Easter Day (Påskedag) Sunday in March or April

Easter Monday (2. Påskedag) Day after Easter

Great Prayer Day (Store Bededag) Fourth Friday after Easter

Ascension Day (Kristi Himmelfartsdag) Sixth Thursday after Easter

Whitsunday (Pinsedag) Seventh Sunday after Easter

Whitmonday (2. Pinsedag) Seventh Monday after Easter

Constitution Day (Grundlovsdag) 5 June

Christmas Eve (Juleaften) 24 December (from noon)

Christmas Day (Juledag) 25 December

Boxing Day (2. Juledag) 26 December

New Year's Eve (Nytårsaften) 31 December (from noon)

Safe Travel

Denmark is a very safe country and travelling here presents no unusual dangers. Travellers should nevertheless be careful with their belongings, particularly in busy places such as Copenhagen's central station.

In cities, you'll need to quickly become accustomed to the busy bike lanes that run beside roads (between the vehicle lanes and the pedestrian pavements). These cycle lanes (and fast-moving cyclists) are easy to wander into accidentally.

Telephone

Phone Codes

➡ All telephone numbers in Denmark have eight digits; there are no area codes. This means that all eight digits must be dialled, even when making calls in the same city.

➡ For local directory assistance dial 🖉118. For overseas enquiries, including for rates and reverse charge (collect) calls, dial 🖉113.

➡ The country code for Denmark is 🖉45. To call Denmark from another country, dial the international access code for the country you're in followed by 🖉45 and the local eight-digit number.

➡ The international access code in Denmark is 🖉00. To make direct international calls from Denmark, dial 🖉00 followed by the country code for the country you're calling, the area code, then the local number.

Mobile Phones

➡ As of June 2017, the EU has ended roaming surcharges for people who travel periodically within the EU. EU residents can use mobile devices when travelling in the EU, paying the same prices as at home.

➡ For non-EU folks, the cheapest and most practical way to make calls at local rates is to purchase a European SIM card and pop it into your own mobile phone (tip: bring an old phone from home for that purpose). Before leaving home, make sure that your phone isn't blocked from doing this by your home network.

➡ If you're coming from outside Europe, also check that your phone will work in Europe's GSM 900/1800 network (US phones work on a different frequency).

➡ You can buy and top-up a prepaid Danish SIM card at supermarkets, kiosks and petrol stations. **Lebara** (www.lebara.dk) and **Lycamobile** (www.lycamobile.dk) are common. The latter can be obtained for free (see the website) and you can top up online.

Payphones

➡ Public phones are elusive in Denmark. There may be a payphone outside the local train or bus station and some bigger attractions, but few others.

➡ You pay by the minute. Phones accept coins, credit cards or prepaid phonecards (available from kiosks and post offices).

Time

➡ As in neighbouring European countries, Denmark is one hour ahead of GMT/UTC in winter, or two hours ahead during daylight saving time (from the last Sunday in March to the last Sunday in October).

➡ During the northern hemisphere summer, Denmark is one hour ahead of London, six hours ahead of New York, and eight hours behind Sydney.

➡ The 24-hour clock system is used for all timetables and business hours.

➡ *Klokken,* which means o'clock, is abbreviated as kl (kl 19.30 is 7.30pm).

➡ The Danes number the weeks of the year – eg schools break for winter holidays in week 7 or 8; many businesses are closed for summer holidays in weeks 29 and 30. See www.ugenr.dk.

Toilets

In towns and cities, public toilets are generally easy to find. There may be a small fee to use the facilities at shopping centres or large train stations.

Tourist Information

Denmark is generally well served by helpful tourist offices and multilingual staff. Each town and region publishes a glossy annual brochure that covers most of the things travellers need to know, and has a website full of sights, accommodation options and practical info. Many now offer a downloadable app and have installed touchscreens around town (at train and bus stations, for example).

The trend in recent times is for information to be obtained online, with shorter staffed hours at tourist offices (though these offices may be open for self-service pick-up of brochures or use of a touchscreen). A few larger towns have done away with physical tourist offices.

Important websites for visitors to Denmark include www.denmark.dk and www.visitdenmark.com. Other official websites covering local areas include the following:

Bornholm (www.bornholm.info)

Copenhagen (www.visitcopenhagen.com)

Funen (www.visitfyn.com)

East Jutland (www.visitaarhus.com, www.visitdjursland.com)

North Jutland (www.visitnordjylland.com, www.toppenafdanmark.com)

West Jutland (www.sydvestjylland.com, www.visitnordvestjylland.com)

Zealand (www.visitnorthsealand.com, www.cphcoastandcountryside.com)

Travellers with Disabilities

➡ Denmark is improving access to buildings, transport and even forestry areas and beaches all the time, although accessibility is still not ubiquitous.

➡ The official www.visitdenmark.com website has a few links for travellers with disabilities – see www.visitdenmark.com/a-z/6244.

➡ A useful resource is God Adgang (Good Access; www.godadgang.dk), which lists service providers who have had their facilities registered and labelled for accessibility.

Visas

Generally not required for stays of up to 90 days. Not required for members of EU or Schengen countries.

Volunteering

➡ Denmark has a very strong tradition of volunteer organisations and a high percentage of Danes do volunteer work.

➡ There is less opportunity for people without knowledge of Danish, but a good place to check is www.volunteering.dk, which tries to bring organisations and volunteers with an international background together.

Work

For EU nationals and EEA citizens, it's relatively easy to relocate to Denmark for work. For non-EU nationals, things aren't so easy. Full details are outlined on www.nyidanmark.dk.

Transport

GETTING THERE & AWAY

Getting to Denmark is simple. The capital, Copenhagen, has worldwide air connections, plus some carriers fly into regional airports. Roads and railways link to Germany and Sweden. Ferries reach five countries.

Entering the Country/Region

Denmark is part of the Schengen agreement. When entering Denmark from a neighbouring country, passports are not usually checked, but you must still have your passport or Schengen-country identification with you. When flying in from outside the Schengen area, passports (and visas where necessary) are checked. Passports must be valid for three months beyond your proposed departure date.

Air

Airports & Airlines

➡ The majority of overseas flights into Denmark land at **Copenhagen Airport** (☑ 32 31 32 31; www.cph.dk; Lufthavnsboulevarden, Kastrup; Ⓜ Lufthavnen, Ⓢ Københavns Lufthavn) in Kastrup, about 9km southeast of central Copenhagen.

➡ A number of international flights, mostly those coming from other Nordic countries or the UK, land at smaller regional airports, in Aarhus, Aalborg, Billund, Esbjerg and Sønderborg.

➡ Dozens of international airlines fly to/from Danish airports; the airport websites have up-to-date information on all the relevant carriers.

➡ **SAS** (☑ 70 10 20 00; www.flysas.com) is the flag carrier of Denmark (and Norway and Sweden).

Land

Denmark has a land border with Germany and a bridge over the Øresund links to Sweden. For comprehensive tips on reaching Denmark overland, see www.seat61.com/denmark.

Bicycle

Cycling into Denmark from Germany is fine but from Sweden the Øresund Bridge doesn't allow bicycles, so you'll need to use the train (bike adds 50% to an adult fare) or one of the ferry routes (modest extra fare).

Bus

The main international bus operator is **FlixBus** (☑ 32 72 93 86; www.flixbus.dk). From Copenhagen, direct overnight routes include Amsterdam (12 hours), Berlin (8¼ hours via Rostock), Cologne (12¼ to 15¼ hours), Frankfurt (15 hours), Oslo (8¾ hours) and Stockholm (9½ hours). With connecting services

---

CLIMATE CHANGE & TRAVEL

Every form of transport that relies on carbon-based fuel generates CO_2, the main cause of human-induced climate change. Modern travel is dependent on aeroplanes, which might use less fuel per kilometre per person than most cars but travel much greater distances. The altitude at which aircraft emit gases (including CO_2) and particles also contributes to their climate change impact. Many websites offer 'carbon calculators' that allow people to estimate the carbon emissions generated by their journey and, for those who wish to do so, to offset the impact of the greenhouse gases emitted with contributions to portfolios of climate-friendly initiatives throughout the world. Lonely Planet offsets the carbon footprint of all staff and author travel.

many other destinations are available, including arrival or departure in/from Aalborg, Aarhus, Roskilde and Odense. FlixBus has dynamic pricing and tickets must generally be prebooked online. Beware that in several cities FlixBus uses stops that are not the main bus stations, so check carefully.

Car & Motorcycle

If you bring a vehicle that is registered in a non-EU country to Denmark, you must take out a border insurance policy. These requirements are outlined on the website of the **Danish Motor Insurers' Bureau** (DFIM; www.dfim.dk).

Car ferries are available from several countries. Alternatively, you can drive to Denmark from Germany (numerous roads) and from Sweden across the remarkable 16km Øresundsbroen (Øresund Bridge; www.oresundsbron.com, car/motorcycle/campervan 410/210/820kr) between Malmö and Copenhagen. That's actually a combination tunnel-island-bridge motorway plus railway.

UK

From exiting the Channel Tunnel it's a little over 900km to the Danish border through France, Belgium, Netherlands and Germany. That's feasible in around 12 hours' of driving, dependent upon traffic conditions.

Train

Eurail and InterRail passes are valid on **Danish national railways** (www.dsb.dk) but must be prepurchased before arrival in Denmark. There's a dizzying variety of other rail passes depending on your age, residence etc, but look at www.railpass.com first and figure out if the pass really saves any money. Always read the small print. High-speed supplements and night trains are rarely included.

Sea

Ferries link Denmark to Norway, Sweden, Germany, Poland (via Sweden), Iceland and the Faroe Islands.

Fares vary wildly, by season and by day of the week, usually highest on summer weekends. Discounts are often available for seniors, children and holders of rail passes or student cards. Travelling by car, most car fares include passengers, but booking well in advance is highly advised, especially in summer and on weekends.

Faroe Islands & Iceland

Smyril Line (www.smyrilline.com) Sails from the Northern Jutland port of Hirtshals to Tórshavn, the capital of the Faroe Islands (38 hours, once weekly year-round, twice weekly in summer peak), and from Hirtshals to Seyðisfjörður (Iceland) via Tórshavn (66 hours, once weekly).

Germany

BornholmerFærgen (www.bornholmerfaergen.dk) Sails from Rønne (on Bornholm) to Sassnitz (3½ to four hours) a handful of times weekly from April to October (daily in July and August).

Scandlines (www.scandlines.dk) Sails from Rødbyhavn (on Lolland) to Puttgarden (45 minutes, every half-hour) and from Gedser (on Falster) to Rostock (1¾ hours, up to 10 daily).

Sylt Ferry (www.syltferry.com) Sails from Havneby (on west-coast Rømø) to the German island of Sylt (40 minutes, up to nine daily).

Norway

Color Line (www.colorline.com) Sails from Hirtshals to Kristiansand (3¼ hours, once or twice daily) and Larvik (3¾ hours, once or twice daily).

DFDS Seaways (www.dfdsseaways.com) Copenhagen to Oslo (17 hours, daily).

Fjordline (www.fjordline.com) Offers a fast catamaran service from Hirtshals to Kristiansand (2¼ hours, two or three services daily mid-May to mid-September). Also sails year-round from Hirtshals to Bergen via Stavanger (Stavanger 10½ hours, Bergen 16½ hours, once daily), and to Langesund (4½ hours, once daily).

Stena Line (www.stenaline.dk) Frederikshavn to Oslo (nine hours, daily).

Poland

Polferries (www.polferries.com) Świnoujście to Ystad in southern Sweden (6½ hours, once or twice daily) with connecting shuttle bus to Copenhagen for for foot passengers.

TT-Line (www.ttline.com) Świnoujście to Rønne (on Bornholm), weekly, summer only.

Sweden

BornholmerFærgen (www.bornholmerfaergen.dk) Rønne (Bornholm) to Ystad (80 minutes, up to nine times daily).

Scandlines (www.scandlines.dk) Helsingør to Helsingborg (20 minutes, up to four sailings an hour).

Stena Line (www.stenaline.com) Sails from Frederikshavn to Gothenburg (3½ hours, up to five times a day) and from Grenaa to Varberg (four to five hours, once or twice daily).

GETTING AROUND

Air

Domestic air traffic is mostly limited to business travellers and people connecting from international flights through Copenhagen, from where there are short-hop connections to Aarhus, Aalborg and Billund on **SAS** (www.flysas.com). **Danish Airport Transport** (DAT; www.dat.dk) operates flights to Bornholm and Midtjylland/Korup while Alsie (www.alsieexpress.dk) serves Sønderborg.

Bicycle

Denmark is the EU's most cycle-friendly country with countless excellent bicycle routes.

➡ To take your bike on ferries and on regional and intercity trains you need to buy a ticket (cykelbillet). Prices vary with distance travelled. From May to August, an advance bike-space reservation (cykelpladsbillet) is also required for IC and ICL trains.

➡ In Copenhagen, bikes go for free on the S-tog suburban train network. However, on the metro you'll need a bike ticket and no bikes are permitted during weekday peak hours.

Hire

➡ Almost every Danish town (and many a village) has bike rental from around 100/400kr per day/week for something basic. Helmets are generally not included (they're not compulsory in Denmark).

➡ A few upmarket hotels have free bikes for guest use.

➡ Copenhagen, Aarhus, Odense and Aalborg have bycykler (town bike) schemes.

Boat

Tunnels and/or bridges link all Denmark's main land masses but ferries can prove quicker than driving where road routes are circuitous. Boats provide important links to populated smaller islands that lack road links. It's a good idea to book car passage in advance at any time of year, but especially on summer weekends.

Bus

➡ Long-distance buses are less frequent and usually slower than trains, but can prove cheaper, considerably so if you book in advance on the **FlixBus** (☑32 72 93 86; www.flixbus.dk) network, which has dynamic pricing. Regular bus options ex-Copenhagen include Aarhus (from 149kr, 3½ to 4½ hours) and Aalborg (from 209kr, 5½ to 6½ hours). These generally drive via Odense (Funen) though one daily service uses the Odden-Aarhus ferry.

➡ **Thinggaard Express** (☑98 11 66 00; www.expressbus.dk) operates Esbjerg-Aalborg trans-Jutland service 980.

➡ Use www.rejseplanen.dk to compare bus and train journey durations.

Car & Motorcycle

➡ Most roads are high quality and well signposted. Except during rush hour, traffic is quite light, even in major cities.

➡ Cyclists often have the right of way: it's essential to check cycle lanes before turning right.

➡ Roads leading out of town centres are named after the main city that they lead to (eg the road heading out of Odense to Faaborg is called Faaborgvej).

➡ Petrol stations, with toilets, baby-changing facilities and minimarkets, are at 50km intervals on motorways.

➡ Other than the Øresund Bridge to Sweden the only toll road is the 18km **Storebælt** (Great Belt; www.storebaelt.dk) motorway bridge-causeway linking Funen and Zealand (car/motorcycle 240/125kr).

Driving Licence

Short-term visitors may hire a car with only their home country's driving licence (so long as the licence is written in Roman script; if not, an international driving licence is necessary).

Fuel

➡ Unleaded petrol and diesel fuel are available. Although prices fluctuate somewhat, per-litre prices at the time of research were around 10kr.

➡ In towns, petrol stations may be open until 10pm or midnight, but there are some 24-hour services. Some have unstaffed 24-hour automatic pumps operated with credit cards.

Hire

➡ Rental cars are relatively expensive in Denmark, but a little research can mean big savings. Walk-in rates start at about 600kr per day for a small car, although naturally the per-day rates drop the longer you rent.

RIDE SHARING

Long-distance ride-share websites/apps within Europe include www.blablacar.com, www.ridefinder.eu or www.gomore.com.

Denmark-specific options can be found at www.samkorsel.dk and www.gomore.dk.

➡ You may get the best deal on a car rental by booking with an international rental agency before you arrive. Be sure to ask about promotional rates, prepay schemes etc. Ensure you get a deal covering unlimited kilometres.

➡ Avis, Budget, Europcar and Hertz are among the largest operators in Denmark, with offices in major cities, airports and other ports of entry. There are very few local budget operators. If you'll be using a rental car for a while, you might consider hiring your car in cheaper Germany and either returning it there afterwards, or negotiating a slightly more expensive one-way deal.

➡ Rental companies' weekend rates, when available, offer real savings. For about 1000kr, you can hire a small car from Friday to Monday, including VAT and insurance. These deals may have restrictions on the amount of kilometres included (often around 300km) – request a plan that includes unlimited kilometres if you'll need it.

Parking

Look out for parking rules and restrictions in the centre of towns and cities.

Parking forbidden Indicated by *Parkering forbudt*, generally accompanied by a round sign with a red diagonal slash.

Paid parking This is indicated by *P-billet*. Parking ticket machines (*billetautomat*) will generally have information available in a few languages, and accept credit cards.

Time-restricted parking Indicated by *P-skive* followed by a number of hours (eg 2 *timer* = two hours). In many areas parking is free of charge but time restricted (and these restrictions are enforced). Use of a parking disc is required – this is a device that looks like a clock, which you place on the dashboard of your car to indicate the time you arrived at a car-parking space.

Discs come standard with rental cars, and are often available from petrol stations and tourist offices.

Road Rules

➡ Drive on the right-hand side of the road.

➡ Cars and motorcycles must have dipped headlights on at all times.

➡ Drivers are required to carry a warning triangle in case of breakdown.

➡ Seat belt use is mandatory. Children under 135cm must be secured with approved child restraint appropriate to the child's age, size and weight.

➡ Motorcycle riders (but not cyclists) must wear helmets.

➡ Speed limits: 50km/h in towns and built-up areas, 80km/h on major roads, up to 130km/h on motorways. Maximum speed for vehicles with trailers: 80km/h. Speeding fines can be severe.

ROAD DISTANCES (KM)

	Aalborg	Copenhagen	Esbjerg	Frederikshavn	Grenaa	Helsingør	Kalundborg	Kolding	Næstved	Nyborg	Odense	Ringkøbing	Rødby	Skagen	Thisted	Tønder	Viborg	Århus (Aarhus)
Aalborg	---																	
Copenhagen	402	---																
Esbjerg	216	298	---															
Frederikshavn	65	465	278	---														
Grenaa	136	367	216	193	---													
Helsingør	443	47	339	506	408	---												
Kalundborg	345	103	241	408	310	139	---											
Kolding	199	230	72	261	164	271	173	---										
Næstved	342	85	238	405	307	125	71	152	---									
Nyborg	274	228	170	337	239	169	71	102	68	---								
Odense	243	165	139	306	208	206	108	71	105	37	---							
Ringkøbing	174	336	81	236	188	377	279	115	276	208	177	---						
Rødby	410	181	306	473	375	221	176	238	105	136	173	344	---					
Skagen	105	505	319	41	233	546	448	302	445	377	346	277	513	---				
Thisted	90	399	185	138	186	440	342	196	339	271	240	123	407	172	---			
Tønder	284	315	77	347	249	356	258	86	255	187	156	148	323	387	252	---		
Viborg	80	323	136	142	100	354	266	119	263	195	164	94	331	183	87	205	---	
Århus (Aarhus)	112	304	153	171	63	345	ferry	101	244	176	145	127	312	212	153	186	66	---

→ Using a hand-held mobile phone while driving is illegal; hands-free use is permitted.

→ It's illegal to drive with a blood-alcohol concentration of 0.05% or more.

→ Motorways have emergency telephones at 2km intervals, indicated by arrows on marker posts. From other telephones, dial ☏112 for emergencies.

Hitching

Hitching is never entirely safe anywhere in the world and we don't recommend it. In Denmark, it's not a common practice, is generally unrewarding and is illegal on motorways.

Local Transport

Local transport in Denmark is of a high standard. There are excellent train, metro and bus options within Copenhagen; outside the capital, larger towns have local bus networks and most small towns have bus connections to their regional hub.

Bus

Nearly every town in Denmark supports a network of local buses, which circulate around the town centre and also connect it with outlying areas. In smaller towns, the local bus terminal is often adjacent to the train station and/or long-distance bus terminal. Cash fares are around 20kr to 25kr per local ride, but daily travel passes may be useful.

Rejsekort

Rejsekort (www.rejsekort. dk) is a rechargeable electronic card ticketing system using whichever fares are

cheaper on most domestic transport. The system is aimed primarily at Danish nationals and registered residents, but visitors can buy Rejsekort Anonymous (nonrefundable 80kr plus minimum first top-up 170kr). If using this for long-distance travel ensure that it's set to 'national journey' (see website).

Taxi

Taxis are typically ordered by phone, but in bigger cities can be found near major shopping centres and at train stations: a lit *fri* sign (or a green light) means you can wave it down.

You can pay by cash or credit card. The tip is included in the fare.

Train

Denmark's reliable railway network extends to most of the country, except the southern islands and a pocket of northwestern Jutland. In these areas, local buses connect towns to the nearest train station.

Most long-distance trains operate at least hourly throughout the day. National operator DSB's main train service typyes include:

InterCity (IC) Modern comforts.

InterCityLyn (ICL) On certain well-travelled routes. Same facilities as InterCity, but with fewer stops.

Regionaltog Regional trains; reservations generally not accepted.

S-tog Greater Copenhagen's urban and suburban network.

Fares & Discounts

Standard train fares work out to be a fraction over 1kr

per kilometre to a maximum total of 503kr.

→ A 30kr seat reservation (*pladsbillet*) is recommended on IC and ICL services.

→ A DSB 1 (1st-class ticket) costs about 50% more than the standard fare, but gives an automatic seat guarantee on IC or ICL services.

Discounts include the following:

Children Under 15s pay half adult fares, under 12s travel free if they are with an adult travelling on a standard ticket (maximum two kids per adult).

Group *'Minigruppe'* offers a 20% discount for groups of three to seven people travelling on the same ticket (minimum two adults). For *'gruppebillet'* (eight or more adults travelling together) contact DSB.

Orange *Orange-billetter* are limited availability discount tickets (as low as 99kr for lengthy IC and ICL journeys – Copenhagen to Aarhus, for example) – although the number of tickets available at that price is limited. For the cheapest fares, buy your ticket well in advance (up to two months before your travel date) and travel outside peak hours Monday to Thursday or Saturday.

Youth (aged 16 to 25) A DSB *Ung Kort* (youth card), valid one year, costs 125kr; allows discounts from 20% to 50%.

Left-Luggage

Many Danish train stations have left-luggage lockers (from 20kr for 24 hours).

Train Passes

Some rail passes, including Eurail and InterRail passes, should be bought before you arrive in the country.

Language

As a member of the Scandinavian or North Germanic language family, Danish is closely related to Swedish and Norwegian. With about 5.5 million speakers, it's the official language of Denmark and has co-official status – alongside Greenlandic and Faroese respectively – in Greenland and the Faroese Islands. Until 1944 it was also the official language of Iceland and today is taught in schools there as the first foreign language. Danish is also a minority language in the area of Schleswig-Holstein in northern Germany, where it has some 30,000 speakers.

Most of the sounds in Danish have equivalents in English, and by reading our coloured pronunciation guides as if they were English, you're sure to be understood. There are short and long versions of each vowel, and additional 'combined vowels' or diphthongs. Consonants can be 'swallowed' and even omitted completely, creating (together with vowels) a glottal stop or stød steudh which sounds rather like the Cockney pronunciation of the 'tt' in 'bottle'. Note that ai is pronounced as in 'aisle', aw as in 'saw', eu as the 'u' in 'nurse', ew as the 'ee' in 'see' with rounded lips, ow as in 'how', dh as the 'th' in 'that', and r is trilled. The stressed syllables are in italics in our pronunciation guides. Polite and informal forms are indicated with 'pol' and 'inf' respectively.

BASICS

Hello.	Goddag.	go·da
Goodbye.	Farvel.	faar·vel
Yes./No.	Ja./Nej.	ya/nai
Please.	Vær så venlig.	ver saw ven·lee
Thank you.	Tak.	taak
You're welcome.	Selv tak.	sel taak
Excuse me.	Undskyld mig.	awn·skewl mai
Sorry.	Undskyld.	awn·skewl

How are you?
Hvordan går det? — vor·dan gawr dey

Good, thanks.
Godt, tak. — got taak

What's your name?
Hvad hedder — va hey·dha
De/du? (pol/inf) — dee/doo

My name is ...
Mit navn er ... — mit nown ir ...

Do you speak English?
Taler De/du — ta·la dee/doo
engelsk? (pol/inf) — eng·elsk

I don't understand.
Jeg forstår ikke. — yai for·stawr i·ke

ACCOMMODATION

Where's a ...?	Hvor er der ...?	vor ir deyr ...
campsite	en camping-plads	in kaam·ping·plas
guesthouse	et gæstehus	it ges·te·hoos
hotel	et hotel	it hoh·tel
youth hostel	et ungdoms-herberg	it awng·doms·heyr·beyrg

Do you have a ... room?	Har I et ... værelse?	haar ee it ... verl·se
single	enkelt	eng·kelt
double	dobbelt	do·belt
How much is it per ...?	Hvor meget koster det per ...?	vor maa·yet kos·ta dey peyr ...
night	nat	nat
person	person	per·sohn

WANT MORE?

For in-depth language information and handy phrases, check out Lonely Planet's *Western Europe Phrasebook*. You'll find it at **shop.lonelyplanet.com**.

DIRECTIONS

Where's the ...?
Hvor er ...? vor ir ...

What's the address?
Hvad er adressen? va ir a·*draa*·sen

Can you show me (on the map)?
Kan De/du vise mig kan dee/doo *vee*·se mai
det (på kortet)? (pol/inf) dey (paw *kor*·tet)

How far (away) is it?
Hvor langt (væk) er det? vor laangt (vek) ir dey

How do I get there?
Hvordan kommer vor·*dan* ko·ma
jeg derhen? yai deyr·*hen*

Turn ...	*Drej ...*	drai ...
at the corner	*ved hjørnet*	vi *yeur*·nedh
at the traffic lights	*ved trafik-lyset*	vi traa·*feek*·lew·set
left	*til venstre*	til *vens*·tre
right	*til højre*	til *hoy*·re

It's ...	*Det er ...*	dey ir ...
behind ...	*bag ...*	ba ...
far (away)	*langt (væk)*	laangt (vek)
in front of ...	*foran ...*	*fo*·ran ...
left	*til venstre*	til *vens*·tre
near (to ...)	*nær (ved ...)*	ner (vi ...)
next to ...	*ved siden af ...*	vi *see*·dhen a ...
on the corner	*på hjørnet*	paw *yeur*·net
opposite ...	*på modsate side af ...*	paw *mohdh*·sa·te *see*·dhe a ...
right	*til højre*	til *hoy*·re
straight ahead	*lige ud*	*li*·e oodh

EATING & DRINKING

What would you recommend?
Hvad kan De/du va kan dee/doo
anbefale? (pol/inf) an·bey·fa·le

What's the local speciality?
Hvad er den lokale va ir den loh·*ka*·le
specialitet? spey·sha·lee·*teyt*

Do you have vegetarian food?
Har I vegetarmad? haar ee vey·ge·*taar*·madh

Cheers!
Skål! skawl

I'd like (the) ..., please.	*Jeg vil gerne have ..., tak.*	yai vil *gir*·ne ha ... taak
bill	*regningen*	*rai*·ning·en
drink list	*vinkortet*	*veen*·kor·tet

SIGNS

Indgang	Entrance
Udgang	Exit
Åben	Open
Lukket	Closed
Forbudt	Prohibited
Toilet	Toilets
Herrer	Men
Damer	Women

menu	*menuen*	me·*new*·en
that dish	*den ret*	den ret

Could you prepare a meal without ...?	*Kan I lave et måltid uden ...?*	kan ee *la*·ve it *mawl*·teedh oo·dhen ...
butter	*smør*	smeur
eggs	*æg*	eg
meat stock	*kød-boullion*	*keudh*·boo·lee·yong

Key Words

bar	*bar*	baar
bottle	*flaske*	*flas*·ke
breakfast	*morgenmad*	*morn*·madh
cafe	*café*	ka·*fey*
children's menu	*børne-menu*	*beur*·ne·mey·new
cold	*kold*	kol
cup	*kop*	kop
daily special	*dagens ret*	*da*·ens rat
dinner	*middag*	*mi*·da
drink	*drink*	drink
food	*mad*	madh
fork	*gaffel*	*gaa*·fel
glass	*glas*	glas
hot	*varm*	vaarm
knife	*kniv*	kneev
lunch	*frokost*	*froh*·kost
market	*marked*	*maar*·kedh
menu	*menu/spisekort*	me·*new*/*spee*·se·kort
plate	*tallerken*	ta·*ler*·ken
restaurant	*restaurant*	res·toh·*rang*
snack	*mellem-måltid*	*me*·lem·mawl·teedh
spoon	*ske*	skey

teaspoon	teske	tey·skey
with	med	me
without	uden	oo·dhen

Meat & Fish

beef	oksekød	ok·se·keudh
chicken	hønsekød	heun·se·keudh
cod	torsk	torsk
eel	ål	orl
fish	fisk	fisk
herring	sild	seel
lamb	lammekød	la·me·keudh
lobster	hummer	haw·ma
meat	kød	keudh
mutton	fårekød	faw·re·keudh
pork	svinekød	svee·ne·keudh
salmon	laks	laks
seafood	skaldyr	skal·dewr
steak	engelsk bøf	eng·elsk beuf
trout	forel/ørred	foh·rel/eur·redh
tuna	tunfisk	toon·fisk
veal	kalvekød	kal·ve·keudh

Fruit & Vegetables

apple	æble	eb·le
apricot	abrikos	a·bree·kohs
banana	banan	ba·nan
beans	bønner	beu·na
cabbage	kål	kawl
carrots	gulerødder	goo·le·reu·dha
cauliflower	blomkål	blom·kawl
cherry	kirsebær	keer·se·ber
corn	majs	mais
cucumber	agurk	a·goork
fruit	frugt	frawgt
leek	porre	po·re
lemon	citron	see·trohn

QUESTION WORDS

How?	Hvordan?	vor·dan
What?	Hvad?	va
When?	Hvornår?	vor·nawr
Where?	Hvor?	vor
Who?	Hvem?	vem
Why?	Hvorfor?	vor·for

mushroom	champignon	sham·peen·yong
nuts	nødder	neu·dha
onion	løg	loy
orange	appelsin	a·pel·seen
peach	fersken	fers·ken
peanut	jordnød	jor·neudh
pear	pære	pe·re
peas	ærter	er·ta
pineapple	ananas	a·na·nas
plum	blomme	blo·me
potato	kartoffel	ka·to·fel
spinach	spinat	spee·nat
strawberry	jordbær	jor·ber
vegetable	grønsag	greun·saa
watermelon	vandmelon	van·mey·lon

Other

bread	brød	breudh
butter	smør	smeur
cake	kage	ka·e
cheese	ost	awst
cream	fløde	fleu·dhe
egg	æg	eg
garlic	hvidløg	veedh·loy
honey	honning	ho·ning
ice	is	ees
jam	syltetøj	sewl·te·toy
noodles	nudler	noodh·la
pepper	peber	pey·wa
rice	ris	rees
salad	salat	sa·lat
soup	suppe	saw·pe
sugar	sukker	saw·ka

Drinks

beer	øl	eul
buttermilk	kærnemælk	ker·ne·melk
coffee	kaffe	ka·fe
(orange) juice	(appelsin-) juice	(aa·pel·seen·) joos
lemonade	citronvand	see·trohn·van
milk	mælk	melk
mineral water	mineralvand/ danskvand	mee·ne·ral·van/ dansk·van
red wine	rødvin	reudh·veen
soft drink	sodavand	soh·da·van
sparkling wine	mousserende vin	moo·sey·ra·ne veen

tea	*te*	tey
water	*vand*	van
white wine	*hvidvin*	veedh·veen

EMERGENCIES

Help!	*Hjælp!*	yelp
Go away!	*Gå væk!*	gaw vek
Call ...!	*Ring efter ...!*	ring ef·ta ...
a doctor	*en læge*	in le·ye
the police	*politiet*	poh·lee·tee·et

It's an emergency!
Det er et nødstilfælde!   dey ir it neudhs·til·fe·le

I'm lost.
Jeg er faret vild.   yai ir faa·ret veel

I'm sick.
Jeg er syg.   yai ir sew

It hurts here.
Det gør ondt her.   dey geur awnt heyr

I'm allergic to (antibiotics).
Jeg er allergisk over   yai ir a·ler·geesk o·va
for (antibiotika).   for (an·tee·bee·oh·tee·ka)

Where's the toilet?
Hvor er toilettet?   vor ir toy·le·tet

SHOPPING & SERVICES

Where's the ...?	*Hvor er ...?*	vor ir ...
ATM	*der en hæve-automat*	deyr in he·ve·ow·toh·mat
bank	*der en bank*	deyr in baank
local internet café	*den lokale internet café*	den loh·ka·le in·ta·net ka·fey
nearest public phone	*den nærmeste telefonboks*	den ner·mes·te te·le·fohn·boks
post office	*der et postkontor*	deyr it post·kon·tohr
public toilet	*der et offentligt toilet*	deyr it o·fent·leet toy·let
tourist office	*turist-kontoret*	too·reest·kon·toh·ret

I'm looking for ...
Jeg leder efter ...   yai li·dha ef·ta ...

Can I have a look?
Må jeg se?   maw yai sey

Do you have any others?
Har I andre?   haar ee aan·dre

How much is it?
Hvor meget koster det?   vor maa·yet kos·ta dey

That's too expensive.
Det er for dyrt.   dey ir for dewrt

NUMBERS

1	*en*	in
2	*to*	toh
3	*tre*	trey
4	*fire*	feer
5	*fem*	fem
6	*seks*	seks
7	*syv*	sew
8	*otte*	aw·te
9	*ni*	nee
10	*ti*	tee
20	*tyve*	tew·ve
30	*tredive*	traadh·ve
40	*fyrre*	fewr·re
50	*halvtreds*	hal·tres
60	*tres*	tres
70	*halvfjerds*	hal·fyers
80	*firs*	feers
90	*halvfems*	hal·fems
100	*hundrede*	hoon·re·dhe
1000	*tusind*	too·sen

What's your lowest price?
Hvad er jeres laveste   va ir ye·res la·ve·ste
pris?   prees

There's a mistake in the bill. (restaurant/shop)
Der er en fejl i   deyr ir in fail ee
regningen/   rai·ning·en/
kvitteringen.   kvee·tey·ring·en

TIME & DATES

What time is it?
Hvad er klokken?   va ir klo·ken

It's (two) o'clock.
Klokken er (to).   klo·ken ir (toh)

Half past (one).
Halv (to). (lit: half two)   hal (toh)

At what time ...?
Hvad tid ...?   va teedh ...

At ...
Klokken ...   klo·ken ...

am (morning)	*om morgenen*	om mor·nen
pm (afternoon)	*om eftermiddagen*	om ef·taa·mi·da·en
pm (evening)	*om aftenen*	om aaft·nen
yesterday	*i går*	ee gawr
today	*i dag*	ee da

ROAD SIGNS

Ensrettet	One Way
Indkørsel Forbudt	No Entry
Motorvej	Freeway
Omkørsel	Detour
Parkering Forbudt	No Parking
Selvbetjening	Self Service
Vejarbejde	Roadworks
Vigepligt	Give Way

tomorrow	i morgen	ee morn
Monday	mandag	man·da
Tuesday	tirsdag	teers·da
Wednesday	onsdag	awns·da
Thursday	torsdag	tors·da
Friday	fredag	fre·da
Saturday	lørdag	leur·da
Sunday	søndag	seun·da

January	januar	ya·noo·ar
February	februar	feb·roo·ar
March	marts	maarts
April	april	a·preel
May	maj	mai
June	juni	yoo·nee
July	juli	yoo·lee
August	august	ow·gawst
September	september	sip·tem·ba
October	oktober	ohk·toh·ba
November	november	noh·vem·ba
December	december	dey·sem·ba

TRANSPORT

Public Transport

Is this the ... to (Aarhus)?	Er dette ... til (Århus)?	ir dey·te ... til (awr·hoos)
boat	båden	baw·dhen
bus	bussen	boo·sen
plane	flyet	flew·et
train	toget	taw·et

What time's the ... bus?	Hvad tid er den ... bus?	va teedh ir den ... boos
first	første	feurs·te
last	sidste	sees·te

next	næste	nes·te
One ... ticket (to Odense), please.	En ... billet (til Odense), tak.	in ... bee·let (til oh·dhen·se) taak
one-way	enkelt	eng·kelt
return	retur	rey·toor

At what time does (the train) arrive/leave?
Hvornår ankommer/ afgår (toget)? — vor·nawr an·ko·ma/ ow·gawr (taw·et)

Does it stop at (Østerport)?
Stopper den/det på (Østerport)? — sto·pa den/dey paw (eus·ta·port)

What's the next station/stop?
Hvad er næste station/ stoppested? — va ir nes·te sta·shohn/ sto·pe·stedh

Please tell me when we get to (Roskilde).
Sig venligst til når vi kommer til (Roskilde). — see ven·leest til nawr vee ko·ma til (ros·kee·le)

Please take me to (this address).
Vær venlig at køre mig til (denne adresse). — ver ven·lee at keu·re mai til (de·ne a·draa·se)

Please stop here.
Venligst stop her. — ven·leest stop heyr

Driving & Cycling

I'd like to hire a ...	Jeg vil gerne leje en ...	yai vil gir·ne lai·ye in ...
bicycle	cykel	sew·kel
car	bil	beel
motorbike	motor-cykel	moh·tor·sew·kel

air	luft	lawft
oil	olie	ohl·ye
park (car)	parkere	paar·key·ra
petrol	benzin	ben·seen
service station	benzin-station	ben·seen·sta·shohn
tyres	dæk	dek

Is this the road to (Kronborg Slot)?
Fører denne vej til (Kronborg Slot)? — feu·ra de·ne vai til (krohn·borg slot)

Can I get there by bicycle?
Kan jeg cykle derhen? — kan yai sewk·le deyr·hen

I need a mechanic.
Jeg har brug for en mekaniker. — yai haar broo for in mi·ka·ni·ka

I've run out of petrol.
Jeg er løbet tør for benzin. — yai ir leu·bet teur for ben·seen

I have a flat tyre.
Jeg er punkteret. — yai ir pawng·tey·ret

Behind the Scenes

SEND US YOUR FEEDBACK

We love to hear from travellers – your comments keep us on our toes and help make our books better. Our well-travelled team reads every word on what you loved or loathed about this book. Although we cannot reply individually to your submissions, we always guarantee that your feedback goes straight to the appropriate authors, in time for the next edition. Each person who sends us information is thanked in the next edition – the most useful submissions are rewarded with a selection of digital PDF chapters.

Visit **lonelyplanet.com/contact** to submit your updates and suggestions or to ask for help. Our award-winning website also features inspirational travel stories, news and discussions.

Note: We may edit, reproduce and incorporate your comments in Lonely Planet products such as guidebooks, websites and digital products, so let us know if you don't want your comments reproduced or your name acknowledged. For a copy of our privacy policy visit lonelyplanet.com/privacy.

OUR READERS

Many thanks to the travellers who used the last edition and wrote to us with helpful hints, useful advice and interesting anecdotes: Alja Gartner, Helle Lassen, Hristina Bodin, Ivan Augsburger, Jonas Hammarberg, Laura Murray, Mathies Jespersen, Monica Kær, Rebecca Morris

WRITER THANKS

Mark Elliott

A very special thank you to the wonderful Sally Cobham for love, company and great insight. En route, many thanks to Elisabeth and Jens in Maribo, Uve Horst in Stege, Mikayl at Skelby, Annette at Knuthenland, Morgens Grønning, Jens and the beer club in Helsingør, motor-mouth pop-up historian Peter Andreas, Klaus at Ringsted church, Stine and her big green heart, Ole Rasmussen at NaturparkÅmosen, Henning Vingborg at Løve Windmill, Kevin at the train museum, Eddie at Midtfyns, Jesper at Flakhaven, David at Faarborg Arest, Michael, Bent and Marianne at Kiss The Frog, Katerin at Søbygaard, Helle and Jacob, Urt and Ties at Insp!

Carolyn Bain

It's always a joy to return to Denmark and spend time with my Danish family, the Østergaards. *Tusind tak*, as ever, for welcoming me back. Warm thanks to my cowriters on this project, Cristian Bonetto and Mark Elliott, for input, and to regional tourism pros Heidi Lindberg and Helle Mogensen for kind assistance. This trip was special for the friendships forged: *mange tak* to Sif Orellana, Catrine Engelgreen, Trine Nissen and especially Mia Sinding Jespersen for *hygge* and heart.

Cristian Bonetto

For their priceless insight, generosity and friendship, *tusind tak* to Martin Kalhøj, Mette Cecilie Smedegaard, Christian Struckmann Irgens, Mads Lind, Mia Hjorth Lunde and Jens Lunde, Mary-ann Gardner and Lambros Hajisava, Sophie Lind and Kasper Monrad, Anne Marie Nielsen, Sanna Klein Hedegaard Hansen and Carolyn Bain. In-house, many thanks to Gemma Graham.

ACKNOWLEDGEMENTS

Climate map data adapted from Peel MC, Finlayson BL & McMahon TA (2007) 'Updated World Map of the Köppen-Geiger Climate Classification', Hydrology and Earth System Sciences, 11, 163344.

Cover photograph: Old Town, Aarhus; Olya Nosenko/500px ©

THIS BOOK

This 8th edition of Lonely Planet's *Denmark* guidebook was researched and written by Mark Elliott, Carolyn Bain and Cristian Bonetto. The previous edition was written by Carolyn Bain and Cristian Bonetto. This guidebook was produced by the following:

Destination Editor Gemma Graham

Product Editors Jenna Myers, Kate Chapman, Genna Patterson

Cartographers Julie Dodkins, Valentina Kremenchutskaya

Book Designer Clara Monitto

Assisting Book Designer Nicholas Colicchia

Assisting Editors Imogen Bannister, Michelle Bennett, Bruce Evans, Alex Knights, Jodie Martire, Anne Mulvaney, Kristin Odijk, Gabbi Stefanos, Sam Wheeler

Cover Researcher Naomi Parker

Thanks to Anne Mason, Claire Naylor, Vicky Smith

Index

Map Legend

Sights

- Beach
- Bird Sanctuary
- Buddhist
- Castle/Palace
- Christian
- Confucian
- Hindu
- Islamic
- Jain
- Jewish
- Monument
- Museum/Gallery/Historic Building
- Ruin
- Shinto
- Sikh
- Taoist
- Winery/Vineyard
- Zoo/Wildlife Sanctuary
- Other Sight

Activities, Courses & Tours

- Bodysurfing
- Diving
- Canoeing/Kayaking
- Course/Tour
- Sento Hot Baths/Onsen
- Skiing
- Snorkelling
- Surfing
- Swimming/Pool
- Walking
- Windsurfing
- Other Activity

Sleeping

- Sleeping
- Camping
- Hut/Shelter

Eating

- Eating

Drinking & Nightlife

- Drinking & Nightlife
- Cafe

Entertainment

- Entertainment

Shopping

- Shopping

Information

- Bank
- Embassy/Consulate
- Hospital/Medical
- Internet
- Police
- Post Office
- Telephone
- Toilet
- Tourist Information
- Other Information

Geographic

- Beach
- Gate
- Hut/Shelter
- Lighthouse
- Lookout
- Mountain/Volcano
- Oasis
- Park
- Pass
- Picnic Area
- Waterfall

Population

- Capital (National)
- Capital (State/Province)
- City/Large Town
- Town/Village

Transport

- Airport
- Border crossing
- Bus
- Cable car/Funicular
- Cycling
- Ferry
- Metro station
- Monorail
- Parking
- Petrol station
- S-Bahn/Subway station
- Taxi
- T-bane/Tunnelbana station
- Train station/Railway
- Tram
- Tube station
- U-Bahn/Underground station
- Other Transport

Routes

- Tollway
- Freeway
- Primary
- Secondary
- Tertiary
- Lane
- Unsealed road
- Road under construction
- Plaza/Mall
- Steps
- Tunnel
- Pedestrian overpass
- Walking Tour
- Walking Tour detour
- Path/Walking Trail

Boundaries

- International
- State/Province
- Disputed
- Regional/Suburb
- Marine Park
- Cliff
- Wall

Hydrography

- River, Creek
- Intermittent River
- Canal
- Water
- Dry/Salt/Intermittent Lake
- Reef

Areas

- Airport/Runway
- Beach/Desert
- Cemetery (Christian)
- Cemetery (Other)
- Glacier
- Mudflat
- Park/Forest
- Sight (Building)
- Sportsground
- Swamp/Mangrove

Note: Not all symbols displayed above appear on the maps in this book

OUR STORY

A beat-up old car, a few dollars in the pocket and a sense of adventure. In 1972 that's all Tony and Maureen Wheeler needed for the trip of a lifetime – across Europe and Asia overland to Australia. It took several months, and at the end – broke but inspired – they sat at their kitchen table writing and stapling together their first travel guide, *Across Asia on the Cheap*. Within a week they'd sold 1500 copies. Lonely Planet was born.

Today, Lonely Planet has offices in Franklin, London, Melbourne, Oakland, Dublin, Beijing and Delhi, with more than 600 staff and writers. We share Tony's belief that 'a great guidebook should do three things: inform, educate and amuse'.

OUR WRITERS

Mark Elliott

Funen; Møn, Falster & Lolland; Zealand Mark Elliott had already lived and worked on five continents when, in the pre-Internet dark ages, he started writing travel guides. He has since authored (or co-authored) around 60 books, including dozens for Lonely Planet. He also acts as a travel consultant, occasional tour leader, video presenter, speaker, interviewer and blues harmonicist. Co-researched with Wil Klass, Elliott's first published work was *Asia Overland*, a ludicrously over-ambitious brick-thick opus covering a whole continent. Designed to aid impecunious English teachers get home cheaply from Japan, it was one of the first guides to help backpackers cross the then-new states of the former USSR. It garnered something of a cult following in its day.

Carolyn Bain

Bornholm; Central Jutland; Northern Jutland; Southern Jutland A travel writer and editor for more than 20 years, Carolyn has lived, worked and studied in various corners of the globe, including Denmark, London, St Petersburg and Nantucket. Her Iceland obsession has led to her setting up a permanent home in Reykjavík. Carolyn's former base was Melbourne, Australia, but she was repeatedly drawn north to cover diverse destinations for Lonely Planet; from dusty outback Australia to luminous Greek islands, by way of Maine's lobster shacks and Slovenia's alpine lakes. The Nordic region stakes a large claim to her heart, with repeated visits to Iceland and Denmark for work and pleasure. Carolyn also wrote the Plan, Understand and Survival Guide chapters.

Cristian Bonetto

Copenhagen; Around Copenhagen Cristian has contributed to over 30 Lonely Planet guides to date, including *New York City*, *Italy*, *Venice & the Veneto*, *Naples & the Amalfi Coast*, *Denmark*, *Copenhagen*, *Sweden* and *Singapore*. Lonely Planet work aside, his musings on travel, food, culture and design appear in numerous publications around the world, including *The Telegraph* (UK) and *Corriere del Mezzogiorno* (Italy). When not on the road, you'll find the reformed playwright and TV scriptwriter slurping espresso in his beloved hometown of Melbourne.

Published by Lonely Planet Global Limited
CRN 554153
8th edition – May 2018
ISBN 978 1 78657 466 4
© Lonely Planet 2018 Photographs © as indicated 2018
10 9 8 7 6 5 4 3 2 1
Printed in China